BLACK AMERICAN WRITERS PAST AND PRESENT:

A Biographical and Bibliographical Dictionary

by
Theressa Gunnels Rush
Carol Fairbanks Myers
Esther Spring Arata

Volume II: J-Z

The Scarecrow Press, Inc.
Metuchen, N. J.   1975

Z 1229
N39 R87
v. 2

THE DICTIONARY [J-Z]

JACKMAN, Marvin   see   MUHAJIR, El

JACKSON, A. J.
POETRY   A Vision of Life and Other Poems.   Hillsborough, O.:
Printed at the Highland news office, 1869.

JACKSON, Angela.   Born 25 July 1951 in Greenville, Mississippi.
Education: Northwestern University; OBAC Writers Workshop.
Currently living in Chicago.   Career: A student at Northwestern,
secretary for OBAC Writers Workshop.   Awards, Honors: 8th
recipient of the Conrad Kent Rivers Literary Award, sponsored
by Black World, August 1973.
POETRY
    Voo Doo/Love/Magic.   Chicago: Third World, 1973.
    (Periodicals): Black Collegian, November-December 1972;
        Black Creation, Winter 1973; Black World, January, Sep-
        tember 1971; January, September 1973; Nommo, Summer
        1972; Anniversary Issue 1973.
REVIEWS
    Published in Black World.
INTERJECTIONS
    "I am a Black woman nationalist attempting through nommo
(the power of the word) to understand life in order to work with
Black people as we work to perfect it."

JACKSON, Aurilda.
POETRY   Untangled.   New York: Vantage, 1956.

JACKSON, Beth.
POETRY   (Anthology): Boyd, Poems by Blacks, vol. 2

JACKSON, Bill.
POETRY   (Periodical): Journal of Black Poetry, No. 12 (1969).

JACKSON, Blyden.   Born 12 October 1910 in Paducah, Kentucky.
Education: B.A., Wilberforce University, 1930; M.A., University of Michigan, 1938; Ph.D., University of Michigan, 1952.
Currently living in Chapel Hill, North Carolina.   Career: Public
school teacher in Kentucky, 1934-45; English professor, Fisk University, 1945-54; Professor of English and Chairman of the Department, Southern University, 1954-62; Dean of the Graduate
School, Southern University, 1962-69; Professor of English, Uni-

versity of North Carolina--Chapel Hill, 1969 to present. Member: Vice President, now defunct Louisville Association of Teachers in Colored Schools, 1940-42; President, Louisville Association of Teachers in Colored Schools, 1942-44; Vice President of College Language Association, 1955-57; President, College Language Association, 1957-59; Vice President, Southern Association of Land Grant Colleges and State Universities, 1968-69; Associate Editor, CLA Journal. Awards, Honors: Julius Rosenwald Fellow, 1947-49; University of Michigan Fellow, 1947-49; Honors Convocation, Michigan, 1948.

CRITICISM AND ESSAYS

"The Blithe Newcomers: A Résumé of Negro Literature in 1954." Phylon 16 (First Quarter 1955): 5-12.

"A Casual People." Friends Intelligencer 102 (27 July 1946): 450-451.

"The Case for American Negro Literature." The Michigan Alumnus Quarterly Review 61 (February 1955): 161-166.

"The College Language Association." PMLA 73 (December 1958): 12-13.

"The Continuing Strain: A Resumé of Negro Literature in 1955." Phylon 17 (First Quarter 1956): 35-40.

Encyclopedia Americana, 1972: articles on Countée Cullen, Paul Laurence Dunbar, Ralph Ellison, and Langston Hughes.

"An Essay in Criticism." Phylon 12 (Fourth Quarter 1950): 338-343.

"Faith Without Works in Negro Literature." Phylon 12 (Fourth Quarter 1951): 378-388.

"Full Circle." Phylon 9 (First Quarter 1948): 30-35.

"The Ghetto of the Negro Novel." The Southern University Bulletin, Creative and Research Issue 12 (February 1956): 62-65.

"A Golden Mean for the Negro Novel." CLA Journal 3 (December 1959): 81-87.

"Immortal Longings," in The Sphinx, between 1940 and 1945.

"Jericho! Jericho!" in The Sphinx, between 1940 and 1945.

"Largo for Adonais." Journal of Negro Education 7 (Winter 1946): 169-175.

"The Negro's Image of the Universe as Reflected in His Fiction." CLA Journal 4 (September 1960): 23-31; also in Turner and Bright, Images of the Negro in America; Singh and Fellowes, Black Literature in America; Chapman, Black Voices.

"The Negro's Negro in Negro Literature." Michigan Quarterly Review 4 (October 1965): 290-295.

"Notes on a Theme." CLA Journal 1 (November 1956): 62-65.

"The Ring and the Book." CLA Bulletin 9 (Spring 1955): 4-5.

"Some Negroes in the Land of Goshen." Tennessee Folklore Society Bulletin 19 (December 1953): 103-107.

"Survey Course in Negro Literature." English Journal 35 (March 1974): 631-636.

"Trends in Contemporary Criticism." The Quarterly Review

of Higher Education Among Negroes 12 (January 1963):
37-42.
"A Word about Simple." CLA Journal 11 (June 1968): 310-
318.
NON-FICTION
  With S. V. Martorana, et al. New Careers and Curriculum
  Change: A Conference Report for the Institute of Higher
  Educational Opportunity of the Southern Regional Educa-
  tion Board (Atlanta, 1968).
REVIEW BY JACKSON
Journal of Negro History, January 1971.

JACKSON, Booker. Born 6 March 1929 in Center Point, Arkansas.
Education: B.A., Philander Smith College, 1956. Currently
living in Little Rock, Arkansas. Career: Worked at the Vet-
erans Administration Hospital in North Little Rock, and for the
post office in Little Rock; was assistant to Editor, Watts Star
Review. Member: South & West, Inc., (charter member);
International Writers Fellowship; World Poetry Society Inter-
continental. Awards, Honors: South and West Poet of the
Year, 1969; Citation from World Poetry Society.
POETRY
  God Looks Down. Fort Smith, Ark.: South & West, 1968.
  The World Needs. Fort Smith, Ark.: South & West, 1972.
  (Periodicals): Cyclotron; American Bard; Voices Internation-
  al; Swordsman Review; Contemporary Poets of Arkansas.
  (Newspapers): Kansas City Star; Denver Post; Arkansas Ga-
  zette; Southwest Times Record.
WORK IN PROGRESS
Presently writing songs.
INTERJECTIONS
"Among my ideals are: An end to man's injustice to man,
human equality. Also, the end of racial prejudice--dignity and
respect in society for the black man...brother-hood."

JACKSON, C. Bernard.
DRAMA With James V. Hatch. Fly Blackbird, 1963.

JACKSON, Claude.
POETRY (Periodical): Journal of Black Poetry, Winter-Spring,
1970.

JACKSON, Elaine.
DRAMA "Toe Jam." In King and Milner, Black Drama Anthology.

JACKSON, Emma Lou. Born in Macon County, Alabama. Educa-
tion: Grammar School. Currently living in Akron, Ohio. Ca-
reer: Housekeeper and writer.
GENRE UNKNOWN
  The Veil of Nancy. New York: Carlton, 1970.
WORK IN PROGRESS
A book on Christianity.

Jackson 414

JACKSON, Eugenia Lutcher. Born in Lake Charles, Louisiana.
Education: Studied at Los Angeles City College and Los Ange-
les Trade Tech College. Currently living in Los Angeles, Cali-
fornia. Career: Writer, producer, composer of music and
lyrics for eleven songs; Founder-Director of Co-Real Artists.
Member: Greater Los Angeles Urban League; Kelly Services,
Inc., Lutheran Church in America Pacific South West Synod;
N.A.A.C.P.; National Urban League; National Association of
Radio Announcers; National Association for Artists and Models.
Awards, Honors: Achievement Certificate for Basic Scientific
Study of People; City of Los Angeles Exemplary Community
Service Citation; Community and Urban League New Thrust
Award.
DRAMA
    Everything Is Everything.
    Life.
INTERJECTIONS
    "Literary and Cultural advantages make it very easy to con-
vey the messages of the heart and mind in a beautiful and dra-
matic fashion, because words and music are just things until
people bring them alive. I am happy for the opportunity to contribute music and the spoken word to this life. I hope that as
much joy is transmitted to the world in hearing and reading
them as I experienced in writing them."

JACKSON, Franklin.
    UNPUBLISHED NOVEL Exerpt in Black Review No. 1. Edited
        by Mel Watkins.

JACKSON, J. Denis. (Julian Moreau).
    WRITINGS The Black Commandos. Atlanta: Cultural Institute
        Press, 1967.

JACKSON, James Thomas.
    NON-FICTION
        (Anthology): Schulberg, From the Ashes.
    POETRY
        (Anthology): Schulberg, From the Ashes.
        (Periodicals): Antioch Review, Fall 1967; poetry has also
            been published in West, Sunday magazine for the Los Ange-
            les Times.
    SHORT STORY
        (Anthology): Schulberg, From the Ashes.

JACKSON, Jesse. Born 1 January 1908 in Columbus, Ohio. Edu-
    cation: Was graduated from high school in Columbus. Cur-
    rently living in New York City. Career: Writer and lecturer.
    Served as visiting associate professor at Appalachian State Uni-
    versity, 1972 and 1974. Member: Author's Guild. Awards,
    Honors: Child Study Association's Award for Call Me Charley;
    commendation by the Council of Christians and Jews for Anchor
    Man.

Jesse Jackson

CHILDREN AND YOUNG ADULTS
   Anchor Man. New York: Harper & Row, 1947*; New York:
      Dell, 1968†.
   With Elaine Landau. Black In America: A Fight for Free-
      dom. New York: Messner, 1973*.
   Call Me Charley. New York: Harper & Row, 1945*; New
      York: Dell, 1967†. large type ed.*
   Charley Starts from Scratch. New York: Harper & Row,
      1958*; New York: Dell, 1968†.
   The Fourteenth Cadillac. New York: Doubleday, 1972*.
   Make a Joyful Noise Unto the Lord: The Life of Mahalia
      Jackson. New York: T. Y. Crowell, 1974*.
   Room for Randy. New York: Friendship, 1957.
   The Sickest Don't Always Die the Quickest. New York:
      Doubleday, 1971*.
   Tessie. New York: Harper & Row, 1968*; New York: Dell,
      1969†.
BIOGRAPHY ON JACKSON
   Commire. Something About the Author, vol. 2.

JACKSON, Jo.
DRAMA Martin and Malcolm.

JACKSON, John Robert.
POETRY With Homer Preston Johnson and Robert Milum Baker.
Twilight Dreams. New York: Exposition, 1950.

JACKSON, Laura F.
POETRY Paradise (Cleveland Park) and Other Poems. Washington: R. L. Pendleton, 1920.

JACKSON, Mae. Born 3 January 1946 in Earl, Arkansas. Education: New School of Social Research. Currently living in Brooklyn, New York. Career: Teacher, Rothschild Junior High School, Brooklyn, New York. Awards, Honors: Conrad Kent Rivers Memorial Award.
POETRY
    Can I Poet with You. Introduction by Nikki Giovanni. New York: Black Dialogue, 1969; Detroit: Broadside, 1972†.
    (Anthologies): Adoff, Black Out Loud; Adoff, The Poetry of Black America: King, Blackspirits.
    (Periodicals): Black World, September 1970; September 1972; Journal of Black Poetry, Fall-Winter 1971; Negro Digest, September 1969.
SHORT STORY
    (Periodical): Negro Digest, June 1969.

JACKSON, R. Orlando.
POETRY (Anthology): Pool, Beyond the Blues.

JACKSON, Richard.
POETRY (Periodical): Journal of Black Poetry, Summer 1972.

JACKSON, Rev. Spencer.
DRAMA
    Come Home, 1969.
    A New Day, 1969.

JACKSON, W. Warner.
NOVEL The Birth of the Martyn's Ghost: A Novel. New York: Comet, 1957.

JACKSON, Will.
POETRY (Anthology): Boyd, Poems by Blacks, vol. 2.

JACOBSON, Harriet Price.
POETRY Songs in the Night. New York: Exposition, 1947.

JACQUES, Geoffrey.
POETRY
    (Periodical): Journal of Black Poetry, Summer 1972.
REVIEW BY JACQUES
    (Periodical): Black World, October 1971.

JAMES, Beauregard (pseud.)
> FICTION
> > The Road to Birmingham. New York: Published for Society
> > of Racial Peace of Washington, D.C., by Bridgehead
> > Books, 1964.

JAMISON, Roscoe Conkling. Born in Winchester, Tennessee, 1888.
> Died 1918. Education: Fisk University.[1]
> POETRY
> > Chords and Discords. n.p., n.d.
> > Negro Soldiers ("These Truly Are the Brave") and Other Po-
> > ems. St. Joseph, Mo.: W. F. Neil, 1918. (Published
> > soon after his death by his friend, Charles Bertram John-
> > son.)[2]
> (Anthology): Johnson, The Book of American Negro Poetry.
> CRITICISM ON JAMISON
> Brawley. The Negro Genius, pp. 238-239.
> _____. The Negro in Literature and Art, p. 110-111.
> Kerlin. Negro Poets and Their Poems, pp. 191-195.
> > [1]Benjamin Brawley, The Negro Genius (New York:
> Dodd, Mead, 1937), p. 240.
> > [2]Ibid.

JANEY, Margaret.
> POETRY (Periodicals): Journal of Black Poetry, Spring 1969;
> Fall-Winter 1971.

JANSSEN, Milton W.
> NOVEL Divided. New York: Pageant Press, 1963.

JARRETTE, Alfred Q.
> NON-FICTION
> > Muslims Black Metropolis. Los Angeles: Great Western
> > Book, 1962.
> > Politics and the Negro. Boston: Vinjano Educational Pub-
> > lishers, 1964.
> NOVEL
> > Beneath the Sky. New York: Weinberg Book Supply, 1949.
> CRITICISM ON JARRETTE
> Hughes. The Negro Novelist, pp. 159-160.

JARRY, Hawke. Born 20 August 1938 in St. Louis, Missouri.
> Education: B.S. (History), Illinois State University, Normal,
> 1964. Currently living in University City, Missouri. Career:
> Traveller and writer. Currently working on a novel and col-
> lection of short stories.
> NOVEL
> > Black Schoolmaster. New York: Exposition, 1970.
> INTERJECTIONS
> > "a) Have always tried to view life universally, and I mean
> every aspect of it. b) Have a deep need to understand man's
> inner drives, if one can be into others through oneself."

JEANETTE, Gertrude.
DRAMA
A Bolt from the Blue, 1952.
Light in the Cellar.
This Way Forward, 1951.

JEFFERS, Lance. Born 1919 in Nebraska.
CRITICISM
"Afro-American Literature, The Conscience of Man." The
Black Scholar 2 (January 1971): 47-53.
"Bullins, Baraka, and Elder: The Dawn of Grandeur in
Black Drama." CLA Journal 16 (September 1972).
POETRY
My Blackness Is the Beauty of This Land. Detroit: Broad-
side, 1970†.
(Anthologies): Adoff, The Poetry of Black America; Brooks,
A Broadside Treasury; Burning Spear; Chapman, Black
Voices; Davis and Redding, Cavalcade; Henderson, Umbra;
Major, The New Black Poetry; Pool, Beyond the Blues;
Simmons & Hutchinson, Black Culture.
(Periodicals): Freedomways, Summer 1966; Negro American
Literature Forum, Spring 1972; Negro Digest, October
1968; Phylon, First Quarter 1958; other poetry in Dasein;
Quarto; Survive; Tamarack Review.

JEFFERSON, Wilson James. Born 1879.
NON-FICTION
Judging the Negro Family. Philadelphia: n.p., 1944.
POETRY
Black Annals. Philadelphia: By the Author, 1929.
Verses. Boston: R. G. Badger, 1909.

JEMMOTT, Claudia E. Born 1949.
POETRY (Anthology): Shuman, A Galaxy of Black Writing.

JENKINS, Deaderick Franklin. Born 8 June 1910 in Pobtotoc Coun-
ty, Mississippi. Education: B.S., Rust College; advanced work
in the Social Sciences at the University of California. Current-
ly living in Los Angeles, California. Career: Publisher of
Fine Books; Songwriter. Awards, Honors: Received the Kent
State University Library Award for It Was Not My World; Per-
sonal Poetry Broadcasts Award.
NON-FICTION
Published in Living Magazine and The Modern Thinker.
NOVELS
It Was Not My World. Los Angeles: By the Author, 1942.
Letters to My Son. Los Angeles: Deaderick F. Jenkins,
1947.
REVIEW: It Was Not My World.
The Negro Yearbook 1941-46, p. 459.
INTERJECTIONS
"One is primarily what he eats, thinks. One is also what
and how he lives."

Deaderick F. Jenkins

JENKINS, Welborn Victor. Born 1879.
   NON-FICTION
      The "Incident" at Monroe, a Requiem for the Victims of July
        25th, 1946, Written at the Scene of the Tragedy. Atlanta,
        Ga.: United Negro Youth of America for the Malcolm-
        Dorsey Memorial Committee, 1948.[1]
   POETRY
      Trumpet in the New Moon and Other Poems. Foreword by
        E. H. Webster. Boston: Peabody, 1934.
        [1]See The New York Times Index, July-December 1946,
      for a listing of articles about this incident.

JENKINS, William H.
   POETRY "Blossoms." Princess Ann, Md.: Princess Anne
      Academy Press, n.d.

JENNINGS, H. A. (Habte Wolde).
   POETRY Enough to Die For. Detroit: Broadside, 1972.

JENRETTE, Corinne McLemore. Born 23 April 1903 in Crockett
   County, Bells, Tennessee. Education: B.S., Tennessee State
   University, 1940; M.S., Tennessee State University, 1953.
   Career: Spent 50 years in the classroom as an elementary

school teacher; published poems several times a year in the
Crockett County Sentinel in Almo, Tennessee. Member: Ten-
nessee Teachers Association; National Education Association;
Worthy Matron of O. E. S. Chapter. Awards, Honors: Received
plaque from the Crockett County School System; Woman of the
Year, Sorority, Lane College.
POETRY
    Just for Fun and Pleasure. New York: Carlton, 1970.
INTERJECTIONS
    "It is hoped that the youth of our nation will become more in-
spired to wisely use some of their leisure time to continue to
read good literature, and to do some creative writing."

JERROD.
    POETRY To Paint a Picture Book. Chicago: Free Black
    Press, 1969.

JESSYE, Eva Alberta. Born 1897 in Coffeyville, Kansas. Education: Was graduated from Western University, 1914. Career:
Taught piano at Muskogee, Oklahoma; served as director of music at Morgan College 1919-1920; managed a training school for
radio artists, New York City.[1] Served on the editorial staff of
the Afro-American for one year; was Director of Music for the
first all-Negro moving picture, Hallelujah, 1929. Was creator
of the radio sketches, "Aunt Mamy's Chilun," and "Four Dusty
Travellers."[2]
NON-FICTION
    My Spirituals. New York: Robbins-Engel, 1927.
POETRY
    (Anthology): Kerlin, Negro Poets and Their Poems.
BIOGRAPHY AND CRITICISM ON JESSYE
    Kerlin. Negro Poets and Their Poems, pp. 139-142, 340.
REVIEW: My Spirituals.
    Bennett, Gwendolyn. Opportunity 5 (November 1927): 338-
    339.
        [1]Robert T. Kerlin. Negro Poets and Their Poems
    (Washington, D. C.: Associated, 1923), p. 340.
        [2]Who's Who in Colored America (Brooklyn, N. Y.:
    Thomas Yenser, 1933), p. 238.

JEWELL, Aander.
    POETRY There Is a Song. New York: Pageant, 1967.

JIGGETTS, Bess. Education: B. A., Morgan State College; John O.
Killens Writer's Workshop (Columbia University); C. C. N. Y.
Master's Program in Creative Writing. Currently living in New
York City. Career: Presently working on a play and conduct-
ing a writer's workshop for young people. Member: The Po-
etry Society of London, Eastern Centre; International Black
Writers.
POETRY
    Soft Souls. New York: Baker Enterprises, n. d.
    (Anthology): Giovanni, Night Comes Softly.

(Periodicals and Newspapers): Black Writer's News; The
News and Observer (Raleigh, North Carolina); Soulbook.

JOANS, Ted. Born in Cairo, Illinois. Education: B.A., Indiana
University, 1951; also educated in "the streets of Harlem/Green-
wich Village/Europe and Africa--meeting and listening (to
learn) to some of the best minds of this generation, both white
as well as Black, and female as well as male. Still laughing,
to keep from lying, thus steel wool!" Career: Painter and
jazzman as well as poet.
BIOGRAPHY
    "The Langston I Knew." Black World 21 (September 1972):
    14-19.
POETRY
    Afrodisia: New Poems by Ted Joans. New York: Hill &
    Wang, 1970*†.
    All of Ted Joans and No More: Poems and Collages. New
    York: Excelsior-Press, 1961.
    A Black Manifesto in Jazz Poetry and Prose. London: Cal-
    dar & Boyars, 1971.
    Black Pow-Wow: Jazz Poems. New York: Hill & Wang,
    1969*†.
    The Truth: A Poem. Amsterdam: Surrealistisch Kabinet,
    1968.
    (Anthologies): Abdul, The Magic of Black Poetry; Adoff,
    Black Out Loud; Adoff, The Poetry of Black America;
    Austin, Fenderson and Nelson, The Black Man and the
    Promise of America; Baker, Black Literature in America;
    Bell, Afro-American Poetry; Bontemps, American Negro
    Poetry; Brooks, A Broadside Treasury; Hayden, Kaleido-
    scope; Henderson, Understanding the New Black Poetry;
    Hollo, Negro Verse; Hughes, The Book of Negro Humor;
    Hughes, New Negro Poets: USA; Hughes and Bontemps,
    The Poetry of the Negro: 1746-1970; Lomax and Abdul,
    3000 Years of Black Poetry; Patterson, A Rock Against
    the Wind; Patterson, An Introduction to Black Literature
    in America; Pool, Beyond the Blues; Randall and Bur-
    roughs, For Malcolm; Simmons and Hutchinson, Black Cul-
    ture; Weisman and Wright, Black Poetry for All Ameri-
    cans.
    (Periodicals): Black World, April 1971; May 1971; Negro Di-
    gest, September 1969; February 1970; Présence Africaine,
    No. 57.
SHORT STORY
    (Anthology): Sanchez, We Be Word Sorcerers.
UNPUBLISHED WORKS
    "I, Black Surrealist (An Autobiography of a Hipster)"; "A
    Black Man Guides Allyall to Africa"; "Niggers from Out of
    Space" (short stories and plays).
INTERJECTIONS
    "Jazz is my religion and surrealism is my point of view. Africa
is the garden of the earth and amerikkka is an office to the factory
of which is found in the cemetery called Europe although amerikkka

itself is the greatest factory for unhip slaves. Black Power in all
its overt forms that lead to the marvelous for Blacks which in
turn germinate the entire human being world like our music
does/which is the classic music of today."

JOHN, Hedley.
WRITINGS Hill Toward Sunset. New York: Carlton, 1969.

JOHNSON, Adolphus.
POETRY
     The Silver Chord. Philadelphia: By the Author, 1915?
CRITICISM ON JOHNSON
     Kerlin. Negro Poets and Their Poems, pp. 104-105.

JOHNSON, Alicia. Born 27 February 1944 in Chicago. Education:
Attended Wilson Junior College; Southern Illinois University;
University of Ghana (Legon, West Africa); University of West
Indies (Mona, Jamaica). Currently living in East St. Louis,
Illinois. Career: Has specialized in Afro-American Arts and
Letters (African, Caribbean and American Art and Literature).
Exhibited art at Southern Illinois University, Gallery 51; held a
one-woman show at Southern Illinois University's Office of Life
and Activities. Presently working with Katherine Dunham and
preparing a study of Katherine Dunham for publication.
POETRY
     Realities vs. Spirits. n.p., By the Author, 1969.
     Two Black Poems. n.p., n.d.
     (Anthologies): Adoff, Black Out Loud; Alhamisi and Wangara,
          Black Arts; Brooks, A Broadside Treasury; Brown, Lee
          and Ward, To Gwen with Love; Coombs, We Speak as Lib-
          erators; Davis and Redding, Cavalcade; Shuman, Nine
          Black Poets; Watkins, Black Review No. 1.
     (Periodicals): Black World, December 1970; Journal of Black
          Poetry, Présence Africaine, #66, #68; Negro Digest, Ap-
          ril 1968; September-October 1968; September 1969; also
          published in Brazilian anthology of poetry and Search Lit-
          erary Magazine.
WORK IN PROGRESS
     A novel, "Ola"; a collection of poems, a book of space and
     form drawings.
INTERJECTIONS
     "Man reacts out of fear of acting not. Man's creativity
     weighs heavily upon his ability to comprehend the timely mag-
     netic forces of the cosmos. If he cannot breathe the rapid air
     of other breathers such as himself he will not survive the
     breath in which he must breathe" (Predictable Precisions, 1972).

JOHNSON, Amelia E. (Mrs. A. E. Johnson). Born 1859 in Maryland. Career: Founded the literary magazine, Joy in 1887.
NOVELS
     Clarence and Corinne; or, God's Way. Philadelphia: Ameri-
          can Baptist Publication Society, 1890.
     The Hazeley Family. Philadelphia: American Baptist Publi-

cation Society, 1894.
Martina Meriden; or, What Is My Motive? Philadelphia:
American Baptist Publication Society, 1901.
BIOGRAPHY ON JOHNSON
Afro-American Press, n.d.
Majors. Noted Negro Women, p. 210.

JOHNSON, Charles. Born 15 December 1949.
POETRY (Anthology): Coombs, We Speak as Liberators.

JOHNSON, Charles Bertram. Born 5 October 1880 in Callao, Ma-
con County, Missouri. Education: Western College; Lincoln
University; University of Chicago. Career: Taught for twenty
years, including eight years at the English Preparatory Depart-
ment of Western College. Became a minister, serving in Mo-
berly, Missouri.1
POETRY
The Mantle of Dunbar and Other Poems, 1918. (Pamphlet.)
Songs of My People. Boston: Cornhill, 1918; facsimile ed.,
Freeport, N.Y.: Books for Libraries*.
Wind Whisperings, 1900 (Pamphlet.)
(Anthologies): Eleazer, Singers in the Dawn; Johnson, The
Book of American Negro Poetry; Kerlin, Negro Poets and
Their Poems; White and Jackson, An Anthology of Verse
by American Negroes.
(Periodicals): Crisis 18 (1919): 183; 20 (1920): 282; 21
(1920): 75; 22 (1921): 120, 223, 258; 25 (1923): 229, 251;
26 (1923): 17; 36 (1929): 85.
BIOGRAPHY AND CRITICISM ON JOHNSON
Kerlin. Negro Poets and Their Poems, pp. 95-99.
White and Jackson. An Anthology of Verse by American Ne-
groes, p. 189.
1Newman Ivey White and Walter Clinton Jackson, An
Anthology of Verse by American Negroes (Durham, N.C.:
Moore, 1924): p. 189.

JOHNSON, Christine C.
POETRY (Anthology): Randall and Burroughs, For Malcolm.

JOHNSON, Clifford Vincent. Born 1936 in Chicago.
SHORT STORY (Anthologies): Hughes, The Best Short Stories
by Negro Writers; Patterson, An Introduction to Black Literature in America.

JOHNSON, Don Allen. (Mustafa). Born 1942 in Chattanooga, Ten-
nessee.
POETRY
(Anthologies): Hughes, New Negro Poets: USA; Hughes and
Bontemps, The Poetry of the Negro: 1746-1970; Singh
and Fellowes, Black Literature in America.

JOHNSON, Doris J.
POETRY
A Cloud of Summer and Other New Haiku. Chicago: Follett,
1967.
SHORT STORY
(Periodical): Negro Digest, November 1967.

JOHNSON, Dorothy Vena. Born in Los Angeles, California. Died
15 July 1970. Education: A.B., University of Southern Cali-
fornia; also attended the University of California Teachers Col-
lege. Career: Taught junior high school in Los Angeles.
Founder of the Allied Arts League. Member: Los Angeles
Creative Writing Teachers Association.
POETRY
(Anthologies): Murphy, Ebony Rhythm; Murphy, Negro Voices.

JOHNSON, Edd.
POETRY (Periodical): Journal of Black Poetry, Spring 1969.

JOHNSON, Eugene.
DRAMA Spaces in Between.

JOHNSON, Evelyn Allen.
WRITINGS My Neighbor's Island. New York: Exposition, 1965.

JOHNSON, Fenton. Born 7 May 1888 in Chicago. Died 1958.
Education: Attended the University of Chicago and Northwestern
University. Career: Had a varied career: taught English at
the State University, Louisville, for one year; served as special
writer for the Eastern Press Association and as acting dramatic
editor for the New York News; published three Negro spirituals
in Monroe and Henderson's The New Poetry; edited The Champion Magazine (a monthly survey of Negro achievement, 1916-
1917?); edited The Favorite Magazine (The World's Greatest
Monthly)[1]; had his plays produced at the Pekin Theatre in Chicago when he was 19;[2] wrote the words for the song "The Banjo
Player" by Abraham Wolk Bender. He has been called "one of
the first Negro revolutionary poets."[3]
NON-FICTION
For the Highest Good. Chicago: The Favorite Magazine,
1920.
POETRY
A Little Dreaming. Chicago: The Peterson Linotyping Co.,
1913; reprint ed., Washington, D.C.: McGrath, 1969*.
Songs of the Soil. New York: By the Author, 1916; reprint
ed., New York: McGrath, 1969*.
Visions of the Dark. New York: By the Author, 1915; fac-
simile ed., Freeport, N.Y.: Books for Libraries*.
(Anthologies): Adoff, The Poetry of Black America; Baker,
Black Literature in America; Blanden, The Chicago An-
thology; Bontemps, American Negro Poetry; Bontemps,
Golden Slippers; Braithwaite, Victory; Braithwaite, An Anthology of Magazine Verse; Brown, Davis and Lee, The

Negro Caravan; Calverton, An Anthology of American Ne-
gro Literature; Chambers and Moon, Right On!; Crawford,
and O'Neil, Today's Poetry; Cullen, Caroling Dusk;
Eleazer, Singers in the Dawn; Hayden, Kaleidoscope;
Hughes and Bontemps, The Poetry of the Negro: 1746-
1970; Johnson, The Book of American Negro Poetry; Ker-
lin, Negro Poets and Their Poems; Kreymborg, Others;
Lomax and Abdul, 3000 Years of Black Poetry; Long and
Collier, Afro-American Writing; Miller, Blackamerican
Literature; Watkins and David, To Be a Black Woman;
White and Jackson, An Anthology of Verse by American
Negroes; Wood, Poets of America.
(Periodicals): Crisis 5 (1913): 240; 7 (1913): 91; 34 (1927):
265; 35 (1928): 14. Also published in The Favorite Mag-
azine; The Liberator; Poetry, A Magazine of Verse.
SHORT STORIES
Tales of Darkest America. Chicago: The Favorite Magazine,
1920; facsimile ed., Freeport, N.Y.: Books for Li-
braries*.
(Periodicals): Crisis 4 (1912): 188; 6 (1913): 292; 13
(1917): 169.
BIOGRAPHY AND CRITICISM ON JOHNSON
Brawley. Negro Genius, pp. 237-248.
Brown. Negro Poetry and Drama, pp. 347-348.
Gloster. Negro Voices in American Fiction, pp. 118, 122-
123.
Kerlin. Negro Poets and Their Poems, pp. 99-104.
Redding. To Make a Poet Black, pp. 86-88.
Wagner. Black Poets of the United States, pp. 172, 179-
183.
White and Jackson. An Anthology of Verse by American Ne-
groes, pp. 160, 224-225.
REVIEWS
A Little Dreaming.
Crisis 7 (1914): 301.
Visions of the Dusk.
Crisis 12 (1916): 69.
[1]Newman Ivey White and Walter Clinton Jackson, An
Anthology of Verse by American Negroes (Durham, N.C.:
Moore, 1968), p. 160.
[2]Countée Cullen, Caroling Dusk (New York: Harper,
1927), pp. 61-62.
[3]James Weldon Johnson, The Book of American Negro
Poetry (New York: Harcourt, Brace & World, 1959), p.
140.

JOHNSON, Frank Arthur.
POETRY Fireside Poems, 1931; rev. memorial ed., edited
by Sarah L. Johnson Swint. New York: Swint's Studio,
1953.

JOHNSON, Fred. Born 1940 in Philadelphia.
POETRY (Anthology): Adoff, The Poetry of Black America.

JOHNSON, Georgia Douglas. Born 10 September 1886 in Atlanta,
Georgia. Died 1966. Education: Atlanta University; Oberlin
Conservatory of Music. Career: Listed as housewife-writer
in the Who's Who of Colored America, 1932, but she also
taught and worked for the government.[1] Her home in Washington, D.C., was a center for Negro literary gatherings.[2] The
Schomburg Collection Catalog indicates that she wrote the words
for the song, "I Want to Die While You Love Me" (music by
Harry T. Burleigh). Member: League of Neighbors; League
for Abolition of Capital Punishment. Awards, Honors: Plumes
was chosen by Opportunity magazine as the best play in the
1927 contest.
DRAMA
    Blue Blood. New York: Appleton, 1927; also in Shay, Frank.
        Fifty More Contemporary One Act Plays, 1928.
    Frederick Douglass. In Richardson and Miller, Negro His-
        tory in Thirteen Plays.
    Plumes: Folk Tragedy. New York: French, 1927; also in
        Calverton, Anthology of American Negro Literature, pp.
        147-156; Locke and Gregory, Plays of Negro Life.
    William and Ellen Craft. In Richardson and Miller, Negro
        History in Thirteen Plays.
    A Sunday Morning in the South: A One-Act Play. Washing-
        ton, n.p., 1924?
POETRY
    An Autumn Love Cycle. Introduction by Alain Locke. New
        York: H. Vinal, 1928; New York: Neal, 1938; facsimile of
        1928 ed., Freeport, N.Y.: Books for Libraries*.
    Bronze. Introduction by W. E. B. Du Bois. Boston: B.J.
        Brimmer, 1922; facsimile ed., Freeport, N.Y.: Books for
        Libraries*.
    The Heart of a Woman and Other Poems. Introduction by
        William Stanley Braithwaite. Boston: Cornhill, 1918; fac-
        simile ed., Freeport, N.Y.: Books for Libraries*.
    Share My World: A Book of Poems. Washington, D.C.: By
        the Author, 1962.
    (Anthologies): Adoff, The Poetry of Black America; Bon-
        temps, American Negro Poetry; Bontemps, Golden Slippers;
        Braithwaite, Anthology of Magazine Verse for 1926; Brown,
        Davis and Lee, The Negro Caravan; Byars, Black and
        White; Calverton, An Anthology of American Negro Litera-
        ture; Cullen, Caroling Dusk; Eleazer, Singers in the Dawn;
        Hayden, Kaleidoscope; Hughes and Bontemps, The Poetry
        of the Negro: 1746-1970; Kerlin, The Voice of the Negro;
        Johnson, The Book of American Negro Poetry; Johnson,
        Ebony and Topaz; Lomax and Abdul, 3000 Years of Black
        Poetry; Locke, The New Negro; Marcus, An Anthology of
        Revolutionary Poetry; Murphy, Ebony Rhythm; Patterson,
        A Rock Against the Wind; White and Jackson, An Anthol-
        ogy of Verse by American Negroes.
    (Periodicals): Mrs. Johnson's poems appeared in The Crisis
        almost every year between 1916 and 1937. For specific
        poems and dates, see Yellin, "An Index of Literary Ma-

terials in The Crisis, 1910-1934: Articles, Belles Lettres, and Book Reviews." Poems were also published in
the years 1935 and 1937.   Other periodicals: Palms, October 1926; Phylon, Second Quarter 1942; Second Quarter
1944; Third Quarter 1948; Third Quarter, Fourth Quarter
1953; First Quarter, Fourth Quarter 1954; First Quarter
1955; Second Quarter, Fourth Quarter 1956; Second Quar-
ter, Fourth Quarter 1958; Voice of the Negro, June 1905;
Voices, Winter 1950.   Poems were also published in The
Liberator and The Worker's Monthly; Journal of Negro
Life.
BIOGRAPHY AND CRITICISM ON JOHNSON
Brawley.   The Negro Genius, pp. 219-220.
_____.   The Negro in Literature and Art, pp. 112-113.
Davis.   The American Negro Reference Book, p. 858.
Dover, C.   "The Importance of Georgia Douglas Johnson."
    Crisis 59 (December 1952): 633-36.
Ebony 4 (February 1949): 41.
Journal of Negro History 51 (July 1966): 237.
Kerlin.   Negro Poets and Their Poems, p. 341.
Mays.   The Negro's God, pp. 184, 226.
Opportunity 5 (July 1927): 204.
Ploski and Kaiser.   The Negro Almanac 2nd ed. , p. 683.
White and Jackson.   An Anthology of Verse by American Ne-
    groes, p. 225.
Who's Who of Colored America, 1932, p. 240.
REVIEWS
An Autumn Love Cycle.
    Bonner, Marita Odette.   Opportunity 7 (April 1929): 130.
    Spencer, Anne.   Crisis 36 (1929): 87.
Bronze: A Book of Verse.
    Locke, Alain.   Crisis 25 (1923): 161.
    Newsome, Effie Lee.   Opportunity 1 (December 1923): 377.
    [1]Harry Ploski and Ernest Kaiser, The Negro Almanac,
2nd ed. (New York: Bellwether, 1971), p. 683.
    [2]James Weldon Johnson, The Book of American Negro
Poetry (New York: Harcourt Brace and World, 1959), p.
181.

JOHNSON, Hall.   Born 12 March 1888 in Athens, Georgia.   Died
    1970.   Education: Atlanta University; Allen University; B. Mus.,
    University of Pennsylvania, 1910; Hahn School of Music; D. Mus.,
    Institute of Musical Art, 1934.   Career: Moved to New York
    in 1914 and played in many orchestras.   Founded the Hall John-
    son Negro Choir in 1925.   Arranged and helped direct the mu-
    sic for Green Pastures, 1930.   Wrote the book and music for
    his own show, Run, Little Chillun!, which opened in 1933.
    Moved to Hollywood in 1935 to make film version of Green Pas-
    tures, and to do the arranging and composing for many other
    plays.[1]   Awards, Honors: Harmon Award, 1931.
    DRAMA
    Run, Little Chillun!, 1933.[2]

BIOGRAPHY AND CRITICISM ON JOHNSON
Abramson. Negro Playwrights in the American Theater, pp.
    49-54.
Hobson, C. "Hall Johnson: Preserver of the Negro Spiritu-
    al." Crisis 73 (November 1966): 480-485.
Hughes and Meltzer. Black Magic, pp. 103, 120, 126, 128,
    134, 135, 223.
Robinson. Historical Negro Biographies, p. 211.
REVIEW
    Run, Little Chillun!
    Carmer, Carl. Opportunity 11 (April 1933): 103.

JOHNSON, Helen Aurelia see COLLINS, Helen Johnson

JOHNSON, Helene. Born 1907 in Boston.
POETRY
    (Anthologies): Adams, Conn and Slepian, Afro-American Lit-
        erature: Poetry; Adoff, The Poetry of Black America;
        Bontemps, American Negro Poetry; Bontemps, Golden
        Slippers; Braithwaite, Anthology of American Verse; Cul-
        len, Caroling Dusk; Hughes and Bontemps, Poetry of the
        Negro: 1746-1970; Locke, The New Negro; Patterson,
        A Rock Against the Wind.
    (Periodicals): Palms, October 1926; also published in Op-
        portunity, Vanity Fair and The Literary Digest.

JOHNSON, Henry Theodore. Born 1857. Died 1910.
NON-FICTION
    (See additional items in The National Union Catalog, Pre-
        1956 Imprints.)
    How to Get On. A Series of Practical Essays for Young and
        Old. Philadelphia: H. J. Greer, 189?
    Johnson's Gems, Consisting of Brief Essays and Disserta-
        tions on Literary, Ethical, Religious and Current Topics.
        n.p., 1901.
    Pulpit, Pew and Pastorate. n.p., 1902. (Lectures prepared
        for students at Phelps Hall Bible Training School, an in-
        stitution connected with Tuskegee Institute.
    Tuskegee Talks. Philadelphia: Press of International Print-
        ing Co., 1902.
POETRY
    Wings of Ebony. Philadelphia: AME Book Concern, 1904.
TALE
    Sinbad the Sailor, An Old Tale Retold. London: n.p., 1899.

JOHNSON, Herbert Clark. Born 1911 in Mattoax, Amelia County,
    Virginia.
POETRY
    Poems from Flat Creek. n.p., n.p., 1943.
    (Anthology): Hughes and Bontemps, The Poetry of the Negro:
        1746-1970.
    (Periodicals): Black World, September 1972; Opportunity,
        August 1939; November 1940.

JOHNSON, Herschell. Born 1948 in Birmingham, Alabama.
POETRY (Anthologies): Coombs, We Speak as Liberators;
Patterson, A Rock Against the Wind.

JOHNSON, Homer Preston.
POETRY With John Robert Jackson and Robert Milum Baker.
Twilight Dreams. New York: Exposition, 1950.

JOHNSON, Hugh G.
POETRY Poems. New York: Comet, 1961.

JOHNSON, James Weldon. Born 17 June 1871 in Jacksonville, Fla.
Died 26 June 1938. Education: A.B. Atlanta University, 1894;
A.M. Atlanta, 1904. He attended Columbia University for three
years; received a Litt.D. degree from Talledega College, Alabama, 1917; attended Howard University, 1923.[1] Career: "Although he was principal of a colored high school at Jacksonville
for several years, and was admitted to the Florida bar which
enabled him to practice law until 1901,[2]..." he finally followed
his strongest propensity and turned author.[3] In 1901, he moved
to New York and collaborated with his brother, J. Rosamond
Johnson, to write light opera for the stage.[4] Combining their
talents, the two brothers wrote Toloso, a satirical comic opera
on the United States imperialism in the Spanish American War.
After spending two summers in New York, James decided to
make his fortune in Tin-Pan-Alley. Together with Bob Cole,
the Johnson brothers produced a steady flow of hit songs: "The
Maiden With the Dreamy Eyes," "My Castle on the Nile," "Under the Bamboo Tree," the "Congo Love Song," and many others.[5]
    In 1906, James began a diplomatic career as an appointed
Consular at Puerto Cabella, Venezuela; in 1909, he was transferred as Consular to Corinto, Nicaragua; in 1912, he was sent
to the Azores. After leaving the Consulate, he joined the
NAACP and became the national secretary from 1916 to 1930.[6]
    At the end of 1930, he resigned as general secretary to
NAACP and accepted the Adam K. Spense chair of Creative Literature at Fisk University. The last few years of his life were
devoted to writing, teaching, and lecturing at Fisk and at New
York University.[7]
    As a writer who had mastered the Spanish language, he trans-
lated the Spanish grand opera, Goyescas into English. The Opera was produced by the Metropolitan Company in 1915.[8] Johnson was also an editorial writer. In fact, he won an editorial
contest conducted by the Philadelphia Public Ledger in 1915.
He was a contributing editor to the New York Age and to various other magazines. Many of his articles were published in
the Encyclopaedia Britannica.[9] His poetry, too, appeared in
such magazines as Century, Independent, and the Crisis.[10]
    He completed his first novel, The Autobiography of an Ex-
Colored Man in 1912; from that time forward he continued to
write books of poetry, Negro spirituals, a history of Black
Manhattan, and an autobiography--his final assessment of the

American racial system. [11]
Of national importance to all Black people, is his "Lift Every Voice and Sing," the "Negro National Hymn--copyrighted, 1900." [12] Teachers taught the words to their students, and typed copies appeared in hymn books throughout the Black nation. Today, it "has become the most widely used song ever composed by a Negro; it is the Negro National Hymn." [13] Johnson was killed in a grade crossing accident, June 26, 1938, while vacationing in Maine. [14]

EDITOR
  The Book of American Negro Poetry. New York: Harcourt
      Brace, 1931.
  The Book of American Negro Spirituals. New York: Viking,
      1940.
  The Second Book of Negro Spirituals. New York: Viking,
      1940.
NON-FICTION
  Along This Way. New York: Viking, 1933*†. (Autobiogra-
      phy.)
  Black Manhattan. New York: Knopf, 1930; reprint ed. , New
      York: Arno*; New York: Atheneum†.
  The Larger Success. Hampton, Va. : Hampton Institute,
      1923. (Commencement Address.)
  Lynching, America's National Disgrace. New York: Nation-
      al Association for the Advancement of Colored People,
      1924.
  Native African Races and Culture. Charlottesville, Va. :
      The Trustees of the John F. Slater Fund. Occasional Pa-
      pers No. 25, 1927.
  Negro Americans, What Now? New York: Viking 1934; re-
      print ed. , New York: Da Capo*.
  Saint Peter Relates an Incident of the Resurrection Day.
      New York: Viking, 1930, 1935.
  Self-determining Haiti. New York: The Nation, 1920.
  (Anthologies): Locke, The New Negro; Long and Collier,
      Afro-American Writing.
  (Periodicals): Century 115 (November 1927-April 1928): 65;
      Survey Graphic 6 (March 1925): 635.
NOVEL
  Autobiography of an Ex-Colored Man. Boston: Sherman,
      French, 1912; New York: Knopf, 1927*; New York: Hill
      & Wang, 1960†. Serialized in Half-Century, November
      1919-December 1920. Excerpts in Davis and Redding,
      Cavalcade; Kendricks and Levitt, Afro-American Voices;
      Patterson, An Introduction to Black American Literature.
POETRY
  Fifty Years and Other Poems. New York: Cornhill, 1917.
  God's Trombones, Seven Negro Sermons in Verse. New
      York: Viking, 1927*†.
  St. Peter Relates an Incident: Selected Poems. New York:
      Viking, 1935.
  (Anthologies): Adoff, I Am the Darker Brother; Adoff, The
      Poetry of Black America; Baker, Black Literature in

America; Bontemps, American Negro Poetry; Bontemps,
Golden Slippers; Brawley, The Negro Genius; Brown, Dav-
is and Lee, The Negro Caravan; Calverton, An Anthology
of American Negro Literature; Davis and Redding, Caval-
cade; Eastman, The Norton Anthology of Poetry; Eleazer,
Singers in the Dawn; Ellman and O'Clair, The Norton An-
thology of Modern Poetry; Emanuel and Gross, Dark Sym-
phony; Faderman and Bradshaw, Speaking for Ourselves;
Ford, Black Insights; Hayden, Kaleidoscope; Henderson,
Understanding the New Black Poetry; Hughes and Bontemps,
Poetry of the Negro, 1746-1970; Johnson, The Book of
American Negro Poetry; Jordan, Soulscript; Kearns, Black
Identity; Kerlin, Negro Poets and Their Poems; Lomax
and Abdul, 3000 Years of Black Poetry; Long and Collier,
Afro-American Writing; Marcus, An Anthology of Revolu-
tionary Poetry; Margolies, A Native Sons Reader; Miller,
Blackamerican Literature; Patterson, A Rock Against the
Wind; Randall, The Black Poets; Walrond and Pool, Black
and Unknown Bards; Watkins, An Anthology of American
Negro Literature.
(Periodicals): Century 106 (May-October 1923): 716; Crisis 5
   (1913): 172; 9 (1915): 239; 10 (1915): 172; 11 (1916): 199;
   15 (1917): 13; 77 (November 1970): 364, 365; 78 (June
   1971): 136-137, 138-139. Negro Digest 9 (January 1951):
   18; New York Times, 1 January 1913; Phylon, 32 (Winter
   1971): 374-382.

SPIRITUALS AND SONGS
   With J. Rosamund Johnson. Lift Every Voice and Sing.
   New York: E. B. Marks, 1921; New York: Hawthorn,
   1970*.

BIOGRAPHY AND CRITICISM ON JOHNSON
   Abramson, Doris E.   "It'll Be Me." In Chametzky and Kap-
      lan, Black and White in American Culture, pp. 380-390.
   Adams, Russell. Great Negroes Past and Present, pp. 107,
      147, 155, 159.
   Amann, Clarence A. "Three Negro Classics--An Estimate."
      Negro American Literature Forum 4 (Winter 1970): 113.
   Anon. "James W. Johnson." (Men of the Month Column)
      Crisis 5 (1913): 171.
   Anon. "The New Secretary of NAACP." Crisis 12 (1920):
      68.
   Bacote, C. A. "James Weldon Johnson and Atlanta Univer-
      sity." Phylon 32 (Winter 1971): 333-343.
   Baker, H. A. "Forgotten Prototype." Virginia Quarterly
      49 (Summer 1973): 433-449.
   Bardolph. The Negro Vanguard, pp. 180, 186, 188, 202-
      203, 206-208, 236, 295.
   Bartlett, Robert M. They Dared to Live. New York: As-
      sociation, 1937, pp. 42-46.
   Barton, Rebecca Chalmers. Witness for Freedom, pp. 221-
      237.
   Bell, Bernard W. "Contemporary Afro-American Poetry as
      Folk Art." Black World 22 (March 1973): 16-26, 74-83.

Bergman. The Chronological History of the Negro in America. Years: 1878, 1895, 1924, 1916, 1926, 1925, 1920, 1923, 1900, 1912, 1913, 1917, 1927, 1934.

Bond, The Negro and the Drama, pp. 39-41.

Bontemps. The Harlem Renaissance Remembered, pp. 11, 21-22, 25, 29, 35, 43-44, 47, 91, 178, 213, 224, 228-229, 231, 233, 236, 245, 247.

"A Brief Biography." Crisis 78 (June 1971): 113.

Butcher, Margaret Just. The Negro in American Culture, pp. 33, 56, 72, 84, 100-103, 197, 218.

Carroll, R.A. "Black Racial Spirit: An Analysis of James Weldon Johnson's Critical Perspective." Phylon 32 (Winter 1971): 344-364.

Collier, Eugenia. "Endless Journey of an Ex-Colored Man." Phylon 32 (Winter 1971): 365-373.

_____. "James Weldon Johnson: Mirror of Change." Phylon 21 (Winter 1960): 351-359.

Copeland, George Edward. "James Weldon Johnson: A Bibliography." Masters Thesis, Pratt Institute, 1951.

Cruse, Harold. The Crisis of the Negro Intellectual, pp. 33-38.

Current, G.B. "James Weldon Johnson--Freedom Fighter." Crisis 78 (June 1971): 116-118.

Dreer. American Literature by Negro Authors, pp. 36-37.

Du Bois, W.E.B. "James Weldon Johnson." Journal of Negro History 52 (April 1967): 128-145; 52 (July 1967): 224-227.

"Editorials on the Death of James Weldon Johnson." Crisis 78 (June 1971): 14-141.

Eppse. The Negro, Too, in American History, pp. 377-379.

Fleming, Robert E. "Contemporary Themes in Johnson's Autobiography of an Ex-Colored Man." Negro American Literature Forum 4 (1970): 120-124, 141.

Garrett, M.P. "Early Recollections of and Structural Irony in The Autobiography of an Ex-Colored Man." Critique 13 (1971): 5-14.

Huggins. Harlem Renaissance, pp. 5, 152-153, 156, 196, 209-210.

_____. "Irony as a Key to Johnson's The Autobiography of an Ex-Colored Man." American Literature 43 (March 1971): 83-96.

Isaacs, Harold R. The New World of Negro Americans. London: Phoenix House, 1963, pp. 82, 138, 232, 339-340.

Jackson, Miles, Jr. "James Weldon Johnson." Black World (June 1970): 55-56.

_____. "Letters to a Friend: Correspondence from James Weldon Johnson to George A. Towns." Phylon 29 (Summer 1968): 182-198.

_____. "Literary History: Documentary Sidelights--James Weldon Johnson and Claude McKay." Negro Digest 17 (June 1968): 25-29.

Jahn. Neo-African Literature, pp. 164, 183, 189, 192, 197, 198, 207, 209-212, 217.
Johnson, J. W. Black Manhattan, pp. 240-243, 266, 273.
Kent, George E. "Patterns of the Renaissance." Black World 21 (June 1972): 13.
Kerlin. Negro Poets and Their Poems, pp. 90-95.
Killens, John O. "Another Time When Black Was Beautiful." Black World 20 (November 1970): 20-36.
Larson, Charles R. "African Afro-American Literary Relationship." Negro Digest 19 (December 1969): 35-42.
Logan, R. W. "James Weldon Johnson and Haiti." Phylon 32 (Winter 1971): 396.
Loggins. The Negro Author, pp. 360, 369-373.
Lotz, Phillip Henry, ed. Rising Above Color. New York: Association. 1935, pp. 16-24.
"Mrs. James Weldon Johnson Discusses Her Husband." New York Times, 12 October 1971, p. 48.
Mitchell. Black Drama, pp. 25, 40-47, 63, 69, 186.
Nall, Torney Otto. Youth's Work in the New World. New York: Association, 1935, pp. 16-24.
Opportunity 2 (November 1924): 330; 5 (January 1927): 21; 6 (February 1928): 46-47; 8 (August 1930): 250; 9 (May 1931); 12 (January 1934): 29; 16 (August 1948): 228; 17 (June 1939): 183; 18 (February 1940): 38-40; 22 (Winter 1944): 26.
Ottley. The Negro in New York, pp. 124, 157, 159, 164, 197, 199, 255, 257, 261, 289.
Redding, Saunders. "The Problems of the Negro Writer." In Chametzky and Kaplan, Black and White in American Culture, pp. 360-371.
Ringel, Frederick J. America as Americans. New York: Harcourt Brace, 1932, pp. 160-165.
Robinson. Historical Negro Biographies, pp. 213-214.
Rollins. They Showed the Way, pp. 88-90.
Smith, Bernard. The Democratic Spirit. New York: Knopf, 1941, pp. 688-689.
Stone, Irving and Richard Kennedy, eds. We Speak for Ourselves. New York: Doubleday, 1950, pp. 274-279.
Tate, Ernest. "The Wit of James Weldon Johnson." Negro History Bulletin 25 (April 1962): 152-154.
Toppin. Biographical History of Blacks in America Since 1528, pp. 172, 336-368.
"Tributes to James Weldon Johnson." Crisis 78 (June 1971): 138-139.
Whalum, W. P. "James Weldon Johnson's Theories and Performance Practices of Afro-American Folksong." Phylon 32 (Winter 1971): 383-395.
Williams. They Also Spoke, pp. 73, 77, 122, 155, 198, 201, 213, 234, 245, 259, 260-261, 268.
Young. Black Writers of the Thirties, pp. 233, 237, 429-433, 149-151, 155-156.
    [1]A. N. Marquis, ed., Who Was Who in America (Chicago: Marquis Co. , 1943), p. 639.

Johnson, J.W. (cont.)   434

²Newman Ivey White and Walter Clinton Jackson, An Anthology of Verse by American Negros (Durham, N.C.: Moore, 1924), p. 171.
³Robert T. Kerlin, Negro Poets and Their Poems (Washington, D.C.: Associated Publishers, 1935), p. 90.
⁴White and Jackson, p. 171.
⁵Richard Barksdale and Keneth Kinnamon, Black Writers of America (New York: Macmillan, 1972), pp. 480-481.
⁶White and Jackson, p. 171.
⁷Barksdale and Kinnamon, p. 481.
⁸Marquis, p. 639.
⁹White and Jackson, p. 171.
¹⁰Marquis, p. 639.
¹¹Barksdale and Kinnamon, pp. 481-82.
¹²"Negro National Hymn," Negro Heritage 1 (1961): 9.
¹³Ibid.
¹⁴Barksdale and Kinnamon, p. 482.

JOHNSON, Jessie Davis.
POETRY Christmas Poems. Washington, D.C.: By the Author, 1937.

JOHNSON, Jesse J. Born 15 May 1914 in Hattiesburg, Mississippi. Education: A.B., Tougaloo College, 1939; LL.B., American Extension School of Law, 1949; M.A., Hampton Institute, 1963. Currently living in Hampton, Virginia. Career: Served with CCC camps in Michigan in the early forties; entered the Army as a private in 1942, retiring in 1962 with the rank of lieutenant colonel. Presently studying (U.S. Army Military Extension courses) and working on books about Blacks in the U.S. military service. Member: Authors Guild, Inc.
AUTOBIOGRAPHICAL NOVEL
Ebony Brass: An Autobiography of Negro Frustration Amid Aspiration. New York: William-Frederick Press, 1967.
EDITOR
The Black Soldier: Documented (1619-1815). Hampton, Va.: Author, Hampton Institute, 1971.
A Pictorial History of Black Servicemen: Air Force, Army, Navy, Marines. Hampton, Va.: By the Author, Hampton Institute, 1970.
A Pictorial History of Black Soldiers: 1619-1969. Hampton, Va.: By the Author, Hampton Institute, 1970.
INTERJECTIONS
Johnson writes "to inspire the young, to encourage the middle aged and to inform the old; and to help cultivate better race relations through better history."

JOHNSON, Joe. Born 1940 in Harlem. Education: B.A., Columbia University; M.A., Teachers College, Columbia University. Currently living in Ramapo, New Jersey. Career: Director of Tutorial Centers, Harlem Education Project, 1962-63; Instructor, Department of Special Programs, City College of New York, 1971-72; Instructor, Department of American Studies,

1971-72 and Assistant Professor, Department of American Studies, Ramapo College of New Jersey, 1972 to present.   Co-Editor, Umbra Magazine; Interviewer, Radio-Television France; Reporter, Harlem Daily and Newark Advance; Corresponding Editor, Dues: Anthology of Earth Writing. Has given poetry read-
ings at numerous colleges and universities, for church and civ-
ic organizations, at Arts festivals and on radio stations WBAI
and WPAT. Member: Modern Language Association; Linguistic
Society of America. Awards, Honors: Dean's List, Columbia
University; French Honors, Columbia University; Bertha Baer
Academic Scholarship, Columbia University.
NON-FICTION
   Interview with William Demby. Black Creation, Spring 1972.
NOVEL EXCERPT
   "Searchin'." Black Creation, Fall 1971.
POETRY
   (Anthologies): Adoff, The Poetry of Black America; Ameri-
      can Black Poetry (Mondodori-Milan, Italy); Gross, Open
      Poetry; Lowenfels, In Time of Revolution; Lowenfels,
      Poets of Today; Welburn, Dues.
   (Periodicals): Liberator; Umbra.
SHORT STORY
   (Anthologies): Reed, Yardbird Reader I; Welburn, Dues.
   (Periodicals): Black Creation, Winter 1972.

JOHNSON, Leanna F.
POETRY (Anthology): Murphy, Ebony Rhythm.

JOHNSON, Mae Smith. Born 1890 in Alexandria, Virginia. Career:
Secretary at the Good Samaritan Orphanage, Newark, New Jer-
sey.
POETRY
   (Anthology): Kerlin, Negro Poets and Their Poems.
   (Periodical): Crisis 38 (1931): 342.

JOHNSON, Maggie Pogue.
POETRY
   Virginia Dreams: Lyrics for an Idle Hour. Tales of the
      Time Told in Rhyme. n. p., 1910.
   Thoughts for Idle Hours. Roanoke, Va.: Stone Printing &
      Mfg. Co., 1915.

JOHNSON, Matthew.
POETRY (Periodical): Black World, December 1973.

JOHNSON, Randall.
POETRY (Periodical): Black World, August 1973.

JOHNSON, Ray.
POETRY (Anthology): Jones and Neal, Black Fire.

JOHNSON, Ruth Brownlee.
POETRY

(Anthology): Murphy, Ebony Rhythm.
(Pamphlet): Life, Lore, Love. n.p., n.d.

JOHNSON, Samuel M. Born 27 July 1899 in Richmond, Virginia.
Currently living in Brooklyn, New York. Career: A retired
Civil Service Clerk. Awards, Honors: Received six medals
and Battle Stars in World War II.
TALES
    Often Back: The Tales of Harlem. New York: Vantage,
    1971.

JOHNSON, William Matthews. Born 5 May 1905 in Greenville, Texas. Education: Studied at the University of Wisconsin-Madison,
1929-35; took special classes in creative writing, literature and
drama at Indiana University, 1939-40, 1946. Currently living
in Indianapolis, Indiana. Career: "I came to writing rather
late in life, 34 years of age, principally as a rebound from the
wreck of efforts to prepare for a career in law, government
and commerce in Liberia, West Africa. In reality, though I
toyed with verse and short prose pieces, say, from the ages of
thirteen to seventeen, I was actually contemptuous of literary
aspirations, particularly versifying. As an aside, I intend to
try my hand again at verse before my strength ebbs away.
    "During the involvements in the two major aims in my life--
becoming a public figure, then a literary worker--I can hardly
say I have followed a vocation. Although I obviously had to re-
sort to some means of livelihood, my efforts have scarcely
meant more to me than that. In the quest for sustenance, I
have worked at all the jobs available in domestic, commercial,
and industrial activities. For five years from 1937 to 1942, I
had a stint as a Recreation Center Director, and from 1942,
until my retirement in 1972, another as a federal civil servant,
with the Defense and later Post Office departments." Presently a free lance writer. Member: Second Christian Church;
Knights of Pythias Lodge; Federated Associated Clubs; The C.
T. Amos Music Study Group. Awards, Honors: Frankenberger
Literary Medal, University of Wisconsin, 1934; Distinguished
Novel, Indiana University Writers' Conference Award, 1968.
NON-FICTION
    "Travel Notes by a Black American Author on Liberia, West
    Africa." Nonaligned Third World Annual 1970. St. Louis,
    Mo.: DHTE International, 1970.
NOVEL
    The House on Corbet Street. New York: William-Frederick
    Press, 1967.
SHORT STORY
    (Periodical): Index Magazine (Indiana University, 1949).
WORK IN PROGRESS
    A play dealing with riots.
INTERJECTIONS
    "Literary creation, to me, is a means of purging one's soul
of impulsive longings and desires; for through it the creator can
achieve a vaster communion with nature and man. The immen-

sity and awesomeness of the universe inspire a mighty incentive for artistic expression. Of the majesties of the universe, man and his nature constitute not the least of them. So, if an artist, through speech, letters, or tools can capture the most minute degree of these qualities, he has achieved a God's plenty of universal inspiration. Let none disdain any being as too low, too mean to exemplify the essential nobleness of mankind."

JOHNSON, Yvette.
POETRY (Periodical): Negro American Literature Forum, Spring 1972.

JOHNSTON, Gary.
POETRY Blind Beggar's Blues. New York: Amuru, 1973†.

JOHNSTON, Percy. Born 18 May 1930 in New York City. Education: A.B., Howard University; M.A., Montclair State College, 1968; additional study at the studio of Claire Heywood (painting and drawing); the studio of David Allentuck (serigraph); the studio of Arnold Eagle (film-making); Saint Peters College; Long Island University; New School of Social Research. Career: Teaching fellow, Howard University, 1960-61; faculty member, Montclair State College, 1968 to present; Adjunct Professor, Essex County College, 1968-69; Editor and Founder, Dasein: Aesthetics, Literature and Philosophy, 1961 to present.
DRAMA
Dawitt II. New York: Rinjohn Productions, 1973.
Emperor Dessalines. New York: Rinjohn Productions, 1973.
John Adams, A Historical Drama, Parts I and II. New York: Rinjohn Productions, 1972.
EDITOR
A Dictionary of Elizabethan English: The Anglo Saxon Language as Spoken and Written During the Tudor, Elizabethan and Jacobean Periods. New York: New Merry Mount Press, 1973.
NON-FICTION
Afro American Philosophies: Selected Readings from Jupiter Hammon to Eugene C. Holmes. Upper Montclair, N.J.: Montclair State College Press, 1970.
Phenomenology of Negritude. New York: New Merry Mount Press, 1973.
POETRY
Concerto for Girl & Convertible. Washington, D.C.: DJH Press, 1961.
'Round 'Bout Midnight. New York: DJH Press, 1973.
Sean Pendragon Requiem: In Memoriam JFK. Appreciatory Note by Robert F. Kennedy. New York: DJH Press, 1964.
(Anthologies): Breman, Sixes and Sevens; Burning Spear; Davis and Redding, Cavalcade; Henderson, Understanding the New Black Poetry; Pool, Beyond the Blues; Lowenfels, In a Time of Revolution.

(Periodicals): Dasein; Présence Africaine, No. 57.
INTERJECTIONS
"Art has only one synonym in English: 'Work!' "

JONES, Alice H.
POETRY
(Anthologies): Coombs, We Speak as Liberators; Patterson,
A Rock Against the Wind.
(Periodical): Negro Digest, September-October, 1968.

JONES, Cornelia.
POETRY (Periodical): Journal of Black Poetry, Summer 1972.

JONES, E. H. Born 8 July 1925 in Holmes County, Lexington, Mississippi. Education: two years of college; on-the-job training;
special schools (secretarial); home study. Currently living in
Washington, D.C. Career: A generalist in business management and technical writing. Presently Special Assistant to Pro-
ject Director of a Comprehensive Neighborhood Health Center,
a position involving speech-writing, preparing reports and other
special projects. Member: Chairman, Commission on Ecu-
menical affairs, Asbury United Methodist Church; Chairman,
Downtown Cluster of Congregations.
DRAMA
Our Very Best Christmas.
POETRY
A Pleasant Encounter and Other Poems. New York: Vantage
1964.
(Periodical): The Washington Afro-American Newspaper, 13
April 1968.
UNPUBLISHED WORK
Novel: "Manifest Destiny."
INTERJECTIONS
"It is my observation that people waste too much energy on
prejudices, hatred, jealousy and deception. If that wasted en-
ergy could be directed towards love, helping or encouraging
others what a great 'together' world this would be. I believe
that all men are brothers under God; with that in mind, and a
true spirit of brotherhood in your heart, there is a freedom
within that is worthy of experiencing and sharing with others.
'A Pleasant Encounter' reflects love in at least two dimensions
--depending upon the state of the mind of the reader. It de-
fined for its author, the dimensions of love sought by here, that
which makes one truly a part of the universe, open to sharing
and forthrightness, and a love far deeper than that manifested
in biological attraction between two persons--which was one dimension in many of the poems. If the reader, however,
probes deeper, he sees the second dimension--which one can
only feel and can never in this world touch."

JONES, Edward Smyth. Born 1881. Education: Harvard University.
See his poem "Cell No. 40, East Cambridge Jail, Cambridge,
Massachusetts, July 26, 1910," which tells how he walked from

the South to New England, seeking a Harvard education.
POETRY
> The Rose That Bloometh in My Heart--and Other Poems.
> Louisville?: n.p., 1908.
> Souvenir Poem: Our Greater Louisville. Louisville? Ky.:
> 1908.
> The Sylvan Cabin: A Centenary Ode on the Birth of Lincoln,
> and Other Verse. Introduction by William Stanley Braith-
> waite. Boston: Sherman, French, 1911; Introduction from
> The New York Times, San Francisco: Taylor & Taylor,
> 1915.
> (Anthologies): Eleazer, Singers in the Dawn; Johnson, The
> Book of American Negro Poetry; Kerlin, Negro Poets and
> Their Poems.
BIOGRAPHY AND CRITICISM ON JONES
> Ebony (June 1953): 63.
> Kerlin. Negro Poets and Their Poems, pp. 163-169.

JONES, Gayl. Born 23 November 1949 in Lexington, Kentucky.
Education: B.A. (English), Connecticut College, 1971; M.A.
(Creative Writing), Brown University, 1973. Currently living
in Providence, Rhode Island. Career: Wrote several short-
length novels while completing an undergraduate degree and doing graduate work. Has also written a book-length poem called
"Chile Woman," which attempts to draw its overall structure
from folk tradition using the improvisational technique of jazz,
the blues-sermon motif. Awards, Honors: Connecticut College
award for best original poem, 1969 and 1970; Frances Steloff
Award for Fiction for "The Roundhouse" (see Panache, edited
by R. B. Frank); scholarship to 1971 Breadloaf Writer's Conference.
POETRY
> (Anthologies): Frank, Panache; Harper, Heartblow: Black
> Veils (forthcoming); Jordan, Soulscript; Welburn, Dues
> 1974; Williams and Harris, Amistad 2.
> (Periodicals): Essence, September 1970; Laureate, 1970;
> Silo, Winter 1969.
SHORT STORY
> (Periodicals): Essence, October 1970; November 1973.
INTERJECTIONS
"I believe that the oral tradition is not only as valid a way
of transmitting culture, but also as valid a source for the artist in terms of form and subject matter--in terms of an artistic tradition. I feel that it's not enough to simply 'encourpo-
rate' folk ways and forms in a structure that's essentially alien
or at counterpoints to that rhythm, vocabulary, world view of
the black community, but the black writer should look to the
oral tradition as a source for the overlying structure as well--
that is, use folk forms to present folk material--a creative expansion and synthesis of such forms as the sermon, blues,
jazz, etc. This would probably eliminate some of those problems of handling of folk material; and by using those forms
that are already at work within the community, be a means of

Gayl Jones (credit: Stevens Studios)

eliciting that same response to black letters, which black music, that never broke with our oral tradition, has. I also believe in authenticity in dialogue, that black writers should rely upon 'heard' sounds, all others being taken for literary formulas. I believe that any individual black consciousness and memory is able to hold within it not only all the language modes of our oral tradition, but also both the intimacies of relationships as well as the consequences of history. For the black man, his very life is a criticism of the society in which he lives--so that the black writer need not 'criticize,' he need only present life as it is. I would eventually like to teach writing technique as it relates specifically to the problems of the black writer."

JONES, Gene-Olivar.
DRAMA No Church Next Sunday.

JONES, Georgia Holloway.
POETRY (Anthology): Murphy, Ebony Rhythm.

JONES, Harold.
POETRY Broadway and Other Poems. n. p., n. d.

JONES, Howard. Born 1941 in New York City.
POETRY (Anthology): Major, The New Black Poetry.

JONES, J. McHenry. Born 30 August 1859 in Gallipolis, Ohio.
Died 1909. Education: Finished high school in 1882. Career:
Became an African Episcopal Methodist Minister, preaching in
small towns along the Ohio River. Began teaching near Pome-
roy, 1882. Became principal of the Lincoln School in Wheeling,
West Virginia, 1883. In 1895 he became a speaker on the
Chautauqua Circuit, and a state officer for the Grand United Or-
der of Odd Fellows. Became President of the West Virginia
Colored Institute in 1898.[1]
NOVEL
    Hearts of Gold: A Novel. Wheeling, W. Va.: Daily Intelli-
        gencer Steam Job Press, 1896; reprint ed., College Park,
        Md.: McGrath, 1969*.
BIOGRAPHY AND CRITICISM ON JONES
    Bone. The Negro Novel in America, pp. 18,32.
    Gloster. Negro Voices in American Fiction, pp. 31-32, 33,
        34, 56, 117.
        [1]Negro History Bulletin 4 (January 1942): 94.

JONES, James Arlington. Born 1936 in Newark, New Jersey.
POETRY
    (Anthology): Shuman, Nine Black Poets.
    (Periodicals): American Bard; Atlantic Monthly; Evergreen
        Review; The Massachusetts Review; Poetry.

JONES, John Hudson.
POETRY (Periodical): Harlem Quarterly, Fall-Winter 1950.

JONES, Joseph.
POETRY (Periodicals): Journal of Black Poetry, Summer
    1972; Negro Digest, August 1961.

JONES, Joshua Henry, Jr. Born 1876 in Orangeburg, South Carolina. Education: Brown University; Ohio State University; Yale
University. Career: Served on the editorial staffs of the Providence News; the Worcester Evening Post; Boston Daily Adver-
tiser; Boston Post; Boston Telegram.[1] Also served as secretary to Mayor James M. Curley of Boston, by whom he was appointed editor of the City Record.[2]
NOVEL
    By Sanction of the Law. Boston: B. J. Brimmer, 1924;
        reprint ed. College Park, Md.: McGrath, 1969*.
POETRY
    The Heart of the World and Other Poems. Boston: Stratford,
        1919.
    Poems of the Four Seas. Boston: Cornhill, 1921; reprint ed.,
        Freeport, N.Y.: Books for Libraries*.
    (Anthologies): Johnson, The Book of American Negro Poetry;
        Kerlin, Negro Poets and Their Poems.

BIOGRAPHY AND CRITICISM ON JONES
Gloster. Negro Voices in American Fiction, pp. 125-127.
Kerlin. Negro Poets and Their Poems, pp. 113-118.
REVIEW
By Sanction of Law.
Dill, A. G. Crisis 28 (1924): 218.
[1]Robert T. Kerlin, Negro Poets and Their Poems
(Washington, D.C.: Associated, 1923), p. 342.
[2]James Weldon Johnson, The Book of American Negro
Poetry (New York: Harcourt, Brace & World, 1959), p.
201.

JONES, Jymi.
POETRY
Guerrilla Warfare in Philly. Elkins Park, Md.: Uhuru Pub-
lications, 1970.
(Anthology): Kendricks, Afro-American Voices.

JONES, Maryer.
POETRY
(Periodical): Negro History Bulletin, October 1962.
BIOGRAPHY ON JONES
Negro History Bulletin 26 (October 1962): 57.

JONES, Oswald.
POETRY (Periodical): Black Dialogue.

JONES, Paulette.
POETRY
(Anthology): Brown, Lee and Ward, To Gwen with Love.
(Periodical): Journal of Black Poetry, Summer 1972.

JONES, Ralph H. Born 4 May 1906 in Philadelphia. Education:
A.B. degree (by legislative decree), Central High School, Philadelphia, 1927; B.S. in Education, Howard University, 1931; also attended University of Pennsylvania, Fels Institute, receiving
certification in Local and State Government; completed seven
courses offered by the F.B.I. Currently living in Philadelphia.
Career: Retired Sergeant of County Detectives, District Attorney's Office (pensioned 1965); General Superintendent, Tindley
Temple United Methodist Church School for 32 years; Director
of Publicity, National Youth Administration, 1935-37. Presently Executive Editor, Philadelphia Tribune; Commentator, Radio
Station WCAU; Cathedral Secretary, United Supreme Council,
Northern Jurisdiction, Ancient Accepted Scottish Rite of Free-
masonry (33rd degree Masons) and Editor of its official publica-
tion, "The Bulletin"; Secretary, Philadelphia Chapter, Howard
University Alumni; Director, Publicity, M. W. Prince Hall Grand
Lodge of Freemasons; Director, Publicity, Imperial Council,
Ancient Egyptian Arabic Order, Nobles of the Mystic Shrine.
Member: N.A.A.C.P., Supreme Council, A.A.S.R.; Member
at large, National Council, Boy Scouts of America to 1974.
Awards, Honors; Received Trophy and Cash Award, National

Ralph H. Jones

Newspaper Publishers Association (2nd Best Editorial, Nationwide, 1972; 3rd Best Editorial, Nationwide, 1973); Freedom
Foundation Medal and Check, Editorial on Freedom, 1952;
Award of Merit, M. W. Prince Hall Grand Lodge of Pennsylvania Free and Accepted Masons, for exceptional public relations service, 1973; Distinguished Service Award, DeMolay Con-
sistory No. 1 (32nd and 33rd Degrees Masons), 1966; Social
Action Award, Nu Sigma Chapter, Phi Beta Sigma, 1964. Wil-
kie Award for distinguished newspaper work, 1946.
NOVEL
      The Pepperpot Man.   New York: Vantage, 1965.

JONES, Robert.
      DRAMA Through Black and Back.

JONES, Roger.
      POETRY (Periodical): Journal of Black Poetry, Spring 1969.

JONES, Rosie Lee Logan see LOGAN, Rosie Lee

JONES, Silas. Born 17 January 1942 in Cynthiana, Kentucky.
      Education: a Theatre Arts major at Los Angeles City College,
      studying screen-writing. Currently living in Los Angeles,

California. Awards, Honors: The Gwendolyn Brooks Literary
Award for Fiction, 1972.
SHORT STORIES
     (Periodicals): Black World, January 1972; March 1973.
WORK IN PROGRESS
     A novel, "The Price of Dirt," and a collection of Black folk
          tales (as opposed to "modern" short stories), "Deliver Us
          from Evil."
INTERJECTIONS
     Mr. Jones is a separatist.

JONES, Tilford.
     POETRY (Anthology): Kerlin, Negro Poets and Their Poems.

JONES, Walter.
     DRAMA
          Dudder Lover, 1972.
          The Boston Party at Annie Mae's House, 1970.
          Fish n' Chips.
          Jazznite, 1968.
          Mae's House, 1970.
          Nigger Nightmare, 1969.
          Reverend Brown's Daughter, 1972.

JONES, Willa Saunders. Born 22 February 1904 in Little Rock,
     Arkansas. Education: Studied voice, piano and organ. Cur-
     rently living in Chicago. Career: Singer, pianist, organist
     for 18 years. Directed the thousand-voice choruses that sang
     at National Baptist Conventions in Chicago, Cleveland, Detroit,
     New York, California and Hot Springs.
     DRAMA
          The Birth of Christ.
          The Call to Arms.
          Just One Hour to Live--for the Dope Addict.
          The Life Boat.
          The Passion Play. (The 1973 Passion Play was the 44th
               annual production.)
          Up from Slavery.

JONES, William H.
     NOVEL The Triangle's End. New York: Exposition, 1954.

JONES, Yorke.[1] Born 1860. Career: Minister.
     NOVEL
          The Climbers: A Story of Sun-Kissed Sweethearts. Chi-
               cago: Glad Tidings, 1912.
     POETRY
          Gold and Incense. Fort Wayne, Ind. : Glad Tidings, 1925.
               [1]The Dictionary Catalog of the Schomburg Collection
          indicates that Jones is a "Negro author," but not an
          "American Negro author."

JOPLIN, Scott. Born 1868 in Texarkana, Texas. Died 1917. Education: Was taught piano, theory and musical history by an old German musician in his home town; continued his studies at George Smith College for Negroes at a much later date. Career: Began by playing piano in the towns and villages of the Mississippi Valley country, arriving at the Silver Dollar saloon in St. Louis in 1885; continued to play in St. Louis and Missouri until 1895 when he toured with his own group, the Texas Medley Quartette. Settled in Sedalia, Missouri, in 1896, playing at the Maple Leaf Club. His Original Rags were published in March 1899, and in that same year the Joplin-Stark partnership was formed: John Stark, the sheet music publisher, bought "Maple Leaf Rag" for 50 dollars and royalties. With the financial success of "Maple Leaf Rag," Joplin gave up playing piano and moved back to St. Louis where he taught music and composition. From 1906-09 he occasionally followed the vaudeville circuit, finally settling in New York City.[1] The last ten years of his life were devoted to the writing and producing of Treemonisha (considered to be "the first demonstrably great American opera") which he was forced to publish at his own expense in 1911. Unable to find a producer, he arranged for a one-night performance in a Harlem hall in 1915, but it failed to attract the financial backing necessary for a full-scale production.[3] By the time of his death, the "ragtime craze" had passed, and his young, Black "heirs" (J. Rosamond Johnson, Tim Brymn, Chris Smith) felt that ragtime music was "low class."[4] On March 29, 1917, a note appeared in the New York Age: "Scott Joplin, composer of the Maple Leaf Rag and other syncopated melodies, is a patient at Ward's Island for mental trouble."[5] Three days later the "King of Ragtime" was dead.

DRAMA
   Guest of Honor, a Ragtime Opera, 1903.[6]
   The Rag-Time Dance (folk ballet), 1903.
   Treemonisha (ragtime opera), 1911. In The Collected Works
      of Scott Joplin. New York: The New York Public Library,
      1971. (World premiere held in Atlanta, January 28 and
      29, 1972 under the direction of Robert Shaw, with Katherine Dunham as stage director.)

BIOGRAPHY AND CRITICISM ON JOPLIN
   Charters, Samuel B. and Leonard Kunstadt. Jazz: A History of the New York Scene. Garden City, N.Y.: Doubleday, 1962, pp. 42, 43-50, 56.
   de Lerma, Dominique-Rene, ed. Reflections on Afro-American Music. Kent, Ohio: Kent State University Press, 1973, pp. 22, 26, 74, 85, 178, 189, 197, 204, 206, 220, 257.
   Drimmer, Melvin. "Joplin's Treemonisha in Atlanta."
      Phylon 34 (June 1973): 197-202.
   Hentoff, Nat and Albert J. McCarthy, eds. Jazz. New York: Rinehart, 1959, pp. 46-49, 51, 53-55, 62, 64, 65, 71, 79, 197, 198.
   Schafer, William J. and Johannes Riedel. "Scott Joplin's Treemonisha." The Art of Ragtime. Baton Rouge: Lou-

isiana State University Press, 1973, pp. 205-225. See also pp. 5-155 passim.

Schuller, Gunther. Early Jazz: Its Roots and...Development.
New York: Oxford University Press, 1968, pp. 24, 33,
144, 146, 177, 216, 282, 283.

Southern, Eileen. The Music of Black Americans: A History. New York: Norton, 1971, pp. 318-322, 330, 331,
332, 354, 509.

Stearns, Marshall W. The Story of Jazz. New York: Oxford University Press, 1956, pp. 71, 141, 144, 146, 181.

Ulanov, Barry. A History of Jazz in America. New York:
Viking, 1950, pp. 47, 79-81.

Walton, Ortiz. Music: Black, White & Blue. New York:
Morrow, 1972, pp. 38, 42-45, 131, 169.

INTERJECTIONS

"Joplin's genius lay in the development of beautifully accented
melodies set against a subtle and highly developed rhythmic
structure."[7]

[1]Eileen Southern, The Music of Black Americans: A
History (New York: Norton, 1971), pp. 318-322.

[2]Melvin Drimmer, "Joplin's Treemonisha in Atlanta,"
Phylon 35 (June 1973): 197-198.

[3]William J. Schafer and Johannes Riedel, The Art of
Ragtime (Baton Rouge: Louisiana State University, 1973),
p. 205.

[4]Samuel B. Charters and Leonard Kunstadt, Jazz: A
History of the New York Scene (Garden City, N.Y.:
Doubleday, 1962), p. 45.

[5]Ibid., p. 49.

[6]Joplin scholars have been unable to locate a copy of
this work.

[7]Ibid., p. 45.

JORDAN, Elsie.
NOVEL Strange Sinner. New York: Pageant, 1954.

JORDAN, June Meyer. Born 9 July 1936 in Harlem, U.S.A. Education: Attended Barnard College and the University of Chicago.
Currently living in New York City. Career: Worked as research associate and writer for the Technical Housing Department of Mobilization for Youth; taught English at City College of
New York and at Connecticut College; taught for the SEEK program at City College of New York; was co-founder and co-director of the Creative Writing Workshop for Children in Brook-
lyn--The Voice of the Children Inc. Has given poetry readings
in schools and colleges around the country and at the Guggenheim Museum. The Academy of American Poets has sponsored
her poetry readings in the New York City public schools. Presently is teaching at Sarah Lawrence College. Awards, Honors:
Received a Rockefeller Foundation Fellowship in Creative Writing, 1969-70, and the Prix de Rome in Environmental Design of
the American Academy in Rome, 1970-71; was nominated for the
National Book Award (His Own Where), 1972. Member: Nation-

al Coalition for Land Reform; American Civil Liberties Union.
CHILDREN AND YOUNG ADULTS
   Fannie Lou Hamer. A Crowell Biography. New York: T.
      Y. Crowell, 1972*.
   His Own Where. New York: T. Y. Crowell, 1971*; New
      York: Dell, 1973†.
   New Room: New Life. New York: T. Y. Crowell, 1974*.
   Who Look at Me. New York: T. Y. Crowell, 1969*.
   Dry Victories. New York: Holt, Rinehart & Winston, 1972*.
   R. Buckminster Fuller. New York: T. Y. Crowell, forth-
      coming.
CRITICISM
   "Young People: Victims of Realism in Books and in Life."
      Wilson Library Bulletin 48 (October 1973): 140-145.
EDITOR
   Soulscript. New York: Simon & Schuster, 1970*†.
   With Terri Bush. Voice of the Children. New York: Holt,
      Rinehart & Winston, 1970*; New York: Washington Square,
      1974†.
   The Voice of the Children: Writings by Black and Puerto
      Rican Young People. New York: Washington Square Press,
      1974†.
NON-FICTION
   "Writing and Teaching." Partisan Review 36 (1969): 478-482.
POETRY
   New Days: Poems of Exile and Return. New York: Emer-
      son Hall, 1973*.
   Some Changes. Black Poets Series. Introduction by Julius
      Lester. New York: Dutton, 1971*†.
   (Anthologies): Adoff, The Poetry of Black America; Harper,
      Heartblow: Black Veils; Howe and Bass, No More Masks;
      King, Blackspirits; Lowenfels, In the Time of Revolution;
      Major, The New Black Poetry; Patterson, A Rock Against
      the Wind; Randall, The Black Poets; Welburn, Dues.
   (Periodicals): Black Creation, Spring 1972; Black World,
      March, September 1973; Essence, October 1973; Freedom-
      ways, Second Quarter 1971; Negro Digest, September 1969;
      Harper's Bazaar, August 1970; Library Journal, 15 April
      1970. Also published in The New York Times; Encore;
      Newsday; American Report; The Nation; Village Voice;
      Partisan Review; Blackstage; Esquire; Chelsea.
WORK IN PROGRESS
   Novel: "Okay Now" (to be published by Simon & Schuster).

JORDAN, Norman. Born 30 July 1938 in Ansted, West Virginia.
   Education: Life. Currently living in Cleveland, Ohio. Career:
   Former playwright-in-residence at Karamu Theatre in Cleveland.
   Participant in the 1967 U. N. International Playwright's Work-
   shop. Presently a technical writer for a business firm. His
   film, "The Life and Works of Norman Jordan," is available
   from the English Department, Case Western Reserve.
   DRAMA
      Cadillac Dreams, 1972.

Destination Ashes, 1971.
In the Last Days, 1971.
POETRY
   Above Maya (to a Higher Consciousness). Cleveland: Jordan
      Press, 1971.
   Destination: Ashes (Four Years with a Black Poet in the
      Ghetto). Cleveland: Jordan Press, 1967; Chicago: Third
      World, 1971†.
   (Anthologies): Adoff, Black Out Loud; Alhamisi and Wangara,
      Black Arts; Chambers and Moon, Right On!; Chapman,
      New Black Voices; Dee, Glow Child; Hughes and Bontemps,
      The Poetry of the Negro: 1746-1970; Jones and Neal,
      Black Fire; King, Blackspirits; Major, The New Black Po-
      etry.
   (Periodicals): Black World, July 1970; Journal of Black Po-
      etry, Spring 1969, Fall-Winter 1971; Negro American Lit-
      erature Forum, Spring 1972; additional poems in Confron-
      tation, Cricket, and Umbra.
INTERJECTIONS
   "I believe that the creation is one with no beginning or end-
ing. But why? or for who?"

JORDAN, W. Clarence. Born in Bardstown, Kentucky.
   POETRY (Anthology): Kerlin, Negro Poets and Their Poems,
      pp. 190-191.

JORDAN, Winifred Virginia.
   POETRY
      (Anthology): Kerlin, Negro Poets and Their Poems.
      (Periodicals): Crisis 20 (1920): 76, 137; 21 (1921): 172.

JOSEPH, Arthur.
   WRITINGS
      Volcano in Our Midst. New York: Pageant, 1952.
      Dark Metropolis. Boston: Meador, 1936.

JOSEPH, Fitzroy G. Born in Trinidad.
   POETRY A Living Expression. New York: Pageant, 1958.

JOSEPH, Raymond A.
   POETRY (Anthology): Brown, Lee and Ward, To Gwen with
      Love.

-K-

KAIN, Gylan.
   DRAMA
      Epitaph to a Coagulated Trinity.
   POETRY
      (Anthology): King, Blackspirits.
   BIOGRAPHY AND CRITICISM ON KAIN
      Harrison. The Drama of Nommo, pp. 56, 222.

KAISER, Ernest. Born 5 December 1915 in Petersburg, Virginia.
Career: See Shockley and Chandler, Living Black American
Authors. pp. 85-86.
CRITICISM
"A Critical Look at Ellison's Fiction and at Social and Lit-
erary Criticism By and About the Author." Black World
22 (December 1970): 53-59.
"The Failure of William Styron." In Clarke, William Sty-
ron's Nat Turner.
"The Literature of Harlem." Freedomways 3 (1963): 276-
291; also in Gayle, Black Expression, pp. 239-254; Shu-
man, A Galaxy of Black Writing.
"The Literature of Negro Revolt." Freedomways 3 (1963):
26-47.
"Literature of the South." Freedomways 4 (1964): 149-167.
"On Heightening the Social Muse." Freedomways 2 (Spring
1962): 119-132.
"Recent Books." Freedomways, in each issue.
"Recent Literature on Black Liberation Struggles and the
Ghetto Crisis (A Bibliographical Survey)." Science and
Society 33 (1969): 168-196.
EDITOR
With Harry A. Ploski. Afro U.S.A.: A Reference Work on
the Black Experience. New York: Bellwether, 1971.
With Harry A. Ploski. The Negro Almanac. New York:
Bellwether, 1971*.
With Harry A. Ploski and Otto J. Lindenmeyer. Reference
Library of Black America, 5 vols. New York: Bellwether,
1971.
NON-FICTION
In Defense of the People's Black and White History and Cul-
ture. New York: Freedomways Magazine, 1970.
(Periodicals): Freedomways, Spring 1961; Fall 1961; Fall
1965; Winter 1969; Harlem Quarterly, Winter 1949-50;
Fall-Winter 1950; Negro Digest, February 1968; Phylon,
Fourth Quarter, 1948.

KALI see GROSVENOR, Kali

KAMP, John.
They Cry for Love. New York: Vantage, 1968.

KARIM, Walidin. Born 14 July 1951 in Philadelphia. Education:
Two years at California State University at Long Beach. Currently living in Compton, California. Career: Presently studying music, "in theory and in application, with the concept that
'music is the Healing Force of the Universe.' " Also working
as a library aid.
POETRY
Hantu: Time and Space, forthcoming.
(Newspapers): Compton Bulletin; Herald Examiner. Also
published in school papers at California State University,
Long Beach, and Northridge.

Walidin Karim (credit: Willie Ford)

INTERJECTIONS
"Under the Light of Love the flowers of Peace and Happiness grow to bear fruit--so that man may share its Joys. The Waters of Life nourish the roots of Wisdom and Understanding.... Blessings of Allah, whereby man may seek His Treasures under the Throne over the Waters, between Heaven and Earth and in the hearts of men. As space breathes, man breathes. And as the sun's vibration fluctuates, Man's heart pulsates with the rhythm of the Universe."

KARIUKI, Joseph.
POETRY (Anthology): Patterson, A Rock Against the Wind.

KATIBU, Cheo.
POETRY (Periodical): Journal of Black Poetry, Summer 1972.

KATIBU, Mwanifunzi.
POETRY (Periodical): Black Theatre, April 1970.

KATIBU, Sultani. Born August 1949 in Newark, New Jersey. Education: Eight years at Fourteenth Avenue Elementary School and four years at West Side High School. Currently living in Newark, New Jersey. Career: Specializes in communications. Presently editor for Jihad Productions.
POETRY
   (Anthology): Alhamisi and Wangara, Black Arts.
   (Periodicals): Black Creation; Black World; Journal of Black Poetry.
   (Newspaper): Black NewArk.
INTERJECTIONS
"As a member of the Committee for Unified NewArk, as a Pan Afrikan Nationalist, as an advocate of Revolutionary Kawaida as taught by Imamu Amiri Baraka and Fanon, and as Chairman of the Committee for Unified NewArk, I believe that Black Art must be (1) Collective, for and about the masses of Black people; (2) Functional, having a revolutionary purpose, and (3) Committing, committing us to the world struggle of Afrikan people."

KAUFMAN, Bob. Born 19 April 1925 in New Orleans.
POETRY
   The Abomunist Manifesto. San Francisco: City Lights Books, 1959.
   Does the Mind Whisper. San Francisco: City Lights Books, 1960.
   Golden Sardine. San Francisco: City Lights Books, 1967†.
   Second April. San Francisco: City Lights Books, 1959.
   Solitudes Crowded with Loneliness. New York: New Direction, 1965†.
   (Anthologies): Adoff, City in All Directions; Adoff, The Poetry of Black America; Bell, Afro-American Poetry; Brinnin and Read, Twentieth Century Poetry; Faderman and Bradshaw, Speaking for Ourselves; Hayden, Kaleidoscope; Hughes and Bontemps, The Poetry of the Negro: 1746-1970; Jordan, Soulscript; Lomax and Abdul, 3000 Years of Black Poetry; Lowenfels, The Writing on the Wall; Major, The New Black Poetry; Miller, Blackamerican Literature; Robinson, Nommo.
   (Periodicals): Beatitude; Umbra.
BIOGRAPHY AND CRITICISM ON KAUFMAN
   Christian, Barbara. "Whatever Happened to Bob Kaufman." Black World 21 (September 1972): 20-29.

Sultani Katibu

KAYE, Philip B. see ADAMS, Alger Leroy

KECKLEY, Elizabeth. Born 1825 in Virginia. Died 1905 in Washington, D.C. Career: Was a slave for 30 years; then became
a well-known "society" dressmaker in Washington,[1] as well as
seamstress and friend of Mary Todd Lincoln. Formed the Con-
traband Relief Society for Freedom during the Civil War.[2]
AUTOBIOGRAPHY
    Behind the Scenes; or Thirty Years a Slave, and Four Years
    in the White House. New York: Carlton, 1868; reprint
    ed., New York: Arno*.[3] Excerpts in Barksdale and Kin-
    namon, Black Writers of America; Brown, Davis and Lee,
    Negro Caravan; Davis and Redding, Cavalcade.
BIOGRAPHY ON KECKLEY
    Barksdale and Kinnamon. Black Writers of America, pp.
    305-307.
    Brown. Homespun Heroines, p. 147.
    Dannett. Profiles of Negro Womanhood, pp. 147-177.
    Davis and Redding. Cavalcade, p. 132.
    Ebony (March 1970): 99.
    Washington, John E. They Knew Lincoln. New York: Dut-
    ton, 1942.
        [1]Arthur P. Davis and J. Saunders Redding, Cavalcade:
    Negro American Writing from 1760 to the Present (Bos-

ton; Houghton Mifflin, 1971), p. 132.
    [2]William L. Katz, Eyewitness: The Negro in American
History (New York, Toronto, London: Pitman, 1967), p.
215.
    [3]A parody was published under the title, Behind the
Seams; by a Nigger Woman Who Took in Work from Mrs.
Lincoln and Mrs. Davis. (New York: 1868), by Betsey X.
Kickley (Nigger).

KEITH, Adolphus. Born 2 June 1939 in Detroit, Michigan. Ca-
reer: Writer.
CHILDREN AND YOUNG ADULTS
    Chaka and the Sacred Snake. Chicago: Third World, 1972†.
INTERJECTIONS
"Life should be lived fully with its ups and downs."

KELLEY, Emma Dunham.
    Megda. By "Forget-me-not." Boston: James H. Earle, 1891;
    1892.

KELLEY, William Melvin. Born 1937 in New York City. Career:
See Ploski, Reference Library of Black America.
CRITICISM
    "The Task of the Negro Writer as Artist." Negro Digest 14
    (April 1965): 64, 78. (Symposium.)
NON-FICTION
    (Periodicals): Negro Digest, January 1967; May 1968; Novem-
    ber 1969; Partisan Review, 1968; The New York Times
    Magazine, 20 May 1960; Mademoiselle, March 1950.
NOVELS
    dem. Garden City, N.Y.: Doubleday, 1967. Excerpts in
    Davis and Redding, Cavalcade; Hicks, Cutting Edges.
    A Different Drummer. New York: Doubleday, 1962. Ex-
    cerpts in Margolies, A Native Sons Reader; Miller, Black-
    american Literature; Kendricks, American Voices.
    A Drop of Patience. Garden City, N.Y.: Doubleday, 1965.
    Dunsfords Travels Everywhere. Garden City, N.Y.: Double-
    day, 1969. Excerpt in Reed, 19 Necromancers from Now.
SHORT STORIES
    Book of Short Stories. Garden City, N.Y.: Doubleday, 1974.
    Dancers on the Shore. Garden City, N.Y.: Doubleday, 1964.
    (Anthologies): Adoff, Brothers and Sisters; Austin, Fender-
    son and Nelson, The Black Man and the Promise of Amer-
    ica; Baker, Black Literature in America; Barksdale and
    Kinnamon, Black Writers of America; Chambers and Moon,
    Right On!; Chapman, New Black Voices; Clarke, Ameri-
    can Negro Harlem; Davis and Redding, Cavalcade; Emanu-
    el and Gross, Dark Symphony; Ford, Black Insights;
    Hughes, The Best Short Stories by Negro Writers; James,
    From These Roots; Kearns, Black Experience; King,
    Black Short Story Anthology; Kostelanetz, The Young Amer-
    ican Writers; Long and Collier, Afro-American Writing;
    Margolies, A Native Sons Reader; Turner, Black Ameri-

can Literature: Fiction.
(Periodical): Black World, October 1970.

BIOGRAPHY AND CRITICISM ON KELLEY

Abrahams, Willie E. "Introduction." dem. New York: Collier Books, 1969.

Anderson, Jervis. "Black Writing: The Other Side." Dissent 15 (1968): 233-242.

George, Felicia. "Black Woman, Black Man." Harvard Journal of Afro-American Affairs 2 (1971): 1-17.

Jarab, Josef. "The Drop of Patience of the American Negro: W. M. Kelley's A Different Drummer (1959), A Drop of Patience (1965)." Philologica Pragensia 12 (1969): 159-170.

Kelley, William Melvin. "Ivy League Negro." Esquire 60 (August 1963): 54-56.

Klotman, Phyllis R. "Examination of the Black Confidence Man in Two Black Novels: The Man Who Cried I Am and dem." American Literature 44 (January 1973).

_____. "The Passive Resistant in A Different Drummer, Day of Absence and Many Thousand Gone." Studies in Black Literature 3 (Autumn 1972): 7-12.

_____. "The White Bitch Archetype in Black Fiction." The Bulletin of the Midwest Modern Language Association 6 (Spring 1973): 96-110.

Nadeau, Robert L. "Black Jesus: A Study of Kelley's A Different Drummer." Studies in Black Literature 2 (Summer 1971): 13-15.

Newquist. "Conversation," pp. 205-214.

Randall, Dudley. "On the Conference Beat." Negro Digest 16 (1967): 89-93.

Schatt, Stanley. "You Must Go Home Again: Today's Afro-American Expatriate Writers." Negro American Literature Forum 7 (Fall 1973): 80-82.

Serebnick, J. "New Creative Writers." Library Journal 84 (1959): 3015.

"Talent's 'New Wave.'" Negro Digest 11 (1962): 43-47.

Whitlow. Black American Literature, pp. 158-161.

"William Melvin Kelley." Negro Digest 11 (October 1962): 44-46.

KELLY, Jo-Ann. Born 16 April 1949 in Philadelphia. Education: Studied playwrighting techniques with T. Dianne Anderson. Currently living in Philadelphia. Career: Songwriter as well as poet and playwright. Has worked with the Freedom Theatre in Philadelphia, studying acting, playwrighting technique, creative writing and poetry. Played the leading role in Dorothy Ahmad's play, "Papa's Daughter." Has given numerous poetry readings at community colleges and work shops. Presently working with a producer-director revising a full-length play for possible off-Broadway production.

DRAMA

A Gift for Aunt Sarah. In Freedom Theater, December-January 1970-71.

Where the Sun Don't Shine.
POETRY
   (Periodical): Black World, May 1972.
UNPUBLISHED WORK
   A book of poems and song poems.
INTERJECTIONS
   "As a young, black creative writer, I feel that there is much
still to be learned; and I intend to keep myself open enough in
order to grow and to learn it.   I believe that what I have chosen
to do (write) is a lovely thing and a hard thing, but loving it like
I do makes it somewhat easier to me and very satisfying and en-
joyable.   I want to create art that people, and especially black
people, can feel and be moved by.   My main goal, however, is
to be a 'playwright' who writes plays that last, with characters
that will never die. In this sense I want to pattern myself after
Lorraine Hansberry and her Raisin in the Sun.   In other words,
I want to take some real black values and set them down.   And,
my philosophy, in the end, is to be daring and to challenge my
audience at all times by first choosing the subjects and themes
that most writers by-pass either out of fear or simply because
they didn't think them to be that important, and then to say
something new and something distinct about these themes."

KELLUM-ROSE, Matthew.
   POETRY (Anthology): Shuman, A Galaxy of Black Writing.

KEMP, Arnold.
   DRAMA
      White Wound, Black Scar.
   NOVELS
      Eat of Me I Am the Savior. New York: Morrow, 1972*.
   POETRY
      (Anthology): Coombs, We Speak as Liberators.
   SHORT STORY
      (Anthology): Coombs, What We Must See.

KENDRICK, Delores.
   POETRY
      (Anthology): Brown, Lee and Ward, To Gwen with Love.
      (Periodicals): Dasein; Four Quarters; Quicksilver; Spirit.

KENNEDY, Adrienne. Born 13 September 1931 in Pittsburgh, Pennsylvania. Education: B.A., Ohio State University; additional
   studies at Columbia University, American Theatre Wing and Circle in the Square Theatre School. Currently living in New Haven,
   Connecticut. Career: Teaching Fellow, Yale University, 1972-
   73. Awards, Honors: Two Rockefeller Grants; Grant from National Endowment for the Arts; The Stanley Award for Playwriting; Obie Award for Funnyhouse of a Negro.
   DRAMA
      A Beast Story, 1966. In Kennedy, Cities in Bezique.
      Cities in Bezique: Two One-Act Plays. New York: Samuel
         French, 1970. (Includes A Beast Story and The Owl An-

swers.)
Funnyhouse of a Negro. In Brasmer and Consolo, Black
    Drama; Oliver and Sills, Contemporary Black Drama;
    Patterson, Anthology of the Negro in American Theater;
    Richards, Best Short Plays of 1970.
With John Lennon and V. Spinetti. The Lennon Play: In His
    Own Write. New York: Simon & Schuster, 1972†.
A Lesson in Dead Language. In Parone, Collision Course.
The Owl Answers. In Hoffman, New American Plays, vol. 2;
    Poet Lore 60 (1965); Kennedy, Cities in Bezique.
A Rat's Mass. In Couch, New Black Playwrights; Poland and
    Mailman, The Off Off-Broadway Book; Smith, More Plays
    from Off Off-Broadway.
The Son, 1970.
Sun. In Owens, Spontaneous Combustion.
BIOGRAPHY AND CRITICISM ON KENNEDY
    Abramson. Negro Playwrights in the American Theatre, pp.
        279, 281, 283.
    Harrison. The Drama of Nommo, pp. 216-220.
    Mitchell. Black Drama, pp. 198-199, 216.
REVIEWS
    Cities in Bezique: New York Times, 13 January 1969, p.
        26; 19 January 1969, sec. 2, p. 3; New Yorker, 25 Janu-
        ary 1969, p. 77.
    Funnyhouse of a Negro: New York Times, 15 January 1964,
        p. 25; New Yorker, 25 January 1964, p. 76.
    In His Own Write: New York Times, 20 June 1968, p. 50;
        9 July 1968, p. 30; 14 July 1968, sec. 2, p. 4.

KENNEDY, Mark.
    NOVEL
        The Pecking Order. New York: Appleton, 1953.
    CRITICISM ON KENNEDY
        Maund. "The Negro Novelist and the Contemporary Ameri-
            can Scene," pp. 28-34.

KENNEDY, Vallejo Ryan.
    POETRY (Anthologies): Schulberg, From the Ashes; Troupe,
        Watts Poets.

KENNER, Peggy. Born 4 November 1937 in Chicago.
    POETRY (Anthology): Brooks, Jump Bad.

KENT, George E. Born 31 May 1920 in Columbus, Georgia. Edu-
    cation: B.S., Savannah State College, 1941; M.A., Boston Uni-
    versity, 1948; Ph.D. Boston University, 1953. Currently living
    in Chicago. Career: Professor and Chairman, Department of
    Languages and Literature; Professor of English and Dean of the
    College--Delaware State College, 1949-1960. Professor and
    Chairman of English, 1960-64; Professor of English and Chair-
    man, Division of Liberal Arts, 1964-70, Quinnipiac College.
    Visiting Professor, 1969-70, Professor of English, 1970 to
    present, University of Chicago. Held Visiting Professorships

(summers) at Wesleyan University, 1965, 1969, 1970; University of Connecticut, 1962-64; Florida A and M University, 1958; Grambling College, 1955. Has presented papers and has served as panelist at innumerable professional meetings and at colleges and universities. Has served as literary consultant for the University of Chicago Press, 1970, and the Macmillan Company, 1971. <u>Member</u>: American Studies Association; College Language Association (Research Committee, Member; Chairman, Committee on Black Studies; Advisory Editor, <u>CLA Journal</u>); Modern Language Association; National Council of Teachers of English (Member, Commission on Literature); Advisory Board, <u>Negro Literature Forum</u>, Indiana University; Fellow, Conference on African and African-American Studies, Atlanta University. <u>Awards, Honors</u>: Distinguished Lecturer, National Council of Teachers of English, 1972.

CRITICISM

"The Art of Fiction: George Lamming, West Indian Novelist." <u>Black World</u>, March 1973.

"Baldwin and the Problem of Being." <u>College Language Association Journal</u> (March 1964): 202-214; reprinted in Gibson, <u>Five Black Writers.</u>

<u>Blackness and the Adventure of Western Culture</u>. Chicago: Third World, 1972*†.

"Ethnic Impact in American Literature." <u>College Language Association Journal</u> 11 (September 1967): 24-37. Excerpt in Chapman, <u>Black Voices</u>, pp. 690-698.

<u>Faulkner and White Racial Consciousness.</u> New York: Emerson-Hall, forthcoming.

"Flight of the Nestling." <u>Negro Educational Review</u> (July, October 1956): 126-133.

"Introduction." <u>Report from Part I: Autobiography of Gwendolyn Brooks</u>. Detroit: Broadside, 1972.

"John Galsworthy, Social Critic." <u>Boston University Graduate Journal</u> (June 1953): 193-194.

"Langston Hughes and Afro-American Folk and Cultural Tradition." In <u>Langston Hughes, Black Genius</u>. Edited by Therman B. O'Daniel. New York: William Morrow, 1971, pp. 183-210.

"On the Future Study of Richard Wright." <u>CLA Journal</u> (June 1969): 366-370. Partial reprint in <u>Mel Watkins, Black Review</u>, No. I. New York: William Morrow, 1971.

"Outstanding Works in Black Literature during 1972." <u>Phylon</u> 34 (December 1973).

"Patterns of the Harlem Renaissance." <u>Black World</u> (June 1972): 13-24. Reprint in Bontemps, <u>Harlem Renaissance Remembered,</u> pp. 27-50.

"The Poetry of Gwendolyn Brooks, Part I." <u>Black World</u> (September 1971): 30-43.

"The Poetry of Gwendolyn Brooks, Part II." <u>Black World</u> (October 1971): 36-48, 68-71.

"Ralph Ellison and Afro-American Folk and Cultural Tradition." <u>College Language Association Journal</u> (March 1970): 265-276.

"Reflections on Stephen Henderson's Understanding the New
Black Poetry: A Review Essay." Black World 23 (Febru-
ary 1974): 51-52, 73-77.
"Search for the Image." Phylon, December 1972.
"Self-Conscious Writers and Black Folk Tradition." A Na-
tional Council of Teachers of English Distinguished Lecture,
given at five colleges, now distributed by the National Coun-
cil--(1111 Kenyon Road, Urbana, Illinois) on Cassette Tape
and printed in The Humanity of English, December 1972,
NCTE publication.
"Shaping up the Field of Black Literature." Black World
(September 1972): 51-52, 87-89. (Review-essay.)
"The Soulful Way of Claude McKay." Black World (Novem-
ber 1970): 37-51.
"Richard Wright." CLA Journal (June 1969): 321-343. Re-
printed in Watkins, Black Review No. I; Baker, Richard
Wright: Critical Essays. New York: Prentice-Hall, 1972.
"The World of Gwendolyn Brooks." Black Books Bulletin
(Winter 1972): 38-41. (Review-essay.)
REVIEWS BY KENT
Also published in The New York Times Book Review; Modern
Philology.
SHORT STORY
(Periodical): Black World, January 1974.

KENYATTA, Damon.
DRAMA The Black Experience, 1971.

KGOSITSILE, Keorapetse William.   Born 1938 in Johannesburg, South
Africa.
CRITICISM BY KGOSITSILE
"Language, Vision and the Black Writer." Black World 21
(June 1972): 25-27. Also in Gayle, Black Expression, pp.
146-147.
"Paths to the Future." In Gayle, The Black Aesthetic. Re-
printed from Negro Digest (September-October 1968).
"Towards Our Theatre: A Definitive Act." Negro Digest 16
(April 1967): 14-16.
EDITOR
The Word Is Here: Poetry from Modern Africa. Garden
City, N.Y.: Doubleday, 1972†.
NON-FICTION
(Periodicals): Black World, June 1971; Journal of the New
African Literature and the Arts, Fall 1966; Negro Digest,
July 1967, May 1968; May 1970.
POETRY
For Melba: Poems. Chicago: Third World, 1970†.
My Name Is Afrika. Introduction by Gwendolyn Brooks.
Garden City, N.Y.: Doubleday, 1971*†.
Spirits Unchained: Paeans. Detroit: Broadside, 1969†.
(Anthologies): Adoff, The Poetry of Black America; Alhami-
si and Wangara, Black Arts; Bell, Afro-American Poetry;
Brooks, A Broadside Treasury; Brown, Lee and Ward,

To Gwen with Love; Henderson, Understanding the New
Black Poetry; Jones and Neal, Black Fire; King, Black-
spirits; Randall and Burroughs, For Malcolm; Robinson,
Nommo.
(Periodicals): Black World, November 1971; November 1972;
September 1973; Journal of Black Poetry, Winter-Spring
1970; Special Issue 1970; Negro American Literature Forum,
Spring 1972; Negro Digest, June 1969; September 1969;
September 1966, other poetry in Black Dialogue; The New
African; Urban Review; Pan African Journal.
SHORT STORY
(Periodical): Negro Digest, October 1969.
BIOGRAPHY AND CRITICISM ON KGOSITSILE
"Interview." Negro Digest, May 1969.

KGOSITSILE, Melba.
SHORT STORY (Periodical): Black Dialogue.

KILGORE, James C. Born 2 May 1928 in Ansley, Louisiana. Education: B.A., Wiley College, 1952; M.A., University of Mis-
souri-Columbia, 1963; additional graduate work at Texas South-
ern University, University of Arkansas-Fayetteville, San Diego
State College, Kent State University. Currently living in Cleveland, Ohio. Career: English instructor, Langston High School,
Hot Springs, Arkansas, 1954-68; English instructor, A.M. and
N. College, Pine Bluff, Arkansas, 1958-59; English instructor,
Fair Lawn High School, Fair Lawn, New Jersey, 1959-60; English instructor, Central High School, Hayti, Missouri, 1960-61;
Employee, University Hospital, Columbia, Missouri, 1961-63;
English instructor, Southwest High School, Kansas City, Missouri, 1963-66; Professor of English, Cuyahoga Community College, Cleveland, Ohio, 1966-72; Adjunct Professor of English
(Afro-American Literature) Akron University, 1972. Read poetry, Cleveland area secondary schools and colleges, and colleges and universities in most sections of the nation, 1969-73;
participant, Annual Ashland College Poetry Festival, 1971;
Workshop Director, International Black Writer's Conference,
1971; Poetry Consultant, Karamu House of Writers' Conference,
1970; Participant, Bread Loaf Writers' Conference, 1971. Member: National Council of Teachers of English; Modern Language
Association of America; Renaissance Society of America; Ohio
Poets' Association; Phi Beta Sigma Fraternity; Lee Road Baptist
Church. Awards, Honors: Fellowships--Case Western Reserve
University, 1964; University of Nebraska, 1966; University of
California-Santa Barbara, 1968; Bread Loaf Writers' Conference,
1971; York University Writers' Conference, 1972.
CRITICISM
"The Case for Black Literature." Negro Digest 18 (July 1969):
22-25, 66-69; also in The World of Informative-Persuasive
Prose. Edited by K. F. McKean and C. Wheeler. New
York: Holt, Rinehart & Winston, 1971.
"Toward the Dark Tower." Black World 19 (June 1970): 14-
17.

James C. Kilgore

NON-FICTION
(Periodical): <u>Cleveland Press</u>, 1969.
POETRY
<u>The Big Buffalo and Other Poems: A Sampler of the Poetry of James C. Kilgore.</u> Cuyahoga, Ohio: Cuyahoga Community College Press, 1970. (Pamphlet.)
<u>A Time for Black Devotion</u>. Ashland, Ohio: Ashland Poetry Press, 1971†.
<u>Midnight Blast and Other Poems</u>. Cleveland, Ohio: King Publishing Co., 1971.
(Anthologies): Boyd, <u>Poems by Blacks</u>; McGovern and Snyder, <u>60 on the 60's</u> (Ashland, Ohio: Ashland Poetry Press, 1970); <u>Poetry Cleveland,</u> (1971 pamphlet); Simmons and Hutchinson, <u>Black Culture</u>; Snyder and McGovern, <u>Read In: Read Out</u> (Ashland, Ohio: Ashland Poetry Press, 1971); <u>The Strong Voice</u> (Ashland Poetry Press, 1972).
(Periodicals): <u>Black Ascensions</u>, Fall 1971; <u>Black World</u>, September 1972; <u>Central Wake</u>, 20 January 1972; <u>Crisis,</u> April 1970; <u>Free Lance,</u> 1971-72; <u>Everyman,</u> Spring 1972; <u>The Green Apple,</u> 1969; Spring 1970; <u>Haiku Highlights,</u> Winter 1967; <u>Phylon,</u> 1968; 1969; Fall 1971; <u>Poets on</u>

Platform, 1970; Prairie Schooner, Summer 1969; Proud
Black Images, Spring 1971.
(Newspapers): Call and Post, 3 July 1971; Kansas City Star,
1967; 1968.
SHORT STORY
(Periodical): Essence, July 1972.
WORK IN PROGRESS
Currently putting together a third book of poetry and a col-
lection of personal material.
BIOGRAPHY ON KILGORE
Contemporary Authors, 33/36.
INTERJECTIONS
"I try to present a positive, humanistic portrait of Black hu-
manity. Although many of my poems and essays are about the
Black American experience, many are simply man-poems, po-
ems that apply to all men anywhere on earth. Although I began
writing in traditional forms, I have changed to using almost always free verse because the form affords me greater freedom
of expression. It allows me the freedom of using words because
they come nearer the truth rather than using words because they
rhyme best."

KILLEBREW, Carl.
POETRY (Anthology): Brooks, A Broadside Treasury.

KILLENS, John Oliver. Born 1916 in Macon, Georgia. Education:
Attended Edward Waters College, Morris Brown College, How-
ard University, Terrell Law School, Columbia University, New
York University. Career: Worked with the National Labor Re-
lations Board in Washington, D.C.; directed the Harlem Writers'
Workshop and the Black Arts Program at Columbia University's
School of the Arts. Served as Writer-in-Residence at Fisk Uni-
versity and at Howard University.
CRITICISM BY KILLENS
"Another Time When Black Was Beautiful." Black World 20
(1970): 20-36.
"The Black Writer and the Revolution." Arts in Society 5
(1968): 395-399.
"The Black Writer Vis-à-Vis His Country." In Gayle, The
Black Aesthetic.
"Broadway in Black and White." African Forum 1 (Winter
1966): 66-70.
"The Confessions of Willie Styron." In Clarke, William Sty-
ron's Nat Turner, pp. 34-44.
"New Creative Writers." Library Journal 79 (15 February
1974): 374.
"Opportunities for Development of Negro Talent." American
Negro Writer and His Roots, pp. 64-70.
DRAMA
With Loften Mitchell. Ballad of the Winter Soldiers, 1965.
Lower than the Angels, 1965.
EDITOR
Trial Record of Denmark Vesey. Boston: Beacon, 1970*†.

John O. Killens (credit: Willard Moore)

NON-FICTION
  Black Man's Burden, 1965; New York: Pocket Books, 1969†.
    Excerpts in Adoff, Black on Black; Ebony, August 1965;
    Negro Digest, August 1965.
  Great Gittin' Up in the Morning: A Biography of Denmark
    Vesey. Garden City, N.Y.: Doubleday, 1972*†.
  (Anthologies): Adoff, Black on Black; Boroff, The State of
    the Nation; Long and Collier, Afro-American Writers;
    Patterson, An Introduction to Black Literature in America
    from 1746 to the Present; Robinson, Nommo.
NOVELS
  Cotillion: Or One Good Bull Is Half the Herd. New York:
    Trident, 1971*; New York: Pocket Books, 1972†. Excerpt
    in Chapman, New Black Voices.
  And Then We Heard the Thunder. New York: Knopf, 1963*.
  'Sippi. New York: Trident, 1967*.
  Youngblood. New York: Dial, 1954*. Excerpt in Hughes,
    The Book of Negro Humor.
SCREENPLAY
  Slaves. New York: Pyramid, 1969.
  Odds Against Tomorrow.

SHORT STORIES
   (Anthologies): Baker, Black Literature in America; Brown,
   Lee and Ward, To Gwen with Love; Clarke, American Ne-
   gro Short Stories; Clarke, Harlem; Ford, Black Insights;
   Hughes, The Best Short Stories by Negro Writers; King,
   Black Short Story Anthology; Singh and Fellowes, Black
   Literature in America.
BIOGRAPHY AND CRITICISM ON KILLENS
   Bigsby. "From Protest to Paradox: The Black Writer at
      Mid-Century," pp. 217-240.
   Broderick. Negro Protest Thought, pp. 348-357.
   Cruse. The Crisis of the Negro Intellectual, pp. 10-562 pas-
      sim.
   Harrison. The Drama of Nommo, p. 147.
   Kent. "The Struggle for the Image," p. 308.
   Killens, John Oliver. "Rappin' With Myself." In Williams
      and Harris, Amistad 2, pp. 97-136.
   Klotman. "The White Bitch Archetype in Contemporary Black
      Fiction," pp. 96-110.
   Mitchell, Loften. Black Drama, pp. 29, 178, 187, 189, 202,
      217, 218, 222.
   _____. "Three Writers and a Dream." Crisis 72 (April
      1965): 219-223.
   New York Times, 2 March 1969, p. 49; 28 March 1969, p.
      42; 27 March 1970, p. 22; 29 May 1972, p. 15.
   Ploski and Kaiser. The Negro Almanac, p. 685.
REVIEWS: The Cotillion:
   Bond, C. Freedomways 11 (1971): 23-25.
   Davis, G. Black World 2 (June 1971): 51-52.
   Fleischer, Leonard. Saturday Review, 6 March 1971, p. 36.
   Frakes, J. R. New York Times Book Review, 17 January
      1971, p. 4.
'Sippi:
   Williams, Ronald. Negro Digest 17 (November 1967): 85-86.
And Then We Heard Thunder:
   Algren, Nelson. New York Herald Tribune Books, 14 April
      1963, p. 8.
   Griffin, J. H. Saturday Review, 26 January 1963, p. 46.
   Negro Digest 12 (April 1963): 71.
Youngblood:
   Butcher, Philip. Midwest Journal 6 (Summer 1954): 78-80.
   Winslow, Henry F. Crisis 61 (October 1954): 511-512.
INTERJECTIONS
   "Art is life and life is art. All art is social, all art is
propaganda, notwithstanding all propaganda is not art. The ulti-
mate purpose of art is to teach man about himself and his rela-
tionship with other men."

KILONFE, Oba (rob penny). Born 1940 in Opelika, Alabama.
   POETRY
      Black Tones of Truth. Pittsburgh: Oduduwa Productions,
         1970.
      (Anthologies): Adoff, Poetry of Black America; Demarest

and Lamdin, The Ghetto Reader; Patterson, A Rock Against
the Wind.
(Periodicals): Black Lines, Spring 1973; also published in
Connections.

KILPATRICK, George A. Born 4 June 1941 in Manhattan, New
York. Education: Attended Brooklyn Community College. Ca-
reer: Employed as an Ophthalmic technician. Working on a
second book of poetry entitled, "Outside Within." Currently liv-
ing in Mount Vernon, New York.
POETRY
A Voice in the Cosmos. New York: Carlton, 1972*.
INTERJECTIONS
When we raise the level of our love act,
We shall raise the level of a child.
When we raise the level of our children,
We shall raise the level of our people.
When we raise the level of our people,
We shall raise the level of a nation.
[excerpt from "Outsiders Within"]

KILPATRICK, Lincoln.
DRAMA With Loretta Leverse. Deep Are the Roots.

KIMBROUGH, Jess.
NOVEL Defender of the Angels. New York: Macmillan, 1969.

KINAMO, Hodari.
POETRY (Periodical): Journal of Black Poetry, Winter-Spring
1970.

KING, Helen H. Born 15 October 1931 in Clarksdale, Mississippi.
Career: See Shockley and Chandler, Living Black American Au-
thors, pp. 90-91.
CHILDREN AND YOUNG ADULTS
Soul of Christmas. Chicago: Johnson, 1972*.
Willy. Garden City, N.Y.: Doubleday, 1971*.
POETRY
(Anthology): Brown, Lee and Ward, To Gwen with Love.

KING, Jefferson.
POETRY Darky Philosophy Told in Rhyme. Chicago: Smith
Jubilee Music Co., 1906.

KING, Leyland.
POETRY (Anthology): Coombs, We Speak as Liberators.

KING, Martin Luther, Jr. Born 15 January 1929 in Atlanta, Geor-
gia. Died 4 April 1968. Education: B.A., Morehouse, 1948;
B.D., Crozer Theological Seminary, 1951; Ph.D., Boston Uni-
versity, 1953; additional study in philosophy at University of
Pennsylvania and Harvard University. Career: Pastor, Dexter
Avenue Baptist Church, Montgomery, Alabama. Became a lead-

ing figure in the civil rights movement in 1955 when he accepted
the presidency of the Montgomery Improvement Association and
led the Montgomery bus boycott. In April 1963, he led his "non-
violent army" in Birmingham, Alabama.   (See his eloquent "Letter from Birmingham Jail.") As president of the Southern
Christian Leadership Council he directed numerous demonstra-
tions, including the voter registration drive in Selma, Alabama,
1965, and the March on Washington, D.C., March 1963.
Awards, Honors: Plafker Award (outstanding student) and the J.
Lewis Crozer Fellowship for graduate study, Crozer Theological
Seminary.   Numerous honorary degrees from colleges and uni-
versities.   Chosen Man of the Year by Time magazine in 1963.
Recipient of the Nobel Peace Prize, 1964. Recipient of the
Judaism and World Peace Award of the Synagogue Council of
America.[1]
NON-FICTION
  America's Greatest Crisis. New York: Transport Workers
    Union of America, AFL-CIO, 1961. (An address.)
  Letter from Birmingham City Jail. Philadelphia: American
    Friends Service Committee, 1963. Excerpts in Fishel and
    Quarles, The Black American; Chace and Collier, Justice
    Denied.
  A Martin Luther King Treasury. Yonkers, N.Y.: Education-
    al Heritage, 1964.
  Measure of a Man. Philadelphia: United Church, 1968†.
  Our Struggle: The Story of Montgomery. New York: Con-
    gress of Racial Equality, 1957.
  Strength to Love. New York: Harper & Row, 1963*.
  Stride Toward Freedom: The Montgomery Story. New York:
    Harper & Row, 1958*†. Excerpt in Chace and Collier,
    Justice Denied; Barksdale and Kinnamon, Black Writers of
    America.
  Where Do We Go from Here: Chaos or Community. New
    York: Harper & Row, 1967*; Boston: Beacon†. Excerpt in
    Davis and Redding, Cavalcade; Ford, Black Insights.
  Why We Can't Wait. New York: Harper & Row, 1964*; New
    York: New American Library, 1964†. Excerpt in Turner
    and Bright, Images of the Negro in America.
SPEECHES
  (For a more complete listing of King's speeches, see Sutton,
    Roberta Briggs and Mitchell, Charity. Speech Index, 4th
    ed. Metuchen, N.J.: Scarecrow, 1972; Reader's Guide to
    Periodical Literature should also be consulted.)
  "The American Dream." (6 June 1961 at Lincoln University,
    Pennsylvania.) In Foner, The Voice of Black America.
  "Give Us the Ballot--We Will Transform the South." (17
    May 1957, Washington, D.C.) In Foner, The Voice of
    Black America.
  "I Have a Dream." (28 August 1963, the March on Washing-
    ton for Civil Rights.) In Foner, The Voice of Black Amer-
    ica; Hill, The Rhetoric of Racial Revolt; Adams, Conn and
    Slepian, Afro-American Literature: Nonfiction.
  "I See the Promised Land." (King's last speech, 3 April

1968, Memphis.) Excerpts in Foner, The Voice of Black America.

"Love, Law and Civil Disobedience." (16 November 1961, the annual meeting of the Fellowship of the Concerned.) Nobel Prize Lecture by the Reverend Martin Luther King, Jr. Oslo, Norway: Harper & Row, 1964.

"A Testament of Hope." Playboy (January 1969). Excerpt in Hughes, From a Black Perspective; Messner, Another View: To Be Black in America.

"A Time to Break Silence." (4 April 1967, Riverside Church, N.Y.C.) In Freedomways 7 (Second Quarter 1967): 104-111; Foner, The Voice of Black America.

BIOGRAPHY AND CRITICISM ON KING
(See Biography Index and Guide to General Periodical Literature for additional listings.)

Adams. Great Negroes Past and Present, pp. 106-107.

Allen, Harold C. Great Black Americans. West Haven, Conn.: Pendulum, 1971, pp. 71-94.

Bartlett. They Stand Invincible, pp. 235-256.

Bennett, Lerone, Jr. What Manner of Man. Chicago: Johnson, 1964.

Bishop, Jim. The Days of Martin Luther King, Jr. New York: Putnam, 1971.

Bleiweiss, Robert M., ed. Marching to Freedom: The Life of Martin Luther King, Jr., 1968; New York: New American Library, 1971.

Boutelle, Paul, ed. Murder in Memphis. Chicago: Path.

Clayton, Edward T. Martin Luther King, Jr.: The Peaceful Warrior. Englewood Cliffs, N.J.: Prentice-Hall, 1968.

Davis, Lenwood G. I Have a Dream...The Life and Times of Martin Luther King, Jr. Brooklyn: Adams, 1969.

"From the Birmingham Jail." Negro History Bulletin 31 (May 1968): 19.

King, Coretta Scott. My Life with Martin Luther King, Jr. New York: Holt, Rinehart & Winston, 1969. Excerpts in Life, 12 September 1969; 19 September 1969.

Lewis, David L. King: A Critical Biography. New York: Praeger, 1970.

Lincoln, C. Eric, ed. Martin Luther King, Jr.: A Profile. New York: Hill and Wang, 1970.

Lomax, Louis E. To Kill a Black Man. Los Angeles, Calif.: Holloway House, 1968.

"Martin Luther King, Jr., and Mahatma Gandhi." Negro History Bulletin 31 (May 1968): 4-5.

Quarles, B. "Martin Luther King in History." Negro History Bulletin 31 (May 1968): 9.

Williams, John A. The King God Didn't Save. New York: Coward, McCann & Geoghegan, 1970.

[1]Current Biography Yearbook (New York: H. W. Wilson, 1965), pp. 220-223.

KING, Woodie, Jr. Born 27 July 1937 in Detroit, Michigan. Education: Wayne State University; Will-O-Way School of Theatre;

Detroit's School of Arts and Crafts Society. Currently living in
New York City. Career: Drama critic for Detroit Tribune,
1959-62; Director, Concept-East Theatre in Detroit, 1960-1963.
Producer: plays by LeRoi Jones, Ed Bullins, Ronald Milner,
and Ben Caldwell, A Black Quartet; LeRoi Jones's Slaveship;
William Mackey's Behold! Cometh the Vanderkellans; Ed Bullin's
In New England Winters; J. E. Franklin's Black Girl; New Black
Poets in America (a three-day festival); The Last Poets in the
motion picture Right On!; other motion pictures: The Game,
Ghetto; Where We Live; You Dig It? and Epitaph. Also produced the record albums: New Black Poets in America (Motown) and Nation Time by LeRoi Jones (Motown). Cultural Arts
Director, Mobilization for Youth, New York City, 1965-70;
films produced under the program won Venice Festival Award,
Oberhavsen Award, International Film Critics Award, the A.
Phillip Randolph Award. Consultant, arts and humanities, Rockefeller Foundation, 1968-70 (responsible for the Black Theatre
survey of 1969; travelled around the country reporting on theatre, and suggesting theatres and playwrights for financial as-
sistance). Artistic Director, Henry Street Settlement, New
York City, 1970 to present. Coordinator of Lower East Side
Workshops. Founder and Co-Director of New Federal
Theatre.

CRITICISM
  "Black Theatre: Present Condition." The Drama Review
    12 (Summer 1968): 117-124. In King and Anthony, Black
    Poets and Prophets.
  "Black Theatre: Weapon for Change." Negro Digest 16
    (April 1967): 35-39.
  "Black Writer's View of Literary Lions and Values." Negro
    Digest 18 (January 1968): 26.
  "The Dilemma of a Black Theater." Negro Digest 19 (April
    1970): 10-15, 86-87.
  "Educational Theater and the Black Community." Black
    World 21 (April 1972): 25-29.
  "Problems Facing Negro Actors." Negro Digest 16 (April
    1966): 53. Also in Patterson, Anthology of the Negro in
    the American Theater.
  "Remembering Langston." Negro Digest 18 (April 1969):
    27-32.

DRAMA
  The Weary Blues, 1966. (Adapted from Langston
    Hughes.)
  Simple Blues, 1967. (Adapted from Langston Hughes.)

EDITOR
  With Ron Milner. Black Drama Anthology. New York: Co-
    lumbia University Press, 1972*; New York: New American
    Library, 1972†.
  With Earl Anthony. Black Poets and Prophets. New York:
    New American Library†.
  Black Short Story Anthology. New York: Columbia Univer-
    sity Press, 1972*; New York: New American Library,
    1972†.

King, W. (cont.)   468

Blackspirits.   New York: Random House, 1972*.
SHORT STORIES
(Anthologies): Hughes, Best Short Stories by Negro Writers;
King, Black Short Story Anthology; Kochman, Rappin' and
Stylin' Out; Sanchez, We Be Word Sorcerers.
(Periodicals): Liberator, August 1965; Negro Digest, August
1962; June 1963; June 1968; Negro History Bulletin, Oc-
tober 1962.

KIRK, Paul.
NOVEL   No Need to Cry.   New York: Carlton, 1967.

KIRKSEY, Van.
DRAMA   The Hassle.

KIRTON, St. Clair.
POETRY   Poetic Creations.   Boston: L. Benn, 1943.

KNIGHT, Barbara Jean.
POETRY   (Anthology): Poems by Blacks, vol. 2.

KNIGHT, Etheridge.   Born 1931 in Corinth, Mississippi.   Career:
See Contemporary Authors, 23/24.
EDITOR
Black Voices from Prison.   New York: Path Press, 1970*†.
POETRY
Belly Song and Other Poems.   Detroit: Broadside, 1972*†.
Poems from Prison.   Preface by Gwendolyn Brooks.   Detroit:
Broadside, 1968†.
(Anthologies): Adoff, Black Out Loud; Adoff, The Poetry of
Black America; Alhamisi and Wangara, Black Arts; Baker,
Black Literature in America; Bell, Afro-American Poetry;
Brooks, A Broadside Treasury; Brown, Lee and Ward,
To Gwen with Love; Chapman, New Black Voices; Colley
and Moore, Starting with Poetry; Ellman and O'Claire, The
Norton Anthology of Modern Poetry; Henderson, Under-
standing the New Black Poetry; Major, The New Black Po-
etry; Miller, Dices and Black Bones; Randall, The Black
Poets; Randall, Black Poetry: A Supplement; Randall and
Burroughs, For Malcolm; Robinson, Nommo; Turner,
Black American Literature: Poetry.
(Periodicals): Black World, March 1972; September 1973;
Journal of Black Poetry, Spring 1969; Negro Digest, July,
September 1965; June 1966; September-October 1968; April
1969; September 1970.
SHORT STORIES
(Anthology): Chapman, Black Voices.
(Periodicals): Negro Digest, December 1965; August 1966;
June 1967; February 1968.   Other poetry and short stories
in Jaguar, Music Journal; Goliards.
BIOGRAPHY AND CRITICISM ON KNIGHT
Lee.   Dynamite Voices, pp. 51-54.
Negro Digest, January 1968; July 1968.
Whitlow.   Black American Literature, pp. 167-170.

KNOX, Jacqueline Lloyd.
    POETRY Bittersweets, a Book of Verse. Philadelphia: Dor-
        rance, 1938.

KNOX, Jean Lindsay.
    POETRY A Key to Brotherhood. New York: Paebar, 1932.

KNUDSEN, K.
    DRAMA There Were Two Tramps Now There Are None.

KOENIG, Laird.
    DRAMA The Dozens, 1969.

KOGER, Earl, Sr. Education: Attended West Virginia State Col-
    lege; John Hopkins University of Maryland. Career: Insurance
    broker and publisher.
    CHILDREN AND YOUNG ADULTS
        Black Mother Goose: Jingles and Rhymes. Baltimore: Earl
            Koger Co., 1969.
        History of the Black Man. Baltimore: Earl Koger Co.,
            1973.
        The Legend of Jocko. Baltimore: Earl Koger Co., 1972.
    INTERJECTIONS
    "History has to be presented in a form which is well-illus-
    trated, inexpensive, and revised and up to date."

KUUMBA. (Barbara A. Briggs).
    POETRY (Periodicals): Journal of Black Poetry; Spring-Sum-
        mer 1970; Summer 1972.

KWARTHER, Stephen. Born 31 January 1950 in Bronx, New York.
    POETRY (Anthology): Jordan, Soulscript.

                            -L-

LACY, Ed.
    SHORT STORY (Anthology): Ford and Faggett, Best Short Sto-
        ries by Afro-American Authors.

LACY, March.
    SHORT STORY (Anthology): Ford and Faggett, Best Short Sto-
        ries by Afro-American Authors.

LADELE X (Leslie Powell).
    POETRY (Anthology): Henderson, Understanding the New Black
        Poetry.

LA GRONE, Oliver. Born in McAlester, Oklahoma. Career: See
    Shockley and Chandler, Living Black American Authors, pp. 93-
    94.
    POETRY
        A Duo-Poem. Written for the Centennial Year of the Emanci-

pation Proclamation. n.p.: By the Author, n.d.
Footfalls: Poetry from America's Becoming. Detroit: Dar-
el Press, 1949.
They Speak of Dawns. Detroit: Brinkley-Leatherman, 1963.
(Anthologies): Chapman, New Black Voices; Hughes, New
Negro Poets: USA; Hughes and Bontemps, Poetry of the
Negro: 1746-1970; Pool, Beyond the Blues; Randall and
Burroughs, For Malcolm.
(Periodical): Negro Digest, March 1966; Negro History Bul-
letin 26 (October 1962): 67, 70, 76, 78-82 (includes a
brief biography.)
REVIEW: Footfalls
Benét, William Rose. Saturday Review, February 1950.

LAINE, Henry Allen. Born 10 January 1869 in College Hill, Ken-
tucky. Education: Attended public schools in College Hill; Be-
rea College. Career: Taught in the district schools of Bran-
field, Kentucky. Member: State Teacher's Association; was
president from 1904-1906.[1]
POETRY
Footfalls. Richmond, Ky.: Cut Rate Printing Co., 1914;
Daily Register Press, 1924; New York: Hobson Book Press,
1947.
(Periodicals): Voice of the Negro (August 1906): 583.
"The Kentuckian," first appeared in the Richmond Kentucky
Pantograph; reprinted in the Louisville Post; read to Gov-
ernor J. C. W. Beckham.[2]
BIOGRAPHY AND CRITICISM ON LAINE
Jones, Paul W. L. "Two Kentucky Poets." Voice of the
Negro (August 1906): 583-588.
　[1]Paul W. L. Jones, "Two Kentucky Poets," Voice of
the Negro (August 1906): 583.
　　[2]Ibid., p. 584.

LAKIN, Mattie T. Born 12 December 1917 in Florence, South Carolina. Education: A.B., North Carolina College at Durham;
M.A., North Carolina College at Durham; additional studies at
North Carolina Central University, North Carolina A. and T.
State University, Appalachian State University, Columbia University, Queens College, Bread Loaf (Vermont), and the University
of Iowa. Currently living in Salisbury, North Carolina. Career: Has taught in Beaufort, South Carolina and in the city
school systems of Durham and Gastonia, North Carolina. Currently Assistant Professor of English at Livingstone College in
Salisbury, North Carolina.
POETRY
Portico of the Temple. Gastonia, N.C.: Minges Printers,
1970.
(Anthologies): American Poetry 1947; Poetry Digest and Anthology, 1950; National Poetry Anthology, 1962, 1963,
1964, 1965, 1966, 1967; also Shuman, A Galaxy of Black
Writing; Lawrence, Rhyme 'N' Rhythm Song Writers and
Poets of Today; Lawrence, Songwriters and Poets of

America.
WORK IN PROGRESS
Editing the poems of slave poet, George Moses Horton, and
writing a book of original character sketches.
INTERJECTIONS
"I Believe in God!
I Believe in life and love.
I Believe in happiness and hard work and the hereafter.
I Believe in sunshine and beauty.
I Believe in people and prosperity.
I Believe in adventure and opportunity.
I Believe in expansion and renewal.
I Believe in the universe and my place in it.
I Believe in the stars and splendid skies, and green
meadows and flowing streams.
I Believe in heights that men may reach.
I Believe in dreams.
I Believe in the spirit of God in man.
I Believe in the ultimate goodness of humanity.
I Believe in myself!"

LALANDE, Athelstan.
POETRY (Anthology): Murphy, Negro Voices.

LAMAR, Thelma.
POETRY (Anthology): Boyd, Poems by Blacks, vol. 2.

LaMARRE, Hazel L. Born 14 May 1917 in Odessa, Missouri.
Died 1973. Education: B.A., University of Kansas, Lawrence,
1930; did post-graduate work at Western Reserve; University of
California-Berkeley. Career: During World War II served
three years with the Women's Army Corps in France and Eng-
land; was a newspaper woman practically all of her working life;
was actively engaged in poetry workshops in Los Angeles; helped
young playwrights. Member of Delta Sigma Theta. Awards,
Honors: Won the Best Youth Page Editor for the Los Angeles
Sentinel Newspaper, awarded by A. N. P., Associated Negro
Press; won the Humanitarian Award presented by the A. M. E.,
1966. [1]
POETRY
Breath in the Worldwind. Los Angeles: Print Rite Printing
Co., 1955.
Il Silenzio, Hollywood, Ca.: Swordsman, 1972.
Half-Past Tomorrow, Hollywood, Ca.: Swordsman, 1973.
(Anthology): Hughes and Bontemps, Poetry of the Negro:
1746-1970.
[1]Information supplied by her husband, René N. LaMarre,
shortly after she passed away.

LAMB, Arthur Clifton. Born 5 May 1909 in Muscatine, Iowa. Ca-
reer: See Directory of American Scholars, 5th ed., 1969.
DRAMA
Black Woman in White, 1941.

The Breeders.
Christy's Citadel. In Intercollegian, April 1956.
The New Window.
Portrait of a Pioneer (one act). In Negro History Bulletin
      12 (April 1949): 162-164.
Roughshod Up the Mountain, 1956.
The Two Gifts: A Christmas Play for Negroes, 1932. In
      Grinnell Plays. Chicago: Dramatic Publishing Co., 1934.

LAMBERT, Calvin S.
      POETRY (Anthology): Murphy, Negro Voices.

LANE, Pinkie Gordon. Born 12 January 1923 in Philadelphia.
      Education: B.A., Spelman College, 1949; M.A., Atlanta Uni-
      versity, 1956; the first black woman to receive a Ph.D. at
      Louisiana State University, 1967. Currently living in Baton
      Rouge. Career: Has been teaching for a number of years and
      is currently a Professor of English at Southern University; has
      given poetry readings at numerous poetry festivals, colleges,
      and universities, high schools, professional meetings, and civic
      group meetings, as well as for television; was appointed perma-
      nent editor of Poems by Blacks, an annual publication of South
      and West, Inc., 1972. Her oil paintings have been exhibited lo-
      cally, and for women's liberation groups. Member: Poetry So-
      ciety of America; Poetry Society of Louisiana; Poetry Society of
      Pennsylvania; National Organization for Women; Delta Sigma
      Theta Sorority; Modern Language Association; National Council
      of Teachers of English; Louisiana Art and Artists' Guild.
      Awards, Honors: Fifth Prize, The National Writers Club, 1969;
      Certificate of Recognition, Southern University Library Staff,
      1970; Certificate of Merit, Tulsa Poets, 1970; Special Honors;
      "Louisiana Women in the Seventies" symposium, 1972. Her
      work is included in The Beinecke Rare Book and Manuscript Li-
      brary of Yale University and the James Weldon Johnson Memor-
      ial Collection of Negro Arts and Letters.
      EDITOR
         Discourses on Poetry: Prose and Poetry by Blacks. Fort
            Smith, Ark.: South & West, 1972.
         Poems by Blacks. Fort Smith, Ark.: South & West, forth-
            coming.
      POETRY
         Wind Thoughts. Fort Smith, Ark.: South & West, 1972.
         (Anthologies): Boyd, Poems by Blacks, vols. 1 and 2; Brown,
            Lee and Ward, To Gwen with Love; Powers, Journeyman
            (published by the Unitarian Fellowship of Baton Rouge);
            Certain Days are Islands (published by the Fellowship
            Church, Baton Rouge); Lane, Discourses on Poetry: Prose
            and Poetry by Blacks.
         (Periodicals): Bardic Echoes, June 1970; Confrontation: A
            Journal of Third World Literature, forthcoming; Energy
            West, 1972; Hoo Doo, 1973; Jeopardy, Spring 1971; March
            1970; Journal of Black Poetry, Fall-Winter 1971; The Last
            Cookie, 1972; Louisiana Review, Summer 1972; Negro

Pinkie Gordon Lane

American Literature Forum, Spring 1972; Pembroke,
1973; The Personalist, July 1963; Phylon, Spring 1969;
Spring 1963; Fall 1961; South and West, Fall 1970-Winter
1971; Summer 1971; Winter 1970; Southern Review, forthcoming; Voices International, Summer 1972; Spring 1972;
Winter 1971.
BIOGRAPHY ON LANE
    Community Leaders and Noteworthy Americans, 1974.
    Dictionary of International Biography, 1974.
    Directory of American Scholars, 1969.
    Personalities of the West and Midwest, 1971, 1972.

LANGE, Ted. Born in Oakland, California. Education: Doing
    theatre in Oakland, Los Angeles, and New York. Currently liv-
    ing in Los Angeles, California. Career: Has acted in Broad-
    way plays (Ain't Supposed to Die a Natural Death and Hair); in
    national tours (Hair); in professional shows, (Visigoths, Golden
    Boy, Big Time Buck White); in Shakespearean plays (Henry VI,
    Part 2, Macbeth, Two Gentlemen of Verona, Midsummer Night's
    Dream, Romeo and Juliet; in Theatre of the Absurd (Rhinoceros,
    The Bald Soprano); in Black plays (Soul Gone Home, Integra-
    tion). Has directed numerous plays including the recent Zodiac
    Theatre (Los Angeles) production of Medea; has taught theatre

arts at George Washington University, at University of California at Davis, at Performing Arts Society of Los Angeles, at
Central City Health Center of Los Angeles. Recently directed
his play, A Foul Movement, in Hollywood. A screenplay, Passing Thru, was filmed in November 1973 by Larry Clarke and
the Film Department at U.C.L.A. in association with the Performing Arts Society of Los Angeles. Presently attending the
American Film Institute as a Directing Fellow and studying
screenwriting. Awards, Honors: Best Actor, San Francisco
City College, 1967.

DRAMA
    Day Zsa Voo.
    A Foul Movement.
    Pig, Male and Young.
    Sounds from a Flute.

NON-FICTION
    (Periodical): Tulane Drama Review.

SCREENPLAYS
    Booker's Back.
    Boss Rain Bow.
    Little Brother.
    Passing Thru.
    Pig, Male and Young.
    Sounds from a Flute.
    Tuned In.

INTERJECTIONS
"Niggers should Do--Don't Talk--Show--Act
    If you disagree, fine, don't bullshit about right or wrong.
    Produce, create, you will Influence
            and spark another
                to move
                    to act
                        to write
                            to see."

LANUSSE, Armand. Born 1812 in New Orleans, Louisiana. Died
    1867. Education: Well-educated, but there is disagreement
    over whether he studied in New Orleans, or in Paris.[1] Career:
    Served as Principal of the Catholic School for Indigent Orphans
    of Color, 1852-1866. Was the leader of the young group of po-
    ets who published in Les Cenelles.[2] Remembered by those who
    knew him as a man of sincerity and integrity, devoted to serv-
    ing his people.[3]

EDITOR
    Les Cennelles. New Orleans, 1845; centennial edition, Ed-
        ward Maceo Coleman, ed. Creole Voices: Poems in
        French by Free Men of Color. Washington, D.C.: Asso-
        ciated, 1945.

NON-FICTION
    Published in L'Union and La Tribune, two prominent newspa-
        pers published by Creoles in Louisiana.

POETRY

(Anthologies): Coleman, Creole Voices; Desdunes, Nos
    Hommes et Notre Histoire; Hughes and Bontemps, The Po-
    etry of the Negro: 1746-1970.
BIOGRAPHY AND CRITICISM ON LANUSSE
    Bergman. The Chronological History of the Negro in Amer-
        ica, p. 184.
    Bone, Robert. "American Negro Poets: A French View."
        Tri-Quarterly No. 4 (1965): 185-195.
    Coleman. Creole Voices, pp. xxvi-xxviii.
    Davis. The American Negro Reference Book, pp. 852-853.
    Desdunes. Nos Hommes et Notre Histoire, pp. 17-32.
    Good, Charles Hamlin. "The First American Literary Move-
        ment." Opportunity 10 (March 1932): 77-79.
    Roussève, Charles Barthélemy. The Negro in Louisiana:
        Aspects of His History and His Literature. New Orleans:
        Xavier University Press, 1937.
    Testut, Charles. Portraits litteraires de la Nouvelle-Or-
        léans. New Orleans: Imprimerie des Veillees, 1850.
    Tinker, Edward Larocque. Creole City: Its Past and Its
        People. New York: Longmans, Green, 1953.
REVIEW: Les Cenelles.
    La Chronique, 30 January 1848.
        [1]According to Edward Larocque Tinker, Lanusse was
    educated in Paris. See Tinker, Creole City: Its Past
    and Its People (New York: Longmans, Green, 1953), p.
    262. Rodolphe L. Desdunes, however, maintains that
    Lanusse visited Paris "only through the prism of his im-
    agination." Desdunes, Our People and Our History, trans.
    Sr. Dorothea O. McCants (Baton Rouge: Louisiana State
    University Press, 1973), p. 13.
        [2]Desdunes provides the following explanation for the
    title, Les Cenelles. "The cenelle is the fruit (small
    berry) of the hawthorn bush: their small volume reflected
    the modesty of its authors. The hawthorn, 'a thorny bush
    with both white and pink flowers,' expressed, I believe,
    the trials of these men who were laboring in an environ-
    ment so alien to their poetic talents" (Ibid., p. 11).
        [3]Ibid., pp. 13-16.

LANUSSE, Numa. 19th century Creole poet, brother of Armand La-
    nusse. Died at the age of 26 from injuries received when
    thrown from a horse.[1]
    POETRY
        (Anthologies): Coleman, Creole Voices; Desdunes, Nos
        Hommes et Notre Histoire.
            [1]Edward Maceo Coleman, ed., Creole Voices: Poems
        in French by Free Men of Color (Washington, D.C.: As-
        sociated, 1945), p. xxv.

LARSEN, Nella. (Mrs. Elmer Imes). Born 1893 in Chicago.
    Died 1963 in Brooklyn. Education: Audited classes at the Uni-
    versity of Copenhagen; earned a certificate in library science
    and a nursing degree in New York.[1] Awards, Honors: Har-

mon Foundation Bronze Medal for Quicksand; Guggenheim Fellowship, 1930.[2]

NOVELS

Passing, 1929; New York: Negro Universities Press, 1969*; New York: Arno, 1970*; New York: Macmillan, 1971†.

Quicksand, 1928; New York: Negro Universities Press, 1969*; New York: Macmillan, 1971†.

SHORT STORY

(Anthology): Smith, Sheila Kay, ed. Mrs. Addis, a Story. New York: The Century Magazine, 1922.

BIOGRAPHY AND CRITICISM ON LARSEN

Bone. The Negro Novel in America, pp. 97, 101, 102-106.

Brawley. The Negro in Literature and Art, pp. 123-124.

Brown. The Negro in American Fiction, p. 142.

Gloster. Negro Voices in American Fiction, pp. 39, 90, 111, 117, 135, 141-146, 194.

Huggins. Harlem Renaissance, pp. 157-161, 189, 236.

Mays. The Negro's God, pp. 220-224, 229.

Redding. To Make a Poet Black, p. 117.

Sato, Hiroko. "Under the Harlem Shadow: A Study of Jessie Fauset and Nella Larsen." In Bontemps, The Harlem Renaissance Remembered, pp. 63-89.

Thornton, Hortense E. "Sexism as Quagmire: Nella Larsen's Quicksand." CLA Journal 16 (March 1973): 285-301.

REVIEWS: Passing

Dawson, M.C. New York Herald Tribune, 28 April 1929, p. 6.

Du Bois, W. E. B. Crisis 36 (1929): 234.

Hyman, Esther. Bookman 69 (June 1929): 427.

Labaree, Mary Fleming. Opportunity 7 (August 1929): 255.

New York Times, 28 April 1929, p. 14.

Seabrook, W. B. Saturday Review of Literature, 18 May 1929, p. 1017.

Quicksand

Bennett, Gwendolyn. Opportunity 6 (May 1928).

Bradford, Roark. Books (New York Herald Tribune), 13 May 1928, p. 522.

Du Bois, W. E. B. Crisis 35 (1928): 202.

Hayden, K. S. Annals of the American Academy of Political and Social Science 140 (November 1928): 345.

New York Times, 8 April 1928, p. 16.

Saturday Review of Literature, 19 May 1928, p. 896.

Walton, Eda Lou. Opportunity 6 (July 1928): 212.

    [1]Miss Larsen was the first Black woman to receive a Guggenheim. See Hortense E. Thornton, "Sexism as Quagmire: Nella Larsen's Quicksand," CLA Journal 16 (March 1973): 285, n.2.

    [2]Ibid., pp. 285-286.

LATIMER, Bette Darcie. Born 1927 in Rochester, New York.

POETRY

(Anthologies): Adoff, The Poetry of Black America; Hughes

and Bontemps, The Poetry of the Negro: 1746-1970.
(Periodical): Phylon, Second Quarter 1948.

LATIMER, Lewis Howard. Born 4 September 1848 in Chelsea, Massachusetts. Career: Enlisted in the Union Navy at the age of
15; studied drafting upon the completion of military service; in-
vented and patented the first incandescent electric light bulb with
a carbon filament. He became an engineer for Edison Company,
and supervised the installation of electric lights in New York,
Philadelphia, Montreal, and London. He wrote the first text
book on the lighting system used by Edison Company.[1]
POETRY
    Poems of Love and Life. n.p., 1925.
BIOGRAPHY ON LATIMER
    Bergman. The Chronological History of the Negro in Amer-
        ica, p. 291.
    Haber. Black Pioneers of Science and Invention, pp. 49-60.
        [1]Harry A. Ploski and Ernest Kaiser, The Negro Al-
        manac (New York: Bellwether, 1971), p. 730.

LATIMORE, Jewel C. see AMINI, Johari

LA TOUR, Lou.
    POETRY The Power and the Glory. Charleston, Ill.: Prairie
        Press, 1967.

LATTON, Vyola Therese.
    WRITINGS The Big Lie. New York: Vantage, 1964.

LAW, John.
    POETRY A Nation in Distress. New York: William-Frederick,
        1972**.

LAWRENCE, Harold see WANGARA, Harun Kofi

LAWRENCE, Joyce Whitsitt see WANGARA, Malaiko Ayo

LAWS, Clarence A.
    POETRY (Anthology): Murphy, Negro Voices.

LAWSON, Edward.
    SHORT STORY (Anthology): Ford and Faggett, Best Short Sto-
        ries by Afro-American Authors.

LEAGUE, Raymond.
    DRAMA Mrs. Carrie B. Phillips, 1971.

LEAKS, Sylvester. Born 11 August 1927 in Macon, Georgia. Education: Studied Accounting at City College of New York; graduated from Cambridge School of Radio Broadcasting. Currently
living in Brooklyn. Career: Former lead dancer with Asadata
Dafora African Dancers and Singers; Public Relations Specialist
for Broadway plays and movies; lecturer on African and Afro-

Sylvester Leaks

American Culture and History; President of Sylvester Leaks Associates, Inc. Member: President, Harlem Writers' Guild.
DRAMA
    Trouble, Blues N' Trouble.
NON-FICTION
    (Periodical): Freedomways, Summer 1963.
POETRY
    (Periodical): Black World, September 1970; March 1973.
SCREENPLAY
    My God, My God Is Dead.
SHORT STORY
    (Anthology): Hughes, The Best Short Stories by Negro
       Writers.
REVIEWS BY LEAKS
    See Freedomways.
WORK IN PROGRESS
    A biography of Malcolm X.
BIOGRAPHY AND CRITICISM ON LEAKS
    Mitchell. Black Drama, pp. 145, 194, 197, 217.
INTERJECTIONS
    "God did not make man; man made God. The black writer
should not overly concern himself with 'truth,' because truth
does not necessarily set one free. Struggle sets one free. If

Whitney J. LeBlanc

---

truth is battered or slaughtered during the black man's struggle
for freedom then let her perish.   Let her perish!   The over-
riding goal of the black writer should be to inform and rectify
black consciousness.   The most costly commodity in the world
is ignorance, and black people have paid dearly for it.   All art
is political--either by omission or commission.   Art does not
grow out of politics.   Politics grow out of art."

LeBLANC, Whitney J. Born 20 June 1931. Education: B.A.,
Southern University, 1954; M.A., State University of Iowa,
1958. Currently living in Baltimore, Maryland. Career: Director, designer, technical director, lighting designer, television director, teacher, producer and playwright.   Stage manager and assistant technical director at Karamu House in Cleveland, 1959; Assistant Professor, Antioch College, where he also was designer for the Antioch Summer Theatre, 1959-64; Associate Professor of Theatre, Howard University, 1964-65; Associate Professor, Towson State, 1955-69.   In 1968 he and his
wife, the dancer, Elizabeth Walton, opened their own theatre--
Theatre U.   In 1969, he designed the original production of
Ceremonies in Dark Old Men for the Negro Ensemble Company.

Also in 1969, he became a television director at the newly op-
ened Maryland Center for Public Broadcasting, directing a dra-
matic series, Our Street, written by Ted Shine. Presently As-
sistant Project Director for Production for a television series
in Life Long Skills for Minority Group High School Students,
Channel 53, WNVT, Annandale, Virginia. Awards, Honors:
Ohio State Award, Arena Players Citation. Member: American
Theatre Association, National Association of Educational Broad-
casters.
DRAMA
   Dreams Deferred.
   It's a Small World.
   The Killing of an Eagle.

LEE, Audrey. Born in Philadelphia. Career: See Contemporary
Authors 25/28.
NOVELS
   The Clarion People. New York: McGraw, 1968.
   The Workers. New York: McGraw, 1969*.
POETRY
   (Periodicals): Essence, May, November 1971; also published
      in The Saturday Evening Post.
SHORT STORIES
   (Anthology): Coombs, What We Must See.
   (Periodicals): Black World, February, December 1969; Oc-
      tober 1970; November 1971; Essence, February 1971.
REVIEW: The Clarion People.
   Giovanni, Nikki. Negro Digest 17 (September-October 1968):
      14-15.
   Levin, M. New York Times Book Review, 19 May 1968, p.
      37.

LEE, Billy.
DRAMA   A Bench in Central Park.

LEE, Don. (Mwalimu Haki R. Maghabuti). Born 23 February 1942.
Education: Wilson Junior College (now Kennedy-King); Roose-
velt University. Career: Taught at Columbia College, Cornell
University, Northeastern Illinois State College, University of Illi-
nois.
CRITICISM BY LEE
   "The Achievement of Gwendolyn Brooks." Black Scholar 3
      (Summer 1972): 32-41.
   "Black Critics." Black World 19 (September 1970): 24-30.
   "Black Poetry: Which Direction?" Negro Digest 17 (Septem-
      ber-October 1968): 27-32.
   "The Black Writer and the Black Community." Black World
      21 (May 1972): 85-86.
   "Black Writer's Views of Literary Lions and Values." Ne-
      gro Digest 17 (January 1968): 44.
   "Black Writing." Journal of Black Poetry, Fall-Winter
      1971.
   "Directions for Black Writers." Black Scholar 1 (December

1969): 53-57.
Dynamite Voices: Black Poets of the 1960's. Detroit:
Broadside, 1971†.
"Toward a Definition: Black Poetry of the Sixties." In
Gayle, The Black Aesthetic.
EDITOR
With Patricia L. Brown and Francis Ward. To Gwen with
Love. Chicago: Johnson, 1971.
NON-FICTION
Europe and Africa: A Poet's View--Part I. Chicago: Insti-
tute of Positive Education, n.d. (Pamphlet.†)
For Black People (and Negroes Too): A Poetic Statement on
Black Existence in America with a View of Tomorrow.
Chicago: Third World, 1968.
From Plan to Planet. Detroit: Broadside, n.d.
(Periodicals): Black Books Bulletin, Summer-Fall 1973; The
Black Position, 1971; Black World, October 1973; Negro
Digest, November 1969; January 1970.
Also published in The Journal of Black History; Evergreen Re-
view; Muhammad Speaks; Free Lance; Nommo; The Chi-
cago Defender; The New York Times.
POETRY
Black Pride. Introduction by Dudley Randall. Detroit:
Broadside, 1968†.
Directionscore: Selected and New Poems. Detroit: Broad-
side, 1971*†.
Don't Cry, Scream. Introduction by Gwendolyn Brooks. De-
troit: Broadside, 1969*†.
For Black People. Chicago: Third World, 1968†.
Think Black. 3rd ed. Detroit: Broadside, 1967†.
We Walk the Way of the World. Detroit: Broadside, 1970*†.
(Anthologies): Adoff, Black Out Loud; Adoff, The Poetry of
Black America; Alhamisi and Wangara, Black Arts; Baker,
Black Literature in America; Barksdale and Kinnamon,
Black Writers in America; Bell, Afro-American Poetry;
Brooks, A Broadside Treasury; Brown, Lee and Ward, To
Gwen with Love; Chapman, New Black Voices; Colley and
Moore, Starting with Poetry; Coombs, We Speak as Lib-
erators; Davis and Redding, Cavalcade; Demarest and Lam-
din, The Ghetto Reader; Ellman and O'Clair, The Norton
Anthology of Modern Poetry; Ford, Black Insights; Gill,
New American and Canadian Poetry; Gross, A Nation of
Nations; Henderson, Understanding the New Black Poetry;
Jordan, Soulscript; King, Blackspirits; Long and Collier,
Afro-American Writing; Major, The New Black Poetry;
Patterson, A Rock Against the Wind; Randall, The Black
Poets; Randall, Black Poetry: A Supplement; Robinson,
Nommo; Simmons and Hutchinson, Black Culture; Turner,
Black American Literature: Poetry.
(Periodicals): Black World, September 1971; July 1972; Sep-
tember 1973; Freedomways, Third Quarter 1971; Journal
of Black Poetry, Spring 1969; Fall-Winter, 1971; Negro
Digest, August, September-October 1968; July, September

1969; January, May 1970.

BIOGRAPHY AND CRITICISM ON LEE

Giddings, Paula. "From a Black Perspective." In Williams and Harris, Amistad 2, pp. 297-318.

Greene, Daniel. "In Prose and Poetry, The New Black Voices." National Observer, 14 July 1969.

Kent. "Struggle for the Image," pp. 312, 319.

Kessler, J. "Comment." Poetry 121 (February 1973): 292-293.

Llorens, David. "Black Don Lee: Writer-in-Residence at Cornell University." Ebony 24 (March 1969): 72-78.

Malkoff. Crowell's Handbook of Contemporary American Poetry, pp. 170-172.

Palmer, R. Roderick. "The Poetry of Three Revolutionists: Don L. Lee, Sonia Sanchez, and Nikki Giovanni." CLA Journal 15 (September 1971); 25-36; also in Gibson, Modern Black Poets.

Redding, Saunders. "The Black Arts Movement in Negro Poetry." The American Scholar 42 (Spring 1973): 330-335.

Shands, Annette Oliver. "The Relevancy of Don L. Lee as a Contemporary Black Poet." Black World 21 (June 1972): 35-48.

REVIEWS: Dynamite Voices.

Zahorski, J. CLA Journal 15 (December 1971): 257-259.

We Walk the Way of the World.

Gant, L. Black World 2 (April 1971): 84-87.

Miller, J. A. Journal of Negro History 56 (April 1971): 153-155.

LEE, Ed.

POETRY (Anthology): Murphy, Ebony Rhythm.

LEE, George Washington.
Born 4 January 1894 in Indianola, Mississippi. Education: B.S., Alcorn A. & I. College. Career: Vice-President, Mississippi Life Insurance Co., 1922-24; District Manager, Atlanta Life Insurance Co., 1927-. Member: National Insurance Association; American Legion; West Tennessee Civic and Political League; Omega Psi Phi; Elks.[1]

NON-FICTION
Beale Street: Where the Blues Began.[2] New York: R.O. Ballou, 1934; reprint ed., Washington, D.C.: McGrath, 1969*.

NOVEL
River George. New York: Macauley, 1937.

SHORT STORY
Beale Street Sundown. New York: Field, 1942.

CRITICISM ON LEE
Gloster. Negro Voices in American Fiction, pp. 238-241.

REVIEW: River George.
Beckwith, E. C. New York Times, 20 June 1937, p. 16.
Bell, Lisle. Books, 18 April 1937, p. 18.

[1]Who's Who in Colored America, 5th ed. (1938-1939-1940).
[2]Mr. Lee's business was situated on Beale Street.

LEE, Harrison Edward.
POETRY Poems for the Day. New York: Comet, 1954.

LEE, James.
DRAMA The Rag Pickers.

LEE, James F.
NOVEL The Victims. New York: Vantage, 1959.

LEE, John Francis. Born 28 May 1873 in Alexandria, Virginia.
Died 1930. Education: A.B., A.M., Livingstone College,
1894-99; S.T.B., Boston University, 1910; American School of
Law, 1923; post-graduate work at Northwestern University.
Career: Editor, Sunday School Literature of the African Meth-
odist Episcopal Zion Church beginning in 1916, Charlotte, North
Carolina. Member: Masons; Woodmen of Union; Galilean
Fisherman, St. Luke's; Knights of Pythias.[1]
NON-FICTION
  Building the Sermon. Atlanta, Ga.: A.B. Caldwell, 1921.
  Studies in the Old Testament and the Book of Genesis in Out-
    line. Charlotte, N.C.: Piedmont Printery, 1927.
POETRY
  Discord and Harmony. n.p., n.d.
  Poems. Norfolk, Va.: Burk & Gregory, Printers, 1905.
  The Prince in Ebony. n.p., 1907.
  What Ye Gene'do Wi' Ham. n.p., n.d.
    [1]Who's Who in Colored America (1927), p. 121.

LEE, John M.
NOVEL Counter Clockwise. New York: Malliet, 1940.

LEE, Maryat.
DRAMA
  Dope (revised version), 1965.
  Four Men and a Monster, 1969.

LEONG, Jeffrey.
POETRY (Anthology): Reed, Yardbird Reader I.

LeROY, Leslie Hurley.
DRAMA Festivities for a New World.

LESLIE, Cy. Born 1921 in St. Croix, Virgin Islands.
POETRY (Anthologies): Major, The New Black Poetry; Simmons and Hutchinson, Black Culture.

LESTER, Julius. Born 1939 in St. Louis, Missouri. Career:
See Contemporary Authors 17/18; Ploski, Reference Library of
  Black America, p. 24.
CHILDREN AND YOUNG ADULTS
  Black Folktales. New York: R. W. Baron, 1969*; New York:
    Grove, 1970†.
  The Knee-High Man and Other Tales. New York: Dial, 1972*.

Long Journey Home: Stories from Black History. New
    York: Dial, 1972*.
To Be a Slave. New York: Dial, 1968*; New York: Dell,
    1970†.
Two Love Stories. New York: Dial, 1972*.
Who I Am. New York: Dial, 1974.
EDITOR
    Seventh Son: The Thoughts and Writings of W. E. B. Du
        Bois. 2 vols. New York: Random, 1971*†.
NON-FICTION
    With Pete Seeger. Folksinger's Guide to the Twelve String
        Guitar as Played by Leadbelly. New York: Quick-Fox,
        n.d. †
    Look Out Whitey--Black Power's Gon' Get Your Mama.
        New York: Dial, 1968*; New York: Grove, 1969†. Ex-
        cerpt in Gold, The Rebel Culture.
    Revolutionary Notes. New York: R. W. Baron, 1969*;
        New York: Grove, 1970†.
    Search for the New Land. New York: Dial, 1969*; New
        York: Dell, 1970†.
    With Rae P. Alexander. Young and Black in America. New
        York: Random, 1970†.
    (Anthologies): Robinson, Nommo; Watkins, Black Review No.
        1.
    (Periodicals): Liberation, October 1968; August-September
        1969; July, October, November, December 1970.
POETRY
    The Mud of Vietnam: Photographs and Poems. New York:
        Folklore Center, 1967.
    (Anthologies): Adoff, The Poetry of Black America; Colley,
        Starting with Poetry; Jordan, Soulscript.
SHORT STORY
    (Anthology): Watkins, Black Review No. 2.
BIOGRAPHY AND CRITICISM ON LESTER
    "Interview." Arts in Society 5 (1968): 228-230.
    Meras, Phyllis. "An Interview with Julius Lester." Nation,
        22 June 1970, pp. 762-763.
REVIEW: Revolutionary Notes.
    Washington, Mary Helen. Negro Digest 19 (February 1970):
        81-84.

LEVY, Lyn.
    POETRY
        Singing Sadness Happy. Detroit: Broadside, forthcoming.
        (Periodicals): Freedomways, Third Quarter 1971; Journal of
            Black Poetry, Fall-Winter 1971.

LEWIS, Angelo. Born 1950 in Oakland, California.
    POETRY
        (Anthologies): Adoff, It Is the Poem Singing Into Your Eyes;
            Adoff, The Poetry of Black America.
        (Periodical): Motive.

LEWIS, Carrie Louise.
    POETRY Polished Pebbles: Poems. New York: Exposition,
        1960.

LEWIS, David. Born 14 January 1939 in Spanish Harlem, New York
    City. Education: He graduated from Murray Hill Vocational
    School in 1957; attended the New School for Social Research.
    Currently living in Bronx, New York. Career: A playwright.
    Awards, Honors: New American Playwrighting Series Award,
    Brooklyn College, 1959.
    DRAMA
        Heaven--I've Been There; Hell--I've Been There Too.
            Bronx, N.Y.: By the Author, 655 Burke Ave., 1972.
        Miss America of 1910.
        One Hundred Is a Long Number.
        Sporty.
        Those Wonderful Folks (Of the First Baptist Church of Jeru-
            salem).
        Wally Dear.
    INTERJECTIONS
        "There is little, if anything, in my maturing years, that
    would point to a writing career. At that time, my whole exist-
    ence was manifested in one giant obsession: playing baseball!...
        "The myth abounds that ghetto children have no really crea-
    tive outlets. Well, that certainly wasn't the case when I was
    growing up.... My wonderful late mother took my sisters and
    I to... The Roxy Theater (my favorite), to Radio City Music
    Hall, to the old Madison Square Garden.... And if we were
    good for the week, my mother would promise to take us down-
    town on either the Third Avenue El or Trolley....
        "This all sounds very romantic and pastoral, I know. As if
    we were solid members of the landed gentry--or at any rate,
    middle-class. In fact, we were never that in terms of income,
    but in outlook and orientation.... We lived in a kind of genteel
    poverty. What a beautiful euphemism for the ordeal!...
        "These kinds of images have left a warm afterglow on my
    life. So in a real sense, every word that I put on paper is
    dedicated to my mother--and by extension, to all Black people."

LEWIS, Dio.
    POETRY (Anthology): Murphy, Ebony Rhythm.

LEWIS, Harry Wythe, Jr.
    POETRY (Anthology): Murphy, Negro Voices.

LEWIS, Jaceylin. Born 14 January 1950 in Huntsville, Alabama.
    POETRY (Anthologies): Boyer, Broadside Annual, 1973;
        Witherspoon, Broadside Annual, 1972.

LEWIS, Julia. Born 12 February in New Orleans, Louisiana. Edu-
    cation: two years of business school. Currently living in Los
    Angeles, California. Career: Bookkeeper and office manager.
    She has recited poetry for KPFK (radio), for IBWC (Chicago),

and for college, library, and community groups.

SHORT STORIES
    Published in Shades of Black.
INTERJECTIONS
    "We should be able to love freely without guilt--not to con-
fuse love with weakness--kindness with foolishness. To be able
to freely forgive and to ask forgiveness--to freely give of ourselves and worldly goods without obligating or being obligated.
Only by knowing and loving ourselves can we know and love oth-
ers--to fight for what is ours without any restraints."

LEWIS, Larry   see   MOGUMBO, Vajava

LEWIS, Leigh.
    POETRY   Murphy, Negro Voices.

LEWIS, Luvester.
    CHILDREN AND YOUNG ADULTS   Jackie.   Chicago: Third
        World, n.d.

LEWIS, Ronald.
    NOVEL   The Last Junkie.   New York: Amuru, 1973†.

LEWIS, Theophilus. Born 4 March 1891 in Baltimore, Maryland.
    Career: Was attracted to the theatre as a teenager. Later, he
    served in World War I; following the war he lived in Detroit for
    three years before moving to New York City in 1922. There,
    he secured a job in the post office. He also wrote drama re-
    views for the Messenger magazine from 1923 to 1927, and for
    the magazine, America, for 20 years.[1]
    CRITICISM
        "If This Be Puritanism." Opportunity (April 1929): 132.
            (Review of Harlem by Rapp and Thurman.)
        "The Negro Actor's Deficit." In Ebony and Topaz, edited by
            Charles S. Johnson.
        "Saga of Bigger Thomas." Catholic World 153 (May 1941):
            201-206.
                [1]Theodore Kornweibel, Jr., "Theophilus Lewis and the
            Theater of the Harlem Renaissance," The Harlem Renais-
            sance Remembered, Arna Bontemps, ed., (New York:
            Dodd, Mead, 1972), pp. 172-173.

LILLY, Octave, Jr. Born 28 April 1908 in New Iberia, Louisiana.
    Education: B.A., New Orleans (now Dillard) University, 1931;
    studied short story writing with Famous Writers School; was a
    writer on Federal Writers Project, Dillard University, 1937-38.
    Currently living in New Orleans. Career: Vice President and
    Director for the Peoples' Insurance Company, a post held since
    1950; past Vice President and member of the National Insurance
    Association; past First Vice President and member of the New
    Orleans Insurance Executives Council; life member and executive
    committee member, N.A.A.C.P. (New Orleans); recording sec-
    retary, Friends of Amistad; New Orleans Urban League; United

Octave Lilly, Jr.

Methodist Church.

POETRY

    Cathedral in the Ghetto and Other Poems. New York: Vant-
      age, 1970.

    (Anthology): Murphy, Negro Voices.

    (Periodicals): Black World, September 1971; September 1972;
      August 1973; Crisis, 1939; May 1972; Freedomways, Third
      Quarter 1973; The Louisiana Weekly; The Negro History
      Bulletin; Opportunity, September, November, December
      1938; August 1939; January 1940; October 1942; June 1943.

WORK IN PROGRESS

    A volume of poems tentatively entitled, "Killer of Dreams
    and Other Poems."

REVIEWS: Cathedral in the Ghetto and Other Poems.
    Freedomways 12 (1972): 345-346.
    Plumpp, Sterling. Black World 11 (September 1971): 95-97.

INTERJECTIONS

    "Just as I believe that there is no such thing as 'black' or
'white' poetry--that poetry has a built-in universality that in
cludes the concerns of all mankind, and transcends the narrow
perspectives of individual racial clans--I reject the notion of

equating estheticism on the basis of the color of men's skins--
on the premise that this is wading in the deepest of fatuous
waters; and in trepidation that such fallacious reasoning consti-
tutes a threat to spiritual and intellectual freedoms, and to the
dignity and equality of man before God."[1]

[1]"Foreword." Cathedral in the Ghetto and Other Poems.
(New York: Vantage, 1970).

LINCOLN, Abbey. Career: See Who's Who of American Women,
8th ed., (1974-1975).
CRITICISM
"The Negro Woman in American Literature." Freedomways
6 (Winter 1966): 11-13.
DRAMA
A Streak o' Lean. Scene from play in Childress, Black
Scenes.
BIOGRAPHY ON LINCOLN
Ebony (June 1957); 27-31; (October 1968): 52-59.

LINDEN, Charlotte E. Born 1859.
POETRY
Autobiography and Poems. 3rd ed. Springfield, O.: n.p.,
1907?
Scraps of Time: Poems. Springfield, O.: By the Author,
n.d.

LINDSAY, Powell. Born 2 September in Philadelphia, Pennsylvania.
Education: Attended St. Paul's Virginia Union University; Yale
University School of Drama. Currently living in Ann Arbor,
Michigan. Career: Executive Director of Suitcase Theatre,
Inc., and the Michigan Youth Troupe touring North America and
Europe in international culture exchange. He produced the Suit-
case Theatre's international tour production reviewing life in
America: "...these truths..." 1970, 1971, 1972, 1973, 1974
(and continuing) editions; "Langston Hughes Looks at Dark Amer-
ica" 1967, 1968, 1969, and "This Is Our America" staged for
the Panorama of Progress at the Michigan State Fairgrounds.
Aside from his dramatic activities, Lindsay was also a Research
Analyst in the Legislative Service Bureau, Michigan State Legis-
lature. Member: International Platform Association; People-
to-People, International; Musical Youth International (Board of
Directors); Baha'f Faith. Awards, Honors: First Prize, Yale
University Drama Tournament, City of New Haven; Citation of
Appreciation, City of Lansing, Michigan; Award for Excellence,
Michigan Education Association, and Michigan Association of
Classroom Teachers for Suitcase Theatre's "outstanding and
uniquely creative contributions to international understanding
among students and citizens"; citations and/or plaques in tribute
to Suitcase Theatre from national and city administrators and
drama societies in England, Wales, Belgium, The Netherlands,
Germany, Finland, Denmark, Sweden, and Canada, as well as
the United States Congress and Michigan State Legislature.

Powell Lindsay

CRITICISM BY LINDSAY
    "We Still Need Negro Theatre in America." Negro History
      Bulletin 27 (February 1964): 112.
DRAMA
    Flight from Fear.
    Young Man from Harlem, 1938.
NON-FICTION
    (Periodicals): The Michigan Challenge (special issues on
      "The Negro in Michigan," 1968, 1969); also published in
      The Michigan Chronicle; The New York Times (a syndi-
      cated newspaper column called "The Curtain Is Up.")
POETRY
    The Negro History Bulletin, October 1962.
BIOGRAPHY AND CRITICISM ON LINDSAY
    Abramson. Negro Playwrights in the American Theatre, p.
      92.
    Hughes and Meltzer. Black Magic, p. 170.
    Mitchell. Black Drama, pp. 105, 113, 114, 139.
INTERJECTIONS
    "Should my motivation be of interest, it's simply to BE--to
DO...to live--to learn--to love--to serve...through Suitcase
Theatre, to give my best to the best I know (as members of
the Bahá'í Faith are guided) to help unify the human family by
eliminating prejudices, so we can all live together more freely
and fully, with world order (as Bahá'u'lláh formulated) for justice, at peace...."

LINDSEY, Kay.
    POETRY (Periodical): Black World, January 1973.

LINEBARGER, A.
    POETRY (Periodical): Journal of Black Poetry, Summer 1972.

LINO.
    POETRY (Anthology): Troupe, Watts Poets.

LINSON, Cornell.
    POETRY (Periodical): Journal of Black Poetry, Summer 1972.

LINYATTA.
    POETRY
      (Anthology): Brooks, Jump Bad.
      (Periodicals): Evergreen Review, Nommo, Tazama.

LIOTAU, M. F. Died 1847. Career: A poet of New Orleans who
    contributed to Les Cenelles (Armand Lanusse, compiler). There
    is no information about his background and career.[1]
    POETRY
      (Anthologies): Coleman, Creole Voices; Desdunes, Nos Hom-
      mes et Notre Histoire.
        [1]Edward Maceo Coleman, ed., Creole Voices: Poems
    in French by Free Men of Color (Washington, D.C.: As-
    sociated, 1945), pp. xxviii-xxix.

LIPSCOMB, C. E.
   DRAMA
      Compromise, 1925.
      Frances, 1925.

LIPSCOMB, Ken. Born in 1921.
   NOVEL Duke Casanova. New York: Exposition, 1958.

LISCOMB, Harry F.
   WRITINGS The Prince of Washington Square. New York:
      Frederick A. Stokes, 1925.

LITTLE, Malcolm see MALCOLM X

LLORENS, David. Born 1939. Died 26 November 1973. Career:
   Worked as a SNCC activist in Mississippi.; as a newspaper re-
   porter in Chicago; as an assistant editor of Negro Digest; as an
   associate editor of Ebony. Was Director of the Black Studies
   Department, University of Washington, at the time of his death.
   CRITICISM
      "Ameer (Leroi Jones) Baraka." Ebony 24 (August 1969): 75-
         78.
      "Black Don Lee." Ebony 24 (March 1969): 72-78.
      "Remembering a Young Talent--Diane A. Oliver." Negro
         Digest 15 (September 1966): 84.
      "Too Young to Die." Negro Digest 15 (February 1966): 49-
         50. (Southern Free Theatre.)
      "Two Busy Writers Who Are Also 'Real.' " Negro Digest
         15 (December 1965): 49-50.
      "What Contemporary Black Writers Are Saying." Nommo 1
         (Winter 1969): 24-27.
      "What Good the Word Without the Wisdom? Or 'English
         Ain't Relevant.' " Black Books Bulletin 1 (Spring-Summer
         1972): 11-15.
      "Writers Converge at Fisk University." Negro Digest 15
         (June 1966): 54-58.
   NON-FICTION
      (Anthology): Jones and Neal, Black Fire.
      (Periodicals): Ebony, March 1966; July, August, October,
         November 1967; January, February, March, June, August,
         December 1968; May 1969; Negro Digest, December 1964;
         December 1965; April 1969.
   POETRY
      (Anthologies): Brooks, A Broadside Treasury; Randall and
         Burroughs, For Malcolm.
      (Periodicals): Black World, September 1970; Negro Digest,
         March 1964; February, September 1966.
   BIOGRAPHY AND CRITICISM ON LLORENS
      Mitchell. Black Drama, pp. 218-219.

LOCKE, Alain LeRoy. Born 13 September 1886 in Philadelphia.
   Died 9 June 1954. Education: Attended the Philadelphia School
   of Pedagogy, 1902-04; A.B., Harvard University, 1907; Rhodes

Scholar, Oxford University (England), 1907-10; additional graduate study in philosophy, University of Berlin, Germany); Ph.D.,
Harvard University, 1918. Career: His positions at several
universities were numerous and varied: at Fisk he was Assistant Professor of Philosophy and Education, 1916-25, did special
Research and Literary work, 1925-27, and became a Research
Professor, in 1927; at Howard University he was Professor of
Philosophy, 1928-1953;[1] in Haiti he was an Inter-American Exchange Professor, 1943; at the University of Wisconsin he became a Visiting Professor from 1945-46, and then became Visiting Professor at the New School for Social Research, 1947.
"With the publication of The New Negro in 1925, Locke became
one of the recognized critical authorities on Negro cultural
achievement."[2] Member: Phi Beta Kappa; Phi Beta Sigma
(honorary); Theta Sigma; Sigma Pi Phi; American Negro Academy; Society for Historical Research; Academie des Sciences
Coloniales (Paris);[3] National Order of Honor and Merit (Haiti);
Honorary Fellow of the Sociedad de Estudios Afro-Cubanos;
Founding Member, Conference on Science, Philosophy and Religion; named to the 1942 Honor Roll of Race Relations.[4]

BIBLIOGRAPHIES BY LOCKE

A Decade of Negro Self-Expression. Charlottesville, Va.:
John F. Slater Fund, 1928.

The Negro in America. Chicago: American Library Assn.,
1933.

CRITICISM BY LOCKE[5]

"American Literary Tradition and the Negro." The Modern
Quarterly 3 (May-June 1926): 215-222.

"Art or Propaganda?" Harlem: A Forum of Negro Life
(November 1928): 12.

"Beauty Instead of Ashes." Nation 18 April 1928, pp. 432-
434.

"Broadway and the Negro Drama." Theatre Arts 25 (1941):
745-752.

"A Critical Retrospect of the Literature of the Negro for
1947." Phylon 9 (1948): 3-11.

"Dawn Patrol: A Review of the Literature of the Negro for
1948." Phylon 10 (1949): 5-13; Part II, 167-172.

"Deep River, Deeper Sea.... A Retrospective Review of
the Literature of the Negro for 1953." Opportunity 14
(1936): 6-10; Part II, 41-46, 53.

"The Drama of Negro Life." Theatre Arts 10 (1926): 701-
706.

"The Eleventh Hour with Nordicism: Retrospective Review
of the Literature of the Negro for 1934." Opportunity 13
(1935): 8-12, 46-48, 59.

"From Native Son to Invisible Man: A Review of the Literature of the Negro for 1952." Phylon 16 (1953): 34-44.

"God Save Reality! Retrospective Review of the Literature
of the Negro: 1936." Opportunity 15 (1937): 8-13, 40-
44.

"The High Price of Integration: A Review of the Literature
of the Negro for 1951." Phylon 13 (1953): 7-18.

"Introduction: The Negro and the American Theatre." In
Gayle, The Black Aesthetic.
"Inventory at Mid-Century: A Review of the Literature of
the Negro for 1950." Phylon 12 (1951): 5-12.
"Jingo, Counter-Jingo and Us--Retrospective Review of the
Literature of the Negro: 1937." Opportunity 16 (1938):
7-11, 27; Part II, 39-42.
"The Message of the Negro Poets." Carolina Magazine 58
(May 1927): 5-15.
"The Negro and the American Theatre." In Isaacs, Theatre:
Essays on the Arts of the Theatre.
"The Negro in American Culture." Carolina Magazine; re-
printed in Watkins, Anthology of American Negro Litera-
ture; Calverton, Anthology of American Negro Literature.
"The Negro in American Literature." New World Writing
No. 1. New York: Mentor, 1952, pp. 18-33.
"The Negro Minority in American Literature." English Jour-
nal 35 (1946): 315-319.
"The Negro: 'New' or Newer." Opportunity 17 (1939): 4-
10; Part II, 36-42.
"Negro Youth Speaks." In Gayle, The Black Aesthetic; Hay-
den, Burrows and Lapides, Afro-American Literature.
"The Negro's Contribution to American Art and Literature."
Annals of the American Academy of Political and Social
Science (November 1928): 234-247.
"1928: A Retrospective Review." Opportunity 7 (January
1929): 8-11.
"Of Native Sons: Real and Otherwise." Opportunity 19
(1941): 4-9, Part II, 48-52.
"Self-Criticism: The Third Dimension in Culture." Phylon
11 (1950): 319-394.
"Steps Toward the Negro Theatre." Crisis 25 (1922): 66-
68.
"Sterling Brown: The New Negro Poet." In Cunard, Negro
Anthology, pp. 111-115.
"This Year of Grace." Opportunity 9 (February 1931): 48-
51.
"We Turn to Prose: A Retrospective Review of the Litera-
ture of the Negro for 1931." Opportunity (February 1932):
40-44.
"Who and What Is 'Negro'? A Retrospective Review of the
Literature of the Negro for 1941." Opportunity 20 (1942):
36-41; Part II, 83-87.
"Wisdom de Profundis: The Literature of the Negro, 1949."
Phylon 11 (1950): 5-14.
EDITOR
Four Negro Poets. New York: Simon & Schuster, 1927.
(Poems by Claude McKay, Jean Toomer, Countee Cullen,
and Langston Hughes, with criticism by Locke.)
The Negro in Art: A Pictorial Record of the Negro Artist
and of the Negro Theme in Art. Washington, D.C.: As-
sociated, 1940; reprint ed., New York: Hacker, 1971*.
The New Negro: An Interpretation. New York: A. and C.

Boni, 1925; New York: Gordon*; New York: Atheneum, 1968; New York: Arno, 1968*; New York: Johnson reprint, 1968*. Excerpts reprinted in Baker, Black Literature in America; Davis and Redding, Cavalcade; Miller, Backgrounds to Blackamerican Literature; Brown, Davis and Lee, Negro Caravan.

With Montgomery Gregory. Plays of Negro Life: A Sourcebook of Native American Drama. New York and London: Harper, 1927; reprint ed., New York: Negro Universities Press*.

With Bernhard J. Stern. When Peoples Meet, a Study in Race and Culture Contacts. New York: Committee on Workshops, Progressive Education Association, 1942; New York: Kinds, Hayden & Eldredge, 1946.

NON-FICTION[6]

"Enter the New Negro." Survey Graphic 6 (March 1925): 631-634.

"Harlem." Survey Graphic 6 (March 1925): 629-630.

The Negro and His Music. Washington, D.C.: Associated, 1936.

Negro Art: Past and Present. Washington, D.C.: Associated, 1936.

"Negro Contribution to America." World Today 12 (June 1929): 225-257.

"Our Little Renaissance." In Johnson, Ebony and Topaz.

Le Role du Negro dans la culture des Amériques. Port-au-Prince: Impr. de l'Etat, 1943.

World View on Race and Democracy: A Study Guide in Human Group Relations. Chicago: American Library Assn., 1943.

BIBLIOGRAPHY OF LOCKE'S WRITINGS

Martin, R. E. "Bibliography of the Writings of Alain Leroy Locke." In The New Negro Thirty Years Afterward: Papers Contributed to the Sixteenth Annual Spring Conference, April 20, 21, and 22, 1955, pp. 89-96. Edited by Rayford W. Logan and others. Washington, D.C.: Howard University Press, 1955.

BIOGRAPHY AND CRITICISM ON LOCKE

Adams. Great Negroes Past and Present, p. 113.

Braithwaite, William Stanley. "Alain Locke's Relationship to the Negro in American Literature." Phylon 18 (1957): 166-173.

Brawley. The Negro Genius, pp. 227-228.

Current Biography (1944), pp. 423-424.

Davis. The American Negro Reference Book.

"Dr. Alain Locke: Editorial." Crisis 61 (June-July 1954): 353.

Emanuel and Gross. Dark Symphony, pp. 73-74.

Gloster. Negro Voices in American Fiction, pp. 105, 114, 134, 171, 183-184, 187, 190, 191, 205, 218, 224, 238.

Hay, Samuel. "Alain Locke and Black Drama." Black World 21 (April 1972): 8-15.

Holmes, Eugene C. "Alain Locke--Philosopher, Critic,

Spokesman." The Journal of Philosophy 54 (1967): 113-118.

————. "Alain Leroy Locke: A Sketch." Phylon 20 (1959): 82-89.

————. "Alain Locke and the New Negro Movement." Negro American Literature Forum 2 (1968): 60-68.

————. "The Legacy of Alain Locke." Freedomways 3 (Summer 1963): 292-306.

Huggins. Harlem Renaissance, pp. 56-60, 79-81, 201-202.

Hughes. The Big Sea, pp. 92-93, 204.

Jet, 16 September 1965, p. 11.

Journal of Negro Education 30 (Winter 1961): 25-34; 34 (Winter 1965): 5-10.

Kallen, Horace M. "Alain Locke and Cultural Pluralism." The Journal of Philosophy 54 (1957): 119-127.

Long, Richard A. "Alain Locke: Cultural and Social Mentor." Black World 20 (November 1970): 87-90.

Negro History Bulletin 26 (May 1963): 240-243.

Ploski. Negro Almanac, pp. 691-692.

Robinson. Historical Negro Biographies, p. 222.

Who's Who in America, (1944-45).

Who's Who in Colored America, 5th ed. (1940).

[1]Who's Who in Colored America, 5th ed. (1940).
[2]Current Biography (1944).
[3]Who's Who in Colored America.
[4]Current Biography.
[5]Materials left by Locke were published by Margaret Just Butcher, The Negro in American Culture (New York: Knopf, 1956).
[6]The reader should consult the Catalog of the Schomburg Collection for a more detailed listing of Locke's essays.

LOCKE, Edward.
POETRY Pause, and Other Poems. New York: Exposition, 1954.

LOCKETT, Reginald. Born 1947 in Berkeley, California.
POETRY
(Anthology): Jones and Neal, Black Fire.
(Periodical): Black World, September 1973.
SHORT STORY
(Periodical): Black World, August 1972.

LOCKETT, Tina. Born 1945 in Pittsburgh, California.
POETRY
(Anthology): Coombs, We Speak as Liberators.
(Periodicals): Negro Digest, March, September-October 1968.

LOCKHART, Theodore.
POETRY In Search of Roots. Philadelphia: Dorrance, 1970.

LOFTIN, Elouise. Born 22 June 1950 in Brooklyn, New York.
Education: Attended New York University. Currently living in
Brooklyn, New York. Career: Has given poetry readings and
lectures at numerous high schools, colleges, and universities as
well as at community functions. Presently is poetry editor for
Black Creation.
POETRY
    Jumbish. New York: Emerson Hall, 1972.
    (Anthologies): Adoff, The Poetry of Black America; Boyer,
      Broadside Annual 1973.
    (Periodicals): Black Creation, Fall 1971; Black World, Sep-
      tember 1973. Other poetry in Confrontation: A Journal of
      Third World Literature; Essence.
WORK IN PROGRESS
    Completing a second volume of poetry, "Dwell Like a Ghost."
INTERJECTIONS
    "Poetry is the expression of feeling and ideas in the most po-
etic form accessible at any particular moment in space. This
may mean at some times a quiet silence or to 'Dwell like a
Ghost.' "

LOFTIS, Norman.
    POETRY Exiles and Voyages. n.p., n.d.

LOFTY, Paul.
    Excerpt from untitled novel in Reed, 19 Necromancers from
    Now.

LOGAN, Rosie Lee. (Rosie Lee Logan Jones). Born 23 October
1924 on a farm in Reagan, Texas. Education: B.S., Paul
Quinn College, 1952; graduate work at Texas Southern University. Currently living in Beaumont, Texas. Career: Teacher
since 1948. Presently involved in a number of activities, including substitute teaching, lecturing, serving as a notary public, working as a book saleslady, coaching students. Has written poetry columns for weekly newspapers, and has had several
plays staged by school and community groups. Member: former member of Pinywoods Writers' Conference. Awards, Honors: Literary Award, Department of English, Paul Quinn College, 1952.
WRITINGS
    "Foot Prints," forthcoming.
    Raindrops and Pebbles, n.p.: Chance-Foster, n.d.
    Tender Clusters. San Antonio: Naylor, 1969. (Poetry.)
    Treasures of Life. Riesel: Riesel Russel, 1945.
INTERJECTIONS
    "When asked by persons from time to time if I have children
I reply 'My brainchildren are my offsprings, to whom I devote
my life. I've given to society no human people; I am my husband's BARREN WIFE.' So it is my contention that books are
true mind reproductions of the (PARENT) WRITER. These children go many places and are before many faces. The manner
by which my literary work is received is quite pleasing to me.

Rosie Lee Logan (Jones)

Scores of young people are inspired to write due to my work."

LOMAX, Almena. Career: See Stein, Blacks in Communications, pp. 92-96.
SHORT STORY
    (Periodical): Harper Magazine, September 1968.

LOMAX, Pearl Cleage. Born 7 December 1948 in Springfield, Massachusetts. Education: Howard University (Playwrighting), 1966-69; Yale University, Summer 1969; B.A. (Drama and Playwrighting), Spelman College, 1971; University of West Indies, Summer Writer's Workshop, 1971; now working toward an M.A. in Afro-American Literature at Atlanta University. Currently living in Atlanta, Georgia. Career: Member of the Field Collection Staff, Martin Luther King, Jr. Archival Library, 1969-70; Assistant Director, Southern Education Program, Inc., 1970-71; Hostess/Interviewer, Black Viewpoints, produced by Clark College for Channel 30, WETV, Atlanta, 1972; Staff Writer/Interviewer, Ebony Beat Journal, WQXI-TV, Channel 11, Atlanta, 1972; Producer/Writer, Ebony Beat Journal and Ebony Beat, WQXI-TV, Channel 11, Atlanta, 1972 to present. Awards, Honors: First Prize for Poetry, Promethan Literary Magazine, 1968.

DRAMA

Duet for Three Voices (one act), 1969.
Hymn for the Rebels (one act), 1968.
The Sale (one act), 1972.

POETRY

We Don't Need No Music. Detroit: Broadside, 1972†.
(Anthologies): Adoff, The Poetry of Black America; Coombs,
We Speak as Liberators; Mahoney and Schmittroth, The
Insistent Present; Patterson, A Rock Against the Wind;
Welburn, Dues.
(Periodicals): Afro-American Review, Fall 1968; Atlanta
University Sampler, 1972 and 1973; The Black Collegian,
vol. 2, 1971; Black Creation, Summer 1972; Black World,
September 1972; Detroit Free Press Magazine, 1967; Es-
sence, July 1973; Journal of Black Poetry, Winter-Spring,
1970; Summer 1972; Ms. Magazine, February 1973;
Readers and Writers Magazine, 1967, 1968.

NON-FICTION

(Periodicals): Essence, August 1972; Pride, September, October, November 1972.

CRITICISM ON LOMAX

Kent. "Outstanding Works," pp. 323-324.

INTERJECTIONS

"I believe that a Black Poet has a responsibility to contribute
his art toward the strengthening and unifying of the Black Nation.   There are several ways that a poet may contribute to the
liberation struggle.   One way is to explore the relationships of
brothers and sisters inside the nation in hopes of reflecting positive values and exposing negative ones.   This is what I hope to
do with my poems.   I hope that the reflection of positive Black
images will help us to see ourselves and eliminate the psychological sickness that we have been infected with after so many
years of slavery and oppression.   I would hope to write healing
poems that show Black people their own beauty as a group and
help to move us from a collection of individuals to a cohesive
force dedicated to the liberation struggle."[1]

1Pearl Lomax, We Don't Need No Music (Detroit:
Broadside, 1972), back cover.

LONG, Doughtry. Born 1942 in Atlanta, Georgia.

POETRY

Black Love, Black Hope. Introduction by Dudley Randall.
Detroit: Broadside, 1971†.
Song for Nia. Detroit: Broadside, 1971†.
(Anthologies): Adoff, The Poetry of Black America; Brooks,
A Broadside Treasury; Patterson, A Rock Against the
Wind; Randall, The Black Poets; Randall, Black Poetry:
A Supplement.
(Periodicals): Black Creation, Spring 1972; Black World, De-
cember 1970; Negro Digest, September 1969; December
1970.

REVIEW: Black Love, Black Hope.

Washington, M. H. Black World 21 (December 1971): 51-52.

LONG, Richard A. (Ric Alexander.) Born 9 February 1927 in
Philadelphia, Pennsylvania. Career: See Shockley and Chand-
ler, Living Black American Authors, p. 101; Contemporary
Authors, 37/40.
CRITICISM BY LONG
    "Alain Locke: Cultural and Social Mentor." Black World
        20 (November 1970): 87-90.
    "Crisis of Consciousness: Reflections of the Afro-American
        Artist." Negro Digest 17 (May 1968): 88-92.
    "Image of Man in James Gould Cozzens." CLA Journal 10
        (June 1967): 299-307.
    "John Heywood, Chaucer, and Lydgate." Modern Language
        Notes 65 (January 1949): 55-56.
    "New Esthetics and the Teacher of Literature." CLA Jour-
        nal 2 (December 1958): 128-133.
    "Weapon of My Song: The Poetry of James Weldon Johnson."
        Phylon 32 (Winter 1971): 374-382.
DRAMA
    Black Is Many Hues, 1969.
    Joan of Arc (folk opera), 1964.
    Pilgrim's Price (sketches), 1963.
    Reasons of State, 1966.
    Stairway to Heaven (gospel opera), 1964.
EDITOR
    With Eugenia Collier. Afro-American Writing: An Anthol-
        ogy of Prose and Poetry. New York: New York Univer-
        sity Press, 1972*†.
    With Albert Berrian. Negritude: Essays and Studies. Hamp-
        ton, Va.: Hampton Institute Press, 1967.
NON-FICTION
    "From African to the New World: The Linguistic Continuum."
        CAAS Papers in Linguistics. Atlanta, Ga.: Center for
        African and Afro-American Studies, 1970?
    "Man and Evil in American Negro Speech." American Speech
        34 (December 1959): 305-306.
    "The Measure and Meaning of the Sixties." Negro Digest 19
        (November 1969): 4. (Symposium.)
    "Toward a Theory of Afro-American Dialects." CAAS Pa-
        pers in Linguistics. Atlanta, Ga.: Center for African
        Studies, 1970?
Non-fiction also published in CLA Journal, September 1970;
    September 1971; African Forum, Spring and Summer 1968.
POETRY
    (Periodicals): Black World, September 1971; June 1973; CLA
        Journal, November 1957; Phylon, 1945; Winter 1972.
REVIEWS BY LONG
    Published in Phylon.

LONG, Worth. Born 1936 in Durham, North Carolina.
    POETRY
        (Anthology): Major, The New Black Poetry.
        (Periodicals): New South, July-August 1964; also in The
            Harvard Advocate.

LORDE, Audre (Rey Domini). Born 18 February 1934 in New York City. Education: National University of Mexico, 1954; B. A., Hunter College, 1959; M. L. S., Columbia University, 1961. Currently living in New York City. Career: Poet-in-Residence, Tougaloo College, 1968; Instructor at Lehman College, Bronx, 1968-70; Instructor of English and Education classes for white teachers in the Ghetto areas; presently teaching at John Jay College, CCNY, (Poetry, Race and the Urban Situation). Awards, Honors: National Endowment for the Arts Grant, 1968, for poetry; currently completing a third book of poetry under a grant from the Cultural Council Foundation.

POETRY
    Cables to Rage. London: Breman, 1970.
    From a Land Where Other People Live. Detroit: Broadside, forthcoming.
    The First Cities. New York: Poets Press, 1968.
    (Anthologies): Adoff, The Poetry of Black America; Bell, Afro-American Poetry; Breman, Sixes and Sevens; Cade, The Black Woman; Chapman, New Black Voices; Colley and Moore, Starting with Poetry; Henderson, Understanding the New Black Poetry; Hughes, New Negro Poets: USA; Jordan, Soulscript; Major, The New Black Poetry; Margolies, A Native Sons Reader; Menarini, I Negri: Poesie E Canti (Rome, 1969): Pool, Beyond the Blues; Wilentz and Weatherly, Natural Process.
    (Periodicals): Black World, July 1970; June, September 1973; Freedomways, Third Quarter 1970; First Quarter 1972; Harlem Quarterly, Fall-Winter 1950; Journal of Black Poetry, Winter 1969; Spring 1969; Fall 1969; Winter-Spring 1970; Massachusetts Review, Winter-Spring 1972; Negro Digest, September 1963; January, February, October 1964; September 1965; March 1966; June, October 1967; September-October 1968; September 1969; Parasite (Paris, 1968; Pen Journal, 1972; Pound, 1968; Présence Africaine, 57; Transatlantic Review #41; Venture Magazine, 1956.

BIOGRAPHY AND CRITICISM ON LORDE
    Contemporary Authors, 25/28
    Gayle. Black Expression, pp. 111-113.
    Randall, Dudley. Negro Digest, September 1968.

LOVE, George. Born in Charlotte, North Carolina.
    POETRY (Anthologies): Adoff, I Am the Darker Brother; Hughes, New Negro Poets: USA.

LOVE, Melvin.
    POETRY War in Heaven and Other Poems. New York: Exposition, 1954.

LOVE, Rose Leary. Career: A teacher from North Carolina.
    POETRY
    Nebraska and His Granny. Tuskegee, Ala.: Tuskegee Institute Press, 1966.
    BIOGRAPHY ON LOVE

501   Love, R. L. (cont.)

"The Leary Family." Negro History Bulletin 10 (November
   1946): 27-34, 47.
Woodson, C. G.   "Women Eligible to Be Daughters of the
   American Revolution." Negro History Bulletin 7 (November 1943): 36, 39.

LOVETT, Jon.
   POETRY (Periodical): Black Dialogue.

LOVINGOOD, Penman.
   POETRY Poems of a Singer. Compton, Ca. : Lovingood Co.,
   1963.

LUBIN, Gilbert.
   NOVEL The Promised Land. Boston: Christopher, 1930.

LUCAS, Curtis. Born 1914.
   NOVELS
      Angel. New York: Lion, 1953.
      Flour Is Dusty. Philadelphia: Dorrance, 1943.
      Forbidden Fruit. New York: Universal, 1953.
      Lila. New York: Lion, 1955.
      So Low, So Lonely. New York: n.p., 1952.
      Third Ward Newark. Chicago: Ziff Davis, 1946.
   CRITICISM ON LUCAS
      Bone. The Negro Novel in America, p. 159.
      Hughes. The Negro Novelist, pp. 76-79, 132-134.

LUCAS, James R. Born in Falmouth, Virginia.
   POETRY (Anthologies): Coombs, We Speak as Liberators;
      Dee, Glow Child; Randall and Burroughs, For Malcolm.

LUCIANO, Felipe. Born 24 November 1947 in Manhattan.
   POETRY
      (Anthologies): Adoff, The Poetry of Black America; King,
         Blackspirits.
      (Periodical): Black Creation, Summer 1972.

LUPER, Luther George, Jr.
   POETRY (Anthology): Murphy, Ebony Rhythm.

LUTOUR, Lou.
   POETRY The Power and the Glory. Charleston, Ill. : Prairie
   Press, 1967.

LYLE, K. Curtis (Kansas Curtis Lyle). Born 13 May 1944 in Los
   Angeles, California. Education: His degrees are somewhat un-
   orthodox, but possibly represent more learning and experience
   than can be gained in many of our academic institutions:
   "B.A., Irrational Institute of Higher Education (English); M.A.,
   Federal Pen Post Office, Leavenworth, Kansas (License Plates);
   M.S., Dysfunctional (Vestigial) Components of Malagasy Land
   Seaweed(s), Malagasy Institute for the Deaf; Ph.D. (Astro-In-

finite-Mystical-Warrier Literature), London School of Nigger
Fiction. Career: Writer-in-Residence, Washington University,
1971-72; S. W. Rollbar Professor of Black Astral Literature,
and Aleister Crowley Fellow (Post-Doctoral) of Mystical War at
Jefferson-Franklin Institute of Magical Reality (St. Louis, Missouri), 1972-73. Presently working on the effacement of all
logical-positivist-conventional-expedient history and conversely
creating the Legend of Fakin Floyd Raintree." Awards, Honors:
Has received major awards, fellowships, money (sort of), and
encouragement, but no cash!

DRAMA
    Days of Thunder, Nights of Violence, 1970.
    Guerrilla Warfare, 1970.
    Minstrel Show, 1970.
    The Processes of Allusion.
    Wichita.

POETRY
    (Anthologies): Adoff, The Poetry of Black America; Chap-
        man, New Black Voices; Troupe, Watts Poets.
    (Periodicals): Black World, September 1973; Journal of
        Black Poetry, Winter-Spring 1970; Summer 1972; Negro
        American Literature Forum. Spring 1972.

INTERJECTIONS
    "About life and art I have ideas, certain theories, no phi-
losophy, and two impressions; that is, I believe life can be
summed up in the immemorial phrase--solve et coagula!!"

LYMAN, James C.
    SHORT STORY (Anthology): James, From These Roots.

LYNCH, Charles Henry. Born 1 November 1943 in Baltimore,
    Maryland. Education: B.A., Kenyon College, 1964; M.A.,
    City College of New York, 1968; Ph.D. candidate, New York
    University. Currently living in Brooklyn. Career: Has taught
    at Brooklyn College, Rutgers University, and New York Univer-
    sity.

POETRY
    (Anthology): Adoff, The Poetry of Black America.
    (Periodicals): Black Creation, December 1970; April 1971;
        Summer 1972; For Now, No. 13, 1972; The Gallery (pub-
        lished by Associated Students of Rutgers University), n.d.;
        Hika (Kenyon College undergraduate quarterly), Fall 1963;
        Spring 1964; Journal of Black Poetry, Spring-Summer
        1972; Liberator, March 1971; Negro American Literature
        Forum, Fall 1973; Pamoja Tutashinda, April 1972; Per-
        spective, Autumn 1971; Readers and Writers, November-
        January 1968; Riverrun, May 1972; W.E.W. Review #6;
        Washington Square Review, Winter 1967; World Order,
        Spring 1971.

UNPUBLISHED WORK
    "Whitman's 1860 Edition of Leaves of Grass: The Confes-
        sional and the Programmatic Poet."

WORK IN PROGRESS

W. T. Lyons

Presently working on dissertation: a critical study of the poetry of Robert Hayden and Gwendolyn Brooks.

LYNN, Eve see REYNOLDS, Evelyn Crawford

LYONS, Leona.
    POETRY (Anthology): Murphy, Negro Voices.

LYONS, Martha E.
    POETRY (Anthology): Murphy, Ebony Rhythm.

LYONS, W. T. Born 10 August 1919 in Griffin, Georgia. Education: B.A. (Magna Cum Laude) Howard University, 1949; additional graduate work in English and Education at Howard University and the University of Pennsylvania. Currently living in Washington, D.C. Career: Served as Staff Advisor, Industrial Relations Liaison Officer, Administrative Assistant, Management Analysis Officer and Head of the Administrative and Planning Division for the Supply and Fiscal Department--U.S. Naval Air Station, and U.S. Naval Air Facility, Washington, D.C.--July 1952-June 1963. Assistant for Manpower Management and Utilization; Consultant to Naval Bureaus, Offices, and Systems Commands; Program Administrator; Project Manager for Management and Industrial Engineering projects--U.S. Naval Personnel Research and Development Laboratory, Washington, D.C.--June 1963 to August 1968; Principal Advisor and Staff Assistant to the Assistant Vice Chief of Naval Operations; Management Analyst and Manpower Analyst--Office of the Chief of Naval Operations, Pentagon--August 1968 to retirement as of June 1973. Author of numerous technical publications, 1964-1969.

POETRY
Soul in Solitude: Poems. New York: Exposition, 1970.

LYTLE, Corinne.
POETRY (Anthology): Murphy, Negro Voices.

-M-

McBAIN, Barbara Mahone.
POETRY
Sugarfields. Detroit: Broadside, 1970.
(Anthologies): Adoff, The Poetry of Black America; Simmons and Hutchinson, Black Culture.
(Periodicals): Journal of Black Poetry, Summer 1972.

MacBETH, Robert.
DRAMA
A Black Ritual. In Drama Review 13 (Summer 1969): 129-130; also in Simmons and Hutchinson, Black Culture.
NON-FICTION
"A Theatre Uptown Please." The Probe 1 (May 1967): 12.
BIOGRAPHY AND CRITICISM ON MacBETH
"MacBeth Speaks." Black Theatre 6 (1972): 14-20. (Interview.)

McBROWN, Gertrude Parthenia. Education: A graduate of Emerson College of Drama; studied in Paris at the Conservatoire National de Music et d'Art Dramatique, and at the Institute Britannique of the Sorbonne. Career: Actress; founder and director of the District of Columbia Children's Theatre and Drama Workshop; member of the Educational Board of the Negro History Bulletin. [1]
DRAMA
Birthday Surprise. In Negro History Bulletin 16 (February 1953).
POETRY
The Picture-Poetry-Book. Washington: Associated, 1935†.
(Children's book.)
RADIO DRAMATIZATION
"Bought with Cookies." Negro History Bulletin 12 (April 1949): 155-156, 165-166.
REVIEW: Picture-Poetry-Book.
Journal of Negro History 21 (April 1936): 225-227.

BIOGRAPHY AND CRITICISM ON McBROWN

Cromwell, Turner and Dykes. Readings from Negro Authors,
pp. 53-54.
[1]Beatrice M. Murphy, Ebony Rhythm (Freeport, N.Y.:
Books for Libraries, 1968), p. 104.

McCALL, James Edward. Born 2 September 1880 in Montgomery,
Alabama. Education: was graduated from Alabama State Normal in 1900; began medical studies at Howard University, but
was forced to abandon career plans when blinded following an
attack of typhoid fever; accompanied by his sister, he began
studies at Albion in 1905. Career: Became a journalist, employed as a special writer for a local white daily in Montgomery;
published The Emancipator; moved to Detroit in 1920 and became city editor and editorial writer for the Detroit Independent.[1]
POETRY
(Anthologies): Cullen, Caroling Dusk; Kerlin, Negro Poets
and Their Poems; Pool, Beyond the Blues.
(Periodicals): Alexander's Magazine, January 1906; Voice
of the Negro, December 1904; March 1905.
BIOGRAPHY AND CRITICISM ON McCALL
Kerlin. Negro Poets and Their Poems, pp. 342-343.
Negro History Bulletin 26 (October 1926): 67.
[1]Countee Cullen, Caroling Dusk (New York: Harper &
Row, 1927), pp. 33-34.

McCALL, Valaida Potter. (W. J. McCall, pseud.).
NOVEL Sunrise Over Alabama. New York: Comet, 1959.

McCLAIN, Ruth Rambo.
POETRY (Periodicals): Journal of Black Poetry, Spring 1969;
also published in Black Dialogue.

McCLAURIN, Irma.
POETRY Black Chicago. New York: Amuru, 1973†.

McCLELLAN, George Marion (McLlelan). Born 29 September 1860
in Belfast, Tennessee. Died 1934. Education: B.A., Fisk
University, 1885; M.A., Fisk University, 1890; B.D., Hartford
(Connecticut) Theological Seminary, 1886. Career: Was both
teacher and chaplain at State Normal School, Normal, Alabama;
pastor at a Congregational Church in Memphis, 1897-1899;[1]
teacher of Latin and English at Central High School, Louisville,
1899-1911; Principal of the Dunbar Public School, Louisville,
1911-1919.[2] He also served as a financial agent, seeking funds
for Fisk University. He moved to Los Angeles in 1924 and devoted his last year to soliciting funds for an anti-tubercular
sanatorium for Black people.[3]
POETRY
Poems. Nashville, Tenn.: A.M.E. Church Sunday School
Union, 1895.
The Path of Dreams. Louisville, Ky.: Morton, 1916; Free-

port, N.Y.: Books for Libraries*.
Songs of a Southerner.   Boston: Press of Stockwell & Chur-
chill, 1896.
(Anthologies): Hughes and Bontemps, The Poetry of the Ne-
gro, 1746-1949; Johnson, The Book of American Negro
Poetry; Kerlin, Negro Poets and Their Poems; Robinson,
Early Black American Poets; White and Jackson, An An-
thology of Verse by American Negroes.
SHORT STORIES
Old Greenbottom Inn, and Other Stories.   Louisville, Ky.:
By the Author, 1906; New York: AMS Press*.
BIOGRAPHY AND CRITICISM ON McCLELLAN
Culp, Daniel Wallace. American Negro: His History and
Literature. New York: Arno Press, 1969, pp. 274-286.
Davis. The American Negro Reference Book, p. 856.
Emanuel and Gross. Dark Symphony, pp. 3, 10.
Gloster. Negro Voices in American Fiction, pp. 68-70.
Redding. They Came in Chains, p. 153.
White and Jackson. Negro Poets and Their Poems, pp. 21,
92-97, 229-230.
     1William H. Robinson, ed. Early Black American Po-
ets (Dubuque, Iowa: William C. Brown, 1969), p. 121.
     2Newman Ivey White and Walter Clinton Jackson, An
Anthology of Verse by American Negroes (Durham, N.C.:
Moore, 1968), p. 92.
     3Robinson, p. 121.

McCLELLAN, Isabelle.
POETRY (Anthology): Murphy, Ebony Rhythm.

McCLUSKEY, John. Born 1944 in Middletown, Ohio.
POETRY
(Periodical): Black World, January 1973.
SHORT STORY
(Anthology): Coombs, What We Must See.

McCORKLE, George Washington.
POETRY Poems of Thought and Cheer. Petersburg, Va.,
n.d.; Washington: Published under the auspices of the National Bureau of Negro Writers and Entertainers, n.d.

McCORMACK, Tom.
DRAMA American Roulette, 1969.

McCOY, Fleetwood M., Jr.
POETRY (Anthology): Murphy, Ebony Rhythm.

McCRAY, Nettie see SALIMU

McDONALD, Gerald.
POETRY (Anthology): Boyd, Poems by Blacks, vol. 2.

MacDONALD, Samuel E.
WRITINGS The Other Girl, with Some Further Stories and Po-
    ems. New York: Broadway, 1903.

McDUFFIE, Eleanor. Born 1920 in Tuscaloosa, Alabama.
POETRY (Anthology): Murphy, Negro Voices.

McELROY, Colleen. Born 30 October 1935 in St. Louis, Missouri.
Education: Ph.D. candidate at the University of Washington,
specializing in Language Arts. Currently living in Seattle. Career: Formerly a Speech Pathologist. Moderator of the twice-
monthly show, "Outlook," KVOS-TV, Bellingham, 1968-71.
Speaker for various civic and professional groups and poetry
reader for groups in the Seattle area. Presently instructor of
English, University of Washington; curriculum specialist and public school consultant, specializing in all forms of language--lan-
guage acquisition and communication with emphasis on cultural
differences and frame of reference. Also editor of the journal,
Dark Waters, 1973.
POETRY
    The Mules Done Long Since Gone. Seattle: Harrison-Ma-
        drona, 1973.
    (Periodicals): December 1971; Essence, March 1972;
        Jeopardy, 1971; Northwest Review, Winter 1972; Poetry
        Northwest, Spring 1972; Poetry Pilot, 1971; South Dakota
        Review, 1971-72; Wild Fennel, 1971; Wormwood Review,
        1971; also published in Black Lines; Black Dialogue;
        Choice.
NON-FICTION
    Speech and Language Development of the Preschool Child.
        Springfield, Ill.: C. C. Thomas, 1972.
INTERJECTIONS
    "We are all in a constant state of change--those changes are
effected by personal experiences and expectations. Throughout
my life, I fight to continue to say--'I am me,' 'I am black,'
'I am female'--that is all that is real."

McFARLAND, Harry Stanley. Born 24 April 1900 in Jamaica, West
Indies. Education: City College of New York and New York
University. Currently living in Brooklyn. Career: Retired
from the business world since 1965. Edited Education, a publi-
cation of the Negro Needs Society, directed the Beginners'
School (private lessons in English). Member: National Associa-
tion for the Advancement of Colored People.
POETRY
    Columbia Speaks. n.p., 1953.
    Growing Up: A Book of Verse. Boston: Meador, 1956.
    Missing Pages: Poems. Boston: Forum, 1962.
    More Missing Pages: A Book of Poems. New York: Carl-
        ton, 1966.
    Passing Through: A Collection of Poems. New York: Mal-
        liet, 1950.
    Some More Missing Pages. New York: Vantage, 1969.

To My Country. n.p., 1953.
Trilogy. New York: Vantage, 1971.
INTERJECTIONS
"My poetry is a record of my passing through this planet, earth."

McFARLANE, Milton.
POETRY (Anthology): Troupe, Watts Poets.

McGAUGH, Lawrence. Born 1940 in Newton, Kansas.
POETRY
A Fifth Sunday. Berkeley: Oyez, 1965†.
Vacuum Cantos. Berkeley: Oyez, 1969†.
(Anthologies): Adoff, Black Out Loud; Adoff, The Poetry of Black America.

McGEE, Maud.
POETRY To Get My Name in the Kingdom Book. Atlanta: By the Author, 1963.

McGEE, Pearl. Born 28 August 1934 in Bastfield, Arkansas.
Education: Was graduated from high school in 1950. Currently living in Los Angeles, California. Career: Community volunteer since 1953; Director and founder of the Pearl McGee Foundation. Awards, Honors: Certificate of Merit, City of Los Angeles; Honorary Ph.D. California State University, 1972; Woman of the Year; Outstanding Volunteer Award.
POETRY
Twenty Two Years on Welfare. n.p., n.d.

McGEE, Perry Honce.
POETRY My Valued Ruby. Washington, Pa.: By the Author, 1920.

McGIRT, James Ephraim. Born in Robeson County, North Carolina. Died 1930 in Greensboro, North Carolina. Education: Was graduated from Bennett College in 1885. Career: Owner and editor of McGirt's Magazine and McGirt's Publishing Company in Philadelphia. Returned to Greensboro where he developed the Star Hair Grower Company into a successful business venture. Became a realtor before his death.[1]
POETRY
Avenging the Maine. A Drunken A.B., and Other Poems. Raleigh: Edward & Broughton, printers, 1899.
For Your Sweet Sake: Poems. Philadelphia: John C. Winston, 1906.
Some Simple Songs, and a Few More Ambitious Attempts. Philadelphia: Larker, 1901.
SHORT STORIES
The Triumphs of Ephraim. Philadelphia: McGirt, 1907.
BIOGRAPHY AND CRITICISM ON McGIRT
Gloster. Negro Voices in American Fiction, pp. 70-71.
Parker, John W. "James E. McGirt: Tarheel Poet."

Crisis 60 (1953): 286-289.
White and Jackson. _An Anthology of Verse by American Negroes,_ p. 230.
  [1]John W. Parker, "James E. McGirt: Tarheel Poet,"
Crisis 60 (1953): 286-289.

McGRIFF, Milton.
  DRAMA _And Then We Heard Thunder,_ 1968. (Based on novel
    by John O. Killens.)

McGUIRE, Lois.
  DRAMA _The Lion Writes,_ 1970.

McIVER, Ray.
  DRAMA
    God Is a (Guess What?), 1968.
  REVIEWS: _God Is a (Guess What?)_
    Kerr, Walter. _The Sunday Times,_ 29 December 1968.
    Sullivan, Dan. _The New York Times,_ 18 December 1968.

MACK, L. V. _Born_ 6 May 1947 in Brooklyn.
  POETRY (Anthologies): Adoff, _The Poetry of Black America;_
    Wilentz and Weatherly, _Natural Process._

MACK, Ron.
  DRAMA _Black Is...We Are,_ 1969.

McKAY, Claude (Eli Edwards, pseud.). _Born_ 15 September 1890 in
  Sunny Ville, Jamaica, W.I. _Died_ 22 May 1948. _Education:_ In
  his earlier years he was self-educated with the help of an elder
  brother, an agnostic school teacher, and Walter Jekyll, an intellectual English resident of Jamaica, a collector of folklore. The
  two men allowed Claude access to their books and he became an
  avid reader of poets and philosophers.[1] Later, in 1912, after
  his arrival in the States, he attended Tuskegee Institute. From
  1912-14 he attended Kansas State College.[2] _Career:_ The young-
  est of eleven children, he was forced to help support the family.
  This he managed to do when he won a cabinet maker's apprenticeship.[3] He also worked the trade of wheelwright and later
  entered in the service of the Jamaican Constabulary, Kingston,
  1909. Attracted to writing, he published two collections of
  verse, _Songs of Jamaica,_ and _Constab Ballads._ The scholarship won for his poetry permitted him to leave for the States in
  1912. From 1912 to 1917 while in the States he attended school,
  became a kitchen helper in New England hotels, and a Pullman
  waiter on trains out of New York.
    In 1917 when the _Seven Arts,_ a literary magazine, published
  two of his sonnets, he finally won literary recognition in America. Following this successful attempt to publish, _Pearson's
  Magazine_ and the _Liberator_ selected and published his poems.
  England also became interested in his poetry, particularly his
  Constab Ballads. While in England, his poems were published
  in _Dreadnought_ and in the _Cambridge Magazine._[4] He remained

in England for a short time, returned to the United States and
accepted an associate editor position on The Liberator. The
wanderlust struck again, and in the years 1921-44 he travelled
in Russia, Germany, Spain, North Africa and France.

His pro-communist leanings made him welcome in Russia and
he was received as a comrade. He read his poems in public
and Pravda published a translation of a poem he wrote in Petro-
grad for May Day, 1923. He continued to travel and to write
in Europe until 1934 when again he returned home to Harlem.
In 1938 he met Ellen Tarry, a Catholic and writer of children's
books who invited him to Friendship House in Harlem. Here
he met the founder, Baroness de Huech. His friendship with
Miss Tarry and the Baroness, and the intellectual-spiritual at-
mosphere in Friendship House, lead him to reflect on his spiritual life, begun earlier while in Spain. On 11 October 1944,
Monsignor Sheil baptized him into the Catholic faith. On 22
May 1948, in a Chicago clinic, he passed away. [6] Awards, Honors: 1912, Medal of the Institute of Arts and Sciences, Jamaica; 1928, the Harmon Gold Award for Literature. [7]

BIBLIOGRAPHY OF McKAY's WORK
> Lopez, Manuel D. "Claude McKay." Bulletin of Bibliogra-
>   phy 29 (October-December 1972): 128-133.

COLLECTED WORKS
> The Dialect Poems of Claude McKay, 2 vols. in 1; facsimile
>   ed., Songs of Jamaica and Constab Ballads. Freeport,
>   N.Y.: Books for Libraries*.
> The Passion of Claude McKay: Selected Poetry and Prose,
>   1912-1948. Edited by Wayne Cooper. New York: Schock-
>   en, 1973.
> (Manuscript Collections)
> Schomburg Collection of Negro Literature and History, New
>   York Public Library.
> Beinecke Rare Book and Manuscript Library, Yale Univer-
>   sity Library.

AUTOBIOGRAPHY
> "Boyhood in Jamaica." Phylon 14 (Second Quarter 1953):
>   134-145. (Supplements A Long Way from Home.)
> A Long Way from Home. New York: Lee Fruman, 1937;
>   New York: Arno*†; New York: Harcourt Brace Jovanovich,
>   1970†.
> My Green Hills of Jamaica, forthcoming from Independent
>   Publishers.
> (Anthology): Barton, Witnesses for Freedom.

NON-FICTION
> Harlem: Negro Metropolis. New York: Dutton, 1940; New
>   York: Harcourt Brace Jovanovich, 1972†.
> (Periodicals): The African (March-April 1938): 197-208;
>   American Mercury 47 (August 1939): 444-450; (September
>   1940): 73-80; Catholic Digest 9 (July 1945): 43-45; Crisis
>   22 (July 1921): 102-103; 27 (April 1924): 259-262; 27 (De-
>   cember 1923): 61-65; (January 1924): 114-118; 28 (Septem-
>   ber 1924): 225-228; Ebony 1 (March 1946): 32; Epistle 11
>   (Spring 1945): 43-45; Jewish Frontier 4 (October 1937):

19-21; 7 (January 1940): 9-11; The Liberator 4 (July 1921):
20-21; 5 (April 1922): 8-9; (March 1922): 20-21; Nation
6 February 1935, pp. 151-153; 3 April 1935, pp. 382-383;
16 October 1937, pp. 399-402; 8 May 1943, pp. 663-665;
Negro History Bulletin 31 (April 1968): 10-11; New Leader
21, 10 September 1938, p. 5; 20 May 1939, pp. 5-6; 11
November 1939, p. 4; 18 February 1939, pp. 2, 5; 18
November 1939, pp. 4, 6; 23 September 1939, p. 4, 7;
10 June 1939, p. 8; 7 December 1940, p. 5; 27 September 1941, p. 5; 30 August 1941, p. 3; 25 October 1941,
p. 4; 15 November 1941, p. 4; 29 November 1941, p. 5;
13 February 1943, p. 4; New York Herald Tribune, 6
March 1932; Opportunity 15 (March 1937): 72-75; 17 (November 1939): 324-328; Worker's Dreadnought, 24 April
1920, p. 2; 7 February 1920, p. 6; 15 September 1920,
p. 6; 14 February 1920, p. 8; 7 August 1920, p. 7; 21
January 1920, pp. 1-2; 2 October 1920, p. 4.

NOVELS
Banana Bottom. New York and London: Harper, 1933;
    Chatham, N. J.: Chatham Bookseller*.
Banjo: A Story without a Plot. New York: Harper, 1929;
    New York: Harcourt Brace Jovanovich, 1970†.
Harlem Glory, forthcoming from Independent Publishers.
Home to Harlem. New York: Harper, 1928; Chatham, N.J.:
    Chatham Booksellers*. Excerpts in Brown, Davis and
    Lee, The Negro Caravan, pp. 196-203; Davis and Red-
    ding, Cavalcade, pp. 295-301.
Romance in Marsailles, forthcoming from Independent Pub-
    lishers.
POETRY
Constab Ballads. London: Watts, 1912. (See "Collected
    Works" for current publication.)
Harlem Shadows: The Poems of Claude McKay. New York:
    Harcourt, Brace, 1922.
Selected Poems. New York: Bookman, 1953; New York:
    Harcourt Brace Jovanovich, 1969†.
Selected Poems of Claude McKay. New York: Twayne,
    1971*.
Songs of Jamaica. Kingston (Jamaica): Gardner, 1912. (See
    "Collected Works" for current publication.)
Spring in New Hampshire and Other Poems. London: Rich-
    ards, 1920.
(Anthologies): Abdul, The Magic of Black Poetry; Adams,
    Conn and Slepian, Afro-American Literature: Poetry;
    Adoff, The Poetry of Black America; Baker, Black Lit-
    erature in America; Barksdale and Kinnamon, Black
    Writers of America; Bell, Afro-American Poetry; Bon-
    temps, American Negro Poetry; Bontemps, Golden Slip-
    pers; Breman, You'd Better Believe It; Brown, American
    Stuff; Brown, Davis and Lee, The Negro Caravan; Calver-
    ton, Anthology of American Negro Literature; Chambers
    and Moon, Right On!; Chametzky and Kaplan, Black and
    White in American Culture; Chapman, Black Voices; Cul-

len, Caroling Dusk; Davis and Redding, Cavalcade; Eleazer, Singers in the Dawn; Ellman and O'Claire, The Norton Anthology of Modern Poetry; Emanuel and Gross, Dark
Symphony; Ford, Black Insights; Hayden, Kaleidoscope;
Hayden, Burrows and Lapides, Afro-American Literature;
Henderson, Understanding the New Black Poetry; Hughes
and Bontemps, The Poetry of the Negro 1746-1970; Johnson, Ebony and Topaz; Johnson, The Book of American Negro Poetry; Jones, From the Roots; Jones, The Blues
People; Jordan, Soulscript; Kearns, Black Identity; Kendricks and Levitt, Afro-American Voices; Locke, The New
Negro; Lomax and Abdul, 3000 Years of Black Poetry;
Margolies, A Native Sons Reader; Miller, Blackamerican
Literature; Patterson, A Rock Against the Wind; Pool, Be-
yond the Blues; Randall, The Black Poets; Simmons and
Hutchinson, Black Culture; Singh and Fellowes, Black Lit-
erature in America; Stanford, I, Too, Sing America, Tur-
ner, Black American Literature: Essays, Poetry, Fiction
and Drama; Walrond and Pool, Black and Unknown Bards;
Watkins, An Anthology of American Negro Literature;
White and Jackson, An Anthology of Verse by American
Negroes; Young, Black Experience.
(Periodicals): Bookman, 62 (September 1925): 67; 63 (June
1926): 450; Cambridge Magazine 10 (Summer 1920): 55-59;
Canadian Forum 12 (November 1931): 68; Catholic Worker
11 (January 1945): 2; 12 (October 1945): 4-5; (July 1945):
4; 12 (January 1946): 3; 13 (May 1946): 5; 14 (July 1947):
2; (October 1947): 8; Crisis 28 (June 1924): 67; 30 (March
1926): 228; 33 (February 1927): 202; 35 (June 1928): 196;
77 (November 1970): 367; Freedomways 1 (Summer 1961):
162; Independent, 27 September 1919, p. 42; Interracial
Review 19 (March 1946): 37; Jet, 23 May 1963, p. 11;
Liberator 2 (September 1919): 25; (July 1919): 6, 20, 21,
46; (April 1919): 14; (March 1919): 6; (August 1919): 46;
3 (February 1920): 7, 12; (May 1920): 48; 4 (March 1921):
24; (July 1921): 6; (August 1921): 7, 10, 11; (October
1921): 6, 7; (December 1921): 9; 4 (January 1922): 23;
(March 1922): 22; (April 1922): 27; (May 1922): 16; (July
1922): 14; 6 (August 1923): 15; Literary Digest, 28 October 1922, p. 33; Nation, 24 March 1926, p. 318; Opportunity 4 (November 1926): 342, 338; 27 (Winter 1949); 9;
Pearson's Magazine 39 (September 1918): 276; 45 (December 1919): 664; 48 (March 1922): 33; The Seven Arts 2
(October 1917): 741-742; Workers' Dreadnought, 10 July
1920, p. 8; 9 October 1920, p. 5; 17 April 1920, p. 2;
19 April 1920, p. 3; 3 July 1920, p. 7; 24 April 1920, p.
1; 3 April 1920, p. 4; 31 July 1920, p. 9; 28 February
1920, p. 7; 19 January 1920, p. 1601.

SHORT STORIES
Gingertown. New York: Harper, 1932; facsimile ed., Freeport, N.Y.: Books for Libraries*.
(Anthologies): Watkins, Anthology of American Negro Literature.

513

McKay, C. (cont.)

BIOGRAPHY AND CRITICISM ON McKAY

Adams. Great Negroes, Past and Present, p. 123.

Anon. "Here Are 20 of America's Most Distinguished Negroes: Politicians, Poets, Musicians, Soldiers." Life, 3 October 1938, p. 58.

Anon. "Details that Budenz Omitted." St. Louis Post Dispatch, 7 February 1953.

Anon. "Did You Know." Crisis 60 (April 1953): 250.

Bardolph. The Negro Vanguard, pp. 202-208.

Barksdale and Kinnamon. Black Writers of America, pp. 489-491.

Barton. Witnesses for Freedom, pp. 135-146.

Bell, Gordon. "Claude McKay, Negro Poet and Novelist." The Daily Gleaner, 8 April 1933.

Bigsby. The Black American Writer, vol. 1, pp. 23, 60, 230, 234, 254.

Bone. The Negro Novel in America, pp. 48, 50, 55, 56, 67-75, 77, 101, 113, 132.

Bontemps. The Harlem Renaissance Remembered, 2-276 passim.

Brawley. Negro Builders and Heroes, pp. 238-239.

_____. The Negro Genius, pp. 241-246.

_____. The Negro in Art and Literature, pp. 117, 119-121.

Broderick. Negro Protest Thought in Twentieth Century Literature, p. 109.

Bronz. Roots of Negro Racial Consciousness: The 1920's: Three Harlem Renaissance Authors, pp. 69-89.

Butcher. The Negro in American Culture, pp. 103, 105, 140.

Cameron, May. "Claude McKay Declares Negro Writers Can Advance Only by Losing Self-consciousness: An Open Letter [to] Claude McKay." New York Post, 22 May 1937.

Cartey, W. "Four Shadows of Harlem." Negro Digest 18 (August 1969): 22-25.

Chametzky and Kaplan. Black and White in American Culture, pp. 344, 346, 350, 369.

Collier, Eugenia. "The Four-Way Dilemma of Claude McKay." Atlanta, Ga.: Center for African and Afro-American Studies, n.d. (Mimeographed.)

_____. "Heritage from Harlem." Black World 20 (November 1970): 52-59.

Conroy, Sister Mary. "The Vagabond Motif in the Writings of Claude McKay." Negro American Literature Forum 5 (1971): 15-23.

Cook and Henderson. The Militant Black Writer, pp. 12, 117.

Cooper, Wayne. "Claude McKay and the New Negro of the 1920's." Phylon 25 (Fall 1964): 297-306; also in Bigsby, The Black American Writer, pp. 53-65.

_____ and Robert C. Reinders. "A Black Briton Comes 'Home': Claude McKay in England, 1920." Race 9 (July 1967): 67-83.

Davis. The American Negro Reference Book, pp. 859-860, 875.

Doherty, Eddie. "Poet's Progress." Extension 41 (September 1946): 5, 46.

Drayton, Arthur D. "McKay's Human Pity: A Note on His Protest Poetry." Black Orpheus (June 1965): 39-48; also in Introduction to African Literature. Edited by Ulli Beier. Evanston: Northwestern University Press, 1967, pp. 76-88.

Dreer. American Literature by Negro Authors, pp. 45-46.

Earley, Stephen B. "Dark Singers." America 69 (3 July 1943): 352-354.

Freeman, Joseph. An American Testament: A Narrative of Rebels and Romantics. New York: Octagon, 1972, pp. 234, 245, 246, 254, 257, 258, 310, 378.

Gayle. Black Expression, pp. 74-254 passim.

Gloster. Negro Voices in American Literature.

Gregory, Horace and M. Zaturenska. History of American Poetry, 1900-1940. New York: Harcourt, Brace, 1946, pp. 393-394.

Hart, Rollin Lynde. "Moscow Champions the Negro Cause." Boston Herald, 30 December 1922.

Jackson, Blyden. "The Essential McKay." Phylon 14 (1953): 216-217.

Jahn. Neo-African Literature, pp. 183, 189, 191, 193, 198, 201-203, 207, 210-212, 217, 243, 272.

Johnson, James Weldon. Black Manhattan, pp. i-xxxiv, 284.

_____. "A Real Poet." New York Age, 20 May 1922.

Kaye, Jacqueline. "Claude McKay's 'Banjo.'" Présence Africaine, no. 73 (1970): 165-169.

Kent, George E. Blackness and the Adventure of Western Culture, pp. 16, 22, 25, 26, 29, 31-52, 55, 114.

_____. "Patterns of the Renaissance." Black World 21 (June 1972): 13.

_____. "The Soulful Way of Claude McKay." Black World 20 (November 1970): 37-51.

Kerlin. Negro Poets and Their Poems, 126-131, 272-273, 298.

Killam, G. D., ed. African Writers on African Writing. Evanston: Northwestern University Press, 1973, p. 104.

Lang, Phyllis Martin. "Claude McKay: Evidence of a Magic Pilgrimage." CLA Journal 16 (June 1973).

Larson, Charles R. "African Afro-American Literary Relationships." Negro Digest 19 (December 1969): 35-42.

_____. "Three Harlem Novels of the Jazz Age." Critique 11 (1969): 66-78.

Libman, Valentina A., comp., Robert V. Allen, trans., Clarence Gohdes, ed. Russian Studies of American Literature. Chapel Hill: University of North Carolina Press, 1969, p. 136.

Margolies, Edward. Native Sons, pp. 40-42.

Meikle, Robert E. "Address on the Poetry of Jamaica." Daily Gleaner, 25 November 1933.

Mphahlele, Ezekiel. Voices in the Whirlwind. New York: Hill & Wang, 1972, pp. 138-139.

Nelson, John Herbert. "Negro Characters in American Literature." Humanistic Studies of the University of Kansas, vol. 4. Lawrence: Kansas University Press, 1932, p. 134.

Ottley and Weatherby. The Negro in New York, pp. 224, 255-257.

Oxley, Thomas L. G. "The Negro in the World's Literature." New York Amsterdam News, 29 February 1928.
_____. "Survey of Negro Literature, 1760-1926." The Messenger 9 (February 1927): 37-39.

"Persons and Achievements to Be Remembered in December." Negro History Bulletin 2 (December 1938): 19.

Pinkney, Alphonso. Black Americans. Englewood Cliffs, N.J.: Prentice-Hall, 1969, pp. 147-149.

Priebe, Richard. "The Search for Community in the Novels of Claude McKay." Studies in Black Literature 3 (Summer 1972): 22-30.

Ramchand. "Claude McKay and Banana Bottom." Southern Review 4 (1970): 53-66.

Redding. They Came in Chains, pp. 256, 263, 266, 285.

Smith, Robert A. "Claude McKay: An Essay in Criticism." Phylon 9 (1948): 270-273.

Stoff, Michael B. "Claude McKay and the Cult of Primitivism." In Bontemps, The Harlem Renaissance Remembered, pp. 126-145.

Taylor, Clyde. "Black Folk Spirit and the Shape of Black Literature." Black World 21 (August 1972): 31-40.

Wagner. Black Poets of the United States, pp. 197-257.

Whitlow. Black American Literature, pp. 76-80.

Young. Black Writers of the Thirties, pp. 141-143, 147, 203-205, 212-216, 223.

[1]Richard Barksdale and Keneth Kinnamon, Black Writers of America (New York: Macmillan, 1972), p. 489.
[2]Sterling Brown, Arthur P. Davis and Ulysses Lee, The Negro Caravan (New York: Citadel, 1941), p. 348.
[3]Arthur P. Davis and Saunders Redding, Cavalcade (Boston: Houghton Mifflin, 1971), p. 292.
[4]Barksdale and Kinnamon, pp. 489-90.
[5]Davis and Redding, p. 292.
[6]Jean Wagner, The Black Poets of the United States (Urbana: University of Illinois Press, 1973), pp. 203-204.
[7]Abraham Chapman, Black Voices (New York: Mentor, 1968), pp. 371-372.

MACKEY, Nathaniel Ernest. Born 25 October 1947 in Miami, Florida. Education: A.B., Princeton, 1969. Currently living in Oakland, California. Career: Presently a doctoral candidate in English at Stanford University, writing a dissertation dealing with Open Field Poetics.
POETRY AND STORIES
Published in Black Arts; Brilliant Corners; Catalyst; Experiment; Nassau Lit; Upstart; Yardbird Review.

WORK IN PROGRESS
   An extended work in poetry called "When Angels Speak of
      Love," planning a magazine, Hambone, having to do with
      song, poetry, love and ta' will ("the exegesis that leads
      the soul back to truth").
INTERJECTIONS
   "Then will appear in the bottom of the vessel the mighty
Ethiopian, burned, calcined, discoloured, altogether dead and
lifeless. He begs to be buried, to be sprinkled with his own
moisture and slowly calcined till he shall arise in glowing form
from the fierce fire. Behold a wondrous restoration and renewal of the Ethiopian! Because of the bath of rebirth he takes a
new name, which the philosophers call the natural sulphur and
their son, this being the stone of the philosophers. And behold
it is one thing, one root, one substance with nothing superflu-
ous added, from which much that was extraneous is taken away
by the magistry of the art. It is the treasure of treasures, the
supreme philosophical potion, the divine secret of the ancients.
Blessed is he that finds such a thing. One that has seen this
thing writes and speaks openly, and I know that his testimony
is true."

MACKEY, William Wellington.
   DRAMA
      Behold! Cometh the Vanderkellans, 1965.
      Billy No Name (musical), 1970.
      Death of Charlie Blackman.
      Family Meeting. In Couch, New Black Playwrights, pp. 247-
         285.
      Love Me, Love Me, Daddy--Or I Swear I'm Gonna' Kill You.
      Requiem for Brother X. In King and Milner, Black Drama
         Anthology.
   REVIEW: Behold! Cometh the Vanderkellans.
      Fuller, Hoyt. Negro Digest 16 (April 1967): 51-52.

McKINSTRY, Charles.
   POETRY (Anthology): Boyd, Poems by Blacks, vol. 2.

McLEAN, Eldon George.
   POETRY (Anthology): Murphy, Ebony Rhythm.

McLEAN, William Alfred, Jr.
   POETRY (Anthology): Adoff, Black Out Loud.

McLEMORE, William P. Born 30 March 1931 in Savannah, Georgia. Career: See Shockley and Chandler, Living Black American Authors, p. 103.

McMORRIS, Thomas.
   POETRY Striving to Win. Boston: Christopher, 1949.

McNEAL, James Harrison.
   POETRY Thoughts in the Negro Experience. Philadelphia:
      Russell Press, 1967.

McNEIL, Dee Dee. Born 17 September 1943 in Detroit, Michigan.
POETRY (Anthologies): Patterson, A Rock Against the Wind;
  Witherspoon, Broadside Annual 1972.

McPHERSON, James Alan. Born 1943 in Savannah, Georgia. Career: See Contemporary Authors, 25/28.
NON-FICTION
  "Indivisible Man." Atlantic 226 (December 1970): 45-60;
    also in Hersey, Ralph Ellison.
SHORT STORIES
  Hue and Cry: Short Stories. Boston: Little, 1969*; New
    York: Fawcett, 1970†.
  (Anthologies): Abrahams, Prize Stories 1970: The O'Henry
    Awards; Chapman, New Black Voices; Foley, Best American Short Stories 1973; Ford, Black Insights; Hayden,
    Burrows and Lapides, Afro-American Literature; Hicks,
    Cutting Edges; Robinson, Nommo.
  (Periodicals): Atlantic, Playboy.
REVIEW: Hue and Cry.
  Hicks, Granville. Saturday Review, 24 May 1969.
  Howe, Irving. Harper 239 (December 1969): 570.
  Llorens, David. Negro Digest 19 (November 1969): 86-87.

McRAE, John C17X.
SHORT STORY
  (Anthology): Sanchez, We Be Word Sorcerers.
  Also published in Sanchez, 360° of Blackness Coming at You.

MADDEN, Will Anthony. Career: Worked with Attorney Louis Nizer for many years.
CHILDREN AND YOUNG ADULTS
  Let's Read a Story About Princess Carolyn. New York: Exposition, 1970.
SHORT STORIES AND DRAMA
  Five More. New York: Exposition, 1963.
  Sextette. New York: Exposition, 1972.
  Two and One: Two Short Stories and a Play. New York:
    Exposition, 1961.

MADGETT, Naomi Long. Born 5 July 1923 in Norfolk, Virginia.
Education: B.A., Virginia State College, 1945; M.Ed., Wayne
State University, 1955; also studied at University of Detroit,
1962-63; and University of Iowa. Currently living in Detroit,
Michigan. Career: Taught in public high schools for 12 years,
initiating courses in Afro-American literature and creative writing; Associate Professor of English (specializing in Afro-American literature and creative writing), Eastern Michigan University, 1965 to present. Frequently lectures on poetry, and
serves as guest lecturer at the University of Michigan. Has
travelled in Europe, Africa, and the Middle East. Awards,
Honors: Recipient of a Mott Fellowship in English at Oakland
University; named Distinguished Teacher of the Year by the
Metropolitan Detroit English Club, 1967.

Naomi Long Madgett

POETRY
One and the Many. New York: Exposition, 1956.
Pink Ladies in the Afternoon. Detroit: Lotus Press, 1973†.
Songs to a Phantom Nightingale. New York: Fortuny's, 1941.
Star by Star: Poems. Detroit: Harlo Press, 1965.
(Anthologies): Adams and Briscoe, Up Against the Wall,
　Mother; Arnfield, et al., Mirror of Men's Minds; Adoff,
　The Poetry of Black America; Bell, Afro-American Po-
　etry; Brooks, Bahn and Okey, Literature for Listening;
　Boyd, Ten by Blacks; Brooks, A Broadside Treasury;
　Chambers and Moon, Right On!; Chapman, Black Voices;
　Chapman, New Black Voices; Davis and Redding, Caval-
　cade; Dreer, American Literature by Negro Authors;
　Drake, Michigan Signatures; Cuban and Roth, Promise
　of America; Fabre, Les Noirs Americains (France); Hay-
　den, Kaleidoscope; Hughes, New Negro Poets: USA;
　Hughes and Bontemps, The Poetry of the Negro: 1746-
　1970; Jordan, Soulscript; Kramer, On Freedom's Side;
　Kytle, The Comp Box; Long and Collier, Afro-American
　Writing; Marandet and Gabriel, Britain America (France);
　Pool, Beyond the Blues; Pettit, Poems to Enjoy; Pettit,
　Poems to Remember; Olsen and Swinburne, Tomorrow
　Won't Wait; Pool, Ik Ben De Nieuwe Neger (The Nether-

lands); Pool and Breman, Afro-Amerikaanse Poezie (The
Netherlands); Randall, The Black Poets; Randall, Black
Poetry: A Supplement; Ryan, Within You, Without You;
Salerno and Meyer, Composition and Literary Form;
Sweeney, World of Challenge, Book 3 (England); Tester,
Black America, Yesterday and Today; Turner, Black
American Literature: Poetry.

(Periodicals): Freedomways, Fall 1961; Journal of Black Po-
etry, Fall-Winter 1971; Negro Digest, April, September,
October 1963; September 1966; September-October 1968;
Phylon, Second Quarter 1945.

Also published in Michigan Challenge; Poetry Digest; American
Pen; Negro History Bulletin; Poetry News-Letter; The
Free Lance; Blue River Poetry Magazine; Missouri School
Journal; The Detroit News; The Michigan Chronicle; The
Norwester; The Virginia Statesman.

TEXTBOOK
    With Ethel Tincher and Henry B. Maloney. Success in Lan-
guage and Literature. Chicago: Follett, 1967.

BIOGRAPHY ON MADGETT
    Contemporary Authors, 33/36.
    Negro History Bulletin 26 (October 1962): 56-57.

REVIEW: Star by Star.
    Randall, Dudley. Negro Digest 15 (September 1966): 51-52.

MAEFIELD, Isaac.
    POETRY (Anthology): Black Poets Write On!

MAHONE, Barbara   see   McBAIN, Barbara Mahone

MAHONEY, William. Born 1 October 1941.
    NON-FICTION
    (Anthology): Jones and Neal, Black Fire.
    NOVEL
    Black Jacob. New York: Macmillan, 1969*.
    REVIEWS: Black Jacob.
    Karp, David. New York Times Book Review, 9 March 1969,
    p. 38.
    Saturday Review, 5 April 1969, p. 39.

MAHR, Allen David. Born 7 January 1910 in Belleville, Illinois.
    Education: Studied writing in adult education, at University
City High School in St. Louis; at St. Louis University, and at
the Missouri University Extension, St. Louis. Also took advanced English courses at McKendree College and Missouri University. Currently living in St. Louis, Missouri. Career:
Postal clerk. His poems have been displayed in St. Louis area
libraries and in Illinois libraries. Seventy-eight poems have
been recorded by Dean Sale under the title, "Tape Talk for the
Blind." Other poems were recorded and sent to Saurashtra University Area English Teachers Association, Rajkot, India. He
has contributed poetry to the memorials of Tom Dooley, John
F. Kennedy, Winston Churchill, Lyndon B. Johnson. Member:

David Mahr

McKendree Writers Conference; St. Louis Poetry Center; Avalon Writers; Arizona Poetry Society. Awards, Honors: Cum Laude, John Masefield Memorial Competition; Book prize for "Dag Hammarsjold" in Manifold's Poems of the Decade Competition; 8th place, Manifold's "Forestry" competition; Honorable mention for "Courage Personified," St. Louis Poetry Concert.
POETRY
 (Anthologies): Ballet on the Wind; Yearbook of Modern Poetry.
 (Periodicals): The Christian, 23 December 1973; Cyclo-Flame, Spring 1969; Spirit/Talk Magazine, September 1972; also published in The Poetry Form, The Hearing Digest, Manifold: A Review of Poetry and the Arts (London): Swordsman; Vision.
BIOGRAPHY ON MAHR
 International Who's Who in Poetry.

MAJOR, Clarence. Born 31 December 1936 in Atlanta, Georgia. Education: Chicago Public Schools. Career: Editor, Coercion Review, 1958-63; Associate Editor, Proof, 1960; Book Review Editor, Anagogic and Paideumic Review, 1960-61; Associate

Clarence Major (credit: Shary J. Skeeter)

Editor, Journal of Black Poetry, 1967-70; Instructor, Academy
of American Poets, Board of Education, New York City, 1968
to present; Instructor at Pennsylvania Advancement School, 1967-
68, at Brooklyn College, 1968-69; at the Center for Urban Education, 1968; Consultant, Cazenovia College Summer Institute,
1969; Visiting Writer, University of Wisconsin-Eau Claire, 1970;
Lecturer at the Guggenheim Museum, at the New School for Social Research and at the University of Rhode Island.[1]

CRITICISM

"Black Criteria." Journal of Black Poetry, Spring 1967;
also in Chapman, Black Voices; Robinson, Nommo.
"Close to the Ground: A Note on Walt Whitman." American
Dialog (1969).
The Dark and Feeling. New York: Third Press, 1974*.
"The Explosion of Black Poetry." Essence June 1972.
"Formula or Freedom." In Studies in Black American Fic-
tion.
"An Interview with Clarence Major and Victor Hernandez
Cruz." In Chapman, New Black Voices.
"Introduction." The New Black Poetry. Edited by Major;
reprinted in Miller, Blackamerican Literature.
"Frank London Brown: A New American Voice." Proof 1
(Summer 1960).
"H.D.: To Preserve the Living Tradition." Anagogic and
Paideumic Review (1961).
"The Poetry of LeRoi Jones: A Critique." Negro Digest
14 (March 1965): 54-56.

EDITOR

The New Black Poetry. New York: International, 1969*†.

NON-FICTION

Dictionary of Afro-American Slang. New York: International,
1970. Published in England as Black Slang (Routledge &
Paul Kegan, 1971).
Slaveship and Relationship. New York: Emerson Hall, forthcoming.
(Periodicals): Anagogic and Paideumic Review, 1961; Black
Orpheus (Nigeria), 1961; Bronze Mirror, 1962; Caw!,
1968; Coercion Review, 1958, 1965; el carno emplumado,
1969; Essence, January 1971; New Left Notes, 23 December 1966, 6 November 1967; Nickel Review, 26 September,
3 October, 10 October, 24 October, 31 October, 7 November, 5 December 1969; 23 January 1970; Proof, Summer
1960; Trace, 1959; The Village Voice, 25 November 1971.

POETRY

Cotton Club. Detroit: Broadside, 1972†.
Human Juices. Omaha: Coercion Press, 1965.
Love Poems of a Black Man. Omaha: Coercion Press, 1964.
Private Line. London: Breman, 1971†; distributed in the
U.S. by Broadside Press.
Symptoms and Madness. New York: Corinth, 1971*†.
The Syncopated Cakewalk. New York: Barlenmir House,
1974.
(Anthologies): Adoff, Black Out Loud; Adoff, The Poetry of

Black America; Baylor and Stokes, Fine Frenzy; Bell,
Modern and Contemporary Afro-American Poetry; Berri-
gan, A Punishment for Peace; Bontemps, American Negro
Poetry; Boyle and Merritt, Urban Adventures; Breman,
You Better Believe It; Chapman, New Black Voices; Clark,
The Real Imagination; Colley and Moore, Starting with Po-
etry; Goodman, The Movement Toward a New America;
Gross, Open Poetry; King, Black Spirits; Lief and Light,
The Modern Age: Literature; Lowenfels, Where Is Viet-
nam?; Major, The New Black Poetry; Miller, Dices or
Bones; Randall, Black Poetry: A Supplement; Randall and
Burroughs, For Malcolm; Reed, Yardbird Reader I; Wil-
entz and Weatherly, Natural Process.
(Periodicals): Altissimo Catamont, 1959; Anagogic and Pai-
deumic Review, Winter 1960; Artesian, 1960; Artpress
Magazine, 1960; Beatitude, February 1960; Beginning,
1966; Black World, September 1971; Blue River, 1955;
Brand X, June 1962; Camels Coming, 1966; Center, 1971;
Chelsea, 1971; Coercion Review, 1960, Spring 1965; Con-
gress, 1967; The Cresset, 1960; Dawn: Young Writer's
Magazine, 1957; Do It, 1966; Down Here, 1967; East and
West (India), 1959; The Editors, May 1966; el carno em-
plumado (Mexico), 1969; Entrails, 1966; Equal-Time, Fall
1972; Essence, February, October 1971, January 1972;
Existeria, 1955, 1956, 1957, 1958; Fallout, Summer 1965;
Fiddlehead (Canada), 1959; Free Lance, 1960, 1965, 1968;
From a Window, June 1965; Galley Sail Review, 1960,
Spring 1965, 1967, 1968; Graffiti, August 1965; Green-
field Review, 1971; Hearse, 1958; A Houyhnhnm's Scrap-
book, 1955; Illuminations, 1969; Journal of Black Poetry,
1966, 1967, 1969; Kauri, March-April, July-August 1965;
Literary Calendar, 1958; Literary Review, 1959; Maga-
zine, 1966; Motive, 1968; Mundas Artium, 1973; National
Guardian, 1967; Negro American Literature Forum, Fall
1972; Letras De Provinica, September-October 1960; New
Athenaeum, 1958; The New Lantern Club Review, Summer
1965; New York Quarterly, Winter 1972; Nickel Review, 6
February 1970; 19 December 1969; Nightshade, 1965; Nomad, 1959, 1960; Ole, May 1966; The Outsider, 1962,
1969; Park Row, 1969; The Pendulum of the Time and the
Arts, March-April 1961; Penny Poems, 1959; Poetaster,
Fall 1968; Poetry Dial/Piggot Banner, 2 July 1965; Po-
etry Digest, 1959; Poetry Fund Journal, 1960; Poetry Review (London), Summer 1972; Quadrant, November-Decem-
ber 1972; Quicksilver, 1960; Red Clay Reader, Fall 1965;
Scrivener, March-April 1965; Soulbook, 1966, 1967; State-
ments, no. 3, 1959; Tautara (Canada, 1970; 'This And...",
October 1965; Thoth, Fall 1972, Fall 1973; Umbra, 1963;
The Unmuzzled Ox, 1973; The View from Here, 1967;
Vigil, 1959; White Dove Review, 1959, 1960; Wild Dog,
March 1965; Works, 1967, 1971, Summer 1972; The World,
1967.   Poetry also published in Aperch; Avalanche; Black
Orpheus; Coffin; '8' Pages; The Fly's Eye; For Now; Hu-

man Voice Quarterly; Input; Intrepid; Jean's Journal;
Letras da Provincia (Brazil); Lili; Manic Press; New
Magazine; Outcast; Poetry Pendulum; The Poets Bulletin;
Showcase; Workshop; Workshop Directory.

NOVELS
All-Night Visitors. New York: Olympia, 1969; University
Place, 1973. Also published in Italy and Germany. Ex-
cerpt in Reed, 19 Necromancers from Now.

REVIEWS BY MAJOR
Published in Black Creation, Black Dialogue, Essence.

SHORT STORIES
(Anthologies): Mayfield, Ten Times Black; Maurice Girodias,
ed. , The New Olympia Reader (Los Angeles: Sherbourne,
1970); Welburn, Dues.
(Periodicals): Black Creation, Summer 1972; Essence, December, 1973.

BIOGRAPHY AND CRITICISM ON MAJOR
Contemporary Authors, 23/24.
Jaffe, Daniel. "A Shared Language in the Poet's Tongue."
Saturday Review, 3 April 1971, pp. 31-32.
Lehmann-Haupt, Christopher. "Books of the Times: On
Erotica." The New York Times, 7 April 1969.
Lowenfels, Walter. "Black Poets." New World Review
(Second Quarter 1969).
O'Brien. Interviews with Black Writers, pp. 125-140.
Welburn, Ron. "All Night Travelers." Nickel Review 3
(September 1969).

REVIEWS: All-Night Visitors.
Miller, Adam David. The Black Scholar 2 (January 1971):
54-56.
Welburn, Ron. Negro Digest (December 1969): 85, 86, 87.
No
Davis, G. The New York Times, 1 July 1973, sec. 8, p.
22.
Walker, Jim. Black Creation 4 (Summer 1973): 44.

Swallow the Lake
McShane, Frank. Poetry 118 (August 1971): 295.
Welburn, Ron. Essence (November 1970).
[1]International Who's Who in Poetry, 3rd ed. (1972-73).

MAJOR, Joseph. Born 1948 in Brooklyn, New York.
POETRY (Anthology): Major, The New Black Poetry.

MALCOLM X (Malcolm Little). Born 19 May 1925 in Omaha, Nebraska. Died 21 February 1965. Education: Read prodigious-
ly while in prison for burglary. Career: Went to Boston in
1941, becoming a procurer, a dope pusher, and an armed rob-
ber after ordinary jobs like waiting table and shining shoes became too dull and routine. While serving a prison sentence he
became interested in the teachings of Elijah Muhammed, and entered the Nation of Islam upon his release from prison. His
dynamic leadership and magnetic personality enabled him to
rise within the organization and extend the boundaries of the

Nation of Islam. However, he fell into disfavor because of his success and was forced to dissociate himself from the Black Muslim movement. Upon his return from a journey to Mecca and Africa he became an orthodox Muslim, adopted the name El Hajj Malik El-Shabazz, and was trying to establish a new Organization of Afro-American Unity at the time of his assassination.

AUTOBIOGRAPHY

With Alex Haley. The Autobiography of Malcolm X. New York: Grove, 1965†. Excerpts in Baker, Black Literature in America; Barksdale and Kinnamon, Black Writers of America; Chambers and Moon, Right On!; Davis and Redding, Cavalcade; Kearn, Black Experience; Kendricks, Afro-American Voices; Margolies, Native Sons Reader; Miller, Blackamerican Literature.

NON-FICTION

Malcolm X on Afro-American History. New York: Pathfinder, 1970.

SPEECHES

Breitman, George, ed. Malcolm X Speaks. New York: Grove, 1965†. Excerpt in Long and Collier, Afro-American Writing.

_____, ed. By Any Means Necessary. New York: Pathfinder, 1972†.

Epps, Archie. The Speeches of Malcolm X at Harvard. New York: Apollo Editions, 1969. New York: Morrow, 1968*.

Goodman, Benjamin, ed. The End of White World Supremacy: Four Speeches. New York: Monthly Reviews, 1971 *†.

BIOGRAPHY AND CRITICISM ON MALCOLM X

Adams. Great Negroes, Past and Present, p. 131.

Adoff, Arnold. Malcolm X. New York: T. Y. Crowell, 1970.

Baldwin, James. One Day When I Was Lost. New York: Dial, 1973. (Based on Alex Haley's The Autobiography of Malcolm X.)

Boulware, M. H. "Minister Malcolm: Orator Profundo." Negro History Bulletin 30 (November 1967): 12-14.

Breitman, George. The Last Year of Malcolm X. New York: Schocken, 1968.

_____, Malcolm X: The Man and His Ideas. New York: Pathfinder, 19.

Broderick. Negro Protest Thought in the Twentieth Century, pp. 357-383.

Clarke, John Henrik. "Malcolm X: The Man and His Times." Negro Digest 18 (May 1969): 23-27.

_____ and others, eds. Malcolm X. New York: Macmillan, 1969.

Cleage, Albert. Myths About Malcolm X.

Curtis, R. The Life of Malcolm X. Philadelphia: MacRae Smith, 1971.

Fax. Contemporary Black Leaders, pp. 1-17.

Goldman, Peter Louis. The Death and Life of Malcolm X.
New York: Harper, 1973.
Haskins, James. Revolutionaries. Philadelphia: Lippincott,
1971, pp. 17-32.
_____, Profiles in Black Power. Garden City, N.Y.:
Doubleday, 1972, pp. 103-122.
Hoyt, Charles A. "The Five Faces of Malcolm X." Negro
American Literature Forum 4 (1970): 107-122.
Jamal, H. A. From the Dead Level: Malcolm X and Me.
. London: Deutsch, 1971.
Larrabee, Harold A. "The Varieties of Black Experience."
New England Quarterly 43 (December 1970): 638-645.
New York Times, 22 February 1965, p. 1.
Ohmann, Carol. "The Autobiography of Malcolm X: A
Revolutionary Use of the Franklin Tradition." American
Quarterly 22 (1970): 131-149.
Parks. Born Black, pp. 51-61.
_____. "Violent End of the Man Called Malcolm X." Life,
5 March 1965, pp. 26-31.
Playboy. Playboy Interviews. Chicago: Playboy Press,
1967, pp. 30-51.
Randall and Burroughs, For Malcolm.
Shabazz, Betty. "Legacy of My Husband, Malcolm X."
Ebony 24 (June 1969): 172-174.
Toppin. Biographical History of Blacks in America, pp. 358-
363.
Warren, R. P. "Malcolm X: Mission and Meaning." Yale
Review 56 (December 1966): 161-171.

MALCOLM, Barbara see NAYO

MALONEY, Clarence J. (Chaka Ja).
DRAMA The Sun Force, 1970.

MARGETSON, George Reginald. Born 1877 in St. Kitts, British
West Indies. Education: Was graduated with honors from the
Bethel Moravian School, 1895. Career: Came to the United
States in 1897, eventually becoming a sanitary engineer in Cam-
bridge, Massachusetts.
NON-FICTION
England in the West Indies. n.p., 1906.
Ethiopia's Flight: The Negro Question, or, The White Man's
Fear. n.p., 1907.
POETRY
The Fledgling Bard and the Poetry Society. Boston: R. G.
Badger, 1916.
Songs of Life. Boston: Sherman, French, 1910; facsimile
ed., Freeport, N.Y.: Books for Libraries*.
(Anthologies): Eleazer, Singers in the Dawn; Johnson, The
Book of American Negro Poetry; Kerlin, Negro Poets and
Their Poems; White and Jackson, An Anthology of Verse
by American Negroes.
BIOGRAPHY AND CRITICISM ON MARGETSON

Brawley. The Negro Genius, pp. 236-237.

Johnson. The Book of American Negro Poetry, pp. 107-108.

Kerlin. Negro Poets and Their Poems, pp. 109-110.

[1]Newman, Ivey White and Walter Clinton Jackson, An Anthology of Verse by American Negroes. (Durham, N.C.: Moore, 1968), p. 168.

MARKS, Jim.

POETRY Vibrations in Sanctuary. Palo Alto, Ca.: Jamal, P.O. Box 424, n.d.

MARRANT, John. Born 1755 in New York. Career: Chaplain of the African Lodge of Masons in Boston. Traveled to England. Served as a missionary in Nova Scotia. Considered "the most picturesque religious devotee among the early Negro writers."[1]

JOURNAL

Journal of John Marrant. London, 1789.

NARRATIVE

A Narrative of the Lord's Wonderful Dealings with John Marrant, a Black.... Taken down from His Own Relation, Arranged, Corrected, and Published by the Rev. Mr. Aldridge. London, 1785; 1802; also in Porter, Early Negro Writing, pp. 427-447.

SERMON

A Sermon: Preached on the 24th day of June, 1789. Being the Festival of St. John the Baptist. Boston, 1789.

BIOGRAPHY AND CRITICISM ON MARRANT

Loggins. The Negro Author in America, pp. 31-34, 95, 374, 411.

[1]Vernon Loggins. The Negro Author in America, 1931. (Port Washington, N.Y.: Kennikot, 1959), pp. 31-32.

MARSHALL, Florence.

POETRY Are You Awake? Lansing, Mich.: Shaw, 1936.

MARSHALL, Lila.

SHORT STORIES (Periodicals): Negro Story, May-June, July-August, October-November, December-January 1944-45.

MARSHALL, Paule. Born 9 April 1929 in Brooklyn, N.Y. Career: See Shockley and Chandler, Living Black American Authors, p. 106.

NOVELS

Brown Girl, Brownstones. New York: Random, 1959; Chatham, N.J.: Chatham Bookseller*; New York: Avon, 1970†.

The Chosen Place, The Timeless People. New York: Harcourt Brace Jovanovich, 1969*.

SHORT STORIES

Soul Clap Hands and Sing. New York: Atheneum, 1961; Chatham, N.J.: Chatham Bookseller*.

(Anthologies): Baker, Black Literature in America; Barksdale and Kinnamon, Black Writers of America; Chapman, Black Voices; Clark, American Negro Short Stories; Clarke,

Harlem; Davis and Redding, Cavalcade; Emanuel and
Gross, Dark Symphony; Ford, Black Insights; David, To
Be a Black Woman; Hughes, The Best Short Stories By
Negro Writers; Long and Collier, Afro-American Writing;
Patterson, An Introduction to Black Literature in America.
(Periodicals): Harper's, October 1962; New World (West In-
dies), 1967; Freedomways, Summer 1964.

CRITICISM BY MARSHALL
"The Negro Woman in American Literature." Freedomways
6 (Winter 1966): 21-25.

BIOGRAPHY AND CRITICISM ON MARSHALL
Barksdale and Kinnamon. The Black Writer of America,
pp. 773-774.
Braithwaite, Edward. "Rehabilitation." Critical Quarterly
13 (Summer 1971); 175-183.
_____. "West Indian History and Society in the Art of
Paule Marshall's Novel." Journal of Black Studies 1
(December 1970): 225-238.
Kapai, Leela. "Dominant Themes and Technique in Paule
Marshall's Fiction." CLA Journal 16 (September 1972):
49-59.
Miller, Adam David. "A Review of Paule Marshall's Brown
Girl, Brownstone." Black Scholar 3 (May 1972): 56-58,
Redding. "Since Richard Wright," pp. 27-28.
Stoelting, Winifred L. "Time Past and Time Present: The
Search for Viable Links in The Chosen Place, The Time-
less People by Paule Marshall." CLA Journal 16 (Sep-
tember 1972): 60-71.
Whitlow. Black American Literature, pp. 139-141.

MARTIN, Chester. Born 17 August 1892 in Utica, New York. Ca-
reer: machinist for 50 years; now retired.
NOVELS
He Was Born, He Died and He Lived. New York: Carlton,
1965.
Middle Years. New York: Carlton, n.d.
INTERJECTIONS
"I think the Watergate is a gross exaggeration of the affair.
Why spend good money on the trials. I can tell you when the
Democrats destroyed votes in 1920 (Harding election)."

MARTIN, Herbert Woodward. Born 4 October 1933 in Birmingham,
Alabama. Education: B.A., University of Toledo, 1964; M.A.,
State University of New York (Buffalo), 1967; M. Litt. (drama),
Bread Loaf School of English, Middlebury College, 1972; also
attended Antioch College and the University of Colorado. Currently living in Dayton, Ohio. Career: Although Woodward
is a classical and folk singer, he is also a specialist in the
16th and 17th century literatures, and in drama; directing, tech-
nicalities, acting, and critical readings of the plays. In the
academic field he was an Assistant Professor of English and the
Poet-in-residence, at Aquinas College from 1969-1970; an Assistant Professor of English at the University of Dayton, and the

Herbert Woodward Martin (credit: Carl Kotheimer)

Poet-in-residence from 1970-1973; a Distinguished Professor at
Central Michigan University, Fall, 1973. He made his Midwest Dramatic Debut narrating Aaron Copland's A Lincoln Portrait. Awards, Honors: Scholarships and fellowships at Antioch College, University of Colorado, Middlebury College's
Bread Loaf Writer's Project.

DRAMA
  Dialogue. In Cahill and Cooper, The Urban Reader.
POETRY
  New York the Nine Million. Grand Rapids, Mich.: Abraca-
    dabra Press, 1969.
  The Shit-Storm Poems. Grand Rapids, Mich.: Pilot Press,
    1972.
  (Anthologies): Adoff, The Poetry of Black America; Hayden,
    Burrows and Lapides, Afro-American Literature; also pub-
    lished in 10 Michigan Poets and Face the Whirlwind.
  (Periodicals): The Activist; Confrontation; Mainstream; Rap;
    Sumac; Trace.
WORK IN PROGRESS
  Editing: "Arias and Silences: Poems for Ezra Pound."
  Poetry: "War to Escape the Body"; "The Persistence of
    the Flesh."
INTERJECTIONS
  "WORK. That sums up much of my philosophy. Read.
Hear. Feel. Touch. Smell. Taste. See. If one does these
things with the heart and mind, and with the sure knowledge
that you ought to write about that with which you are familiar,
then you will have less trouble being a writer. I think one
needs to be familiar with practically EVERYTHING. It sure
helps when reading other authors, and it will help the beginning
writer with understanding the technical problems he faces, and
how to solve many of those problems. Poetry for me is the
re-making of experiences: all of the anguish, joy and love. I
feel one must be individual and specific before you can be universal, if that is finally of any importance."

MARTIN, Rose Hinton.
  POETRY Endearing Endeavors. New York: Pageant, 1960.

MARTINEZ, Maurice M. (Marty Most.) Born 1934 in New Orleans.
  POETRY
    New Orleans Blues. n.p.: By the Author, 1964.
    (Anthology): Hughes and Bontemps, Poetry of the Negro:
      1746-1970.

MARVIN X see MUHAJIR, El

MASK, W. E.
  POETRY Whispers from heaven and melodies of the heart.
    Washington: By the Author, n.d.

Clifford Mason

MASON, B. J.
    NOVEL The Jerusalem Freedom Manufacturing Co. New York:
        Paperback Library, 1971.

MASON, Clifford. Born 5 March 1932 in Brooklyn. Education:
    B.A. (English), Queens College, 1958. Currently living in New
    York City. Career: Taught junior high school English in Man-
    hattan, 1958-1966; during this period also taught adult education
    classes, 1959-1960, English to the foreign born, 1960-1961,
    English for Operation Second Chance, 1962-1963, and English to
    professional emigres, 1963-1964. Served as Chairman of the
    English Department, 1965-1966. Has appeared on television as
    panelist, interviewer, and drama critic. His radio show, Clif-
    ford Mason on Theatre, ran from June 1967 to August 1968.
    Taught a survey course in Black poetry and prose, and a semi-
    nar on Black theatre and related topics at Manhattanville Col-
    lege for two years. Wrote four pamphlets for the Wiley & Sons
    Springboard Series, 1968 (historical fiction on Blacks in Amer-
    ica). Currently an Assistant Professor at Rutgers University,
    literary critic, freelance writer, drama critic and playwright.
    Member: Dramatists Guild, Actors Equity, New Dramatists

Committee. Awards, Honors: $1000 first prize for Gabriel.
CRITICISM
  "Black Writer's Views on Literary Lions and Values." Ne-
     gro Digest 17 (January 1968): 47.
  "Jean Toomer's Black Authenticity." Black World 20 (No-
     vember 1970): 70-76.
  "Ralph Ellison and the Underground Man." Black World 20
     (December 1970): 20-26.
DRAMA
  Gabriel. In King and Milner, Black Drama Anthology.
  Jimmy X (one act), 1971.
  Sister Sadie, 1970.
  Midnight Special.
NON-FICTION
  (Periodicals): Live, 8 May 1970; New York Sunday Times,
     9 April 1967; 10 September, 10 December 1967.
REVIEWS BY MASON
  Published in New York Magazine; New York Amsterdam
     News; New York Times Book Section.
INTERJECTIONS
  "The black cultural tradition in America is a priceless one,
springing from the confluence of great mother Africa (sub-
merged in the New World but never destroyed), and the Anglo-
Saxon, Western European overflow. We, as blacks in America,
still don't realize this, that we are the citizens of the world,
and as such should never have to play the role of the proverbi-
al crabs in a barrel."

MASON, Leo J. Born 1947 in Detroit, Michigan.
  POETRY (Anthology): Henderson, Understanding the New Black
     Poetry.

MASON, Mason Jordan (pseud.)
  POETRY
  The Blue-Green Whale. Ranches of Taos, N. Mex.: Motive
     Press, 1952.
  The Constipated Owl. Eureka, Calif.: Hearse Press, 1962.
  Dream in Heliotrope. Ranches of Taos, N. Mex.: Motive
     Press, 1952.
  Lambent Fugue. n.p., By the Author, 1948?
  A Legionere. Eureka, Calif.: Hearse Press, 1959.
  The Mules That Angels Ride. Eureka, Calif.: Hearse Press,
     n.d.
  Mussolini Has Met His End in the Mad House. Ranches of
     Taos, N. Mex.: Motive Press, 1952.
  Notebook 23. Ranches of Taos, N. Mex.: Motive Press,
     1949.
  The Twenty-third of Love. Eureka, Calif.: Hearse Press,
     1958.
  A Wild Population of Drosophila. Ranches of Taos, N. Mex.:
     Motive Press,
  (Anthology): Hughes and Bontemps, The Poetry of the Negro:
     1746-1970.

(Periodical): <u>Phylon</u>, Second Quarter, 1952.

MASSEY, Joe C. <u>Born</u> 1892.
   POETRY <u>Singing Stars: Verses.</u> New York: Greenwich,
      1961.

MATHEUS, John Frederick. <u>Born</u> 10 September 1887 in Keyser,
   West Virginia. <u>Education</u>: A.B. <u>cum laude</u>, Western Reserve
   University, 1910; A. M. , Columbia University, 1921; additional
   study at the Sorbonne, Paris, 1925; University of Chicago,
   1927. <u>Currently living in</u> Charleston, West Virginia. <u>Career</u>:
   Professor of Latin and Modern Foreign Languages, Florida Ag-
   ricultural and Mechanical College, 1911-1922. Professor and
   Head, Department of Romance Languages, West Virginia State
   College, 1922-1953. Spent six months in Liberia as Secretary
   to Dr. Charles S. Johnson, American member of the International Commission of Inquiry to Liberia, 1930. Director for
   the teaching of English in the national schools of Haiti, 1945-
   1946. While in Haiti, prepared and broadcasted: (1) progressive
   lessons in English (weekly); (2) a broadcast on American music.
   Has served as visiting professor at eight colleges. Has travelled extensively in Cuba, Europe, Haiti, Africa, Mexico, and
   South America. <u>Member</u>: College Language Association (Treasurer since 1942); West Virginia State Teachers' Association
   (Chairman of the Modern Foreign Language Section since 1932);
   American Association of Teachers of French (President of the
   West Virginia Chapter 1949 and 1950); Modern Language
   Teachers' Association (President of the West Virginia Chapter,
   1952-53); American Association of University Professors; West
   Virginia Association of Higher Education; American Association
   of Teachers of Spanish and Portuguese; El Instituto Internacion-
   al de Estudios Adro-americanos of Mexico City; National Lexi-
   cographic Board (Consultant in Romance Languages); American
   Academy of Language Research; Sigma Delta Pi (National Hon-
   orary Society for Students of Spanish); Sigma Pi Phi; Alpha Phi
   Alpha; the Kanawha County Association for the United Nations.
   <u>Awards, Honors</u>: "Officier de l'Ordre Nationale 'Honneur et
   Merite' " (decoration from the Haitian Government); Annual
   Achievement Award, Tau Chapter of Kappa Alpha Psi, 1951;
   Short Story Award, <u>The Crisis</u> contest, 1926; award for best re-
   view of the year, <u>The Journal of Negro History,</u> 1936.
   CRITICISM BY MATHEUS
      "African Footprints in Hispanic-American Literature." <u>The</u>
         <u>Journal of Negro History</u> 23 (July 1939).
      "An Estimate of Mercer Cook's <u>Five French Negro Authors.</u>"
         <u>Negro History Bulletin</u> 7 (January 1944): 86, 94.
      "Lady Windermere's Fan." <u>Dramatis Personae</u> 34 (1927): 11.
      "The Poetry of Haiti." <u>Opportunity,</u> October 1927.
      "Some Aspects of the Negro Interpreted in Contemporary
         American and European Literature." In Cunard, <u>Negro</u>
         <u>Anthology,</u> p. 83.
      "The Theatre of Jose Joaquin Gamboa." <u>College Language</u>
         <u>Association Bulletin</u> (Spring 1951).

John F. Matheus

DRAMA
>   Black Damp. In Caroline Magazine 49 (April 1929).
>   'Cruiter. In Locke and Gregory, Plays of Negro Life; Miller,
>   Blackamerican Literature; Cromwell, Turner, and Dykes,
>   Readings from Negro Authors.
>   Ouanga. (A drama and a libretto, music by Clarence Cam-
>   eron White), 1929-31. World Premiere held in South
>   Bend, Indiana, June 10 and 11, 1949.
>   Ti Yvette. In Richardson, Plays and Pageants from the Life
>   of the Negro.

EDITOR
>   With W. Napoleon Rivers. Georges by Alexander Dumas,
>   pere. Washington, D.C.: Associated, 1936.

NON-FICTION
>   (Periodicals): CLA Journal, June 1972 (article about Ouan-
>   ga.); Opportunity, July 1926, October, 1941; The Quarter-
>   ly Review of Higher Education Among Negroes, July 1934,
>   October 1942; Modern Language Journal, November 1937;
>   Bulletin of the Association of American Colleges, October
>   1941.

POETRY
  (Anthologies): Brown, Davis and Lee, Negro Caravan; Cook
    and Bellegarde, The Haitian-American Anthology; Cullen,
    Caroling Dusk; Patterson, A Rock Against the Wind.
  (Periodicals): The Carolina Magazine, May 1928; Negro Di-
    gest, July, 1947, Opportunity, September 1934.
REVIEWS BY MATHEUS
  Published in Opportunity; The Journal of Negro History; The
    Race; Color; The America; The Negro Educational Review.
SHORT STORIES
  A Collection of Short Stories.   Edited by Leonard Slade, Jr. ,
    Kentucky: n. p. , 1974.
  (Anthologies): Locke, The New Negro; Brown, Davis and
    Lee, Negro Caravan; Johnson, Ebony and Topaz; Cromwell,
    Turner and Dykes, Readings from Negro Authors; Boyle,
    Vail and Conarain, 365 Days, A Book of Short Stories, Cal-
    verton, Anthology of American Negro Literature.
  (Periodicals): Opportunity, May 1925; April, July, October,
    1926, August 1928; December 1929; July 1931; February
    1936; August 1937; The Crisis, December 1926; November
    1931; The Chronicle, June 1931; The Arts Quarterly, July-
    September 1937.
WORK IN PROGRESS
  An autobiography.
INTERJECTIONS
  "I have a creative literary bias.   Beginning in high school,
  inspired by Poe, Longfellow, Heine, I published poems in the
  two newspapers of Steubenville, Ohio.   In college I fell under
  the spell of Shakespeare, Maupassant, the Russian writers, Ro-
  bert Burns, Paul L. Dunbar, W. E. B. Du Bois, Grey's Elegy.
  My wife was psychic.   Thru her I became a student of Theoso-
  phy, Swedenborg, Spiritualism.   I found Bahaism.   I believe
  that the Mind is master over Matter."
BIOGRAPHY AND CRITICISM ON MATHEUS
  Bardolph.   The Negro Vanguard.   pp. 223, 317, 318.
  Bond.   The Negro and the Drama, pp. 112, 193.
  Brawley.   The Negro Genius, pp. 262-263, 284.
  Cullen.   Caroling Dusk, p. 60.
  Leaders in Education.
  Who's Who in America.
  Who's Who in American Education.
  Who's Who in Colored America.
  Who's Who in the West.
  Who's Who in West Virginia.

MATHIS, Sharon Bell.   Born 26 February 1937 in Atlantic City,
  New Jersey.   Education: B.A., Morgan State College, 1958.
  Currently living in Washington, D.C.   Career: A special edu-
  cation teacher at Stuart Junior High School in Washington, D.C.;
  Writer-in-Resident at Howard University; writes a monthly col-
  umn, "Ebony Junior Speak!" in Ebony Jr. magazine.   Member:
  Board of Advisors, Lawyer's Committee, D. C. Commission on
  the Arts; former head of the Children's Division of the D. C.

Black Writer's Workshop. Awards, Honors: Council on Inter-
racial Books for Children Award, 1970, for Sidewalk Story;
Teacup Full of Roses was selected as an ALA Notable Book of
1972; Bread Loaf Writers Conference fellow, 1970.
CHILDREN AND YOUNG ADULTS
   Brooklyn Story. New York: Hill & Wang, 1970.
   Listen for the Fig Tree. New York: Viking, 1974*.
   Ray Charles: A Biography. New York: T. Y. Crowell,
      forthcoming.
   Sidewalk Story. New York: Viking, 1971*; New York: Avon,
      1973†.
   Teacup Full of Roses. New York: Viking, 1972*; New York:
      Avon, 1973†.
SHORT STORY
   (Periodicals): Black World, June 1973; Essence, March
      1972; also published in Tan.
REVIEW: Teacup Full of Roses.
   Black World 22 (August 1973): 86.

MATTHEWS, Ralph.
   SHORT STORY (Anthology): Ford and Faggett, Best Short Sto-
      ries by Afro-American Writers.

MATURA, Mustapha.
   DRAMA Black Pieces. n.p.: Calder and Boyars, n.d. (in-
      cludes As Time Goes By.)

MAXEY, Bob.
   POETRY (Anthology): Coombs, We Speak as Liberators.

MAYFIELD, Julian. Born 6 June 1928 in Greer, South Carolina.
   Education: attended Lincoln University (Pennsylvania). Currently living in Guyana. Career: Actor; journalist; producer;
   founding editor of The African Review (Accra, Ghana); aide to
   President Kwame NKrumah, 1926-66; W. E. B. Du Bois Distinguished Visiting Fellow at Cornell University, 1970-71; also lectured at New York University, and taught a two-week seminar
   course in Black Techniques of Survival at the State University
   of New York--Cortland.
   CRITICISM
      "And Then Came Baldwin." Freedomways 3 (Spring 1963):
         143-155.
      "Black Writer's Views on Literary Lions and Values." Ne-
         gro Digest 17 (January 1968): 16.
      "Crisis or Crusade: An Article-Review of Harold Cruse's
         Crisis of the Negro Intellectual." Negro Digest 17 (June
         1968): 10-24.
      "Into the Mainstream and Oblivion." African Forum, 1960.
         Also in The American Negro Writer and His Roots; Baker,
         Black Literature in America, pp. 415-418; Gayle, Black
         Expression, pp. 271-275; Gross, A Nation of Nations;
         Emanuel and Gross, Dark Symphony.
      "The Negro Writer and the Stickup." Boston University Jour-

nal 1 (Winter 1969): 11-16.

"Tale of Two Novelists." Negro Digest 14 (June 1965): 70-72.

"You Touch My Black Aesthetic and I'll Touch Yours." In Gayle, The Black Aesthetic.

DRAMA
417. Scene in Childress, Black Scenes.
The Other Foot (one act), 1950.
A World Full of Men (one act), 1952.

EDITOR
The World Without the Bomb: The Papers of the Accra Assembly. Accra: The Secretariat of the Accra Assembly, 1963.

Ten Times Black: Stories from the Black Experience. New York: Bantam, 1972†.

NON-FICTION
(Anthology): Roger H. Klein, ed. Young American Abroad. (New York: Harper & Row, 1963.)

(Periodicals): Freedomways, Summer 1961, Black Scholar, July-August 1973; Commentary, April 1961; other articles in Puerto Rico World Journal; The African Review (Accra); Commentary; The New Republic; The Nation; Freedom.

NOVELS
The Hit. New York: Vanguard, 1957*; Belmont-Tower, 1970†.
The Grand Parade. New York: Vanguard, 1961*. (Published as Nowhere Street, New York: Warner Paperback Library, n.d.)
The Long Night. New York: Vanguard, 1958*.

SCREENPLAYS
Uptight.
Christophe.

SHORT STORIES
(Anthology): Mayfield, Ten Times Black.
(Periodical): Black World, February 1972.

WORK IN PROGRESS
Autobiography: "Which Way Does the Blood Red River Run?"

BIOGRAPHY AND CRITICISM ON MAYFIELD
Contemporary Authors, 13/14.
Cruse. The Crisis of the Negro Intellectual, pp. 373-38, 382, 384, 387-389, 509-510.
Lacy, Leslie Alexander. "African Responses to Malcolm X." In Black Fire. Edited by Jones and Neal, pp. 34-37.
"A Letter from Tom Feelings to Julian Mayfield." Black World 2 (August 1971): 26-34.
Mitchell. Black Drama, pp. 139, 155, 189.
O'Brien. Interviews with Black Writers, pp. 141-151.

REVIEWS: The Grand Parade.
Blotner, Joseph. New York Times Book Review, 19 (June 1961): p. 26.
Graham, Shirley. Freedomways 1 (Summer 1961): 218-223.
Redding, Saunders. New York Herald Tribune Books, 9 (July 1961): p. 9.

Mayfield, J. (cont.)   538

The Hit.
    Hughes, Langston. New York Herald Tribune Book Review,
      20 (October 1957): p. 12.
    Millstein, Gilbert. New York Times 29 (December 1957):
      p. 4.

MAYHAND, Ernest A.
    POETRY (Anthology): Schulberg, From the Ashes.

MAYS, Benjamin E. Born 1 August 1895 in Epworth, South Caro-
    lina. Career: See Shockley and Chandler, Living Black Amer-
    ican Authors, pp. 108-109.
    CRITICISM BY MAYS
      The Negro's God, as Reflected in His Literature, 1938; New
        York: Atheneum, 1968*; New York: Russell & Russell,
        1968*.
    NON-FICTION
      Born to Rebel: An Autobiography. New York: Scribner's,
        1971.
      Disturbed About Man. Richmond, Va.: John Knox, 1969*.
      With Joseph W. Nicholson. The Negro's Church, 1933. rev.
        ed. New York: Friendship Press, 1964; New York: Negro
        Universities Press, 1969*; New York: Russell & Russell,
        1969*.
      Seeking to Be Christian in Race Relations. rev. ed., New
        York: Friendship Press, 1965†.
      (Periodicals): Negro Digest; Journal of Religious Thought;
        Sepia; Crisis; Phylon.
      "Why I Am a Life Member (NAACP)." Crisis 63 (February
        1956): 96.
      "Why I Believe There Is a God." Ebony 17 (December 1961):
        139.
    BIOGRAPHY ON MAYS
      "America's Ten Most Powerful Negroes." Our World 10
        (April 1955): 48-55.
      Ebony 26 (July 1971): 88-92.
      Interview. Arts in Society 5 (1968): 279.
      Jet, 22 April 171, p. 17.
      Thurman, Howard. Why I Believe There Is a God. Chicago:
        Johnson, 1969, p. 2.

MAYS, Willie.
    MYSTERY With Jeff Harris. Danger in Center Field. Larch-
      mont, N.Y.: Argonaut, 1963.

MAZARD, Marie.
    POETRY Funny Girl. Kilburn, England: By the Author, 81
      Callcott Road, n.d.

MBEMBE (Milton Smith). Born 7 December 1946 in Kansas City,
    Missouri.
    POETRY (Anthology): Boyer, Broadside Annual, 1973.

MBERI, A. S. K.
    POETRY (Periodical): Journal of Black Poetry, Winter-Spring
       1970.

MEADDOUGH, R. J., III. Born 1935 in New York City.
    SHORT STORIES
       (Anthologies): Adoff, Brothers and Sisters; Clarke, Harlem;
          Hughes, The Best Short Stories By Negro Writers; Mirer,
          Modern Black Stories.
       (Periodicals): Freedomways, Fall 1967.
    REVIEWS BY MEADDOUGH
    Published in Freedomways, 1971.

MEANS, Sterling M.
    POETRY
       The Black Devils, and Other Poems. Louisville, Ky.: Pente-
          costal, 1919.
       The Deserted Cabin, and Other Poems. Louisville, Ky.:
          Pentecostal, 1919.
       (Anthology): Kerlin, Negro Poets and Their Poems.
    CRITICISM ON MEANS
       Kerlin. Negro Poets and Their Poems. p. 238.

MEBANE, Mary Elizabeth. Born 26 June in Durham, North Caro-
    lina. Education: A.B. (Music and English), North Carolina
    College at Durham, 1955; M.A. (English), University of North
    Carolina, 1961; Ph.D. in English, University of North Carolina
    at Chapel Hill, 1973. Currently living in Orangeburg, South
    Carolina. Career: Has taught high school in Durham, North
    Carolina; has taught in the Freshman-Sophomore English Pro-
    gram at the University of North Carolina; has been a Visiting
    Professor of Black Literature at the University of South Caro-
    lina; presently Associate Professor of English, South Carolina
    State College. Her major area of specialization is American
    Literature with a minor in Romantic and Victorian Literature.
    INTERJECTIONS
    "In my writings I want to portray accurately sensory impres-
    sions, moods, states of mind. The key word is 'accurate.' "
    NON-FICTION
       (Anthology): Harrison E. Salisbury, ed. The Eloquence of
          Protest: Voices of the Seventies. Boston: Houghton Miff-
          lin, 1972.
       (Newspaper): New York Times.
    SHORT STORY
       (Anthology): Shuman, A Galaxy of Black Writing.

MEDLEY, Lloyd J., Jr. Born 9 October 1949 in New Orleans,
    Louisiana. Education: B.A. in English, Louisiana State Uni-
    versity, 1971; work in progress for M.A. in Special Education,
    Louisiana State University; other educational experience re-
    ceived with the Blkartsouth Writer's Workshop and the Free
    Southern Theatre's Writer's Workshop. Currently living in
    New Orleans. Career: Participated in dramatic productions

and poetry reading sessions while in college, where he was also a member of the Black Student Association and a worker in
various phases of community organizations. Now serving as a
contributing editor on a final issue of NKOMBO, a Black literary publication, and reviewing articles for Expressions, a new
review of the Black Arts. Currently teaching in Special Education and working as a professional photographer. Awards, Honors: Dudley Randall Award for the best poem published for the
first time in Black World. Member: Free Southern Theatre's
Writer's Workshop.
POETRY
> (Periodical): Black World, September 1971; Journal of
> Black Poetry, Summer 1972; NKOMBO, March, June,
> 1971.

MELANCON, Norman. Born 6 November 1939 in Paincourtville,
Louisiana. Education: B.A., Dillard University, 1962; M.Ed.,
Nicholls State University, 1969; M.S., Loyola University, 1972.
Currently living in Paincourtville, Louisiana. Career: Spe-
cializes in elementary and secondary education. Taught for the
past nine years in the public schools of Assumption Parish;
currently teaching seventh and eighth grade science. Member:
Louisiana Education Association, National Education Associa-
tion, Assumption Parish Education Association.
POETRY
> Birth of a Slave Child. Los Angeles: National Poetry Press,
> 1968.
> I'll Just Be Me: Poems for Young and Old. New York:
> Exposition, 1967.
> (Periodical): Fall College Poetry Biennial.
INTERJECTIONS
"My philosophy may be stated in this poem:
> If I could walk, as the Master taught
> If I could love, as I ought.
> If I could give a helping hand to my fellow-man
> If I could sing, a well sung song, to life,
> Someone, as I travel along.
> So, I could cry, like apostle Paul
> > O! Death, where is thy sting,
> > O! Grave, where is thy Victory!"

MELFORD, Larry. Born in Brooklyn, New York. Education:
attended Pratt Institute in Brooklyn and evening sessions at
Columbia University; now attending Fordham University (evening sessions). Currently living in New York City. Career:
Employed as a program evaluator for the City of New York
while working on a collection of short stories and a novel. Has
read several of his short stories at public gatherings and on
radio; and has participated in the John Oliver Killens Writer's
Workshop at Columbia University for two years.
SHORT STORIES
> (Periodical): Black Creation.

WORK IN PROGRESS
   Novel: "Ironjaw"
   Short stories dealing with Manhattan's Lower East Side during the 1960's.
INTERJECTIONS
   "If I have any philosophical approach to writing it is somewhat similar to Ryunosuke Akutagawa's approach to his short
story 'The Spider's Thread.' In the story Akutagawa goes full
circle from an ideal situation down into the depths of hell only
to return again to the ideal situation. In some of my stories I
like to touch on similar conditions and its effect on the character involved. As a black writer I consider that the ideal condition within a Black artist is not just Blackness, but rather that
the artist is coming from the fundamental plateau of being 'both'
Black and Beautiful."

MENARD, John Willis. Born 1838. Died 1893.
   POETRY Lays in Summer Lands. Washington, D.C.: n.p.,
      1879. (Includes a biographical preface by F. G. Barba-
      does.)

MENKEN, Adah Isaaks. Born 1835. Died 1868.
   POETRY
      Infelicia. New York: H. L. Williams, 1868; Philadelphia:
         Lippincott, 1868; London: Chatto & Windus, 1888.
      See also: Deltwyn, Mrs. Agnes Proctor. Echoes from
         Shadow-land. New York: Alliance, 1900; republished as
         Believest Thou This. Chicago: M. A. Donahue, 1913.
         (Preface states that "These poetic messages were received
         clair-audiently from a source external to the writer,
         claiming to be the spirit of Adah Isaaks Menken, and are
         the sequelae to a volume of poems issued before the de-
         mise of that writer under the title of 'Infelicia'."

MENKITI, Ifeanyi. Born in 1940, Onitsha, Nigeria. Education:
   B.A., Pomona College, 1964; M.S., Columbia University, 1965;
   M.A., New York University, 1968; now working toward Ph.D.,
   Harvard University. Currently living in Cambridge, Massachusetts. Career: Teacher and writer, specializing in poetry with
   special interest in the area of philosophy; has given poetry readings in the New York City public schools under the auspices of
   the Academy of American Poets; other readings given at Columbia University, Brooklyn College, Long Island University, and
   at the Harvard Advocate.
   POETRY
      Affirmations. Chicago: Third World, 1971.
      (Anthologies): Gross, Open Poetry; other poetry in Lacy and
         Makward, eds. Contemporary African Literature. (New
         York: Random House, 1972); in W. Kgositsile, ed. The
         World Is Here: Poetry from Modern Africa. (Garden
         City, N.Y.: Doubleday, 1973.).
      (Periodicals): Transition; Journal of Black Poetry; Nigeria
         Magazine; Stony Brook; Sewanee Review; Chelsea; Sumac;

Okike; Southwest Review; African Arts; Pan African Journal; Bitterroot; Shantih; Evergreen Review.

MERCER, Will.
PLAY with Richard Grant, The Southerners (1904).

MERIWETHER, Louise M. Born in Haverstraw, New York.
CHILDREN AND YOUNG ADULTS
Don't Ride the Bus on Monday: The Rosa Parks Story.
Englewood Cliffs, N.J.: Prentice-Hall, 1973*.
Heart Man: Dr. Daniel Hale Williams. Englewood Cliffs,
N.J.: Prentice-Hall, 1972*.
The Freedom Ship of Robert Smalls. Englewood Cliffs, N.J.:
Prentice-Hall, 1971*.
NOVEL
Daddy Was a Number Runner. Englewood Cliffs, N.J.:
Prentice-Hall, 1970; New York: Pyramid, 1971.
CRITICISM BY MERIWETHER
"Amen Corner." Negro Digest 14 (January 1965): 40
"James Baldwin: Fiery Voice of the Negro Revolt." Negro
Digest 12 (August 1963): 3-7.
NON-FICTION
(Periodical): Negro Digest, October 1965.
SHORT STORY
(Periodicals): Antioch Review, Fall 1967; Essence, June
1971.
(Anthologies): Clarke, Harlem; King, Black Short Story Anthology; Watkins, Black Review No. 2.
BIOGRAPHY AND CRITICISM ON MERIWETHER
"Daddy Was a Number Runner." Ebony 25 (July 1970): 98-
103.
Schulberg. "Black Phoenix." p. 281.
REVIEWS: Daddy Was a Number Runner
Giovanni, Nikki. Black World 19 (July 1970): 85-86.
King, Helen. Black World 19 (May 1970): 51-52.
Marshall, Paule. New York Times Book Review, 28 June
1970, p. 3.
Sissman, L. E. New Yorker 11 (July 1970): p. 77.

MERRITT, Alice Haden. Born 1905.
POETRY
Dream Themes and Other Poems. Philadelphia: Dorrance,
1940.
Psalms and Proverbs: A Poetical Version. Philadelphia:
Dorrance, 1941.
Whence Waters Flow: Poems for All Ages from Old Virginia. Richmond, Va.: Dietz Press, 1948.

MERRIWEATHER, Angela.
SHORT STORY (Anthology): Shuman, A Galaxy of Black Writing.

MERRIWEATHER, Claybron William.
POETRY
  Goober Peas. Boston: Christopher, 1932.
  The Pleasures of Life, Lyrics of the Lowly, Essays and
    Other Poems. Hopkinsville, Ky.: New Era Printing Co.,
    1931.
  Sun Flowers; Lyrics of Sunshine and Other Poems. Hopkins-
    ville, Ky.: New Era Printing Co., 1938.

MESCHI, Howard.
  SHORT STORY (Anthology): Ford and Faggett, Best Short Sto-
    ries by Afro-American Writers.

MEYER, Annie Nathan.
  DRAMA
    Black Souls, 1932.
  SHORT STORY
    (Periodical): Crisis, January 1935.

MEYER, June see JORDAN, June Meyer

MICHEAUX, Oscar. Born 1884. Died in 1951. Career: Founded
  the Oscar Micheaux Corporation, becoming the first Black film
  producer with the first all-Black company.[1] Over a 30-year
  period he produced 34 pictures, most of which were designed
  for Negro audiences. As a novelist he wrote melodramas which
  would appeal to the masses, and he arranged extensive promotional tours to introduce each new book. He agreed to sell the
  screen rights to his novel, The Homesteader, only if he were
  permitted to direct the film version. After his offer was rejected, he was able to enlist enough support from his fans to
  make the film, which appeared in 1919. His films emphasized
  Black bourgeois interests and outlooks, failing to focus on the
  problems of the ghetto or racial strife; nevertheless, he took
  films a long step beyond the Hollywood servant-jester stereotype.[2]
NOVELS
  The Case of Mrs. Wingate. New York: Book Supply Co.,
    1945.
  The Conquest; The Story of a Negro Pioneer, by the Pioneer.
    Lincoln, Nebr.: Woodruff, 1913, reprint ed., Washington,
    D.C.: McGrath*; also available on microfiche: The Mi-
    crobook of American Civilization. Chicago: Library Re-
    sources, 1971. (LAC 15812.)
  The Forged Note; a Romance of the Darker Races. Lincoln,
    Nebr.: Western Book Supply, 1915.
  The Homesteader. Sioux City, Ia.: Western Book Supply,
    1917, reprint ed., Washington, D.C.: McGrath*.
  The Masquerade, an Historical Novel. New York: Book Sup-
    ply Co., 1947. (Plagiarizing C. W. Chesnutt's novel The
    House Behind the Cedars.)
BIOGRAPHY AND CRITICISM ON MICHEAUX
  Bone. The Negro Novel in America, p. 49.

Gloster. Negro Voices in American Fiction, pp. 84-89.
Half-Century (May 1919): 13-14.
Hughes. The Negro Novelist, pp. 35-36, 130-133, 226, 268.
    [1]Peter M. Bergman, The Chronological History of the
Negro in America (New York: Harper & Row, 1969), p.
375.
    [2]Donald Bogle, Toms, Coons, Mulattoes, Mammies,
and Bucks (New York: Viking, 1973), pp. 109-116.
    [3]According to Bone, The Negro Novel in America, p.
258, The Homesteader and The Wind from Nowhere are
virtually the same as The Conquest.

MICOU, Regina see IFETAYO, Femi Funmi

MIDDLETON, Henry Davies.
    POETRY
        Dreams of an Idle Hour. Chicago: Advocate, 1908.
        (Periodical): The Voice of the Negro, March 1906, Decem-
            ber, May 1904.
    SHORT STORY
        (Periodical): Half Century, November 1917; March, April
            1918.
    VIGNETTE
        (Periodical): Voice of the Negro, May 1906.

MILES, Cherrilyn.
    DRAMA
        Eleanora.
        To Each His Own.
        X Has No Value, 1970.

MILLER, Adam David. Born 8 October 1922 in Orangeburg, South
    Carolina. Education: M.A., University of California at Berke-
    ley; Advanced study in dramatic literature and U.S. cultural and
    literary history, University of California at Berkeley. Current-
    ly living in Berkeley, California. Career: Actor (stage and
    screen); Producer-director (stage); producer (television); co-or-
    dinator, actor, and director at the Aldridge Players/West in
    San Francisco; correspondent, San Francisco Bay Area, Black
    Theatre; Founding Editor, The Graduate Student Journal; organ-
    izer and member of Black-English Teachers. Currently teach-
    ing Black literature and composition at Laney College while work-
    ing on a film and a new anthology of Black poets; also prepar-
    ing a radio program of poetry. "The Imaged World," KPFA-
    FM. Awards, Honors: 1973 Award of Merit, California Associ-
    ation of Teachers of English; Artist-in-residence, University of
    Western Michigan (Arts and Ideas), 1969.
    CRITICISM
        "It's a Long Way to St. Louis: Notes on the Audience for
            Black Drama." The Drama Review 12 (Summer 1968):
            147-150.
        "News from the San Francisco East Bay." Black Theatre
            No. 4 (1970): 5.

"Some Observations on a Black Aesthetic." In Gayle, The
   Black Aesthetic.
EDITOR
   Dices or Black Bones: Black Voices of the Seventies. Bos-
      ton: Houghton Mifflin, 1970*.
POETRY
   (Anthologies): Adoff, The Poetry of Black America; Chap-
      man, New Black Voices; Miller, Dices and Black Bones;
      Simmons and Hutchinson, Black Culture.
REVIEWS BY MILLER
   Published in Black Scholar.
INTERJECTIONS
   "We more fortunate ones owe it to ourselves and to the world
not to despair but to do everything in our power to move the
work of human liberation along."

MILLER, Clifford Leonard.
   DRAMA
      Wings Over Dark Waters. New York: Great-Concord, 1954.
   POETRY
      Imperishable the Temple. Mexico City: By the Author, 1963.
      Haunting Voice, n.p., n.d.
      (Anthologies): Murphy, Ebony Rhythm; Pool, Beyond the
         Blues.

MILLER, Ezekiel Harry. Born 1890.
   NOVEL The Protestant. Boston: Christopher, 1933.

MILLER, Henry Jefferson. Born 1877.
   Blasted Barriers: Views of a Reporter in Story and Song.
      Boston: Christopher, 1950.

MILLER, Jeannette.
   POETRY (Anthology): Murphy, Negro Voices.

MILLER, Jeffrey.
   DRAMA
      The Last Ditch Junkie.
      Who Dreamed of Attica.

MILLER, Kelly. Born 23 July 1863 in Winnsboro, South Carolina.
   Died 1939. Education: Some work at Johns Hopkins University,
   1887-89; A.M., Howard University, 1901; LL.D., Howard University, 1903. Career: Entered government service while a
   student at Howard. Taught mathematics at Washington University in 1890, becoming Dean of the College of Arts and Sciences.[1] His great popularity and widespread activities helped
   to popularize Black history.[2] Member: Academy of Political
   and Social Science; American Social Science Association; N.E.A.;
   Walt Whitman International Fellowship; American Negro Academy;
   N.A.A.C.P.
   NON-FICTION
      See Directory Catalog of the Schomburg Collection or the

National Union Catalog Pre-1956 Imprints for listings of Miller's non-fiction publications.

(Anthologies): Calverton, Anthology of American Negro Literature; Ford, Black Insights; Miller, Backgrounds to Black American Literature; Thorpe, Black Historians.

POETRY

(Periodicals): Voice of the Negro, December 1905.

PROSE POEM

Kerlin, Negro Poets and Their Poems.

SHORT STORY

(Periodical): Voice of the Negro, November, 1905.

BIOGRAPHY AND CRITICISM ON MILLER

Bardolph. The Negro Vanguard, pp. 128, 160, 176-177, 179, 180, 251.

Bergman. The Chronological History of the Negro in America, p. 428.

Brawley. The Negro in Literature and Art, pp. 106-107, 150.

_____. The Negro Genius, pp. 169-170.

Davis. The American Negro Reference Book, pp. 556-557.

Journal of Negro History (July 1960): 182-197.

Kerlin. Negro Poets and Their Poems, p. 343.

Mays. The Negro's God, pp. 152-164, 167, 187, 197-200.

Meier, August. Journal of Negro Education (Spring 1960): 121-127.

_____. Negro Thought in America, pp. 62-63, 177, 183, 188, 198, 199, 213-217, 245, 260, 265, 267.

Negro History Bulletin 24 (November 1960): 42-43.

Thorpe. Black Historians, p. 152.

Who's Who in Colored America, 5th ed. (1938-1939-1940).

Young. Black Writers of the Thirties, pp. 6-13, 58-59; 236-237.

[1]Who's Who in Colored America, 3rd ed. (1930-1931-1932).

[2]Earl E. Thorpe. Black Historians (New York: William Morrow, 1971), p. 152.

MILLER, Larry see KATIBU, Sultani

MILLER, Laura Ann.

DRAMA

The Cricket Cries (one act), 1967.

The Echo of a Sound (one act), 1968.

Fannin Road, Straight Ahead, 1968.

Git Away from Here Irvine, Now Git, 1969.

MILLER, Lois.

POETRY (Anthology): Boyd, Poems by Blacks, Vol. 2.

MILLER, May (Mrs. John Sullivan). Born in Washington, D.C. Education: B.A., Howard University; additional work at American University and Columbia University. Currently living in Washington, D.C. Career: A former teacher of speech and dramatics, Frederick Douglass High School, Baltimore, Maryland. Has served as reader, panelist, lecturer, and guest poet at Monmouth College, at University of Wisconsin--Milwaukee, and at the Phillips Exeter Academy. Recorded for the Library of Congress Collection of Poets Reading Their Own Works, 1972. Worked for three years as coordinator for performing poets under the auspices of Friends of the Arts in the Public Schools of the District of Columbia. Member: Commission on the Arts of the District of Columbia (Chairman of Literature).

DRAMA
>Christophe's Daughters (one act). In Richardson and Miller, Negro History in Thirteen Plays.
>Graven Images (one act). In Richardson, Negro History in Thirteen Plays.
>Harriet Tubman (one act). In Richardson, Negro History in Thirteen Plays.
>Riding the Goat (one act), 1929. In Richardson, Plays and Pageants from the Life of the Negro.
>Samory (one act). In Richardson and Miller, Negro History in Thirteen Plays.
>Scratches (one act). In Carolina Magazine 49 (April 1929).
>Sojourner Truth (one act). In Richardson and Miller, Negro History in Thirteen Plays.

EDITOR
>With Willis Richardson. Negro History in Thirteen Plays. Washington, D.C.: Associated Publishers, 1935.

POETRY
>Into the Clearing. Washington, D.C.: Charioteer Press, 1959.
>The Clearing and Beyond. Washington, D.C.: Charioteer Press, 1973*.
>With K. L. Lyle and M. Rubin. Lyrics of Three Women. Baltimore: Linden Press, 1964.
>Poems. Thetford, Vermont: Cricket Press, 1962.
>(Anthologies): Davis and Redding, Cavalcade, Lowenfels, Poets of Today; Pool, Beyond the Blues.
>(Periodicals): Phylon, First Quarter 1950; First Quarter 1951; Fourth Quarter 1959; Also published in The Antioch Review; Cafe Solo; Common Ground; The Crisis; Energy West; The Nation; The New York Times; Poetry; Alan Swallo's P.S.; Writer; American University; World Order.

SHORT STORY
>(Periodical): Opportunity, Summer 1945.

CRITICISM ON MILLER
>Brawley, The Negro Genius, p. 284.

INTERJECTIONS
>"I am dedicated to a far-reaching scope for art, always believing in who I am and the direction in which I am going."

MILLICEN, Arthenia Bates   see   BATES, Arthenia

MILNER, Ron.   Born 1938 in Detroit.
CRITICISM BY MILNER
>"Black Magic: Black Art." Negro Digest 16 (April 1967): 8-12.

"Black Theatre--Go Home." Negro Digest (April 1968); also
in Gayle, The Black Aesthetic.

"Black Writer's Views on Literary Lions and Values." Negro Digest 17 (January 1968): 45.

DRAMA
(M)ego and the Green Ball of Freedom, 1972.
The Monster. In Negro Digest 19 (November 1969): 63; also
in Alhamisi and Wangara, Black Arts, pp. 52-70; Robin-
son, Nommo.
The Warning--A Theme for Linda, 1969. In Black Quartet;
excerpt in Negro Digest 18 (April 1969): 53-68.
What the Winesellers Buy, 1972.
Who's Got His Own, 1966. In King and Milner, Black Drama
Anthology.

EDITOR
With Woodie King. Black Drama Anthology. New York:
Columbia University Press, 1972*; New York: New Amer-
ican Library, 1971†.

NON-FICTION
(Anthology): King and Anthony, Black Poets and Prophets.

SHORT STORY
(Anthology): Hughes, The Best Short Stories by Negro
Writers.

BIOGRAPHY AND CRITICISM ON MILNER
Bigsby. The Black American Writer, vol. 2, pp. 199-200.
Harrison. The Drama of Nommo, p. 26.
Mitchell. Black Theatre, p. 223.
"A New Playwright." Negro Digest 15 (October 1966): 49-50.

REVIEWS: Who's Got His Own.
Crisis 74 (January-February 1967): 31-34.
Crisis 74 (October 1967): 423.

What the Wineseller Buys.
Gottfried, Martin. Woman's Wear Daily, 19 February 1974.
Wilson, Edwin. The Wall Street Journal, 21 February 1974.

MIMS, Harley.
UNPUBLISHED NOVEL
"Memoirs of a Shoeshine Boy," excerpt in Antioch Review,
Fall 1967.

SHORT STORY
(Anthology): Schulberg, From the Ashes.

BIOGRAPHY AND CRITICISM ON MIMS
Schulberg. "Black Phoenix," pp. 280-281.

MINUS, Marian.
SHORT STORY (Periodical): Crisis, September 1940.

MISSICK, Rupert.
POETRY Naked Moon. New York: Graham Publications, 1970.

MITCHELL, Joe.
POETRY (Periodical): Black World, December 1972.

MITCHELL, Leroy E., Jr. Born in Detroit, Michigan.
　　SHORT STORY
　　　(Periodical): Negro History Bulletin, October 1962.
　　BIOGRAPHY AND CRITICISM ON MITCHELL
　　　Negro History Bulletin 26 (October 1962): 69.

MITCHELL, Loften. Born 15 April 1919 in Harlem. Education:
　　B.A., Talladega College, 1943; M.A., Columbia University,
　　1951; special studies at City College of New York, Union Theo-
　　logical Seminary, and General Theological Seminary. Currently
　　living in Binghamton, New York. Career: Has served as a
　　social investigator for the City of New York Department of Wel-
　　fare, specializing in Gypsy cases; as program director for a
　　senior citizen's day center; as public relations officer for pro-
　　grams for Older Persons; as a member of committee writing
　　papers for the first White House Conference on Aging; Co-pro-
　　ducer of several professional plays; Publicity officer for the
　　Jewish Federation of Welfare Services. Assisted with special
　　programs for Harlem Preparatory School; edited special mater-
　　ials such as the NAACP Freedom Journal; wrote filmscripts for
　　Young Man of Williamsburg (1954), Integration: Report One
　　(1961), I'm Sorry (1962), The Vampires of Harlem (1972); also
　　wrote for radio and television: Friendly Advisor (a daily pro-
　　gram for WWRL, New York, 1954), The Later Years (for
　　WNYC, 1950-1962), special programs for WLIB, WWRL, Chan-
　　nel 13, WNBC and other major stations; prepared two special
　　programs: Readings from the Work of a Harlem Playwright
　　(performed by Ossie Davis in Westchester County, November,
　　1972), and Come Back to Harlem (a benefit performance at
　　Loew's Victoria, produced by Brock Peters). Contributed es-
　　says to The Oxford Companion to the Theatre and to the Enci-
　　clopedia Della Spetla Colo. Adjunct Associate Professor of Eng-
　　lish at Long Island University, 1969, and at New York Univer-
　　sity, 1970; Lecturer in Theatre and Afro-American Studies,
　　State University of New York at Binghamton, 1971 to present;
　　guest lecturer for enumerable university and civic groups.
　　Awards, Honors: John Simon Guggenheim Memorial Award for
　　Creative Writing in the Drama, 1958-59; Special Award from
　　Harlem Cultural Council, 1969; Special Award from the Church
　　of Our Savior, Yonkers, New York, 1972. Collections: Loften
　　Mitchell Collection established at Talladega College; Loften Mit-
　　chell Collection of Plays and Essays at Schomburg Collection
　　(New York City Library); Collection of Plays for the State Uni-
　　versity of New York at Binghamton.
　　CRITICISM BY MITCHELL
　　　Black Drama: The Story of the American Negro in the The-
　　　　atre. New York: Hawthorn, 1966*†.
　　　"Fishing--on and off Broadway." Crisis 76 (June-July 1969):
　　　　250-252.
　　　"Harlem Reconsidered." Freedomways 4 (Fall 1964): 465-
　　　　478.
　　　"I Work Here to Please You." In Gayle, The Black Aes-
　　　　thetic.

"The Negro Theatre and the Harlem Community." Freedom-
    ways 3 (Summer 1963): 384-394; also in Gayle, Black Ex-
    pression, pp. 148-158; Patterson, Anthology of the Negro
    in the American Theatre.
"The Negro Writer and His Materials." In The American
    Negro Writer and His Roots. pp. 55-60; also in Patter-
    son, An Introduction to Black Literature in America.
"On the 'Emerging' Playwright." In Bigsby, The Black
    American Writer, vol. 2, pp. 129-136.
"Three Writers and a Dream." The Crisis 72 (1965): 219-
    223.

DRAMA
    The Afro-Philadelphian, 1970.
    And the Walls Came Tumbling Down.
    With Irving Burgie. Ballad for Bimshire (musical), 1963.
    Ballad of a Blackbird (musical), 1968.
    With John Oliver Killens. Ballad of the Winter Soldiers,
        1964.
    The Bancroft Dynasty, 1948.
    The Cellar, 1947.
    Collected Plays. New York: Emerson Hall, forthcoming.
    The Final Solution to the Black Problem in the United States
        of America; or, The Fall of the American Empire, 1970.
    Horse's Play.
    Land Beyond the River, 1957. Cody, Wyoming: Pioneer Dra-
        ma Service, 1963; also in Adams, Conn and Slepian, Afro-
        American Literature: Drama; Scene in Childress, Black
        Scenes.
    The Phonograph, 1961.
    Sojourn to the South of the Wall.
    Star of the Morning. New York: Free Press, 1965; also in
        King and Milner, Black Drama Anthology.
    Tell Pharoah, 1967. New York: Negro University Press,
        1970.
    The World of a Harlem Playwright, 1968.
NON-FICTION
    Harlem, My Harlem. New York: Emerson Hall, 1973.
    (Anthology): Clarke, Harlem, U.S.A.
    (Periodical): Crisis, February, April 1965; October 1966;
        December 1968; February, June-July, November 1969;
        March 1970. Also published in the New York Times, New
        York Amsterdam News; The Episcopalian; The Sun Bulle-
        tin.
NOVEL
    The Stubborn Old Lady Who Resisted Change. New York:
        Emerson Hall, 1973*.
REVIEWS BY MITCHELL
    Published in Crisis.
SCREENPLAY
    The Vampires of Harlem, 1973. (To be filmed by Vanguard
        Productions)
WORK IN PROGRESS
    Drama: "The Prosecution of the Criminals Against Human-

ity." (Tentative title)
BIOGRAPHY AND CRITICISM ON MITCHELL
Abramson. Negro Playwrights in the American Theatre,
pp. 204-221.
Arts in Society 5 (1968): 230-232.
Bigsby, C.W.E. "Three Black Playwrights: Loften Mitchell,
Ossie Davis, Douglas Turner Ward." In Bigsby, The
Black Writer in America, vol. 2, 137-155.
Ploski. Reference Library of Black America, p. 26.
Redding, Saunders. "Literature and the Negro." Contempo-
rary Literature 9 (Winter 1968): 130-135.
INTERJECTIONS
" 'In my Father's house are many mansions'--and to me that
means there is room for all on this earth. I believe in total
freedom for all and 'before I'll be a slave, I'll be buried in my
grave and go home to my Lord and be free.' "

MIZELL, Don A.
POETRY (Anthologies): Black Poets Write On!; Coombs, We
Speak as Liberators; Patterson, A Rock Against the Wind.

MKALIMOTO, Ernie. Born 1942 in California.
CRITICISM
"Revolutionary Black Culture: The Cultural Arm of Revolu-
tionary Nationalism." Negro Digest 19 (December 1969):
11-17.
POETRY
(Anthology): Major, The New Black Poetry.

MOGUMBO, Vajava (Larry Lewis).
Assassin Poems by Vajava Mogumbo and Brothers. Detroit:
Black Graphics International, 1970.

MOLETTE, Barbara. Born 1940.
DRAMA
With Carlton Molette. Booji Wooji, 1971; revised as screen-
play.
With Carlton Molette and Charles Mann. Doctor B. S. Black.
In Encore 13 (1970).
With Carlton Molette. Rosalee Pritchett. New York: Dra-
matists Play Service, 197; also in Barksdale and Kinna-
mon, Black Writers of America, p. 824.

MOLETTE, Carlton W., II. Born 23 August 1939 in Pine Bluff,
Arkansas. Education: B.A., Morehouse College, 1959; graduate study at University of Kansas City; M.A., University of
Iowa, 1962; Ph.D., Florida State University, 1968. Currently
living in Atlanta, Georgia. Career: Actor, technician, designer, director, or playwright in more than 75 productions;
Assistant Director of the Little Theatre, Tuskegee Institute,
1960-1961; Designer-Technical Director, Des Moines Community Playhouse, 1962-63; Assistant Professor of Technical Production and Design, Howard University, 1963-1964; Assistant

Professor and Technical Director (1964-1967), Associate Professor (1967-1969), Florida A. & M. University; Associate Professor, Spelman College, 1969 to present; Program Director, Summer Drama Workshop (Matching funds provided through a grant from the National Endowment for the Arts), 1973. Has been associated with many Atlanta University Center Programs; as scenic designer/prop manager for the feature film, Together for Days, 1971; produced a 15-minute weekly television program entitled FAMU FORUM, WFSU-TV, Channel 11, Tallahassee, 1968-69. Frequently serves as theatre consultant, workshop coordinator or speaker for theatre conferences, colleges, universities, and the U.S. Army. Awards, Honors: Ford Foundation Early Admission Scholarship to Morehouse College, 1955-1959. Graduate Fellowship in Theatre, University of Kansas City, 1959-1960; Carnegie Foundation Grant, Florida State University, 1966-1968; Atlanta University Center Faculty Research Grant, 1970-1971. Member: The Dramatists Guild, American Theatre Association (past Vice Chairman of the Black Theatre Project), National Association of Dramatic and Speech Arts (past Editor of Encore), United States Institute for Theatre Technology.

CRITICISM BY MOLETTE
"Afro-American Ritual Drama." Black World 22 (April 1973).

DRAMA
With Barbara Molette. Booji Wooji, 1971; revised as screenplay.
Boosie, 1972.
With Barbara Molette and Charles Mann. Doctor B.S. Black. In Encore 13 (1970).
With Barbara Molette. Rosalie Pritchett. New York: Dramatists Play Service; also in Barksdale and Kinnamon, Black Writers of America.
Rosche, 1970.

BIOGRAPHY AND CRITICISM ON MOLETTE
Barksdale and Kinnamon, Black Writers of America, p. 824.

MONROE, Isabelle.
POETRY (Anthology): Murphy, Negro Voices.

MONTAGUE, W. Reginald. Born 30 January 1938 in Brooklyn.
NOVEL Ole Man Mose: A Novel of the Tennessee Valley. New York: Exposition, 1957.

MONTE, Eric.
DRAMA Revolution.

MOODY, Christina.
POETRY A Tiny Spark. Washington: Murray Brothers Press, 1910.

MOODY, David Reese.
SHORT STORY (Anthology): Schulberg, From the Ashes.

MOON, Albert.
   SHORT STORY (Anthology): Ford and Faggett, Best Short Stories by Afro-American Writers.

MOORE, Birdell Chew.
   SHORT STORY (Anthology): Schulberg, From the Ashes.

MOORE, David (Amus Mor).
   POETRY
      The Coming of John. Chicago, n. p., 1969.
      (Anthology): King, Blackspirits.
      (Periodical): Negro Digest, September 1969.

MOORE, Elvie.
   DRAMA
      Angela Is Happening, 1971.
      Bring the House Down.

MOORE, John P.
   SHORT STORY (Anthology): Ford and Faggett, Best Short Stories by Afro-American Writers.

MOORE, La Nese B.
   POETRY Can I Be Right? New York: Vantage, 1971.

MOORE, Mal.
   DRAMA Where? 1971.

MOORE, Raymond L.
   POETRY Visions of Reality and Other Poems. Chicago: Free Black Press, 1969.

MOORE, Robert E.
   POETRY
      (Anthology): Street Verses in Some Righteousness (Manna House Anthology, 1971).
      (Periodicals): Black Sports Magazine, July 1973, October 1973.
   UNPUBLISHED WORK
      With Linda Baron. "Rocksteady."

MOORELAND, Wayne. Born 1948.
   POETRY (Anthology): Adoff, The Poetry of Black America.

MOORER, Lizelia Augusta Jenkins.
   POETRY
      Prejudice Unveiled, and Other Poems. Boston: Roxburgh, 1907.
      (Periodical): Voice of the Negro, February 1904.

MOR, Amus   see   MOORE, David

MORALES, Aida.
DRAMA With James V. Hatch and Larry Garvin. The Conspiracy, 1970.

MOREAU, Julian see JACKSON, J. Denis

MORELAND, Charles King, Jr. Born 1945 in Yazoo City, Missis-
sippi.
EDITOR
Watts Writers and Poets, n.p., n.d.
POETRY
(Anthology): Shuman, A Galaxy of Black Writing.
(Periodicals): Black World, September, 1970; Negro Digest,
September 1969.
SHORT STORY
(Periodical): Negro Digest, June 1969.

MORGAN, James H. Born 1916 in Kirkwood, Missouri. Education: Attended schools in Kirkwood, Webster Groves, and St.
Louis, Missouri. Currently living in Rock Hill, Missouri.
Career: Served in the U.S. Army, 1941-1945, where as a non-
commissioned officer he was awarded a Certificate of Eligibility
for Chemical Warfare, the American Theatre Campaign Badge,
the American Service Medal, The Good Conduct and Pacific Cam-
paign Medals, and The Bronze Star. Has worked with the South-
western Bell Telephone Company since 1945, and has been ac-
tively engaged in many civic organizations. Member: First
Baptist Church of Webster Groves, Missouri; Life Member,
The Poetry Society.
POETRY
Poems by Candlelight and The Flare of a Match: Poems
Composed and Written for Encouragement and Entertain-
ment. New York: Vantage, 1967.
WORKS IN PROGRESS
A Second book of poems and stories for television.

MORRIS, Earl J.
NOVEL The Cop. New York: Exposition, 1951.

MORRIS, Isaac.
DRAMA The Secret Place.

MORRIS, James Cliftonne. Born 18 December 1920 in Talladega,
Alabama. Education: Talladega College; B.S. (Professional
Writing), Columbia University; M.A. (Secondary and Junior College education in English), Teachers College, Columbia University. Currently living in Springfield Gardens, New York. Career: Has taught in the New York City school system for twen-
ty-one years; has served as English Department Chairman, 1956
present; has taught Black literature and English composition at
Queensborough Community College, 1968 to present. Awards,
Honors: Teacher of the Day Award, Radio Station WMCA, New
York City; his poetry was selected for Christmas Day reading,

BBC, London, 1963; he represented the New York City Board
of Education Junior High School Division for the Board of Edu-
cation-Community television show, Channel 7, January 1970.
Member: Black Poets Reading (lectures on radio and television); Vice President, New York City Association of Teachers
of English, Junior High School Division.
POETRY
> Cleopatra and Other Poems.   Jericho, N.Y.: Exposition,
> 1955.
> From a Tin-Mouthed God to His Brass-Eared Subject. New
> York: Greenwich, 1966.
> (Anthologies): Brown, Lee and Ward, To Gwen with Love;
> Pool, Beyond the Blues; Weisman and Wright, Black Po-
> etry for All Americans.

SHORT STORY
> (Anthology): Short Story Scene (forthcoming).

UNPUBLISHED WORK
> Poetry: "Olympus Levelled."
> Aphorisms: "Shavings from a Mental Block."

INTERJECTIONS
"The only truth is human consideration for one's own desire
and concern for every other man on earth............Poetry is
life attempting to reveal itself in its honest form............
Each voice deserves an audience--nothing more, nothing less
............I feel guilty if I do not 'get into' a poem or a poem idea each week. Verse is my life itself."

MORRIS, John David.
POETRY Nature's Meditations; a Book of Verses.   Toledo,
> Ohio: By the Author, 1922.

MORRIS, Myra Estelle.
POETRY (Anthology): Murphy, Negro Voices.

MORRIS, Stanley.
POETRY (Anthology): Pool, Beyond the Blues.

MORRISON, C. T.   Born 1936.
NOVEL The Flame in the Icebox: An Episode of the Vietnam
> War. New York: Exposition, 1968.

MORRISON, Toni.   Born 18 February 1931 in Lorain, Ohio.   Education: B.A., Howard University, 1953; M.A., Cornell University, 1955. Currently living in New York City. Career: Former professor, English and humanities, at Texas Southern University and at Howard University. Editor at Random House,
1965 to present.
NON-FICTION
> "Behind the Making of the Black Book." Black World 23
> (February 1974): 86-90.

NOVELS
> The Bluest Eye. New York: Holt, Rinehart and Winston,
> 1970*; New York: Pocket Books, 1972†.

Sula. New York: Knopf, 1974*; also published in Redbook, January 1974.
REVIEWS: The Bluest Eye.
Frankel, Haskel. New York Times Book Review, 1 November 1970, p. 46.
Loftin, Elouise. Black Creation 3 (Fall 1971); 48.
Wilder, C.M. CLA Journal 15 (December 1971): 253-255.

MORRISON, William Lorenzo.
POETRY
Dark Rhapsody: Poems. New York: Henry Harrison, 1945.
(Anthology): Murphy, Ebony Rhythm.

MORSE, George Chester. Born 1904 in Orange, New Jersey.
NON-FICTION
(Periodicals): The Independent, Commonweal, Outlook, The World Tomorrow, The Protestant, Negro Digest, The Negro History Bulletin.
SHORT STORY
(Periodical): Crisis, December 1941.

MOSES, Gilbert. Born 20 August 1942 in Cleveland, Ohio. Education: Oberlin College; The Sorbonne; New York University.
Currently living in New York City. Career: Director for stage and film. Member: Directors Guild of America; S.S.D.I.C.
Awards, Honors: Obie Award, Drama Desk Award, Tony Nomination.
CRITICISM
With John O'Neal. "Dialogue: The Free Southern Theatre." Tulane Drama Review 9 (Summer 1965): 63-76.
DRAMA
Roots. In Dent, Schechner and Moses, The Free Southern Theater.
EDITOR
With Thomas C. Dent and Richard Schechner. The Free Southern Theater by the Free Southern Theater. Indianapolis: Bobbs-Merrill, 1969.
NON-FICTION
(Periodical): International Theatre Institute magazine.
BIOGRAPHY AND CRITICISM ON MOSES
"Dialogue: The Free Southern Theater." Tulane Drama Review 9 (Summer 1965): 63-76.
Harrison. The Drama of Nommo, pp. xiii, 197.
Interview. Black Creation, Winter 1972.

MOSLEY, Joseph M., Jr. Born 1935 in Philadelphia.
POETRY (Anthology): Major, The New Black Poetry.

MOST, Marty see MARTINEZ, Maurice M.

MOTLEY, Dennis. Born 1950.
POETRY (Anthology): Shuman, A Galaxy of Black Writing.

Gilbert Moses directing.

MOTLEY, Willard. <u>Born</u> 14 July 1912 in Chicago. <u>Died</u> 4 March
1965 in Mexico City. <u>Career</u>: Left his middle class home to
work as a migratory laborer, ranch hand, cook and shipping
clerk; also worked as a photographer, radio script writer, interviewer for the Chicago Housing Authority, and writer for the
Office of Civil Defense. He bicycled, hitch-hiked and travelled
by jalopy back and forth across the United States, and then settled in Chicago's West Madison Street skid row to continue his
study of humanity. His first book, <u>Knock on Any Door</u>, placed
him among the leading naturalistic novelists. In 1952 he moved
to Mexico. At the time of his death, he had been living alone

in the hills above Mexico City, writing a book tentatively entitled, "My House Is Your House," which dealt with the influx
of tourists into a small Mexican town.[1]

NOVELS
> Knock on Any Door. New York: Appleton-Century, 1947;
>   New York: New American Library†.
> Let No Man Write My Epitaph. New York: Random House,
>   1958*.
> Let Noon Be Fair. New York: Putnam, 1966.
> Tourist Town. New York: Putnam, 1965.
> We Fished All Night. New York: Appleton-Century-Crofts,
>   1951.

BIOGRAPHY AND CRITICISM ON MOTLEY
> Bardolph. The Negro Vanguard, pp. 194, 295, 373, 376-
>   379.
> Baylis, John F. "Nick Romano: Father and Son." Negro
>   American Literature Forum 3 (Spring 1969): 18-21.
> Bigsby. "From Protest to Paradox: The Black Writer at
>   Mid-Century," pp. 217-240.
> Bone. The Negro Novel in America, p. 169, 178-180.
> Davis. The American Negro Reference Book, pp. 875-877.
> Ford, Nick Aaron. "Four Popular Negro Novelists." Phy-
>   lon 15 (1954): 29-39.
> Gelfant, Blanche Housman. The American City Novel. Nor-
>   man: University of Oklahoma Press, 1954.
> Giles, James R. and Jerome Klinkowitz. "The Emergence
>   of Willard Motley in Black American Literature." Negro
>   American Literature Forum 6 (Summer 1972): 31-34.
> Hughes. The Negro Novelists, pp. 148, 178-193, 197, 243-
>   247, 251, 253, 261-262, 273-274, 277.
> "Knock On Any Door." Look, 30 September 1947, pp. 21-31.
> Maund, Alfred. "The Negro Novelist and the Contemporary
>   American Scene." Chicago Jewish Forum 12 (Fall 1954):
>   28-34.
> New York Times, 5 March 1965, p. 30. (Obituary.)
> Ploski and Kaiser. The Negro Almanac, p. 688.
> Rideout, Walter Bates. The Radical Novel in the United
>   States, 1900-1954. Cambridge: Harvard University Press,
>   1956, pp. 292-300.
> Turpin. "Evaluating the Work of Contemporary Novelists,"
>   pp. 59-60.
> "Willard Motley." Ebony 2 (September 1947): 47-50.
> Wood, Charles. "The Adventure Manuscript: New Light on
>   Willard Motley's Naturalism." Negro American Literature
>   Forum 6 (Summer 1972): 35-39.
>> [1]New York Times, 5 March 1965, p. 30.

MSHAIRI, Tauhid.
> POETRY (Periodical): Journal of Black Poetry, Spring 1969.

El MUHAJIR (Marvin X; Marvin Jackman). Currently living in San
    Francisco. Career: Directory of Your Black Educational The-
    atre, Inc. of San Francisco; contributing editor to the Journal

of Black Poetry; associate editor of Black Theatre magazine;
also taught at Fresno State University and the University of
California, Berkeley. Awards, Honors: Writing grants from
Columbia University and the National Endowment for the Arts.
CRITICISM
  "Interview with Ed Bullins." In Bullins, New Plays from the
    Black Theatre.
  "Islam and Black Art: An Interview with LeRoi Jones."
    Negro Digest 18 (January 1969): 4-10; also in Alhamisi
    and Wangara, Black Arts.
  "Manifesto: The Black Educational Theatre of San Francis-
    co." Black Theatre 6 (1972): 30-35.
DRAMA
  The Black Bird, A Parable by Marvin X. San Francisco:
    Julian Richardson, n.d.; also in Bullins, New Plays from
    the Black Theatre, pp. 109-118.
  Come Next Summer.
  Flowers for the Trashman, or Take Care of Business. In
    Drama Review 12 (Summer 1968); also in Jones and Neal,
    Black Fire.
  The Resurrection of the Dead. In Black Theatre 3 (1969).
  The Trial.
NON-FICTION
  (Periodicals): Black Scholar, April-May 1971; February
    1973; Journal of Black Poetry, Summer 1973.
POETRY
  Black Man Listen: Poems and Proverbs. Detroit: Broad-
    side, 1969.
  Fly to Allah: Poems. Fresno: Al Kitab Sudan, 1969.
  Woman--Man's Best Friend. San Francisco: Al Kitab Sudan
    & Rene Productions, 1973†.
  The Son of Man. Fresno: Al Kitab Sudan Publications, n.d.
  (Anthologies): Brooks, A Broadside Treasury; Jones and
    Neal, Black Fire; Simmons and Hutchinson, Black Culture.
  (Periodicals): Black Scholar, April-May 1971; Journal of
    Black Poetry, Spring 1969; Winter-Spring 1970; Negro Di-
    gest, September 1969.
WORK IN PROGRESS
  Non-Fiction: "Black Man in the Americas," discourses on
    the history, culture, and art of Black people in the West-
    ern Hemisphere.
REVIEW: Black Man Listen
  Sanchez, Sonia. Negro Digest 19 (April 1970): 51-52.

MUHAMMAD, Abdullah. Currently living in Brooklyn. Career:
Has travelled extensively, working with Black Student Unions
across the country and giving poetry readings. His works have
been printed in SiSi Kwa SiSi, Afro-American Student Association at Fordham University.
POETRY AND ESSAYS
  Conscious Black Communication. Brooklyn: EAST Publica-
    tions, 1972.

MULET, Paul.
DRAMA
Jimmy, Jr.
Portraits in Blackness.
The Scabs.
This Piece of Land.

MULLER-THYM, Thomas. Born 23 December 1948.
SHORT STORY (Anthology): Coombs, What We Must See.

MUNGIN, Horace. Born 5 August 1941 in Young's Island, South
Carolina. Education: After many years of street education, is
now enrolled at Fordham University. Currently living in New
York City. Career: Joined the army in 1960, spending two
years in Germany with the 82nd Airborne Division. Upon re-
turning home, he became interested in community affairs and
helped to create the Lincoln Square Community Betterment
League, serving as business manager; has also served as Chair-
man of the Promoter's Five, an investment group. Presently
employed as a conductor for the New York Transit Authority.
POETRY
Dope Hustler Jazz. n.p.: Free Spirit Press, 1968.
How Many Niggers Make Half a Dozen. n.p.: Free Spirit
Press, n.d.
Now See Here, Homer. n.p.: Free Spirit Press, 1969.
(Anthologies): Adoff, Black Out Loud; Robinson, Nommo.
WORK IN PROGRESS
"I am presently working on a novel concerning those of us
Black people who live by their wits. The theme will be how
Black people become rich living outside of society (that is--
some Black people)."
INTERJECTIONS
"The Black artist's first responsibility is to the awareness
of the Black mind--then to his art. And when the time has
come he can then become an individual and go in the direction
the soul of his art takes him."

MURAPA, Rukudzo. Born in Zimbabwe, Rhodesia.
NON-FICTION
(Periodicals): Black World, July 1970; October 1971; Negro
Digest, May 1969.
POETRY
(Anthology): Brown, Lee and Ward, To Gwen with Love.

MURPHY, Beatrice M. Born 12 June 1908 in Monessen, Pennsylvania. Career: See Shockley and Chandler, Living Black American Authors, p. 114.
EDITOR
Ebony Rhythm, 1948; facsimile ed., Freeport, N.Y.: Books
for Libraries, 1968*.
Negro Voices: An Anthology of Contemporary Verse. New
York: Henry Harrison, 1938; Ann Arbor, Mich.: University Microfilms, 1971*.

Today's Negro Poets: An Anthology by Young Negro Poets.
New York: Messner, 1970.
POETRY
With Nancy L. Arnez.   Home Is Where the Heart Is.   n. p. ,
n. d.
Love Is a Terrible Thing.   New York: Hobson, 1945.
With Nancy L. Arnez.   The Rocks Cry Out.   Detroit: Broad-
side, 1969†.
(Anthologies): Bontemps, Golden Slippers; Hughes and Bon-
temps, The Poetry of the Negro, 1746-1970.
(Periodical):   Crisis 35 (1928): 158.
REVIEW: The Rocks Cry Out.
Giovanni, Nikki.   Negro Digest 18 (August 1969): 97-98.

MURRAY, Albert.   Born 12 May 1916 in Nokomis, Alabama.   Education: B. S. (Education), Tuskegee Institute, 1939; M. A. , (English), Tuskegee Institute, 1948; additional work at the University
of Michigan, Northwestern University, University of Paris, Air
Force University, and Ohio State University.   Currently living
in New York City.   Career: Taught undergraduate composition
and literature at Tuskegee Institute, 1940-43; 1946-51.   Directed
college little theatre and served as consultant to local radio programs (Tuskegee) on jazz.   Taught at the Graduate School of
Journalism, Columbia University, 1968; served as O'Connor Professor of Literature, Colgate University, 1970 and 1973; as Visiting Professor of Literature, University of Massachusetts, 1971;
as Paul Anthony Brick Lecturer, University of Missouri, 1972.
Was Base Level Plans and Training Officer during World War II;
taught geopolitics and other AFROTC subjects; served as staff
training officer, command level, Southern Air Material Area
(North Africa and the Middle East); and as Personnel Services
Officer, Los Angeles area.   Also lectured on jazz and Ameri-
can arts for American Consul in Morocco; planned and conducted
cultural orientation programs for Americans overseas; conducted
briefings in psychological warfare.   Present status: Major
USAF, retired.
CRITICISM
"Something Different, Something More."   In Hill, Anger, and
Beyond, pp. 112-137.
NON-FICTION
The Hero and the Blues.   The Paul Anthony Brick Lectures,
Ninth Series.   Columbia: University of Missouri Press,
1973*.
The Omni-Americans.   New York: Outerbridge, 1970*.
South to a Very Old Place.   New York: McGraw Hill, 1972*.
(Periodicals):   Life, 3 July 1964; The New Leader, 7 Decem-
ber 1964; 21 June 1965; 17 January 1965; 17 January 1966;
9 May 1966; 3 December 1967.
NOVEL
Trainwhistle Guitar.   New York: McGraw-Hill, 1974*.
REVIEWS BY MURRAY
Published in Bookweek and Book World.

Albert Murray

SHORT STORIES
   (Anthologies): Bambara, Tales and Stories; Clarke, Ameri-
      can Negro Short Stories; Emanuel and Gross, Dark Sym-
      phony; Margolies, A Native Sons Reader, New World Writ-
      ing IV.
WORK IN PROGRESS
   "The Story Teller as Blues Singer."
   Also, a novel about the adventures of a young man who in-
      terrrupts his college education to play bass fiddle in a
      jazz band.
BIOGRAPHY AND CRITICISM ON MURRAY
   Beauford, Fred. "Conversation with Al Murray." Black
      Creation 3 (Summer 1972): 26-27.
   Sheppard, R. Z. "Soul: Straight Up, No Ice." Time, 10
      January 1972, p. 65.

MURRAY, Henry Clifford.
  POETRY The Sight of Dawn. New York: Exposition, 1959.

MURRAY, Pauli. Born 1910 in Baltimore, Maryland. Career:
  See Who's Who of American Women, 1st ed. (1958-1959).
  NON-FICTION
    Proud Shoes: The Story of an American Family, 1956; re-
      print ed., Spartanburg, S.C.: Reprint*. Excerpt in Hill,
      Soon One Morning.
  POETRY
    Dark Testament and Other Poems. Norwalk, Conn.: Silver-
      mine, 1970*†.
    (Anthologies): Adoff, The Poetry of Black America; Bon-
      temps, American Negro Poetry; Hughes and Bontemps,
      Poetry of the Negro 1746-1970; Patterson, A Rock Against
      the Wind.
    (Periodicals): Challenge, March 1934; May 1935; Crisis,
      January, December 1939; 1940; October 1967; November
      1970; Opportunity, February, July 1934; June 1938; other
      poetry in Common Ground, South Today, Saturday Review.
  BIOGRAPHY ON MURRAY
    Afro-American, 20 January 1968.
    Diamonstein, Barbaralee. Open Secrets. New York: Viking,
      1972, pp. 289-294.
    Ploski. Negro Almanac, p. 699.

MURRAY, Samuel M., Jr.
  SHORT STORY (Anthology): Sanchez, We Be Word Sorcerers.

MWANDISHI, Kuweka.
  POETRY (Anthology): Black Poets Write On!

MYERS, Gayther.
  DRAMA Teachers Teaching.

MYERS, Walter D. Born 12 August 1937 in Martinsburg, West
  Virginia. Education: Attended New York City College. Cur-
  rently living in New York City. Career: Senior Trade Book
  Editor, Bobbs-Merrill, 1970 to present. Awards, Honors:
  Council on Interracial Books for Children Award for Where
  Does the Day Go, 1968.
  CHILDREN AND YOUNG ADULTS
    The Dancers. New York: Parents Magazine Press, 1972*.
    The Dragon Takes a Wife. Indianapolis: Bobbs-Merrill,
      1972.
    Where Does the Day Go? New York: Parents Magazine
      Press, 1969.
    The World of Work. Indianapolis: Bobbs-Merrill, n.d.
  NON-FICTION
    (Periodical): Black Creation, Winter 1973.
  SHORT STORIES
    (Anthologies): Coombs, What We Must See; Sanchez, We Be
      Sorcerers.

(Periodicals): Black Creation, Fall 1971; Black World, March 1971.
INTERJECTIONS
"About life: I just stumble along the best I can. Don't really know enough to have developed a philosophy. My general impression is that it's the best thing I've known."

MYLES, Glenn. Born 1933 in Carthage, Texas.
POETRY (Anthologies): Major, The New Black Poetry; Miller, Dices and Black Bones; also published in Yardbird Reader I.

-N-

NAILOR, Alexander J.
POETRY Divinely Inspired Message Poems. n.p.: By the Author, 1922.

NASH, Mary Nell.
POETRY (Anthology): Boyd, Poems by Blacks, vol. 2.

NAYO (Barbara Malcomb).
DRAMA
Fourth Generation, 1969.
POETRY
I Want Me a Home. New Orleans: Blkartsouth, 1969.
(Anthologies): Chapman, New Black Voices; Simmons and Hutchinson, Black Culture.

NAZEL, Joseph, Jr. Born 5 June 1944 in Berkeley, California.
Education: A.B., University of Southern California, 1972. Currently living in Los Angeles, California. Career: Social worker. Instructor in Afro-American Studies at the University of Southern California; Writer of an adventure series for Pinnacle Books (New York) and for Holloway House (Los Angeles).
NOVELS
The Iceman, USA. Los Angeles: Holloway House, forthcoming.
My Name Is Black. New York: Pinnacle Books, 1973†.
SHORT STORY
(Periodical): Grass Roots Forum.
UNPUBLISHED WORKS
Folktales: "Spider's Magic Web."
Novel: "Wee Willie Weasel and the Root Working Man."
Poetry: "Drum Talk"; "Ain't Nuthin' in Graveyards But Dead Folks"; "Home Ground in the Bottom."
INTERJECTIONS
"Through the arts we will learn the truth."

NEAL, Gaston. Born 1934.
POETRY (Anthology): Jones and Neal, Black Fire.

NEAL, Larry. Born 1937 in Atlanta, Georgia.
CRITICISM BY NEAL
"Any Day Now: Black Art and Black Liberation." Ebony 24

(August 1969): 54-58, 62.

"The Black Arts Movement." Drama Review 12 (Summer 1968): 29-39; also in Bigsby, The Black American Writer, vol. 2, pp. 187-202; Davis and Redding, Cavalcade, pp. 797-810; Singh and Fellowes, Black Literature in America; Gayle, The Black Aesthetic.

"The Black Writer's Role--James Baldwin." Liberator 6 (April 1966): 10.

"Black Writer's Views on Literary Lions and Values." Negro Digest 17 (January 1968): 35.

"Cultural Front." Liberator 5 (June 1965): 26.

"Cultural Nationalism and Black Theatre." Black Theatre, no. 1 (1968): 8-10.

"The Development of LeRoi Jones." Liberator 6 (January 1966): 20; 6 (February 1966): 18.

"Eatonville's Zora Neale Hurston: A Profile." In Watkins, Black Review No. 2.

"Ellison's Zoot Suit." Black World 20 (December 1970): 31-52.

"The Ethos of the Blues." Black Scholar 3 (Summer 1972): 42-48.

"Some Reflections on the Black Aesthetic." In Gayle, The Black Aesthetic.

"Toward a Relevant Black Theatre." Black Theatre, no. 4 (1970): 14-15.

"Uncle Rufus Raps on the Squared Circle." Partisan Review 39 (1972): 44-62.

DRAMA
The Suppression of Jazz, 1970.

EDITOR
With LeRoi Jones. Black Fire: An Anthology of Afro-American Writing. New York: Morrow, 1968.

NON-FICTION
(Anthology): Jones and Neal, Black Fire.
(Periodicals): Brooks, The Black Position, 1971; Ebony, August 1969; Negro Digest, March 1967; January 1970.
Analytical Study of Afro-American Culture. n.p., 1972.

POETRY
Black Boogaloo (Notes on Black Liberation). San Francisco: Journal of Black Poetry Press, 1969.
Hoodoo Hollerin. n.p.: Bepop Ghosts, 1971.
(Anthologies): Afro-Arts Anthology; Alhamisi and Wangara, Black Arts; Baker, Black Literature in America; Brooks, A Broadside Treasury; Chapman, New Black Voices; Henderson, Understanding the NewBlack Poetry; Jones and Neal, Black Fire; Jordan, Soulscript; King, Blackspirits; Major, The New Black Poetry; Miller, Blackamerican Literature; Randall, The Black Poets; Randall and Burroughs, For Malcolm; Simmons and Hutchinson, Black Culture.
(Periodicals): Black World, September 1970; July 1972; Journal of Black Poetry, Winter-Spring, 1970; Negro Digest, March, September 1966; January, September 1969; poetry also in Black Dialogue and Umbra.

SHORT STORY
>(Anthologies): Jones and Neal, Black Fire; Robinson, Nom-
>mo.

BIOGRAPHY AND CRITICISM ON NEAL
>Anderson, Jervis. "Black Writing--The Other Side." Dis-
>sent (May-June 1968): 233-242.
>Harrison. The Drama of Nommo, pp. 33-229, passim.

NEELY, Bennie E.
DRAMA Sue.

NELSON, Alice Moore Dunbar see DUNBAR-NELSON, Alice Moore

NELSON, Annie Greene.
NOVEL
>After the Storm. Columbia, S.C.: Hampton, 1942.
>The Dawn Appears. Columbia, S.C.: Hampton, 1944.

NELSON, Clydell O.
POETRY (Anthology): Boyd, Poems by Blacks, vol. 2.

NELSON, David.
POETRY
>Black Impulse. 2nd ed. Brooklyn: Drum, 1969?
>(Anthologies): Dee, Glow Child; King, Blackspirits.

NELSON, Robert J.
POETRY (Periodical): Journal of Black Poetry, Winter-Spring
>1970.

NEWSOME, Mary Effie Lee. Born 19 January 1885 in Philadelphia.
Education: Wilberforce University, 1901-04; Oberlin College,
1904-05; Academy of Fine Arts, 1907-08; University of Pennsyl-
vania, 1911-14. Career: Editor of "The Little Page" for chil-
dren, The Crisis magazine. Organized the Boys of Birming-
ham Club in 1925. Lived most of her life in Wilberforce,
Ohio. [1]
CHILDREN AND YOUNG ADULTS
>Gladiola Gardens. Washington, D.C.: Associated, 1940.
>>(Poetry.)
>(Periodical): Opportunity 3 (December 1925): 372.
NON-FICTION
>(Periodicals): Crisis 10 (1915): 89; Phylon, First Quarter
>1944.
POETRY
>(Anthologies): Agree, R., How to Eat a Poem and Other
>>Morsels (New York: Pantheon, 1967); Bontemps, American
>>Negro Poetry; Bontemps, Golden Slippers; Cullen, Carol-
>>ing Dusk; Hughes and Bontemps, The Poetry of the Negro,
>>1746-1970.
>(Periodicals): Crisis 13 (1917): 219; 16 (1918): 269; 17
>>(1918): 17; 24 (1922): 265; 25 (1922): 57; 26 (1923): 68; 29
>>(1925): 113; 31 (1925): 65; 32 (1926): 136, 247; 34 (1927):

48, 84, 158, 190, 193; 37 (1930): 130; 38 (1931): 15, 162, 306, 414; 39 (1932): 216, 349; 40 (1933): 110; 41 (1934): 180; 48 (1941); Opportunity 4 (1926): 127; Phylon, Fourth Quarter 1940; First Quarter 1941; First Quarter 1942.
SHORT STORIES
    (Periodicals): Crisis 35 (1928): 331; Opportunity 4 (April 1926): 126-127; 5 (April 1927): 117.
BIOGRAPHY ON NEWSOME
    Negro History Bulletin 10 (February 1947).
        1Who's Who in Colored America, 5th ed. (1938-1939-1940).

NEWTON, Tengemana.
    POETRY (Periodical): Journal of Black Poetry, Summer 1972.

NGATHO, Stella.
    POETRY (Anthology): Boyd, Poems by Blacks, vol. 2.

NICHOL, James W.
    DRAMA Home, Sweet Home, 1969.

NICHOLAS, A. X.   Born 1943 in Mobile, Alabama.
    CRITICISM BY NICHOLAS
        "A Conversation with Dudley Randall." Black World 21 (December 1971): 26-34.
    EDITOR
        Poetry of Soul. New York: Bantam, 1971†.
        Woke Up This Mornin' Poetry of the Blues. New York: Bantam, 1973†.
    POETRY
        (Anthology): Coombs, We Speak as Liberators.
        (Periodical): Negro Digest, September 1969.

NICHOLAS, Michael. Born 1941 in Mobile, Alabama.
    POETRY
        Watermelons Into Wine. n. p. , 1968.
        (Anthology): Major, The New Black Poetry.
        (Periodicals): Journal of Black Poetry, Summer 1972.

NICHOLES, Marion.
    POETRY
        Life Styles. Detroit: Broadside, 1971†.
        REVIEWS: Life Styles
        Kent. "Struggle for the Image," p. 315.
        Spody, James G. Black Books Bulletin 1 (1973): 42-43.

NICHOLS, Constance.
    POETRY (Anthology): Murphy, Ebony Rhythm.

NICHOLS, James Emanuel.
    POETRY Verse Fragments. New York: Vantage, 1958.

NICHOLSON, Carol.
POETRY (Anthology): Boyd, Poems by Blacks, vol. 2.

NODELL, Albert Charles.
DRAMA A River Divided, 1964.

NOLTE, Donald Eugene.
POETRY (Anthology): Boyd, Poems by Blacks, vol. 2.

NORFORD, George.
DRAMA
    Head of the Family, 1950.
    Joy Exceeding Joy, 1939.
CRITICISM ON NORFORD
    Mitchell. Black Drama, pp. 106, 107, 113.

NUGENT, Bruce. Born 1905 in Washington, D.C.
POETRY
    (Periodicals): Opportunity, October 1925; Palms, October
    1926.
SHORT STORY
    (Anthology): Locke, The New Negro.

-O-

OCCOMY, Marita Bonner see BONNER, Marita

O'DANIEL, Therman B. Born 9 July 1908 in Wilson, North Caro-
    lina. Education: A.B., Lincoln University, 1930; M.A., Uni-
    versity of Pennsylvania, 1932; summer school study at Harvard
    University, University of Chicago, University of Pennsylvania,
    Pennsylvania State College, University of Ottawa; Ph.D., Uni-
    versity of Ottawa, 1956. Currently living in Baltimore, Mary-
    land. Career: Held various positions at Allen University: In-
    structor, 1933-34; Assistant Professor, 1934-35; Associate Pro-
    fessor, 1935-36; Professor of English and Head of the Division
    of Languages and Literature, 1936-37; Dean of the Liberal Arts
    College, 1937-40; Acting President, March to July, 1939. At
    Fort Valley State College he served as Associate Professor of
    English, 1940-43; Professor of English, 1943-55; Acting Admin-
    istrative Dean and Acting Registrar, 1945-46; Director of Sum-
    mer School, 1946; Head of the English Department, 1946-52;
    Registrar and Director of Summer School, 1952-55. He served
    as Associate Professor of English at Dillard University, 1955-
    56. Since 1956 he has been at Morgan State College, serving
    as Assistant Professor of English, 1956-63; Director of Summer
    School, 1962 and 1963; Associate Professor of English, 1963-
    67; Professor of English, 1967 to present. Since 1957 he has
    edited the CLA Journal. Member: Modern Language Associa-
    tion; The National Council of Teachers of English; The College
    English Association; The College Language Association (life
    member); The National Educational Association (life member);

The Melville Society; The Association for the Study of Negro
Life and History, Inc.; Society for the Study of Southern Literature. Awards, Honors: General Education Board Fellowship,
1936-37; Ford Foundation Fellowship, 1951-52; Alice E. Johnson Memorial Fund Award from the Black Academy of Arts and
Letters, 1972, for the CLA Journal.
CRITICISM BY O'DANIEL
    "The CLA Journal." CLA Journal 1 (November 1957): 1-2.
    "Cooper's Treatment of the Negro." Phylon 8 (Second Quar-
      ter 1947).
    "Emerson as a Literary Critic." CLA Journal 8 (Septem-
      ber 1964): 21-43; 8 (December 1964): 157-189; 8 (March
      1965): 246-276.
    "Francis Bacon's Literary Theory." Allen University Bulle-
      tin 1 (October 1938).
    "The Friendship of Irving and Dickens, With a Note on Their
      Views of England and America." Allen University Bulle-
      tin 3 (January 1940).
    "Herman Melville as a Writer of Journals." CLA Journal 4
      (December 1960): 94-105.
    "The Image of Man as Portrayed by Ralph Ellison." CLA
      Journal 10 (June 1967): 277-284.
    "An Interpretation of the Relationship of the Chapter Entitled
      'The Symphony' to Moby Dick as a Whole." Allen Univer-
      sity Bulletin 2 (January 1939); reprinted in CLA Journal
      (September 1958).
    "Introduction." The Blacker the Berry by Wallace Thurman.
      New York: Collier Books, 1970.
    "James Baldwin: An Interpretive Study." CLA Journal 7
      (September 1963): 37-47.
    "A Langston Hughes Bibliography." CLA Bulletin 3 (Spring
      1951).
    "Lincoln's Man of Letters." Lincoln University Bulletin 67
      (Langston Hughes Issue, 1964): 9-12.
  EDITOR
    James Baldwin: A Critical Evaluation. New York: Morrow,
      forthcoming.
    Langston Hughes, Black Genius: A Critical Evaluation, New
      York: Morrow, 1971*†.

ODARO, (Barbara Jones). Born 22 June 1946.
    POETRY
      (Anthology): Jones and Neal, Black Fire.
      (Periodical): Harlem Youth Unlimited Quarterly.

ODELL, Albert Charles. Born 13 June 1922 in Baton Rouge, Lou-
    isiana. Career: See Shockley and Chandler, Living Black
    American Authors, p. 120.

ODEN, G. C. (Gloria Catherine Oden). Born 30 October 1923 in
    Yonkers, New York. Education: B.A., Howard University,
    1944; J.D., Howard University, 1948; additional graduate work
    in American Studies at New York University, 1969-71. Current-

ly living in Baltimore, Maryland. Career: Visiting Lecturer, State University of New York at Stony Brook; Lecturer, New School of Social Research; Senior Project Editor in mathematics and science, and Project Director for secondary language arts, Holt, Rinehart and Winston Publishers; Senior Editor, Institute of Electrical and Electronic Engineers and the American Institute of Physics. Presently Assistant Professor, English Department, University of Maryland, Baltimore County. She is one of three poets subject of an educational film, Poetry Is Alive and Well and Living in America, distributed overseas by Media Plus, Inc., New York). She has given poetry readings at numerous high schools, libraries, colleges and universities, and at the Guggenheim Museum. Awards, Honors: Received two awards from the John Hay Whitney Foundation for creative writing; a fellowship to Yaddo, Saratoga Springs, New York; a fellowship to Breadloaf Writers Conference, Vermont.

CRITICISM BY ODEN
   "Literature and Politics--The Black Investment." New School
      Bulletin 23 (16 November 1965): 1, 4.

NON-FICTION
   (Anthologies): Atherton, Pauline, Humanization of Knowledge
      in the Social Sciences (Syracuse: School of Social Science,
      1972); Chametzky and Kaplan, Black and White in Ameri-
      can Culture (reprinted from Massachusetts Review, Spring-
      Summer 1965).

POETRY
   The Naked Frame: A Love Poem and Sonnets. New York:
      Exposition, 1952.
   (Anthologies): Adoff, The Poetry of Black America; Bell,
      Afro-American Poetry; Bontemps, American Negro Poetry;
      Hayden, Kaliedoscope; Hughes, New Negro Poets: USA;
      Hughes, La Poésie Negro-Américaine; Hughes and Bon-
      temps, The Poetry of the Negro, 1746-1970; Miller,
      Blackamerican Literature; Patterson, A Rock Against the
      Wind; Williams, Beyond the Angry Black.
   (Periodicals): Saturday Review; The Poetry Digest; The Half
      Moon.
Also published in Downbeat and Sin Nihon Bugaku.

ODEN, Thomas Hildreth   see   BURLEIGH, Benny

OFFORD, Carl.   Born 1910 in Trinidad.
   NOVELS
      The Naked Fear.   New York: Ace, 1954.
      The White Face.   New York: McBride, 1943.
   SHORT STORY
      (Anthology): Clarke, American Negro Short Stories.
   CRITICISM ON OFFORD
      Hughes.   The Negro Novelist, pp. 84-86, 212-215.

OGILVIE, D. T.
   POETRY   (Anthology):   Major, The New Black Poetry.

OGLETREE, Carolyn. <u>Born</u> 13 February 1948 in Birmingham, Alabama. <u>Education:</u> B.A., Magna Cum Laude, California State
University--San Francisco, 1972; M.S., California State Univer-
sity--San Francisco, 1974. <u>Currently living in</u> San Francisco.
<u>Career:</u> Art teacher, tutor and counselor, San Francisco Black
Writer's Workshop, 1968 to present; EOP Student Counselor,
California State University, 1969-72; counselor for unwed mothers and problem teenagers, YWCA, Oakland, 1972; Equal Opportunity Intern, Office for Civil Rights/HEW, Summer 1973;
Graduate Assistant, California Youth Authority, San Francisco,
1973-present. Worked with the San Francisco Black Writer's
Workshop and Laney College to provide cultural enrichment
programs for prisoners. <u>Member:</u> Black Students Psychological Association; Youth Guidance Volunteer Auxiliary; African
Historical Society; American Personnel and Guidance Association; National Advisory Board of San Francisco Black Exposition; N.A.A.C.P.; California Personnel and Guidance Association; American Rehabilitation Counselors Association; Community Counselors and Workers for Survival; Bayview Self-Help
Incorporated; Professional Black Women--University of California, Berkeley.
NON-FICTION
    Published in <u>The Rehab. Review</u> (California State University,
    San Francisco.)
POETRY
    (Periodical): <u>Black Art Writer's Literary Magazine</u>, First
    Quarter 1971.
INTERJECTIONS
    "Life is but a small segment of time; therefore you must
use it wisely."

O'HIGGINS, Myron. <u>Born</u> 1918 in Chicago, Illinois.
POETRY
    With Robert Hayden. <u>The Lion and the Archer</u>. Nashville,
    Tenn.: Hemphill Press, 1949.
    (Anthologies): Adoff, <u>I Am the Darker Brother</u>; Adoff, <u>The
    Poetry of Black America</u>; Bontemps, <u>American Negro Po-
    etry</u>; Hayden, <u>Kaleidoscope</u>; Hughes and Bontemps, <u>The
    Poetry of the Negro, 1746-1970</u>; Lowenfels, <u>Poets of To-
    day</u>.
BIOGRAPHY ON O'HIGGINS
    "Poets." <u>Ebony</u> 4 (February 1949): 41.

OJENKI, (Alvin Saxon, Jr.). <u>Born</u> 17 May 1947 in Los Angeles,
California. <u>Education:</u> Mis-educated at Los Angeles City College; studied at the New Communicators School of Cinemaphotog-
raphy. <u>Currently living in</u> Los Angeles. <u>Career:</u> Besides
writing poetry, he is involved in tutoring science and mathematics, in film-making, and "in probing the depths of the universe."
POETRY
    (Anthologies): Adoff, <u>The Poetry of Black America</u>; Schul-
    berg, <u>From the Ashes</u>; Troupe, <u>Watts Poets</u>.

(Periodicals): <u>Antioch Review</u>, Fall 1967; <u>Black World</u>, December 1967.

INTERJECTIONS

"The poet is a mystic in tune with the rhythms and vibrations of his worlds; therefore his vision penetrates far beyond the veil of appearances and, depending on the strength of his focus and concentration, he is able to gaze upon the awesome but lovely features of reality. He is a 'Magician' in that he uses words to evoke images in the minds of others, thereby hooking the listener and reader of his work to a fresh look of reality; so because he deals with essence rather than with form he communes with God more than most men; ergo others consider him a madman, a holy one, a restless spirit enshrined in flesh."

BIOGRAPHY AND CRITICISM ON OJENKI

Schulberg. "Black Phoenix," pp. 279, 281.

OJI, Abayome see WAKEFIELD, Jacques

OKPAKU, Joseph O. O. <u>Born</u> 24 March 1943 in Lokoja, formerly Northern Nigeria. <u>Education:</u> B.S. (Civil Engineering), Northwestern University, 1965; M.S. (Structural Engineering), Stanford University, 1968; Ph.D., (thesis pending), Dramatic Literature and Theatre History, Stanford University. <u>Currently living in</u> New York City. <u>Career:</u> Instructor, Stanford University, 1969; Associate Professor of Literature, Sarah Lawrence College, 1970-72; Lecturer on drama, aesthetics, criticism, social problems and current affairs at colleges in the U.S., Africa, and Europe; Writer for radio; Founder, editor and publisher of <u>Journal of the New African Literature and the Arts</u>; President and publisher of the Third Press--Joseph Okpaku Publishing Co., Inc., New York City. <u>Member:</u> International PEN Club; International Platform Association. <u>Awards, Honors:</u> Fellowship, African Scholarship Program of American University; second prize, essay competition, western Region, 1960; second prize, BBC African Drama Competition for <u>Virtues of Adultery</u>, 1966; fellowship for study at the University of Warsaw, 1969.

DRAMA

<u>Born Aside the Grave</u>, 1966.

<u>The Frogs on Capitol Hill</u> (an adaptation of Aristophanes' The Frogs).

<u>The Virtues of Adultery</u>, 1966.

NON-FICTION

<u>African Mythology.</u> New York: T. Y. Crowell, 1971.

With Ferdinand Jones. <u>Anatomy of White America,</u> forthcoming.

<u>New African Literature and the Arts</u>, vols. 1, 2 and 3. New York: T. Y. Crowell, 1970, 1971, 1972*†. (Editor.)

<u>Nigeria: Dilemma of Nationhood</u>. Westport, Conn.: Greenwood, 1971*; New York: Third, 1974†.

<u>Verdict: The Exclusive Picture Story of the Trial of the Chicago 8</u>. New York: Third, 1970*†.

(Periodicals): <u>Africa Report</u>, October 1968; November 1969;

Author's Guild Bulletin; Frankfurter Allgemeine Zeitung, August 1969; Présence Africaine, 1969; Publishers Weekly, 15 March 1971; 15 November 1971. Also published in the Chicago Sun-Times.

REVIEWS BY OKPAKU
Published in Black World and Essence.

SHORT NOVEL
"Under the Iroko Tree." In The Literary Review (Summer 1968).

BIOGRAPHY AND CRITICISM ON OKPAKU
Contemporary Authors 29/32.
Who's Who in America.

OLATUNJI, Ade.
POETRY (Periodical): Journal of Black Poetry, Summer 1972.

OLIVER, Diane. Born 1943 in Charlotte, North Carolina. Died 1966. Education: A.P., University of North Carolina--Greensboro; Writers Workshop of the University of Iowa. [1] Career: Guest editor of Mademoiselle, 1964; teacher's aid, Operation Head Start. Awards, Honors: O'Henry Award for Short Stories; Honorable Mention, Mademoiselle's fiction competition. [2]

SHORT STORIES
(Anthologies): Adoff, Brothers and Sisters; Chambers and Moon, Right On! Abrahams, Wm., Prize Stories of 1967: The O'Henry Awards (Garden City, N.Y.: Doubleday, 1967); Margolies, A Native Sons Reader; Watson, R. and G. Ruark, The Greensboro Reader (University of North Carolina Press, 1968).
(Periodicals): Negro Digest, November 1965; July 1966; March 1967; Red Clay Reader, Fall 1965; Sewanee Review, Spring 1966.

BIOGRAPHY ON OLIVER
Llorens, David. "Remembering a Young Talent." Negro Digest 15 (September 1966): 88-89.
    [1]Miss Oliver was killed in an automobile accident a few days before she would have received her master's degree. David Lorens, "Remembering a Young Talent," Negro Digest 15 (September 1966): 89.
    [2]Ibid., pp. 88-89.

OLIVER, Georgiana.
POETRY (Anthology): Murphy, Negro Voices.

OLIVER, James B.
SHORT STORY (Periodical): Black World, March 1972.

OLOGBONI, Tejumola (Rockie D. Taylor). Born 1945 in Salina, Kansas.
POETRY
Drum Song. Introduction by Gwendolyn Brooks. Milwaukee: n.p., 196?.
(Anthologies): Chapman, New Black Voices. Brown, Lee

Ologboni, T. (cont.)

and Ward, To Gwen with Love.

OLU, Niyonu.
POETRY (Periodical): Journal of Black Poetry, Summer 1972.

OLUMOLA, Olubiyi.
POETRY (Periodical): Journal of Black Poetry, 1969.

O'NEAL, John.
CRITICISM
"Black Arts: Notebook." In Gayle, The Black Aesthetic.
With Gilbert Moses. "Dialogue: The Free Southern Theatre."
Tulane Drama Review 9 (Summer 1965): 63-76.
"Motion in the Ocean: Some Political Dimensions of the Free
Southern Theatre." Drama Review 12 (Summer 1968): 70-
77.
"Problems and Prospects." Negro Digest 16 (April 1966): 4.
"The Status of the Negro Actor." Drama Critique 12 (Spring
1964): 96.
DRAMA
Black Power, Green Power, Red in the Eye, 1972.
Hurricane Season, 1973.
With the Southern Free Theatre Workshop. Where Is the
Blood of Your Fathers, 1971.
POETRY
(Anthology): Chapman, New Black Voices.

O'NEILL, Richard.
POETRY (Anthology): Black Poets Write On!

ORMES, Gwendolyn.
DRAMA
Ome-Nka.
Untitled.

OVERBY, Beatris.
POETRY (Anthology): Murphy, Negro Voices.

OVERSTREET, Cleo.
NOVEL
The Boar Hog Woman. Garden City, N.Y.: Doubleday, 1972*.
REVIEW: The Boar Hog Woman
Foot, A. C. Book World, 28 May 1972, p. 440.

OWENS, Daniel Walter. Born 14 July 1948 in Malden, Massachusetts. Education: Certificate in Computer Programming, Bryant and Stratton Junior College, 1968; attended Boston State College, 1968; B.A. (English), University of Massachusetts at Boston, 1971; attended Yale Graduate School of Drama-Playwright-
ing, 1971; Harvard Graduate School of Education. Currently living in Roxbury, Massachusetts. Career: Has had varied work
experience with Manpower Inc., as a morgue attendant, mail
clerk and dishwasher. Also served as counselor for the Re-

source Opportunity Center in New Haven, Connecticut; as messenger for the Deaconness Hospital in Boston; as teacher-director of summer programs; as assistant educational director for the Store Front Learning Center in Boston, 1969-71; as coordinator of Columbia Point Summerthing, 1969, and as associate director of Roxbury Summerthing, 1971.   Lecturer on Black Theater at Boston University and Boston College; Resident Playwright for the New African Company of Boston, summer 1969; Director of Playwrights Workshop National Center of Afro-American Artists, 1970-71; producer of his own plays, New Haven and Boston, 1972; Associate editor of Viewpoint, a Black student publication at the University of Massachusetts; Writer for Brotherlove, Channel 7, Boston 1972.   Member: Board of Directors of the Roxbury Ecumenical Center, 1969; advisor to the Youth Fellowship of Emmanuel Baptist Church of Malden, 1967; President, Youth Council of N.A.A.C.P., Malden-Everett, 1963-65.   Awards, Honors: One of 12 playwrights selected for the Eugene O'Neill Theater Program, 1973.

DRAMA

The Box, 1969.
Bus Play, 1972.
Clean, 1970.
Imitatin' Us, Imitatin' Us, Imitatin' Death, 1971.
Joined, 1970.
Misunderstanding, 1972.
Nigger, Nigger Who's the Bad Nigger, 1969.
Refusal, 1972.
What Reason Could I Give, 1973.
Where Are They? 1972.

POETRY

(Anthology): Murphy, Today's Negro Voices.
(Periodical): Journal of Black Poetry, 1969.

INTERJECTIONS

"I believe that the Gods (Allah) have given me a talent, another eye, and it is up to me to use them towards an affirmation of life.   I write about love, about communication, about the tyrannies and oppression that a person subjects his or her ownself to as well as those imposed from outside.   I am not a prophet or visionary but only a creation of the Gods, whose only wish is that someday each man will be a man in all senses of the word."

OWENS, Rev. John Henry.
POETRY (Anthology): Murphy, Ebony Rhythm.

OYAMO (Charles F. Gordon). Born 1943 in Lorain, Ohio.
DRAMA

The Barbarians.
The Advantage of Dope.
The Breakout. In King and Milner, Black Drama Anthology.
The Chimpanzee.
The Entrance--A Journey.
His First Step.

Lovers, 1969.
The Revelation.
The Thieves, 1970.
Willie Bignigga.
POETRY
    (Anthology): Major, The New Black Poetry.

-P-

PAGE, Daphne Diane.
    POETRY (Anthology): Henderson, Understanding the New Black
        Poetry.

PAISLEY, John Walter.
    POETRY The Voice of Mizraim. New York: Neale, 1907.

PALMER, Vernon U. Born 27 March 1930 in New York City. Edu-
    cation: B.A. (Economics), New York University--Washington
    Square College of Liberal Arts, 1962. Currently living in
    Brooklyn, New York. Career: A systems programmer and
    coder for a leading data processing organization in New York
    City.
    POETRY
        The New Grand Army: Poems. New York: Vantage, 1965.
    UNPUBLISHED WORK
        Two volumes of poetry.
    INTERJECTIONS
    "A true poet of classical standards can greet each day with
    boundless optimism when he feels that his personal sacrifices
    for his art from day to day will one day be consumed by the
    world in a romantic explosion of concerned recognition that there
    is one man within it who loves. Writing can be an escape to
    reality; mortality must surely be more than physical existence
    and a glimpse of immortality (as Swedonborg discovered)."

PANNELL, Lynn K.
    DRAMA
        Conversation.
        It's a Shame, 1971.

PARKER, Gladys Marie.
    POETRY (Anthology): Murphy, Ebony Rhythm.

PARKER, Patricia.
    POETRY (Anthology): Miller, Dices and Black Bones.

PARKS, Alma.
    POETRY
        (Periodical): Negro History Bulletin, October 1962.
    BIOGRAPHY ON PARKS
        Negro History Bulletin 26 (October 1962): 56-57.

PARKS, Gordon. Born 30 November 1912 in Fort Scott, Kansas.
Education: A.F.D., Maryland Institute; Doctor of Humane Letters, Boston University; Doctor of Humane Letters; Fairfield
University; Doctor of Literature, Kansas State University; Doctor of Humane Letters, St. Olaf's College, 1973. Currently living in New York City. Career: Journalist; photographer for
Federal Security Agency, 1942-43, and for Life magazine, 1948-
72; consultant for Hollywood productions; film director of three
documentaries on Black ghetto life for NET; writer, producer,
director of The Learning Tree, 1969, and other motion picture
productions in the United States and Europe; composer whose
compositions have been premiered in Vienna and Philadelphia.
Awards, Honors: honorary degrees as listed above; The Julius
Rosenwald Fellowship, 1941; other awards: National Conference
of Christians and Jews, 1964; the Philadelphia Museum of Art,
1964; the Syracuse University School of Journalism, 1963; the
New York Art Directors Club, 1963-64; the American Society of
Magazine Photographers, 1963; the Missouri School of Journal-
ism, 1964; the Photographic Society of America; the Rochester
Institute of Technology, 1962; the Frederick W. Brehm Award,
1962; University of Miami, 1964; 57th Spingarn Medal, 1972.
AUTOBIOGRAPHY
   Choice of Weapons. New York: Harper & Row, 1966*†; New
      York: Berkley†; New York: Noble, 1968†.
NON-FICTION
   Born Black. Philadelphia: Lippincott, 1971*.
NOVEL
   The Learning Tree. New York: Harper & Row, 1963*;
      Greenwich, Conn.: Fawcett, 1970†. Excerpt in Austin,
      Fenderson and Nelson, The Black Man and the Promise of
      America.
POETRY
   Gordon Parks: A Poet and His Camera. New York: Viking,
      1968*.
   Gordon Parks: Whispers of Intimate Things. New York:
      Viking, 1971*.
   In Love. Philadelphia: Lippincott, 1971*.
BIOGRAPHY AND CRITICISM ON PARKS
   Contemporary Authors.
   Crisis, October 1972. (Acceptance Speech upon receipt of the
      57th Spingarn Medal.)
   Ebony (July 1946): 25.
   "Gordon Parks Releases Second Movie." Crisis 78 (July
      1971): 162.
   Harnan, Terry. Gordon Parks: Black Photographer and
      Film Maker. Champaign, Ill.: Garrard, 1972.
   Interview. Black Creation, Winter 1972.
   Negro Digest (January 1944): 41-42.
   Parade, 23 June 1968.
   Robinson. Historical Negro Biographies, p. 243.
   Toppin. Biographical History of Blacks in America Since
      1528, pp. 381-384.
   Turk, Midge. Gordon Parks. New York: Crowell, 1971.

Wolf, William. Cue, 9 August 1969.
REVIEWS: The Learning Tree
    Berry, Faith. Crisis 70 (December 1963): 634-635.
    Hentoff, Nat. New York Herald Tribune, 25 August 1963,
        p. 6.

PARKS, Valerie.
    POETRY
        (Anthology): Murphy, Negro Voices.
        (Periodicals): Negro Story, October-November 1944; Decem-
        ber-January 1944-45.

PARRISH, Clarence R.
    NOVEL Images of Democracy (I Can't Go Home). New York:
        Carlton, 1967.

PARRISH, Dorothy.
    POETRY (Periodical): Black Art Writer's Literary Magazine,
        First Quarter 1971.

PATTERSON, Charles. Born 29 October 1941.
    DRAMA
        Black Ice. In Jones and Neal, Black Fire.
        Legacy. In Reed, 19 Necromancers from Now.
        The Super, 1965.
    POETRY
        (Anthology): Major, The New Black Poetry.

PATTERSON, Harry Wilson.
    POETRY Gems of the Soul; Book of Verse and Poetic Prose.
        Washington, D.C.: Murray Brothers, 1935.

PATTERSON, James. Born 1933 in Moscow, Russia.
    POETRY (Anthology): Randall and Burroughs, For Malcolm.

PATTERSON, Jesse F.
    POETRY (Anthology): Murphy, Ebony Rhythm.

PATTERSON, Lindsay. Born in Bastrop, Louisiana. Education:
    Attended Morehouse Parish Training School in Bastrop; Atkins
    High School in Winston Salem, N.C.; received B.A. (English)
    from Virginia State College. Career: Information Specialist
    and correspondent for the Stars and Stripes in Europe for the
    U.S. Army; feature writer and managing editor of The Patton
    Post, United States Special Troops, United States Army Head-
    quarters in Heidelberg, Germany; Editorial assistant to Lang-
    ston Hughes; Columnist for the Associated Negro Press; Special
    Publicity Writer on the film, Uptight, for Jules Dassin and Para-
    mount Pictures. Also worked for Pan American World Airways
    and Harrison Advertising Agency. Has been guest lecturer at
    numerous colleges and universities. Awards, Honors: Nation-
    al Foundation on the Arts and Humanities (cash award); Mac-
    Dowell Colony (three fellowships); Edward Albee Foundation (two
    fellowships).

CRITICISM
> A Critical Study of the Best Black Playwrights. New York:
> Dodd, Mead, forthcoming.
> "Langston Hughes, An Inspirer of Young Writers." Free-
> domways 8 (Spring 1968): 179-181.

EDITOR
> Anthology of the American Negro in the Theatre. Interna-
> tional Library of Negro Life and History. New York:
> Publishers, 1967.
> Black Theater: A 20th-Century Collection of the Work of Its
> Best Playwrights. New York: Dodd, Mead, 1971*.
> Black Films and Film-makers: A Comprehensive Anthology
> from Stereotype to Superhero. New York: Dodd, Mead,
> 1973*.
> Introduction to Black Literature in America, From 1746 to
> the Present. International Library of Negro Life and His-
> tory. New York: Publishers, 1968.
> The Negro in Music and Art. International Library of Negro
> Life and History. New York: Publishers, 1967.
> A Rock Against the Wind: Black Love Poems. New York:
> Dodd, Mead, 1973*.

ESSAYS AND REVIEWS
> Published in The New York Times; Columbia University For-
> um; In Black America; Saturday Review; Negro History
> Bulletin; Writer's Yearbook.

SCREENPLAY
> Roper.

SHORT STORIES
> (Anthologies): Barbour, Russel B., ed. Black and White
> Together (Philadelphia: United Church, 1967); Coombs,
> What We Must See; Hughes, The Best Short Stories by Ne-
> gro Writers; Patterson, An Introduction to Black Litera-
> ture in America.
> (Periodicals): Essence; One Magazine; The Voice.

WORK IN PROGRESS
> Autobiography: "Diary of an Aging Young Writer: An Auto-
> biography."
> Novel: "T-baby."

PATTERSON, Orlando. Born 5 June 1940 in Jamaica, West Indies.
Education: B.Sc. (Economics), London University, 1962; Ph.D.,
(Sociology), London University, 1965; A.M. (Honorary), Harvard
University, 1971; additional study at the University of the West
Indies and the London School of Economics. Currently living in
Cambridge, Massachusetts. Career: Assistant Lecturer in Sociology, The London School of Economics, 1965-67; Researcher,
sponsored by the London Institute of Race Relations, Summer
1966; Consultant and Tutor in Sociology for the management of
training program, 1966-67; Lecturer in Sociology, The University of the West Indies, Mona Campus, Jamaica, 1967-70; Associate Professor of Afro-American Studies, Harvard University,
1970-71; Research Fellow, Center for the Behavioral Sciences,
Harvard University, 1971; Allston Burr Senior Tutor, Leverett

Orlando Patterson

House, Harvard University, 1971-73; Senior Scholar, The Educational Development Center and Professor of Sociology, Harvard University, 1971 to present. <u>Member</u>: Editorial Board, <u>New Left Review</u>, 1965-66; The Technical Advisory Council to the Prime Minister of Jamaica, 1972 to present. <u>Awards, Honors</u>: Jamaica Government Exhibition Scholar, University College of the West Indies, 1959; Commonwealth Scholarship to the London School of Economics, London University, 1962-65; Fictional Prize, Dakar Festival of Negro Arts, 1965.

CRITICISM
    "Baldwin as Stylist and Moralist: Critical Assessment of the Essays of James Baldwin." <u>New Left Review</u> 26 (Summer 1964).
    "Twilight of a Dark Myth: Assessment of the Social Philosophy and Poetry of Negritude." <u>The Times Literary Supplement</u> (Special Commonwealth Edition), 16 September 1965.

NON-FICTION
    <u>The Sociology of Slavery</u>. Cranbury, N.J.: Fairleigh Dickinson University Press, 1969*.
    (Anthologies): Brewster, H., <u>The Development Problem in St. Vincent</u> (I.S.E.R.); Foner, <u>Slavery in the New World</u>; <u>Race and Immigration: A New Society Studies Reader</u> (1970).

(Periodicals): <u>American Scholar</u>, Winter 1973-74; <u>The British Journal of Sociology</u>, June 1966; <u>Harvard Educational Review</u> 41 (1971); <u>Harvard Journal of Afro-American Affairs</u>, No. 2, 1971; <u>New Left Review</u>, May-June 1965; <u>New Society</u>, November 1964; September 1966; June 1969; <u>The New Statesman</u>, 8 March 1968; <u>The Public Interest</u>, Spring 1972; Spring 1973; <u>Race</u>, 1968; <u>Social and Economics Studies</u>, September 1970.

NOVELS

<u>The Children of Sisyphus.</u> London: Hutchinson, 1964; Boston: Houghton Mifflin, 1965; published as <u>Dinah.</u> Elmhurst, N.Y.: Pyramid Books, 1968.

<u>An Absence of Ruins.</u> London: Hutchinson, 1967.

<u>Die the Long Day.</u> New York: Morrow, 1972*; Philadelphia: Curtis, 1973†.

REVIEWS BY PATTERSON

Published in <u>Caribbean Quarterly</u>; <u>Social and Economic Studies; Population Studies</u>; <u>New World Quarterly</u>; <u>The American Anthropologist</u>; <u>The Times Literary Supplement</u>; <u>The Manchester Guardian</u>; <u>The New Statesman</u>.

SHORT STORIES

(Anthology): A. Salkey, <u>Stories from the Caribbean</u> (United Kingdom: Elek Books, 1965).

(Periodicals): <u>The Jamaica Journal</u> No. 2 (1968); <u>New Left Review</u>, September-October 1965.

TEXTBOOK

<u>Black in White America: Historical Perspectives.</u> New York: Macmillan, forthcoming.

INTERJECTIONS

"Liberal and cosmopolitan in cultural and social affairs. Left of center politically. Conservative on educational matters."

PATTERSON, Raymond Richard. <u>Born</u> 14 December 1929 in New York City. <u>Education</u>: A.B., Lincoln University, 1951; M.A., New York University, 1956; additional study at Wagner College, Columbia University and Hunter College. <u>Currently living in</u> Merrick, New York. <u>Career</u>: 1956-58, Children's Supervisor, Youth House for Boys; 1958-59, Instructor in English, Benedict College, South Carolina; 1959-68, Teacher of English, New York City Public Schools, 1968 to present; Lecturer in English, The City College, City University of New York. His poetry can be heard on the recording, <u>Tough Poems for Tough People</u> (Caldman Records) and seen in the filmstrip, <u>Black Poetry</u> (Warren Schoat). <u>Member:</u> National Council of Teachers of English. <u>Awards, Honors</u>: Borestone Mountain Poetry Award, 1950; Poet-in-Residence, Minneapolis Public Schools, Spring 1969; National Endowment for the Arts Award, 1970; Library of Congress Poetry Reading, 1971.

POETRY

<u>Twenty-Six Ways of Looking at a Black Man, and Other Poems.</u> New York: Award Books, 1969†.

(Anthologies): Adoff, <u>Black Out Loud</u>; Adoff, <u>City in All Directions</u>; Adoff, <u>I Am the Darker Brother</u>; Adoff, <u>The</u>

Poetry of Black America; Baylor and Stokes, Fine Frenzy;
Breman, Sixes and Sevens; Brooks, A Broadside Treasury;
Chapman, New Black Voices; Coombs, We Speak as Lib-
erators; Eisenberg, Not Quite Twenty; Hughes, New Negro
Poets: USA; Hughes, La Poesie Negro-Américaine, Hughes
and Bontemps, The Poetry of the Negro: 1746-1970; Jor-
dan, Soulscript; Lowenfels, The Writing on the Wall; Ma-
jor, The New Black Poetry; Michel, Headway; Pool, Be-
yond the Blues; Randall and Burroughs, For Malcolm;
Robinson, Nommo; Weisman and Wright, Black Poetry for
All Americans.
(Periodicals): Chicago Tribune Magazine, 22 November 1970;
The Minnesota Review, March 1970; Negro Digest, Septem-
ber-October 1968; Scholastic Voices; 2 February 1970; 16
November 1970; October 1972; Scholastic Scope, 6 Decem-
ber 1971; The Transatlantic Review, Winter-Spring 1972;
Sumac, Fall 1968; Phylon, Third Quarter 1957; Présence
Africain, no. 57.
BIOGRAPHY ON PATTERSON
Contemporary Authors.

PATTERSON, Thomas.
SHORT STORY (Anthology): Ford and Faggett, Best Short
Stories by Afro-American Writers.

PAULDING, James E. Born 1935.
NOVEL Sometime Tomorrow. New York: Carlton, 1965.

PAWLEY, Thomas. Born 5 August 1917 in Jackson, Mississippi.
Career: See Shockley and Chandler, Living Black American Au-
thors, p. 123; Contemporary Authors, 29/32.
CRITICISM
"The Black Theatre Audience." Players 46 (August-Septem-
ber 1971): 257-261.
"The First Black Playwrights." Black World 21 (April 1972):
16-24.
DRAMA
Crispus Attucks, 1947.
FFV, 1963.
Freedom in My Soul (one act), 1938.
Judgment Day (one act), 1938. In Brown, Davis and Lee,
The Negro Caravan.
Messiah (eight scenes), 1948.
Smokey (one act), 1939.
The Tumult and the Shouting, 1969.
Zebedee, 1949.
EDITOR
With William R. Reardon. The Black Teacher and the Dra-
matic Arts: A Dialogue, Bibliography and Anthology.
New York: Negro Universities Press, 1970*.
POETRY
(Periodicals): Crisis, 1935; Phylon, Second Quarter, Fourth
Quarter, 1943; Second Quarter 1944; First Quarter 1945;
First Quarter 1946.

PAYNE, Rev. Daniel A. <u>Born</u> 24 February 1811 in Charleston,
North Carolina. <u>Died</u> 1893. <u>Education:</u> Attended the Miner's
Moralist Society in Charleston, North Carolina and the Gettys-
burg, Pennsylvania, Lutheran Seminary.[1] <u>Career:</u> Served a
shoemaker's apprenticeship for a few months; was a carpenter
four years and a tailor for nine months; at the age of 21 began a day school with three pupils who paid 50 cents each;
taught slaves at night; at the age of 22, erected a plain building and taught until April 1835 when the Charleston legislature
passed a law against schools for Black children; started a private school in Philadelphia in 1840.[2] Became a bishop of the
A.M.E. Church in 1852. Payne organized the first Black pastor's association in the District of Columbia; laid the foundation for the Home and Foreign Mission Society; established the
Bethel Literary Association in Washington, D.C.,[3] and founded
other literary societies and groups for the self-improvement of
Blacks;[4] visited the White House and urged Lincoln to sign the
bill for emancipation, 1862; persuaded the A.M.E. Church to
purchase Wilberforce, a Black school established in 1856 by
the A.M.E. Church; served as president of Wilberforce for 16
years.[5]

AUTOBIOGRAPHY

<u>Recollections of Seventy Years.</u> Edited by C. S. Smith.
    Compiled by Sarah C. Bierce. Introduction by Rev. F. J.
    Grimke. Nashville, Tenn.: The A.M.E. Sunday School
    Union, 1888.
(Anthology): Brown, Davis and Lee, <u>The Negro Caravan.</u>

NON-FICTION

<u>Bishop Payne's First Annual Address to the Philadelphia An-
nual Conference of the A.M.E. Church.</u> 16 May 1853.
    Philadelphia: C. Sherman, 1853.
<u>Education of the Ministry.</u> Washington: n.p., n.d.
<u>Historical Sketch of Wilberforce University.</u> Xenia, O.:
    n.p., 1879.
<u>History of the African Methodist Episcopal Church in the
United States of America.</u> Edited by C. S. Smith. Nash-
ville, Tenn.: A.M.E. Sunday School Union, 1891.
<u>Sermons Delivered Before the General Conference of the A.
M.E. Church, Indianapolis, Indiana,</u> May 1888. Steno-
graphically Reported. Edited by Rev. C. S. Smith.
Nashville, Tenn.: A.M.E. Sunday School Union, 1888.
<u>A Treatise on Domestic Education.</u> Cincinnati: Cranston &
Stowe, 1885.

POETRY

<u>The Pleasures and Other Miscellaneous Poems.</u> Baltimore:
Sherwood, 1850.
(Anthology): Robinson, <u>Early Black American Poets,</u> p. 50.

BIOGRAPHY AND CRITICISM ON PAYNE

Adams. <u>Great American Negroes Past and Present,</u> p. 83.
Brawley. <u>Negro Builders and Heroes,</u> pp. 95-103.
_____. <u>Negro Genius,</u> pp. 74-80.
Brown, Davis and Lee. <u>The Negro Caravan,</u> pp. 732-733.
Coam, Josephine R. <u>Daniel Alexander Payne, Christian</u>

Educator. Philadelphia: A. M. E. Book Concern, 1935.

Cromwell, John Wesley. The Negro in American History; Men and Women Eminent in the Evolution of the American of African Descent. Washington, D. C.: The American Negro Academy, 1914, pp. 115-125.

Holly, James Theodore. A Vindication of the Capacity of the Negro Race for Self Government. n. p. , 1857.

Killan, C. "Wilberforce University, The Reality of Bishop Payne's Dream." Negro History Bulletin 34 (April 1971): 83-87.

Loggins. The Negro Author in America, pp. 233-456 passim.
Negro History Bulletin 1 (February 1938): 5-6.

Ploski. Reference Library of Black America, vol. 3, p. 27.

Prince, W. H. The Stars of African Methodism. Portland, Ore.: n. p. , 1916.

Redding. The Lonesome Road, pp. 25, 26, 29, 32-38, 53, 61, 62, 68, 74, 80-81, 145.

Robinson. Early Black American Poets, pp. 50-51.

Robinson. Historical Negro Biographies, p. 106.

Simmons. Men of Mark, pp. 1078-1085.

Smith, Charles Spencer. A History of the African Methodist Episcopal Church; Being a Volume Supplemental to a History of the African Methodist Episcopal Church, by Daniel Payne, D. D. LL. D. , Late one of its Bishops, Chronicling the Principal Events in the Advance of the African Methodist Episcopal Church from 1856 to 1922. Philadelphia: Book Concern of the A. M. E. Church, 1922.

Smith David. Biography of Rev. David Smith of the A. M. E. Church; Being a Complete History, Embracing over Sixty Years' Labor in the Advancement of the Redeemer's Kingdoms on Earth. Including "The History of the Origin and Development of Wilberforce University." Xenia, O.: Xenia Gazette Office, 1881.

Toppin. A Biographical History of Blacks in America Since 1528, pp. 384-385.

White, Lulla G. "Daniel Payne." Negro History Bulletin 6 (May 1943): 175-177.

[1]Edgar A. Toppin, A Biographical History of Blacks in American Since 1528 (New York: David McKay, 1969, 1971), p. 384.

[2]John Wesley Cromwell, The Negro in American History (Washington: The American Negro Academy, 1914), pp. 115-117.

[3]Ibid. , pp. 119-125.

[4]Sterling A. Brown, et al. , The Negro Caravan (New York: Dryden, 1941), p. 732.

[5]Ibid. , pp. 732-733.

PAYNTER, John H. Born 1862. Died 1947.
NON-FICTION
Fifty Years After. New York: Margent, 1940.
Fugitives of the Pearl. Washington, D. C.: Association, 1930; reprint ed. , New York: A. M. S. , 1970*.

Horse and Buggy Days with Uncle Sam. New York: Margent, 1943.
Joining the Navy; or Abroad with Uncle Sam. Hartford, Conn.: American, 1895.
Slave Narrative.

PEACE, Ernest E. Born 16 December 1890 in Henderson, North Carolina. Education: A.B. and M.A., Howard University. Career: Lived in Washington, D.C., most of his life; taught school there.[1]
POETRY
    (Anthology): Murphy, Negro Voices.
BIOGRAPHY AND CRITICISM ON PEACE
    Opportunity 5 (July 1927): 205, 313.
        [1]Beatrice Murphy, ed., Negro Voices (New York: Henry Harrison, 1938), p. 124.

PEARSON, Bernard.
POETRY (Periodical): Journal of Black Poetry, Spring 1969.

PEKTOR, Irene Mari.
POETRY
    Golden Banners. Boston: Christopher, 1941.
    War or Peace? Oceano, Ca.: Harbison & Harbison, 1939.

PENNY, Rob see KILONFE, Oba

PERKINS, Charles.
NOVEL Portrait of a Young Man Drowning. New York: Simon & Schuster, 1962.

PERKINS, Eugene. Born 13 September 1932 in Chicago. Education: B.S., George Williams College, 1961; M.S., George Williams College, 1964. Currently living in Chicago. Career: Group worker, Ada S. McKinley House, 1959-60; Group Worker, Fuman Settlement House, 1960-63; Extension Worker, Chicago Boys Club, Chicago Youth Development Project, 1963; Program Director, Henry Horner Chicago Boys Club, 1963-66; Instructor, Central YMCA College, 1968-69; Lecturer, Roosevelt College (Black Experience in Literature), Summer 1969; Workshop Instructor, South Side Community Art Center, 1967 to present. Also taught creative writing at Cook County Jail, 1970-present; Helen Robinson Library, 1970-present; Farragut High School, 1969-70; Pontiac Prison, 1970-present. Has served as consultant to the YMCA National Outreach Program; for the Literary Magazine, School District 10, Chicago Public Schools; For Educational Television, School District 10; for Art & Soul Gallery; for the Museum of Afro-American History. Has lectured at more than thirty colleges and universities throughout the country and for the Adult Education Program of Chicago and Ebony Talent, Incorporated. Also editor and publisher of the Free Black Press; editor of Black Expression, a Journal of Literature and Art. Member: Founder of the Association for the Development

Eugene Perkins

of Black Children.   Awards, Honors: Special Award, Council
on Interracial Books for Children, for Ghetto Fairy, 1972.
CRITICISM BY PERKINS
    "Black Theater and Community Expression." Inner City
       Studies Journal (North Eastern State College), Summer
       1970.
    "Black Theater as Image Maker." Black Books Bulletin 1
       (Spring-Summer 1972): 24.
    "Black Theater in Chicago." Chicago Sun-Times.
    "Black Writers and Liberation Movement." Illinois English
       Bulletin, 1968.
    "Changing Status of Black Writers." Black World 19 (June
       1970): 18-23.
    "New Voices in Black Culture." Panorama Magazine (Chi-
       cago Daily News), 7 December 1968.
DRAMA
    Black Is So Beautiful.
    Cry of the Black Ghetto.
    Ghetto Fairy (A Play for Children).
    The Image Makers, 1972.
    Maternity Ward.
    Turn a Black Cheek.
EDITOR
    Black Expressions: Anthology of New Black Poets. Chicago:
       YMCA, 1967.
    Poetry of Prison. Chicago: DuSable Museum of Afrikan
       American History, 1972.
NON-FICTION
    Home Is a Dirty Street: The Social Oppression of Black
       Children. Chicago: Third World, 1973.
POETRY
    An Apology to My African Brother. Chicago: Adams Press,
       1965.
    Black Is Beautiful. Chicago: Free Black Press, 1968.
    Silhouette. Chicago: Free Black Press, 1970.
    West Wall. Chicago: Free Black Press, 1969. (Photogra-
       phy by Roy Lewis.)
    (Anthologies): Alhamisi and Wangara, Black Arts; Brown,
       Lee and Ward, To Gwen with Love; Perkins, Black Ex-
       pression; Simmons and Hutchinson, Black Culture. Also
       published in Anthology of Black Creations and Port of Chi-
       cago Poets.
    (Periodicals): Freedomways, Winter 1966; Fourth Quarter
       1971; Negro Digest, November 1963; January 1966; Sep-
       tember-October 1968; also published in Journal of Black
       Poetry; Liberator.
WORK IN PROGRESS
    A book on the development of Afrikan children; a play on
       Cinque; a book of children's poems and plays.
BIOGRAPHY AND CRITICISM ON PERKINS
    Lee. Dynamite Voices, pp. 41-43.
    Washington, Cleve. "Perkins Pulls the Plug on Electric
       Niggers." Black Books Bulletin 1 (1973): 21-23.

REVIEW: Silhouette
    Plumpp, Sterling.   Black Books Bulletin 1 (Winter 1972):
    46-48.

INTERJECTIONS
    "Life and Art are interrelated. For man is a product of his
culture, and therefore his art helps to mold his total development. As a Black Artist, this is particularly important because
of white America's attempt to destroy his original Afrikan culture. A Black writer should use his craft as a means to rede-
fine his culture and as a political instrument to shape and control it."

PERKINS, Minnie Louise.
    POETRY A String of Pearls. Chicago: By the Author, 1945.

PERRY, John Sinclair.
    POETRY Voice of Humanity: Song of the New World. Boston:
        Christopher, 1952.

PERRY, Julianne. Born 1952 in Durham, North Carolina.
    POETRY
        (Anthology): Adoff, The Poetry of Black America.
        (Broadside): "Black Song." Detroit: Broadside, n.d.

PERRY, Leslie.
    DRAMA
        The Minstrel Show, 1970.
        The Side Show, 1971.

PERRY, Manokai.
    DRAMA The House That Was a Country.

PERRY, Margaret. Born 15 November 1933 in Cincinnati, Ohio.
    Career: See Shockley and Chandler, Living Black American
    Authors, pp. 123-124.
    CRITICISM
        Bio-Bibliography of Countée Cullen, 1903-1946. New York:
        Negro Universities Press, 1970*.

PERRY, Richard. Born 13 January 1944 in Bronx, New York.
    Education: B.A. (English), City College of New York, 1970;
    M.F.A. (Writing), Columbia University, 1973. Currently living
    in New York City. Career: Teaches English and Black Litera-
    ture at Pratt Institute. Presently working on a second novel.
    NOVEL
        Changes. Indianapolis: Bobbs-Merrill, 1974*.
    SHORT STORY
        (Periodical): Black Creation, Spring, Summer 1972.

PERRY, Robert N., Jr.
    POETRY (Anthologies): Murphy, Ebony Rhythm; Murphy,
        Negro Voices.

PERRY, Shauneille.
  DRAMA
    Mio, 1971.
  BIOGRAPHY ON PERRY
    Ebony 28 (April 1973): 107.

PETERSON, Geraldine.
  POETRY (Anthology): Boyd, Poems by Blacks.

PETERSON, Josephine. Born 7 April 1950 in Camden, New Jersey.
  Education: Attended Temple University and California State Uni-
  versity. Currently living in San Francisco. Career: Current-
  ly an "employee of Black America"; a "student of life" and a
  student at California State University seeking a degree in biology
  for medical research. Member: University Poetry Workshop;
  Black Writer's Workshop; Community Poetry Center. Awards,
  Honors: President's List, California State University.
  POETRY
    (Periodical): E.O.P. Third World Journal (California State
      College/University publication), June 1973.
  WORK IN PROGRESS
    A collection of poetry entitled "This Child Is Going to Live!"

PETERSON, Louis. Born 1922 in Hartford, Connecticut.
  DRAMA
    Crazy Horse Have Jenny Now.
    Entertain a Ghost, 1962.
    Joey (teleplay).
    Take a Giant Step. New York: French, 1954†; Also in
      Ford, Black Insights; Patterson, Black Theater; Turner,
      Black Drama in America; Kronenberger, The Best Plays
      of 1953-54 (a condensation).
  BIOGRAPHY AND CRITICISM ON PETERSON
    Abramson. Negro Playwrights in the American Theatre, pp.
      221-238.
    Arts in Society 5 (1968): 234-235. (Interview.)
    Bardolph. The Negro Vanguard, pp. 292, 374, 376, 378,
      413.
    Harrison. The Drama of Nommo, pp. 170-171.
    "Louis Takes a 'Giant Step.'" Our World 9 (January 1954):
      45-48.
    Mitchell. Black Drama, pp. 163-166.
    Turpin, Waters E. "The Contemporary American Negro
      Playwright." CLA Journal 9 (September 1965): 16-18.

PETRIE, Phil W. Born 1937.
  POETRY (Anthology): Abdul, The Magic of Black Poetry.

PETRY, Ann Lane. Born 1911 in Old Saybrook, Connecticut. Education: Ph.G., University of Connecticut, 1931. Currently living in Old Saybrook, Connecticut. Career: Pharmacist, 1931-
  38; advertising saleswoman and writer for the Amsterdam News,
  1938-41; reporter and women's page editor for People's Voice,

1941-44; journalist and teacher.   Member: P. E. N.; Authors
Guild; Author's League of America; Screen Writers Guild of
America West.   Awards, Honors: Houghton Mifflin Literary
Fellowship, 1945; Best American Short Story for 1946; "Like a
Winding Sheet. "

AUTOBIOGRAPHY

"My Most Humiliating Jim Crow Experience." Negro Digest
4 (June 1946): 63-64.

CHILDREN AND YOUNG ADULTS

The Drugstore Cat. New York: T. Y. Crowell, 1949.

Harriet Tubman: Conductor on the Underground Railway.
New York: T. Y. Crowell, 1955*; New York: Pocket
Books†.

Legends of the Saints. New York: T. Y. Crowell, 1970*.

Tituba of Salem Village. New York: T. Y. Crowell, 1964*.

CRITICISM

"The Novel as Social Criticism." The Writer's Book, Edited
by Helen Hull. New York: Harper, 1950, pp. 31-39.

NON-FICTION

(Periodicals): Holiday, April 1949; The Horn Book, April
1965; Negro Digest, March 1945; March 1947.

NOVELS

Country Place.   Boston: Houghton Mifflin, 1947; Chatham,
N. J. : Chatham Booksellers*.

The Narrows. Boston: Houghton Mifflin, 1953; Chatham
Booksellers*; New York: Pyramid, 1971†.

The Street. Boston: Houghton Mifflin, 1946; New York:
Pyramid†. Excerpt in Demarest and Lamdin, The Ghetto
Reader; Negro Digest, March 1946.

NOVELLA

In Darkness and Confusion. In Seaver, Cross-Section; Chapman, Black Voices; Chambers and Moon, Right On!

SHORT STORIES

Miss Muriel and Other Stories. Boston: Houghton Mifflin,
1971*.

(Anthologies): Baker, Black Literature in America; Barks-
dale and Kinnamon, The Black Writer in America; Clarke,
American Negro Short Stories; Clarke, Harlem; Foley,
The Best American Short Stories 1946; Hill, Soon One
Morning; James, From These Roots; Shea, Strange Bar-
riers.

(Periodicals): Crisis, December 1943; May, November 1945;
Holiday, April 1949; The Magazine of the Year, August,
October 1947; The New Yorker, 25 October 1958; 29 May
1965; Opportunity, October 1947; Phylon, Fourth Quarter
1944; Redbook, May 1967.

BIOGRAPHY AND CRITICISM ON PETRY

Adams, George R. "Riot as Ritual: Ann Petry's 'In Darkness and Confusion.' " Negro American Literature Forum
6 (Summer 1972): 54-57.

Barksdale and Kinnamon. Black Writers of America, pp.
762-763.

Bone. The Negro Novel in America, pp. 180-185.

Cherry, Thomas and Willis. Portraits in Color: The Lives of Colorful Negro Women, pp. 146-147.

"The Common Ground." The Horn Book 41 (April 1965): 147-151.

Contemporary Authors 7/8.

DeMontreville, Doris and Donna Hill. Third Book of Junior Authors. Wilson, 1972, pp. 223-224.

Dempsey, David. "Uncle Tom's Ghost and the Literary Abolitionist." Antioch Review 6 (1946): 442-448.

Greene, Marjorie. "Ann Petry Planned to Write." Opportunity 24 (April-June 1946): 78-79.

"Has Anybody Seen Mrs. Dora Dean?" New Yorker, 25 October 1958, pp. 41-48.

Hughes. The Negro Novelist, pp. 160-163.

Ivy, James W. "Ann Petry Talks About First Novel." Crisis 53 (February 1946): 48-49.

_____. "Mrs. Petry's Harlem." Crisis 53 (1946): 436.

Littlejohn. Black on White, pp. 154-156.

Maund. "The Negro Novelist and the Contemporary American Scene," pp. 28-34.

O'Brien. Interviews with Black Writers, pp. 153-163.

"On the Author." New York Herald Tribune, 16 August 1953, p. 3.

Richardson. Great American Negroes, pp. 150-162.

Robinson. Historical Negro Biographies, pp. 235-236.

REVIEWS: Miss Muriel and Other Stories.

Kazin, Alfred. Saturday Review, 2 October 1972, pp. 34-35.

The Country Place.

Butcher, Margaret J. W. Journal of Negro Education 17 (1948): 169.

The Narrows.

Bontemps, Arna. Saturday Review, 22 August 1953, p. 11.

PFISTER, Arthur. Born 20 September 1949 in New Orleans, Louisiana. Education: B.A., Tuskegee Institute; M.A., Creative Writing), John Hopkins University, 1971. Career: Painter, musician and actor as well as writer; staff writer for the Tuskegee Progressive Times; a member of the now defunct Free Southern Theatre's BlkArtSouth workshop; a former member of the Tuskegee Institute "Little Theatre"; a former library editor of the Tuskegee Institute newspaper; has taught at Southern University; was Writer-in-Residence at Texas Southern University; has read his poetry at many universities and colleges. Awards, Honors: Recipient of a National Endowment for the Arts "Discovery Grant."

POETRY

Bullets, Beer Cans, Pieces and Things. Detroit: Broadside, 1971†.

(Anthologies): Brooks, A Broadside Treasury; Coombs, We Speak as Liberators; King, Blackspirits; Boyd, Poems by Blacks, vol. 1.

(Broadsides): "Granny Black Poet." Detroit: Broadside, n.d.

(Periodicals): Journal of Black Poetry, Fall-Winter 1971;
Negro American Literature Forum, Spring 1972.   Also
published in Black World; Ebony; Writers Digest; Pegasus
College Poetry; The Tuskegee Progressive Times; The
Campus Digest; The Southern University Digest; The Min-
nesota Review; NKOMBO; Subterraneans; The Human Voice
Quarterly; The Saint Andrews Review; SOULBOOK 9; The
Black Collegian; The Forward Times; Roots; High Em-
pires; The Louisiana Weekly.

INTERJECTIONS
"Life is only or should only be practical application of and
conjunction with art."

PHARR, Robert Dean.   Born 5 July 1916 in Richmond, Virginia.
NOVELS
The Book of Numbers.   Garden City, N.Y.: Doubleday, 1969;
New York: Avon, 1970†.
S. R. O.   Garden City, N.Y.: Doubleday, 1971*.
SHORT STORIES
(Anthology): Chapman, New Black Voices.
(Periodical): New York Magazine, 22 September 1969.
CRITICISM ON PHARR
Whitlow.   Black American Literature, pp. 165-167.
REVIEWS: The Book of Numbers.
Gross, R. A.   Newsweek, 16 June 1969, p. 98.
Levin, Martin.   New York Times Book Review, 27 April
1969, p. 36.
S. R. O.:
Bryant, Jerry.   Nation, 13 November 1971, p. 536.
Carew, Jan.   New York Times Book Review, 31 October
1971, p. 7.

PHILIP, Wayne (pseud. Dawad).   Born 18 October 1947 in Trinidad,
West Indies.   Education: Quit school at the age of 15, but con-
tinued his education as an artist/poet on a day-to-day basis.
Currently travelling.   Career: An artist/poet touring the world,
reading from his works at universities.   Awards, Honors: Let-
ters of recognition from around the world, including Princess
Anne's and Harvey Scribner's.
POETRY
The Dawadian.   n.p., n.d.
INTERJECTIONS
"Am not necessarily a contemporary writer or as such a
black literature writer; I prefer seeing myself as a 'Black man
poet.'   My writings are folk style as in seeing myself as the
instrument for 'life' commentary."

PHILLIPS, Frank Lamont.   Born 13 April 1953 in Eloy, Arizona.
POETRY
(Anthologies): Boyer, Broadside Annual 1973; Colley and

Moore, Starting with Poetry.
(Periodical): Essence, January 1974.

PHILLIPS, Jane. Born 1944.
NOVEL
Mojo Hand. New York: Trident Press, 1969; New York:
Pocket Books, 1969†.
POETRY
(Periodical): Black World, August 1973.

PHILLIPS, Waldo.
POETRY Poetry Is Proflection. Los Angeles: Compton Coun-
seling Center, 1965.

PICKENS, William. Born 15 January 1881 in Anderson County,
South Carolina. Died 1954. Education: Attended Talladega College; A.B., Yale University, 1904; Diploma from British Espe-
ranto Association, 1906; A.M., Fisk University, 1908; Litt.D.,
Selma University, 1915.1 Career: As a child, Pickens moved
frequently and worked on farms instead of going to school, but
was finally able to attend school and work full time near Little
Rock, Arkansas.2 Served as instructor of Latin and German,
1904-1909, and as Professor of Greek, Latin and German, 1909-
1914, Talladega College; Professor of Greek and sociology,
Wiley College; 1914-1915; Dean, Morgan State College, 1915-20;3
also served as vice president of Morgan State College. Suc-
ceeded James Weldon Johnson as field secretary of the N.A.A.
C.P.; joined the United States Treasury Department, 1941, and
was advisor and consultant of minority affairs for numerous federal agencies;4 served as president of the Alabama State Teacher's Association.5 Awards, Honors: Earned scholarships during all four years at Yale; won the Ten Eyck Oratorical Competition and received 50 dollars from the glee club, numerous
congratulatory letters, a check from the sister of Theodore
Roosevelt, and three 50-dollar gold certificates from "an unknown well-wisher" for this victory.6 Graduated from Yale with
Phi Beta Kappa honors and was offered an American-European
tour as an award for his high scholastic achievements, but de-
clined;7 listed in Who's Who in Colored America.
AUTOBIOGRAPHY
Bursting Bonds and The Heir of Slaves. Boston: Jordan &
More, 1923.
The Heir of Slaves; An Autobiography. Boston and New York:
Pilgrim, 1911.
NON-FICTION
Abraham Lincoln, Man and Statesman. Talladega, Ala.:
n.p., 1910; reprint ed., New York: n.p., 1930.
Frederick Douglass and the Spirit of Freedom. Boston:
Arakelynn, reprint ed., New York, n.p., 1931.
Fifty Years of Emancipation. n.p., 1913.

The New Negro, His Political, Civil and Mental Status.
New York: Neale, 1916; New York: AMS Press*; Westport,
Conn.: Negro Universities Press*.

Papers of the American Negro Academy...Read at the Nine-
teenth Annual Meeting of the American Negro Academy...
Washington, D.C., December 28th and 29th, 1915. Washington, n.p., 1916.

The Ultimate Effects of Segregation and Discrimination. The
Seldom Thought on the Negro Problem. n.p., 1915.

(Anthologies): Barton, Witnesses for Freedom: Negro Americans in Autobiography; Eleazer, Singers in the Dawn;
Strong, Sydney Dix, ed., What I Owe My Father (Introduction by James E. West. New York: Holt, 1931).

(Periodicals): Journal of Negro Education 34 (Spring 1966):
106-113; Crisis 57 (June 1950): 370-371; also published in
Opportunity.

SHORT STORIES
American Aesop, Negro and Other Humor. Boston: Jordan
& Moore, 1926; New York: AMS Press, 1969*.

The Vengeance of the Gods and Three Other Stories of Real
American Life. Introduction by John Bishop Hurst. Phil-
adelphia: The A.M.E. Book Concern, 1922; facsimile ed.,
Freeport, N.Y.: Books for Libraries*.

BIOGRAPHY AND CRITICISM ON PICKENS
Boris, Joseph J. Who's Who in Colored America: A Bio-
graphical Dictionary of Notable Living Persons of Negro
Descent in America. vol. 1. New York: Who's Who in
Colored America Corp., 1927.

Christmas. Negroes in Public Affairs and Government, pp.
308-309.

"Do You Remember...William Pickens?" Negro Digest 9
(January 1951): 17-18.

Gloster. Negro Voices in American Fiction, pp. 123-125.

Jet, 9 April 1964, p. 11.

Opportunity 19 (August 1941): 238-239.

Robinson. Historical Negro Biographies, pp. 236-237.

Writer's Program of New York City. Biographical Sketches.
Research Studies Compiled by Workers of the Writer's
Program of the Work Projects Administration in New York
City, for Negroes of New York. New York: n.p., 1938-
1941.

REVIEW: The Vengeance of the Gods.
Crisis 25 (1934): 37.

[1]Joseph J. Boris, Who's Who in Colored America, vol.
1 (New York: Who's Who in Colored America, 1927), p.
158.

[2]Richard Bardolph, The Negro Vanguard (New York:
Vintage, 1959), p. 184.

[3]Boris, p. 158.

[4]Bardolph, p. 346.

[5]Boris, p. 158.

[6]Bardolph, p. 188.

[7]Ibid., p. 188.

PINN, Willard.
POETRY (Periodical): Journal of Black Poetry, Spring 1969;
Winter-Spring 1970.

PINSON, Dave.
POETRY Studies in Black and White. New York: Vantage,
1966.

PITCHER, Oliver. Born 1924? in Massachusetts.
DRAMA
The Bite, 1970.
The One. In Milner and King, Black Drama Anthology.
Snake! Snake! A Play. New York?: New York Poets The-
atre?, 1961? (Typescript.)
POETRY
Dust of Silence. San Francisco: Troubador, 1960.
(Anthologies): Adoff, The Poetry of Black America; Bon-
temps, American Negro Poetry; Hayden, Kaleidoscope;
Hughes, New Negro Poets: USA; Lomax and Abdul,
3000 Years of Black Poetry; Pool, Beyond the Blues.
(Periodicals): Negro Digest, June 1965; Présence Africaine,
No. 57; also published in The Tiger's Eye; Totem; Points
of Light; Umbra.
BIOGRAPHY AND CRITICISM ON PITCHER
Mitchell. Black Drama, p. 136.

PITTS, Gertrude.
NOVEL Tragedies of Life. Newark: By the Author, 1939.

PITTS, Herbert Lee.
POETRY (Anthology): Coombs, We Speak as Liberators.

PITTS, Lucia Mae.
DRAMA
Let Me Dream.
POETRY
With Tomi Carolyn Tinsley and Helen C. Harris. Triad.
n.p.: By the Authors, December 1945.
(Anthologies): Murphy, Ebony Rhythm; Murphy, Negro
Voices.
(Periodicals): Challenge, March 1934; May 1935; Opportunity,
November 1942.

PLANT, Phillip Paul.
DRAMA
Different Strokes for Different Folks.
Switcharoo.

PLATO, Ann. Career: Was a member of the Colored Congregational Church in Hartford, Connecticut in 1841;[1] was not active
in anti-slavery activities; only one anti-slavery piece in her
book.[2]

POETRY AND PROSE
  Essays Including Biographies and Miscellaneous Pieces in
    Poetry and Prose. Introduction by Rev. James W. C.
    Pennington. Hartford: By the Author, 1841.
  (Anthology): Robinson, Early Black American Poets.
BIOGRAPHY AND CRITICISM ON PLATO
  Loggins. The Negro Author in America, pp. 248-249.
  Robinson. Early Black American Poets, p. 113.
        1William H. Robinson, ed., Early Black American Po-
    ets (Dubuque, Iowa: William C. Brown, 1969), p. 113.
        2Vernon Loggins, The Negro Author in America (Port
  Washington, New York: Kennikat Press, 1959), p. 249.

PLOMER, William.
  DRAMA I Speak of Africa, 1964.

PLUMPP, Sterling Dominic. Born 30 January 1940 in Clinton,
  Mississippi. Education: St. Benedict's College, 1960-62;
  B. A., Roosevelt University, 1970; has 30 hours credit toward
  M. A. Two years in the army, seven years with the Chicago
  Main Post Office and 34 years as a Black Man have also con-
  tributed to his education. Currently living in Chicago. Career:
  Teaching Black literature at the University of Illinois, Chicago
  Circle, and developing a blueprint for training artists and
  teachers to teach the arts.
NON-FICTION
  Blueprint for Developing Young People's Workshops. Chi-
    cago: Institute of Positive Education, n. d. (Pamphlet.)
POETRY
  Black Rituals. Chicago: Third World, 1972†.
  Half Black, Half Blacker. Chicago: Third World, 1970†.
  Portable Soul. Chicago: Third World, 1969†.
  (Anthologies): Adoff, The Poetry of Black America; Brown,
    Lee and Ward, To Gwen with Love; Simmons and Hutch-
    inson, Black Culture.
  (Broadside): "Muslim Men." Detroit: Broadside, n. d.
  (Periodicals): Black World, June, September 1971; Septem-
    ber 1973; Journal of Black Poetry, Special Issue 1970;
    Summer 1972; Negro Digest, September-October 1968;
    September 1969.
REVIEW: Half Black, Half Blacker.
  Gant, L. Black World 2 (April 1971): 84-87.
INTERJECTIONS
  "I love life and people and therefore I place living life to its
  highest form as the greatest work of art. I am not impressed
  with Gods or their Messengers or Prophets. I feel every man
  as God is allowed to live life to its fullest. For me, there is
  nothing beyond the enjoyment of living, therefore I fear the in-
  ability to live my life more than I fear the loss of my life or
  death. I'm of this world and when I'm gone I shall become a
  part of this world."

POLITE, Allen.
   POETRY
     (Anthology): Hughes, New Negro Poets: USA.
     (Periodical): Présence Africaine.

POLITE, Carlene Hatcher. Born 28 August 1932 in Detroit. Career: See Contemporary Authors, 23/24.
   NON-FICTION
     (Periodical): Mademoiselle, January 1968.
   NOVEL
     The Flagellants. New York: Farrar, Straus & Giroux, 1967*. Excerpts in Robinson, Nommo; Watkins and David, To Be a Black Woman.
   BIOGRAPHY ON POLITE
     Lottman, H. R. "Authors and Editors." Publishers Weekly, 12 June 1967, 20-21.

POLK, Elaine D. R.
   POETRY Dreams at Twilight: Religious Meditations in Verse and Prose. New York: Exposition, 1965.

POLLARD, Freeman. Born 1922.
   NOVEL Seeds of Turmoil: A Novel of American PW's Brainwashed in Korea. New York: Exposition, 1959.

POLLARD, Will.
   POETRY (Anthology): Boyd, Poems by Blacks, vol. 2.

PONTIFLET, Sudan.
   DRAMA
     Five Black Men.
     The Preacher's Son.

POOLE, Tom. Born 1938 in Ashville, North Carolina.
   POETRY (Anthologies): Adoff, Black Out Loud; Major, The New Plack Poetry.

POPCORN.
   POETRY (Anthology): Reed, Yardbird Reader I.

POPEL, Esther A. W.
   POETRY
     A Forest Pool. Washington: Modernistic Press, 1934.
     (Periodicals): Opportunity, January, April, September 1925; August 1929; November 1931; October 1933; April, December 1934.
   BIOGRAPHY ON POPEL
     Cromwell, Turner and Dykes. Readings from Negro Authors, pp. 48-49.

POPULUS, Auguste. Career: A mason by trade who later made a fortune speculating in state warrants with information furnished him by a carpetbag state treasurer.[1]

POETRY
   (Anthology): Desdunes, Nos Hommes et Notre Histoire.
BIOGRAPHY ON POPULUS
   Coleman. "Preface." Creole Voices, p. xxix.
   Desdunes. Nos Hommes et Notre Histoire, pp. 76-77.
      1Charles Hamlin Good, "The First American Literary
   Movement," Opportunity 10 (1932): 76-79.

PORTER, Curtiss E.
   POETRY (Periodical): Black Lines.

PORTER, Dorothy. Born 1905 in Washington, D.C. Career: See
   Shockley and Chandler, Living Black American Authors, p. 128.
   BIBLIOGRAPHIES
      "Early American Negro Writings: A Bibliographic Study."
         Papers of the Bibliographic Society of America 39 (1945):
         192-268.
      North American Negro Poets: A Bibliographic Checklist of
         Their Writings 1760-1944. Hattiesburg, Miss.: Book
         Farm, 1945*.
      A Working Bibliography on the Negro in the United States.
         Ann Arbor: University Microfilms, 1968*.
   CRITICISM
      "Padre Domingos Caldas Barbosa: Afro-Brazilian Poet."
         Phylon (Third Quarter 1951): 264-271.
      "Some Recent Literature Pertaining to the American Negro."
         Wilson Library Bulletin 9 (June 1935): 569-570.
   EDITOR
      With others. Negro Protest Pamphlets: A Compendium.
         New York: Arno, 1969*†.
      Early Negro Writing 1760-1837. Boston: Beacon, 1971*.
   NON-FICTION
      (Periodicals): African Studies Bulletin, January 1959; Jour-
         nal of Negro Education, 1936; Winter 1952; Journal of Ne-
         gro History, April 1935; Negro History Bulletin, April
         1953; Phylon, Fourth Quarter 1947.

PORTER, George Washington. Born 1849.
   AUTOBIOGRAPHY
      Autobiography of George Washington Porter. Reminiscences,
         Observations and Writings. Punxsutawney, Pa.: Spirit,
         1929.
   POETRY
      Race Poems...; containing poems of race progress, Easter
         festivals, Christmas time, and other miscellaneous writ-
         ings, intended to inspire hope in the Negro people.
         Clarksville, Tenn.: By the Author, n.d.
      Streamlets of Poetry. Philadelphia: A.M.E. Book Concern,
         1912.

PORTER, John.
   POETRY In Spite of Handicaps: A Book of Verse. New York:
      Comet, 1959.

599   Porter

PORTER, Timothy. Born 1946 in Woodstock, Maryland.
  POETRY (Anthology): Coombs, We Speak as Liberators.

PORTMAN, Julie.
  DRAMA With Bryant Rollins. Riot, 1968.

POSEY, Cecil James.
  POETRY A Message from Noah and Other Poems. New York:
    Henry Harrison, 1946.

POSEY, Edwin.
  POETRY The Voice of the Negro in South Carolina. Columbia,
    S.C.: Crescent, 1917.

POSTON, Ted (Theodore Roosevelt Augustus Major Poston). Born
  4 July 1906 in Hopkinsville, Kentucky. Died January 1974 in
  Brooklyn. Education: A.B., Tennessee State College, 1928;
  additional study at New York University in editorial and short-
  story writing.[1] Career: Began his career on his family's newspaper, The Contender, in Hopkinsville. Later, while working as
  a waiter on the Pennsylvania Rail Road, he wrote a column for
  the Pittsburgh Courier. In 1929, he received his first full-time
  newspaper job with the Amsterdam News, becoming city editor
  in 1934. When he joined the New York Post he became the
  first Black to work full time for a New York daily.[2] In September, 1940, he moved to Washington working as public relations consultant for the National Advisory Defense Commission
  and the Office of Production Management; the War Production
  Board and the War Manpower Commission. He then became
  chief of the Negro News Desk in the News Bureau, Office of
  War Information.[3] His byline appeared in the New York Post
  over a period of 33 years.[4] Member: Omega Psi Phi Fraternity; Washington Chapter of the Newspaper Guild.
  AUTOBIOGRAPHY
    "My Most Humiliating Jim Crow Experience." Negro Digest
      2 (April 1944): 55-56.
  NON-FICTION
    (Periodicals): Ebony, December 1952; Negro Digest, Febru-
      ary 1946, July, October 1947; July 1949; January 1950;
      March 1962; also published in the New Republic, Saturday
      Review, The Nation, Survey.
  SHORT STORIES
    (Anthologies): Brown, Davis and Lee, The Negro Caravan;
      David, Black Joy; Hughes, The Best Short Stories by Ne-
      gro Writers.
  Vignette:
    Adoff, Black on Black; Moon, Primer for White Folks; Wat-
      kins, Anthology of American Negro Literature.
      [1]Sylvester C. Watkins, ed., Anthology of American Ne-
    gro Literature (New York: Modern Library, 1944), p. 474.
      [2]M. L. Stein, Blacks in Communications (New York:
    Messner, 1972), pp. 55-56.
      [3]Watkins, pp. 474-475.
      [4]Time, 21 January 1974, p. 43.

POTTER, Valaida (Pseud. W. J. McCall).
NOVEL Sunrise Over Alabama. New York: Comet, 1959.

POWE, Blossom.
POETRY
(Anthology): Dee, Glow Child; Schulberg, From the Ashes;
Simmons and Hutchinson, Black Culture; Troupe, Watts
Poets.
(Periodical): Negro American Literature Forum, Fall 1970.
SHORT STORY
(Anthology): Schulberg, From the Ashes.

POWELL, Adam Clayton, Sr. Born 5 May 1865 in Franklin County,
Virginia. Died 1953. Education: D.D. Virginia Union University, 1904; D.D., Virginia Seminary and College, 1904; D.D.,
Howard University. 1924; attended Yale Divinity School. Career:
As a young man, worked in the coal mines and as a janitor
while attending school;[1] served as pastor of Emanuel Baptist
Church, New Haven, Connecticut, 1893-1908, and the Abyssinian
Baptist Church, New York City;[2] served as director of the N.A.
A.C.P.; was an influential Republican leader, but switched to
Roosevelt in 1936, many New York Blacks following him.[3]
Member: Masons; Knights of Pythias; Odd Fellows; and Alpha
Phi Alpha Fraternity.[4]
AUTOBIOGRAPHY
Against the Tide, An Autobiography. New York: R. R. Smith,
1938.
NON-FICTION
Palestine, and Saints in Caesar's Household. New York: R.
R. Smith, 1939.
Patriotism and the Negro. New York: Beehive, 1918.
Riots and Ruins. New York: R. R. Smith, 1945.
(Periodicals): Negro Digest 8 (May 1950): 19-21; 9 (April
1951): 10-13.
NOVEL
Picketing Hell; A Fictitious Narrative. New York: W. Malliet, 1942.
PAMPHLETS
"Broken But Not Off."
"Colored Man's Contribution to Christianity."
"The Kind of Christianity Needed to Construct the World."[5]
BIOGRAPHY AND CRITICISM ON POWELL
Adams. Great Negroes Past and Present, p. 87.
Boris, Joseph J. Who's Who in Colored America: A Biographical Dictionary of Notable Living Persons of Negro
Descent in America, vol. 1, New York: Who's Who in
Colored America Corp., 1927.
Christmas. Negroes in Public Affairs and Government.
Richardson. Great American Negroes, pp. 185-193.
Robinson. Historical Negro Biographies.
[1]Richard Bardolph, The Negro Vanguard (New York:
Vintage Books, 1959), p. 145.
[2]Joseph J. Boris, Who's Who in Colored America, vol.

601   Powell, A.C. (cont.)

1 (New York: Who's Who in Colored America Corp., 1927),
   p. 161.
   [3]Bardolph, p. 145.
   [4]Boris, p. 162.
   [5]Joseph J. Boris, Who's Who in Colored America, vol.
   2 (New York: Who's Who in Colored America Corp., 1932),
   p. 343.

POWELL, Geneva.
   FOLKTALES (Anthology): Bambara, Tales and Stories.

POWELL, Leslie see LADELE X

POWELL, William I.
   POETRY (Anthology): Murphy, Ebony Rhythm.

PRESTON, Tony.
   DRAMA Rags and Old Iron, 1972.

PRETTO, Clarita C. Born in the Virgin Islands.
   NOVEL The Life of Autumn Holliday. New York: Exposition,
      1958.

PRETTYMAN, Quandra.
   POETRY (Anthologies): Adams, Conn and Slepian, Afro-Amer-
      ican Literature: Poetry; Adoff, Black Out Loud; Adoff,
      The Poetry of Black America.

PRICE, E. Curmie.
   POETRY
      The State of the Union. n.p.: Sono Nis Press, 1971.
      (Periodical): Journal of Black Poetry, Spring 1969.

PRIESTLEY, Eric John. Born 16 December 1943 in Los Angeles,
   California. Education: Informal--the street. Formal--A.B.
   (Psychology), California State College-Los Angeles, 1970. Currently living in Alhambra, California. Career: Presently a
   pre-med student.
   POETRY
      (Anthologies): Coombs, We Speak as Liberators; Troupe,
         Watts Poets.
   SHORT STORY
      (Anthology): Coombs, What We Must See.
   INTERJECTIONS
      "Life is very hard in this country. It is especially hard for
   black folks. Tell me, can you understand this? Whites say get
   a good education so you can get the better job, etc. Then why
   is it most of the brilliant young blacks, especially males, who
   are college graduates, are walking around looking for a job?
   Folks be lying, don't they? Why?"

PRIME, Cynthia.
   POETRY The Sour and the Sweet. New York: William Fred-
      erick, 1972.

PRIMUS, Marc.
  DRAMA
    With B. Banks. High John De Conquer, 1969.
  EDITOR
    Black Theatre: A Resource Directory. New York: The Black
      Theatre Alliance, n.d.

PRINGLE, Ronald J.
  DRAMA
    Dead Flowers on a Great Man's Grave.
    Deep Roots.
    The Fall of the Chandelier.
    Feed the Lion.
    The Finger Meal. In Reed, 19 Necromancers from Now.
    The Lesser Sleep.
    The Price.

PRITCHARD, Gloria Clinton.
  POETRY Trees Along the Highway. New York: Comet, 1953.

PRITCHARD, Norman Henry II. Born 22 October 1939 in New York
  City. Education: B.A., (with Honors in Art History and
  Speech), Washington Square College, 1961; graduate study at the
  Institute of Fine Arts, New York University, 1961-63, and at
  Columbia University, 1962. Currently living in New York City.
  Career: A vocalist, whose "vocalization is manifested in a
  trance state, and is not unlike chanting and speaking in tongues";
  may be heard on two recordings--Destinations: Four Contemporary American Poets (compiled and edited by W. F. Locas, Essence Records, 1964-65); New Jazz Poets (edited by Walter Lowenfels, Broadside Records, 1967). Has given numerous public
  readings and interviews for colleges, universities, literary societies as well as for radio and television. Poet-in-Residence
  at Friends Seminary, 1968-to present, and instructor for a poetry workshop at the New School for Social Research, 1969-to
  present. Co-Chairman of the National Standing Committee on
  Poetry for the American Festival of Negro Arts, 1963-64.
  POETRY
    The Matrix: Poems 1960-1970. New York: Doubleday, 1970.
    EECCHHOOEESS. New York: New York University Press,
      1971*.
    (Anthologies): Adoff, The Poetry of Black America; Chap-
      man, New Black Voices; Kostelanetz, In Youth; Lowenfels,
      In a Time of Revolution; Major, The New Black Poetry;
      Miller, Dices and Black Bones.
    (Periodicals): Negro Digest, June, September 1965; May,
      September 1966; also published in The East Village Other;
      Liberator; Hudson Review; Poetry Northwest, Umbra.
  SHORT STORY
    (Anthology): Reed, Yardbird Reader I.
  WORK IN PROGRESS
    "Origins: An Anthology of Transreal Writing"; "The Mundus"
      (novel); "Poems 1970-75."

Norman Henry Pritchard II (credit: David Perry Jenks)

INTERJECTIONS
"Transreal is a word which visited me in the autumn of 1967 while making initial probes into a work which I entitled 'Origins: a contribution to the monophysiticy of form.' The concept of transreality is indistinguishable from that which is totality--it is indeed that which is. As regards cultural phenomena it is manifest in literature, dance, music, painting, sculpture, architecture, etc."

PROPES, Arthur.
SHORT STORY (Anthology): Ford and Faggett, Best Short Stories by Afro-American Writers.

PRYOR, George Langhorne.
NOVEL Neither Bond Nor Free. New York: J. S. Ogilvie, 1902.

PRYOR, Philip Louille.
POETRY
Broken Strings and Other Things. n.p., n.d.
Lyrics of Life, Love, Laughter. Toledo: Pioneer, 1945.

PUCKETT, G. Henderson.
FICTION One More Tomorrow. Vantage, 1959.

PURVIS, T. T.
SHORT STORIES Hager, The Singing Maiden, with Other Stories and Rhymes. Philadelphia: Walton, 1881.

-Q-

QUESTY, Joanni. Born in New Orleans. Died 1869. Education: Regarded as one of the most learned men of his time. Career: Taught Spanish, French, and English at the Catholic School for Indigent Orphans, where Armand Lanusse was principal; spent his last years as chronicler for La Tribune de la Nouvelle Orléans.[1]
NON-FICTION
La Tribune de la Nouvelle Orléans.
L'Album Littéraire.
POETRY
(Anthologies): Coleman, Creole Voices; Desdunes, Nos Hommes et Notre Histoire.
L'Almanach pour Rire.
UNPUBLISHED NOVEL
"M. Paul."
BIOGRAPHY AND CRITICISM ON QUESTY
Coleman. Creole Voices, p. xxix-xxx.
Desdunes. Nos Hommes et Notre Histoire, pp. 34-35.
Good. "The First American Literary Movement," p. 78.
Testut, Charles. Portraits litteraires de la Nouvelle-Orléans. New Orleans: Imprimerie des Veillees, 1850

[1]Charles Hamlin Good, "The First American Literary
Movement," Opportunity, 10 (March 1932): 78.

QUIGLESS, Helen. Born 16 July 1944 in Washington, D.C. Edu-
cation: Attended Putney School, Vermont and Bard College;
A.B., Fisk University, 1966; M.S. in Library Service, Atlanta
University, 1968. Currently living in Tarboro, North Carolina.
Career: Librarian.
POETRY
    (Anthologies): Murphy, Today's Negro Voices; Major, The
    New Black Poetry; Randall and Burroughs, For Malcolm.
    (Newspapers): The Fisk Herald.

-R-

RAGLAND, J. Farley. Born 24 August 1904 in South Boston, Virginia. Education: Phar.C., Howard University, 1929; also attended Virginia State College, Hampton Institute, Virginia Union
University, University of Richmond. Currently living in Lawrenceville, Virginia. Career: A former instructor of science
at St. Paul's College and in the public school system of Halifax
County, Virginia. Was feature columnist for the Journal and
Guide, and for Afro-American newspapers for many years; Was
Poetry Editor for Spotlighter, a New York magazine; presently
writes weekly columns in poetry and prose for the Brunswick
Times Gazette (Lawrenceville) and the South Boston News (Virginia); also editor of two Southside Virginia newspapers: Banner and Beacon (Lawrenceville), and the Digest Reporter
(Petersburg and vicinity). He composed the words and music
for the alma mater song of the Virginia State School at Hamp-
ton. In 1959 he became a minister in the Baptist Church, officially licensed by the Bannister District Association of Baptist
Churches of Virginia. He is now pastor of the Bethlehem Baptist Church of Chase City, Virginia, and a pharmacist at the
Campus Pharmacy in Lawrenceville, and at Rangland's Drug
Store in South Boston, which he owns and operates. Awards,
Honors: Composed "Arise Unto Your Song," which was the
prize-winning theme song for the National Negro Exposition in
Chicago in 1940; another song, "Now Is the Time," was winner
of the Carl Murphy Prize in a pep song contest sponsored at
Virginia State College by the Afro-American newspapers in
1949.
POETRY
    Muses in Black. New York: Edmonds, forthcoming.
    Rhymes of the Times: Poems. New York: Malliet, 1946.
    Stepping Stones to Freedom: Poems of Pride and Purpose.
        Richmond, Va.: Quality Printing Co., 1960.
    (Anthologies): Murphy, Ebony Rhythm; Murphy, Negro
        Voices; Pool, Beyond the Blues.
    (Periodical): Freedomways, Spring 1961.

REVIEW: Rhymes of the Times
    Parker, John W. Journal of Negro Education 16 (1947): 69-
    70.
INTERJECTIONS
    "I definitely believe in the Christian Theory; I believe that
    God always works in the affairs of men."

RAHMAN, Aishah.
    DRAMA Lady Day, 1972.

RAHMAN, Yusef (Roland Stone).
    POETRY
        Two Poems: Transcendental Blues; Acceleration. n.p.:
            Am God Publishing Co., 1966?
        (Anthology): Jones and Neal, Black Fire.
        (Periodicals): Journal of Black Poetry, Fall-Winter 1971;
            Summer 1972.

RAINEY, H.
    POETRY (Periodical): Black Dialogue.

RAMSEY, Leroy L. Born 12 November 1923 in Meridian, Missis-
    sippi. Education: B.S., Jackson State College, 1952; Ed.M.,
    Boston University, 1956; M.A., New York University, 1967;
    Ph.D., New York University, 1972. Currently living in West
    Hempstead, New York. Career: Adjunct Professor of History,
    Hofstra University, 1966-69; EOC Poverty Program Director,
    Roosevelt, New York, 1968; Coordinator, Minority Group Pro-
    gram, Graduate School of Public Administration, New York Uni-
    versity, 1970-71; Nassau County Consultant on Black History,
    1971; Model Cities Program Director, New Rochelle, New York,
    1971-72; Director of Minority Affairs, University of Nebraska,
    Lincoln, Nebraska, 1972-73; Presently chairman, Education
    Committee, Nassau County Human Rights Commission; Chief of
    the Bureau of Educational Integration, New York State Education
    Department, Albany. Member: American Society of Public Ad-
    ministrators; United Federation of Teachers; Nassau County Hu-
    man Rights Commissioner; Kappa Alpha Psi Fraternity; Key
    Women of America (Honorary). Awards, Honors: Martin Luther
    King Fellow; Louis E. Lomax Memorial Award; National Casual-
    ty Fellow; National Commission on Safety Education (NEA, Wash-
    ington, 1960).
    NON-FICTION
        (Periodical): Hofstra Review, Fall 1970.
        (Newspapers): Freeport, 1970; Long Island Catholic, 1970-
            71 series; Newsday; Westbury Times, May 1970.
    NOVEL
        The Trial and the Fire. New York: Exposition, 1967. (In-
            cludes three stories.)
    WORK IN PROGRESS
        Three books in preparation.

RANAIVO, Flavien (Miriam Koshland).
    POETRY (Anthology): Patterson, A Rock Against the Wind.

RANDALL, Dudley. Born 14 January 1914 in Washington, D.C.
    Education: B.A., Wayne State University, 1949; M.A. (Library
    Science), University of Michigan, 1951. Currently living in De-
    troit. Career: Ford Motor Company, 1932-37; U.S. Post Of-
    fice, 1937-51. Librarian at Lincoln University (Missouri), 1951-
    54, at Morgan State College, 1954-56, and at Wayne County Fed-
    eral Library System, 1959-69. Since 1969, he has been li-
    brarian and Poet-in-Residence at the University of Detroit. In
    1965, he founded Broadside Press, publishing poetry, antholo-
    gies, broadsides, posters, records, and tapes of poets reading
    their own poems. In 1966, he visited Paris, Prague and the
    Soviet Union with a delegation of black artists; in 1970 he vis-
    ited Ghana, Togo and Dahomey.
CRITICISM BY RANDALL
    "The Black Aesthetic in the Thirties, Forties, and Fifties."
        In Gayle, The Black Aesthetic.
    "Black Bards and White Reviewers." In Brooks, The Black
        Position, pp. 3, 15.
    "Black Emotion and Expression." American Librarian 4
        (February 1973): 86-90.
    "Black Poetry." In Gayle, Black Expression, pp. 109-114.
    "An Interview with Frank Marshall Davis." Black World
        23 (January 1974): 37-48.
    "New Books for Black Readers." Publishers Weekly, 22 Oc-
        tober 1973, pp. 48-51.
    "The Poets of Broadside Press: A Personal Chronicle."
        Black Academy Review 1 (Spring 1970): 40-47.
    "Ubi Sunt and Hic Sum." Negro Digest 14 (Sept. 1965): 73-76.
EDITOR
    Black Poetry: A Supplement to Anthologies Which Exclude
        Black Poets. Detroit: Broadside, 1969*†.
    The Black Poets. New York: Bantam, 1971†.
    With Margaret G. Burroughs. For Malcolm: Poems on the Life
        and Death of Malcolm X. Detroit: Broadside, 1967, 2nd ed.
        1969*†.
NON-FICTION
    (Periodicals): Negro Digest, August 1966; November 1967.
POETRY
    After the Killing. Chicago: Third World, 1973.
    Cities Burning. Detroit: Broadside, 1968.
    Love You. 2nd ed. London: Paul Breman, 1971†. Dis-
        tributed by Broadside Press.
    More to Remember: Poems of Four Decades. Chicago:
        Third World, 1971†.
    With Margaret Danner. Poem Counterpoem. rev. ed. De-
        troit: Broadside, 1969†.
    (Anthologies): Abdul, The Magic of Black Poetry; Adams,
        Conn and Slepian, Afro-American Literature: Poetry;
        Adoff, Black Out Loud; Adoff, I Am the Darker Brother;
        Adoff, The Poetry of Black America; Alhamisi and

Dudley Randall (credit: Kwadwo Olu Akpan)

Wangara, Black Arts; Baker, Black Literature in America;
Barksdale and Kinnamon, Black Writers of America; Bell,
Afro-American Poetry; Bontemps, American Negro Poetry;
Breman, You'd Better Believe It; Brooks, A Broadside
Treasury; Brown, Lee and Ward, To Gwen with Love;
Chambers and Moon, Right On!; Chapman, Black Voices;
Chapman, New Black Voices; Davis and Redding, Caval-
cade; Ellman and O'Clair, The Norton Anthology of Modern
Poetry; Emanuel and Gross, Dark Symphony; Faderman
and Bradshaw, Speaking for Ourselves; Ford, Black In-
sights; Hayden, Kaleidoscope; Hayden, Burrows and La-
pides, Afro-American Literature; Henderson, Understand-
ing the New Black Poetry; Hughes, New Negro Poets:
USA; Hughes, La Poesie Negro Americaine; Hughes and
Bontemps, Poetry of the Negro: 1746-1970; Kearns,
Black Identity; Major, The New Black Poetry; Patterson,
A Rock Against the Wind; Pool, Beyond the Blues; Randall,
Black Poetry: A Supplement; Randall, The Black Poets;
Simmons and Hutchinson, Black Culture; Ten: A Detroit
Anthology; Turner, Black American Literature: Poetry;
Weisman and Wright, Black Poetry for All Americans.

(Broadsides): "Ballad of Birmingham" (1965); "Dressed All in
Pink" (1965); "Booker T. and W. E. B." (1966); "Green
Apples" (1972). Detroit: Broadside.
(Periodicals): Black World, September, December 1962;
March, July, September 1964; February, June, August,
September 1965; January, April, May, August, September
1966; January, May, November 1967; January 1968; Sep-
tember 1969; September 1970; April 1971; September 1972;
February, September 1973; Essence, February, April 1971;
May 1973; Journal of Black Poetry, Fall-Winter 1971;
Midwest Journal, Winter 1952-53; Negro History Bulletin,
October 1962; also published in the Beloit Poetry Journal,
Peninsula Poets.
SHORT STORY
(Periodical): Negro History Bulletin, October 1962.
BIOGRAPHY AND CRITICISM ON RANDALL
Black Books Bulletin 1 (Winter 1972): 23-26. (Interview.)
Contemporary Authors, 25/28.
Kent. "Struggle for the Image," pp. 312-313.
Negro History Bulletin 26 (October 1962): 67-68.
Nicholas, A. X. "A Conversation with Dudley Randall."
Black World 21 (December 1971): 26-34.
Redding, Saunders. "The Black Arts Movement in Negro Po-
etry." The American Scholar 42 (Spring 1973): 330-335.
Who's Who in the Midwest, 1973-74.
REVIEWS: Cities Burning.
Giovanni, Nikki. Negro Digest 18 (September 1969): 96.
Welburn, Ron. Negro Digest 19 (December 1969): 94-95.

RANDALL, Florence.
CHILDREN AND YOUNG ADULTS
The Almost Year. New York: Atheneum, 1971*.
Haldane Station. New York: Harcourt Brace Jovanovich,
1973*.
Place of Sapphires. New York: Fawcett, 1971, 1973†.

RANDALL, James A., Jr. Born 3 December 1938 in Detroit,
Michigan. Education: A.B., University of Michigan, 1960.
Currently living in Brooklyn. Career: Journalist and photographer with the Public Information Office of the U.S. Navy; Staff
writer, book reviewer and military editor for the Flint Journal;
contributing editor for Time magazine's Canadian edition, based
in Montreal; Presently a contributing editor for Time in New
York City. A painter as well as writer; an exhibit of his work
was held at the DeWaters Art Museum, Flint, Michigan. Awards,
Honors: Recipient of the Major Avery Hopwood Award for Po-
etry, University of Michigan.
NON-FICTION
(Periodicals): New York magazine; World magazine.
POETRY
Cities and Other Disasters. Detroit: Broadside, 1973†.
Don't Ask Me Who I Am. Detroit: Broadside, 1970.
(Anthologies): Brooks, A Broadside Treasury; Lane, Face

James Randall, Jr. (credit: David Gahr)

the Whirlwind; Pool, Ik Ben de Nieuwe Neger; Randall, The Black Poets.

(Periodicals): Journal of Black Poetry, Fall-Winter 1971; also published in Michigan Voices; Arts in Society; First Soundings.

WORK IN PROGRESS
"Bloodsonnets." "Blackboy (A Fable)." "The Nixon Songs & Other Comics."

RANDALL, Jon. Born 26 March 1942 in Detroit. Education: Attended the University of Michigan for one year; B.S., Wayne State University, 1969. Currently living in Evansville, Indiana. Career: U.S. Navy, 1961-65; Harper Hospital, 1965-66; manager, Special Marketing Projects, Mead Johnson Laboratories, 1969-present. Member: Evansville Community Awareness Committee; Board of Directors, Evansville Family and Children's

Service; Adult Advisor, Poetry and Drama, Neighborhood Youth
Corps.[1]
POETRY

> Blackheart Blues. Detroit: Broadside, 1974.
> (Anthologies): Lane, Face the Whirlwind; Patterson, A Rock
>   Against the Wind; Witherspoon, Broadside Annual 1972.
> (Broadside): "Indigoes." Detroit: Broadside, 1973.
> (Periodical): Black Creation, Winter 1973.
>   [1]Leaonead Pack Bailey, ed., Broadside Authors and
>   Artists (Detroit: Mich.: Broadside), 1974.

RANDOLPH, Jeremy.
DRAMA

> Blow Up in a Major. New York: Amuru, 1972†.
> Cartouche. New York: Amuru, 1973†.
> Negro Mama, Black Son. New York: Amuru, 1973†.
> Rock Baby Rock While de Darkies Sleep. New York: Amu-
>   ru, 1973†.
> To the Slave Mountain Alone. New York: Amuru, 1973†.

POETRY

> Fight to Be Free. New York: Amuru, 1973†.
> Poems II. New York: Rannick Playwrights, 1971.
> Sez Me a Southern Nigga. New York: Amuru, 1973†.

OTHER WRITING

> Sleeping Jurors, A Nodding Judge, A Ladder-Climbing D.A.
>   Make the White Court System a Circus for a Black Veter-
>   an. New York: Amuru, 1973†.

RANDOLPH, Loretta.
POETRY (Periodical): Journal of Black Poetry, Fall-Winter
    1971.

RAPHAEL, Lennox.
CRITICISM

> With Steve Cannon and James Thompson. "A Very Stern
>   Discipline." Harper's 234 (March 1967): 76-95. (An ex-
>   change with Ralph Ellison.)

DRAMA

> Blue Soap.
> Che. North Hollywood, Ca.: Contact Books, 1969.

NON-FICTION

> (Periodical): Negro Digest, November 1963.

NOVEL EXCERPT

> "Tales for Poor Ulysses." Reed, 19 Necromancers from
>   Now.

POETRY

> (Anthologies): Adoff, The Poetry of Black America; Major,
>   The New Black Poetry; Wilentz and Weatherly, Natural
>   Process.

SHORT STORY

> (Anthology): Reed, Yardbird Reader I.

RASHIDD, Amir. Born 1943 in Cleveland, Ohio.
    POETRY (Anthology): Major, The New Black Poetry.

RASHIDD, Niema.
    CRITICISM
    "Black Theatre in Detroit." Black Theatre no. 4
        (1970): 3.
    POETRY
        (Anthology): Major, The New Black Poetry.

RASMUSSEN, Emil Michael. Born 1893.
    NOVEL
        The First Night. New York: Wendell Malliet, 1947.
    CRITICISM ON RASMUSSEN
        Hughes. The Negro Novelist, pp. 148-149.

RASUL, Sha'ir.
    POETRY (Periodicals): Black World, March 1971; Freedom-
        ways, 1970; Journal of Black Poetry, Summer 1972.

RATCLIFFE, Theodore P.
    POETRY Black Forever More. Okolona, Miss.: Okolona Indus-
        trial School, 1939.

RAULLERSON, Calvin H. Born 1920 in Utica, New York.
    POETRY (Anthology): Lincoln University Poets.

RAVELOMANANTSOA, Glen Anthony. Born 12 July 1948 in Omaha,
    Nebraska. Education: B.A., Creighton University, 1970; addi-
    tional study in modern advertising at the University of Nebraska,
    1971. Currently living in Omaha, Nebraska. Career: Reporter,
    The Omaha World-Herald, 1968-70; presently a copywriter for
    Mutual of Omaha. Studied acting at the Omaha Community Play-
    house, and studied modern dance and ballet at Beth Gaynes
    Dance Studio in Omaha. Appeared in numerous college and com-
    munity theatre productions. Member: Afro-Academy of Dra-
    matic Arts, Omaha.
    DRAMA
        19th Nervous Breakdown.
        Obsolete Bird.
        Resurrections and Kingly Rites.
    NON-FICTION
        (Newspaper): The Omaha World-Herald.
    REVIEWS BY RAVELOMANANTSOA
        Published in The Omaha World-Herald.
    INTERJECTIONS
    "The primary problem for young Black writers who want to
    learn and to improve their craft is a lack of encouragement and
    opportunity. Should a black writer choose the approach of higher
    education (college), he or she generally must hold a job to get
    through school. This cuts deeply into the amount of time the
    writer can give to exercising his skills. Whereas, any young
    white writers I know are supported by their parents or, at the

least, have access to greater number of grants to pursue writing. Where does this leave the young black who doesn't even
go on to college, but want to write?"

RAVEN, John.   Born 22 June 1936 in Washington, D.C.
   POETRY
      Blues for Momma and Other Low Down Stuff.   Detroit:
         Broadside, 1970†.
      (Anthologies): Brooks, A Broadisde Treasury; Randall, The
         Black Poets.
   REVIEW: Blues for Momma and Other Low Down Stuff.
      Adams, Jeannette.   Black Books Bulletin 1 (1973): 39-40.

RAY, Henrietta Cordelia.   Born 1850.   Died 1916.   Education:
   Graduated from New York University, and Sauveuer School of
   Languages.[1]   Career: Taught at Grammar School No. 80 in
   New York City while Charles L. Reason was principal; encour-
   aged the antislavery work of her father.
   NON-FICTION
      With Florence Ray, Sketch of the Life of the Rev. Charles B.
         Ray. New York: n.p., 1887.
   POETRY
      Commemoration Ode on Lincoln: Written for the Occasion of
         the Unveiling of the Freed-Man's Movement in Memory of
         Abraham Lincoln, April 4, 1876.   New York: J. J. Little,
      Poems.   New York: Grafton, 1910.
      Sonnets.   New York: J. J. Little, 1893.
      (Anthologies): White and Jackson, An Anthology of Verse by
         American Negroes; Wilson, Joseph Thomas, ed.   Emanci-
         pation, Its Course and Progress from 1481 B.C. to 1885
         A.D.   (Washington, D.C.: Gibson Brothers, 1876).
   REVIEW: Poems.
      Fauset, Jessie.   Crisis 4 (1912): 183.
         [1]William H. Robinson, Early Black American Poets
      Dubuque, Iowa: William C. Brown, 1969), p. 138.

RAZAF, Andy (Andreamanentania Paul Razafinkeriefo).   Born 1895
   in Washington, D.C.   Career: Started writing lyrics as a teen-
   age elevator operator in Washington, D.C.   Wrote dozens of
   globally known hits, including "Blackbirds," "Keep Shuffling,"
   "Connie's Hot Chocolates," "S'posin'," "Honeysuckle Rose,"
   "Memories of You," "Ain't Misbehavin'," "My Fate Is in Your
   Hands," "Massachusetts," "In the Mood," "Keeping Out of Mis-
   chief Now," "Gee, Baby, Ain't I Good to You?" "You're Lucky
   to Me," "How Can You Face Me?" and "I'm Gonna Move to the
   Outskirts of Town"; wrote patriotic songs also; worked with
   Thomas "Fats" Waller and composed a number of tunes now
   considered standard favorites; also collaborated with Johnny
   Finke on numerous songs; wrote a column, "Time Out for Thinking," for a Los Angeles Weekly; appeared regularly on radio
   programs; has completed more than 150 songs;[2] Period Records
   issued an LP album of his works, sung by Maxine Sullivan; be-

came one of the ranking figures of the American Society of
Composers, Authors and Publishers; in 1950, was stricken by
a still unexplained paralysis that left him paralyzed from the
waist down.

DRAMA
        Hot Chocolates, 1929.

POETRY
        (Anthology): Kerlin, Negro Poets and Their Poems.
        (Periodicals): Contributed poetry frequently to the Negro
        World, the Newspaper organ of the Universal Negro Im-
        provement Society;[3] Crisis January 1939; 1940; Negro Di-
        gest, October 1951.

BIOGRAPHY AND CRITICISM ON RAZAF
        "Do You Remember...Andy Razaf?" Negro Digest 9 (Oc-
        tober 1951): 11-12.
        Feather, Leonard. "The Lonely Wait of Andy Razaf." Ne-
        gro Digest 11 (March 1962): 75-77.
        Kerlin. Negro Poets and Their Poems, p. 199.
        "Mr. Tin Pan Alley." Our World 8 (July 1953): 38-39.
        Sepia 12 (May 1963): 61-64.
        "Wheel Chair Composer." Ebony 13 (March 1958): 73-74.
                [1]"Do You Remember--Andy Razaf?" Negro Digest 9
        October 1951): p. 12.
                [2]"Wheel Chair Composer," Ebony 13 (March 1958): p.
        73.
                [3]Robert T. Kerlin, Negro Poets and Their Poems
        (Washington, D.C.: Associated, 1923), p. 199.

REARDON, William R.
        DRAMA
                Never Etch in Acid, 1969.
        EDITOR
                With Thomas Pawley. The Black Teacher and the Dramatic
                Arts: A Dialogue, Bibliography and Anthology. New
                York: Negro Universities Press, 1970*.

REASON, Arthur Wesley.
        POETRY Poems of Inspiration for Better Living. New York:
        Exposition, 1959.

REASON, Charles D. Born 1818 in New York City. Died 1898.
        Education: Attended the African Free School which was estab-
        lished by the New York Manumission Society in 1787; also at-
        tended the Theological Seminary of the Protestant Episcopal
        Church. Career: Began his teaching career at age 14 because
        he had finished the studies offered at the African Free School.[1]
        While teaching, he took private lessons in mathematics and his
        excellent work earned for him the reputation of a great scholar;
        was later appointed as a professor at the Central College at Mc-
        Grawville, New York; resigned in 1882 to become head of the
        Institute of Colored Youth in Philadelphia. This institute was
        established by Reason with money left for that purpose by Rich-
        ard Humphreys, a Quaker. The school later came to be known

as Chency State Normal School in Chester, Pennsylvania.[2]
NON-FICTION
   Manuscript Letter from Reason to Alexander Crummel, dated
      March 1873. In the Schomburg collection of the New York
      Public Library.[3]
   (Anthology): Autographs for Freedom, (1854), pp. 11-15.
   (Periodicals): Liberator, 4 January 1850.
POETRY
   (Anthologies): Crummell, A Eulogy on the Life and Charac-
      ter of Thomas Clarkson; Robinson, Early Black American
      Poets; Simmons, Men of Mark.
   Autographs for Freedom (1854), pp. 221-229.
BIOGRAPHY AND CRITICISM ON REASON
   Kerlin. Negro Poets and Their Poems, pp. 24-25.
   Loggins, The Negro Author, His Development, pp. 129, 234-
      235, 395, 396, 429, and 438.
   Payne, Daniel A. (Bishop). Recollections of Seventy Years,
      edited by C. S. Smith. Compiled by Sarah C. Bierce.
      Introduction by Rev. F. J. Grimke. Nashville, Tenn.:
      The A. M. E. Sunday School Union, 1888.
   Robinson. Early Black American Poets, p. 72.
   Robinson. Historical Negro Biographies, p. 114.
   Roy, J. H. "Teacher," Negro History Bulletin 16 (June
      1953): 204-205.
   Simmons. Men of Mark, pp. 1105-1112.
      [1]J. H. Roy, "Teacher," Negro History Bulletin 16
   (June 1953): 205.
      [2]Ibid.
      [3]Vernon Loggins, The Negro Author in America (Port
   Washington, N.Y.: Kennikat, 1959), p. 395.

REDD, Ronnie.
   SHORT STORY (Periodical): Black Creation, Winter 1973.

REDDING, Saunders (Jay Saunders Redding). Born 13 October 1906
   in Wilmington, Delaware. Education: Ph.B., Brown Univer-
   sity, 1928; M.A., Brown University, 1932; additional study at
   Columbia University, 1933-34. Currently living in Ithaca, New
   York: Career: Taught at Morehouse College, 1928-31; at
   Louisville Municipal College, 1934-38; at Southern University
   1936-38; at North Carolina State Teachers College, 1938-43; at
   Hampton Institute, 1943-66. Served as visiting professor at
   Brown University 1949-50; as Rosenfeld Lecturer at Grinnell
   College; as AMSAC lecturer in Africa. Presently is Ernest I.
   White professor of American Studies and Humane Letters at
   Cornell University, and special consultant for the National Endowment for the Humanities. Member: College Language Association; American Folklore Society; Association for Study of
   Negro Life and History; American Society of African Culture
   (past-president); Phi Beta Kappa. Served on the editorial board
   of The American Scholar, 1953-63, and 1970 to present; as a
   fellow in the cooperative program in the Humanities, Duke University and the University of North Carolina, 1964-65; on the

Redding, S. (cont.) 616

board of fellows, Brown University. Awards, Honors: Rockefeller Foundation Fellowship, 1940; for travel in the south (re-
sulting in the book, No Day of Triumph, which won the Mayflower Award for distinguished writing, 1944); Guggenheim fellowships, 1945-46, and 1959-60; distinguished service award,
National Urban League; U.S. State Department lecturer in India,
1952; participant, U.S. Commission, World Festival of Negro
Art, 1964-66; has been awarded honorary degrees: D. Litt.,
Brown University, Virginia State College; L.H.D., Hobart College.

AUTOBIOGRAPHY
"My Most Humiliating Jim Crow Experience." Negro Digest
3 (December 1944): 43-44.
No Day of Triumph. New York: Harcourt, Brace, 1942; excerpts in Chapman, Black Voices; Cromwell, Turner and
Dykes, Readings from Negro Authors; Watkins, Anthology
of American Negro Literature; Watkins, Black Joy.

CRITICISM BY REDDING
"The Alien Land of Richard Wright." In Hill, Soon One
Morning, pp. 48-59; also in Gibson, Five Black Writers.
"American Negro Literature." The American Scholar 18
(1949): 137-148; also in Gayle, Black Expression; Hayden,
Burrows and Lapides, Afro-American Literature.
"The Black Arts Movement in Negro Poetry." The American
Scholar 42 (Spring 1973): 330-335.
"The Black Revolution in American Studies." American Stud-
ies: An International Newsletter 9 (Autumn 1970): 3-9.
"Contradictions de la littérature négro-américaine." Présence
Africaine Nos. 27-28 (August-November 1959): 11-15.
"The Fall and Rise of Negro Literature." American Scholar
(Spring 1949); reprinted in Negro Digest 7 (September 1949):
41-51.
"Literature and the Negro." Contemporary Literature 9
(Winter 1968): 130-135.
"The Negro Author: His Publisher, His Public, and His
Prose." Publishers Weekly 147 (1945): 1284-1288.
"The Negro Writer and American Literature." In Hill,
Anger, and Beyond.
"The Negro Writer and His Relationship to His Roots." The
American Negro Writer and His Roots; also in Patterson,
An Introduction to Black Literature in America; Baker,
Black Literature in America; Chapman, Black Voices;
Davis and Redding, Cavalcade; Long and Collier, Afro-
American Writing.
"The Negro Writer: The Road Where." Boston University
Journal 17 (Winter 1969): 6-10.
"The Negro Writer--Shadow and Substance." Phylon 11 (1950):
371-373.
"Negro Writing in America." The New Leader 42 (16 May
1960): 8-10.
"The New Negro Poet in the Twenties." In Gibson, Modern
Black Poets.
"The Problems of the Negro Writer." Massachusetts Review

6 (Autumn 1964): 57-70; reprinted in Chametzky and Kaplan, Black and White in American Culture.
"Since Richard Wright." African Forum 1 (Spring 1966): 21-31.
To Make a Poet Black. Chapel Hill, N.C.: University of North Carolina Press, 1939; "The Forerunners" is reprinted in Gayle, Black Expressions.

EDITOR
With Arthur P. Davis. Cavalcade: Negro American Writing from 1760 to the Present. Boston: Houghton Mifflin, 1971†.
With Ivan Early Taylor. Reading for Writing. New York: Ronald, 1952.

NON-FICTION
An American in India: A Personal Report on the Indian Dilemma and the Nature of Her Conflicts. Indianapolis: Bobbs-Merrill, 1954.
The Lonesome Road: Biographical History of Black America. Garden City, N.Y.: Doubleday, 1958*†.
The Negro. Washington, D.C.: Potomac Books, 1967*.
On Being Negro in America. Indianapolis: Bobbs-Merrill, 1951. Excerpts in Austin, Fenderson and Nelson, The Black Man and the Promise of America; Gayle, Bondage, Freedom and Beyond; Turner and Bright, Images of the Negro in America.
They Came in Chains: Americans from Africa, 1950; rev. ed. Philadelphia: Lippincott, 1973*.
(Periodicals): American Mercury, November 1942; American Scholar, Spring 1963; Atlantic Monthly, March 1943; Negro Digest, December 1942; April, November, December 1943; January, February, November 1944; Survey Graphic, August 1944.

NOVEL
Stranger and Alone. New York: Harcourt, Brace, 1950; excerpt in Ford, Black Insights.

SHORT STORY
(Periodical): The Negro Quarterly, Fall 1942.

BIOGRAPHY AND CRITICISM ON REDDING
Arts in Society 5 (Summer-Fall 1968); 273-274. (Interview.)
Bardolph. The Negro Vanguard, pp. 308, 373, 375-376, 378, 380.
Bergman. The Chronological History of the Negro in America, pp. 349-350.
Bone. The Negro Novel in America, pp. 1-2, 164n., 171.
Contemporary Authors, 4.
Current Biography, 1969, pp. 355-357.
Davis and Redding. Cavalcade, p. 438.
Freeman, Ethel. Harlem Quarterly 1 (Spring 1950): 49-50.
Hill. Anger, and Beyond, p. 216.
Hughes. The Negro Novelist, pp. 107-112, 228-230.
Jet, 21 April 1960, pp. 12-18.
Ploski. Reference Library of Black America, p. 29.
Robinson. Historical Negro Biographies, p. 241.

REVIEWS: Stranger and Alone.
Butcher, Philip. Journal of Negro Education 27 (1958): 486-487.
Ellison, Ralph. New York Times, 19 February 1950, p. 4.
Lovell, John, Jr. Journal of Negro Education 20 (1951): 67-69.
Petry, Ann. Saturday Review of Literature, 25 February 1950, p. 18.
Rosenberger, Coleman. New York Herald Tribune, 19 February 1950, p. 7.

REDDY, T. J. Born 6 August 1945 in Savannah, Georgia. Currently at Northern Carolina Central Prison in Raleigh. Career: Griot; artist; former draft counselor for Black youth; free lance writer.
POETRY
(Anthology): Shuman, A Galaxy of Black Writing.
(Periodicals): The Red Clay Reader; Southern Poetry Review.
WORK IN PROGRESS
Book of poetry scheduled for publication, 1974, by Vintage Press of Random House.
BIOGRAPHY ON REDDY
New York Times, 4 February 1974, p. 28.
INTERJECTIONS
"Born Black enuf to warrant superior attitude to white anemia having survived centuries of atrocities. Art--its genesis is related to the people who need life. Ideas--to not separate my creations from black people--poets--dancers--musicians--rhythmiticians--who inspired my work. Theory--the more positive images are portrayed concerning liberation, the more liberated black people will become. Black Aesthetics--the concept of purpose and relevancy, which must be related to the survival of our beauty as a black people."

REDMOND, Eugene B. Born 1 December 1937 in St. Louis, Missouri (raised in East St. Louis, Illinois). Education: B.A., Southern Illinois University, 1964; M.A., Washington University, 1966. Currently living in Sacramento, California. Career: U.S. Marine Corps, 1958-61. Associate Editor, East St. Louis Beacon, 1962-63; Associate Editor, East St. Louis Evening Voice, 1962-63; Held concurrent positions on student newspaper, Southern Illinois University, 1961-64; and appointed editor-in-chief of Alestle in 1963; Contributing editor, 1963-65, and executive editor, 1965-67, East St. Louis Monitor; Director, Project Headstart, Grace Hill Settlement House, 1966-67; publicist/proposal writer, St. Louis Human Development Corporation, Summer 1965; research assistant, 50-year Population Projection for Illinois, Southern Illinois University, Fall-Winter 1966; teacher and counselor, Experiment in Higher Education, Southern Illinois University, 1967-68; Poet-in-Residence and Director of Language Workshops, Southern Illinois University, 1968-69; Senior Consultant, Katherine Dunham Performing Arts Training Center, 1967-69, (acted, wrote, directed, and supervised writing and drama

Eugene B. Redmond

departments. Visiting lecturer in Afro-American Literature,
Webster College, Summer 1968; consultant and visiting lecturer
to 30-college consortium (Regional Council for International Education), 1970-71; Writer-in-Residence and lecturer in Afro-
American Studies, Oberlin College, 1969-70; member of con-
sulting team for designing Black Studies programs in public,
private, and community institutions, 1967-71; English professor
and poet-in-residence, Ethnic Studies, California State Univer-
sity-Sacramento, 1970-present; visiting Writer-in-Residence,
Southern University (Baton Rouge), Summers 1971 and 1972;
Editor and publisher of Black River Writers; Editor, special
Black poetry edition of Negro American Literature Forum,
Spring 1972. Member: Institute of the Black World; Black
World Foundation; Intercontinental Biographical Association;
World Poetry Society Intercontinental; International Platform
Association; International Poetry Association; Editorial Board,
Black Anthology Project, 1972-74; American Newspaper Guild;
Northern California Folk Arts Association; Black English Teach-
ers of Northern California; California Association of Afro-Amer-
ican Educators; Sacramento Area Black Educators; International
Black Writers Conference. Awards, Honors: Selected as one
of the outstanding college students in America, Chicago Tribune,
1963; named outstanding collegiate of the year, Pro-eight Social

Civic Club, East St. Louis, 1963; cited for special recognition, Illinois Governor's Committee on Literacy and Learning, 1963; was the subject of a series of articles on Black arts and Black political awareness, St. Louis Post-Dispatch, 1968; received the "Merit Award" for outstanding community service, Sacramento's Progressive Twelve Social Club, 1972; cited for cultural and political enhancement, mayor of East St. Louis and the Community Schools, 1972; received first prize, Annual Festival of Arts Poetry Contest, Washington University, 1965; Honorable Mention, Annual Norma Lowery Memorial Poetry Contest, 1965-66; First Prize, Annual Freelance Poetry Contest, 1966; Honorable Mention, Annual Wednesday Club Senior Original Verse Contest, 1968; Resolution (for literary and community service), California State Assembly, 1974; Writing grant, California State University--Sacramento, Spring Semester 1973.

CRITICISM BY REDMOND

"The Black American Epic: Its Roots, Its Writers." Black Scholar 2 (January 1971): 15-22.

"Five Black Poets: Book Reviews." Parnassus: Poetry in Review, Spring-Summer 1974.

"How Many Poets Scrub the River's Back?" Confrontation: A Journal of Third World Literature, Spring 1971.

"Indigenous Struggle Pays Off." Focus/Midwest, (Fall 1968): 40-45.

"Into the Canaan of the Self." Introduction to "Afro-American Literature" section. Sunbursts: Third World Voices. Edited by Quincy Troupe and Rainer Schulte. New York: Random House, 1974.

"Introduction." 'Ark of Bones' and Other Stories by Henry Dumas, 1970, 1974.

"Introduction." Negro American Literature Forum, Spring 1972.

"It Is, Again, About Respect and Hard Work." Nickel Review 4 (6 February 1970): 8.

"Olajunji: Controlled Center in a Rhythmic and Ritualistic Deluge." Fine Arts (February 1970): 8-9.

"A Planter of Trees." Introduction to When I Know the Power of My Black Hand by Lance Jeffers. Detroit: Broadside, 1974.

"Today's Black Woman: Is She Scurrying from Sun to Sun?" National Beauticians Directory (Summer 1969): 12-13.

"What the Poet Is." Sou'Wester (Spring 1964): 33-35.

Also see editorials, columns and reviews of literature and art published in the East St. Louis (Illinois) Monitor, 1965 to 1970.

DRAMA

The Face of the Deep, 1971.

Kwanza: A Poetic Ritual in 7 Movements, 1973.

The Night John Henry Was Born, 1972.

With Katherine Dunham. Ode to Taylor Jones, 1967-68.

Poets with the Blues, 1971.

River of Bones, 1971.

Shadows Before the Mirror, 1965.

Will I Still Be Here Tomorrow?: A Eulogistic Ritual, 1972.
EDITOR
   With Hale Chatfield. "Ark of Bones" and Other Stories by
      Henry Dumas. Carbondale: Southern Illinois University
      Press, 1970; New York: Random House, 1974.
   Play Ebony Play Ivory by Henry Dumas. New York: Random
      House, 1974.
   With Hale Chatfield. Poetry for My People by Henry Dumas.
      Carbondale: Southern Illinois University Press, 1970.
   Sides of the River: A Mini-Anthology of Black Writing.
      Oberlin, O.: By the Author, 1969.
POETRY
   Bloodlinks and Sacred Places. East St. Louis, Ill.: Black
      River Writers, 1973. (Lp. recording.)
   Consider Loneliness as These Things. Italy: Centro Studi E
      Scambi Internogionali, 1973.
   In a Time of Rain and Desire. East St. Louis, Ill.: Black
      River Writers, 1973.
   River of Bones and Flesh and Blood. East St. Louis, Ill.:
      Black River Writers, 1971.
   Sentry of the Four Golden Pillars. East St. Louis, Ill.:
      Black River Writers, 1970.
   Songs from an Afro/Phone. East St. Louis, Ill.: Black River
      Writers, 1972.
   A Tale of Time and Toilet Tissue. East St. Louis, Ill.:
      Black River Writers, 1968. (Pamphlet.)
   A Tale of Two Toms. East St. Louis, Ill.: Black River
      Writers, 1969.
   (Anthologies): Adoff, The Poetry of Black America; Boyd,
      Poems by Blacks, vol. 1; Boyd, Poems by Blacks, vol. 2;
      Chapman, New Black Voices; Generation (Los Angeles:
      Idlewild, 1970); Gersehl, Words among America; Gross,
      Open Poetry; Henderson, Understanding the New Black Po-
      etry; Lane, Poems by Blacks, vol. 3; Major, The New
      Black Poetry; Murphy, Today's Negro Voices; Poetry
      Pageant (Washington, D.C., 1970); Nancy Prichard, ed.,
      Voices (Boston: Houghton Mifflin, 1970); Redmond, Sides of
      the River; Shuman, A Galaxy of Black Writing; Clyde Tay-
      lor, Vietnam and Black America (Garden City, N.Y.:
      Doubleday, 1973); Troupe and Schulte, Sunbursts: Third
      World Voices; Venice Poetry Company Presents (Los Ange-
      les: Venice Poetry Co., 1972); White and Schwartz, Tam-
      bourine.
   (Periodicals): The Activist, Winter 1969; Aim, Spring 1969;
      Afro-American Affairs, November 1970; American Dialog,
      Autumn 1971; Black Liberator, November 1970; Black
      Lines, Fall 1971; Black Orpheus, 1968; Black Writers News,
      May-June 1973; The Commuter, November 1970; Confronta-
      tion, June 1970; June 1972; Discourses on Poetry, 1972;
      Free Lance, December 1965; Journal of Afro-American Is-
      sues, May 1974; Journal of Black Poetry, Fall-Winter 1971;
      Metro-East Journal, September 1970; Mill Creek Intelli-
      gencer (St. Louis, Mo.), February 1969; Negro Digest/

Black World, January 1970; Oberlin Review, December
1969; Poet, December 1973; February, April 1974; Re-
flections, Spring 1966; Rumble, March 1974; South and
West: An International Quarterly, Winter-Spring 1972;
Sou'Wester, Spring 1964; Fall 1968; Uhuru News (St.
Louis, Mo.), June 1969.

WORK IN PROGRESS
   Criticism: "The Black American Epic"; "Handbook to Black
      Poetry: A Critical Student-Teacher Guide"; "To Reed &
      Rite: Using Poetry to Develop Ritual Theatre."
   Poetry: "The Eye in the Ceiling: New and Selected Poems";
      "Into the Canaan of the Self" (Lp recording); "Kwanza: A
      Poetic Ritual in 7 Movements"; Nodding in a Nightmare
      Called America"; "To Amplify a Sigh."
   Editor: Collected prose and poetry of Henry Dumas; poetry
      of Harold "Wine" Carrington.
   Other: A critical biography of Henry Dumas; a script adap-
      tation of Henry Dumas' "Ark of Bones" and Other Stories.

BIOGRAPHY AND CRITICISM ON REDMOND
   Atkinson, Bev. "Resident Poet Eugene Redmond Called
      'Leading Black Neologist.' " The State Hornet (Calif.
      State Univ.), 11 December 1973, p. 4.
   Corbett, Michael Y. "Redmond's Poetry." The Sacramento
      Observor (Entertainment Section), 29 November-5 Decem-
      ber 1973.
   Craig, Paul. "Poetry Column." The Sacramento Bee "Val-
      ley Leisure," 19 March 1972, p. 13.
   Elelstein, Stewart I. "Artists in Their Residences." Ober-
      lin Alumni Magazine (May 1970): 20-21.
   Gorman, Bertha. "Aiwa! Aiwa! Aiwa!" Sacramento Bee,
      12 February 1971, p. 2.
   Gray, Bill. "Redmond: Black Poet as Political Commenta-
      tor." Metro-East Journal, 9 September 1970, p. 33.
   Johnson, Al. " 'Hipsofical' Poet Enjoys Rap." Richmond
      (Va.) News Leader, 26 February 1970, p. 13.
   Medovoy, George. "How to Save Poetry by Forgetting the
      Leisure Class." Sacramento Union Weekender Magazine,
      19 January 1974, p. 4.
   Passman, Arnie. "Redmond Rap." Berkeley Barb, 18-20
      January 1974, p. 14.
   "Poetry: Eugene Redmond." Poetry Center Speaker (St.
      Louis), April-May 1974.
   Price, Ann. " 'Face of the Deep' Stunning Work." Morning
      Advocate (Baton Rouge, La.), 28 July 1971, p. 13-A.
   Robertson, Byron. "Poems of 'Black Unstance.' " The
      Sacramento Bee, Valley Leisure, 3 June 1973, p. 15.
   Slattery, Tom. "Redmond at CCC." The Commuter (Cuya-
      hoga Community College, 6 November 1970, pp. 6-7.
   See also: International Who's Who in Poetry, 1972, 1973;
      Directory of American Scholars, 1974; Outstanding Com-
      munity Leaders and Noteworthy Americans, 1974; Outstand-
      ing Educators of America, 1973; The Writers Directory,
      1974; Yearbook of the Intercontinental Biographical Asso-
      ciation, 1974.

REDMOND, L. C., Jr.   see   ANTARAH, Obi

REDWOOD, John.
  DRAMA
    But I Can't Go Alone.
    The Dragon's Tooth (one act).   In Richardson, The King's
      Dilemma and Other Plays for Children.
    The Elder Dumas.   In Richardson and Miller, Negro History
      in Thrteen Plays.
    The Flight of the Natives.
    A Ghost of the Past (one act).   In Locke and Gregory, Plays
      of Negro Life.
    The Gypsy's Finger Ring (one act).   In Richardson, The
      King's Dilemma and Other Plays for Children.
    Hope of the Lonely.
    The Imp of the Devil (one act).
    In Menelek's Court (one act); 1935.   In Richardson and Mil-
      ler, Negro History in Thirteen Plays.
    The Jail Bird (one act).
    Joy Rider.
    The King's Dilemma and Other Plays for Children.   New
      York Exposition, 1956.
    Man of Magic (one act).   In Richardson, The King's Dilem-
      ma and Other Plays for Children.
    The Man Who Married a Young Wife (one act).
    Miss or Mrs. (one act), 1941.
    Mortgaged, 1923.
    Near Calvary (one act).   In Richardson and Miller, Negro
      History in Thirteen Plays.
    The New Santa Claus (one act).   In Richardson, The King's
      Dilemma and Other Plays for Children.
    The Nude Siren (one act).
    A Pillar of the Church (one act).

REED, Clarence.
  POETRY
    Not Forever Tears.   Newark, N.J.: Jihad, 1967.
    The Ship Was Called Jesus.   New York: B & G, n.d.
    (Anthologies): Jones and Neal, Black Fire; King, Blackspir-
      its.
    (Periodical): Journal of Black Poetry, Winter-Spring 1970.

REED, Ishmael.   Born 22 February 1938 in Chattanooga, Tennessee.
  Education: largely self-taught.   Currently living in Berkeley,
  California.   Career: Writer, university lecturer; director of
  the Yardbird Publishing Co., Inc.   Member: P.E.N.; Authors
  Guild of America; The Ninth Generation of Artists.   Awards,
  Honors: Honorary Priest of the Paratheo-Anametamystikhood
  of Eris Esoteric.
  CRITICISM BY REED
    "Black Artist: 'Calling a Spade a Spade.'"   Arts 41 (May
      1967): 48-49.
    "Can a Metronome Know the Thunder or Summon a God?"

Reed, I. (cont.) 624

In Reed, 19 Necromancers from Now; Gayle, The Black
Aesthetic.
"Introduction." Yardbird Reader, vol. 1.
"Too Hot for Scanlan's?" Nickel Review (April 1971): 6-7.
EDITOR
19 Necromancers from Now. Garden City, N.Y.: Doubleday,
1970.
With others. Yardbird Reader, vol. 1. Berkeley: Yardbird,
1972.
NON-FICTION
(Periodical): Essence, January 1971.
NOVELS
The Free-Lance Pallbearers. Garden City, N.Y.: Double-
day, 1967. Excerpts in Ford, Black Insights; Robinson,
Nommo.
Mumbo Jumbo. Garden City, N.Y.: Doubleday, 1972*; New
York: Bantam, 1973†.
Yellow Back Radio Broke-Down. Garden City, N.Y.:
Doubleday, 1969; New York: Bantam, 1972†. Excerpt in
Hicks, Cutting Edges.
POETRY
catechism of a neoamerican hoodoo church. London: Breman,
1970†. Distributed by Broadside Press.
Chattanooga. New York: Random, 1973*†.
Conjure: Selected Poems, 1963-1970. Boston: University of
Massachusetts Press, 1972*†.
(Anthologies): Adoff, The Poetry of Black America; Chap-
man, New Black Voices; Eastman, The Norton Anthology
of Poetry; Hayden, Burrows and Lapides, Afro-American
Literature; Hughes and Bontemps, Poetry of the Negro:
1746-1970; Jordan, Soulscript; Lowenfels, A New American Anthology; Lowenfels, In a Time of Revolution; Lowen-
fels, Poets of Today; Lowenfels, Where Is Vietnam?; Low-
enfels, The Writing on the Wall; Major, The New Black
Poetry; Miller, Dices or Black Bones; Quasha and Rothen-
berg, America: A Prophecy; Randall, The Black Poets;
Reed, Yardbird Reader, vol. 1.
(Periodical): Black World, September 1970; September 1973;
Negro Digest, September 1966; November 1969; also pub-
lished in Umbra; The Friends Seminary Review; Cricket;
Poetry India; Scholastic Magazine; Liberator.
BIOGRAPHY AND CRITICISM ON REED
Ambler, Madge. "Ishmael Reed: Whose Radio Broke Down?"
Negro American Literature Forum 6 (Winter 1972): 125-
131.
Beauford, Fred. "Conversation with Ishmael Reed." Black
Creation 4 (1973): 12-15.
Bush, Roland. "Werewolf of the Wild West." Black World
23 (January 1974): 51-52, 64-66.
Contemporary Authors, 23/24.
Ford, Nick Aaron. "A Note on Ishmael Reed: Revolutionary
Novelist." Studies in the Novel 3 (Summer 1971): 180-
189.

"An Interview with Ishmael Reed." Journal of Black Poetry
1 (Summer-Fall 1969): 72-75.
O'Brien. Interviews with Black Writers, pp. 165-183.
Test, George A. "The Cliche as Archetype." Satire News-
letter 7 (Fall 1969): 79.
Whitlow. Black American Literature, pp. 154-157.
REVIEWS: Chattanooga.
New Republic, 24 November 1973, p. 25.
The Free-Lance Pallbearers.
Woodford, John. Negro Digest 18 (Fall 1969): 68-69.
Mumbo Jumbo.
Baker, Houston A., Jr. Black World 22 (December 1972):
63.
Bryant, J. H. Nation, 25 September 1972, p. 245.
Edwards, T. R. New York Review of Books, 5 October 1972,
p. 23.
Friedman, Alan. New York Times Book Review, 6 August
1972, p. 1.
Major, Clarence. Black Creation 4 (Fall 1972): 59-61.
Yellow Back Radio Broke-Down.
Fioforo, Tam. Negro Digest 19 (December 1969): 95-97.
Fleischer, Leonore. Book World, 10 August 1969, p. 3.
Sissman, L. E. New Yorker, 11 October 1969, p. 200.

REED, Kathleen.
POETRY (Anthology): Boyd, Poems by Blacks, vol. 2.

REED, Michael E.
POETRY (Anthology): Boyd, Poems by Blacks, vol. 2.

REESE, Sarah Carolyn. Born in Logansport, Indiana.
POETRY
(Anthologies): Brooks, A Broadside Treasury; Hughes and
Bontemps, Poetry of the Negro: 1746-1970; Patterson,
A Rock Against the Wind.
(Broadside): "Letter from a Wife." Detroit: Broadside,
1967.

REEVES, Donald St. George. Born 23 September 1952 in Detroit,
Michigan. Education: B.S., Cornell University, 1973. Currently living in Queens Village, New York. Career: Editorial
writer for the New York Times. Former news reporter for
Metromedia TV 5, taping news concerning black youth; writer
and editor for Harlem Sports Foundation and Harlem School District; teacher's aid for Headstart program; Neighborhood Youth
Corps worker; track coach for Harlem Sports Foundation; Harlem Summer Olympics. Currently writing a series of articles
for Newsweek, Ebony and Saturday Review, as well as working
with a Cornell professor in compiling information on the practices of the Fair Employment Practices Commission. Member:
Board of Advisors, Foundation for Change; Board of Advisors,
Dayton Ohio Center for High School Students' Rights. Awards,
Honors: Bernard de Voto Breadloaf Writer's fellow; Hackett

Donald Reeves

Medal for Oratory; Telluride Scholastic Scholarship.
AUTOBIOGRAPHY
    Notes of a Processed Brother.   New York: Pantheon, 1971*;
        New York: Avon, 1973†.
NON-FICTION
    (Periodicals): Ebony, March 1973; Seventeen, September
        1972.
    (Newspaper): New York Times, 17 May 1971; 11 March
        1972; 28 April 1972.
BIOGRAPHY AND CRITICISM ON REEVES
    Contemporary Authors, 37/40.
    Interview. Saturday Review, August 1972.
REVIEW: Notes of a Processed Brother.
    Gitlin, Todd. Nation, 10 April 1972, p. 470.
    Nordberg, R. B. Best Sellers, 1 February 1972, p. 489.
    Prescott, P. S. Newsweek, 31 January 1972, p. 80.
INTERJECTIONS
    "My philosophical views are primarily shaped by the writings
of Frantz Fanon. Most of my energies are directed against
(physically & philosophically) institutional racism and for the
recognition of human value and dignity."

REID, Hazel.
DRAMA
 H. E. W. Down the People.
 Midnight Maze.

REILLY, J. Terrence. Born 16 February 1945 in the Bronx, New
 York. Education: B.A., Harpur College; M.F.A., Cornell
 University; candidate for Ph.D., Cornell University. Currently
 living in Owego, New York. Career: Teaching literature and
 writing at the University of the State of New York-Owego; is in-
 volved in playwrighting, acting and directing; is hosting a radio
 program. Member: Board of Directors of the Foundation for
 Research in Afro-American Creative Arts. Awards, Honors:
 Playwright-in-Residence, Black Masquers Guild.
DRAMA
 Black! Poughkeepsie, N.Y.: Myra House, 1973.
 Bogey.
 Enter at Your Own Risk.
 Jejune Ju Ju.
 Montage: An All Black Play.
 Waiting on the Man.
INTERJECTIONS
 "Art is a means of vivifying reality, clarifying truth, educat-
ing in an entertaining manner. Black Art must be committed to
manifesting the character, concerns and aspirations of Black
people, or Black skinned persons, individually and collectively."

RENDER, Sylvia Lyons. Born 1913 in Atlanta, Georgia. Career:
 See Shockley and Chandler, Living Black American Authors, p.
 134.
CRITICISM
 Eagle with Clipped Wings: Form and Feeling in the Fiction
  of Charles Waddell Chesnutt. Ann Arbor: University Micro-
  films, 1963.
EDITOR
 The Short Fiction of Charles W. Chesnutt. Washington,
  D.C.: Howard University Press, 1974.

REYNOLDS, Barbara A.
NON-FICTION
 (Periodicals): Ebony, July 1969; Essence, December 1971;
  Journal of Human Relations, First Quarter 1964.
POETRY
 (Anthology): Brown, Lee and Ward, To Gwen with Love.

REYNOLDS, Evelyn (Eve Lynn).
POETRY
 No Alabaster Box. Philadelphia: Alpress, 1936.
 To No Special Land: A Book of Poems. Introduction by Mary
  McLeod Bethune. New York: Exposition, 1953.
CRITICISM ON EVE LYNN
 Brawley. The Negro Genius, p. 265.

RHODES, Hari. Born 10 April 1932 in Cincinnati, Ohio. Career:
See Contemporary Authors, 19/20.
NOVEL
A Chosen Few. New York: Bantam, 1965.

RHONE, Trevor.
DRAMA Smile Orange.

RICHAM, Carl.
DRAMA Brown Buddies, 1930.

RICHARDS, Beah.
DRAMA
One Is a Crowd, 1971.
BIOGRAPHY AND CRITICISM ON RICHARDS
Mitchell. Black Drama, p. 204.

RICHARDS, Edward.
POETRY
(Anthology): Ebony Rhythm.
(Periodical): Crisis, 1948.

RICHARDS, Elizabeth Davis.
POETRY The Pedlar of Dreams and Other Poems. New York:
W. A. Bodler, 1928.

RICHARDS, Nathan A. Born in Kingston, Jamaica.
POETRY
(Anthologies): Burning Spear; Henderson, Understanding the
New Black Poetry.
(Periodical): Dasein.

RICHARDSON, Alice I. Born in St. Louis, Missouri.
SHORT STORY (Anthology): Coombs, What We Must See.

RICHARDSON, Beulah.
POETRY
A Black Woman Speaks of White Womanhood, of White Su-
premacy, of Peace: A Poem. New York: American Wom-
en for Peace, 1951.
(Periodical): Freedomways, Summer 1962.
BIOGRAPHY ON RICHARDSON
Freedomways 4 (Winter 1964): 58-75.

RICHARDSON, Mel.
DRAMA The Break, 1969.

RICHARDSON, Nola. Born 12 November 1936 in Los Angeles, California. Education: Attended junior college. Currently living in
Inglewood, California. Career: A word processing supervisor
in secretarial and administration areas. Presently preparing a
one-woman show and writing health poems.

NON-FICTION
Published in Community Health News.
POETRY
When One Loves. Millbrae, Ca.: Celestial Arts, 1974†.
INTERJECTIONS
"I believe writing is a necessary means of self therapy."

RICHARDSON, Senora.
POETRY (Anthology): Simmons and Hutchinson, Black Culture.

RICHARDSON, Willis. Born 5 November 1889 in Wilmington, North
Carolina. Education: Graduate of Dunbar High School; studied
poetics, versification, and dramaturgy with a correspondence
school. Career: Now retired after 43 years with the United
States Bureau of Engraving and Printing in Washington, D.C.
(1911-1954). Began writing in 1920 and is well-known as the
first Black playwright to have a serious play produced on the
Broadway stage (The Chip Woman's Fortune, presented in 1923).
He has devoted much of his time and talent to writing plays and
editing collections for use by elementary and secondary school
children. Member: Authors League of America; Dramatists
Guild; Harlem Cultural Council; National Association for the Ad-
vancement of Colored People. Awards, Honors: Amy Spingarn
Prize for drama, 1925 and 1926; Edith Schwarb Cup, Yale Univer-
sity Theater, 1928.
CRITICISM BY RICHARDSON
    "Characters." Opportunity 3 (June 1925): 183.
    "The Hope of a Negro Drama." Crisis 19 (1919): 338.
    "The Negro and the Stage." Opportunity 2 (October 1924):
    310.
    "The Unpleasant Play." Opportunity 3 (September 1925): 282.
DRAMA
    The Amateur Prostitute.
    Antonio Maceo (one act). In Richardson and Miller, Negro
        History in Thirteen Plays.
    Attucks, The Martyr. In Richardson and Miller, Negro His-
        tory in Thirteen Plays.
    Bold Lover (one act).
    Bootblack Lover.
    The Broken Banjo. In Crisis 31 (1926): 167, 225; also in
        Barksdale and Kinnamon, Black Writers of America.
    The Brown Boy (one act).
    The Brownie's Book, 1921.
    The Chip Woman's Fortune, 1923. In Turner, Black Drama
        in America; Patterson, Anthology of the American Negro
        in the Theater.
    Compromise (A Folk Play). In Locke, The New Negro, pp.
        168-195.
    The Curse of the Shell Road Witch (one act).
    The Danse Calinda. In Locke and Gregory, Plays of Negro
        Life.
    The Dark Haven (one act).
    The Deacon's Awakening: A Play in One Act. In Crisis 20

(1920): 10.
The Rider of the Dream. In Locke and Gregory, Plays of
   Negro Life.
Rooms for Rent (one act).
(Anthologies): Plays also published in Dreer, American Lit-
   erature by Negro Authors; Cromwell, Readings from Ne-
   gro Aughors; Shay, Fifty More Contemporary Plays.
POETRY
   Echoes from the Negro Soul. San Antonio, Texas: Alamo
      Printing Co., 1926.
   (Periodical): Crisis 26 (1923).
SHORT STORY
   (Periodical): Crisis, July 1967.
BIOGRAPHY AND CRITICISM ON RICHARDSON
   Barksdale and Kinnamon. Black Writers of America, pp.
      638-639.
   Bond. The Negro and the Drama, pp. 76, 166-167.
   Brawley. The Negro Genius, pp. 271, 282-284.
   Hughes and Meltzer. Black Magic, pp. 123, 124.
   Mitchell. Black Drama, pp. 83-84.
   Opportunity 2 (October 1924), 317.
   Who's Who in Colored America, 1940.
INTERJECTIONS
   "Since I am a playwright I am mainly interested in stage
plays; but I have been greatly disappointed to note that all the
Black professional groups continue to stage plays depicting the
lives and actions of characters in the lowest tenth of our race,
the pimps, the prostitutes, the dope pushers, the street walkers
and the corner dudes. They fail to note that there exists among
us a better class of respectable, educated, refined families with
interesting problems of their own.
   "Before my first play, The Chip Woman's Fortune was staged
on Broadway in 1923, Black actors were put upon the stage to
be laughed at. Now, they are put upon the stage to be pitied or
scorned.
   "I have several plays about better class, respectable, Afro-
American families, but the Black professional actors and producers have ignored them. They fail to realize that the most
people who go to see plays on the stage are middle or upper
class and would enjoy seeing plays about people similar to themselves, plays with plots and characters with whom they have
empathy.

RIDHIANA.
   POETRY (Anthologies): Dee, Glow Child; Major, The New
      Black Poetry; Troupe, Watts Poets.

RIDOUT, Daniel Lyman.
   POETRY Verses from a Humble Cottage. Hampton, Va.:
      Hampton Institute Press, 1924.

RIGGINS, Roger.
   POETRY (Periodical): Umbra.

RILEY, Clayton.
  CRITICISM
    "The Black Arts." Liberator 5 (April 1965): 21.
    "Clayton Riley on the Black Critic." Black Creation 3 (Sum-
      mer 1972).
    "Introduction." A Black Quartet. New York: New American
      Library, 1970, pp. vii-xxiii.
    "The Negro and the Theatre." Liberator 7 (June 1967): 20;
      7 (July 1967): 20; 8 (August 1967): 21.
    "On Black Theatre." In Gayle, The Black Aesthetic.
  NON-FICTION
    "The Death Horse Rides Our Harlems." Black World 2 (Ap-
      pril 1971): 37-38.
  REVIEWS:
    Published in Liberator.
  SHORT STORY
    (Anthology): Clarke, Harlem.

RILEY, Constantia E.
  POETRY (Anthology): Murphy, Ebony Rhythm.

RILEY, James W.
  POETRY In Memory of Departed Friends. Washington: Murray
    Bros. Press, 1914.

RILLIEUX, Victor Ernest. Born 1845. Died 5 December 1898.
  Career: Apparently a poor man whose prolific writings (poems,
  songs, odes, satires, translations) have been lost.[1]
  POETRY
    (Anthologies): Coleman, Creole Voices; Desdunes, Nos Hom-
      mes et Notre Histoire.
  BIOGRAPHY ON RILLIEUX
    Desdunes. Nos Hommes et Notre Histoire, pp. 80-81.
      [1]Edward Maceo Coleman, ed., Creole Voices: Poems
      in French by Free Men of Color (Washington, D.C.: As-
      sociated, 1945), p. xxx.

RIQUET, Nicol. Born in New Orleans, 19th century. Career: A
  cigar-maker by trade who served as ghost-writer for famous
  contemporaries and as song-writer for the youth of his day.[1]
  POETRY
    (Anthologies): Coleman, Creole Voices; Desdunes, Nos Hom-
      mes et Notre Histoire.
      [1]Edward Maceo Coleman, ed., Creole Voices: Poems
      in French by Free Men of Color (Washington, D.C.: As-
      sociated, 1945), pp. xxx-xxxi.

RIVERS, Conrad Kent. Born 1933 in Atlantic City, New Jersey.
  Died 1968. Education: A.B., Wilberforce University, 1955;
  also studied at Indian University, Chicago Teachers College,
  and Temple University. Career: Served in the Armed
  Forces; taught school in Chicago. Black World has established an annual Conrad Kent Rivers Poetry Award in his

honor.
CRITICISM
    "Black Writer's Views on Literary Lions and Values."
       Negro Digest 17 (January 1968): 17.
    "Langston Hughes, and the Fantasy of Harlem." Negro
       Digest 13 (September 1964): 72-76.
    "The Poetry of Gwendolyn Brooks." Negro Digest 13
       (June 1964): 67-68.
DRAMA
    To Make a Poet Black.
NON-FICTION
    (Periodical): Negro Digest 15 (March 1966): 54-58.
POETRY
    Dusk at Selma. n.p., 1965.
    Perchance to Dream, Othello. Wilberforce, O.: Wilber-
      force University Press, 1959.
    The Still Voice of Harlem. London: Breman, 1968. Dis-
      tributed in the U.S. by Broadside Press.
    These Black Bodies and This Sunburnt Face. Cleveland:
      Cleveland Free Lance Press, 1962.
    The Wright Poems. London: Breman, 1973. Distributed in
      the U.S. by Broadside Press.
    (Anthologies): Adams, Conn and Slepian. Afro-American
      Literature: Poetry; Adoff, The Poetry of Black Amer-
      ica; Baker, Black Literature in America; Barksdale
      and Kinnamon, Black Writers of America; Bell, Afro-
      American Poetry; Bontemps, American Negro Poetry;
      Breman, Sixes and Sevens; Brooks, A Broadside
      Treasury; Hayden, Kaleidoscope; Henderson, Under-
      standing the New Black Poetry; Hughes, Negro Poets:
      USA; Hughes and Bontemps, Poetry of the Negro:
      1746-1970; Major, The New Black Poetry; Pool, Be-
      yond the Blues; Randall, The Black Poets; Randall
      and Burroughs, For Malcolm; Simmons and Hutchinson,
      Black Culture.
    (Periodicals): Negro Digest, 12 (September 1963: 56; 14
      (May 1965): 19, 72; 15 (September 1966): 75. Also
      published in Kenyon Review; Antioch Review; Free
      Lance; Ohio Poetry Review; Signet.
SHORT STORIES
    (Anthology), Hughes, Best Short Stories by Negro
      Writers.
    (Periodicals): Negro Digest 13 (April 1964): 55-58, 15
      (October 1966): 53-56.
BIOGRAPHY AND CRITICISM ON RIVERS
    Adoff. The Poetry of Black America, p. 534.
    Baker. Black Literature in America, p. 439.
    Bontemps. American Negro Poetry, pp. 176-177.
    Hayden. Kaleidoscope, pp. 204-207.
    Kent. "Outstanding Works...," pp. 324-325.
    Lee, Don L. Dynamite Voices, pp. 35-40.
    _____. Negro Digest 17 (August 1968): 94-97.
    Raphael. "For a Poet I Know: Conrad Kent Rivers."

Negro Digest 15 (September 1966): 69.

Singh and Fellowes. Black Literature in America, p. 347.

[1] Robert Hayden. Kaleidoscope (New York: Harcourt Brace, and World, 1967), p. 204.

RIVERS, Louis (Paul Mulet, pseud.) Born 18 September 1922 in Savannah, Georgia. Education: B.S., Savannah State College, 1946; M.A., New York University, 1949; working toward Ph.D., Fordham University; additional study at Hunter College; New York University; Yale University; Brette Warren-Howard Di Silva Dramatic Workshop, New York City; Catholic University of America. Currently living in Brooklyn. Career: English teacher and department chairman, Center High School, Waycross, Georgia, 1946-49; Instructor, West Virginia State College, 1950-51; Instructor, Yesoda Hatorah Yeshivah, Bronx, 1951-52; Instructor, Southern University, 1952-53; Assistant Professor, Tougaloo Southern Christian College, 1953-57; teacher, Junior High School 162, Brooklyn, 1958-68; teacher, Chofetz Chaim Yeshivah, New York City, 1960-63; consultant and program designer for ASPIRA's tutorial program, New York City, 1966; drama coach and consultant for Voices, Incorporated, 1966; consultant and program designer for Youth in Action's tutorial program, Bedford-Stuyvesant, 1967; consultant and program designer for Knickerbocker-Wyckoff community services, Bushwick, Brooklyn, 1969; In-service instructor, N.Y.C. Board of Education, 1966-69; member of National Advisory Subcommittee of Urban-Rural School Development Program, Washington, D.C., 1969 to present; teacher of Philosophy of Design, Parsons College of Fashion and Design, 1969 to present. Also served as panelist for New York City Council of English Teachers, 1968; and for the New York State English Council, Syracuse, 1970. Presently, Assistant Professor in Developmental Writing at New York City Community College, Brooklyn. Member: Sambda Xi Chapter of Kappa Delta Pi (education honor society). Awards, Honors: John Hay Whitney Fellow in Creating Writing.

DRAMA
Madam Odum, 1973.
Mr. Randolph Brown.
Purple Passages.
A Rose for Lorraine.
The Scabs. In First Stage: A Quarterly of New Drama (Purdue University), Fall, 1962.
Seeking.

NON-FICTION
With Jim and Marilyn Birkley. Pattern Practices to Learn to Write by. New York: College Skills, 1972.

INTERJECTIONS
"I think; I believe it; I live it. My writing reflects it, amplifies it--A Man is greater than the society or world which has shaped him and he deserves the longest, healthiest, wealthiest and happiest journey from womb to the tomb. This applies to

Louis Rivers

all mankind, and a man must never accept anything less even when another man might think it is necessary if he, the other man, is to realize the objective of his singular journey."

ROACH, Freddie.
    DRAMA Soul Pieces, 1969.

ROBBIN, William Allston.
    POETRY Elbowroom! Elbowroom! New York: Vantage, 1965.

ROBERSON, Arthur.
    DRAMA
        Don't Leave Go My Hand, 1965.
        In the Shadow of Ham, 1968.
        Melanosis, 1969.
        Run Sweet Child to Silence, 1968.

ROBERSON, Ed (Charles Edwin Roberson). Born 1939 in Pittsburgh, Pennsylvania.

POETRY
When Thy King Is a Boy: Poems.   Pittsburgh: University of
Pittsburgh Press, 1970*†.
(Anthologies): Adoff, The Poetry of Black America; Chapman,
New Black Voices; Hughes and Bontemps, The Poetry of
the Negro: 1746-1970; New Directions 22.
(Periodical): Atlantic.

ROBERSON, Sadie L.
SHORT STORIES Killer of the Dream: Short Stories.   New
York: Comet, 1963.

ROBERSON, William.
DRAMA
The Anger of One Young Man, 1959.
The Passing Grade, 1958.

ROBERTS, D. L.
POETRY Tremolo: Poems.   New York: Exposition, 1956.

ROBERTS, Martin Younger.
POETRY A Reconstruction of Me.   n.p.: Red Dust, n.d.

ROBERTS, Roberta.
POETRY (Anthology): Black Poets Write On.

ROBERTS, Victoria.
DRAMA A Time to Laugh, 1971.

ROBINSON, Billy "Hands."
SHORT STORY (Periodical): Black Scholar, September 1971.

ROBINSON, Daniel.
POETRY (Anthology): Boyd, Poems by Blacks, vol. 2.

ROBINSON, Etholia Arthur.
POETRY
(Anthology): Murphy, Ebony Rhythm.
(Periodical): Opportunity, Winter 1947.

ROBINSON, Eugene E.
POETRY Inspirations.   New York: Vantage, 1958.

ROBINSON, Garrett.
DRAMA Land of Lem, 1971.

ROBINSON, J. Terry.
WORKS White Horse in Harlem.   New York: Pageant, 1965.

ROBINSON, Rose.
NOVEL
Eagle in the Air.   New York: Crown, 1969; New York:
Bantam, 1971.

Robinson, R. (cont.)   636

SHORT STORY
(Periodical): Essence, August 1971.

ROBINSON, T. L. Born 6 July 1946 in Mississippi.
POETRY (Anthology): Coombs, We Speak as Liberators.

ROBINSON, William Henry. Born 1922 in Newport, Rhode Island.
Career: See Shockley and Chandler, Living Black American Authors, pp. 136-137.
CRITICISM
   Early Black American Poets. Dubuque, Iowa: William C.
      Brown, 1969†.
   Early Black American Prose. Dubuque, Iowa: William C.
      Brown, 1970†.
   Major Black American Literature, forthcoming.
EDITOR
   Nommo: A Modern Anthology of Black Africa and Black
      American Literature. New York: Macmillan, 1972.

RODGERS, Carolyn M. Born in Chicago, Illinois. Career: See
Shockley and Chandler, Living Black American Authors, p. 137.
CRITICISM
   "Black Poetry--WhereIt's At." Negro Digest 18 (September
      1969): 7-16; also in Kochman, Rappin' and Stylin' Out, pp.
      336-345.
   "Breakforth. In Deed." Black World 19 (September 1970):
      13-22.
   "The Literature of Black." Black World 19 (June 1970): 5-
      14.
   "Uh Nat'chal Thing--THE WHOLE TRUTH--US." Black World
      20 (September 1971): 4-14.
POETRY
   For Flip Wilson. Detroit: Broadside, 1971.
   Now Ain't That Love. Detroit: Broadside, 1970.
   Paper Soul. Introduction by Hoyt W. Fuller. Chicago: Third
      World, 1968.
   Songs of a Black Bird. Chicago: Third World, 1969†.
   2 Love Raps. Chicago: Third World, 1969. (Broadside.)
   (Anthologies): Adoff, The Poetry of Black America; Alhamisi
      and Wangara, Black Arts; Brooks, A Broadside Treasury;
      Brooks, Jump Bad; Brown, Lee and Ward, To Gwen with
      Love; Coombs, We Speak as Liberators; Giovanni, Night
      Comes Softly; Henderson, Understanding the New Black Poetry; King, Blackspirits; Long and Collier, Afro-American
      Writing; Patterson, A Rock Against the Wind; Randall, The
      Black Poets; Robinson, Nommo; Wilentz and Weatherly,
      Natural Process.
   (Broadsides): "Now Ain't That Love?" (1970); "Long Rap"
      (1971); "For H. W. Fuller" (1971). Detroit: Broadside.
   (Periodicals): Black World, June 1973; Journal of Black Poetry, Spring 1969; Negro Digest, September-October 1968;
      September 1969.

SHORT STORIES
   (Anthology): Adoff, Brothers and Sisters.
   (Periodicals): Negro Digest, August 1967; June 1969.
REVIEWS BY RODGERS
   Published in Negro Digest.
BIOGRAPHY AND CRITICISM ON RODGERS
   Lee. Dynamite Voices, pp. 54-60.

RODGERS, Loretta.
   POETRY (Anthologies): Patterson, A Rock Against the Wind;
   Sanchez, 360° of Blackness Coming at You.

ROE, Helene.
   POETRY Teach Me to Live. n.p., 1963?

ROGERS, Alex. Career: Songwriter.
   DRAMA
      With J. A. Shipp. Abyssinia, 1906.
      Baby Blues, 1919.
      With J. A. Shipp. Bandanna Land, 1908.
      With Harry Cort. Charlie, 1923.
      With Leubrie Hill. Dark Town Follies, 1913.
      With Harry Cort and George Stoddard. Go-Go, 1923.
      With J. A. Shipp and Paul Laurence Dunbar. In Dahomey,
         1902.
      With J. A. Shipp and Bert Williams. Mr. Lode of Koal,
         1909.
      With Eddie Hunter. My Magnolia, 1926.
      With Henry Creamer. The Old Man's Boy, 1914.
      This and That, 1919.
      With Henry Creamer. The Traitor, 1912.
   BIOGRAPHY AND CRITICISM ON ROGERS
      Hughes and Meltzer. Black Magic, p. 88.
      Mitchell. Black Drama, pp. 40, 48, 50, 51, 61, 71.

ROGERS, David.
   DRAMA If That's Where It's at Baby, I'm Not Going, 1969.

ROGERS, Elymas Payson. Born 1814. Died 1861. Career: Served
   as a Presbyterian Minister in Newark, New Jersey; taught in
   the public schools in Rochester, New York; was an abolitionist,
   but became disillusioned because of the treatment of Blacks in
   the United States and moved to Africa where he died of a fever
   a few days after landing in 1861.[1]
   NON-FICTION (Sermon)
      Minutes of the Second Presyberian And Congregational Con-
         vention. New York: 1858, pp. 15-19.
   POETRY
      A Poem of the Fugitive Slave Law. Newark, N.J.: A. S.
         Holbrook, 1855.
      The Repeal of the Missouri Compromise Considered. New-
         ark, N.J.: A. S. Holbrook, 1856.

BIOGRAPHY AND CRITICISM ON ROGERS
> Brown, W. W. The Black Man, His Antecedents, His Genius, and His Achievements. New York and Boston: n.p. , 1863, pp. 272, 274.
> Loggins. The Negro Author in America, pp. 239-241, 396, 433, 438.
>   [1]William H. Robinson, Early Black American Poets (Dubuque, Iowa: William C. Brown, 1969), p. 60.

ROGERS, J. Overton.
> POETRY Blues and Ballads of a Black Yankee, A Journey with Sad Sam. New York: Exposition, 1965.

ROGERS, Joel Augustus. Born September 1883 in Jamaica. Died 1966. Career: Rogers came to the United States in 1906 and became a citizen in 1917. As a jouranlist for the Pittsburgh Courier, he covered Haile Selassie's coronation as Emperor of Ethiopia in 1930. He became the first Black war correspondent by reporting the Italo-Ethiopian war; wrote an illustrated feature, "Your History," for the Pittsburgh Courier and a column of criticism for the Messenger magazine. Member: American Geographical Society; The Academy of Political Science;[1] Société d'Anthropologie in Paris, France. [2]
NON-FICTION
> Africa's Gift to America: The Afro-American in the Making and Saving of the United States. New York: By the Author, 1959; with new supplement: Africa and Its Potentialities (civil war centennial ed.) New York: By the Author, 1961.
> The Approaching Storm and How It May Be Averted. An Open Letter to Congress and the 48 Legislatures of the United States of America. From the National Equal Rights League of America. Chicago: By the Author, 1920.
> As Nature Leads; an Informal Discussion of the Reason Why Negro and Caucasions Are Mixing in Spite of Opposition. Chicago: M.A. Donohue, 1919.
> Mature Knows No Color-line; Research into the Negro Ancestry in the White Race. New York: By the Author, 1952.
> 100 Amazing Facts about the Negro; With Complete Proof. A Short Cut to the World History of the Negro. New York: F. Hubner, 1934.
> Facts about the Negro. Pittsburgh: Lincoln Park Studios, 1960.
> From Superman to Man. n.p. , 1917; reprint ed. , Chicago: The Godspeed Press, 1917; Chicago: By the Author, 1917; New York: Lenox, 1924; New York: By the Author, 1941; reprint of 1917 ed. , Freeport, N.Y. : Books for Libraries*.
> The Ku Klux Spirit; A Brief Outline of the History of the Ku Klan Past and Present. New York: The Messenger, 1923.
> The Maroons of the West Indies and South America. n.p. , 1921.
> The Mongrel World; A Study of Negro-Caucasian Mixing Throughout the Ages in All Countries. Chicago: By the Author, 1927.

The Real Facts about Ethiopia. New York: By the Author,
    1936.
Sex and Race; Negro-Caucasian Mixing in All Ages and All
    Lands. New York: By the Author, 1940-1944.
World's Greatest Men of Color. New York: By the Author,
    1935, 1946.
Your History from the Beginning of Time to the Present.
    Pittsburgh: The Pittsburgh Courier, 1940.
(Periodicals):
"Civil War Centennial, Myth and Reality." Freedomways 3
    (Winter 1963): 7-18.
"Jim Crow Hunt." (Book Review of Roi Ottley's No Green
    Pastures: The Negro in Europe Today). Crisis 58 (No-
    vember 1951): 589-592.
    Also published in The American Mercury and Survey Graphic.
NOVELS
Blood Money. n.p., 1923.
The Golden Door. n.p., 1927.
She Walks in Beauty. Los Angeles: Western, 1963.
BIOGRAPHY AND CRITICISM ON ROGERS
Boris, Joseph J. Who's Who in Colored America, vols. 1,
    2 and 3. New York: Who's Who in Colored America
    Corp., 1927, 1932, 1940.
Brown, Davis and Lee. The Negro Caravan, p. 173.
Jet, 8 September 1966.
"Joel Rogers Records History of Negroes." Sepia 7 (Decem-
    ber 1959): 59.
"Negro Historian and Journalist Dies in March, 1966 in New
    York City at the Age of 85." Journal of Negro History
    51 (July 1966): 236.
Ploski. The Negro Almanac, rev. ed., pp. 693-694.
The Truth Seeker (April 1945): 60.
Writer's Program of New York City. Biographical Sketches.
    Research Studies compiled by the workers of the Writers
    Program of the Work Project's Administration in New
    York City for Negroes of New York. New York: n.p.,
    1938-1941.
REVIEWS
Africa's Gift to America: The Afro-American in the Making
    and Saving of the U.S. Crisis 67 (April 1960): 268.
From Superman to Man
Du Bois, W. E. B. Crisis 28 (1924): 218.
    [1]Harry A. Ploski and Ernest Kaiser. The Negro Al-
    manac (New York: The Bellwether Co., 1971), p. 691.
    [2]Thomas Yenser, ed. Who's Who in Colored America
    (Brooklyn: Thomas Yenser, 1940), p. 449.

ROKER, Myntora J. Born in Little Rock, Arkansas.
    POETRY (Anthology): Murphy, Negro Voices.

ROLLINS, Bryant. Born 13 December 1937 in New York City.
    Education: B.A., English, Northeastern University, 1960.
    Currently living in New York City. Career: Copy Boy for

the Boston Post (now defunct) and the Boston Globe, 1955-61.
Assistant Sports Publicity Director, Boston University, 1961-
62. Newspaper reporter, Boston Globe, 1962-65. Stringer,
Time magazine and Newsweek magazine, 1963-66. Co-founder
and editor of the Bay State Banner, a community newspaper
serving the Black community of Greater Boston and the general
civil rights community of Eastern Massachusetts, 1965-66. Coordinator of Afro-American History Curriculum Program at Education Development Centers, Newton and Cambridge, Massachusetts, 1966-67. Director of Economic Development, The New
Urban League of Boston, and Co-Director of the Joint Commu-
nity-University Center for Innercity Change, 1967-69; Vice
President, H. Carl McCall & Associates: Consultants in Urban
Affairs, 1969-71; Executive Editor, New York Amsterdam News,
1971-72; Administrator, The Michele Clark Fellowship Program
of Minority Journalists, Graduate School of Journalism, Columbia University, 1973-. Awards, Honors: N. A. A. C. P. Scholarship, 1955; Joseph Ford Scholarship, 1959; Annual Poet of the
Year Award, Northeastern University, 1959; 1969 Obie to the
OM Theater Workshop for Riot.

DRAMA
   With Julie Portman. Riot, 1968.
NOVEL
   Danger Song. Garden City, N.Y.: Doubleday, 1967†.
   Goin Down Slow. Garden City, N.Y.: Doubleday, forthcom-
      ing.
POETRY
   (Anthology): American Anthology of College Poetry, 1959.

ROLLINS, Charlemae Hill. Born 1897 in Yazoo City, Mississippi.
   Career: See Commire, Something About the Author, 3; Con-
   temporary Authors, 138; The Magic World of Books (Chicago:
   Science Research Associates, 1954).

BIOGRAPHY
   Famous American Negro Poets. New York: Apollo Editions,
      1971†.
   Famous Negro Entertainers of Stage, Screen and Television.
      New York: Dodd, Mead, 1967*.
   They Showed the Way: Forty American Leaders. New York:
      T. Y. Crowell, 1964*.
EDITOR
   Call of Adventure. New York: Crowell-Collier, 1962. (Short
      Stories.)
   Christmas Gif'. Chicago: Follett, 1965*.
NON-FICTION
   We Build Together: A Reader's Guide to Negro Life and Lit-
      erature for Elementary and High School Use. Urbana,
      Ill.: National Council of Teachers of English, 1967†.

ROLLINS, Lamen.
   NOVEL The Human Race a Gang. New York: Carlton, 1965.

ROPER, Moses. Born about 1816 in Caswell County, North Carolina. [1] Education: Attended University College in London. Career: As a child Roper was sold from master to master, was
exposed to numerous floggings, attempted to escape many times
and was severely punished after each attempt. During one escape attempt, he was reunited with his mother after a ten
years' absence, but was hunted down by slave catchers and giv-
en severe punishment. In July 1834, he finally obtained his
freedom by posing as an Indian and fleeing to Savannah. [2]
    While working in the Eastern section of the United States,
Roper was converted to Christianity and his Christian support-
ers provided him with letters of recommendation to English
friends, enabling him to go to England to seek employment in
November 1835. [3] While in England, he attended the University
College at London in order to prepare for missionary work in
the West Indies and Africa. Little is known about Roper's
later life. [4]

AUTOBIOGRAPHY

A Narrative of the Adventures and Escape of Moses Roper
from American Slavery. Preface by Rev. T. Price.
Berwick-upon-Tweed: The Warder Office, 1837; reprint
eds., 1839; London: Harvey & Sarton, 1848; reprint with
brief introduction by Maxwell Whiteman, Philadelphia: Merrihew and Gunn, 1883; 1969.

BIOGRAPHY AND CRITICISM ON ROPER

Barksdale and Kinnamon. Black Writers of America, p.
209.

Loggins. The Negro Author in America, pp. 103-104, 382,
418.

Nichols, Charles H., Jr. Many Thousands Gone: The Ex-
slaves Account of Their Bondage and Freedom. Leiden,
1963, pp. xiii, xiv, 1, 19, 36, 39, 65, 94.
    [1]Richard Barksdale and Keneth Kinnamon, Black Writers
of America (New York: Macmillan, 1972), p. 209.
    [2]Moses Roper, A Narrative of the Adventures and Es-
cape of Moses Roper from American Slavery. (Philadelphia: Merrihew and Gunn, 1838).
    [3]Ibid.
    [4]Ibid.

ROSEBROUGH, Sadie Mae.
    NOVEL Wasted Travail. New York: Vantage, 1951.

ROSS, G. H.
    NOVEL Beyond the River. Boston: Meador, 1938.

ROSS, John M.
    DRAMA
        Aztec Qzin, 1968.
        One Clear Call. Nashville, Tenn.: Fisk University, 1936.
        Rho Kappa Epsilon. Nashville, Tenn.: Fisk University, 1935.
        Strivin', 1937.
        Dog's Place.

House or No House, 1967.
I Will Repay, 1963.
The Purple Lily.
Half Caste Moon.
The Sword, 1948.
Wanga Doll. New Orleans, La.: Dillard University, 1954.

ROWE, George Clinton.
POETRY
A Noble Life. A Memorial Souvenir of Rev. Jos. C. Price.
Charleston, South Carolina, 1887.
Our Heroes: Patriotic Poems on Men, Women and Sayings
of the Negro Race. Charleston, S.C.: Walker Evans &
Cogswell, Printers, 1890.
Thoughts in Verse. Charleston, S.C.: n.p., 1887.

ROWLAND, Ida.
POETRY
Lisping Leaves. Philadelphia: Dorrance, 1939.

ROYAL, A. Bertrand. Born 24 May 1911 in Williamston, South
Carolina. Education: B.S., Claflin College, 1936; M.D., Me-
harry Medical College, 1944. Currently living in Newark, New
Jersey. Career: Physician.
NOVEL
Which Way to Heaven? New York: Vantage, 1970.
INTERJECTIONS
"I have felt a need to picture in the minds of our newer gen-
erations some ·indication of the necessity that they appreciate
that what they are able to receive from the American Dream is
borne on the backs of their forebears whose vitality would not
permit Negro descendants to follow the course of the American
Indian, OBLIVION."

ROYSTER, Philip M. Born 31 July 1943 in Chicago, Illinois. Career: See Shockley and Chandler, Living Black American Authors, pp. 139-140.
POETRY
The Back Door. Chicago: Third World, 1971.
(Periodicals): Journal of Black Poetry, Summer 1972; also
published in Cadence and Liberator.

ROYSTER, Sandra. Born 11 September 1942 in Chicago. Career:
See Shockley and Chandler, Living Black American Authors,
p. 140.
POETRY
(Anthologies): Patterson, A Rock Against the Wind; Wither-
spoon, Broadside Annual 1972.
(Periodical): Black World, April 1972.

RUSS, George B. Born 31 September 1914 in Wilmington, North
Carolina. Education: Studied writing through correspondence
courses. Currently living in Durham, North Carolina. Career:

A. Bertrand Royal

Writes for <u>The Carolina Times</u>, a weekly Black publication in Durham; also works as a chef. Presently developing Bunting-Russ Enterprise, a channel for advertising and distributing Black authors' books. Has written serial stories and semi-feature stories about people and events for newspaper publication. <u>Member</u>: Union Baptist Church.

NOVEL
   <u>Over Edom, I Lost My Shoe</u>. New York: Carlton, 1970.
UNPUBLISHED WORK
   "Hidden Among the Stuff, Justice Lies Sleeping."
   "Black Is Honest--Yaller Steals."
   "Aha! Now You See."
INTERJECTIONS
   "The fortune I planned to amass writing short pieces never materialized. So, out of despair I salvaged hope and dreamed of writing a Best-seller Novel--this dream hangs in the balance. The autumn years of my life find me adding wisdom to self-discipline; understanding to knowledge and enjoyment in the discovery of skills I never knew were really at my finger-tips. It's amazing how the writer finds excuses to continue the grinding task of weaving words into fabrics."

RUSSELL, Beth Duvall.
POETRY
On Earth As It Is. Boston: Christopher, 1963.
(Periodical): Phylon, Fourth Quarter 1954; Fourth Quarter
1955; Second Quarter 1956; Second Quarter 1957.

RUSSELL, Charlie. Born 10 March 1932 in Monroe, Louisiana.
Education: B.S. (English), University of San Francisco, 1959;
M.S.W., New York University, 1966. Currently living in New
York City. Career: Counselor, SEEK program, City College
of New York, 1967 to present. Also, lecturer, Livingston Col-
lege of Rutgers University; founder, Onyx Publications; column-
ist, Manhattan Tribune. Wrote script, "The Black Church" for
ABC-TV, and "A Man Is Not Made of Steel," for WGBH-TV.
Filmscript of Five on the Back Hand Side was released by
United Artists in 1973.
DRAMA
Five on the Back Hand Side. New York: Samuel French,
1970.
With Barbara Ann Teer. Revival!
NON-FICTION
"LeRoi Jones Will Get Us All in Trouble." Liberator 4
(August 1964): 18.
Also published in Negro Digest, May 1967.
NOVELLA
A Birthday Present for Kathelyn Kenyatta. New York: Mc-
Graw-Hill, forthcoming.
SHORT STORY
(Anthologies): Cahill and Cooper, The Urban Reader; Hughes,
The Best Short Stories by Negro Writers.
(Periodicals): Liberator, November 1964.
BIOGRAPHY AND CRITICISM ON RUSSELL
Harris, Jessica B. "National Black Theatre." Drama Re-
view 16 (December 1972): 39-45.
Harrison. The Drama of Nommo, pp. 176, 223.

-S-

SABB, Elijah.
POETRY (Anthology): Boyd, Poems by Blacks, vol. 2.

ST. CLAIR, Wesley.
DRAMA The Station, 1969.

ST. JOHN, Primus. Born 1939.
POETRY
(Anthologies): Adoff, The Poetry of Black America. Also in
Agenda for Survival. Edited by Harold W. Helfrich, Jr.
New Haven: Yale University Press, 1970; and in Poems
and Perspectives. Edited by Robert H. Ross and William
Stafford. New York: Scott Foresman, 1971.
(Periodicals); Concerning Poetry; Poet-Lore; Poetry North-
west.

SALAAM, Iyshaa.
  POETRY (Periodicals): Journal of Black Poetry, 1969; Fall-
    Winter 1971.

SALAAM, Kalamu ya (Val Ferdinand). Born 3 March 1947 in New
  Orleans. Education: Working on an A.B. degree in Business
  Administration. Currently living in New Orleans. Career:
  Specializes in writing critical reviews and plays. Presently is
  director of BLKARTSOUTH in New Orleans; Co-editor/Publisher
  of NKOMBO; Managing Editor of Black Collegian; Editor/Pub-
  lisher of Expressions (a national review of the Black arts published by Pyramid Press, Inc.). Awards, Honors: Recipient
  of the 1971 Wright Award for Criticism.
  CRITICISM
    "Annual Black Theatre Round-Up: New Orleans." Black
      World 21 (April 1972): 40-44.
    "The Dashiki Project Theatre, We Are the Theater." Black
      Theater No. 3 (1969): 4-6.
    "News from BlkArtSouth." Black Theater No. 4 (1970): 4.
    "On Black Theater in America: A Report." Negro Digest
      19 (April 1970): 23-31.
  DRAMA
    Black Liberation Army (one act), 1969.
    Cop Killer (one act), 1968.
    Happy Birthday, Jesus (one act), 1968.
    Homecoming (one act), 1969.
    Mama (one act), 1968.
    The Picket (one act), 1968.
    With Tom Dent. Song of Survival (one act), 1969.
  POETRY
    The Blues Merchant. New Orleans: BlkArtSouth, 1969.
    (Anthologies): Chapman, New Black Voices; Simmons and
      Hutchinson, Black Culture.
    (Periodical): Journal of Black Poetry, Summer 1972.
  REVIEWS
    Published in Black World.
  SHORT STORY
    (Anthologies): Coombs, What We Must See; Sanchez, We Be
      Sorcerers.
  INTERJECTIONS
    "The Black artist at best is a translator of the wonderful-
  ness that is Black life. Black art is a recreation or represen-
  tation of Black life. That's all. Everything else is particulars
  and not essences. Except to say Black people. Afrikan people!
  Got to be free. Afrika must be free! We need a better life.
  Later for art without a better life. Our people need to live a
  better life. That's all. That's all."

SALGADO, Lionel. Born 1928.
  POETRY
    The Songs of the Flowers with No Names. n.p.: By the Au-
      thor, n.d.
    (Anthology): Shuman, A Galaxy of Black Writing.

SALIMU (Nettie McCray).
  DRAMA Growin' Into Blackness. In Bullins, New Plays from
    the Black Theatre, pp. 195-200.

SAMPSON, John Patterson. Born 1837. Career: Was presiding
  elder of the New England Conference of the A.M.E. Church.
  DRAMA
    The Disappointed Bride; or, Love at First Sight. Hampton,
      Va.: Hampton School Steam Press, 1883.
    Jolly People. In Plays, Poems and Miscellany (Schomburg
      Collection).
  LECTURES
    "The Importance of Evangelical Unity in Sunday School Work,
      Regardless of Race or Denomination." Ocean Grove,
      N.J.: n.p., n.d. (In Schomburg Collection).
    How to Live a Hundred Years. Providence: Excelsior Print,
      1909. Also in Articles and Addresses by Negroes (Schom-
      burg Collection).

SAMUEL, Aaron.
  POETRY A Helping Hand. New York, 1905.

SAMUELS, Calvin Henry McNeal.
  POETRY Me. New York: Comet, 1954. (Also includes prose.)

SANCHEZ, Sonia. Born 9 September 1934 in Birmingham, Alabama.
  Career: See Shockley and Chandler, Living Black American Au-
  thors, p. 142; Contemporary Authors, 33/36.
  CHILDREN AND YOUNG ADULTS
    Adventures of Small Head, Square Head and Fat Head. New
      ed. New York: Third, 1973*.
    It's a New Day: Poems for Young Brothas & Sistuhs. De-
      troit: Broadside, 1971*†.
  DRAMA
    The Bronx Is Next (one act). In The Drama Review 12 (Sum-
      mer 1968). Also in Davis and Redding, Cavalcade.
    Malcolm/Man Don't Live Here No Mo. In Black Theatre 6
      (1972): 24-27.
    Sister Son/ji (one act), 1969. In Bullins, New Plays from
      the Black Theater.
    Un Huh, But How Do It Free Us, 1973.
  EDITOR
    Three Hundred and Sixty Degrees of Blackness Comin' at
      You. n.p.: 5X Publishing Co., 1971.
    We Be Word Sorcerers. New York: Bantam, 1973†.
  POETRY
    Blues Book for Blue Black Magical Women. Detroit: Broad-
      side, 1974.
    Homecoming: Poems. Detroit: Broadside, 1968†.
    Love Poems. New York: Third, n.d. *†
    We a BaddDDD People. Introduction by Dudley Randall, De-
      troit: Broadside, 1970*†.
    (Anthologies): Adoff, Black Out Loud; Adoff, The Poetry of

Black America; Afro-Arts Anthology; Alhamisi and Wangara, Black Arts; Barksdale and Kinnamon, Black Writers of America; Bell, Afro-American Poetry; Brooks, A Broadside Treasury; Brown, Lee and Ward, To Gwen with Love; Chapman, New Black Voices; Coombs, We Speak as Liberators; Davis and Redding, Cavalcade; Henderson, Understanding the New Black Poetry; Jones and Neal, Black Fire; Jordan, Soulscript; King, Blackspirits; Major, The New Black Poetry; Patterson, A Rock Against the Wind; Quasha and Rothenberg, America: A Prophecy; Randall, The Black Poets; Randall, Black Poetry: A Supplement; Randall and Burroughs, For Malcolm; Robinson, Nommo; Simmons and Hutchinson, Black Culture; Wilentz and Weatherly, Natural Process.

(Periodicals): Black Scholar, January-February 1970; Black World, September 1970; September 1972; January 1974; Journal of Black Poetry, Spring 1969; Fall-Winter 1971; Massachusetts Review, Winter-Spring 1972; Negro Digest, September 1966, December 1967; September-October 1968; Nickel Review, 6 February 1970; also published in Black Dialogue.

SHORT STORY
(Anthologies): Coombs, What We Must See; Sanchez, We Be Word Sorcerers.

BIOGRAPHY AND CRITICISM ON SANCHEZ
Clarke, S. "Sonia Sanchez and Her Work." Black World 2 (June 1971): 44-46.
Harrison. The Drama of Nommo, pp. 86, 145.
Kent. "Struggle for the Image," p. 315.
Lee. Dynamite Voices, pp. 48-51.
Malkoff. Cromwell's Handbook of Contemporary American Poetry, pp. 276-277.
Palmer, R. Roderick. "The Poetry of Three Revolutionists: Don L. Lee, Sonia Sanchez, and Nikki Giovanni. CLA Journal 15 (September 1971): 25-36.
Walker, Barbara. "Sonia Sanchez Creates Poetry for the Stage." Black Creation 5 (Fall 1973): 12-13.

SANDERS, Tom.
NOVEL Her Golden Hour. Houston: By the Author, 1929.

SANJULO.
POETRY (Periodical): Journal of Black Poetry, Summer 1972.

SARTEN, Lavon.
POETRY My Poetry Stands to Challenge. New York: Paeber, 1950.

SARVER, Ruth E.
POETRY (Anthology): Murphy, Ebony Rhythm.

SAUNDERS, J. Pamela.
POETRY (Anthology): Black Poets Write On!

SAUNDERS, Ruby Constance X. Born 24 August 1939 in Alexandria, Virginia. Education: B.S., Hampton Institute (Chemistry and Mathematics), 1961; graduate student at Howard University (organic research chemist), 1964-65. Also trained with the Howard Players theatre group (acting and dancing), the Negro Ensemble Company's Playwright Workshop (acting, playwrighting and directing), and the Clark Center of the Performing Arts dancer's workshop. Currently living in Alexandria, Virginia. Career: Teacher; organic chemist; dancer, actress of stage and screen; recording artist.
DRAMA
    Goddamn, Judy (one act), 1969.
NON-FICTION
    (Periodicals): Black Collegiate; Black News.
POETRY
    (Anthologies): Coombs, We Speak as Liberators; Patterson, A Rock Against the Wind.
INTERJECTIONS
    "My philosophy is Islam--I am a follower of the Honorable Elijah Muhammad, Messenger of Allah."

SAVAGE, Eudora V.
POETRY Vibrations of My Heartstrings. New York: Exposition, 1944.

SAVOY, Willard. Born 1916.
NOVEL Alien Land. New York: E. P. Dutton, 1949; New York: New American Library, 1950.

SCHAEFER, Lotus.
POETRY (Anthology): Boyd, Poems by Blacks, vol. 2.

SCHUYLER, George Samuel. Born 25 February 1895 in Providence, Rhode Island. Career: See Who's Who in Colored America, 1940.
AUTOBIOGRAPHY
    Black and Conservative. New Rochelle, N.Y.: Arlington, 1966.
    With Josephine Schuyler. "Does Interracial Marriage Succeed?" Negro Digest 3 (June 1945): 15-17.
CRITICISM BY SCHUYLER
    "Forty Years of 'The Crisis.'" Crisis 58 (March 1951): 163-164.
    "The Negro Art Hokum." The Nation 122 (1926): 662-663.
    "The Van Vechten Revolution." Phylon 11 (1950): 362-368.
    "What's Wrong with Negro Authors." Negro Digest 8 (May 1950): 3-7.
NON-FICTION
    Fifty Years of Progress in Negro Journalism. Pittsburgh: Pittsburgh Courier, 1950.
    (Anthologies): Calverton, An Anthology of American Negro Literature; Schmalhausen, Samuel Daniel, Behold America! (New York: Farrar & Rinehart, 1931); Watkins, Anthology

of American Negro Literature.

(Periodicals: Crisis, June 1942; The Modern Quarterly,
Fall 1940; Negro Digest, November 1942; May 1943;
March, June, December 1944; May 1945; February, Sep-
tember 1947; November 1948; May 1949; June, November
1951. Also published in World Tomorrow, The Nation,
The New Masses; The Debunker; American Mercury; The
Messenger; Common Ground; Pittsburgh Courier.

Black No More: Being an Account of the Strange and Wonderful Workings of Science in the Land of the Free A.D.
1933-1940. New York: Macauley, 1931; reprint ed., College Park, Md.: McGrath, 1969*; New York: Macmillan,
1970†. Excerpts in Brown, Davis and Lee, Negro Caravan; Miller, Blackamerican Literature.

Slaves Today, A Story of Liberia. New York: Brewer, Warren & Putnam, 1931; reprint ed. College Park, Md.: Mc-
Grath, 1969*; New York: AMS Press, 1969*.

POETRY
(Periodical): Crisis, 1935.

SHORT STORY
(Periodical): Negro Digest, April 1950.

BIOGRAPHY AND CRITICISM ON SCHUYLER
Bone. The Negro Novel in America, pp. 89-92.
Davis, Allison. "Our Negro Intellectuals." Crisis 35 (1928):
268.
"George S. Schuyler: Iconclast." Crisis 72 (October 1965):
484-485.
Gloster. Negro Voices in American Fiction, pp. 155-157.
Jahn. Neo-African Literature, pp. 199-200.
Schuyler, Josephine. "17 Years of Mixed Marriage." Negro
Digest 4 (December 1946): 61-65. (Condensed from Amer-
ican Mercury, March 1946.)
Schuyler, Philippa. "Meet the George Schuylers: America's
Strangest Family." Our World 6 (April 1951): 22-26.
Whitlow. Black American Literature, pp. 96-100.
Williams. Give Birth to Brightness, pp. 81-83.
Winslow, H. F. "George S. Schuyler: Fainting Traveler."
Midwest Journal 5 (Summer 1953): 24-45.

REVIEW: Black No More.
W. E. B. Du Bois. Crisis 38 (1931): 100.

SCOTT, Addie.
SHORT STORY (Periodical): Negro Story, December-January
1944-45.

SCOTT, Carolyn Patricia.
POEMS AND SHORT STORIES The Boogaloo Child. San Francisco: Julian Richardson, n.d.

SCOTT, Emory Elrage.
POETRY Lyrics of the Southland. Chicago: Wilton Press,
1913.

SCOTT, Jimmie.
 DRAMA Money, 1969.

SCOTT, John.
 DRAMA
  The Alligator.
  I Talk with the Spirits.
  Karma's Call.
  Play Division.
  Ride a Black Horse, 1971.

SCOTT, Johnie. Born 8 May 1946 in Cheyenne, Wyoming. Education: Harvard University, 1964-65; East Los Angeles College 1965-66; B.A., Stanford University, 1970; M.A., Stanford University, 1973; American Film Institute, 1973. Currently living in Inglewood, California. Career: Editorial Intern, Newsweek, 1968-70; Correspondent, Time, 1972-73. Presently Director of Affairs, Afro-West: Theatre of the Black Arts; Special Assistant to Present, Watts Community Housing Corp.; Administrative Assistant to Assemblyman Leon Ralph (Dem.--55th District, California State Legislature); General Co-ordinator, Frederick Douglass House Foundation. Also screenwriter, director and producer (first film was The Manchild, 1971); intern director, Across 110th Street, American Film Institute, 1972. Poetry-in-concert performances were held at Stanford University with leaders of the "new Music": with Cecil Taylor, 1967; with Roscoe Mitchell, 1967; With Sun-Ray, 1968. Awards, Honors: Emmy Nomination, The Angry Voices of Watts, 1966.
NON-FICTION
 (Anthologies): Robinson, Nommo; Schulberg, From the Ashes.
POETRY
 (Anthologies): Coombs, We Speak as Liberators; Major, The New Black Poetry; Patterson, A Rock Against the Wind; Schulberg, From the Ashes; Simmons and Hutchinson, Black Culture.
 (Periodical): Antioch Review, Fall 1967.
INTERJECTIONS
 "Read the biographical chapter, "Johnie," in DON'T SHOOT--WE ARE YOUR CHILDREN! by J. Anthony Lukas (Random House, 1971)--this will give a fair idea of where I was at until 1970-71. Now I will only say that I want to make art my life, and my life a reflection of my art--so that art exists so far as I am concerned in the 'functional' (i.e., the liberating, emancipating--not 'protesting') world.... Art is a tool for social change."
BIOGRAPHY AND CRITICISM ON SCOTT
 Schulberg. "Black Phoenix," pp. 281-282.
 Scott, Johnie. "How It Is: My Home Is Watts." Harper (October 1966): 47-48; correction, January 1967.

SCOTT, Lewis E. Born 7 September 1947 in Cordele, Georgia. Education: Majoring in Fine Arts (English) at Trenton State College. Currently living in Bordentown, New Jersey. Career:

Johnie Scott (credit: Ah King)

Correction Officer, Yardville Youth Correction and Reception
Center. Continues to read his works for college and community
groups locally and out-of-state, and to write a bi-monthly col-
umn for The Black Journal (Trenton, New Jersey). Member:
Delaware Valley Poetry Society; International Black Writers' Conference, Inc.
POETRY
    A Collection of Works. Trenton, N. J.: Commercial Printing
        Co., 1973. (Includes Prose.)
    The Coming of Lewis E. Scott. Trenton, N. J.: Commercial
        Printing Co., 1972.
INTERJECTIONS
    "My writings exemplify man's search for his own identity.
Once man has some knowledge of who and what he is, he real-
izes that he is dealing with three elements: himself, time and
his understanding of the first two elements."

SCOTT, Lionel F.
    POETRY (Periodical): Umbra.

SCOTT, Nathan A., Jr. Born 24 April 1925 in Cleveland, Ohio.
    Education: A.B., University of Michigan, 1944; B.S., Union
    Theological Seminary, 1946; Ph.D., Columbia University, 1949;

Nathan Scott

Currently living in Chicago. Career: Presently Professor of Theology and Literature, and Chairman of the Theology and Literature, and Chairman of the Theology and Literature Field in the Divinity School of the University of Chicago; Professor in the Department of English of the University of Chicago; Priest of the Episcopal Church; Canon Theologian of the Cathedral of St. James, Chicago; Kent Fellow of the Society for Religion in Higher Education; Co-editor of The Journal of Religion. Member: Chicago Board of Directors, Society for Arts, Religion and Culture; Trustee, Seabury-Western Theological Seminary; Fellow, School of Letters, Indiana University; Society for Religion in

Higher Education (Kent Fellow); American Philosophical Association; Modern Language Association. Awards, Honors: Litt.D., Ripon College, 1965; L.H.D., Wittenberg University, 1965; D.D., Philadelphia Divinity School, 1967; S.T.D., General Theological Seminary, 1968; Litt.D., Saint Mary's College, Notre Dame, 1969.

CRITICISM

Albert Camus, 1962; New York: Hillary House, 1969†.

"Auden's Subject: The Human Clay, The Village of the Heart." In Scott, Four Ways of Modern Poetry.

"The Bias of Comedy and the Narrow Escape into Faith." In Comedy: Meaning and Form. Edited by Robert W. Corrigan. San Francisco: Chandler, 1965.

"The Broken Center: A Definition of the Crisis of Values in Modern Literature." In Symbolism in Religion and Literature. Edited by Rollo May. New York: George Braziler, 1960. Also in A Casebook on Existentialism. Edited by William V. Spanos. New York: Thomas Y. Crowell, 1966.

The Broken Center: Studies in the Theological Horizon of Modern Literature. New Haven: Yale University Press, 1966.

"Catholic Novelist's Dilemma." Christian Century, 1 August 1956, pp. 901-902. (A review article about Graham Green's The Quiet American.)

"The Collaboration of Vision in the Poetic Act: The Religious Dimension." Cross Currents (Spring 1957); also in The Christian Scholar (December 1957); Literature and Belief. Edited by M. H. Abrams. New York: Columbia University Press, 1958.

"The 'Conscience' of the New Literature." National Identity: Papers Delivered at The Commonwealth Literature Conference, University of Queensland, Brisbane, 9th-15th August 1968, pp. 251-283. Edited by K. L. Goodwin. London and Melbourne: Heineman. Also in The Shaken Realist: Essays in Modern Literature in Honor of Frederick J. Hoffman. Edited by Melvin J. Friedman and John B. Vickery. Baton Rouge, La.: Louisiana State University Press, 1970.

Craters of the Spirit: Studies in the Modern Novel: Washington, Cleveland: Corpus Books, 1968.

"The Dark and Haunted Tower of Richard Wright." Graduate Comment 7 (1964): 92-99; also in Hemenway, The Black Novelist, pp. 72-87; Gayle, Black Expression, pp. 296-310; Gibson, Five Black Writers.

"Dostoevski--Tragedian of the Modern Excursion into Unbelief." In Scott, The Tragic Vision and the Christian Faith, pp. 189-210.

Ernest Hemingway. Grand Rapids: Eerdmans, 1966†.

"The Example of George Orwell." The Christian Century, 20 July 1959, pp. 107-110.

"Flannery O'Connor's Testimony--the Pressure of Glory." In The Added Dimension: The Mind and Art of Flannery O'Connor. Edited by Melvin J. Stiedman and Lewis A. Lawson. New York: Fordham University Press, 1966.

"Graham Greene: Christian Tragedian." In Graham Greene: Some Critical Considerations. Edited by Robert O. Evans. Lexington: University of Kentucky Press, 1967.

"Judgment Marked by a Cellar: The American Negro Writer and the Dialect of Despair." University of Denver Quarterly 2 (Summer 1967): 5-35; also in Davis and Redding, Cavalcade, pp. 821-842; and in The Shapeless God: Essays on Modern Fiction. Edited by Harry J. Mooney, Jr., and Thomas F. Staley. Pittsburgh, Pa.: University of Pittsburgh Press, 1968.

"Kafka's Anguish." In Scott, Forms of Extremity in the Modern Novel.

"Literary Imagination and the Victorial Crisis of Faith: The Example of Thomas Hardy." Journal of Religion 40 (October 1960): 267-281.

"Man in Modern Literature." Criterion 4 (Autumn 1965): 419-422.

"Meaning of the Incarnation for Modern Literature." Christian Century 8 December 1958, pp. 173-175.

Modern Literature and the Religious Frontier. New York: Harper, 1958.

Nathanael West. Grand Rapids, Mich.: Eerdmans, 1971†.

Negative Capability: Studies in the New Literature and the Religious Situation. New Haven: Yale University Press, 1969*.

"New Heavens, New Earth--the Landscape of Contemporary Apocalypse." Journal of Religion 53 (January 1973): 1-35.

"No Point of Purchase." Kenyon Review 23 (Spring 1961): 337-343. (Review-Article of Richard Wright's Eight Men.)

"Poetry, Religion and the Modern Mind." Journal of Religion 33 (July 1953): 182-197.

"Prolegomenon to a Christian Poetic." Journal of Religion 35 (October 1955): 191-206.

Rehearsals of Discomposure: Alienation and Reconciliation in Modern Literature. New York: King's Crown Press of Columbia University Press, 1952; London: John Lehmann Ltd., 1952.

"Relation of Theology to Literary Criticism." Journal of Religion 33 (October 1953): 266-277.

"Religious Symbolism in Contemporary Literature." In Religious Symbolism. Edited by F. Ernest Johnson. New York: Harper, 1955.

Samuel Beckett, 1963; reprint ed. New York: Hillary House, 1965†.

"Search for Beliefs: Fiction of Richard Wright." University of Kansas City Review 23 (October-December 1956): 131-138.

"Society and Self in Recent American Literature." The Union Seminary Quarterly Review 18 (May 1963): 377-392; also in Emanuel and Gross, Dark Symphony, and in The Search for Identity: Essays on the American Character. Edited by Roger L. Shinn. New York: Harper, 1964.

"T. S. Eliot's The Cocktail Party." Religion in Life 20 (1951): 274-285.

"The Theatre of T. S. Eliot." In Scott, Man in the Modern Theatre.

Three American Moralists: Mailer, Bellow, and Trilling. new ed. Notre Dame, Ind.: University of Notre Dame, 1973*†.

The Unquiet Vision: Mirrors of Man in Existentialism. New York: World, 1969.

"Warren: The Man to Watch." Christian Century, 29 February 1956, pp. 272-273. (A Review-Article on Robert Penn Warren.)

The Wild Prayer of Longing: Poetry and the Sacred. New Haven: Yale University Press, 1971*.

EDITOR

Adversity and Grace: Studies in Recent American Literature. Chicago: University of Chicago Press, 1968*.

The Climate of Faith in Modern Literature. Naperville, Ill.: Allenson, 1964.

Forms of Extremity in the Modern Novel. Richmond: John Knox Press, 1965†.

Four Ways of Modern Poetry. Richmond: John Knox Press, 1965.

Man in the Modern Theatre. Richmond: John Knox Press, 1965†.

The Modern Vision of Death. Richmond: John Knox Press, 1967.

The New Orpheus: Essays Toward a Christian Poetic. New York: Sheed & Ward, 1964*†.

The Tragic Vision and the Christian Faith. New York: Association Press, 1957.

NON-FICTION

Reinhold Niebuhr. Minneapolis: University of Minnesota Press, 1963†.

(Anthologies): Conflicting Images of Man. Edited by William Nicholls. New York: Seabury Press, 1966; Man and the Movies. Edited by W. R. Robinson. Baton Rouge: Louisiana State University Press, 1967; The Scope of Grace. Edited by Philip Hefner. Philadelphia: Fortress Press, 1964; Religion and Contemporary Western Culture. Edited by Edward Cell. New York: Nashville: Abingdon Press, 1967; Holy Laughter. Edited by M. Conrad Hyers. New York: Seabury Press, 1969; Christian Faith and the Contemporary Arts. Edited by Finley Eversole. New York-Nashville: Abingdon Press, 1962.

(Periodicals): Centennial Review; Chicago Review; Christian Century; Christian Scholar; Christianity and Crisis; Cross Currents; Journal of Religious Thought; London Magazine; New Scholasticism; Religion in Life; Review of Metaphysics; Thought.

BIOGRAPHY AND CRITICISM ON SCOTT

Allchin, A. M. "Reflections on Nathan A. Scott, Jr.: After the Death of God." Theology 75 (July 1972): 361-368.

Noel, D. C. "Nathan Scott and the Nostalgic Fallacy: A
Close Reading of Theological Criticism." Journal of the
American Academy of Religion 38 (December 1970): 347-
366. (Scott's response to Noel, March 1971; Noel's reply,
June 1971.)

Schueter, P. "Post-Modern Temper of Recent Literature:
Nathan Scott on Art and Sacrament." Journal of Religion
53 (January 1973): 104-116.

Terry, R. F. "To Stay with the Question of Being: A Con-
sideration of Theological Elements in the Criticism of
Nathan A. Scott, Jr." Anglican Theological Review 55
(January 1973)˙ 3-27.

"Wasteland Observed." Newsweek, 25 July 1966, p. 84.

SCOTT, Raleigh Alonzo.
POETRY Scott's Poetic gems...; a Choice Collection of His
Best Poems, Including his Great Masterpiece and Prize
Winners: Echoes of Emancipation, The World Safe for
Democracy, Count the Negro In, Uncle Sam's Dream, How
Aunt Dinah "got by," etc., etc. Opelika, Ala.: J. B.
Ware, Agent, 1918.

SCOTT, Seret. Born 1 September 1947 in Washington, D.C. Education: studied at North Carolina College (one year) and at New
York University (three years). Currently living in New York
City. Career: An actress who began writing because the roles /
parts for young black women were not satisfactory. Included in
her acting performances are: a tour with the Free Southern
Theatre, Mississippi and Louisiana, 1969; an off-Broadway pre-
sentation of Baraka's Slave Ship, followed by a European tour of
the show, 1970; a tour of various shows in New York State Pri-
sons, 1971-72. Presently appearing with the Hartford State
Company in My Sister, My Sister. Member: Actors Equity As-
sociation; Screen Actors Guild.
DRAMA
  Funnytime, 1972.
  No, You Didn't, 1972.
  Wine and Cheese, 1970.
INTERJECTIONS
"I have always been concerned with becoming a woman...that
small space between growing up and growing old. Womanhood is
the subject of all my work."

SCOTT, Sharon. Born 29 April 1951 in Chicago.
POETRY
  (Anthologies): Brown, Lee and Ward, To Gwen with Love;
    Brooks, Jump Bad.
  (Periodicals): Black World, September 1970; September 1971.

SCOTT-HERON, Gil. Born 1 April 1949 in Chicago, Illinois. Education: B.A., Lincoln University (Pennsylvania), 1970; M.A.,
Johns Hopkins University, 1972. Career: Vocalist and pianist
presently collaborating with Brian R. Jackson, composer. Heads

an eight-piece band called "Midnight," which has performed at
the San Francisco and New York Expos and on television. His
albums (Small Talk at 125th and Lennox, Pieces of a Man, Tree
Will) are produced by Flying Dutchman Ltd. Member: Black
Academy of Arts and Letters. Awards, Honors: fellowship,
Johns Hopkins University.
NOVELS
    The Nigger Factory. New York: Dial, 1972*.
    The Vulture. Derby, Conn.: Belmont Tower, 1971†.
POETRY
    Small Talk at 125th and Lennox: A Collection of Black Po-
        ems. New World, 1970.
    REVIEW: The Vulture.
    Gant, L. Black World 2 (July 1971): 96-98.
    Welburn, Ron. Essence 1 (February 1971): 73.

SCREEN, Robert Martin.
    NOVEL We Can't Run Away from Here. New York: Vantage,
        1958.

SEBREE, Charles.
    DRAMA
        With W. Greer Johnson. Mrs. Patterson, 1954. In Hewes,
            Best Plays of 1954-1955.
    BIOGRAPHY AND CRITICISM ON SEBREE
        Butcher. The Negro in American Culture, p. 204.
        Mitchell. Black Drama, p. 167.

SEILER, Conrad.
    DRAMA
        Darker Brother.
        End of the World.
        Sweet Land, 1935.

SEJOUR, Victor (Juan Victor Séjour Marcon-Ferrand). Born 1817
    in New Orleans.[1] Died 1874 in Paris. Education: attended
Saint Barbe Academy in New Orleans; was sent to Paris in 1836
to complete his formal education. Career: at the age of 17 he
read his poems before La Société des Artisans, a social and
benevolent organization of Creoles. With two other young poets
(Armand Lanusse and Pierre Dalcour), he published the first
American Negro poetry anthology, Les Cenelles, in 1845.[2] In
Paris he became acquainted with Alexandre Dumas and Emile
Augier, and thus developed an interest in drama. His heroic
poem, "Le Retour de Napoleon," brought him to the attention
of the French public. His first play, Diegarias, produced in
1844, was followed by 20 other dramas. However, his melodramas eventually went out of vogue, and he died in a charity
ward of a Paris hospital.[3]
DRAMA
    Les Aventuriers. Paris: Michel-Lévy frères, 1860. (The
        Adventurers.)
    André Gérard. Paris: Michel-Lévy frères, 1857.

L'Argent du diable. Paris: Michel-Lévy frères, 1857. (The
  Devil's Coin.)
La Chute de Séjan. Paris: Michel-Lévy frères, 1849. (The
  Fall of Sejanus.)
Compère Guillery. Paris: Michel-Lévy frères, 1860. (Friend
  Guillery.)
Diégarias. Paris: C. Tresse, 1844.
With Théodore Barrière. Les Enfants de la Louvre. Paris:
  Michel-Lévy frères, 1856. (The Kids of the Louvre.)
Les Fils de Charles-Quint. Paris: Michel-Lévy frères, 1864.
  (Charles Quint's Sons.)
Le Fils de la nuit. Paris: Michel-Lévy frères, 1856. (Son
  of the Night.)
Les Grands Vassaux. Paris: Michel-Lévy frères, 1859.
La Madone des roses. Paris: Michel-Lévy frères, 1869.
  (Our Lady of the Roses.)
Le Marquis Caporal. Paris: Michel-Lévy frères, 1856. (The
  Corporal Is a Marquis.)
With Jules Brésil. Le Martyr du coeur. Paris: Michel-Lévy
  frères, 1858.
Les Massacres de la Syrie, 1856; Paris: J. Barbre, 1860.
  (Syrian Massacre.)
Les Mystères du Temple. Paris: Michel-Lévy frères, 1862.
  Also in La Renaissance (New Orleans), 21 September 1862.
Les Noces vénitiennes. Paris: Michel-Lévy frères, 1855.
  (The Venetian Wedding.)
Le Paletot brun. Paris: Michel-Lévy frères, 1860. (The
  Brown Coat.)
Richard III, 1852; Paris: Michel-Lévy frères, 1870. Also in
  La Semaine (New Orleans), 1853.
La Tireuse de cartes. Paris: Michel-Lévy frères, 1860.
  (The Fortune Teller.)
Le Vampire.
Les Volontaires de 1814. Paris: Michel-Lévy frères, 1862.
  (The 1814 Volunteers.)

POETRY
Le Retour de Napoleon. Paris: Dauvin et Fontaine, 1841.
  (The Return of Napoleon.) Reprinted in les Cenelles; in
  Desdunes, Nos Hommes et Notre Histoire; and in Robinson,
  Early Black American Poets.

BIOGRAPHY AND CRITICISM ON SEJOUR
Brisbane, Era Mae. Théâtre de Victor Séjour. Master's
  thesis, Hunter College, 1942.
Coleman, Edward Maceo. Creole Voices: Poems in French
  by Free Men of Color. Washington, D.C.: Associated,
  1945, pp. xxxii-xxxiii.
Daley, T. A. "Victor Séjour." Phylon 4 (First Quarter
  1943): 5-16.
Davidson, J. W. The Living Writers of the South; 1869.
  Ann Arbor: Finch.
Davis. The American Negro Reference Book, p. 852.
Désdunes, R. L. Nos Hommes et Notre Histoire. Montreal:
  Arbour & Dupont, 1911, pp. 38-43.

Dictionary of American Biography, vol. 16, pp. 565-566L.
Le Figaro, September 24 and 25. (Obituary)
Le Gaulois, 22 September 1874.
Gautier, Theophile. Histoire de l'art dramatique en France
    depuis vingt-cinq ans. Paris: Magnin, Blanchard, 1858-
    1859. 6 vols.
Robinson. Early Black American Poets, pp. 157-163.
Rousseve, Charles B. The Negro in Louisiana. New Or-
    leans: Xavier University Press, 1937.
Searight, Sarah. New Orleans. New York: Stein & Day,
    1973, p. 111.
Tinker, Ed. L. Les Écrits de Langue Française en Louisi-
    ane au XIXe siecle. Paris: H. Champion, 1932.
    [1]T. A. Daley, "Victor Séjour," Phylon 4 (First Quarter
    1943): 5. Daley verified this date in the archives of the
    St. Louis Cathedral in New Orleans.
    [2]John P. Davis, The American Negro Reference Book
    (Englewood Cliffs, N.J.: Prentice-Hall, 1966), p. 852.
    [3]Wilhelmina Robinson, Historical Negro Biographies
    (New York: Publishers, 1967), p. 123.

SELF, Charles.
    DRAMA
        The Smokers, 1968.
    SHORT STORY
        (Anthology): Watkins, Black Review No. 2.

SENNA, Carl. Born 13 April 1944 in Jennings, Louisiana. Educa-
    tion: A.B., Boston University; M.A., Columbia University
    Graduate School of the Arts. Currently living in Jamaica Plains,
    Massachusetts. Career: Writing, editing and teaching at the
    University of Massachusetts, specializing in literary criticism,
    philosophy and journalism.
    CRITICISM
        "Black Boy" Notes. Lincoln, Neb.: Cliff's Notes†.
    EDITOR
        The Fallacy of I.Q. New York: Third Press, 1973*.
        Parachute Shop Blues and Other Poems. New Orleans:
            Xavier University Press, 1972. (Poetry.)
    SHORT STORY
        (Anthology): Shuman, A Galaxy of Black Writing.

SEULL, Malchus M.
    POETRY
        The Black Christ and Verse. Los Angeles: By the Author,
        1957.

SEWARD, Walter Eddie. Born 1891.
    POETRY Negroes Call to the Colors, and Soldiers Camp-life
        Poems. Athens, Ga.: Knox Institute Press, 1919.

SEXTON, Wendell P. Born 28 March 1928 in Kansas City, Mis-
    souri. Education: B.S., Central State University, 1954; addi-

Sexton, W. P. (cont.) 660

tional work at Miami University (Guidance), University of Indiana (Elementary Education), University of Chicago (Black History), University of Missouri (Elementary Education), Texas Southern University (Law), and University of Denver (Black History). Currently living in Houston, Texas. Career: Educational therapist; teacher of mentally retarded and fifth and sixth grade children; administrator at Continental Printing; presently Community Consultant for Greta (3-4-5 Club), Channel 8, University of Houston. Member: Alpha Phi Omega, Parliamentarians, Toastmasters International, National Writers Club.

NON-FICTION
Why Should I Love the White Man. Denver, Colo.: 1970.

WORK IN PROGRESS
A children's book; a book of poetry; a Black history series.

INTERJECTIONS
"Psychologists say that children normally spend much of their time in playful fantasy; then our history books should relate to the whole child. We should appeal to his fantasy and still give him historical facts. This is what I am trying to do in my Black History books."

SHABAZZ, Turhan Abdul (Raymond O. Casey). Born 1937.
POETRY Black Poetry for Every Occasion. Pittsburgh: Oduduwa Productions, 1970?

SHABAZZ, Zakariah.
POETRY Portrait of a Poet. 2nd ed. San Francisco: By the Author, 629 Broderick St., 1970.

SHACKLEFORD, Otis M. Born 1871.
FICTION
Lillian Simmons, or, The Conflict of Sections. Kansas City, Mo.: Burton, 1915.
POETRY AND ESSAYS
Seeking the Best. Dedicated to the Negro Youth. Kansas City, Mo.: Franklin Hudson, 1909.
BIOGRAPHY AND CRITICISM ON SHACKLEFORD
Bone. The Negro Novel in America, p. 18.
Gloster. Negro Voices in American Fiction, pp. 92-93.
Jahn. Neo-African Literature, p. 184.

SHACKLEFORD, Theodore Henry. Born 1887.
POETRY
Mammy's Cracklin' Bread and Other Poems. Philadelphia: I. W. Klopp, 1916.
My Country and Other Poems. Philadelphia: I. W. Klopp, 1918. (Includes all the poems from Mammy's Cracklin' Bread.)
BIOGRAPHY AND CRITICISM ON SHACKLEFORD
Kerlin. Negro Poets and Their Poems, p. 244.

SHACKLEFORD, William H.
POETRY

Pearls in Prose and Poetry. Nashville, Tenn.: National Baptist Publishing Board, 1907.
Poems. Nashville, Tenn.: African Methodist Episcopal Sunday School Union Press, 1915.
NON-FICTION
Sunday School Problems. Nashville, Tenn.: A.M.E. Sunday School Union, 1925.

SHAED, Dorothy Lee Louise.
POETRY (Anthology): Murphy, Negro Voices.

SHANGO, Chaka Aku see COLEMAN, Horace W.

SHARP, Saundra. Born 21 December 1942 in Cleveland, Ohio. Education: B.S., Bowling Green State University, 1964. Currently living in New York City. Career: Singer and actress as well as poet. Played "Netta" in J. E. Franklin's Black Girl (off-Broadway), and "Prissy" in Gordon Park's film, The Learning Tree. Other appearances include Hello, Dolly!; Black Quartet; Five on the Black Hand Side; Poetry Now; To Be Young, Gifted and Black. She has performed with the Theatre for the Forgotten, the Al Fann Theatrical Ensemble, Poets and Performers, and radio plays for the New York City Board of Education's station, WNYE. She is currently being seen as "Cathy" on "Our Street," a dramatic television series produced in Baltimore, Maryland, for the PBS network; she also wrote a script for the show: "The Way It's Done," Summer 1973. As a pop singer she has done TV and night clubs in Mexico, the West Indies, Baltimore Playboy Club, and has appeared with the Jimmy Owens Quartet, the Sammy Benskin Trio, Danny Holgate, Jimmy Radcliffe, and the Bob Cunningham Trio. She heads Togetherness Productions, a theatrical company established to focus attention on young Black creative artists. She also reads the works of Black writers on albums produced by Scholastic magazine.
POETRY
From the Windows of My Mind. New York: Togetherness Productions, 1970.
In the Midst of Change. New York: Togetherness Productions, 1972.
(Anthologies): Abdul, The Magic of Black Poetry; Coombs, We Speak as Liberators; Patterson, A Rock Against the Wind.
(Periodicals): Black Creation, Fall 1971; Black World, September 1972.

SHAW, Doris Ann. Born 1943.
POETRY (Anthology): Shuman, A Galaxy of Black Writing.

SHAW, Edna.
POETRY (Anthology): Murphy, Negro Voices.

SHAW, Letty M. Born 1926.
NOVEL Angel Mink. New York: Comet, 1957.

SHAW, O'Wendell.
NOVEL
Greater Need Below. Columbus: Bi-Monthly Negro Book
Club, 1936.
SHORT STORY
(Periodical): Negro Story, May-June 1944.
BIOGRAPHY AND CRITICISM ON SHAW
Gloster. Negro Voices in American Fiction, pp. 92-93.

SHEBA see EARLEY, Jackie

SHELLEY, William
POETRY From This Dark House: Poems of a Black Teacher.
New York: Paulist Press, 1970.

SHEPARD, John H.
POETRY Poems to Remember Always. New York: Greenwich,
1965.

SHEPP, Archie. Born 24 May 1937 in Fort Lauderdale, Florida.
Career: See The Encyclopedia of Jazz in the Sixties by Leonard
Feather. New York: Horizon, 1966.
DRAMA
Junebug Graduates Tonight! 1967. In King and Milner, Black
Drama Anthology.
Revolution, 1968.
BIOGRAPHY AND CRITICISM ON SHEPP
Abramson. Negro Playwrights in the American Theatre, pp.
281-283.
Balliett, W. "Jazz." New Yorker, 6 April 1968, p. 147.
Nation, 27 March 1967, pp. 411-412.
"New Jazz." Newsweek, 12 December 1966, p. 104.
Patterson. "A Profile-Interview: Archie Shepp." Black
World 23 (November 1973): 58-61.
Walden, Daniel. "Black Music and Cultural Nationalism:
The Maturation of Archie Shepp." Negro American Lit-
erature Forum 5 (Winter 1971): 150-153.
Williams, M. "Problematic Mr. Shepp." Saturday Review
12 November 1966, p. 90.

SHERMAN, Jimmie.
DRAMA
A Ballad from Watts.
POETRY
(Anthology): Schulberg, From the Ashes.
BIOGRAPHY AND CRITICISM ON SHERMAN
Schulberg. "Black Phoenix," p. 280.
Sherman, Jimmie. "From the Ashes: A Personal Reaction
to the Revolt of Watts." Antioch Review, Fall 1967, pp.
285-293. (Includes poetry.)

SHIELDS, Ruth E.
   POETRY   When God's Fire Comes.   New York: Carlton, 1969.

SHINE, Ted.   Born 26 April 1936 in Baton Rouge, Louisiana.   Education: B.A., Howard University, 1953; M.A., State University of Iowa, 1958; Ph.D., University of California-Santa Barbara, 1973.   Currently living in Prairie View, Texas.   Career: Has taught and lectured at northern and southern universities; presently teaching at Prairie View A & M University.   His soap opera, "Our Street," was produced by the Maryland Center for Public Broadcasting for three years.
   DRAMA
      Bat's Out of Hell, 1955.
      The Coca-Cola Boys (one act), 1969.
      Cold Day in August (one act), 1950.
      Comeback After the Fire, 1969.
      Contribution (one act), 1969.   In Brasmer and Consolo, Black
         Drama.
      Dry August, 1952.
      Entourage Royale (musical), 1958.
      Epitaph for a Bluebird, 1958.
      Flora's Kisses (one act), 1969.
      Hamburgers at Hamburger Haven Are Impersonal (one act),
         1969.
      Idabel's Fortune (one act), 1969.
      Jeanne West (musical), 1968.
      Miss Victoria (one act), 1965.
      Morning, Noon and Night, 1964.   In Reardon and Pawley,
         The Black Teacher and the Dramatic Arts.
      Plantation (one act), 1970.
      Pontiac (one act), 1967.
      A Rat's Revolt, 1959.
      Revolution, 1968.
      Sho' Is Hot in the Cotton Patch (one act), 1951.   In Encore
         Magazine 12 (1967):   Produced by the Negro Ensemble
         Company under the title Miss Weaver, 1968.
      Shoes (one act), 1969.   In Encore Magazine 12 (1969); scene
         in Childress, Black Scenes.
      Waiting Room (one act), 1969.
   EDITOR
      With James V. Hatch.   Black Theater, U.S.A.: Forty-Five
         Plays by Black Americans.   Free Press, 1974*.
   INTERJECTIONS
      "Although my area of specialization is playwriting I feel that I am foremost a teacher.   As a Texan I feel that I have an obligation--particularly to the Black youth of this State--to seek out, encourage, and develop that talent which will one day make us all proud."

SHIPMAN, Willie B.
   DRAMA   Pepper, 1972.

SHIPP, J. A.   Career: Actor as well as playwright.
   DRAMA
      With Will Marian Cook. The Policy Players, 1900.
      With Alex Rogers and Bert Williams. Mr. Lode of Koal,
         1909.
      With Alex Rogers and Paul Laurence Dunbar. In Dahomey,
         1902.
      With Alex Rogers. Abyssinia, 1906; Bandanna Land, 1908;
         Senegamian Carnival, 1898.

SHOCKLEY, Ann Allen. Born in Louisville, Kentucky. Career:
   See Shockley and Chandler, Living Black American Authors, pp.
   144-145.
   AUTOBIOGRAPHY
      "A Soul Cry for Reading." The Black Librarian in America.
         Edited by E. J. Josey. Metuchen, N.J.: Scarecrow,
         1970, pp. 225-233.
   CRITICISM
      "Pauline Elizabeth Hopkins: A Biographical Excursion Into
         Obscurity." Phylon 33 (Spring 1972): 22-26.
   EDITOR
      With Sue Chandler. Living Black American Authors: A Bio-
         graphical Dictionary. New York and London: Bowker,
         1973*.
   NOVEL
      Loving Her. Indianapolis: Bobbs-Merrill, 1974*.
   SHORT STORIES
      (Periodicals): Negro Digest, July 1950; October 1962; May
         1964; December 1967; July 1969; January, November 1971;
         Black World, March 1974.

SHOEMAN, Charles H.
   POETRY A Dream and Other Poems. Ann Arbor, Mich.:
      n.p., 1895. (Schomburg Collection.)

SHORE, Herbert L.
   SHORT STORY (Periodical): Phylon 22 (Fourth Quarter 1961).

SHORES, Minnie T.
   NOVELS
      Americans in America. Boston: Christopher, 1966.
      Publicans and Sinners. New York: Comet, 1960.

SHORTER, Lynn. Born 1946.
   POETRY
      (Anthology): Hayden, Burrows and Lapides, Afro-American
         Literature.
      (Periodical): Journal of Black Poetry.

SHUAYB, Omar A. Born 6 January 1940 in McCrory, Arkansas.
   Education: Attended Kennedy-King and Chicago State University.
   Currently living in Chicago. Presently an insurance broker and
   student. Member: OBAC Writers' Workshop; African-Ameri-

can History Roundtable; Treasurer, Masjid of Islam.
POETRY
(Periodical): Black World, April 1973.

SILVERA, Edward S. Born 1906 in Jacksonville, Florida. Died
1937. Education: Studied at Lincoln University and Howard University. Career: Was a member of the varsity basketball
squad at Lincoln and the Colored Junior Tennis Champion of
New Jersey in 1924; studied medicine at Howard University and
practiced in New York up to the time of his death. His poems
appeared in various magazines, including The Crisis and Opportunity.[1]
POETRY
(Anthologies): Adams, Conn and Slepian, Afro-American Literature: Poetry; Cullen, Caroling Dusk; Hughes and Bontemps, The Poetry of the Negro: 1746-1970; Lincoln University Poets; Weisman and Wright, Black Poetry for All
Americans.
(Periodicals): Crisis, 1926; 1927; 1928; 1929; 1931.
BIOGRAPHY AND CRITICISM ON SILVERA
Kerlin. Negro Poets and Their Poems, pp. 210-211.
[1]Robert Kerlin, Negro Poets and Their Poems, (Washington, D.C.: Associated, 1923, 1935), p. 210.

SILVERA, Frank.
CRITICISM
"Toward a Theatre of Understanding." Negro Digest 18
(April 1969): 33-35.
DRAMA
Unto the Least, 1938.
BIOGRAPHY AND CRITICISM ON SILVERA
Hughes and Meltzer. Black Magic, pp. 203, 214, 227, 236,
295.

SIMMONS, Dan. Born 21 August 1923 in Blackstone, Virginia.
Education: B.A., Howard University, 1950; M.A., Howard Uni-
versity, 1951; doctoral study for Ph.D., New York University.
Currently living in St. Albans, New York. Career: Adjunct
Assistant Professor at Pace University, teaching Black History
and Black Literature; District Supervisor, West Side High School,
New York City.
POETRY
(Anthology): Coombs, We Speak as Liberators.
(Periodicals): Negro Digest, September-October, 1968; Sep-
tember 1969. Also published in the N.A.A.C.P. Journal,
Moonlight Review, Jet, Pace, Amsterdam News.
INTERJECTIONS
"I feel that literature is a vital form of communication. It
describes the aspirations, the frustration and anger of a people
in a given era. It also points out joy, though it be brief. For
the Black man, and the Black poet, his life seldom reflects joy
without reservation."

SIMMONS, Gerald L., Jr.   Born 1944 in Memphis, Tennessee.
POETRY
 Ex-Posures in Black.   Detroit: Ulozi Photographics, 1968.
 (Anthology): Major, The New Black Poetry.

SIMMONS, Herbert Alfred.   Born 29 March 1930 in St. Louis, Mis-
 souri.   Career: See Contemporary Authors, 3.
NOVELS
 Corner Boy.   Boston: Houghton Mifflin, 1957.
 Man Walking on Egg Shells.   Boston: Houghton Mifflin, 1962.
    Excerpt in Negro Digest, January 1962.
POETRY
 (Anthology): Major, The New Black Poetry.
REVIEW: Corner Boy.
 Jet, 25 February 1960, pp. 4-5.

SIMMONS, James W.   Born 15 September 1919 in Greenwood, Mississippi.   Education: B.S., Jackson State College, 1946; M.Ed.,
 Atlanta University, 1947; M.A., New York University, 1949;
 Professional Diploma, Columbia University, 1952; Doctorate from
 the College of Metaphysics, 1953; Ed.D., Laurence University,
 1973.   Currently living in Clarksdale, Mississippi.   Career: A
 rural elementary teacher, Washington County, Greenville, Mississippi, 1939-41.   After an army career, he became a social
 worker in the Department of Welfare, Brooklyn, 1952-54.   Began college teaching in the Department of Education and Psychology, Mississippi Valley State College, 1954; also served as Director and Supervisor of the MVSC Testing Center, 1955-70; Visiting Professor of Psychology and Dean of the Community College
 Adult Program, Saints Junior College, Lexington, Miss., 1969-
 72.   Presently, Professor of Education and Psychology, Mississippi Valley State College.   Member: Jackson State College
 Alumni Association; Steward and Choir Conductor at Friendship
 A.M.E. Church (Clarksdale); State Musician for the M W Stringer Grand Lodge; 32° Mason; National Mental Hygiene Association (State Chapter).   Awards, Honors: Military Essay Prize,
 1944; National Science Foundation Grant (Beloit College), 1965;
 selected as one of the top ten Black Americans Past and Pres-
 ent (WABG-TV Channel 6 presentation), 1972; D.Litt., Eastern
 Nebraska Christian College (for the book, Poetical and Philosoph-
 ical Expressions), 1973.   Fellow, Intercontinental Biographical
 Association (England).
POETRY
 Poetical and Philosophical Expressions.   New York: Exposi-
    tion, 1971.
 Thoughts from My Mind.   New York: Exposition, 1962.
UNPUBLISHED WORK
 "Relationship of Esteem Values with Intelligent Quotient and
    and Grade Point Averages."   (Doctoral Dissertation, Laur-
    ence University, 1973).
BIOGRAPHIES ON SIMMONS
 American Association of Choral Conductors, 1965.
 Dictionary of International Biography, 1973.

James W. Simmons

Mississippi Authors, 1963.
Outstanding Educators of America, 1970, 1972.
Personalities of the South, 1971, 1973.
Two Thousand Men of Achievement, 1972.
Who's Who in American Education, 1962.
INTERJECTIONS
"Hardly a man has ever lived who at some time or another,
failed to ask himself this question: 'What am I here for?'
Though philosophical in nature, it may take a volume for some
people and a few lines for others to answer this question. It
would include a gamut from the pipe fitter to the philosopher.

Since we are dealing with the works of arts, I shall limit this discourse to its segments. In essence, it would read like this: Maybe I could paint a picture that would glow like the sunset on the San Francisco Bay Bridge. Maybe I could sing like a mockingbird until the willows bow their heads and weep. Perhaps I could write a poem or line that will find its way into the pages of time. So when the golden leaves are turned, I could speak to generations yet unborn and say to them 'live on' and make your contribution, so that you may reap the eternal joys that make a life worth living."

SIMMONS, Judy Dothard. Born 28 August 1944 in Westerly, Rhode Island. Education: B.A., University of California at Sacramento, 1970. Currently living in New York City. Career: A pianist, singer and songwriter, but primarily a poet who is currently a staff supervisor for American Telephone and Telegraph Company. Played leading roles under the direction of Imamu Amiri Baraka when he was Visiting Professor at the University of California, San Francisco. Her poetry can be heard on tapes: "Judith's Blues" (Broadside) and "Black Box," edited by Etheridge Knight (Washington, D.C.). Awards, Honors: Honorable Mention (6th prize), Benet Narrative Poem Contest, Poet Lore Quarterly, for "Generations," 1971. Superior Achievement Award, National Council of Teachers of English, 1959.
POETRY
    Judith's Blues. Detroit: Broadside, 1973†.
    (Anthologies): Henderson, Understanding the New Black Poetry; Watkins, Black Review No. 2.
WORK IN PROGRESS
    Book of poetry forthcoming from Emerson Hall Publishers.
INTERJECTIONS
    "Art and life are not the same--a distinction Americans have not learned yet, e.g. Hollywood love concepts, revolutionary rhetoric art which neither feeds nor frees. But art is necessary to the spirit of man, and an artist has a rather awesome responsibility--to represent or transmute life experiences in a way which will not mislead, but, instead will clarify and encourage others to live more fully. Also, an artist must have a bit of courage--she has to live with the record of her errors and evolution in public."

SIMPKINS, Edward.
    SHORT STORY
       (Periodical): Negro History Bulletin, October 1962.
    BIOGRAPHY ON SIMPKINS
       Negro History Bulletin 26 (October 1962): 72.

SIMPKINS, Thomas V. Born 28 November 1898 in Weburn, Massachusetts. Education: Forced to terminate premedical studies at the time of his father's death; has always been a prolific reader. Currently living in Bronx, New York. Career: Has served as a blacksmith apprentice, a worker in explosive manufacture, a professional boxer, a postal clerk, a tailor. Pres-

Thomas V. Simpkins (credit: Hearns Photo Studio)

ently retired, devoting full time to reading and writing. Member: a Freemason.
POETRY
    ABC's of Birds and Bees. New York: Vantage, 1965.
    Rhyme and Reason. Boston: Christopher, 1949.
    Rhymes of the Ring and Potpourri. Brooklyn: Pageant-Poseidan, 1972.

SIMPSON, Joshua McCarter.
    POETRY The Emancipation Car. Zanesville, Ohio: Sullivan and Brown, 1874.

SIMS, Cleveland.
    POETRY (Anthology): Troupe, Watts Poets.

SIMS, Lefty.
    POETRY (Anthology): Jones and Neal, Black Fire.

SIMS, Lillian.
    POETRY Collection of Poems. Chicago: By the Author, 1971.

SIRRAH, Leumas.
    POETRY (Anthologies): Schulberg, From the Ashes; Troupe, Watts Poets.

SISSLE, Noble. <u>Born</u> 1889.
DRAMA
With Lew Peyton. <u>Chocolate Dandies</u>, 1924 (musical).
With Eubie Black, Aubrey Lyles and Flournay Miller. <u>Shuf-</u>
<u>fle Along of 1933</u>, 1932 (musical).
BIOGRAPHY AND CRITICISM ON SISSLE
Hughes and Meltzer. <u>Black Magic</u>, pp. 69, 71, 88, 97. 99,
101.
Kimball, Robert and William Bolcom. <u>Reminiscing with</u>
<u>Sissle and Blake</u>. New York: Viking, 1973.
Mitchell. <u>Black Drama</u>, 76-77, 83.

SKEETER, Sharyn Jeanne. <u>Born</u> 12 July 1945 in New York City.
<u>Education</u>: B.A., City College of New York, 1966; additional
study at the French Institute, 1967, and at C.C.N.Y., 1966-68,
1973. <u>Currently living in</u> New York City. <u>Career</u>: Teacher,
New York Public Schools, 1966-68. Editorial Assistant in the
Fiction and Poetry Department, <u>Mademoiselle</u>, 1969. Poetry,
Fiction and Book Review Editor, <u>Essence</u>, 1970 to present.
Has travelled in Europe, the Caribbean and Canada. <u>Member</u>:
American Society of Magazine Editors; Authors League; Fellow,
International Poetry Society.
CRITICISM
"Black Women Novelists." In Welburn, <u>Dues.</u>
"Black Women Writers: Levels of Identity." <u>Essence</u>, May
1973.
"Reprints of Afro-American Classics." <u>Essence</u>, May 1972.
POETRY
(Periodicals): <u>Black Creation,</u> Spring 1971; <u>Essence,</u> July
1970; February 1971; <u>Works,</u> Winter 1972; <u>The Thirteenth</u>
<u>Moon,</u> Summer 1973.
REVIEWS
Published in <u>Essence</u>, <u>Black Creation</u> and <u>Review</u>.

SKINNER, Theodosia B.
SHORT STORIES
<u>Ice Cream from Heaven.</u> New York: Vantage, 1962.
REVIEW
Heidkamp, Mary Jean. <u>Community</u> 23 (December 1963): 12.

SLAY, Johnnie Bea.
SHORT STORY (Anthology): Shuman, <u>A Galaxy of Black Writ-</u>
<u>ing.</u>

SLIM, Iceberg see BECK, Robert

SMALLWOOD, Will.
POETRY (Anthology): Murphy, <u>Ebony Rhythm</u>.

SMITH, Abram G. F. <u>Born</u> 1916; <u>Died</u> 1935. <u>Education</u>: Attended
Temple University. I
POETRY
(Anthology): Murphy, <u>Negro Voices</u>.

[1]Beatrice Murphy, Negro Voices (New York: Henry Harrison, 1938), p. 141.

SMITH, Arthur Lee. Born 1942.
    POETRY
        The Break of Dawn. Philadelphia: Dorrance, 1964.
    EDITOR
        Language, Communication, and Rhetoric in Black America.
            New York: Harper & Row, 1972†.
        With Andrea Rich. Rhetoric of Revolution. Moore, n. d. *
        With Stephen Robb. The Voice of Black Rhetoric: Selections.
            Rockleigh, N.J.: Allyn & Bacon, 1971†.

SMITH, Barry.
    POETRY (Anthology): Black Poets Write On!

SMITH, Daniel.
    A Walk in the City. Cleveland: World, 1972.

SMITH, David.
    POETRY Lawd Spoke to Me from a Red Sky. n.p., 196?

SMITH, Demon.
    DRAMA Private Huckleberry, 1972.

SMITH, Djeniba.
    DRAMA Please Reply Soon, 1971.

SMITH, Frances Laurence.
    POETRY Wishful Thinking: Poems. 2nd ed. Baltimore: Garland Press, 1953.

SMITH, George Lawson.
    Transfer. New York: Vantage, 1970.

SMITH, Ivory H.
    POETRY With Isabelle Tolbert. Life Lines: a Collection of
        Inspiring Poetry and Prose. Charlotte, N.C.: n.p., 1952.

SMITH, J. Augustus.
    DRAMA
        Just Ten Days, Louisiana, 1933.
        With Ben Morell. Turpentine, 1936.
    BIOGRAPHY ON SMITH
        Mitchell. Black Drama, p. 102.

SMITH, J. Pauline.
    POETRY "Exceeding Riches" and Other Verse. Detroit: n. p.,
        1922.

SMITH, James Edgar.
    POETRY (Anthology): Murphy, Ebony Rhythm.

SMITH, Jean Wheeler. Born 1942 in Detroit, Michigan.
CRITICISM
"Black Writer's Views on Literary Lions and Values." Negro Digest 17 (January 1968): 20.
SHORT STORIES
(Anthology): Jones and Neal, Black Fire.
(Periodicals): Black World, June 1971; Negro Digest, January, November 1967; June 1968.

SMITH, Joe (pseud.)
SCIENCE FICTION Dagmar of Green Hills. New York: Pageant, 1957.

SMITH, John Caswell. Born 14 March 1907 in Montclair, New Jersey.
NON-FICTION
(Periodical): Opportunity, June 1937; March 1941.
SHORT STORIES
(Anthologies): Brickel, Prize Stories of 1947: The O'Henry Awards; Clarke, American Negro Short Stories.
BIOGRAPHY ON SMITH
Opportunity 15 (September 1937): 283; 25 (Summer 1947): 157.

SMITH, Jules Wynn.
POETRY (Anthology): Murphy, Ebony Rhythm.

SMITH, Laura E.
POETRY (Anthology): Murphy, Negro Voices.

SMITH, Linwood.
POETRY (Anthology): Brown, Lee and Ward, To Gwen with Love.

SMITH, Lucy.
POETRY
With Sarah Wright. Give Me a Child. Philadelphia: Kraft, 1955.
No Middle Ground: A Collection of Poems. Philadelphia: Philadelphia Council of the Arts, Sciences and Professions, 1952.
(Anthologies): Hughes, New Negro Poets: U.S.A.; Hughes and Bontemps, The Poetry of the Negro: 1746-1970; Singh and Fellowes, Black Literature in America.

SMITH, Mary Carter.
POETRY (Anthology): Hughes and Bontemps, The Poetry of the Negro: 1746-1970.

SMITH, Maurice.
Who Cares. New York: Carlton, 1968.

SMITH, Nannie M. (Nannie M. Travis). Born 20 November 1893 in Lawrenceville, Virginia. Education: B.A., Howard Univer-

sity, 1931; M.A., Columbia University, 1938; additional graduate work at the University of Chicago and Pennsylvania State
University. Currently living in Fayetteville, North Carolina.
Career: Elementary school teacher and superintendent for nine
years in Brunswick Co., Virginia, in Norfolk, Virginia, and in
Rocky Mount, North Carolina. Instructor of English, Fayetteville State Teacher College (now Fayetteville State University),
1932-58. Member: N.A.A.C.P.; National Geographic Society;
American Association of Retired Persons; Zeta Phi Beta Sorority.
POETRY
    (Anthology): Murphy, Ebony Rhythm.
    (Periodicals): Opportunity, September 1940; also published in
        the Norfolk Journal and Guide; Afro-American; Christian
        Leader; North Carolina Teacher's Record.

SMITH, Otis. Born 29 August 1939 in Alabama. Education: attended Daniel Payne Junior College, Los Angeles City College,
workshops and creative writing classes, as well as studying
many years on his own. Career: Presently a creative writing
instructor at the Watts Writers Workshop; a member of the
Watts Prophets poetry group; a lecturer at major colleges in
California; a songwriter and a composer of verses for greeting
cards. Member: American Federation of Television and Radio
Artists; Screen Writers Guild of America (West). Awards, Honors: Poetry album, Rappin Black in a White World nominated
for the N.A.A.C.P. image of the year award; co-authored
and starred in the T.V. documentary, Victory Will Be My Moan,
nominated for Emmy Award.
POETRY
    The Rising Sons--Wisdom and Knowledge. Los Angeles, Ca.:
        Morgan Enterprises, 1973.
UNPUBLISHED WORK
    A book of proverbs; a book of form poems (shipp-o-letts); a
        book of poetry about life and the Black Experience.
WORK IN PROGRESS
    Non-fiction: a textbook about the basic fundamentals of crea-
        tive writing from a Black perspective; a book for children
        on how to care for teeth.
INTERJECTIONS
    "Each effort won't be a great effort
        but each effort should be your best
    In order to gain the most from your ability
        and hopefully attain success
            love, peace and happiness."

SMITH, Welton. Born 1940 in Houston, Texas.
DRAMA
    The Roach Riders.
POETRY
    Penetration. San Francisco: Journal of Black Poetry Press,
        1972.
    (Anthologies): Adoff, The Poetry of Black America; Hughes

and Bontemps, The Poetry of the Negro, 1746-1970; Jones
and Neal, Black Fire; King, Blackspirits; Major, The New
Black Poetry; Randall, The Black Poets.
(Periodicals): Journal of Black Poetry, 1969; 1970.
BIOGRAPHY AND CRITICISM ON SMITH
"Interview." Journal of Black Poetry, Fall-Winter 1971, p.
95.
Kent. "Struggle for the Image," p. 313.

SMITH, William Gardner.   Born 1926 in Philadelphia, Pennsylvania.
CRITICISM BY SMITH
"The Negro Writer: Pitfalls and Compensations." Phylon
(1950): 297-303.   Also in Bigsby, The Black American
Writer, vol. 1; Gayle, Black Expressions, pp. 288-295;
Hemenway, The Black Novelist, pp. 196-204.
NON-FICTION
Return to Black America.   Englewood Cliffs, N.J.: Prentice-
Hall, 1970.
(Periodical): Phylon, Second Quarter 1950.
NOVELS
Anger at Innocence. New York: Farrar, Straus, 1950.
The Last of the Conquerors.   New York: Farrar, Straus,
1948; excerpt in Negro Digest, November 1948.
South Street. New York: Farrar, 1954.
The Stone Face. New York: Farrar, Straus, 1963.
BIOGRAPHY AND CRITICISM ON SMITH
Bigsby. "From Protest to Paradox: The Black Writer at
Mid-Century," pp. 217-240.
Bone. The Negro Novel in America, pp. 157, 159, 176-178
Bryant, Jerry H. "Individuality and Fraternity: The Novels
of William Gardner Smith." Studies in Black Literature
3 (Summer 1972): 1-8.
Butcher. The Negro in American Culture, p. 145.
Schatt, Stanley. "You Must Go Home Again: Today's Afro-
American Expatriate Writers." Negro American Litera-
ture Forum 7 (Fall 1973): 80-82.

SMITHERMAN, Geneva. Born 10 December 1940 in Brownsville,
Tennessee. Education: B.A. (English), Wayne State University,
1960; M.A. (English), Wayne State University, 1962; Ph.D.,
University of Michigan, 1969. Currently living in Cambridge,
Massachusetts. Career: Specializes in Black English and American Social Dialects with focus on applying the theoretical find-
ings of this field to the education of Blacks and other minorities.   Taught Afro-American Literature at Wayne State University; was also involved in training and preparation of teachers
in the College of Education at Wayne State.   Has presented papers and has served as panelist and consultant on various aspects of Black English at professional conferences and at numerous universities. Wayne State representative to Community Culture Project, sponsored by New Detroit and Wayne State, 1968.
Currently teaching in the Afro-American Studies Department at
Harvard University. Member: National Council of Teachers of

English Commission on the English Curriculum; Member of the
Executive Committee of the Conference on College Composition
and Communication, and the Conference's Task Force on Lan-
guage and Dialects; Chairman of the Black Literature Section,
Midwest Modern Language Association, 1972; invited to serve as
Contributing Editor (with regular column) for English Journal,
September 1973 to June 1974. Awards, Honors: University of
Michigan Pre-Doctoral Fellowship, 1968.

CRITICISM

"Ed Bullins/Stage One: Everybody Wants to Know Why I
    Sing the Blues." Black World 23 (April 1974): 4-13.
"The Power of the Rap: The Black Idiom and the New Black
    Poetry." Twentieth Century Literature 19 (October 1973):
    259-274.

EDITOR

Down Nigger Paved Streets by William A. Thigpen. Detroit:
    Broadside, 1972†.

NON-FICTION

"After Bi-Dialectalism--What?" National Council of Teachers
    of English (Cassette Recording Series, February 1973).
"The Black Idiom and White Institutions." Negro American
    Literature Forum 5 (Fall 1971): 88-91.
The Black Idiom: Soul and Style. New York: Harper & Row,
    forthcoming.
"The Black Idiom: What the English Curriculum Bees Need-
    in," Arizona English Bulletin, April 1973.
"Black Power Is Black Language." In Simmons and Hutchin-
    son, Black Culture.
"Class Anxiety, Racism, and the American Consciousness Re-
    flected in Language." In Williams, Black English.
"English Teacher, Why You Be Doing the Things You Don't
    Do?" English Journal 61 (January 1972): 59-65.
" 'God Don't Never Change': Black English from a Black
    Perspective." College English, March 1973.
"The Legitimacy of the Black Idiom." National Council of
    Teachers of English (Cassette Recording Series, March
    1972.)
"Soul 'n Style." English Journal 63 (February 1974): 16-17;
    (March 1974): 14-15.
"White English in Blackface or, Who Do I Be?" Black Schol-
    ar 4 (May-June 1973): 32-39.

INTERJECTIONS

"Art is for the people. While the artist certainly imposes
his individual vision upon his materials, only the people can
validate the artistic integrity and authenticity of his work. Un-
fortunately, traditional Western art has been devoted to the pursuit of the complex and obscure which only that artist and a lim-
ited set of 'elite' individuals can understand. Fortunately, the
contemporary Black artist is salvaging this dying tradition by
taking art back where it belongs--to the people."

SMYTHWICK, Charles A., Jr.
NOVEL
False Measure: A Satirical Novel of the Lives and Objectives
of Upper Middle-Class Negroes. New York: William-Frederick, 1954.

SNAVE, Eimas.
DRAMA
Little Dodo.
The Park on 14th Street.
Skin Deep.

SNEAD, Edward. Born 9 August 1910 in Cambridge, Maryland.
Education: B.A., Fisk University, 1941; M.A., Fisk University, 1952; Diplome d'Etudes, the Sorbonne (Paris), 1953; Cer-
tificat de Scolarité, L'Université de Caen (France), 1953; additional work toward Ed.D., University of Pennsylvania. Currently living in Grambling, Louisiana. Career: Taught foreign languages and graduate education; served as Dean of Men, Butler
College, 1952. Taught French and Spanish, Alabama State College, 1953-62. Taught French, Spanish and German, Grambling
College, 1963 to present. Recently prepared a research project,
entitled "A Study of the Status of Modern Foreign Language Programs in the Predominantly Negro High Schools of Louisiana,"
for use by the Louisiana State Department of Education. Has
composed numerous musical compositions, some with the direct
purpose of improving international relations between the U.S.
and Ecuador, Cuba, and Germany. Before entering the teaching
profession, he played the jazz circuit with such big names as
Jimmie Lunchford, Cootie Williams, Billie Holiday, Wilbur de
Paris, Snub Mosely, the Carolina Cottonpickers, Tab Smith, etc.
Several of his compositions have been recorded. He presently
plays bass in jazz bands, as well as devoting considerable time
serving on drug awareness programs, lecturing, and presenting
original poetry. Member: American Association of Teachers
of German; Southeastern Conference on Latin American Studies;
Modern Language Association; New Jersey Academy of Sciences;
Broadcast Music, Incorporated; New Orleans Jazz Club; American Federation of Musicians. Was elected to serve on the Editorial Board of the Revue de Louisiane (a publication of the Council for the Development of French in Louisiana), 1971. Has also served on the National Screening Committee for the Institute
of International Education. Awards, Honors: Fulbright Fellowship Grant for Study in France, 1953; 1st Prize Award, musical
division of the Deep South Writers Conference, for "Swamp
Girl."
NON-FICTION
(Periodicals): American-German Review, 1965; Americas,
June 1962; Foreign Language Quarterly (Alabama State College), 1956; 1957; 1958; 1959; Southeastern Latin American-
ist, December 1970; September 1971.
POETRY
(Anthology): Ingersoll and Jopp, An Anthology of Eastern

Ed Snead

   Shore Literature (forthcoming from Tidewater Publishers).
UNPUBLISHED WORK
   Poetry: Negro-oriented poems, Harlem poems, folk poems,
      anti-narcotic poems, dialect poems, existentialistic poems.
WORK IN PROGRESS
   Poetry: "Harlem Estate and Other Poems."

SNELLINGS, Roland see TOURE, Askia Muhammed

SOLOMON, Phillip. Born 1954 in Brooklyn.
   POETRY (Anthologies): Jordan, Soulscript; Jordan and Bush,
      The Voice of the Children.

SOUTHERLAND, Ellease.
   POETRY (Periodicals): Black World, May 1972; Journal of
      Black Poetry, Winter-Spring 1970; Fall-Winter 1971.

SPADY, James
POETRY (Anthology): Black Poets Write On.

SPEARMAN, Aurelia L. P. Childs.
POETRY What Christmas Means to Us. New York: Carlton, 1964.

SPELLMAN, A. B. Born August 1935 in Elizabeth City, North Carolina.
POETRY
The Beautiful Days. New York: Poets Press, 1965.
(Anthologies): Adoff, The Poetry of Black America; Bell, Afro-American Poetry; Henderson, Understanding the New Black Poetry; Hollo, Negro Verse; Hughes, New Negro Poets: USA; Jones and Neal, Black Fire; Major, The New Black Poetry; Miller, Dices and Black Bones; Pool, Beyond the Blues; Randall, The Black Poets.
NON-FICTION
Black Music: Four Lives. Schocken, 1970†. (Original title, Four Lives in the Bepop Business, 1966.)
(Anthology): Jones and Neal, Black Fire.
(Periodicals): Ebony, August 1969; Negro Digest, November 1969; also published in Nation, Jazz, and Downbeat.

SPENCE, Eulalie
DRAMA
Fool's Errand. New York: Samuel French, 1927.
Foreign Mail. New York: Samuel French, 1927.
Help Wanted. In Saturday Evening Quill (Boston), April 1929.
Her (one act), 1927.
The Hunch (one act), 1927.
The Starter. In Locke and Gregory, Plays of Negro Life.
Undertone (one act), In Carolina Magazine 49 (April 1929).
BIOGRAPHY AND CRITICISM ON SPENCE
Mitchell. Black Drama, p. 88.

SPENCE, Raymond.
NOVEL Nothing Black But a Cadillac. New York: Putnam, 1969.

SPENCE, Tomas. Born in Jamaica.
NOVEL With Eric Heath. Martin Larwin. New York: Pageant, 1954.

SPENCER, Anne. Born 6 February 1882 in Southern Virginia. Education: Graduated from the secondary division of the Virginia Seminary and College (Lynchburg), 1899. Career: Began her career as a librarian at Dunbar High School in Lynchburg, in the early twenties, where she worked for 20 years. She also began publishing poetry in the early twenties.
POETRY
(Anthologies): Barksdale and Kinnamon, Black Writers of America; Bontemps, American Negro Poetry; Brown, Davis,

and Lee, Negro Caravan; Cullen, Caroling Dusk; Davis and
Redding, Cavalcade; Eleazer, Singers in the Dawn; Ellman
and O'Clair, Norton Anthology of Modern Poetry; Hayden,
Kaleidoscope; Hughes and Bontemps, The Poetry of the Ne-
gro: 1746-1970; Johnson, Book of American Negro Poetry;
Patterson, An Introduction to Black Literature in America
from 1746 to the Present; Untermeyer, American Poetry
Since 1900.
(Periodicals): Crisis, 1920; 1923; 1929; November 1970; Op-
portunity, December 1927; Palms, October 1926; Survey
Graphic, March 1925.
BIOGRAPHY AND CRITICISM ON SPENCER
Brown, Sterling. "Contemporary Negro Poetry, 1914-1936."
Negro Poetry and Drama, pp. 65-66. Also in Watkins,
Anthology of American Negro Literature, pp. 248-249.
Kerlin. Negro Poets and Their Poems, pp. 156-158.
INTERJECTIONS
"Mother Nature, February, forty-five years ago forced me on
the stage that I, in turn might assume the role of a lonely child,
happy wife, perplexed mother--and so far, a twice resentful
grandmother. I have no academic honors, nor lodge regalia. I
am a Christian by intention, a Methodist by inheritance, and a
Baptist by marriage. I write about some of the things I love.
But have no civilized articulation for the things I hate. I proud-
ly love being a Negro woman--It's so involved and interesting.
We are the PROBLEM--the great national game of TABOO."
(From Caroling Dusk, edited by Countée Cullen, p. 47.)

SPENCER, Gilmore.
SHORT STORY (Anthology): Ford and Faggett, Best Short Stories by Afro-American Writers.

SPENCER, Mary Etta.
NOVEL
The Resentment. Philadelphia: A.M.E. Book Concern, 1921.
SHORT STORY
(Periodical): Opportunity, October 1929.
CRITICISM ON SPENCER
Bone. The Negro Novel in America, p. 49.

SPENSLEY, Philip.
DRAMA The Nitty Gritty of Mr. Charlie, 1969.

SPRIGGS, Edward S. Born 6 December 1934 in Cleveland, Ohio.
POETRY
(Anthologies): Alhamisi and Wangara, Black Arts; Afro-Arts
Anthology; Brooks, A Broadside Treasury; Jones and Neal,
Black Fire; Randall, Black Poetry: A Supplement; Randall
and Burroughs, For Malcolm.
(Periodicals): Journal of Black Poetry, Spring 1969; Winter-
Spring 1970; also published in Black Dialogue.

STANBACK, Thurman W.
DRAMA A Change Has Got to Come, 1969.

STANFORD, Theodore.
POETRY
(Anthology): Murphy, Ebony Rhythm.
(Periodicals): Crisis, 1934; 1935; Harlem Quarterly, Fall-
Winter 1950; Negro Story, October-November 1944.

STAPLES, Shirley. Born in Bessemer, Alabama.
POETRY (Anthology): Coombs, We Speak as Liberators.

STATEMAN, Norman Hills.
POETRY (Anthology): Murphy, Ebony Rhythm.

STEELE, Richard.
DRAMA The Matter of Yo Mind.

STEELE, Shirley (Nubia).
POETRY (Periodical): Journal of Black Poetry, Spring 1969.

STEPHANY see FULLER, Stephany

STEPHENSON, Tyrone.
POETRY (Anthology): Black Poets Write On.

STEPTOE, John. Born 14 September 1950 in Brooklyn.
CHILDREN AND YOUNG ADULTS
Birthday. New York: Holt, Rinehart & Winston, 1972*.
Stevie. New York: Harper & Row, 1969*.
Train Ride. New York: Harper & Row, 1971*.
Uptown. New York: Harper & Row, 1970*.

STERN, Harold.
NOVEL Blackland. Garden City, N.Y.: Doubleday, 1970; Belmont-Tower, 1971†.

STEVENS, Ruby.
POETRY (Anthology): Murphy, Negro Voices.

STEVENS, Sandra. Born 1950.
POETRY (Anthology): Shuman, A Galaxy of Black Writing.

STEVENSON, C. Leigh.
SHORT STORY (Anthology): Ford and Faggett, Best Short Stories by Afro-American Writers.

STEVENSON, Jose.
POETRY (Anthology): Boyd, Poems by Blacks, vol. 2.

STEVENSON, William A. III see ADELL, Ilunga

STEWARD, Austin. <u>Born</u> 1794.
AUTOBIOGRAPHY
Twenty-two Years a Slave, and Forty Years a Freeman; Embracing a correspondence of several years, while president of Wilberforce Colony, London, Canada West. Rochester, N.Y.: W. Alling, 1857. Reprint, 1859.

STEWART, James T.
CRITICISM
"The Development of the Black Revolutionary Artist." In Jones and Neal, <u>Black Fire</u>; also in Hemenway, <u>The Black Novelist.</u>
DRAMA
Abganli and the Hunter (Why No One Ever Tells the Truth to Women). In <u>Black Lines</u> 2 (Fall 1971): 43-45.
The Gourd Cup (A Play Spoken with Song and Dance for Little Children). In <u>Black Lines</u> 2 (Fall 1971): 51-52.
How Men Came into the World (How the Lesser Gods Came into the World). In <u>Black Lines</u> 2 (Fall 1971): 48-51.
JoJo, The Story Teller: A Play for Children. In <u>Black Lines</u> 2 (Fall 1971): 52-54.
The Messenger of God (Mamu's Ways Are Just). <u>Black Lines</u> 2 (Fall 1971): 45-48.
POETRY
Nommo. Seattle, Wash.: Harrison-Madrona Center, 3425 E. Denny Way, n.d.
(Anthologies): Alhamisi and Wangara, <u>Black Arts</u>; Jones and Neal, <u>Black Fire.</u>
(Periodical): <u>Journal of Black Poetry</u>, Summer 1972.

STEWART, Ollie.
NON-FICTION
(Periodicals): <u>Opportunity</u>, December 1933; March 1936.
SHORT STORY
(Anthology): Ford and Faggett, <u>Best Short Stories by Afro-American Writers.</u>

STEWART, Ron.
DRAMA With Neal Tate. <u>Sambo (A Nigger Opera)</u>, 1969.

STILES, Thelma Jackson. <u>Born</u> 10 December 1939 in Monroe, Louisiana. <u>Education</u>: B.A., University of California-Berkeley, Cal., 1961. <u>Currently living in</u> Oakland, California. <u>Career</u>: Associate Editor, <u>New Lady</u> Magazine; copywriter, Sage-Allen & Co.; English Instructor, Sunset High, Hayward, California; Instructional Television Scriptwriter, Litton Industries (researching and writing Enrichment and Afro-American History Series, documentary films, and Job Corps commercials). Presently Senior Writer, Audio-Visual Section, Training Department of Wells Fargo Bank.
DRAMA
No One Man Show (one act), 1972.

Thelma Stiles (credit: Procopio Calado)

NON-FICTION
   (Periodical): New Lady Magazine.
INTERJECTIONS
   "Writing is both an obsessive struggle for recognition and a
futile attempt to exorcise the vague anguish that mocks every
pursuit.... The black woman catches hell."

STILL, James. Born 1812 in Jew Jersey. Education: Self-edu-
   cated. Career: Practiced medicine in Medford, New Jersey for
   thirty years.
AUTOBIOGRAPHY
   Early Recollections and Life of James Still. Philadelphia:
      Lippincott, 1877.
BIOGRAPHY AND CRITICISM ON STILL
   Baskin and Runes. Dictionary of Black Culture, pp. 419-
      420.

Fishman, George M. "Letter to the Editor." Negro History
    Bulletin 25 (April 1962): p. 154.
Griscom, L. E. "Dr. James Still, 'Doctor of the Pines' of
    Medford, New Jersey and Brother of the Famed Organizer
    of The Underground Railroad." Camden Courier Post,
    April 1961.
    [1]George M. Fishman, "Letter to the Editor," Negro
    History Bulletin 25 (April 1962): 154.

STILL, William. Born 1821 in Burlington County, New Jersey.
Died 1902. Career: Still was born free only because his parents had escaped separately from Maryland's Eastern Shore to
New Jersey. As a young man, he became a clerk in the office
of the Philadelphia Anti-Slavery Society, and in this capacity,
was frequently involved in forwarding Black passengers to safety
in Canada. He also aided the survivors of the Harper's Ferry
debacle in their escape from Virginia. From 1850 to 1860, he
compiled numerous case histories about fugitive slaves involved
in 1001 situations and disguises for his 1872 publication of Underground Railroad Records. In 1861 he organized a social, civil
and statistical clearing house to collect and preserve historical
material relating to Blacks. Twenty years later, he founded the
first YMCA branch for Blacks. [1]
SLAVE NARRATIVES
    A Brief Narrative of the Struggle for the Rights of the Col-
    ored People of Philadelphia in the City Railway Cars; and
    a Defense of William Still, Relating to his Agency touching
    the passage of the Late Bill, etc. Philadelphia: Merri-
    hew and Son, Printers, 1867.
    The Underground Rail Road. A Record of the facts, Authentic
    Narratives, Letters, etc., Narrating the hardships, Hair-
    breadth Escapes and Death Struggles of the Slaves in their
    Efforts for Freedom and Related by Themselves, and others,
    or witnessed by the author; Together with Sketches of some
    of the Largest Stockholders, and Most Liberal Aiders and
    Advisers of the Road. Philadelphia: Porter and Coates,
    1872. Reprint, Arno Press, 1968.
    (Anthologies): Brown, Davis and Lee, The Negro Caravan;
    Davis and Redding, Cavalcade; Woodson, The Mind of the
    Negro as Reflected in His Letters.
NON-FICTION
    A Tribute of Gratitude to the Honorable H. B. Lowry, State
    Senator, Pennsylvania. Philadelphia: J. B. Rogers Company
    Printers, 1869. (Three volumes.)
BIOGRAPHY AND CRITICISM ON WILLIAM STILL
    Brown, Davis and Lee, The Negro Caravan, pp. 784-785.
    Davis and Redding. Cavalcade, p. 125.
    Ploski. Reference Library of Black America: Literature and
    Art.
        [1]Henry A. Ploski, The Reference Library of Black Amer-
    ica: Literature and Arts, (New York: Bellwether, 1971),
    p. 30.

STOCKARD, Sharon.
  DRAMA
    Edifying Further Elaborations on the Mentality of a Chore,
      1972.
    Proper and Fine, 1969.

STOKES, Deborah.
  POETRY (Anthology): Weisman and Wright, Black Poetry for
    All Americans.

STOKES, Glenn.
  POETRY (Anthology): Coombs, We Speak as Liberators.

STOKES, Herbert (Damu).
  DRAMA
    The Man Who Trusted the Devil Twice. In Bullins, New
      Plays from the Black Theater.
    The Uncle Toms (one act). In The Drama Review 12 (Sum-
      mer 1968).

STOKES, Tony.
  SHORT STORIES Short Stories by Tony Stokes. New York:
    Rannick Amuru, 1973*.

STONE, Chuck (Charles Sumner Stone). Born 21 July 1924 in St.
  Louis, Missouri. Education: A.B., Wesleyan University, 1948;
  M.A., University of Chicago, 1950. Currently living in Hart-
  ford, Connecticut. Career: In Education--Field Representative,
  World Politics Adult Discussion Programs, 1952-56; Lecturer
  in Journalism, Columbia College, Chicago, Illinois, 1963-64;
  John T. Dorrance Visiting Professor in Government, Trinity Col-
  lege, Conn., 1969; Director of Minority Affairs, Educational
  Testing Service, Princeton, N.J., 1970-72; Lecturer in Sociol-
  ogy, Antioch-Putney Graduate School of Education, Philadelphia
  Center, 1973. In Politics--Special Assistant to Rep. Adam Clay-
  ton Powell, Chairman, Education and Labor Committee, U.S.
  House of Representatives, 1965-67; Education Research Special-
  ist to Rep. Robert N. C. Nix, Sr., Chairman, Subcommittee on
  Postal Operations, U.S. House of Representatives, 1968. In
  Journalism and Communications--White House Correspondent and
  Editor, Washington Afro-American, 1960-63; Editor-in-Chief,
  Chicago Daily Defender, 1963-64; Commentator on the "Today"
  Show, NBC-TV, 1969-70. In International Affairs--Overseas
  Representative, CARE for Egypt, Gaza, and India, 1956-57; As-
  sociate Director, American Committee on Africa, New York,
  1960. Presently a columnist for the Philadelphia Daily News,
  syndicated nationally by Universal Press Syndicate. Member:
  Board of Trustees, Wesleyan University; State Board of Colleges
  and University Directors, Pennsylvania; Steering Committee, National Workshop on Testing in Education and Employment; National Conference of Black Political Scientist; Fellow and Founding
  Member of the Black Academy of Arts and Letters; Contributing

Editor, the Black Scholar magazine; Board of Advisors, Contact
magazine; Creative and Visual Arts Panel, American Revolution
Bicentennial Commission, D.C. Awards, Honors: Alpha Man
of the Year, Alpha Phi Alpha Fraternity, Philadelphia, Pa.,
1973; Politician-in-Residence, Morgan State College, Institute
for Political Education, 1969; Outstanding Citizen of the Year,
CORE, Chicago Chapter, 1964; Annual Distinguished Citizen's
Award, Frontiers International, Inc., D.C., 1963; Journalist
of the Year, Capital Press Club, Washington, D.C., 1961.
NON-FICTION
    Black Political Power in America. New York: Dell, 1970†.
    Tell It Like It Is. New York: Pocket Books, 1970†.
    (Anthologies): Barbour, The Black Power Revolt; Chrisman
       and Hare, Contemporary Black Thought: The Best of the
       Black Scholar; Rose, et al., Through Different Eyes.
    (Periodicals): Black Scholar, December 1969; November 1971.
NOVEL
    King Strut. Indianapolis: Bobbs-Merrill, 1970.
REVIEWS: King Strut
    Blackwell, Angela. Black Scholar 3 (February 1972): 58-59.

STONE, Leroy.
    POETRY
       (Anthologies): Burning Spear; Henderson, Understanding the
         New Black Poetry; Pool, Beyond the Blues.
       (Periodicals): Dasein.
    NON-FICTION
    Published in Downbeat and Metronome.

STOREY, Ralph.
    DRAMA Doww, 1971.

STOWERS, J. Anthony.
    POETRY The Aliens. San Francisco: White Rabbit, 1967.

STOWERS, Walter H. (Sanda). Born 1859.
    NOVEL
       With W. H. Anderson. Appointed. Detroit: Detroit Law
         Printing, 1894.
    CRITICISM ON STOWERS
    Bone. The Negro Novel in America, p. 32.

STRONG, Romaner Jack.
    DRAMA
       A Date with the Intermediary, 1968.
       A Direct Confrontation in Black (one act), 1968.
       Mesmerism of a Maniac, 1967.
       Metamorphisms (one act), 1966.
       The Psychedelic Play or a Happening (one act), 1967.

STROUD, Welvin see DUST

STUCKEY, Sterling (Sterling X). Born 1932 in Memphis, Tennessee.
   CRITICISM
     "Franklin London Brown." In Chapman, Black Voices.
     "Through the Prism of Folklore: The Black Ethos in Slavery."
       Massachusetts Review 9 (Summer 1968): 417-437.
   POETRY
     We Righteous Builders of the Black Nations. Chester, Pa.:
       Pyramid, 1971.
     (Broadside): The Honorable Elijah Muhammad. Chester,
       Pa.: New Pyramid, n.d.
   NON-FICTION
     The Ideological Origins of Black Nationalism. Boston: Bea-
      con, 1974†.

SUBLETTE, Walter (S. W. Edwards, pseud.) Born 6 September
   1940 in Chicago. Education: B.A., University of Illinois-Chi-
   cago Circle Campus; M.A., University of Illinois Circle Campus.
   Career: Writer and editor. Awards, Honors: Charles McEl-
   vey award for poetry; guest reader at the University of Chicago
   (downtown), at Long Island University (Bayville), at the Univer-
   sity of Illinois, and at the University of Wisconsin-Madison.
   DRAMA
     Natural Murder, 1973.
   NOVEL
     Go Now In Darkness. Chicago: Baker, 1964.
     I'm Sorry, But That's What Happened. Toronto: McClelland
       & Stewart, forthcoming.
   POETRY
     Resurrection on Friday Night. Chicago: Swallow, forthcom-
      ing.
   UNPUBLISHED WORK
     Poetry: "Naked Exile"; "Preludes."
   INTERJECTIONS
     "On the radio
     The news come at you
     Like a parade of cripples
     That never ends."

SUDAN, Nazzam Al. Born 1944 in Fowles, California.
   DRAMA
     Flowers for the Whiteman or Take Care of Business, 1967.
   POETRY
     (Anthology): Major, The New Black Poetry.

SUDAN, Omar Mali see HOAGLAND, Everett

SULLIVAN, May Miller see MILLER, May

SUMMERS, Debra E.
   POETRY (Anthology): Black Poets Write On.

SUMMERS, Lucy Cooper.
   POETRY 99 Patches. New York: Carlton, 1969.

SUN RA
    POETRY
        (Anthologies): Adoff, The Poetry of Black America; Jones
        and Neal, Black Fire.
        (Periodical): Negro Digest, March 1968.

SUTHERLAND, Christopher. Born 27 July 1932 in Newark, New
    Jersey. Education: Was graduated from Seward Park High
    School in New York City. Career: Has been writing poetry
    since the age of 16.
    POETRY
        (Anthology): Dudley Randall, ed. Bet You Ain't, Bet You
        Can't (to be published by Broadside Press, 1974).
        (Newspapers): Rochester Democrat and Chronicle; Buffalo
        Challenger.
    INTERJECTIONS
    "The Black Aesthetic is not an assumption but a fact and we
    as poets must write to that extent, but we must also remember
    not to simply embellish, but write to teach and to inform as
    well as to entertain."

SUTHERLAND, Efua.
    DRAMA Ananse Swore an Oath, Spring 1972.

SWANCY, André D. Born 13 July 1935 in Kansas City, Kansas.
    Education: Studied at Washington State Art Center; Academy of
    Lighting Arts; University of Kansas. Currently living in Kansas
    City, Kansas. Career: Staff assistant in the Theatre Depart-
    ment, University of Kansas. Presently a lighting consultant;
    co-director of Children's Creative Pre-School; graphic artist;
    poet; printer.
    POETRY
        Reflections. Kansas City: NIEU, 1969.
    INTERJECTIONS
    "Love Self
    Love Earth
    Love Man"
    "To be as one with all things"
    "In order to understand the universe/man you must first un-
    derstand yourself."

SWANN, Darius Leander.
    DRAMA
        A Choral Drama: The Circle Beyond Fear. New York:
        Friendship, 1960.
        The Crier Calls: A Drama for Verse Choir. New York:
        Friendship, 1956.
        A Desert, a Highway: A One-Act Play. New York:
        Friendship, 1963.
        I Have Spoken to My Children: A One-Act Play for Verse
        Chorus. New York: Friendship, 1957.
        A House for Marvin: A One-Act Play About Discrimination
        in Housing. New York: Friendship, 1957.

POETRY
The Answers: A Piece for a Verse Choir. New York:
Board of Foreign Missions of the Presbyterian Church in
the USA, 1953.

SYDNOR, W. Leon.
NOVEL Veronica. New York: Exposition, 1956.

-T-

TALBOT, Dave.
NOVEL The Musical Bride. New York: Vantage, 1962.

TAPIA, Jose. Born 12 September 1942 in Santurce, Puerto Rico.
Education: B.A., Fordham University, 1964; studied one year
at Fordham Law School. Currently living in Amsterdam, The
Netherlands. Career: Specializes in musical theatre. His mu-
sical pageant, Kenya, was presented at P.S. 29, New York City,
1969; a musical mystery play E G O, premiered in Amsterdam,
1970; a musical comedy, Welcome Aboard the Space Ship
O.R.G.Y., was previewed in Dordrecht, 1971; he also contribu-
ted to the off-Broadway musical, Thoughts, which premiered at
Theatre Lys, March 1973. Presently working on a full-length
opera, Sunny Explode.
DRAMA
E G O (musical comedy).
Kenya (musical mystery play).
Outrage (musical).
Satin Man (musical).
Welcome to the Space Ship O.R.G.Y.

TARRY, Ellen. Born 1906 in Birmingham, Alabama. Career: See
Ward and Marquardt, Authors of Books for Young People; Dan-
nett, Profiles of Negro Womanood, vol. 2, pp. 247-254.
AUTOBIOGRAPHY
The Third Door: The Autobiography of an American Negro
Woman, 1955; New York: Guild, 1966; reprint ed. New
York: Negro Universities Press, 1971*.
CHILDREN AND YOUNG ADULTS
Hezekiah Horton. New York: Viking, 1942.
Janie Belle. New York: Garden City.
Katherine Drexel, Friend of the Neglected. New York: Far-
rar, Straus & Cudahy, 1958.
Martin de Porres, Saint of the New World. New York: Far-
rar, Straus & Cudahy, 1958.
With Marie H. Ets. My Dog Rinty. New York: Viking,
1946*.
The Runaway Elephant. New York: Viking, 1950.
Young Jim: The Early Years of James Weldon Johnson. New
York: Dodd, Mead, 1967*.

Jose Tapia (credit: Ruud Gerritsen)

TARTER, Charles L. Born 1907.
  NOVEL Family of Destiny. New York: Pageant, 1954.

TATE, Eleanora E. Born 16 April 1948 in Canton, Missouri.
  NON-FICTION
    (Anthology): Guy, Children of Longing.
  POETRY
    (Anthology): Witherspoon, Broadside Annual 1972.
  Also published in Healthways Magazine and The Lutheran
    Magazine.

TATE, Neal. <u>Born</u> 17 November in Yonkers, New York. <u>Educa-tion</u>: B.S., New York University, 1955; also studied at Manhat-tan School of Music and Juilliard School of Music. <u>Career</u>: Specializes in theatre music and the training of singers and mu-sicians. Currently developing the talents of underprivileged chil-dren in Kingston, Jamaica, and hopes to continue this work in the Caribbean and South America. Working on a text book, <u>Audile Concept of Orchestration,</u> and a book on the training of children in the theatre arts.

DRAMA
    <u>No More Dragons to Kill.</u>
    With Ron Steward. <u>Sambo: A Black Opera with White Spots,</u> 1969.
    <u>Searchin'</u> (musical).
    <u>Surprise</u> (musical).
    <u>You Gotta Deal With It</u> (musical).

INTERJECTIONS
    "I believe there is a need for self expression, in varying de-grees, in everyone. To find it in the young and give it a set-ting in which it can express itself can lead to his or her emo-tional maturity and is the very basis of all theatre."

TAYLOR, David.
    POETRY (Anthology): Murphy, <u>Negro Voices.</u>

TAYLOR, Gloria Lee.
    POETRY <u>Dreams for Sale.</u> New York: Exposition, 1953.

TAYLOR, Jeanne.
    DRAMA
        <u>House Divided,</u> 1968.
    NON-FICTION
        "On Being Black and Writing for Television." <u>Negro Ameri-can Literature Forum</u> 4 (Fall 1970): 79-82.
        (Anthologies): Schulberg, <u>From the Ashes;</u> Simmons and Hutchinson, <u>Black Culture.</u>
    SHORT STORIES
        (Anthologies): Chapman, <u>New Black Voices;</u> Schulberg, <u>From the Ashes.</u>
        (Periodical): <u>Antioch Review,</u> Fall 1967.
    BIOGRAPHY AND CRITICISM ON TAYLOR
        Schulberg. "Black Phoenix," p. 281.

TAYLOR, Margaret Ford. <u>Born</u> in Detroit, Michigan.
    DRAMA
        <u>Hotel Happiness,</u> 1972.
        <u>I Want to Fly.</u>
    POETRY
        (Periodical): <u>Negro History Bulletin,</u> October 1962. (In-cludes brief biography.)

TAYLOR, Mervyn.
    POETRY

(Anthologies): Patterson, <u>A Rock Against the Wind</u>; Sanchez, <u>360° of Blackness Coming at You.</u>
(Periodical): <u>Black Creation,</u> Spring 1972.

TAYLOR, Prentiss, Jr. <u>Born</u> 17 December 1951 in Chicago.
NON-FICTION
   (Periodical): <u>Black World,</u> May 1973.
POETRY
   (Anthologies): Brown, Lee and Ward, <u>To Gwen with Love;</u>
      Witherspoon, <u>Broadside Annual 1972.</u>
   (Periodicals): <u>Black World,</u> August 1972; <u>Journal of Black
      Poetry,</u> Summer 1972; also published in <u>Blackout; Libera-
      tor; L'Ouverture.</u>

TAYLOR, Rockie D. see OLOGBONI, Tejumola

TEAGUE, Bob.
CHILDREN AND YOUNG ADULTS
   <u>Letters to a Black Boy.</u> New York: Walker, 1968*; Lancer,
      1972†.
   <u>Adam in Blunderland.</u> Garden City, N.Y.: Doubleday, 1971*.
DRAMA
   With Langston Hughes. <u>Soul Yesterday and Today,</u> 1969.

TEER, Barbara Ann. <u>Born</u> 18 June 1937 in St. Louis, Missouri.
<u>Career:</u> See <u>Who's Who of American Women</u>, 1974-75.
CRITICISM
   "The Great White Way Is Not <u>Our</u> Way." <u>Negro Digest</u> 17
      (April 1968): 21-29.
   "To Black Artists, with Love." <u>Negro Digest</u> 18 (April 1969):
      4-8.
DRAMA
   <u>A Revival: Change! Love! Organize!</u>, 1972.
SCREENPLAY
   <u>Rise/A Love Poem for a Love People.</u>

TERRELL, Robert L.
NON-FICTION
   (Periodicals): <u>Commonweal; Eye; The Guardian; Evergreen
      Review.</u>
POETRY
   (Anthology): Coombs, <u>We Speak as Liberators.</u>
   (Periodicals): <u>Black World,</u> September 1970; November 1971;
      <u>Negro Digest,</u> September-October 1968, September 1969.

TERRELL, Vincent.
DRAMA
   <u>Sarge,</u> 1970.
   <u>Will It Be Like This Tomorrow,</u> 1972.

TERRY, Lucy (Mrs. Prince). <u>Born</u> 1730 in Africa. <u>Died</u> 1821.
<u>Career:</u> Taken in captivity, she was sold to Ensign Ebenezer
   Wells at the age of five; baptized in 1735; admitted to the fellow-

ship of the Church in 1744.[1] She remained a slave in the
Wells' household in Deerfield, Massachusetts[2] where she worked
until Obijah Prince, a free Negro, bought her freedom and mar-
ried her.[3] Lucy, her husband and family, later settled in the
village of Guilford, Vermont. Guilford's records in the Bureau
of Census reveal that Obijah and Lucy were among the 16 negroes who purchased land and settled in the village. Lucy,
noted for her rhymes and stories, acquired a reputation as a
remarkable storyteller, and her home became the meeting place
for all the young people of the village.[4] She also possessed an
unusual ability for oratory which served her well on two recorded occasions: once, to persuade the Board of Trustees of Williams College to permit her son to enter the school,[5] and thus
become one of the first American Blacks to attempt to break the
color line;[6] later, to argue her own case before the supreme
court when forced to sue Colonel Eli Bronson for his attempt to
claim part of her land.[7] Awards, Honors: In 1746, she quali-
fied for the honor of being the first black poet of North America
by writing a verse account of an Indian raid--"Bars Fight."[8]
POETRY
    "Bars Fight."[9]
    (Anthologies): Hughes and Bontemps, The Poetry of the Ne-
        gro: 1746-1970; Patterson, An Introduction to Black Lit-
        erature in America; Randall, The Black Poets; Robinson,
        Early Black American Poetry.
BIOGRAPHY AND CRITICISM ON TERRY
    Baskin, Wade and Richard N. Runes. A Dictionary of Black
        Culture. New York: Philosophical Library, 1973, p. 430.
    Emanuel and Gross. Dark Symphony, p. 9.
    Garrett, Romeo B. Famous First Facts About Negroes.
        New York: Arno, 1972, p. 98.
    Greene, Lorenzo Johnston. The Negro in Colonial New Eng-
        land. New York: Columbia, 1942, pp. 242-243, 248; cf.
        Prince, Lucy Terry, pp. 314-315.
    Hughes and Meltzer. A Pictorial History of the Negro in
        America, p. 36.
    Katz, Bernard. "A Second Version of Lucy Terry's Early
        Ballad." Negro History Bulletin 29 (Fall 1966): 183-184.
    Katz, William Loren. Eyewitness: The Negro in American
        History. New York: Pitman, 1967, p. 24, 37.
    Sheldon, George. A History of Deerfield, Massachusetts,
        vol. 1. Greenfield, Mass.: Press of E. M. Hall, 1895-
        96, pp. 545-549.
        _____. "Slavery in Old Deerfield." The New England Maga-
        zine 8 (March 1893): 49-60.
    Toppin. A Biographical History of Blacks in American Since
        1528, p. 58.
    Wright, Martha R. "Bijah's Luce of Guilford." Negro His-
        tory Bulletin 27 (April 1965): 152-153, 159.
            [1]Bernard Katz. "A Second Version of Lucy Terry's
    Early Ballad?" Negro History Bulletin 29 (Fall 1966):
    183.
            [2]Langston Hughes and Milton Meltzer, eds. A Pictor-

ial History of the Negro in America (New York: Crown, 1963), p. 36.

[3]Katz, p. 184.

[4]Martha R. Wright. "Bijah's Luce of Guilford," Negro History Bulletin 27 (April 1965): 153.

[5]Lorenzo Johnston Greene. The Negro in Colonial New England (New York: Columbia, 1942), pp. 314-315.

[6]Wright, p. 159.

[7]Greene, p. 315.

[8]Wade Baskin and Richard N. Runes. Dictionary of Black Culture (New York: Philosophical Library, 1973), p. 430.

[9]Greene, p. 242. (The Poem is the fullest and best contemporary version of that struggle; the original has been lost but a secondary copy follows on pp. 242-243. Cf. Bernard Katz, fn. 1.)

THELWELL, Mike. Born 1938 in Jamaica, West Indies.
    CRITICISM
        "Back with the Wind: Mr. Styron and the Reverend Turner." In Clarke, William Styron's Nat Turner.
        "Mr. William Styron and the Reverend Turner." Massachusetts Review 9 (Winter 1968): reprinted in Chatmetzky and Kaplan, Black and White in American Culture.
        "The Turner Thesis." Partisan Review 35 (Summer 1968): 403-414.
    SHORT STORIES
        (Anthologies): Chapman, New Black Voices; Hughes, Best Short Stories by Negro Writers; Patterson, An Introduction to Black Literature in America; The American Literary Anthology I.
        (Periodicals): Negro Digest, January 1964; also published in Short Story International; Story Magazine.

THIERRY, Camille. Born October 1814 in New Orleans. Died 13 April 1875 in Bordeaux, France. Education: Was tutored privately and later attended day school. Career: According to Coleman,[1] Thierry was a successful businessman who was able to retire at a young age and pursue literary interests. Another source indicates that he was "unfit" for the drudgery of business, and soon squandered in Paris the small fortune his father left him. He then withdrew to Bordeaux and concentrated on writing.[2]
    POETRY
        Les Vagabonds; poésies américaines. Paris: E. Lemerre, 1874. (Précédé d'une notice biographique, par l'auteur des "Souvenirs de la Louisiane."
        (Anthologies): Desdunes, Nos Hommes at Notre Histoire; Lanusse, Creole Voices.
    BIOGRAPHY AND CRITICISM ON THIERRY
        Bardolph. The Negro Vanguard, pp. 77, 78.
        Caulfield, Ruby Van A. The French Literature of Louisiana. New York: Institute of French Studies, Columbia Univer-

sity, 1929. (Ph.D. thesis.)
Desdunes, R. L. <u>Nos Hommes et Notre Histoire.</u> Montreal:
Arbour & DuPone, 1911, pp. 44-47.
<u>Dictionary of American Biography,</u> vol. 13, pp. 417-418.
Lanusse, Armand, comp. <u>Creole Voices: Poems in French</u>
<u>by Free Men of Color.</u> Edited by Edward Maceo Coleman,
1845; Washington, D.C.: Associated, 1945, xxxiv-xxxv.
Mercier, Armand. <u>Comptes Rendus de l'Athénée Louisianais,</u>
1 January 1878, p. 135.
Tinker, E. L. <u>Les Cenelles: Afro-American Poetry in Lou-</u>
<u>isiana.</u> New York: By the Author, 1930.
<u>Les Écrits de Langue Francaise en Louisiane aux XIX</u>e
<u>Siècle.</u>
      1Edward Maceo Coleman, ed., <u>Creole Voices</u> (Washing-
ton, D.C.: Associated, 1945), pp. xxxiv-xxxv.
      2<u>Dictionary of American Biography,</u> vol. 13, pp. 417-
418.

THIGPEN, William A., Jr. <u>Born</u> 25 July 1948 in Detroit. <u>Died</u>
13 April 1971. <u>Career:</u> An honors student and star athlete;
was attending Wayne State University at the time of his death.
<u>POETRY</u>
      <u>Down Nigger Paved Streets.</u> Detroit: Broadside, 1972†.
      (Compiled and edited by Geneva N. Smitherman.)
      (Anthology): Witherspoon, <u>Broadside Annual 1972.</u>
<u>REVIEW:</u> <u>Down Nigger Paved Streets</u>
      Spady, James G. <u>Black Books Bulletin</u> 1 (1973): 42-43.

THOMAS, Abel Charles (Iron Grey).
      <u>POETRY</u> <u>The Gospel of Slavery.</u> New York: T.W. Strong,
      1864.

THOMAS, Charles Columbus. <u>Born</u> 10 September (Virgo) in Mc-
Alester, Oklahoma. <u>Education:</u> B.A., Langston University;
M.F.A. (Theatre), Brooklyn College of the City University of
New York; working on doctorate at CUNY. <u>Currently living in</u>
New York City. <u>Career:</u> Taught at Lefferts Junior High School
and served as chairman of the music and drama departments.
Presently Assistant Professor and Director of the Institute of
African and Afro-American Studies, Richmond College of the City
University of New York. Also a musician, conductor, vocalist,
dancer and actor, working with the Screen Actors Guild and the
Chuck Davis Dance Company. Director of Music for "The Missa
Luba," and performer with the Afro-American Folkloric Troupe
at City Center, at Town Hall, at various colleges and universi-
ties, and on educational television. <u>Member:</u> Kappa Delta Pi
Educational Honor Society; Kappa Kappa Psi Honorary Band Fra-
ternity; Alpha Kappa Mu Honor Society; Omega Psi Phi Frater-
nity; Big Brothers; Screen Actors Guild; National Academy of
Recording Arts & Sciences; Jazz Interactions. <u>Awards, Honors:</u>
Research award, City University of New York (African Studies);
Afro-Arts Cultural Award (Dance).

Charles Columbus Thomas

POETRY
The Black Brother Goose: Rinds for Revolution.   New York:
    Wilhelmina Publications, 1971.
(Anthologies): Coombs, We Speak as Liberators; also in
    Probes: An Introduction to Poetry.   (Edited by W. K. Har-
    lan. New York: Macmillan, 1973).

THOMAS, Charles Cyrus.
POETRY
    A Black Lark Caroling.   Dallas, Tex.: The Kaleidograph
        Press, 1936.
    Sweet Land of Liberty.   Ravenna, Ohio: By the Author, 1937.
    Young Bough Blossoming.   Hollywood, Calif.: n.p., 1954?

THOMAS, D. Gatewood.
POETRY   (Anthology): Murphy, Ebony Rhythm.

THOMAS, Fatisha.
  DRAMA
      Choice of Worlds Unfilled.
      It's Been a Long Time Comin'.
      Twenty Year Nigger.
  SHORT STORY
      (Periodical): Black Creation, Spring 1972.

THOMAS, James Henry.
  POETRY Sentimental and Comical Poems. Nashville, Tenn.:
      National Baptist Publishing Board, 1913.

THOMAS, Joyce.
  POETRY Bittersweet. San Jose, Calif.: Firesign, 1973.

THOMAS, Lorenzo. Born 31 August 1944 in the Republic of Pana-
  ma. Education: B.A. (English literature), Queens College,
  1967; graduate work at Pratt Institute. Currently living in
  Houston, Texas. Career: Participated in Poetry-in-the-Schools
  programs in New York City and Westchester, New York; Writer-
  in-Residence, Black Arts Center, Houston; creative writing
  teacher, Ethnic Arts Program of the Black Arts Center, 1973 to
  present; Writer-in-Residence, Texas-Southern University, 1973.
  Translator of Vietnamese poetry: THO TU VIET-NAM. Awards,
  Honors: Poet's Foundation Award, 1966; Committee on Poetry
  grant, 1973. Member: Grants Committee, Coordinating Council of Literary Magazines.
  POETRY
      Dracula. n.p.: Angel Hair Books, 1973.
      Fit Music. n.p.: Angel Hair Books, 1972.
      Sound Science. n.p.: Sun Be/Am Assoc., forthcoming.
      (Anthologies): Adoff, The Poetry of Black America; Chapman,
          New Black Voices; Jones and Neal, Black Fire; Reed,
          Yardbird Reader, I.
      (Periodicals): Angel Hair; Art & Literature; C: A Journal
          of Poetry; El Corno Emplumado; Floating Bear; The Mas-
          sachusetts Review; Liberator; Umbra.
  INTERJECTIONS
      "The surf records the music of one sphere
      Displacing space and mass on other worlds
      But this is OURS.
      And all our effort now must be
      To Make our world a better world."

THOMAS, Richard W. Born 2 April 1939 in Detroit, Michigan.
  Education: B.A., Michigan State University, 1970; M.A., Michigan State University, 1971; presently working on Ph.D. in History at University of Michigan. Currently living in Okemos,
  Michigan. Career: Taught Black History for a community
  course at Northern High Freedom School in Detroit, 1969-70;
  designed and taught "Third World Education" for minority students at Michigan State University, 1970; worked on committee
  for the Tri-Ethnic Curriculum Project sponsored by the Michi-

gan Catholic Conference, 1970; taught History and Social Change
to community aides in Pontiac, Michigan, 1972; worked for television show, "Perspectives in Black," WMSB in East Lansing;
also reviewed books for the program, "Richard's Corner." Has
given numerous lectures on Black history, Black labor history
and revolutionary ethics for university and community groups.
Presently teaching Afro-American History at the University of
Michigan and Michigan State University.

NON-FICTION
    (Anthology): To Improve Learning, An Evaluation of Instruc-
       tional Technology. Edited by Sidney G. Tickton. New
       York: R. R. Bowker, 1971.
    (Periodical): Mazungumzo, Fall 1970; Winter 1970.

POETRY
    (Anthologies): Adoff, The Poetry of Black America; Boyer,
       Broadside Annual 1973; Drake, Michigan Signatures;
       Hughes and Bontemps, The Poetry of the Negro: 1746-
       1970; Jones and Neal, Black Fire; King, Blackspirits;
       Patterson, A Rock Against the Wind; Shuman, A Galaxy
       of Black Writing; Shuman, Nine Black Poets.
    (Periodicals): Negro Digest, September 1969; New City, May
       1968; Red Cedar Review, May 1969; World Order, Fall
       1968; Zeitgeist, Autumn 1966; also in Black Spirits Maga-
       zine; Colloquy.

INTERJECTIONS
"I feel art should have its own social responsibility, that the
artist is not entirely a free agent. He lives in society, par-
takes of its benefits, therefore, he should contribute much more
than his subjectivity. He should build visions of what humans
can become and lead the way."

THOMAS, Stan.
DRAMA In the City of Angels.

THOMAS, Will. Born 1905.
AUTOBIOGRAPHY
    The Seeking. New York: Wyn, 1953.
CRITICISM
    "Negro Writers of Pulp Fiction." Negro Digest 8 (July
       1950): 81-84.
NOVEL
    God Is for White Folks. New York: Creative Age, 1947.
       (Published under the title, Love Knows No Barriers. New
       York: New American Library, 1951.) Excerpt in Negro
       Digest, November 1947.
SHORT STORY
    (Periodical): Crisis, June 1946.
CRITICISM ON THOMAS
    Bone. The Negro Novel in America, pp. 166-167.
    Hughes. The Negro Novelist, pp. 140-142, 233-234.
REVIEW: The Seeking
    Dodson, Owen. "But Not Transformed." New Republic, 27
       July 1953.

THOMPSON, Aaron Belford.
  POETRY
    Echoes of Spring. Rossmoyne, O.: By the Author, 1901.
    Harvest of Thoughts. Introduction by James Whitcomb Riley.
      Indianapolis, Ind.: By the Author, 1907.
    Morning Songs. Rossmoyne, O.: By the Author, 1899.
  CRITICISM ON THOMPSON
    White and Jackson. An Anthology of Verse by American Ne-
      groes, pp. 232-233.

THOMPSON, Clara Ann.
  POETRY
    A Garland of Poems. Boston: Christopher, 1926.
    Songs from the Wayside. Rossmoyne, O.: By the Author,
      1908.
  CRITICISM ON THOMPSON
    White and Jackson. An Anthology of Verse by American Ne-
      groes, p. 233.

THOMPSON, Dorothenia Tinsley.
  POETRY Three Slices of Black. Chicago: Free Black Press,
    1972.

THOMPSON, Eloise Bibb see BIBB, Eloise

THOMPSON, Garland Lee (Aquarius). Born 14 February 1938 in
  Muskegee, Oklahoma, (Oregon-grown). Education: "Ray Brad-
  bury told me to take a few writing courses and get out! That's
  what I had already done!" Currently living in New York City.
  Career: Spent one season at the University of Oregon doing mu-
  sicals, then 13 seasons in Hollywood. First picture: South Pacific; first play: Simply Heavenly, a musical by Langston
  Hughes. Wrote several children's plays, and made a film for
  children. His first play, "Sisyphus and the Blue-Eyed Cyclops,"
  was presented by Studio-West with actors Paul Winfield and
  D'Urville Martin. Then he moved to New York as stage manager for Gordoné's No Place to Be Somebody, and to present
  Sisyphus at the Negro Ensemble Co., with actors Al Freeman,
  Jr., Adolph Caesar, and William Jay. Vinnette Carroll's Urban
  Arts Corp., presented his second play, Papa Bee on the D
  Train, followed by productions at the Black Theatre Alliance
  Festival and the Actors Studio--New York. Production stage
  manager, River Niger, Brooks Atkinson Theatre, 1973. Mem-
  ber: Directors and Playwrights Unit, Actors Studio; Founder of
  the Frank Silvera Writers Workshop and the Black Theatre Al-
  liance. Awards, Honors: 42nd Annual One Act Tournament,
  D.C., for Sisyphus.
  DRAMA
    Sisyphus and the Blue-Eyed Cyclops.
    Papa Bee on the D Train.
  WORK IN PROGRESS
    Drama: "The Incarnations of Reverend Good Black Dress."

INTERJECTIONS
"I am a Theatre Communications specialist. I write, direct,
and produce works for the Theatre. 'If one doesn't make one's
presence felt in one's own Time, one negates one's reason...
uh...raison d'être.' I am working in a form which I call:
Black Astra plays, illusory mind pieces of nonordinary reality.
It means illusions on illusion and hallucinations, but 'concrete
although unordinary, aspects of the reality of every day life.'
B. A. T. or Black Astra Theatre, a different level of consciousness." (Quotes from Sisyphus and the Blue-Eyed Cyclops.)

THOMPSON, Glen. Born 1955 in Brooklyn.
POETRY (Anthologies): Jordan, Soulscript; Jordan and Bush,
    The Voice of the Children.

THOMPSON, James W. Born 21 December 1935 in Detroit.
POETRY
    First Fire: Poems, 1957-1960. London: Breman, 1970.
    This Is Not the Name. London: Breman, 1970.
    (Anthologies): Adoff, The Poetry of Black America; Coombs,
    We Speak as Liberators; King, Blackspirits; Pool, Beyond
    the Blues; Randall, The Black Poets.
    (Periodicals): Antioch Review, Spring-Summer 1972; Es-
    sence, March 1974; Negro Digest, September, October
    1965; September 1966; November 1967; August, September
    1969; September 1970; Negro History Bulletin, October
    1962; Présence Africaine, No. 57.
SHORT STORIES
    (Anthology): King, Black Short Story Anthology.
BIOGRAPHY ON THOMPSON
    Negro History Bulletin 26 (October 1962): 67-68.

THOMPSON, Jim. Born 1906.
    Nothing But a Man. New York: Popular Library, 1970†.
    The Undefeated. New York: Popular Library, 1969†.

THOMPSON, Joseph.
    POETRY Songs of Caroline. Chicago: By the Author, 1936.

THOMPSON, Julius Eric. Born 15 July 1946 in Vicksburg, Missis-
    sippi.
    POETRY
    Hopes Tied Up in Promises. Philadelphia: Dorrance, 1970*.
    (Periodicals): Black World, September 1970; Negro Digest,
    September, October 1965; September 1966; November
    1967; August, September 1969.
    REVIEW: Hopes Tied Up in Promises.
    Plumpp, S. Black World 2 (February 1971): 64-65.

THOMPSON, Larry. Born 1950 in Seneca, South Carolina.
    DRAMA
    A Time to Die (a skit).

POETRY
(Anthologies): Adoff, Black Out Loud; Adoff, It Is the Poem
   Singing Into Your Eyes.
(Periodical): Negro Digest, September-October 1968.

THOMPSON, Priscilla Jane.
POETRY
   Ethiope Lays. Rossmoyne, O.: By the Author, 1900.
   Gleanings of Quiet Hours. Rossmoyne, O.: By the Author,
   1907.
CRITICISM ON THOMPSON
   White and Jackson. An Anthology of Verse by American Ne-
   groes, p. 233.

THOMPSON, Samuel.
SHORT STORIES
   (Anthology): Mirer, Modern Black Stories.
   (Periodical): Freedomways, Spring 1962.

THORNE, Anna V.
DRAMA Black Power Every Hour, 1970.

THORNHILL, Lionel L. Born 1 February 1897 in British Guiana,
S.A. Education: Attended high school in Georgetown, and studied at night classes, Morris High School, New York City. Currently living in Bronx, New York. Career: A former composi-
tor in the printing industry and, for many years, a dining-car
waiter with the Pennsylvania Railroad. Two scenarios have been
published by Universal Scenario Co. (Hollywood). Presently re-
tired, devoting full time to writing. Member: Vice-President,
Happy Hours Club (Senior Citizens of St. Mary's Church, Bronx).
Awards, Honors: Pennsylvania Railroad Honor Roll.
SHORT STORIES
   The Huge Steel Bolt and Other Stories and Poems. New
      York: Vantage, 1966. (Published under the title, The Love
      Thief. New York: Graphicopy, 1973.)
   (Periodical): Education (a Harlem publication).
UNPUBLISHED WORK
   Novels: "Souls of a Rich Family"; "Youth--God and Love."
INTERJECTIONS
   "To be successful, one must be unswervingly persistent. Ac-
tivity is the key to Longevity; hence one must have a hobby
whether retired or not. Parents should make it imperative that
their child or children have a spiritual foundation, without which
their offspring is headed for delinquency, and utter destruction,
as example of which is portrayed in the poem: 'The Culprit or
The Spoiled Boy,' a sad story which was told to me by my
mother when I was clinging to her apron strings. A man and
wife should not depend on sex to bind them together, but rather
strive to develop a oneness in their marital lives. One should
be thankful for God's gifts; not worship them instead of Him.
Give...and it will be given unto you. Happiness is striving to
make the other fellow happy in any manner you can. Never en-

vy the other fellow for his good fortune. Look about you. You
also have been given something. Be thankful for that which you
have. You'll sleep better at nights."

THORNTON, George Bennett.
POETRY
    Great Poems. 2nd ed. Wilberforce, O.: By the Author,
      1948.
    Selections from Thornton. Wilberforce, O.: n.p., 1954.

THORUP, Lester W.
NOVEL Came the Harvest. New York: Carlton, 1966.

THURMAN, Howard.
POETRY The Greatest of These. Mills College, Calif.:
    Eucalyptus Press, 1944.

THURMAN, I. M.
POETRY (Anthology): Murphy, Negro Voices.

THURMAN, Wallace. Born 1902 in Salt Lake City, Utah. Died
1934. Education: Attended the University of Utah for two years,
and the University of Southern California for an additional two
years. Career: Went to Harlem, and became involved in numerous literary activities. Became a reader at Macaulay Publishing Company, and was soon appointed Editor-in-Chief of the
Macaulay staff. Edited two literary magazines, Harlem and
Fire! According to Langston Hughes, he died of tuberculosis in
the charity ward at Bellevue Hospital.[1]
CRITICISM BY THURMAN
    See The Messenger, April to September 1926.
    "Negro Artists and the Negro." New Republic 52 (1927): 37-
      39.
    "Negro Poets and Their Poetry." Bookman 67 (1928): 555-
      561.
    "Nephews of Uncle Remus." Independent 119 (1927): 296-298.
DRAMA (With William Jourdan Rapp)
    Harlem: A Melodrama of Negro Life in Harlem. (Original-
      ly called "Black Belt.") 1929. In the James Weldon John-
      son Collection of Yale University Library.
    Jeremiah, The Magnificent, 1930.
    Savage Rhythm, 1932.
    Singing the Blues, 1931.
NON-FICTION
    (Periodicals): The World Tomorrow 10 (November 1927):
      465-467; Haldeman-Julius Quarterly, October-November-
      December 1924.
NOVELS
    The Blacker the Berry: A Novel of Negro Life. New York:
      Macaulay, 1929; reprint ed., New York: Arno Press,
      1969*; New York: AMS Press, 1969*; New York: Collier
      Books, 1969†.
    Infants of the Spring. New York: Macaulay, 1932.

With Abraham L. Furman. The Interne. New York: Ma-
cauley, 1932.
(Anthologies): Brown, Davis and Lee, The Negro Caravan;
Calverton, Anthology of American Negro Literature.
SHORT STORIES
(Anthologies): Barksdale and Kinnamon, The Black Writer of
America; Turner, Black American Literature: Fiction.
(Periodical): The Messenger.
SKETCHES
(Periodicals): "Cordelia the Crude, a Harlem Sketch," Fire!
1 (1929): 5. (The basis for the play, Harlem.)
BIOGRAPHY AND CRITICISM ON THURMAN
Abramson. Negro Playwrights in the American Theatre, pp.
32-43.
Atkinson, Brooks. New York Times, 3 March 1929.
Bond. The Negro and the Drama, pp. 117-118.
Bone. The Negro Novel in America, pp. 91-94.
Brawley. The Negro Genius, pp. 264, 280.
Bontemps. The Harlem Renaissance Remembered, pp. 15,
19, 46, 48, 50, 64, 97-98, 101, 147-170, 173, 194, 213,
214, 234, 268.
Crisis 39 (September 1932).
Gloster. Negro Voices in American Fiction, pp. 168-172.
Harrison. The Drama of Nommo, pp. 178-180.
Haslam, Gerald. "Wallace Thurman: A Western Renais-
sance Man." Western American Literature 6 (Spring
1971): 53-59.
Henderson, Mae Gwendolyn. "Portrait of Wallace Thurman."
In Bontemps, The Harlem Renaissance Remembered, pp.
147-170.
Hughes. The Big Sea, pp. 233-238, 241.
Lewis, Theophilis. Opportunity (April 1929).
Mitchell. Black Drama, pp. 86-87.
New Yorker, 2 March 1929.
O'Daniel, Therman B. "Introduction." The Blacker the
Berry. New York: Macmillan, 1970, pp. ix-xix.
Opportunity 13 (January 1935), 38-39. (Editorial.)
Rapp, William Jourdan and Wallace Thurman. "Detouring
Harlem to Times Square." New York Times, 7 April
1929, sec. 10, p. 4.
Skinner, R. Dana. Commonweal, 6 March 1929.
West, Dorothy. "Elephant's Dance." Black World 20 (No-
vember 1970): 77-85.
Who's Who, 1926.
Young. Black Writers of the Thirties, pp. 134, 142, 143,
205, 209-212, 214.
REVIEW: The Blacker the Berry
Du Bois, W. E. B. Crisis 36 (1929): 234.
    [1]Therman B. O'Daniel, "Introduction," The Blacker the
Berry (New York: Macmillan, 1970), pp. xii-xiii.

TILLMAN, Katherine Davis.
DRAMA

Aunt Betsy's Thanksgiving.   Philadelphia: A. M. E. Book Concern, n. d.
Fifty Years of Freedom; or, From Cabin to Congress.
    Philadelphia: A. M. E. Book Concern, 1910.

TINNER, Bernadine.
    POETRY (Anthology): Black Poets Write On.

TINSLEY, Tomi Carolyn.
    POETRY
        With Helen C. Harris and Lucia Mae Pitts.   Triad.   n. p.:
            By the Authors, December 1945.
        (Anthology): Murphy, Ebony Rhythm.

TIWONI, Habib.   Born 22 December 1939 in St. Thomas, Virgin Islands. Education: Studied Journalism at the New School for
    Social Research, 1970, and Sociology and Anthropology at Universidad Nacional Autónoma de Mexico, 1971. Currently living
    in New York City. Career: Presently engaged in political
    journalism for an interisland/international Caribbean pamphlet;
    gives feature readings and recitals for high school groups; employed as a social worker at Friendly Homes, Inc., a boys'
    home in the Bronx; is a second degree Shorim-Ryu (Okinawan
    Karate) Sensei. Now in the process of forming an inter-island
    Caribbean Poets Co-operative. Member: Calliope, an assemblage of Westbeth-based poets.
    POETRY
        Attacking the Moncada of the Mind.   New York: El Pueblo
            News Service, 1971.
        (Periodical): The Black American.
    BIOGRAPHY AND CRITICISM ON TIWONI
        "Interview." Caribbean Daily, Sunday, 15 July 1973.
    INTERJECTIONS
        "Where I want to arrive at poetically is the point at which
        the humanism expressed in my work can be the catalyst that
        stimulates interisland/internationalism among Caribbeans and
        other oppressed peoples in the diaspora."

TODD, Joe.   Born in Flint, Michigan.
    POETRY (Anthology): Brown, Lee and Ward, To Gwen with
        Love.

TODD, Walter E.
    POETRY
        Poetry: Fireside Musings. Washington: Murray Bros., 1908-9.
        Gathered Treasures. Washington: Murray Bros., 1912,
            1914.
        A Little Sunshine. Washington: Murray Bros., 1917.

TOLBERT, Isabelle   see   SMITH, Ivory H.

TOLSON, Melvin Beaunorus. Born 6 February 1900 in Moberly,
    Missouri. Died 29 August 1966. Education: Attended Fisk

Habib Tiwoni

University, 1919; was graduated with honors from Lincoln University (Pennsylvania), 1923; studied at Columbia University.
Career: Taught English and Speech, Wiley College, 1924-47; joined the faculty at Langston University, 1947; appointed Avalon Foundation Creative Writing Professor, Tuskegee Institute, 1965-66. Involved in numerous other activities: coached the Wiley College Debate Teams, served as Mayor of Langston, Oklahoma; directed the Dust Bowl Theatre; wrote a column, "Cabbages and Caviar" for the Washington Tribune; organized sharecroppers in Southern Texas. Awards, Honors: Won first place in the National Poetry Contest sponsored by the American Negro Exposition in Chicago, 1939; Omega Psi Phi Award for Creative Writing, 1945; appointed Poet Laureate of Liberia, January 1947; Bess Hokim Award, Poetry Magazine, 1951; awarded Doctor of Letters, Lincoln University (Pennsylvania), 1954; admitted to Knighthood of the Order of the Star of Africa, 1954; appointed

permanent Bread Loaf Fellow in Poetry and Drama, 1954;
awarded Doctor of Humane Letters, Lincoln University (Penn-
sylvania); elected to the New York Herald Tribune Book Review
Board; awarded the District of Columbia Citation and Award for
Cultural Achievement in Fine Arts; received American Academy
of Arts and Letters grant, 1966. [1]
DRAMA
  Black Boy, 1963.
  Black No More, 1952. (Adaptation of Schuyler's book.)
  The Fire in the Flint, 1952. (Adaptation of Walter White's
    book.)
  The Moses of Beale Street.
  Southern Front.
POETRY
  Harlem Gallery; Book 1, The Curator. New York: Twayne,
    1965.
  Libretto for the Republic of Liberia. New York: Twayne,
    1953.
  Rendezvous with America. New York: Dodd, 1944.
  (Anthologies): Adams, Conn and Slepian, Afro-American Lit-
    erature: Poetry; Adoff, Poetry of Black America; Baker,
    Black Literature in America; Bell, Afro-American Poetry;
    Bontemps, American Negro Poetry; Brown, Davis, and Lee,
    The Negro Caravan; Cuney, Hughes and Wright, Lincoln
    University Poets; Davis and Redding, Cavalcade; Drachler,
    African Heritage; Emanuel and Gross, Dark Symphony;
    Ford, Black Insights; Hayden, Kaleidoscope; Henderson,
    Understanding the New Black Poetry; Hill, New Writings
    by American Negroes, 1940-1962; Hughes and Bontemps,
    Poetry of the Negro: 1746-1970; Kearns, Black Identity;
    Lomax and Abdul, 3000 Years of Black Poetry; Long and
    Collier, Afro-American Writers; Miller, Blackamerican
    Literature; Miller, Dices or Black Bones; Murphy, Negro
    Voices; Randall, The Black Poets; Robinson, Nommo; Sim-
    mons and Hutchinson, Black Culture: Reading and Writing
    Black.
  (Periodicals): Negro Digest 9 (September 1951): 51; Negro
    History Bulletin 34 (April 1971): 88; Midwest Journal 1
    (Winter 1948): 80-82; Phylon (Fourth Quarter 1943).
BIBLIOGRAPHY ON TOLSON
  Flasch, Joy. Melvin B. Tolson. New York: Twayne, 1972,
    pp. 159-169.
BIOGRAPHY AND CRITICISM ON TOLSON
  "Appointed to the Avalon Foundation Chair in the Humanities
    at Tuskegee Institute." Journal of Negro History 51 (Jan-
    uary 1966): 67.
  Baskin and Runes. Dictionary of Black Culture, pp. 435.
  Brooks, Gwendolyn. "Book Review." Negro Digest 14 (Sep-
    tember 1965): 51-52.
  Benét, William Rose. "Two Powerful Negro Poets." Satur-
    day Review, 24 March 1945, p. 45.
  Fabio, Sarah Webster. "Who Speaks Negro?" Negro Digest
    16 (December 1967): 54-58.

Flasch, Neva Joy. "Humor and Satire in the Poetry of Melvin B. Tolson." Satire Newsletter 7 (1969): 29-36.

_____. Melvin B. Tolson. New York: Twayne, 1972.

Hill, Herbert. "In Memory of M. B. Tolson...1900-1966." Tuesday (November 1966): 26.

"In Memory of Melvin B. Tolson." Negro Digest 15 (October 1966): 55.

Kerlin. Negro Poets and Their Poems, pp. 325-326.

McCall, Dan. "The Quicksilver Sparrow of Melvin B. Tolson." American Quarterly 18 (1966): 538-542.

"Negro Poet Died September 2, 1966 in Dallas, Texas at the age of 66." Journal of Negro History 51 (January 1966): 315.

Ramsaran, J. A. "The Twice-Born Artists' Silent Revolution." Black World 2 (May 1971): 58-67.

Randall, Dudley. "Melvin B. Tolson: Portrait of a Poet as Racounteur." Negro Digest 15 (January 1966): 54-57.

"Reception Given for M. Tolson by the Detroit Branch of the Association for the Study of Negro Life and History." Negro History Bulletin 30 (April 1967): 14.

Redding. "Since Richard Wright," pp. 30-31.

Shapiro, Karl. "Melvin B. Tolson, Poet." Book Week, New York Herald Tribune, 10 January 1965; reprint in Negro Digest 14 (May 1965): 75-77.

_____. "Review." Negro Digest 14 (May 1964): 75-77.

_____. "Introduction." Harlem Gallery. New York: Collier, 1965.

Tate, Allen. "Preface to Libretto for the Republic of Liberia." Poetry 76 (1950): 216-218.

Thompson, D. G. "Tolson's Gallery Brings Poetry Home." Negro History Bulletin 29 (1965): 69-70.

Tolson, Melvin. "A Poet's Odyssey." In Hill, Anger and Beyond, pp. 181-203. (Interview conducted by M. W. King.)

Turner, Lorenzo D. "Words for a Vast Music." Poetry 86 (June 1955): 174-176.

Walcott, Ronald. "Ellison, Gordone, and Tolson: Some Notes on the Blues, Style and Space." Black World 22 (December 1972): 4-29.

[1]Joy Flasch. Melvin B. Tolson (New York: Twayne, 1972), pp. 15-17.

TOMLIN, Henry.
POETRY Varied Verses. n.p.: By the Author, 1937.

TONEY, Ieda Mai.
POETRY The Young Scholar and Other Poems. Boston: Meador, 1951.

TOOMER, Jean. Born 26 December 1894 in Washington, D.C. Died 30 March 1967. Education: Attended the University of Wisconsin in 1914 and the City College of New York in 1917-18. Career: After spending two years at the above colleges, he wrote numerous sketches, poems, short stories and pieces of criticism for such periodicals as The Double Dealer of New Orleans, Broom, The Crisis, The Liberator, The Little Review, The Modern Review, Nomad, Prairie, S 4 N, and Adelphi (London). His four months as principal of a high school in Sparta, Georgia enabled him to acquire a tremendous awareness of the humanity of the rural Blacks of Georgia, and he based his book Cane, 1923, on this experience. However, despite the racial pride which is evident in Cane, he denied being a part of the Black race and passed as a white man. When asked about his race after his second marriage to a white woman, he reportedly answered: "I really do not know whether I have Negro blood in me or not."[1] Perhaps this skepticism was the result of his indoctrination to Unitism, a religion based on the philosophy of Gurdjieff, the Russian mystic. During the summer of 1924, he was initiated to Unitism at the Gurdjieff Institute in Fountainebleau, France. After traveling extensively and living with writers and artists in various areas of the United States, he moved to Bucks County, Pennsylvania and became a Quaker. He also served as a reader of a Friends Meeting House.[2]

AUTOBIOGRAPHY

"Chapters from Earth-Being, An Unpublished Autobiography." Black Scholar 2 (January 1971): 3-13.

A Fiction and Some Facts. By the Author, 1931.

"Outline of Autobiography." (Unpublished ms., ca. 1934.) Toomer papers, Fisk University Library.

NON-FICTION

Essentials: Definitions and Aphorisms. Chicago: The Lakeside Press, 1931.

The Flavor of Man. Philadelphia: Young Friends Movement of the Philadelphia Yearly Meetings, 1949. (William Penn Lecture, 1949, delivered at Arch Street Meeting House, Philadelphia.)

Living Is Developing: Psychological Series No. I. (Mill House Pamphlets.) Doylestown, Pa.: n.p., 1937.

"Race Relations and Modern Society." Princeton, N.J.: Brownwell,| 1929. Problems in Modern Society, ed. Baker.

Work Ideas I: Psychological Series No. 2 (Mill House Pamphlets.) Doylestown, Pa.: n.p., 1937.

NOVELLA

"York Beach." In The New American Caravan, pp. 12-83. Edited by Alfred Kreymbourg and others. New York: Macaulay, 1929.

POETRY

Cane. New York: Boni & Liveright, 1923.[3]

(Anthologies): Adams, Conn and Slepian, Afro-American Literature: Poetry; Adoff, Poetry of Black America; Baker, Black Literature in America; Barksdale and Kinnamon, Black Writers of America; Bell, Afro-American Poetry; Bontemps, American Negro Poetry; Brown, Davis and Lee, The Negro Caravan; Calverton, Anthology of American Negro Literature; Cullen, Caroling Dusk; Davis and Redding,

Toomer, J. (cont.)   708

Cavalcade; Hayden, Kaleidoscope; Hughes and Bontemps,
Poetry of the Negro: 1746-1970; Jordan, Soulscript; Lo-
max and Abdul, 3000 Years of Black Poetry; Margolies,
A Native Sons Reader; Miller, Blackamerican Literature;
Randall, The Black Poets; Watkins and Davis, To Be a
Black Woman: Portraits in Fact and Fiction.
(Periodicals): Crisis 23 (1922): 261; 24 (1922): 65.

SHORT STORIES
(Anthologies): Second American Caravan: A Yearbook of
American Literature. (Edited by Kreymborg, Mumford,
Rosenfeld. New York: Macaulay, 1928.) Also published
in the following: Adams and Briscoe, Up Against the Wall,
Mother: On Women's Liberation; Baker, Black Litera-
ture in America; Brown, Davis and Lee, The Negro Cara-
van; Calverton, Anthology of American Negro Literature;
Chambers and Moon, Right On!; Davis and Redding, Caval-
cade; Emanuel and Gross, Dark Symphony; Ford, Black In-
sights; Hayden, Burrows and Lapides, Afro-American Lit-
erature: An Introduction; Hill, Soon One Morning; Hughes,
The Best Short Stories by Negro Writers; Kreymborg, The
New American Caravan; Kreymborg, The Second American
Caravan; Simmons and Hutchinson, Black Culture: Reading
and Writing Black; Turner, Black American Literature:
Fiction.

BIBLIOGRAPHY OF TOOMER'S WORK
Turner. In a Minor Chord, pp. 140-143. (Includes unpublished works.)

BIOGRAPHY AND CRITICISM ON TOOMER
Abcarian, Richard and Maroin Klotz, eds. Literature: The
Human Experience, pp. 477-480.
Ackley, Donald G. "Theme and Vision in Jean Toomer's
Cane." Studies in Black Literature 1 (Spring 1970): 45-65.
Armstrong, John. "The Real Negro," New York Tribune, 14
October 1923, p. 26. Also in Durham, Studies in Cane,
pp. 27-28.
Barksdale and Kinnamon. Black Writers of America, pp.
500-502.
Bell, Bernard. "A Key to the Poems in Cane." CLA Jour-
nal 14 (March 1971): 251-258.
Bigsby. The Black American Writer: Fiction.
Bone, Robert. "Jean Toomer." The Negro Novel in Amer-
ica, pp. 80-89.
Bontemps, Arna. The Harlem Renaissance Remembered, pp.
1-2, 38-39, 51-62, 64-65, 67-268 passim.
_____. "Introduction to the 1969 Edition of Cane." New
York: Harper & Row, 1969. Also in Durham, Studies in
Cane.
_____. "The Negro Renaissance." Sewanee Review 30 (22
March 1947): 12-13, 44.
_____. "The Negro Renaissance: Jean Toomer and the Har-
lem Writers of the 1920's." Anger and Beyond, ed., Her-
bert Hill, pp. 20-36. Also Durham, Studies in Cane, pp.
75-88.

Braithwaite, William Stanley. "The Negro in Literature."
Crisis 28 (September1924): 210.
Brown, Sterling. The Negro in American Fiction, p. 153.
Bruno, Lasker. "Doors Opened Southward," Survey 51 (1
November 1923): 190-191.
Cancel, Rafael A. "Male and Female Inter-relationship in
Toomer's Cane. Negro American Literature Forum, pp.
25-31.
Chase, Patricia. "The Women in Cane." CLA Journal 14
(March 1971): 259-273.
Cullen, Caroling Dusk, pp. 93-94.
Davis and Redding. Cavalcade, pp. 285-291.
Dillard, Mabel. "Behind the Veil of Jean Toomer's Esthetic."
In Durham, Studies in Cane, pp. 2-10.
Du Bois, W. E. B. and Alain Locke. "The Younger Literary
Movement." Crisis 27 (1924): 161-163.
Duncan, Bowie. "Jean Toomer's Cane: A Modern Black Or-
acle." CLA Journal 15 (March 1972): 323-333.
Durham, Frank. "Jean Toomer's Vision of the Souther Ne-
gro." Southern Humanities Review 6 (Winter 1972): 13-
22. Also in Durham, Studies in Cane, pp. 102-113.
_____. "The Poetry Society of South Carolina's Turbulent
Year: Self Interest, Atheism, and Jean Toomer." South-
ern Humanities Review 5 (Winter 1971): 76-80.
_____. The Merrill Studies in Cane. Columbus, O.:
Charles E. Merrill, 1971.
Emanuel, James A. "The Challenge of Black Literature:
Notes on Interpretation." The Black Writer in Africa and
the Americas, pp. 85-100.
Farrison, W. Edward. "Jean Toomer's Cane Again." CLA
Journal 15 (March 1972): 295-302.
Fischer, William C. "The Aggregate Man in Jean Toomer's
Cane." Studies in the Novel 3 (Summer 1971): 190-215.
Frank, Waldo. "Forward to the 1923 Edition of Cane." In
Toomer, Cane. New York: Liveright Publishers, 1923.
Also in Durham, Studies in Cane, pp. 18-19.
Fullenwider, S. P. "Jean Toomer: Lost Generation, or Ne-
gro Renaissance?" Phylon 27 (Fourth Quarter 1966): 396-
403. Also in Durham, Studies in Cane, pp. 66-74.
Gloster, Hugh M. "Jean Toomer." Negro Voices in Ameri-
can Fiction, pp. 128-130. Also in Durham, Studies in
Cane, pp. 53-56.
Goede, William J. "Jean Toomer's Ralph Kabnis: Portrait
of the Negro Artist as a Young Man." Phylon 30 (Spring
1969): 72-85.
Graham, James N. "Negro Protest in America 1900-1955:
A Bibliographical Guide." South Atlantic Quarterly 67
(Winter 1968): 94-107.
Grant, Sister Mary Kathryn. "Images of Celebration in
Cane." Negro American Literature Forum 5 (1971): 32-
34, 36.
Gross, T. L. "The Negro Awakening: Langston Hughes,
Jean Toomer, Rudolph Fisher, and Others." In Gross,

The Heroic Ideal in American Literature, pp. 137-147.

Harrison. *The Drama of Nommo*, pp. 26, 112-118, 165.

Hill, *Anger and Beyond*, pp. 20-28.

Holmes, Eugene. "Jean Toomer--Apostle of Beauty." *Opportunity* 10 (August 1932): 252-254, 260. Also in Durham, *Studies in Cane*, pp. 45-50.

Huggins. *Harlem Renaissance*, pp. 179-187.

Hughes. *Best Short Stories by Negroes*, pp. 505-506.

Innes, Catherine L. "The Unity of Jean Toomer's *Cane*." *CLA Journal* 15 (March 1972): 306-322.

"Just Americans." *Time* 19 (28 March 1932): 19. Also in Durham, *Studies in Cane*, pp. 15-17.

Kerlin. *Black Poets and Their Poems*, pp. 283-284.

Kraft, James. "Jean Toomer's *Cane*." *Markham Review* 2 (October 1970): 61-63.

Krasny, Michael J. "Design in Jean Toomer's *Balo*." *Negro American Literature Forum* 7 (Fall 1973): 103-106.

Lieber, Todd. "Design and Movement in Cane." *CLA Journal* 13 (September 1969): 35-50.

Littlejohn, David. 'Before Native Son: The Renaissance and After," *Black on White*. Also in Durham, *Studies in Cane*, pp. 100-102.

Locke, Alain. *Four Negro Poets*. New York: Simon & Schuster, 1927.

_____. "From *Native Son* to *Invisible Man*: A Review of the Literature." *Phylon* 14 (First Quarter 1953): 34. Also in Durham, *Studies in Cane*, pp. 56-57.

Ludington, C. J., Jr. "Four Authors View the South." *Southern Humanities Review* 6 (Winter 1972): 1-4.

McKeever, Benjamin F. "*Cane* as Blues." *Negro American Literature Forum* 4: 61-63.

Margolies. *Native Sons*.

Mason, Clifford. "Jean Toomer's Black Authenticity." *Black World* 20 (January 1971): 70-76.

Mellard, James M. "Symbolism and Demonism: The Lyrical Mode in Fiction." *Southern Humanities Review* 7 (Winter 1973): 37-51.

Miller. *Blackamerican Literature*, pp. 373-381, 767-778.

Munson, Gorham B. "The Significance of Jean Toomer." *Opportunity* 3 (September 1925): 262-63. Also in Durham *Studies in Cane*, pp. 96-100. Also in Munson, *Destinations: A Canvas of American Literature Since 1900*. Chicago: Sears, 1928, pp. 178-186, including two additional paragraphs.

Nower, Joyce. "Fooling Master." *Satire Newsletter* 7 (Fall 1969): 5-10.

Redding, Saunders. "The New Negro." *To Make a Poet Black*, pp. 104-106. Also in Durham, *Studies in Cane*, pp. 51-52.

Reilly, John M. "The Search for Black Redemption: Jean Toomer's *Cane*." *Studies in the Novel* 2 (1970): 312-324.

Robinson, Clayton. "Gillmore Millen's *Sweet Man*: Neglected Classic of the Van Vechten Vogue." *Forum* (Houston), 8

(Fall-Winter 1970): 32-35.

Rosenfeld, Paul. "Jean Toomer." Men Seen: Twenty-Four Modern Authors. New York: Dial Press, 1925, pp. 227-233. Also in Durham, Studies in Cane, pp. 93-95.

Scruggs, C. W. "Mark of Cain and the Redemption of Art: A Study in Theme and Structure of Jean Toomer's Cane." American Literature 44 (May 1972): 276-291.

Singh, Raman K. "The Black Novel and Its Tradition." Colorado Quarterly 20 (Summer 1971): 23-29.

Stein, Marion L. "The Poet-Observer and 'Fern' in Jean Toomer's Cane." Markham Review 2 (October 1970): 64-65.

Thompson, Larry E. "Jean Toomer: As Modern Man." In Bontemps, The Harlem Renaissance Remembered, pp. 51-62.

Turner, Darwin T. "And Another Passing." Negro American Literature Forum (Fall 1967): 3-4.

_____. "The Failure of a Playwright." CLA Journal 10 (June 1967): 308-318. Also in Durham, Studies in Cane, pp. 89-92.

_____. In a Minor Chord: Three Afro-American Writers and Their Search for Identity. Urbana: Southern Illinois University Press, 1971.

_____. "Jean Toomer's Cane; Critical Analysis." Negro Digest 18 (January 1969): 54-61.

Wagner. Black Poets of the United States, pp. 259-281.

Waldron, Edward E. "The Search for Identity in Jean Toomer's 'Esther' " CLA Journal 14 (March 1971): 277-280.

Westerfield, Hargis. "Jean Toomer's 'Fern': A Mythical Dimension." CLA Journal 14 (March 1971): 274-276.

Whitlow. Black American Literature, pp. 80-83.

Who's Who in America 17 (1932-33).

REVIEWS: Cane

Du Bois, W. E. B. "The Younger Literary Movement." The Crisis 27 (February 1924): 161-162. Also in Durham, Studies in Cane, pp. 40-41.

Gregory, Montgomery. "A Review of Cane." Opportunity 1 (December 1923): 374-375. Also in Durham, Studies in Cane, pp. 35-36.

Kerlin, Robert T. "Singers of New Songs." Opportunity 4 (May 1926): 162. Also in Durham, Studies in Cane, pp. 51-52.

"Literary Vaudeville: A Review of Cane." Springfield Republican, 3 December 1923, p. 9. Also in Durham, Studies in Cane, p. 34.

Littell, Robert. "A Review of Cane." The New Republic 37 (26 December 1923): 126. Also in Durham, Studies in Cane, pp. 32-33.

"A Review of Cane." Boston Transcript, 15 December 1923, p. 8. Also in Durham, Studies in Cane, p. 31.

"A Review of Cane." Time, 24 March 1930.

[1]Kansas City American, 22 November 1934. Quoted by

Toomer, J. (cont.)   712

> Jean Wagner, Black Poets of the United States. Trans-
> lated by Kenneth Douglas (Urbana: University of Illinois
> Press, 1973), p. 260.
> [2]Langston Hughes. Best Short Stories by Negro Writers
> (Boston: Little, Brown, 1967), pp. 505-506.
> [3]Cane is classified as "Poetry" by Jean Wagner. See
> his discussion in Black Poets of the United States, pp.
> 265-266.

TOOMEY, Richard E. S. Career: 1st lieutenant, U.S. Infantry,
from Tennessee.[1]
POETRY
> Thoughts for True Americans. Introduction by Paul Laurence
> Dunbar. Washington: Neale, 1901.
> > [1]Newman Ivey White and Walter Clinton Jackson, An
> > Anthology of Verse by American Negroes (Durham, N.C.:
> > Moore, 1968), p. 234. Includes brief discussion of the
> > poems.

TOURE, Aishah Sayyida Mali.
> POETRY (Anthology): Patterson, A Rock Against the Wind.

TOUSSAINT, Richard.
> DRAMA Three Black Ghettos, 1969.

TOWNS, George A. Education: Atlanta University Class of 1894.
Career: Taught at Atlanta University for 34 years, and at Fort
Valley State College for nine years.
DRAMA
> The Sharecroppers.
NON-FICTION
> (Periodicals): Phylon, Second Quarter 1942; Second Quarter
> 1948.
POETRY
> (Periodicals): Opportunity, December 1938; March 1939;
> Phylon, Second Quarter 1943; Third Quarter 1945; Third
> Quarter 1950.

TOWNSEND, Willa A.
> DRAMA Because He Lives. Nashville: Sunday School Pub-
> lishers, Board of the National Baptist Convention, 1924.

TRACY, Robert Archer.
> FICTION
> The Sword of Nemesis. New York: Neale, 1919.
> REVIEW
> Fauset, Jessie. Crisis 20 (1920): 80.

TRAVIS, Nannie M. see SMITH, Nannie Traver

TRAYLOR, Mark.
> POETRY (Anthology): Black Poets Write On.

Cornelius V. Troup

TRENIER, Diane.
 DRAMA Rich Black Heritage, 1970.

TRENT, Helen.
 POETRY My Memory Gems.   Salisbury, N.C.: Livingstone
  College, 1948.

TROUP, Cornelius V. Born 7 February 1902 in Brunswick, Georgia,
  Education: A.B., Morris Brown College, 1925; M.A., Atlanta
  University, 1937; Ph.D., Ohio State University, 1947; LL.D.,
  Wilberforce University, 1949; LL.D., Morris Brown College,

1959; LL.D., Atlanta University 1965. <u>Currently living in</u> Atlanta, Georgia. <u>Career</u>: Head of Commercial Department,
Morris Brown College, 1925-27; Principal, Risley High School,
Brunswick, Georgia, 1928-39; Registrar, Fort Valley State College, 1939-45; President Fort Valley State College, 1945-66;
Director, Talent Research Project, Coppin State College, Maryland, 1966-67; Consultant, Southern Regional Office, National Urban League, 1972; presently retired. <u>Member</u>: National Education Association; Phi Beta Sigma Fraternity; Frontiers International; Phi Delta Kappa; Alpha Kappa Mu; Mason; and Georgia
Association of Educators.

EDITOR

 <u>Distinguished Negro Georgians</u>. Dallas: Royal, 1962.

POETRY

 (Anthologies): Manfield, M.A., <u>Music Unheard: An Anthol-</u>
  <u>ogy of Hitherto Unpublished Verse</u>. (New York: H. Harrison, 1939); Murphy, <u>Ebony Rhythm</u>; Murphy, <u>Negro Voices</u>.

BIOGRAPHY ON TROUP

 <u>Contemporary Authors</u>, 9/10.
 <u>Leaders in Education</u>, 3rd ed.

TROUPE, Quincy. <u>Born</u> 23 July 1943 in New York City. <u>Educa-</u>
<u>tion</u>: A.A., Grambling College, 1963; B.A., Los Angeles City
College, 1968. <u>Currently living in</u> New York City. <u>Career</u>:
Taught creative writing at the Watts Writers Workshop, 1966-
68; creative writing and Black literature at U.C.L.A., 1968 and
at the University of Southern California, 1968. Director of the
Malcolm X Center in Los Angeles, summers of 1969 and 1970.
Director of the John Coltrane Summer Festivals in Los Angeles,
1969 and 1970. Taught creative writing and Third World literature, Ohio University, 1969-72; currently teaching Third World
literature at Richmond College. Has served as editor for numerous publications: <u>Watts Poets & Writers</u>, House of Respect
Publishers, 1968; Associate Editor of <u>Shrewd Magazine</u>, Los
Angeles, 1968; Editor of <u>Confrontation: A Journal of Third</u>
<u>World Literature</u>, published at Ohio University, from 1970 to
present; guest editor of two special issues of the <u>Mundus Artium</u>,
a Black poetry issue and a Black fiction issue, 1973. <u>Awards,</u>
<u>Honors</u>: International Institute of Education grant for travel
throughout Africa, 1972.

EDITOR

 <u>Third World Voices: An Anthology</u>. New York: Random,
  forthcoming.
 <u>Watts Poets: A Book of New Poetry and Essays</u>. Los Angeles: House of Respect, 1968.

NOVEL

 <u>The Legacy of Charlie Footman</u>. New York, Random, forthcoming.

POETRY

 <u>Ash Doors</u>. New York: Random, forthcoming.
 <u>Embryo Poems 1967-1971</u>. New York: Barlenmuir House,
  1972.
 (Anthologies): Adoff, <u>The Poetry of Black America</u>; Chap-

A. John Turner

man, New Black Voices; Coombs, We Speak as Liberators;
King, Blackspirits; Major, The New Black Poetry; Patterson, A Rock Against the Wind; Reed, Yardbird Reader I;
Watkins, Black Review No. 2.
(Periodicals): Antioch Review, Fall 1967; Black Creation,
Spring 1972; Black World, September 1970; Essence, March
1974; Negro American Literature Forum, Spring 1972; also
published in Umbra; Mediterranean Review; Concerning Poetry; Sumac; New Directions 22.
INTERJECTIONS
"Art must be innovative, expansive, stimulating, truth seeking, uplifting, and beautiful. My life has been essentially what
life is all about; living, joyous, and otherwise."

TURNER, A. John. Born 1 August 1914 in Birmingham, Alabama.
Education: Real Estate training at Lunbleau School of Real Estate, 1960; attended Simmons Institute, 1965. Career: General
door-to-door salesman, 1950. Real Estate salesman, 1960-67.
Founder of "Institute of Self Fulfillment," an institution designed
to teach the science of personal achievement, 1968. Owner of
the largest Black-owned furniture store in the downtown section
of Compton, California, 1969-73. Presently a teacher at the
"Institute of Self Fulfillment."

POETRY
The Dark Singer. East St. Louis, Ill.: By the Author, 1940.
Interlude. St. Louis, Mo.: Cathrell Printing Co., 1934.
Seven Sacred Poems. St. Louis, Mo.: By the Author, 1946.
The Song I Sing. New York: Exposition, 1964.

TURNER, Allen Pelzer. Born 1889.
Oakes of Eden. New York: Exposition, 1951.

TURNER, Claire.
POETRY (Anthology): Murphy, Negro Voices.

TURNER, Darwin. Born 7 May 1931 in Cincinnati, Ohio. Education: B.A., University of Cincinnati, 1947; M.A., University of Cincinnati, 1949; Ph.D., University of Chicago, 1956. Currently living in Washington, D.C. Career: Assistant Professor of English at Clark College, 1949-51, and at Morgan State College, 1952-57; Professor and Chairman of the English Department at Florida A. & M. State University, 1957-59, and at North Carolina A. & T. State University, 1959-66; Dean of the Graduate School at North Carolina A. & T., 1966-70; Visiting Professor of English, University of Wisconsin, 1969; Professor of English, University of Michigan, 1970-71; Graduate Record Board, 1971 to present; Dean, College of Liberal Arts, Howard University, 1971 to present; Visiting Professor, University of Hawaii, Summer, 1971. Member: Executive Committee, Conference on College Composition and Communications, 1967-69; Consultant in English and Afro-American Studies for high schools, colleges, private foundations, federal agencies; Trustee, National Council of Teachers English Research Foundation, 1970 to present; President, College Language Association, 1964-65; Chairman, Committee on Education of Minority Groups, 1969, and Director-at-large, 1967-70; National Council of Teachers of English, 1971 to present. Awards, Honors: American Council of Learned Societies grant, 1965; North Carolina-Duke Universities Co-operative Program in the Humanities fellowship; Phi Beta Kappa; Alpha Phi Alpha; Theta Alpha Phi; Lambda Iota Tau.
CRITICISM
"Afro-American Literary Critics." Black World 19 (July 1970): 54-67; also in Gayle, The Black Aesthetic.
"Ambivalent Values in Recent Best-Sellers." Journal of Human Relations 9 (Autumn 1960): 48-57.
"The Black Playwright in the Professional Theatre of the United States of America, 1858-1949." In Brasmer and Consolo, Black Drama, pp. 1-18.
"The Failure of a Playwright." CLA Journal 10 (June 1967): 308-318.
"Frank Yerby as Debunker." Massachusetts Review 9 (1968): 569-577; in Hemenway, The Black Novelist, pp. 62-71.
In a Minor Chord: Three Afro-American Writers and Their Search for Identity. Carbondale, Ill.: Southern Illinois University Press, 1971*.
"Jean Toomer's Cane: Critical Analysis." Negro Digest 18

(January 1969): 54-61.

"Langston Hughes as a Playwright." CLA Journal 11 (June 1968): 297-309.

"The Literary Presumptions of Mr. Bone." Negro Digest 16 (August 1967): 54-65.

"Literature and Society's Values." English Journal 60 (1971): 577-586.

"The Negro Dramatist's Image of the University." CLA Journal 5 (December 1961): 106-120; also in Chapman, Black Voices; Miller, Backgrounds to Blackamerican Literature; Patterson, Anthology of the American Negro in the Theatre; Turner and Bright, Images of the Negro in America.

"The Negro Novel in America: In Rebuttal." CLA Journal 10 (December 1966): 122-134.

"The Negro Novelist and the South." Southern Humanities Review 1 (1967): 21-29.

"Negro Playwrights and the Urban Negro." CLA Journal 12 (September 1968): 19-25.

"The Outsider: Revision of an Idea." CLA Journal 12 (June 1969): 310-321.

"Past and Present in Negro American Drama." Negro American Literature Forum 2 (Summer 1968): 26-27.

"Paul Laurence Dunbar: The Rejected Symbol." Journal of Negro History 52 (January 1967): 1-13; also in Hemenway, The Black Novelist, pp. 33-45.

"A Primer for Critics." CLA Journal 8 (March 1965): 217-224.

"Sight in Invisible Man." CLA Journal 13 (March 1970): 258-264.

"Smoke from Melville's Chimney." CLA Journal 7 (December 1963): 107-113.

"The Teaching of Afro-American Literature." College English 31 (1970): 666-670.

Theory and Practice in the Teaching of Literature by Afro-Americans. Urbana, Ill.: National Council of Teachers of English, 1971†.

"View of Melville's 'Piazza.'" CLA Journal 7 (September 1963): 56-62.

EDITOR

Afro-American Writers. New York: Appleton-Century-Crofts, 1970†.

Black American Literature: Essays. Indianapolis: Bobbs-Merrill, 1969†.

Black American Literature: Fiction. Indianapolis: Bobbs-Merrill, 1969†.

Black American Literature: Poetry. Indianapolis: Bobbs-Merrill, 1969†.

Black American Literature: Essays, Poetry, Fiction, Drama. Indianapolis: Bobbs-Merrill, 1969*†.

Black Drama in America: An Anthology. Greenwich, Conn.: Fawcett, 1971†.

With Jean M. Bright. Images of the Negro in America. Indianapolis: Heath, 1965†.

With Philip Thompson. <u>Responding: Five.</u> Boston: Ginn,
  1973*.
With others. <u>Voices from the Black Experience: African</u>
  <u>and Afro-American Literature.</u> Boston: Ginn, 1972†.

NON-FICTION
  (Periodicals): <u>Journal of Negro History,</u> Winter-Spring 1962;
  January 1967.

POETRY
  <u>Katharsis.</u> Wellesley, Mass.: Wellesley Press, 1964.
  <u>One Last Word.</u> Greensboro, N.C.: n.p., 1964.
  (Anthologies): Hughes and Bontemps, <u>Poetry of the Negro:</u>
  1746-1970; Major, <u>The New Black Poetry;</u> Patterson, <u>A</u>
  <u>Rock Against the Wind;</u> Shuman, <u>A Galaxy of Black Writ-</u>
  <u>ing.</u>
  (Periodicals): <u>Journal of Human Relations,</u> Summer, Winter,
  1960.

REVIEWS BY TURNER
  Published in <u>Journal of Negro History; CLA Journal.</u>

BIOGRAPHY ON TURNER
  <u>Arts in Society</u> 5 (1968): 281-282.
  <u>Contemporary Authors,</u> 21/22.

TURNER, Dennis.
  DRAMA <u>Charlies Was Here and Now He's Gone.</u>

TURNER, Rev. J.M. <u>Born</u> 1 February 1834 in Abbeville, South
  Carolina. <u>Died</u> 8 May 1915. <u>Career:</u> Was ordained Deacon,
  1860, Elder, 1862; was installed as pastor of Israel Church,
  Washington 1863; was appointed Army Chaplain of the Negro
  Troops by President Lincoln, 1863; was assigned to the Georgia
  Office of Freedman's Bureau; assisted in founding the Republican
  Party in Georgia; appointed Post Master at Macon by President
  Grant; served as U.S. Customs Inspector and as a government
  detective; was manager of the African Methodist Episcopal Book
  concern, Philadelphia, 1876; served as Church Bishop, 1880-
  1892; was chancellor of Morris College for 12 years; introduced
  African Methodism in South and West Africa; advocated the return of Blacks to Africa; founded several periodicals including
  the <u>Southern Christian Recorder,</u> 1889, and <u>Voice of Missions,</u>
  1892.[1] <u>Awards, Honors:</u> honorary degree from the University
  of Pennsylvania.[2]

NON-FICTION
  <u>The Barbarous Decision of the U.S. Supreme Court.</u> Atlanta,
  Ga.: By the Author, 1893.
  <u>The Black Man's Doom.</u> Philadelphia: J. B. Rogers, 1896.
  <u>The Conflict for Civil Rights.</u> Washington, D.C.: n.p., 1871.
  <u>The Genius and Theory of Methodist Policy.</u> Philadelphia:
  Publication Department of A.M.E. Church, 1885.
  With Charles W. Elliot and Rev. W. Spencer Carpenter.
  <u>The Negro in Slavery, War and Peace.</u> Philadelphia: A.
  M.E. Book Concern, 1913.
  <u>Respect Black: His (Turner's) Writings and Speeches.</u> Edwin S. Redkey, ed. New York: Arno Press, 1971.

Wrote Introduction to Simmons, Men of Mark.
(Anthologies): Singleton, George A.   The Romance of Afri-
can Methodism (New York: Exposition Press, 1952): Prince,
W. H.   The Stars of the Century of African Methodism
(Portland, Oregon, 1916).
(Periodicals); Augusta Colored American, 13 June 1966;
Christian Recorder, 23 July 1891; Washington Post, 25 Jan-
uary 1895; also Contributed frequently to the AME Church's
national weekly paper and his sermons were often quoted
by the white press. [3]
    [1]Dumas Malone, Dictionary of American Biography (New
York: Charles Scribner's Sons, 1936), p. 65.
    [2]Wade Baskin and Richard N. Runes, Dictionary of
Black Culture.   (New York: Philosophical Library, 1973),
p. 441.
    [3]Edwin S. Redkey, Black Exodus (New Haven: Yale Uni-
versity Press, 1969), p. 24.

TURNER, Joseph.
    DRAMA   The Scheme.

TURNER, Lucy Mae.
    POETRY
       'Bout Cullud Folkses.   New York: Harrison, 1938.
    BIOGRAPHY AND CRITICISM ON TURNER
       The Negro History Bulletin (March 1955): 129, 132, 145; al-
       so (April 1955): 155-158.

TURNER, Peter.
    Black Heat.   New York: Belmont, 1970.

TURNER, Raymond.   Born in San Pedro, California.
    POETRY
       (Anthology): Coombs, We Speak as Liberators.

TURNER, Vernon (Kitabu).
    POETRY
       The Book of Kitabu.   New York: Amuru, 1973†.
       (Periodicals): Freedomways, Fourth Waurter 1971; Second
       Quarter 1973.

TURPIN, Waters Edward.   Born 1910 in Oxford, Massachusetts.
    Died 1968.   Education: Attended Morgan State College; Ph.D.,
    Teacher's College, Columbia.   Career: Did investigation for a
    Harlem housing project.   Was professor and football coach at
    Storer College, Harper's Ferry.   Was English professor, Lin-
    coln University and Professor, Morgan State College, 1950-
    1968.   Awards, Honors: Rosenwald Fellowship for creative writ-
    ing. [1]
    CRITICISM BY TURPIN
       "The Contemporary American Negro Playwright." CLA Jour-
          nal 9 (1965): 12-24.
       "Evaluating the Work of Contemporary Negro Novelists."

Negro History Bulletin 11 (December 1947): 59-61.
"Four Short Fiction Writers of the Harlem Renaissance:
Their Legacy of Achievement." CLA Journal 11 (September 1967): 59-72.
NOVELS
O Canaan! New York: Doubleday, Doran, 1939.
The Rootless. New York: Vantage Press, 1957.
These Low Grounds. New York: Harper, 1937.
(Anthologies): Excerpts in Ford, Black Insights; Brown, Davis and Lee, Negro Caravan.
BIOGRAPHY AND CRITICISM ON TURPIN
Fleming, Robert E. "Overshadowed by Richard Wright:
Three Black Chicago Novelists." Negro American Literature Forum 7 (Fall 1973): 75-79.
Ford, Nick Aaron. Black Insights. Waltham, Mass.: Ginn, 1971, pp. 85-86.
_____. "In Memoriam: Tribute to Waters E. Turpin (1910-1968)." CLA Journal 12 (March 1969): 281-282.
Gloster. Negro Voices in American Fiction, pp. 244-248.
INTERJECTIONS
"...I believe the present-day writer can follow the lead of
André Malraux in his Man's Fate: namely, since the writer of
today must be sensitive to mass movements, his character may
epitomize man's response to his society, each character an individual and at the same time a means of making clear a reaction to the social scene."[2]

[1]Nick Aaron Ford, "In Memoriam: Tribute to Waters
E. Turpin (1910-1968)," CLA Journal 12 (March 1969),
pp. 281-282.
[2]Nick Aaron Ford, Black Insights (Waltham, Mass.:
Ginn, 1971), p. 85.

TUTT, J. Homer.
DRAMA (with Salem Whitney)
Children of the Sun.
Darkest Americans.
Deep Harlem.
De Gospel Train, 1941.
Exprsident of Liberia.
George Washington Bullion Abroad.
His Excellency the President.
Mayor of Newton.
My People.
Oh Joy.
Up and Down.

TWITT, Nathaniel I.
POETRY (Anthology): Murphy, Ebony Rhythm.

TWITTY, Countess W.
POETRY (Anthology): Murphy, Ebony Rhythm.

TYLER, Ephraim David.
    POETRY Tyler's Poems of Everyday Life.   Shreveport, La.:
        n.p., n.d.

-U-

ULLMAN, Marvin.
    DRAMA And I Am Black, 1969.

UNDERHILL, Irvin W. Born 1 May 1868 in Port Clinton, Pennsyl-
    vania. Education: Irregular schooling. Career: Assisted his
    father who was captain of a canal boat, and at the age of 38
    lost his sight. [1]
    POETRY
        The Brown Madonna and Other Poems.   Philadelphia: n.p.,
            1929.
        Daddy's Love and Other Poems.   Philadelphia: A.M.E. Book
            Concern, 1916.
    BIOGRAPHY AND CRITICISM ON UNDERHILL
        Kerlin.   Negro Poets and Their Poems, pp. 184-186.
            [1]Robert T. Kerlin, Negro Poets and Their Poems.
        (Washington, D.C.: Associated Publishers, 1923, 1935),
        p. 345.

-V-

VALE, Coston.
    POETRY (Anthology): Murphy, Negro Voices.

VALLEJO see KENNEDY, Vallejo Ryan

VANCE, Bobbye Marie Booker.   Born 16 June 1943 in New York
    City. Education: B.S., Bishop College, 1968; M.A., Atlanta
    University, 1973. Currently living in Atlanta, Georgia. Ca-
    reer: Assistant Physical Therapist, Chelsea Soldiers' Home,
    Chelsea, Mass., 1962-63; Nurse, Bishop College Infirmary,
    Dallas, 1965-66; Preschool Teacher, Searcy's Youth Foundation,
    Dallas; Teacher, Project Head Start, Boston, 1968; Inner City
    Kindergarten Teacher, Boston Public School System, 1968-69;
    Supervisor and Instructor, Child Development Department, At-
    lanta Area Technical School, 1970-72. Presently a kindergarten
    teacher in the Atlanta public schools. Member: NAEYC, 1972-
    73; Delta Sigma Theta Sorority; Greater Greenbriar Community
    Association; YWCA.
    SCREENPLAY
        With Samuel Vance.   Rip Off.
    UNPUBLISHED WORK
        Novel: "Rip Off."
        Collection of Poems.
    INTERJECTIONS
        "Writing provides an excellent avenue through which I can

hold on to my innermost ideas and impressions and review them as the days and months pass."

"Every Black person is capable of writing a best seller. Our day-to-day confrontation with mere existence provides more entertainment and information than anything labelled 'fiction.' What we must do is help our Brothers and Sisters 'get it together' on paper!"

VANCE, Samuel. <u>Born</u> 15 March 1939 in Douglas County, Georgia. <u>Education:</u> Three years of computer science in technical school. <u>Career:</u> Instructor ROTC, Rutgers University, 1967-68; Senior Programmer, 5th U.S. Army Hg. Data Processing Center, Fort Sheridan, Illinois, 1968-69; Senior Programmer Analyst, Grady Memorial Hospital, 1969-72; Programmer, Metropolitan Atlanta Rapid Transit Authority, 1972 to present. <u>Awards, Honors:</u> Purple Heart and Silver Star.
NON-FICTION
   <u>The Courageous and the Proud.</u> New York: Norton, 1970*.
SCREENPLAY
   <u>The Measure of a Man.</u>
   With Bobbye Vance. <u>Rip Off.</u>
UNPUBLISHED WORK
   Novels: "Rip Off"; "Triumph without Glory."
INTERJECTIONS
   "Where there is no vision, the people perish. I believe that a man should be treated like a man until he proves to you that he should be treated otherwise. If that is his wish, let it be granted."

VANDERPUIJE, Nii Akrampahene. <u>Born</u> 1925 in Liberia.
   <u>NOVEL</u> <u>The Counterfeit Corpse.</u> New York: Comet, 1956.

VAN DYKE, Henry. <u>Born</u> 3 October 1928 in Allegan, Michigan. <u>Education:</u> B.A., University of Michigan, 1953; M.A., University of Michigan, 1955. <u>Currently living in</u> New York City. <u>Career:</u> Associate editor, University Engineering Research Institute, Ann Arbor, 1956-58; Correspondent, Crowell-Collier-Macmillan Publishers, 1959-67. <u>Awards, Honors:</u> Recipient, Avery Hopwood Award, University of Michigan, 1954; Guggenheim Award in Creative Writing, 1971.
NOVELS
   <u>Blood of Strawberries.</u> New York: Farrar, Straus & Giroux, 1965.
   <u>Dead Piano.</u> New York: Farrar, Straus & Giroux, 1971*.
   <u>Ladies of the Rachmaninoff Eyes.</u> New York: Farrar, Straus & Giroux, 1965; New York: Manor Books, 1973†.
SHORT STORY
   (Anthology): Patterson, <u>An Introduction to Black Literature in America.</u>
REVIEWS
   <u>Blood of Strawberries</u>: Hicks, Granville. <u>Saturday Review,</u> 4 January 1969.
   <u>Dead Piano</u>: Loftin, Eloise. <u>Black Creation</u> 2 (Winter 1972):

54-55.
Ladies of the Rachmaninoff Eyes: Hicks, Granville, Satur-
    day Review, 12 June 1965.

VANDYNE, William J.
POETRY
    Revels of Fancy. Boston: Grant, 1891.
CRITICISM ON VANDYNE
    White and Jackson. An Anthology of Verse by American Ne-
    groes, p. 234.

VAN PEEBLES, Melvin. Born 21 August 1932 in Chicago, Illinois.
    Career: Creator-Producer in various media, "specializing in
    Freedom--Education--Black"; has produced ten short films, and
    four feature films (Story of a Three Day Pass; Watermelon Man;
    Sweet Sweetback's Baadasssss Song; Don't Play Us Cheap). His
    six record albums are Brer Soul; Ain't Supposed to Die a Natur-
    al Death; Watermelon Man; Serious as a Heart Attack; Sweet
    Sweetback's Baadasssss Song; Don't Play Us Cheap.
DRAMA
    Ain't Supposed to Die a Natural Death. New York: Bantam,
        1973†.
    Don't Play Us Cheap. New York: Bantam, 1973†.
NOVELS
    A Bear for the FBI. New York: Trident, 1968*. Excerpt in
        Adoff, Brothers and Sisters. (Also published in France.)
    Un américain en enfer. Translated by Paule-Eygénie Truf-
        fert. Paris: Éditions Denoël, 1965. (Also published in
        Mexico.)
    La Fête à Harlem. Paris: J. Martineau, 1967.
    Le Permission. Paris: J. Martineau, 1967.
SHORT STORIES
    Le Chinois du XIVe. Paris: le Gadenet, 1966.
BIOGRAPHY AND CRITICISM ON VAN PEEBLES
    Bailey, Peter. "Annual Round-Up: Black Theater in Amer-
        ica." Black World 21 (April 1972): 31-36.
    Bauerle, R. F. "The Theme of Absurdity in Melvin Van
        Peebles' A Bear for the FBI." Notes on Contemporary
        Literature 1 (September 1971): 11-12.
    Coleman, Horace W. "Melvin Van Peebles." Journal of
        Popular Culture 5 (Fall 1972): 368-384. (Interview with
        introduction.)
    Gussow, M. "Baadasssss Success of Melvin Van Peebles."
        New York Times Magazine, 20 August 1972, pp. 14-15.
    Harrison. The Drama of Nommo, pp. 145-147, 148, 169,
        226.
    Hewes, Henry. "The Ain'ts and the Am Nots." Saturday
        Review, 13 November 1971, pp. 10, 12.
    Higgins, C. "Meet the Man Behind the Sweetback Movie."
        Jet, 1 July 1971, pp. 54-58.
    "Interview." Black Creation (Fall 1971).
    "Power to the Peebles." Time, 16 August 1971, p. 47.
    "Scobie, W. I. "Supernigger Strikes." London Magazine

(April-May 1972): 111-116.
"Sweet Song of Success." Newsweek, 21 June 1971, p. 89.
Wolf, William. "B**da****s Peebles." Milwaukee Journal
    Magazine, 17 September 1972, pp. 33-35.

VAN SCOTT, Glory.
CHILDREN AND YOUNG ADULTS
    Baba and the Flea. Philadelphia: Lippincott, 1972*.
DRAMA
    Miss Truth. (A poetic suite on Sojourner Truth.)

VASHON, George B. Born 1820?[1] Died 5 October 1878. Educa-
tion: A.B. Oberlin College, 1844; M.A., Oberlin College, 1849.
Career: Professor of Belles Lettres at Central College, Mc-
Grawville, New York. Denited admittance to the bar in Wash-
ington, D.C. Taught at Howard University. Went to Haiti
where he taught at College Faustin, returning to the U.S. in
1850. Served as principal in a Black school in Pittsburgh,
Pennsylvania. Practiced law in Syracuse, New York. Went to
Mississippi in 1878 where he contracted Yellow Fever.[2]
LETTER
    Published in the Liberator, 27 August 1859; reprinted in
    Woodson, The Mind of the Negro as Reflected in His Let-
    ters.
NON-FICTION
    (Periodical): Afro-American Magazine 1 (July 1859): 204-
    208.
POETRY
    Vincent Ogé." In Griffiths, Julia, ed. Autographs for Free-
    dom, vol. 2.[3] Auburn; Alden, Beardsley; Richester:
    Wanzer, Beardsley, 1854, pp. 44-60. Also in Brawley,
    Early Negro American Writers; Robinson, Early Black
    American Poets.
BIOGRAPHY AND CRITICISM ON VASHON
    Bergman. The Chronological History of the Negro in Amer-
    ica, pp. 113-114, 187.
    Brawley. Early Negro American Writers, pp. 261-282.
    _____. Negro Genius, pp. 84-87.
    Brown. Homespun Heroines, pp. 133-134.
    Brown, William Wells. The Black Man: His Antecedents,
    His Genius, and His Achievements. New York: T. Hamil-
    ton; Boston: R. F. Wallcut, 1863, pp. 223-227.
    Delany, Martin Robinson. The Condition, Elevation, Emigra-
    tion and Destiny of the Colored People of the United States.
    Philadelphia: By the Author, pp. 119-120.
    Langston, John Mercer. From the Virginia Plantation to the
    National Capitol. Hartford, Conn.: American, 1894, pp.
    74-76.
    Loggins. The Negro Author, pp. 235-238.
    Robinson. Early Black American Poets, pp. 166-167.
    Wagner. Black Poets of the U.S.A., p. 22.
        [1]Jean Wagner gives 1822 as Vashon's birthdate. See
    Black Poets of the United States, p. 22.

[2]Benjamin Brawley, Early Negro American Writers
(Chapel Hill: University of North Carolina Press, 1935),
pp. 261-263.
[3]Bergman states that "Victor Ogé was published "in Vashon's anthology, Autographs of Freedom." According to
Schomburg Collection, Autographs for Freedom, vol. 2,
was edited by Julia Griffiths and published in 1854.

VASSA, Gustavus see EQUIANO, Olaudah

VAUGHN, James. Born 1929 in Xenia, Ohio.
    POETRY (Anthologies): Bontemps, American Negro Poetry;
        Hughes, New Negro Poets, USA; Hughes and Bontemps,
        Poetry of the Negro: 1746-1970.

VAUGHN, Naomi Evans.
    POETRY (Anthologies): Murphy, Ebony Rhythm; Murphy, Negro
        Voices.

VAUGHT, Estella.
    Vengeance Is Mine. New York: Comet, 1959.

VERNE, Berta (pseud.)
    NOVEL Elastic Fingers. New York: Vantage, 1969.

VERTA MAE see GROSVENOR, Verta Mae

VESEY, Paul see ALLEN, Samuel

VOGLIN, Peter.
    NOVEL Now You Lay Me Down to Sleep. Dallas: n.p., 1962.

VOTEUR, Ferdinand.
    DRAMA The Right Angle Triangle, 1939.

VROMAN, Mary Elizabeth. Born 1923 in Buffalo, New York; was
    raised in the West Indies. Died 1967. Education: B.A., Ala-
    bama State College. Career: Taught at Camden Academy in
    Camden, Alabama. Served as technical advisor for the film,
    Bright Road, which was based on her short story, "See How
    They Run." Member: Screen Writers' Guild. Awards, Honors:
    Christopher Award for Inspirational Magazine Writing.[1]
    NON-FICTION
        Shaped to Its Purpose: Delta Sigma Theta, The First Fifty
            Years. New York: Random House, 1965.
        (Periodicals): Ladies Home Journal, September 1951; Febru-
            ary 1957; National Education Association Journal, October
            1951.
    NOVELS
        Esther. New York: Bantam, 1963.
        Harlem Summer. New York: Putnam, 1967.
    POETRY
        (Periodical): Ladies Home Journal, January 1954.

SCREENPLAY
   Bright Road, MGM. (Based on short story, "See How They
      Run." Ladies Home Journal, June 1951.
SHORT STORIES
   (Anthology): Hughes, Best Short Stories by Negro Writers.
   (Periodicals): Freedomways, Spring 1962; Spring 1963;
      Ladies Home Journal, June 1951.
BIOGRAPHY AND CRITICISM ON VROMAN
   Bachner, Saul. "Black Literature: The Junior Novel in the
      Classroom--Harlem Summer." Negro American Literature
      Forum 7 (Spring 1973): 26-27.
   New York Times, 30 April 1967, p. 86. (Obituary.)
   "Writing School Marm: Alabama Teacher Finds Literary,
      Movie Success with First Short Story." Ebony (July 1952):
      23-28.

-W-

WAKEFIELD, Jacques (Abayome Oji).
   POETRY
      Lub. n.p.: Bruthers Hue Man Publications, 1971.
      (Anthologies): Coombs, We Speak as Liberators; Jones and
         Neal, Black Fire.
      (Periodicals): Black Creation, Winter 1973; also published in
         Journal of Black Poetry.

WALCOTT, Brenda. Born 12 July 1938 in Brooklyn, New York.
   Education: M.Ed., Harvard University, 1973. Currently living
   in Cambridge, Massachusetts. Career: Presently a graduate
   student at Harvard University in Education Media. Wrote "A
   Child's World," a video show on children and poetry, produced
   at Harvard Educational Media Center.
   DRAMA
      The Black Puppet Show.
      Fantastical Fanny.
      Look Not Upon Me.
      Temporary Lives.
   WORK IN PROGRESS
      Novel: "My Man--Jones."
   INTERJECTIONS
      "I just try to keep on pushing, growing, and producing."

WALDEN, Islay. Born 1849. Died 1884.
   POETRY
      Walden's Miscellaneous Poems. Washington, D.C.: Reed &
         Woodward, Printers, 1872. Revised ed., 1873.
      Walden's Sacred Poems, with a Sketch of his Life. New
         Brunswick, N.J.: Terhune & Van Anglen's Press, 1877.
   RITUAL
      Ritual of the Golden Circle. Washington, D.C.: Cunningham
         & Brashears, 1875.

Alice Walker (credit: Lilian Kemp)

CRITICISM ON WALDEN
   White and Jackson. An Anthology of Verse by American Negroes, pp. 234-235.

WALKER, Alice. Born 9 February 1944 in Eatonton, Georgia.
   Education: Attended Spelman College, 1961-63; A.B., Sarah
   Lawrence College, 1965. Career: Teacher of Black Studies at
   Jackson State College, 1968-69, and at Tougaloo College, 1970-
   71. Lecturer in Literature and Writing at Wellesley College,
   1972-73; Lecturer in Literature by Black Women Writers, University of Massachusetts, 1973. Currently a Fellow at the Rad-

cliffe Institute, working on a second novel. Member: Board of
Trustees, Sarah Lawrence College; Sponsor, with Mel Leventhal, annual writing award to honor black women writers of the
twenties and thirties, Tougaloo College. Awards, Honors:
First Prize, The American Scholar essay contest, 1967; Merrill Fellowship for Writing, 1966-67; Scholar, Bread Loaf, 1966;
Fellow, the McDowell Colony, 1967; National Endowment for the
Arts Grant, 1969, for The Third Life of Grange Copeland; Radcliffe Institute Fellowship (with appointment by the Harvard Corporation), 1971-73.

CRITICISM
"The Black Writer and the Southern Experience." New South
25 (Fall 1970): 23-26.
"Black Writer's Views on Literary Lions and Values." Negro Digest 18 (January 1968): 13.
"Something to Do with Real Life." The Harvard Advocate
(Winter 1973). Interview with Eudora Welty.
"The Unglamorous but Worthwhile Duties of the Black Revolutionary Artist, or of the Black Writer Who Simply Works
and Writes." The Black Collegian, 1971.
"Women on Women." The American Scholar (Fall 1972).
Interview with Lillian Hellman, pp. 599-627.

CHILDREN AND YOUNG ADULTS
Langston Hughes. New York: T. Y. Crowell, 1973*.

NON-FICTION
(Periodicals): The American Scholar, 1967; The Black Sholar, January-February 1970; Moderator, 1966; Redbook,
September 1971.

NOVEL
The Third Life of Grange Copeland. New York: Harcourt
Brace Jovanovich, 1970*; condensed in Redbook, May 1971.

POETRY
Once: Poems. New York: Harcourt Brace Jovanovich,
1968*.
Revolutionary Petunias and Other Poems. New York: Harcourt Brace Jovanovich, 1973*.
(Anthologies): Adoff, The Poetry of Black America; Hayden,
Burrows, and Lapides, Afro-American Literature; Kaplan,
Voices of the Revolution; Patterson, A Rock Against the
Wind.
(Periodicals): The Activist, 1966; Black World, November
1970; Essence, July 1972; Freedomways, Fourth Quarter
1971; Ms.; Umbra, 1967-68.

SHORT STORIES
In Love and Trouble: Stories of Black Women. New York:
Harcourt Brace Jovanovich, 1973*.
(Anthologies): Bambara, Tales and Stories; Ferguson, Images of Women in Literature; Hughes, The Best Short Stories by Negro Writers; King, Black Short Story Anthology;
Sanchez, We Be Word Sorcerers.
(Periodicals): Brother, 1969; Denver Quarterly, Summer
1967; Essence, September 1971; Freedomways, Summer
1968; 1972; Harper's, March 1972; April 1973; Ms., Au-

gust 1972; July 1973; Negro Digest, June 1968; Red Clay
Reader, No. 7 (1970).

BIOGRAPHY AND CRITICISM ON WALKER

Contemporary Authors, 37/40.

O'Brien. Interviews with Black Writers, pp. 185-211.

O'Leary, Donald J. Freedomways 9 (Winter 1969): 70-73.
(Ms. Walker's response included.)

Smith, Barbara. "The Souls of Black Women." Ms. 2 (February 1974): 42-43, 78.

REVIEWS: The Third Life of Grange Copeland

Plumpp, Falvia. Black Books Bulletin 1 (Fall 1971): 26-27.

Revolutionary Petunias and Other Poems

Black World 22 (September 1973): 51.

INTERJECTIONS

"I believe that art is the medium through which spiritual energy is transferred, and is therefore as necessary to a person's
mind and spirit and soul as food is to the body."

WALKER, Claude, Jr.
Sabih. New York: Carlton, 1966.

WALKER, David. Born 28 September 1785 in Wilmington, North
Carolina. Died 28 June 1830. Education: Informal. Career:
Walker was the son of a free mother and slave father. As a
free man, he traveled extensively in the South during his youth,
and his travels combined with his reading convinced him that
American slavery was the cruelest form of bondage that the
world had ever seen. He moved to Boston in 1827 and established a second-hand clothing business there. Was Boston agent
for Freedom's Journal, America's first Black Newspaper. Wrote
for Rights of all, another abolitionist publication. His appeal
"caused so much consternation that it was rumored a price had
been placed on Walker's life..., and when the author was found
dead outside his second-hand clothes shop in 1830, there were
few who doubted that he had died a violent death."[1]

ESSAYS

Walker's Appeal in Four Articles Together with a Preamble
to the Colored Citizens of the World, but in Particular and
Very Expressly for Those of the United States. Boston:
David Walker, 1830.

(Anthologies): Adams, Conn and Slepian, Afro-American Lit-
erature; Baker, Black Literature in America; Bennett,
Pioneers in Protest; Brawley, Early Negro American
Writers; Davis and Redding, Cavalcade; Loggins, The Ne-
gro Author; Redding, To Make a Poet Black; Robinson,
Early Black American Prose; Woodson, The Mind of the
Negro as Reflected in his Writings (Letter); Fishel and
Quarles, The Black American; Miller, Blackamerican Lit-
erature.

(Periodical): Liberator, 22 January 1831.

BIOGRAPHY AND CRITICISM ON WALKER

Aptheker, Herbert. One Continual Cry. New York: Humanities Press, 1965.

Baker. <u>Black Literature in America,</u> p. 426.
Baskin and Runes. <u>Dictionary of Black Culture,</u> p. 457.
Brawley. <u>Early Negro American Writers.</u>
Davis. <u>American Negro Reference Book,</u> p. 587.
Eaton, Clement. "A Dangerous Pamphlet in the Old South."
   <u>Journal of Southern History,</u> August 1936.
Loggins. <u>The Negro Author,</u> pp. 85-90.
Redding. <u>To Make a Poet Black,</u> pp. 20, 21.
Wiltse, Charles M., ed. <u>David Walker's Appeal.</u>   New
   York: Hill and Wang, 1965.
   [1]Houston A. Baker, Jr., <u>Black Literature in America</u>
   (New York: McGraw-Hill, 1971), p. 426.

WALKER, Drake. <u>Born</u> 15 February 1936 in Birmingham, Alabama.
   <u>Education:</u> Attended the High School of Music and Art in New
   York City; was an art major at New York University. <u>Currently</u>
   <u>living in</u> Brooklyn, New York. <u>Career:</u> Presently directing and
   producing four motion pictures which he has also written. <u>Mem-</u>
   <u>ber:</u> WGA; SAG; DGA.
   NOVEL
      <u>Buck and the Preacher.</u>   New York: Popular Library, 1971.
   SCREENPLAYS
      <u>Buck and the Preacher</u> (Columbia Pictures, 1969-70).
      <u>Henry O. and Jimmy D</u> (Drapat Productions, 1974-75).
      <u>The Joust</u> (Drapat Productions, 1975-76).
      <u>The Prodigals</u> (Drapat Productions, 1974).
   INTERJECTIONS
      "The only way that black people of the arts are going to at-
   tain the respect and proper stature in the arts is going to be
   through hard work and a strong will and determination.
      "I do not believe that the black artist should sit back and
   hope that the white arts will give due respect to them 'IN DUE
   TIME.'
      "There is so much that we have to bring to the public in gen-
   eral. I don't believe that we have to wait for the approval of
   other societies. I also think that with a positive attitude in this
   direction that we will also get the proper BLACK support that is
   definitely necessary. Blacks supporting blacks and not confined
   to wait for the approval of whites. This is not intended to be-
   little the white arts, but simply to say that if we are to get
   ahead, then we must make our own goals and stride strongly in
   that direction."

WALKER, Evan.
   DRAMA
      <u>Coda for the Blues,</u> 1968.
      <u>Dark Light in May</u> (one act), 1960.
      <u>East of Jordan,</u> 1969.
      <u>The Message</u> (one act), 1969.
      <u>A War for Brutus,</u> 1958.
   SHORT STORIES
      (Anthologies): Coombs, <u>What We Must See</u>; King, <u>Black Short</u>
         <u>Story Anthology</u>; Mayfield, <u>Ten Times Black</u>; Sanchez, <u>We</u>

Be Word Sorcerers.
(Periodical): Black World, May 1970.

WALKER, George.
   DRAMA
      With Bert Williams. Sons of Ham, 1899.
   BIOGRAPHY AND CRITICISM ON WALKER
      Hughes and Meltzer. Black Magic, pp. 46, 47, 51, 54, 56,
         59, 286, 337.
      Johnson. Black Manhattan, pp. 95, 102, 103, 104-108, 109,
         110, 114, 119-120, 127, 171, 172, 174, 178, 185, 187.
      Mitchell. Black Drama, pp. 1, 40, 42, 44, 47, 48-53, 60.

WALKER, James Robert.
   POETRY
      Be Firm My Hope. New York: Comet, 1955.
      Menus of Love. New York: Carlton, 1963.
      Speak Nature. New York: Carlton, 1965.

WALKER, Joseph.
   DRAMA
      With Josephine Jackson. The Believers, 1968. In Guernsey,
         Best Plays of 1967-1968.
      The Harangues, 1969.
      The Hiss.
      Ododo, 1968. In King and Milner, Black Drama Anthology;
         Best Short Plays of 1970. (Music written by Dorothy Din-
         roe.)
      The River Niger. New York: Hill & Wang, forthcoming.
      Themes of the Black Struggle, 1970.
      Yin-Yang, 1973.
   NON-FICTION
      (Periodical): Essence, October 1973.
   REVIEWS: Ododo
      Barnes, Clive. New York Times, 25 November 1970.
      Johnson, H. A. Black World 2 (April 1971): 47-48.
      Kerr, Walter. The Sunday Times, 6 December 1970.
   The River Niger
      New Yorker, 16 December 1972, p. 86.
      Times, 1 January 1973, p. 64.

WALKER, Margaret (Mrs. F. J. Alexander). Born 7 July 1915 in
   Birmingham, Alabama. Education: A.B., Northwestern University, 1935; M.A., University of Iowa, 1945; Ph.D., University
   of Iowa, 1965. Currently living in Jackson, Mississippi. Career: Taught at Livingstone College, 1941-42 and 1945-46; at
   West Virginia State College, 1942-43; at Jackson State College
   since 1949. Currently Director of the Institute for the Study of
   History, Life and Culture of Black People. Visiting Professor
   of Creative Writing at Northwestern University, Spring 1969; on
   the Lecture Platform, National Concert and Artists Corporation,
   1943-48; member of the program of the Cape Cod Writers Conference at Craigville, Summer 1967; has held innumerable speak-

ing engagements and poetry readings at colleges, universities, churches, women's clubs, civic organizations, radio and television. Member: National Council of Teachers of English; Modern Language Association; Poetry Society of America; American Association of University Professors; Alpha Kappa Alpha Sorority; National Education Association. Awards, Honors: Yale Award for Younger Poets, 1942; Rosenwald Fellowship for Creative Writing, 1944; Ford Fellow, Yale University, 1954, Fund for the Advancement of Education; Houghton-Mifflin Literary Fellowship, 1966; Mable Carney SNEA Plaque for Scholar-Teacher of the Year, 1966; AKA Citation, 1966, Alpha Kappa Alpha National Sorority Inc.; Citation for Achievement, The Mississippi Valley State College; Citation, New Orleans Urban League Guild, 1968 (presented the key to the City of New Orleans by Mayor Victor Schiro); member of the Honor Roll of Race Relations, Schomburg Collection, New York City Library; Guest at the New York Herald Tribune Book and Author Luncheon, November 1942; appeared at the Book and Author Luncheon for Newsday, Garden City, New York, October 1966.

CRITICISM BY WALKER
"Black Writer's Views on Literary Lions and Values." Negro Digest 17 (January 1968): 23.
How I Wrote Jubilee. Black Paper Series. Chicago: Third World, 1972†.
"The Humanistic Tradition of Afro-American Literature." American Libraries 1 (October 1970): 849-854.
"New Poets." Phylon 11 (1950): 345-354; also in Gayle, Black Expression, pp. 89-99.

NON-FICTION
With Nikki Giovanni. A Poetic Equation: Conversations Between Nikki Giovanni and Margaret Walker. Washington, D.C.: Howard University Press, 1974.
(Periodicals): Education Age, May 1967; Negro Digest, 1951.

NOVEL
Jubilee. Boston: Houghton Mifflin, 1966*. Excerpt in Chambers and Moon, Right On!; Tri-Quarterly, Winter 1964-65.

POETRY
For My People. Younger Poets Series No. 41, 1942; reprint ed. New Haven, Conn.: Yale University Press, 1968*.
October Journey. Detroit: Broadside, forthcoming.
Prophets for a New Day. Detroit: Broadside, 1970†.
(Broadside): "Ballad of the Free for Malcolm X." Detroit: Broadside, 1966.
(Anthologies): Adams, Conn and Slepian, Afro-American Literature: Poetry; Adoff, Black Out Loud; Adoff, The Poetry of Black America; Baker, Black Literature in America; Barksdale and Kinnamon, Black Writers of America; Bell, Afro-American Poetry; Bontemps, American Negro Poetry; Brooks, A Broadside Treasury; Brown, Davis and Lee, The Negro Caravan; Brown, Lee and Ward, To Gwen with Love; Chapman, Black Voices; Davis and Redding, Cavalcade; Emanuel and Gross, Dark Symphony; Ford, Black Insights; Hayden, Kaleidoscope; Hayden, Burrows and La-

pides, Afro-American Literature; Henderson, Understand-
ing the New Black Poetry; Hughes and Bontemps, Poetry of
the Negro: 1746-1970; Jordan, Soulscript; Kearns, The
Black Experience; Kendricks, Afro-American Voices; Ker-
lin, Negro Poets and Their Poems; Long and Collier, Afro-
American Writing; Miller, Blackamerican Literature; Pat-
terson, An Introduction to Black Literature in America;
Pool, Beyond the Blues; Pool, Ik Zag Hoe Zward Ik Was
(The Netherlands); Randall, The Black Poets; Randall,
Black Poetry: A Supplement; Randall and Burroughs, For
Malcolm; Rollins, Famous American Negro Poets; Singh
and Fellowes, Black Literature in America; Turner, Black
American Literature: Poetry; Walrond and Pool, Black and
Unknown Bards; Weisman and Wright, Black Poetry for All
Americans; Williams, Beyond the Angry Black.
(Periodicals): Crisis, 1934, November 1970; Negro Story,
July-August 1944; New Challenge, Fall 1937; Opportunity,
May, June, August, November 1938; January 1939; 1942;
Phylon, Fourth Quarter 1944; Third Quarter, 1952; Poetry,
1938; 1939; Poetry Magazine, 1937; Virginia Quarterly,
1955.

BIOGRAPHY AND CRITICISM ON WALKER
Bardolph. The Negro Vanguard, pp. 374, 377, 378, 379.
Barksdale and Kinnamon. Black Writers of America, pp.
  635-636.
Current Biography (1943).
Gayle. Black Expression, 36, 85-86, 93, 110, 223, 225,
  239,254.
Giddings, Paula. " 'A Shoulder Hunched Against a Sharp Con-
  cern': Some Themes in the Poetry of Margaret Walker."
  Black World 21 (December 1971): 2-25.
Littlejohn. Black on White.
Malkoff. Crowell's Handbook of Contemporary American Po-
  etry, pp. 319-322.
Opportunity 20 (December 1942): 372.
Ploski and Kaiser. The Negro Almanac, pp. 694, 696.
"Poets." Ebony 4 (February 1949): 41.
Randall, Dudley. "The Black Aesthetic in the Thirties, For-
  ties and Fifties." In Gayle, The Black Aesthetic.
Rollins. Famous American Negro Poets.
Shockley and Chandler. Living Black American Authors, p.
  164.
Whitlow. Black American Literature, pp. 136-139.
Williams. American Black Women, pp. 36, 48, 50, 87-88,
  130.
Who's Who of American Women, 8th ed. (1974-1975).
Young. Black Writers of the Thirties, pp. 167, 197-201.

REVIEWS: Jubilee
Barrow, William. Negro Digest 16 (February 1967): 93-95.
Buckmaster, Henrietta. Christian Science Monitor, 29 Sep-
  tember 1966, p. 11.
Carvlin, Evanne. Community 26 (February 1967): 13.
Chapman, Abraham. Saturday Review, 24 September 1966,
  p. 43.

Dykeman, Wilma. New York Times Book Review, 25 September 1966, p. 52.
Maroney, Sheila. Crisis 73 (November 1966): 493.
Times Literary Supplement, 29 June 1967, p. 583.

WALKER, Thomas Hamilton Beb. Born 1873.
NOVELS
Revelation Trial and Exile of John in Epic. Gainesville,
Fla.: Pepper, 1912.
Bebbly, or, The Victorious Preacher. Gainesville, Fla.:
Pepper, 1910.
J. Johnson, or "The Unknown Man": An Answer to Mr.
Thos. Dixon's "Sins of the Fathers." DeLand, Fla.: E.
O. Painter Printing, 1915.
NON-FICTION
History of Liberia. Boston: Cornhill, 1921.
The Presidents of Liberia. Jacksonville, Fla.: Mintz Printing Co., 1915.

WALKER, Victor Steven. Born 19 July 1947 in Chicago.
SHORT STORY (Anthology): Chapman, New Black Voices.

WALKER, William A. Career: Founded Coffee 'n' Confusion, a
privately run workshop for poetry, jazz, and folk music, Washington, D.C.; organized a repertoire filmmaking company.
DRAMA
Aurw Hell and Spanish Prison Reform.
POETRY
Poem Book No. 10 of Every Day Life Poetry. Chicago,
1943.
Poem Book of Inspirational Thoughts. Chicago: By the Author, 1940.
Walker's Book of Original Poems. Chicago: Jones, 1939.
Walker's Everyday Life Poetry Book. Chicago: S. W. White,
1936.
Walker's Humorous Poem Book. Chicago: By the Author,
1940.
Walker's No. 1 All Occasion Poem Book. New York: Exposition, 1940.
Walker's No. 2 All Occasion Poem Book. Chicago: By the
Author, 1944.
Walker's No. 8 Poem Book. Chicago: By the Author, 1942.
Walker's No. 9 Poem Book. Chicago: By the Author, 1943.

WALLACE, Elisabeth West.
NOVEL Scandal at Daybreak. New York: Pageant, 1954.

WALLER, Effie.
POETRY
Songs of the Months. New York: Broadway, 1904.
Rhymes from Cumberland. New York: Broadway, 1909.

WALMSLEY, Dewdrop.
  DRAMA Genius in Slavery (one act). New York: Amuru, 1973†.

WALROND, Eric. Born 1898 in Georgetown, British Guiana. Died
  1966. Education: studied with private tutors, 1913-16; attended
  College of the City of New York, 1918-21; studied at Columbia
  University for one year. Career: was employed with the Health
  Department in Christobal; worked as a reporter for the Star and
  Herald, 1916-18. Walrond arrived in New York City in 1918.
  Served as Associate Editor of The Brooklyn and Long Island In-
  former, and The Negro World, 1923; Business Manager for Op-
  portunity, 1925-27.[1]
  EDITOR
    With Rosey E. Pool. Black and Unknown Bards. Aldington,
      Kent (England): Hand and Flower Press, 1958.
  NON-FICTION
    (Periodicals): Current History, February, September 1923;
      The Independent, January 1925; The New Republic, Novem-
      ber 1922.
  SHORT STORY
    Tropic Death. New York: Boni & Liveright, 1926; New York:
      Macmillan, 1954, 1972.
    (Anthologies): Barksdale and Kinnamon, Black Writers of
      America; Brooks, Kreyborg, Mumford and Rosenfeld, The
      American Caravan; Calverton, Anthology of American Ne-
      gro Literature; Emanuel and Gross, Dark Symphony;
      Hughes, Best Short Stories By Negro Writers; James,
      From the Roots; O'Brien, Best Short Stories.
    (Periodicals): Opportunity, August, September, November
      1923; January, June 1924; June, July 1925; March 1927;
      The Smart Set, September 1923. Also published in All
      Star Weekly; The New Age; The Saturday Review of Litera-
      ture; Success Magazine; Vanity Fair.
  BIOGRAPHY AND CRITICISM ON WALROND
    Barksdale and Kinnamon. Black Writers of America.
    Brawley. The Negro in Literature and Art, pp. 118-119.
    _____. Negro Genius.
    Brown. The Negro in American Fiction, p. 145.
    Emanuel and Gross. Dark Symphony.
    Gloster. Negro Voices in American Fiction, pp. 181-183,
      194-195.
    Redding. To Make a Poet Black, p. 118.
    Wagner. Black Poets of the U.S.A., pp. 302-303.
  REVIEWS: Tropic Death
    Du Bois, W. E. B. Crisis 33 (1927): 152.
    Herrick, Robert. The New Republic, 10 November 1926, p.
      332.
    Hughes, Langston. "Marl-Dust and West Indian Sun." New
      York Herald Tribune Books, 5 December 1926, p. 9.
        [1]Alain Locke, ed., The New Negro (New York: Boni,
      1925), pp. 415-416.

WALTON, Bruce (Mtu Weusi).
POETRY (Anthology): Brown, Lee and Ward, To Gwen with Love.

WAMBLE, Thelma. Born 9 January 1916 in Fort Smith, Arkansas. Career: See Shockley and Chandler, Living Black American Authors, p. 165.
NOVELS
All in the Family. New York: New Voices, 1953.
Look Over My Shoulder. New York: Vantage, 1969.

WANDICK, W. D.
POETRY (Anthology): Brown, Lee and Ward, To Gwen with Love.

WANGARA, Harun Kofi (Harold G. Lawrence). Born 14 December 1928 in Detroit.
EDITOR
With Ahmad Alhamisi. Black Arts. Detroit: Broadside, 1970.
POETRY
(Anthology): Simmons and Hutchinson, Black Culture.
(Periodical): Negro Digest, June 1962.
NON-FICTION
(Anthology): Alhamisi and Wangara, Black Arts.
(Periodical): Crisis, June-July 1962.
SHORT STORY
(Periodical): Negro History Bulletin, October 1962; also published in Journal of Black Poetry, Our Heritage Series, The Siren (Ghana), Uhuru.
BIOGRAPHY ON WANGARA
Negro History Bulletin 26 (October 1962).

WANGARA, Malaiko Ayo (Joyce Whitsitt Lawrence).
POETRY
(Anthologies): Alhamisi and Wangara, Black Arts; Brooks, A Broadside Treasury; Chambers and Moon, Right On!; Major, The New Black Poetry; Randall and Burroughs, For Malcolm.
(Periodical): Negro Digest, September 1964; May, June 1966.

WARD, Douglas Turner. Born 1931 in Burnside, Louisiana.
CRITICISM
"Needed: A Theatre for Black Themes." Negro Digest 17 (December 1967): 34-39.
"American Theatre: For Whites Only?" In Patterson, Anthology of the American Negro in the Theater. (Originally published in The New York Times, 14 August 1966.)
DRAMA
Brotherhood. In King and Milner, Black Drama Anthology.
Happy Ending. New York: Dramatist Play Service, 1968.
Also in Couch, New Black Playwrights; Oliver and Sills, Contemporary Black Drama; Liberator 4 (1964): 18.
Day of Absence. New York: Dramatists Play Service, 1968;

also in Brasmer and Consolo, Black Drama; Couch, New
Black Playwrights; Hayden, Burrows and Lapides, Afro-
American Literature; Miller, Blackamerican Literature;
Oliver and Sills, Contemporary Black Drama; Scenes in
Childress, Black Scenes; Simmons and Hutchinson, Black
Culture.
The Reckoning, 1969.
Two Plays. New York: Third, 1971*†.
BIOGRAPHY AND CRITICISM ON WARD
  Abramson. The Negro Playwright in the American Theatre,
    pp. 279-281.
  Harrison. The Drama of Nommo, pp. 174-176, 207, 228-
    229.
  Hughes and Meltzer. Black Magic, pp. 222-249 passim.
  "Interview." Black Creation, Winter 1972.
  Klotman, Phyllis R. "The Passive Resistant in A Different
    Drummer, Day of Absence and Many Thousands Gone."
    Studies in Black Literature 3 (Autumn 1972): 7-12.
  Mitchell. Black Drama, pp. 209-211, 215, 216.
  Patterson, James E. "The Negro Ensemble Company."
    Players 47 (June-July 1972): 224-229.
  Peavy. "Satire and Contemporary Black Drama," pp. 47-48.

WARD, Ella J. Mayo.
  POETRY
    Purple Wings: A Book of Verse. Charlottesville, Va.: The
      Michie Co., 1941.
    Bougainvillea and Desert Sand. Charlottesville, Va.: The
      Michie Co., 1942.

WARD, Francis. Born 11 August 1935 in Atlanta, Georgia. Education: B.A. (English) Morehouse College, 1958; M.A. (Journalism), Syracuse University, 1961; Member of Kuumba Workshop
  since Spring 1968. Currently living in Chicago, Illinois. Career: Presently a News Reporter, Los Angeles Times, Chicago
  Bureau, and an instructor (Writers Division), the Kuumba Workshop. Has had eight years of experience as news reporter with
  the Atlanta Daily World, Jet, Ebony Magazine, and the Chicago
  Sun-Times. Member: United Black Journalists (Chicago): Kuumba Workshop (Chicago).
  CRITICISM
    With Val Gray Ward. "The Black Artist--His Role in the
      Struggle." Black Scholar 2 (January 1971): 23-32.
    With Val Gray Ward. "Theatre Round-Up: Chicago." Black
      World 21 (April 1972): 37.
  DRAMA
    The Life of Harriet Tubman.
  EDITOR
    With Patricia L. Brown and Don L. Lee. To Gwen with Love.
      Chicago: Johnson, 1970.
  NON-FICTION
    "Superfly"--A Political and Cultural Condemnation by the Ku-
      umba Workshop. Chicago: Institute of Positive Education,

n.d. (Pamphlet.)
(Anthology): Brown, Lee and Ward, To Gwen with Love.
(Periodicals): Black Scholar, October 1973; Black World.
INTERJECTIONS
"Black art and Black life are inseparable; Black artists have
a permanent responsibility to the liberation struggle; Blackness
permeates the work of every Black artist whatever his political
or philosophical persuasion."

WARD, Matthew.
NOVEL The Indignant Heart. New York: New Books, 1952.

WARD, Theodore. Born 15 September 1902 in Thibodeaux, Louisi-
ana.
CRITICISM
"Five Negro Novelists: Revolt and Retreat." Mainstream 1
(Winter 1947): 100-110.
"Our Conception of the Theatre and Its Function." In Taylor,
People's Theatre in Amerika, pp. 188-190.
"The South Side Center of the Performing Arts, Inc." Black
Theatre No. 2 (1969): 3-4.
"Why Not a Negro Drama for Negroes by Negroes?" Current
Opinion 72 (1922): 639-640.
DRAMA
Big White Fog: A Negro Tragedy, 1937. Excerpt in Brown,
Davis and Lee, The Negro Caravan.
The Daubers. Scene in Childress, Black Scenes.
Falcon of Adowa.
John Brown, Act 1, Scene 4 in Masses and Mainstream 2 (Oc-
tober 1949).
Our Lan'. In A Theatre in Your Head. Edited by Kenneth
Rowe. (New York: Funk and Wagnall, 1960.) Also in
Turner, Black Drama in America.
Sick and Tired.
Whole Hog or Nothing.
BIOGRAPHY AND CRITICISM ON WARD
Abramson. Negro Playwrights in the American Theatre, pp.
109-284 passim.
Hughes and Meltzer. Black Magic, pp. 124, 199.
Mitchell, Black Drama, pp. 113-114, 133-134.
Turner. Black Drama in America: An Anthology, p. 115.

WARD, Thomas Playfair.
NOVELS
The Clutches of Circumstances. New York: Pageant, 1954.
The Right to Live. New York: Pageant, 1953.
The Truth that Makes Men Free. New York: Pageant, 1955.

WARD, Val Gray.
CRITICISM
With Francis Ward. "The Black Artist--His Role in the
Struggle." Black Scholar 2 (January 1971): 23-32.
With Francis Ward. "Theatre Round-Up: Chicago." Black

World 21 (April 1972): 37.
POETRY
    (Anthology): Brown, Lee and Ward, To Gwen with Love.

WARDLOW, Exavier X Lowtricia.
    SHORT STORY (Anthology): Sanchez, We Be Word Sorcerers.

WARING, Robert L.
    NOVEL
        As We See It. Washington, D.C.: C. F. Sudworth, 1910.
    CRITICISM ON WARING
        Gloster. Negro Voices in American Fiction, pp. 73-74.

WARNER, Samuel Jonathan. Born 1896.
    NON-FICTION
        Self-Realization and Self Defeat. New York: Grove, 1966.
        The Urge to Mass Destruction. New York: Grune & Strat-
            ton, 1957.
    NOVEL
        Madam President-Elect: A Novel. New York: Exposition,
            1956.

WARREN, Alyce. Born 1940 in Sampson County, South Carolina.
    Career: See Shockley and Chandler, Living Black American Au-
    thors, p. 166.
    WRITINGS
        Into These Depths. New York: Vantage Press, 1968.

WARREN, Lloyd.
    POETRY (Anthology): Murphy, Ebony Rhythm.

WARRICK, Calvin Horatio.
    POETRY
        The Black Rose and Other Poems. Kansas City, Mo.: Ray-
            mond Youmans, 1935.
        Gossip's Row. Kansas City: Quality Printing Co., 1925.
        The True Criteria and Other Poems. Kansas City, Mo.:
            The Sojourner Press, 1924.

WASHINGTON, Bob.
    POETRY S.N.C.C. "ers" They Probe Down to the C.O.R.E.
    Newark, N.J.: Power Press, 1968.

WASHINGTON, Booker T. Born 5 April 1856 in Roanoke, Virginia. [1]
    Died 14 November 1915. Education: B.A., Hampton Institute,
    1875; M.A. Wayland Seminary, Washington, D.C., 1879. Career:
    Was Secretary to General Armstrong after graduation from
    Hampton Institute; was waiter at a summer hotel in Connecticut;
    taught at a Black school in Waldon, West Virginia; was in charge
    of the Indian dormitory and night school at Wayland Seminary,
    1897; started many forms of rural extension work; founded Na-
    tional Negro Health Week, 1914; the National Negro Business
    League, 1900; and Tuskegee Institute, 1881. Awards, Honors:

Was graduated with honors from Hampton Institute, 1875;[2] was awarded an honorary M.A. degree from Harvard; was awarded an honorary Doctor of Laws degree from Dartmouth College;[3] his bust which was designed by the distinguished Black sculptor, Richmond Barthé, stands today in New York University's Hall of Fame.[4]

AUTOBIOGRAPHY

The Story of My Life and Work. Naperville, Illinois and Toronto, Ont.: J. L. Nichols, 1901; revised in 1915.

Up from Slavery. New York: Doubleday, Page and Co., 1901 (published Serially in the Outlook, 1900).

Working with the Hands: Being a Sequel to "Up from Slavery" Covering the Author's Experiences in Industrial Training at Tuskegee. New York: Doubleday, Page, 1904.

NON-FICTION

Black Belt Diamond: Gems from the Speeches, Addresses, and Talks to Students by Booker T. Washington and arranged by Victoria Earle Matthews. New York: Fortune & Scott, 1898.

Character Building: Being Addresses Delivered on Sunday Evenings to the Students of Tuskegee Institute. New York: Doubleday, Page, 1902.

Education of the Negro. Albany, N.Y.: J.B. Lyon, 1900; 1904.

Frederick Douglass. Philadelphia and London: G. W. Jacobs, 1907.

The Future of the American Negro. Boston: Small, Maynard, 1899.

With Robert E. Pack. The Man Farthest Down: A Record of Observation and Study in Europe. New York: Doubleday, Page, 1912.

My Larger Education. New York: Doubleday, Page, 1911.

The Negro in Business. Boston and Chicago: Hertel, Jenkins, 1907.

The Negro in the South. Philadelphia: G. W. Jacobs, 1907.

One Hundred Selected Sayings of Booker T. Washington. Montgomery, Ala.: Wilson, 1923.

Putting the Most Into Life. New York: T. Y. Crowell, 1906.

Sowing and Reaping. Boston: L.C. Page, 1900.

The Story of Slavery. Dansville, N.Y.: F. A. Owen; Chicago, Ill.: Hall & McCreary, 1913.

The Story of the Negro, 2 vol. New York: Doubleday, Page, 1909.

Tuskegee and Its People. New York: D. Appleton, 1905.

AUTOBIOGRAPHY AND NON-FICTION IN ANTHOLOGIES

Adams, Conn, and Slepian, Afro-American Literature: Non-Fiction; Baker, Black Literature in America; Calverton, Anthology of American Negro Literature; Chace and Collier, Justice Denied; David, Black Joy; Davis and Redding, Cavalcade; Dodds, I Too Sing America; Ford, Black Insights; Kendricks, Afro-American Voices; Messner, Another View: To Be Black in America; Miller, Blackamerican Literature; Rollins, Christmas Gif'; Turner and Bright,

Images of the Negro in America.
BIOGRAPHY AND CRITICISM ON WASHINGTON
Adams. Great Negroes Past and Present.
Amann, Clarence A. "Three Negro Classics--An Estimate."
Negro American Literature Forum 4 (Winter 1970): 113-
119.
"Biography of Booker T. Washington." Negro History Bulle-
tin 24 (December 1960): 68.
"Booker T. Washington and the Ulrich Affair of March 19,
1911, in New York City." Phylon 30 (Fall 1969): 286-302.
Brawley. The Negro Genius, pp. 161-165.
_____. Negro Builders and Heroes, pp. 147-157.
Brown, Davis and Lee. Negro Caravan, p. 673.
Carmer, Carl. Cavalcade of America. New York: Crown,
1956, pp. 304-307.
Christmas, Walter. Negroes in Public Affairs, pp. 244-249.
"Contemporary Opposition." Journal of Negro History 45
(April 1960): 103-115.
Drinker, Frederick E. Booker T. Washington: The Master
Mind of a Child of Slavery, 1915; reprint ed., New York:
Negro Universities Press*.
Du Bois, W. E. B. "Of Mr. Booker T. Washington and Oth-
ers." In The Souls of Black Folk.
Dunaway, Philip. Turning Point. New York: Random, 1958,
pp. 221-234.
Gloster. Negro Voices in American Fiction.
Graham, Shirley. Booker T. Washington. New York: Mess-
ner, 1955.
Harlan, Louis R. et al, eds. The Booker T. Washington
Papers, 3 vols. Urbana: University of Illinois Press,
1972, 1973.
Hawkins, Hugh. Booker T. Washington and His Critics.
Boston: D.C. Heath, 1962.
Holsey. Booker T. Washington's Own Story of His Life and
Work, Including an Authoritative Sixty-Four Page Supple-
ment. Atlanta, Ga. and Naperville, Ill.: J. L. Nichols,
1915.
Johnson, Charles S. "The Social Philosophy of Booker T.
Washington." Opportunity (April 1928).
Larson, Charles. "The Deification of Booker to Washington."
Negro American Literature Forum 4 (Winter 1970): 125-
126.
Matthews, Basil. Booker T. Washington: Educator and In-
terracial Interpreter. College Park, Md.: McGrath, 1970.
Meiers. American Story, pp. 248-253.
Miller. Backgrounds to Blackamerican Literature, pp. 255-
271.
Peterson. Treasury of the World's Greatest Speeches, pp.
633-634.
Ploski. Reference Library of Black America, pp. 613-615.
"Riot in Boston--1903." Journal of Negro Education 31
(Winter 1962): 16-24.
Robinson. Historical Negro Biographies, p. 141.

Rollins. <u>They Showed the Way</u>, pp. 141-142.

Rudwick, Elliot. "Booker T. Washington and His Relations with the NAACP." <u>Journal of Negro Education</u> 29 (Spring 1960): 134-144.

Simmons. <u>Men of Mark</u>, pp. 1027-1030.

Spencer, Samuel R., Jr. <u>Booker T. Washington and the Negro's Place in American Life.</u> Boston: Little, Brown, 1955.

Sterling. <u>Lift Every Voice</u>, pp. 1-26.

Stratton. <u>Negroes Who Helped Build America,</u> pp. 68-76†.

Thornbrough, Emma Lou, ed. <u>Booker T. Washington.</u> Englewood Cliffs, N.J.: Prentice-Hall, 1969.

"Uncle Tom or Wooden Horse." <u>Journal of Negro History</u> 49 (October 1964): 240-255.

Wesley. <u>Quest for Equality,</u> pp. 75-76.

Who's Who, 1901.

[1]Emma Lou Thornbrough, ed., <u>Booker T. Washington</u> (Englewood Cliffs, N.J.: Prentice-Hall, 1969), p. 26.

[2]Dumas Malone, <u>Dictionary of American Biography,</u> (New York: Charles Scribner's Sons, 1936), pp. 506-507.

[3]Basil Matthews, <u>Booker T. Washington,</u> (College Park, Md.: McGrath, 1969), p. 99.

[4]<u>Ibid.</u>, p. 312.

WASHINGTON, Dell.
   POETRY
      (Anthology): <u>We Speak as Liberators.</u>
   STORIES
      Published in <u>Sequoia</u> and <u>Black on Black</u> (Stanford Publications).

WASHINGTON, Doris V.
   <u>NOVEL</u> <u>Yulan.</u> New York: Carlton, 1964.

WASHINGTON, Hazel L.
   POETRY
      (Anthology): Murphy, <u>Ebony Rhythm.</u>
      (Periodicals): <u>Phylon,</u> Second Quarter, Third Quarter 1949; First Quarter, 1951.

WASHINGTON, Raymond. <u>Born</u> 21 April 1942 in New Orleans, Louisiana.
   POETRY
      <u>Vision from the Ghetto.</u> New Orleans: BlkArtSouth, 1969.
      (Anthology): Chapman, <u>New Black Voices.</u>

WASHINGTON, Sam.
   <u>DRAMA</u> <u>A Member of the Fateful Gray,</u> 1969.

WATERS, George Hutch.
   <u>POETRY</u> <u>Africa in Brooklyn.</u> New York: Amuru, 1973†.

WATERS, Shirley A.
POETRY Psalms of a Black Woman. Los Angeles: Hopkins-
Thomas, 1969.

WATKINS, Gordon. Born 24 December 1930 in Baltimore, Maryland. Education: B.S., in Music, Juilliard School of Music;
M.S. in Music, Juilliard School of Music; also attended Katherine Dunham School of Dance; Hunter College Graduate Theatre
Department (Playwriting and Directing); New School for Social
Research (Filmmaking); Jarahal School of Music (Voice). Currently living in New York City. Career: Writer, director,
producer, composer for film, television and theatre; actor in
numerous television, Broadway and off-Broadway performances.
Has given concerts as a classical concert artist; has performed
in nightclubs, and as an opera singer in the United States and
Asia; served as director-instructor at Rutgers University; as
producer-director-writer for the film, I Love Harlem, 1970;
as producer for WCBS-TV, 1970-71. Produced, wrote and
staged the 90-minute drama special, Caught in the Middle. Producer-director-writer for WNBC's New York Illustrated series,
What Happened to Brownsville; President, The Touissaint Group,
Inc., a Black-owned film, television, radio and theatre production corporation which produces for the entertainment, industrial, educational, and government markets. Composed original
music for his drama, A Lion Roams the Streets, and for Ed
Bullins' plays, A Son Come Home and How Do You Do? He has
also composed miscellaneous songs. Awards, Honors: Ohio
State Award: Citation for Caught in the Middle; National Asso-
ciation of Television Program Executives! Program Excellence
for Performing Arts, Citation for Caught in the Middle.
DRAMA
A Lion Roams the Streets. n.p.: Breakthrough Press, n.d.
Sojourner Truth (poetic drama).
NON-FICTION
(Anthology): Clarke, Harlem U.S.A.
(Periodical): Freedomways, Spring 1964.
SCREENPLAYS
Jockey.
Tom Gideon and His Friends.
INTERJECTIONS
'The potential of the mass communications media to educate
and influence the moral climate is limitless. The contemporary
American society is rife with tensions which produce dangerous-
ly destructive energies. Many of these tensions may be justly
attributed to an emotional and intellectual orientation drawn from
myths and derogatory stereotypes projected by the mass communications media. The art form has always been a powerful catalyst because by its very nature, it must couple mystical emotional experience and intellectual stimulation. People who have
proven immune to dialectic or intellectual presentations can be
moved by sympathetic dramatic presentations, perhaps to self
analysis and open communication. Sensitive and knowledgeable
film and television productions which depict all of the facets of

Black life could be vital catalysts in the effort to improve the quality of daily life for minority citizens in the United States and the world. Without adequate media exposure there can be no lasting change in modern society."

WATKINS, Lucian Bottow. Born 1879 in Chesterfield, Virginia. Died 2 February 1921. Education: Attended Virginia Normal and Industrial Institute, Petersburg. Career: Taught school and was a soldier in World War I.[1]
POETRY
    The Old Log Cabin. Fort D. Russell, Wyoming: The
      Printery, 1910.
    Voices of Solitude, Poems Written and Composed by Lucian
      B. Watkins. Chicago: M.A. Donohue, 1903.
    Whispering Winds, n.p., n.d.
    (Anthologies): Kendricks, Afro-American Voices; Kerlin, Ne-
      gro Poets and Their Poems.
    (Periodicals): Crisis, 1916; 1917; 1918; 1919.
BIOGRAPHY AND CRITICISM ON WATKINS
    Brawley, Negro Genius, p. 239.
    Kerlin. Negro Poets and Their Poems, pp. 268-270, 345.
    [1]Robert T. Kerlin, Negro Poets and Their Poems
(Washington, D.C.: Associated, 1923), p. 345.

WATKINS, Richard T.
    NOVEL EXCERPT "My Man Quick-Sand." Black Creation 5
      (Fall 1973): 4-8.

WATKINS, Violette Peaches.
    POETRY My Dream World of Poetry: Poems of Imagination,
      Reality and Dreams. New York: Exposition, 1955.

WATSON, Frieda K.
    POETRY Feelin's. Los Angeles: A Kirzna Publication, 5314
      Crenshaw, 1971.

WATSON, Harmon C. Born 1943 in Baltimore, Maryland.
    DRAMA
      Clown in Three Rings.
      Those Golden Gates Fall Down. In Ford, Black Insights.
      Toy of the Gods, 1964.

WATSON, Lydia see WHITE, E. H.

WATSON, Nana.
    POETRY Reap the Harvest. New York: William-Frederick,
      1952.

WATSON, Roberta Bruce. Born 16 August 1911 in Bessemer, Ala-
    bama. Education: Attended the New School of Social Research. Currently living in New York City. Career: Recently retired after eighteen years with the National Bureau of Economic Research and three years as clerk-typist at The Book Press.

Presently devoting full time to writing; plans to return to acting in the theatre.

NOVEL
   Closed Doors. New York: Exposition, 1967.

UNPUBLISHED WORK
   A novel and a play.

INTERJECTIONS
   "While in High School I was given an assignment to write a short story. My English teacher (white) gave me A+ and encouraged me to study Journalism and Literary subjects and become a writer. I never forgot that--now I finally have the time."

WEATHERLY, Tom. Born 3 November 1942 in Scottsboro, Alabama. Education: Morehouse College; Alabama A and M University; St. Mark's Poetry Project; Order of Natural Process. Currently living in Brooklyn. Career: Worked with the Natural Process Workshop in East Harlem, New York Parks Department (under grant from State Council on Arts and the National Endowment for the Arts), 1968-69, and with the Natural Process Workshop for Teachers and Writer's Collaborative, 1968-69. Adjunct Instructor in Art Department, Rutgers University; Poet-in-Residence, Bishop College, 1970-71. Conducted a seminar, "Criticism of Black Poetry," Grand Valley State College (National Poetry Festival), 1971. Poet-in-Residence, Morgan State College, 1971-72; Director, Natural Process Workshop, St. Mark's Church-in-the Bouwerie Poetry Project, 1971-72; Teacher, seventh grade poetry, E. S. Webb School, Westchester, N.Y., 1972. Has held readings at many high schools, colleges and universities, including Bryn Mawr, Morehouse, Harvard, Colgate, Tuskegee, C.U.N.Y., Rutgers, Talladega, and Clark.

EDITOR
   With Ted Wilentz. Natural Process. New York: Hill & Wang, 1970*†.

POETRY
   With Ken Bluford. Climate. Philadelphia: Middle Earth Books, 1972. (Pamphlet.)
   With Ken Bluford. Stream. Philadelphia: Middle Earth Books, 1972. (Pamphlet.)
   MauMau American Cantos. New York: Corinth, 1969†.
   Thumbprint. Philadelphia: Telegraph Books, 1973†.
   (Anthologies): Adoff, The Poetry of Black America; Wilentz and Weatherly, Natural Process; Quasha and Rothenberg, America: A Prophecy.
   (Periodical): Umbra.

INTERJECTIONS
   "Natural process: a poet is human/human, half mortal, half divine, and half oxymoron--Read the poems 'cause poet's theories are theories."

WEAVER, Edwin Earl.
   POETRY The American. New York: Exposition, 1945.

Charles Lewis Webb

WEAVER, Eleanor.
POETRY (Anthology): Murphy, Negro Voices.

WEBB, Charles Lewis. Born 7 November 1918 in Connellsville,
Pennsylvania. Education: A.A., Storer College; B.S., Coppin
State College; M.S., Morgan State College; advanced graduate
study at University of Massachusetts; Temple University; Johns
Hopkins University. Currently living in Joppa, Maryland. Career: Served in World War II in the Southwest Pacific; served
in Korea during the Korean conflict as captain in the Medical
Corps. Presently a teacher in the Baltimore Public School Sys-
tem, and Instructor, Harford Community College, Bel Air,
Maryland. Member: Corpus Christi Chapter, Knights of Col-
umbus (Third Degree); Board of Directors, Harford Opera The-
ater; Vice-Chairman, Board of Directors for the Harford Cen-
ter for the Retarded; American Legion Post 318; Public School
Teachers Association; Maryland State Teachers Association;
Baltimore Teachers Union. Awards, Honors: National Science
Foundation Grant to Educational Development Center, Newton,
Massachusetts, 1970.
NOVEL
    Sasebo Diary. New York: Vantage, 1964.

INTERJECTIONS
"The American black has emerged in this decade of social
change with something more than a second-class citizenship.
He is seen in more than just isolated instances in government,
the professions, business, and education. These fields are not
new to him; however, the proportion of blacks in these positions
is greater than ever. The holding of responsible positions are
not instances of "he made it." His contributions are a viable
element in the American Dream. I feel that when the charla-
tans are removed from the scene of the masses and reality is
faced, a significant progressive inroad may be made from within."

WEBB, Frank J. Born and reared in Philadelphia.
    NOVEL
        The Garies and Their Friends. With a Preface by H. B.
            Stowe. London: Routledge, 1857; New York: Arno, 1969*.
    SHORT STORIES
        (Periodical): The New Era (January-February 1870): 1-4;
            (March-April 1870): 12-15.
    BIOGRAPHY AND CRITICISM ON WEBB
        Bone. The Negro Novel in America, pp. 10, 26, 31.
        Davis, Arthur P. "The Garies and Their Friends: A Neg-
            lected Pioneer Novel." CLA Journal 13 (September 1969):
            27-34.
            _____. "Introduction." The Garies and Their Friends by
            Frank J. Webb. New York: Arno, 1969.
        De Vries, James H. "The Tradition of the Sentimental Nov-
            el in The Garies and Their Friends." CLA Journal 17
            (December 1973): 241-249.
        Fleming, Robert E. "Humor in the Early Black Novel."
            CLA Journal (December 1973): 256-257, 259-260.
        Gloster. Negro Voices in American Fiction, pp. 25, 27, 29,
            260.
        Loggins. The Negro Author in America, pp. 149-151.

WEBBER, Cleveland.
    POETRY Africa, Africa, Africa. Introduction by David Moore.
        Chicago: Artistic Press, 4710 South Cottage Grove, 1969.

WEBER, Adam.
    DRAMA
        Spirit of the Living Dead, 1969.
        To Kill or Die, 1969.

WEBSTER, Bill. Born 12 June 1931 in Crowley, Louisiana. Edu-
    cation: B.A. degree. Currently living in Oakland, California.
    Career: Presently serving as Assistant Superintendent of
    Schools, Oakland, California.
    NOVEL
        One by One. Garden City, N.Y.: Doubleday, 1972*.
    REVIEW: One by One
        Book List, 15 December 1972, p. 381.

Bill Webster (credit: Cleveland Glover)

INTERJECTIONS
"Life is a journey through a maze of conflicts and/or dichot-
omies, and art merely portrays (whether musical, graphic or
literary) those conflicts.   In short, art portrays life--be it beautiful or sordid."

WEBSTER, Carter.
    POETRY (Anthology): Murphy, Ebony Rhythm.

WEEKS, Alan. Born in Brooklyn, New York.
    POETRY (Anthology): Coombs, We Speak as Liberators.

WEEKS, Ricardo.
    POETRY
        Freedom's Soldier and Other Poems. Foreword by Lawrence
            D. Reddick. New York: Malliet, 1947.
        (Anthology): Murphy, Ebony Rhythm.
        (Periodical): Harlem Quarterly, Winter 1949-50; Spring 1950;
            Negro Story, July-August, October-November 1944.
    SHORT STORY
        (Periodical): Negro Story, March-April 1945.
        Also published in Poetry Lore; The Pittsburgh Courier; The
            Amsterdam News; The Washington Tribune; The New York
            Age; The New Jersey Herald; Color.

WELBURN, Ron. Born 30 April 1944 in Bryn Mawr, Pennsylvania.
    Education: B.A., (Psychology and English Literature), Lincoln
    University, 1968; M.A. (Creative Writing), University of Ari-
    zona, 1970. Currently living in Syracuse, New York. Career:
    Instructor in English and Humanities, LIFT Program, Lincoln
    University, 1966-67; Teaching Assistant, Department of English,
    University of Arizona, 1969-70. Musician and composer as
    well as writer and teacher. Has held poetry readings and work-
    shops for numerous community and university groups; has lec-
    tured for various university and community groups. Served as
    musical director for jazz concerts (1966-68) and as leader of
    the Ron Welburn Ensemble (Syracuse University students). In-
    structor, Afro-American Studies Program, Syracuse University,
    1970 to present; Visiting Writer-in-Residence, Auburn Correc-
    tional Facility, Auburn, New York, 1972; Adjunct-Instructor,
    Department of English, Onondaga Community College, Syracuse,
    1972-73; Poet-in-Residence, Lincoln University (March 1973).
    Member: Alpha Phi Alpha Fraternity, Inc.; Duke Ellington So-
    ciety; American Association of University Professors. Awards,
    Honors: Lincoln University: Journalism Key, 1966-67, Edward
    S. Silvera Award for Poetry, 1966-67 and 1967-68; William
    Eichelberger Award for Prose, 1966-67; Amy T. Lockett Me-
    morial Prize for Outstanding Service to Campus and Community,
    1968; Class of 1899 Prize for English Studies, 1968; Who's Who
    Among Students in American Universities and Colleges, 1967-
    68; Southern Graduate Study Fellow, 1968-70.
    CRITICISM
        "The Black Aesthetic Imperative." In Gayle, The Black Aes-
            thetic.
    EDITOR
        Dues I: An Annual of New Earth Writing. New York: Em-
            erson Hall, 1974*.
        Dues II: An Annual of New Earth Writing. New York: Em-
            erson Hall, 1974*.
    NON-FICTION
        (Anthology): Watkins, Black Review No. 2.
    POETRY
        Peripheries: Selected Poems. Greenfield Center, N.Y.:
            Greenfield Review Press, 1972.
        Along the Estabon Way. New York: Emerson Hall, 1974.

Moods, Bright and Indigo: Poems. Knoxville: Carpetbag
Press, 1973.
(Anthologies): Adoff, The Poetry of Black America; Chapman, New Black Voices; Jones and Neal, Black Fire;
Major, The New Black Poetry.
(Periodicals): Black World, September 1972; July 1973;
Essence, July 1971; Journal of Black Poetry, Summer
1972; Negro Digest, September-October 1968; September
1969; Nickel Review, 6 February 1970; 30 March 1970;
also published in The Angry I (Muskingham College); Ax-
iom; The Daily World; Levels (Syracuse University);
America Sings: College Poetry, 1967-68; Pegasus; Col-
lege Poetry 1964-68; The Tongue (University of Arizona);
Umbra/Blackworks; Greenfield Review; BIM (Barbados);
Rhythm.
REVIEWS BY WELBURN
Published in Essence, Nickel Review.
SHORT STORIES
(Anthologies): Cassill, Intro 3; Welburn, Dues I and Dues II.
(Periodicals): Essence, October 1971; also published in Ax-
iom; Greenfield Review; Hoo-Doo 1; The Tongue.
WORK IN PROGRESS
Short Stories: "Devon Hill."
Poetry: "Thumbin' a Ride: Selected Poems 1964-67";
"Brownup, and Other Poems."
Criticism: "Caravans: Music Critiques."
INTERJECTIONS
"In my poetry especially I often metaphorize nature and wild-
life (particularly species of birds) as 'black experiences.' I
support black control of black images, production and distribu-
tion. Music (as listener and performer) feeds my creative writ-
ing--is my first life. Favorite writers: (early) Umbra group;
Audre Lorde, Felix Tchicaya U'Tamse, Austin C. Clarke,
George Lamming, Clarence Major. I respect Faulkner's crafts-
manship."

WELLS, Jack Calvert.
NOVEL
Out of the Deep. Boston: Christopher, 1958.
POETRY
(Anthology): Murphy, Ebony Rhythm.

WELLS, Moses Peter.
SHORT STORIES
Three Adventurous Men. New York: Carlton, 1963.
NON-FICTION
Faults of the World. New York: Carlton, 1962.
Working for Progress. New York: Carlton, 1963.

WESLEY, Richard. Born 11 July 1945 in Newark, New Jersey.
Education: B.F.A., Howard University, 1967. Currently living
in Newark, New Jersey. Career: Playwright-in-Residence,
New Lafayette Theatre, 1973; Guest Lecturer, Wesleyan Univer-

sity; Guest Lecturer, Manhattanville College. Has written
scripts for stage, screen, and television. Awards, Honors:
Drama Desk Award for Outstanding Playwrighting for The Black
Terror, 1972.
CRITICISM BY WESLEY
"An Interview with Playwright Ed Bullins." Black Creation
4 (Winter 1973): 8-10.
"Black Theater in Harlem." Black World 21 (April 1972):
47-48, 70-74.
DRAMA
Ace Boon Coon.
Another Way, 1969.
The Black Terror, 1971.
Gettin' It Together, 1970.
Headline News, 1970.
Knock, Knock, Who Dat, 1970.
The Past Is the Past, 1973.
Springtime High (one act), 1968.
The Streetcorner, 1970.
Strike Heaven On the Face, 1973.
BIOGRAPHY AND CRITICISM ON WESLEY
Bentley, E. R. "White Plague and Black Terror." In The-
atre of War. Edited by E. R. Bentley.
REVIEWS: The Black Terror
Black Theatre 6 (1972): 36-37.
Gottfried, Martin. Women's Wear Daily, 11 November 1971.
Jones, Martha M. Black Creation 3 (Spring 1972): 12, 14.
Kroll, Jack. Newsweek, 29 November 1971.
Watts, Richard. New York Post, 11 November 1971.

WESS, Deborah Fuller.
POETRY (Anthology): Murphy, Ebony Rhythm.

WEST, Donald.
POETRY (Anthology): Boyd, Poems by Blacks, vol. 2.

WEST, Dorothy. Born 1910 in Boston.
CRITICISM
"Elephant's Dance: A Memoir of Wallace Thurman." Black
World 20 (November 1970): 77-85.
EDITOR
Challenge and New Challenge (periodicals published in the
1930's).
NOVEL
The Living Is Easy. Boston: Houghton Mifflin, 1948; reprint
ed., New York: Arno, 1970*. Excerpt in Hill, Soon One
Morning.
SHORT STORIES
(Anthologies): Clarke, Harlem; Hughes, The Best Short Sto-
ries by Negro Writers.
(Periodicals): Opportunity, July 1926; May 1934; October
1940.
Also published in the Boston Post; Saturday Evening Quill.

BIOGRAPHY AND CRITICISM ON WEST
Bardolph. The Negro Vanguard, pp. 467-468.
Bone. The Negro Novel in America, pp. 187-191.
Hughes. The Negro Novelist, pp. 115, 123, 124, 228.
Opportunity 4 (June 1926): 189.
Whitlow. Black American Literature, pp. 121-122.

WEST, John B.
MYSTERY NOVELS
Bullets Are My Business.　New York: New American Library, 1960.
Cobra Venom.　New York: New American Library, 1960.
Death on the Rocks.　New York: New American Library, 1961.
An Eye for an Eye.　New York: New American Library, 1959.
Never Kill a Cop.　New York: New American Library, 1961.
A Taste for Blood.　New York: New American Library, 1960.

WEST, William.
Corner.　New York: Carlton, 1964.

WHEATLEY, Harriet.
POETRY (Periodical): Black World, September 1973.

WHEATLEY, Phillis. Born on the western coast of Africa, about
the year 1753 or 54, and was transported to a slave ship. She
was about seven years old when she was aboard a ship which
landed in Boston. She was put up for sale in 1761.[1] She was
purchased by John Wheatley, a tailor from Boston, to serve as
an attendant to his wife Susannah.[2] Died 5 December 1784.
Education: She was educated at home in the Wheatley household
where she was taught to read and write. She read mostly from
the Bible, Ovid, and the Latin books of mythology. She was
probably 13 years old when she began to write poetry.[3] Her
health began to fail and on the recommendation of the family
physician she was sent abroad on a voyage to England in 1773.
The publication of a poem in 1770 brought her some notice.
Although the poem was on the death of a famous preacher,
George Whitefield, Phillis had addressed the poem to the Countess of Huntington. In 1773, it was the Countess who aided Phillis in meeting many notables of English society. When she left
England in 1773, preparations were well underway for the publication of her book of poems.[4] Shortly after her arrival in Boston, Mrs. Wheatley passed away. Following her death, Phillis
received an offer of marriage from John Peters. Peters was a
fluent writer, a ready spender, and an intelligent Black man. A
grocer by trade, he often pleaded the cause of the Black man
before the tribunals of the State. Phillis, about twenty-five at
the time of her marriage, became ill. The marriage itself was
not satisfactory and the life she led with Peters proved too much
a strain.[5] When Boston fell to the British, she and her husband fled to Wilmington and remained there until it was safe to

return to Boston. Because of the attitudes of her husband, she and her three children suffered from both poverty and social estrangement. Before the winter of 1783-84, the two older children died; in 1784, Peters was jailed. On December 5, 1784, Phillis Wheatley Peters died in Boston; her third child followed her in death in time to be buried with her in a grave whose location has since been lost to the world.[6]

The Boston Magazine, December 1784, p. 630 noted her death as follows: "Mrs. Phillis Peters (formerly Phillis Wheatley [sic]." In the same issue, in The Poetical Essays section, appeared the following, "Elegy On the Death of a Late Celebrated Poetess," pp. 619-620. The poem was signed, Horatio, State St., December 1784. "Of special interest is the poet's focus on Phillis as an accepted Boston poetess and not merely as a freak that resulted from a slave's having encountered fortuitous circumstances."[7]

"Her reputation was kept alive by antislavery writers and publicists of succeeding decades, who well knew the symbolic value of an unmixed Negro slave girl from Africa who had displayed such literary talent, and who had been officially received by no less a personage than General George Washington."[8]

POETRY

An elegiac poem, on the death of that celebrated divine, and eminent servant of Jesus Christ, the late Reverend and pious George Whitefield, Chaplain to the right Honorable the Countess of Huntingdon, etc, etc. Who made his exit from this transitory state, to dwell in the celestial realms of bliss, on Lord's-day, 30th of September 1770, when he was seiz'd with a fit of asthma, at Newbury-Port, near Boston in New England. In which is a condolatory address to his noble benefactress the worthy, and pious Lady Huntingdon; and the orphan-children in Georgia; who with many thousands, are left, by the death of this great man, to lament the loss of a father, and benefactor. By Phillis, a servant girl 17 years of age, belonging to Mr. J. Wheatley, of Boston; and has been but 9 years in this country from Africa. Boston: sold by Ezekial Russell, in Queen-Street, and John Boyles, in Marlboro Street, 1770. (Broadside.)

Life and Works of Phillis Wheatley, Containing her Complete Poetical Works, Numerous Letters, and a Complete Biography of this Famous Poet of a Century and a Half Ago, by G. Herbert Renfro. Also a Sketch of the Life of Mr. Renfro, by Leila Amos Pendleton. Washington: Robert L. Pendleton, 1916, facsimile ed., Freeport, N.Y.: Books for Libraries*; Miami: Mnemosyne†.

Memoir and Poems...Dedicated to the Friends of the Africans. 2nd ed. Boston: Light & Horton, 1835; 3rd ed., Boston: I. Knapp, 1838; facsimile of 1838 ed., Freeport, N.Y.: Books for Libraries*.

Poems... Edited by Charlotte R. Wright. Philadelphia: The Wrights, 1930.

Poems and Letters. First collected ed., Charles Fred Heart-

man, ed. With an appreciation by Arthur A. Schomburg.
New York: By the Editor, 1915; Freeport, N.Y.: Books for
Libraries*.

Poems on Various Subjects, Religious and Moral. Boston: A.
Bell, 1773; 2nd ed. Philadelphia: W. Woodward, 1801;
3rd ed., Cleveland: Revell: 1886; New York: AMS Press*.

(Anthologies): Barksdale and Kinnamon, Black Writers of
America; Brawley, Early Negro American Writers; Braw-
ley, The Negro Genius; Brown, Davis and Lee, Negro
Caravan; Brown, Homespun Heroines; Calverton, An An-
thology of American Literature; Chambers and Moon, Right
On!; Davis and Redding, Cavalcade; Eleazer, Singers in
the Dawn; Faderman and Bradshaw, Speaking for Ourselves;
Ford, Black Insights; Halsam, Forgotten Pages of Ameri-
can Literature; Hayden, Kaleidoscope; Hughes and Bontemps,
The Poetry of the Negro, 1746-1973; Johnson, Ebony and
Topaz; Lomax and Abdul, 3000 Years of Black Poetry;
Long and Collier, Afro-American Writing; Miller, Black-
american Literature; Patterson, Introduction to Black Lit-
erature in America; Porter, Early Negro Writing; Randall,
The Black Poets; Robinson, Early Black American Poets;
White and Jackson, An Anthology of Verse by American
Negroes.

(Periodicals): Negro History Bulletin 6 (February 1943): 117-
118; 25 (January 1962): 91-92; Phylon 14 (1953): 191-198.

BIOGRAPHY AND CRITICISM ON WHEATLEY

Adams. Great Negroes Past and Present, pp. 140, 147-148.

Ahuma, S. Memoirs of West African Celebrities 1700-1850.
Liverpool: D. Marples, 1905.

Allen, William G. Wheatley, Banneker and Horton. Boston:
Laing, 1849.

Anon. Negro History Bulletin 1 (February 1938): 6.

_____. Negro History Bulletin 3 (April 1940): 107.

_____. Negro History Bulletin 3 (November 1940): 46.

Bardolph. The Negro Vanguard, pp. 32-34, 54, 83, 184.

_____. "Social Origins of Distinguished Negroes 1770-1865."
Journal of Negro History 40 (July 1955), 226.

Barksdale and Kinnamon. Black Writers of America, pp. 38-
40.

Baskin and Runes. Dictionary of Black Culture, p. 468.

Belock, M. "Biographical Sketches of Men of Color." Educational Forum 34 (January 1970): 212-213.

Bennett, M. W. "Negro Poets." Negro History Bulletin 9
(May 1946): 171-172.

Bergman. The Chronological History of the Negro in America, pp. 28, 38, 54, 59.

Borland, Kathryn Kilby and Helen Ross Speicher. Phillis
Wheatley: Young Colonial Poet. Indianapolis: Bobbs-Merrill, 1968.

Brawley. Early Negro American Writers, pp. 31-36.

_____. Negro Builders and Heroes, pp. 19-24.

_____. The Negro Genius, pp. 17-19, 28-32, 73, 90.

_____. The Negro in Literature and Art, pp. 12, 15-37,

138, 182.

Brown, Hallie Q. Homespun Heroines. New York: Books for Libraries, pp. 5-10.

Bruce, John Edward. Tracts for the People. New York: n.p., 18--? (Tract #13.)

Butcher. The Negro in American Culture, pp. 24, 96, 170.

Child, Maria L. The Freedman's Book. New York: Arno, 1968, pp. 86-93.

Cook, Mercer and Stephen E. Henderson. The Militant Black Writer, pp. 84-85, 87-88.

Cromwell, John Wesley. The Negro in American History. Washington: The American Negro Academy, 1914, pp. 77-85.

Dannett. Profiles of Negro Womanhood, pp. 32-39.

Davis, Arthur. "Personal Elements in the Poetry of Phillis Wheatley." Phylon 14 (Second Quarter 1953): 191-198.

Davis. The American Negro Reference Book, pp. 23, 766, 850-851.

Dean, Charles, ed. Letters of Phillis Wheatley, the Negro Slave Poet of Boston. Boston: Privately Printed, 1864.

Dobbler, Lavinia and Edgar A. Toppin. Pioneers and Patriots. New York: Doubleday, 1965, pp. 30-50.

Du Bois, W. E. B. The Gift of Black Folk.

Eleazer, Robert B., comp. Singers in the Dawn. Atlanta, Ga.: Commission on Interracial Cooperation, Inc., 1934, pp. 3-4.

Eppse. The Negro, Too, in American History. New York: National Educational Publishers, 1939, pp. 106-107.

"Facing Facts to be Celebrated During Negro History Week." Negro History Bulletin 2 (February 1939): 38.

Fauset, Arthur Huff. For Freedom. Philadelphia: Franklin, 1927, pp. 21-28.

Fishel and Quarles. The Black in America, pp. 7, 37, 70, 367.

Gayle. Black Expression, pp. 62-72, 109, 116, 125, 190-191, 203-204, 210, 212, 223, 225.

Graham, Shirley. 'The Story of Phillis Wheatley." Negro Digest 8 (December 1949): 85-97.

_____. Story of Phillis Wheatley. New York: Messner, 1949.

Greene. The Negro in Colonial New England, pp. 63, 243-245.

Hammon, Jupiter. "An Address to Miss Phillis Wheatley, an Ethiopian Poetess in Boston who Came from Africa at Eight Years of Age, and Soon Became Acquainted with the Gospel of Jesus Christ." Hartford, Conn.: By the Author, 1778.

Haynes, Mrs. Elizabeth Ross. Unsung Heroes. New York: Du Bois and Dill, 1921, pp. 167-177.

Holmes, Wilfred. "Phyllis Wheatley." Negro History Bulletin 6 (February 1943): 117-118.

Hughes, Langston. Famous American Negroes. New York: Dodd, Mead, 1954.

Isaacs. The New World of Negro Americans, p. 58.

Johnson. Black Manhattan, pp. 261-262.

Kuncio, R. C. "Some Unpublished Poems of Phillis Wheatley." New England Quarterly 43 (June 1970): 287-299.

Lecointe-Marsillacs. 'Le More-Locke." Londres et Paris, 1789, p. 169.

Library of American Literature, vol. 3. "Literature of the Revolution, 1765-1787." New York: Webster, 1891, pp. 504-505.

Loggins. The Negro Author, pp. 5-411 passim.

Lossing, Benson John. Eminent Americans. New York: Mason, 1856, pp. 249-250.

Mather, Samuel. Who Was Who in America: Historical Volume (H) 1607-1896. Chicago: Marquis, 1963, p. 338.

Mason, Julian D., Jr. The Poems of Phillis Wheatley. Chapel Hill: University of North Carolina Press, 1966.

Matson, Lynn R. "Phyllis Wheatley--Soul Sister?" Phylon 33 (Fall 1972): 222-230.

Mays. The Negro's God, pp. 103-106, 109, 246.

Montgomery, Gregory. "The Spirit of Phillis Wheatley." Opportunity 11 (June 1924): 181-182.

Morrison, Allen. "Phylis Wheatley." Ebony (August 1966): 90.

"Negro Poets, Singers in the Dawn." Negro History Bulletin 2 (November 1938): 10.

Nell, William. Colored Patriots of the American Revolution. New York: Arno, 1968, pp. 64-73.

Ovington, Mary White. Phillis Wheatley--A Play. New York: Schulte, 1932.

Oxley, Thomas L. G. "Survey of Negro Literature, 1760-1926." The Messenger 9 (February 1927): 37-39.

Pinkney, Alphonso. Black American. Englewood Cliffs, N.J.: Prentice-Hall, 1969, pp. 140-146.

Porter, Dorothy B. "Early American Negro Writings: A Bibliographical Study." The Papers of the Bibliographical Society of America 30 (Third Quarter 1945): 261-266.

_____. North American Negro Poets: A Bibliographical Checklist of Their Writings--1760-1944. Hattiesburg, Miss.: The Brook Farm, 1945, pp. 78-83.

Proceedings of the Massachusetts Historical Society, 1863-1864, vol. 8, pp. 267-279.

Quarles, Benjamin. "Black History's Early Advocates." Negro Digest 19 (February 1970): 4-9.

_____. "A Phillis Wheatley Letter." Journal of Negro History 34 (October 1949): 462-464.

Redding. They Came in Chains, pp, 59, 61, 145.

Remond, Charles Lennox. "Phillis Wheatley." Negro History Bulletin 1 (February 1938): 6.

Renfro, G. Herbert. Life and Works of Phillis Wheatley. Washington, D.C.: Pendleton, 1916.

Ricketson, Daniel. The History of New Bedford, Bristol County, Massachusetts. New Bedford: By the Author, 1858, pp. 262-264.

Rollins. Famous American Negro Poets, pp. 18-21.
_____. They Showed the Way, pp. 143-145.
Roy, J. H. "Know Your History." Negro History Bulletin 21 (January 1958): 87.
Seeber, Edward D. "Phillis Wheatley." Journal of Negro History 24 (July 1939): 259-262.
Shockley, Ann Allen. "The Negro Woman in Retrospect: A Blueprint for the Future." Negro History Bulletin 29 (December 1965): 55-56.
Sterling, Dorothy. Speak Out in Thunder Tones. New York: Doubleday, 1973, pp. 42-44, 382.
Tasker, William W. "Panorama of American Literature." Daye (1947): 46-47.
Thatcher, Benjamin B. Memoir of Phillis Wheatley, a Native African and a Slave. Boston, 1834.
Thorpe, Dr. Earl E. "African Thought in Negro Americans." Negro History Bulletin 23 (October 1959): 5.
Toppin. A Biographical History of Blacks in America Since 1528, pp. 59-60, 155, 451-453.
Turner. Black American Literature: Essays, Poetry, Fiction, Drama, p. 165.
Turner, Lorenzo Dow. "Anti-Slavery Sentiments in American Literature." Journal of Negro History 14 (October 1949): 388-389.
Untermeyer, Louis, ed. American Poets from the Beginning to Whitman. New York: Harcourt Brace, 1931, p. 307.
Weglin, Oscar. "Was Phillis Wheatley America's First Negro Poet? The Literary Collector Press (August 1904): 117-118.
Weight, Glenn S. "The Anniversary of Phyllis Wheatley Remains an Inspiration to All." Negro History Bulletin 25 (January 1962): 91-92.
Wheatley, Hannibal Parish. Genealogy of the Wheatley Family. Farmington, N.H.: Thomas, 1902.
White and Jackson. An Anthology of Verse by American Negroes, pp. 3, 4-5, 27-28, 220-225, 230-231, 235.
Williams, George W. History of the Negro Race in America from 1619-1880, vol. 1, New York: Arno, 1968, pp. 197-202.
Williams, Ora. American Black Women in the Arts and Sciences, pp. xvi, 25.
Wilson, G. R. "The Religion of the American Negro Slave: His Attitude Towards Death." Journal of Negro History 8 (January 1923): 44-45.
Woodson, Carter G. "Phillis Wheatley."
_____. The Mind of the Negro as Reflected in Letters Written During the Crisis 1800-1860, pp. xvi-xxi.
Workman, W. D. "Historical Group Aids the Negro." Negro History Bulletin 24 (April 1961): 159.

[1]G. Herbert Renfro, Life and Works of Phillis Wheatley (Washington, D.C.: Pendleton, 1916), p. 9.
[2]Julian Mason, Jr., The Poems of Phillis Wheatley

(Chapel Hill: University of North Carolina Press, 1966), p. xii.

[3]Charles Fred Heartman, Phillis Wheatley (Florida: Mnemosyne, 1969), p. 10.

[4]Mason, pp. xiv-xv.

[5]Heartman, pp. 12-13.

[6]Mason, pp. xv-xvi.

[7]Ibid., pp. xvi-xviii.

[8]"Phillis Wheatley," Negro Heritage 4 (1965): 60.

[9]For a more complete listing of Phillis Wheatley's work, consult Dorothy Porter, North American Negro Poets: A Bibliographic Checklist of Their Writings 1760-1944 (Hattiesburg, Miss.: Brook Farm, 1945), pp. 78-83.

WHEELER, Benjamin. Born 1854. Died 1919.
  EDITOR
    Cullings from Zion's Poets. Mobile? Ala.: n.p., 1907.
  NON-FICTION
    The Varick Family. Mobile? Ala.: n.p., 1907.
  REVIEW: Cullings from Zion's Poets
    White and Jackson. An Anthology of Verse by American Negroes, p. 236.

WHEELER, Charles Enoch. Born 1909.
  POETRY (Anthology): Hughes and Bontemps, The Poetry of the Negro, 1746-1970.

WHERRY, Sam.
  POETRY (Anthology): Boyd, Poems by Blacks, vol. 2.

WHIPPER, Leigh. Education: Attended Harvard University. Career: Actor.
  DRAMA
    With Billy Mills. Yeah Man, 1932.
    With J. C. Johnson. Runnin' De Town, 1930.
    With Porter Grainger. De Board Meetin', 1925.
    With Porter Grainger. We'se Risin', 1927.
  NON-FICTION
    (Anthology): United Artists Corporation, The Picture Hollywood Said Could Never Be Made. n.p., 1940, p. 11.
    (Articles about the motion picture, Of Mice and Men, by John Steinbeck.)
  BIOGRAPHY ON WHIPPER
    Bond. The Negro and the Drama, pp. 44, 102, 128.
    Hughes and Meltzer. Black Magic, pp. 113, 197, 302, 319.

WHITAKER, Christine D.
  POETRY The Singing Teakettle: Poems for Children. New York: Exposition, 1956.

WHITAKER, Patrick W. Born 1946.
  POETRY (Anthology): Shuman, A Galaxy of Black Writing.

WHITE, Alberta. Born in Providence, Rhode Island. Education:
Attended Los Angeles City College. Currently living in Los
Angeles. Career: Lived in the Virgin Islands for five years,
lecturing at a junior college and a junior high school on crea-
tive writing and Black literature. Served as poetry editor for
Liberator and for Watts Times, and published a poetry maga-
zine. Presently is writing a series for daytime television with
Wesley Gale. Awards, Honors: Our Authors' Study Club--
Ossie D. Wright Award.
POETRY
    (Periodicals): The Angeles Magazine; Poetry of the West;
        Southwest Wave (Los Angeles).
UNPUBLISHED WORK
    Poetry: "Silent Drums."

WHITE, Charles Frederick. Born 1876.
NON-FICTION
    With C. J. Perry, B. F. Lee, and R. R. Wright, Jr. Who's
        Who in Philadelphia: A Collection of Thirty Biographical
        Sketches of Philadelphia People...together with cuts and
        information of some of their leading institutions and or-
        ganizations. Philadelphia: A. M. E. Book Concern, 1912.
POETRY
    Plea of the Negro Soldier and a Hundred Other Poems.
        Easthampton, Mass.: Press of Enterprise Printing Co.,
        1908.

WHITE, Edgar. Born in the West Indies. Education: Attended
New York University and Yale University. Currently living in
New York City. Career: Currently studying architecture.
CHILDREN AND YOUNG ADULTS
    Omar at Christmas. New York: Lothrop, 1973*.
    Sati, the Rastifarian. New York: Lothrop*.
DRAMA
    The Burghers of Calais, 1971.
    The Cathedral at Chartres (one act), 1969.
    The Crucificado: Two Plays. New York: Morrow, 1973*†.
    Les Femmes Noirs.
    Fun in Lethe, 1970.
    La Gente.
    The Life and Times of J. Walter Smintheus, 1970.
    The Mummer's Play (one act), 1969.
    Ode to Charlie Parker.
    Seigismundo's Tricycle. In Watkins, Black Review No. 1.
    The Wonderful Year, 1971.
    Underground: Four Plays. New York: Morrow, 1970*†.
SHORT STORIES
    (Anthologies): Coombs, What We Must See; King, Black
        Short Story Anthology.
SKETCH
    "Novel." In Yardbird Reader I.

WHITE, James Wilson.
   POETRY White's Poems. Washington: n.p., 1925.

WHITE, Joseph. Born 2 December 1933 in Philadelphia. Career:
   See Shockley and Chandler, Living Black American Writers, p.
   169.
   DRAMA
      The Leader (one act), 1969. In Jones and Neal, Black Fire.
      Ole Judge Mose Is Dead (one act). In The Drama Review
         12 (Summer 1968).
   POETRY
      (Anthology): Adoff, The Poetry of Black America; Afro-Arts
         Anthology; Burning Spear; Lowenfels, Poets of Today.
      (Periodical): Dasein.
   SHORT STORIES
      (Periodical): Liberator.
   BIOGRAPHY AND CRITICISM ON WHITE
      Harrison. The Drama of Nommo, pp. 128, 147, 162.
      Peavy. "Satire and Contemporary Black Drama." Satire
         Newsletter 7 (Fall 1969): 45-47.

WHITE, Lucy.
   DRAMA The Bird Child. In Locke and Gregory, Plays of Ne-
      gro Life.

WHITE, Michyle.
   POETRY (Anthology): Coombs, We Speak as Liberators.

WHITE, Thomas J. Born 1933.
   NOVEL To Hell and Back at Sixteen. New York: Carlton,
      1970.

WHITE, Wallace.
   SHORT STORY (Anthology): Coombs, What We Must See.

WHITE, Walter Francis. Born 1 July 1893 in Atlanta, Georgia.
   Died 21 March 1955. Education: Attended Atlanta public
   schools and graduated from Atlanta High School in 1912; and
   the College in 1916. Career: At 13, he observed the Atlanta
   race riots and from this experience was encouraged to fight
   against riots, lynchings and social injustices. In fact he brazen-
   ly entered many communities to investigate the lynchings and to
   gather the facts about the race riots.[1] His early employment
   was working as a bellboy and as an insurance agent. On February 1, 1918 he received an invitation to become an assistant
   secretary for the NAACP[2] to work with James Weldon Johnson.
   He accepted the position and served in this capacity from 1918-
   1931. For four decades he devoted himself to the work of the
   NAACP, even at the risk of being lynched.[3] He travelled more
   than 400,000 miles in the United States and Europe. He attended the Pan-African Congress held in 1921 in England, Belgium and France. In 1927 he went to France for a year of
   writing and studying as a Guggenheim Fellow.[4] When he re-

turned to the States, he continued to lobby for anti-lynching legislature and fought against racism in the defense industry and
in the armed services. He also advised the American delega-
tion at the founding of the United Nations. [5]

White found time to investigate the serious problems that
plagued the Black communities, to give broadcasts, write speeches and confer with people of all races to bring men together for
harmonious living. "He labored dangerously, heroically and
nobly in behalf of civil human, political, and social rights for
colored people and all other people."[6] On July 2, 1937 he was
honored by the NAACP in New York for his investigations of
lynchings, and his lobbying for federal anti-lynching laws.[7]

In March 1934, President Roosevelt appointed him as a member of the Advisory Council for the Government of the Virgin Islands. He resigned the position in May 1935. In 1935 he was
appointed chairman of the Harlem Low Cost Housing Project.
Member: American Center of the P.E.N. Club Board of Visitors of New York Training School for Boys. Awards, Honors:
He was awarded the Spingarn Medal for his personal investigations of lynchings and race riots and for his remarkable tact,
skill and persuasiveness in lobbying for Federal Anti-Lynching
law. In 1927 he received a Guggenheim Fellowship. His first
novel, Fire in the Flint, has been published in England, France,
Germany, Russia, Norway, Denmark, and Japan. [8] Just before
his death, he finished a study, assessing the racial situation in
America, How Far the Promised Land?

NON-FICTION

The American Negro and His Problems. Girard, Ka.: Hal-
deman & Julius, 1927.

Civil Rights: Fifty Years of Fighting. Pittsburgh: Pittsburgh
Courier, 1950.

How Far the Promised Land? New York: Viking, 1955; New
York: AMS Press*.

A Man Called White. New York: Viking, 1948; London: V.
Gallansz, 1949; reprint ed., New York: Arno, 1969*.
(Autobiography.)

The Negro's Contribution to American Culture. Girard, Ka.:
Haldeman-Julius, 1928.

A Rising Wind. Garden City, N.Y.: Doubleday & Doran,
1945; reprint ed., New York: Negro Universities Press*.

Rope and Faggot: A Biography of Judge Lynch. New York:
Knopf, 1929; New York: Arno, 1969*†.

(Periodicals): Crisis 57 (August-September 1951): 434-440,
502-506; 62 (April 1955): 227-229; Ebony 7 (July 1952):
47-48; 6 (February 1951): 78-84; Negro Digest 4 (December 1945): 23-24; 8 (December 1949): 37-40; 8 (March
1950): 8-9; (February 1951): 84-85; New York Post, 22
April 1944; Our World 6 (January 1951): 29-31; Palms 4
(October 1926): 3-7; Survey Graphic (1942): 472-474.

NOVELS

The Fire in the Flint. New York: Knopf, 1924; L'etincelle.
Trans. by Marguerite Humbert-Zeller. Paris: Librairie
Plon, 1928; New York: Negro Universities Press*.

Flight. New York: Knopf, 1926; reprint ed., New York: Negro Universities Press*.

BIOGRAPHY AND CRITICISM ON WHITE

Adams, Julius Jackson. The Challenge. New York: Malliet, 1949.

Adams. Great Negroes Past and Present. pp. 107, 122, 147.

Bardolph. The Negro Vanguard, pp. 181, 185-86, 188, 202, 204, 207-209, 217, 246, 292, 302, 323, 329-332.

Baskin and Runes. Dictionary of Black Culture, p. 470.

Bergman. The Chronological History of the Negro in America, pp. 257, 335, 434, 486, 499.

Bigsby. The Black American Writer, vol. 1, p. 234.

Bone. The Negro Novel in America, pp. 97, 99-101.

Bontemps. The Harlem Renaissance Remembered, pp. 11, 43, 69, 91, 224, 238.

Brawley. The Negro Genius, pp. 221-222.

_____. The Negro in Art and Literature, pp. 124-125.

Brown, Davis and Lee. The Negro Caravan, pp. 181-189.

Butcher. The Negro in American Culture, pp. 139, 213, 215, 217, 226.

Cannon, Poppy. A Gentle Knight, My Husband Walter White. New York: Rinehart, 1956.

_____. "Love That Never Died." Ebony 12 (January 1957): 17-20.

Chalmers, Allan Knight. They Shall Be Free. New York: Doubleday, 1951. (Introduction by Walter White.)

Chametzky and Kaplan. Black and White in American Culture, pp. 345.

Davis. The American Negro Reference Book, pp. 67, 635, 874, 872.

Embree. 13 Against the Odds, pp. 71-95.

Fishel and Quarles. The Black American, pp. 447, 449-451, 467, 469, 476.

Gayle. Black Expression, pp. 181, 243, 254.

Goldstein. Black Life and Culture in the United States, pp. 171, 186.

Hornsby, Alton, Jr. The Black Almanac. Woodbury, N.Y.: Barron's Educational Services, 1973, pp. 64, 81.

Hughes. The Negro Novelist, pp. 36, 138, 235.

Isaacs. The New World of Negro Americans, pp. 28, 29, 43-44, 74.

Johnson. Black Manhattan, pp. 274-275.

Kahn, E. J. "Frontal Attacks." New Yorker, 4 September 1948, pp. 28-32; 11 September 1948, pp. 38-40.

Kent. Blackness and the Adventure of Western Culture, p. 29.

"Life Story of Walter White." Our World 10 (January 1957): 48-52.

Lomax, Michael A. "Fantasies of Affirmation: The 1920 Novel of Negro Life." CLA Journal 16 (December 1972): 232-246.

Lotz, Phillip Henry. Rising Above Color. New York: Association Press; New York: Fleming Revell, 1943, pp. 105-112.

Macy, John Albert, ed. American Writers on American Literature. New York: Liveright, 1931, pp. 442-451.

Mays. The Negro's God, pp. 209-210, 216, 225.

Mitchell. Black Drama, pp. 36, 107.

Ottley and Weatherby. The Negro in New York, pp. 175, 240, 255, 257.

Ovington, Mary White. Portraits in Color. New York: Viking, 1927.

Patterson, Robert, Mildred Mebal and Laurence Hill. On Our Way. New York: Holiday House, pp. 362-372.

Pinkney, Alphonso. Black Americans. Englewood Cliffs, N.J.: Prentice-Hall, 1969, p. 149.

Ploski and Kaiser. The Negro Almanac, pp. 212, 698.

Redding. The Lonesome Road, pp. 243, 249, 272, 274, 320, 327.

_____. They Came in Chains, pp. 223, 257-258, 264, 273, 281, 283, 285-286, 293, 297, 300-301.

Richardson. Great American Negroes, pp. 207-213.

Robinson. Historical Negro Biographies, pp. 260-261.

"Story of Walter White." Newsweek, 8 October 1948, p. 88.

Tischler, Nancy M. Black Masks, p. 87.

Toppin. A Biographical History of Blacks in America Since 1528, pp. 172, 200, 204, 455-459.

Turner. Afro-American Writers, p. 76.

"Walter White." Crisis 62 (April 1955): 227-229.

"Walter White Funeral." Crisis 62 (April 1955): 229-232.

"Walter White." Opportunity 3 (February 1925): 58; 15 (July 1937): 219.

"White Will Be Read." Newsweek, 21 October 1946, pp. 74-75.

Woodson, Carter G. and Charles W. Wesley. The Negro in Our History. New York: Associated, 1922, pp. 627, 736.

Villard, O. G. "Walter White: Courageous Statesman." Crisis 56 (January 1949): 18-19.

Young. Black Writers of the Thirties, pp. 73, 96, 203.

REVIEWS: Fire in the Flint

Du Bois, W. E. B. Crisis 29 (1924): 25.

Flight

Waring, Nora. Crisis 32 (1926): 142.

Van Vechten, Carl. New York Herald Tribune Books, 11 April 1926, p. 3.

[1]Obituary, Journal of Negro History 40 (July 1955): 296.

[2]Mary Ovington White, Portraits in Color (Freeport, N.Y.: Books for Libraries, 1955), p. 104.

[3]Richard Barksdale and Keneth Kinnamon, Black Writers of America (New York: Macmillan, 1972), p. 581.

[4]Sylvestre C. Watkins, Anthology of American Negro Literature (New York: Modern Library, 1944), p. 477.

[5]Barksdale and Kinnamon, p. 581.

[6]Obituary [note 1], p. 298.

White, W. F. (cont.)   764

> [7]Alton Hornsby, Jr. The Black Almanac (Woodbury, N.Y. : Barron's Educational Series, Inc., 1973), p. 64.
> [8]Watkins, pp. 477-478.

WHITFIELD, Cupid Aleins.
POETRY   Poems of Today. Quincy, Fla.: n.p., 1893.

WHITFIELD, James M. Born 10 April 1822 in Exeter, New Hampshire. Died 1878.[1] Education: Informal. Career: Was a barber, but gave up this work after his America and Other Poems appeared in 1853; promoted immigration to Central America; assisted in sponsoring the National Emigration Convention of Colored Men; championed the cause of Black separatism;[2] edited a newspaper, The Repository.[3]
POETRY
> America and Other Poems. Buffalo, N.Y.: J. S. Leavitt, 1853.
> A Poem. San Francisco: San Francisco Elevator Office, 1867.
> Poems. n.p., n.d., 1846.
> With F. Douglas, W. J. Watkins. Arguments Pro and Con, On the Call for a National Emigration Convention to be held in Cleveland, Ohio, August 1854. Detroit: Matthew T. Newsom, 1854.
> Emancipation Oration, San Francisco, 1867.
> (Anthologies): Blair, The Destiny of the Races of this Continent; Brown, Davis and Lee, Negro Caravan; Griffith, Autographs for Freedom; Randall, The Black Poets; Robinson, Early Black American Poets; Woodson, The Mind of the Negro.

LETTERS AND POETRY
> (Periodicals): Elevator, 11 January 6 December 1867; 10 April, 14 August 1868; 6 May 1870; Frederick Douglass Paper, 22 January, 12 November, 17 December 1852; 8 July 1853; 29 February 1856; Liberator, 18 November 1853; The North Star, 10 August, 14 December, 21 December 1849; 5 March, 12, 22 April 1850; Pacific Appeal, August 1862; 23 May 1863.

BIOGRAPHY AND CRITICISM ON WHITFIELD
> Brawley. Negro Genius, pp. 80-83.
> Brown, Davis and Lee. Negro Caravan, p. 290.
> Loggins. The Negro Author: His Development in America to 1900, pp. 241-245.
> Miller. Blackamerican Literature, pp. 207-211, 768.
> Robinson. Early Black American Poets, p. 39.
> Sherman, J. R. "James Monroe Whitfield, Poet and Emigrationist: A Voice of Protest and Despair." Journal of Negro History 57 (April 1972): 169-176.
> Wagner. Black Poets of the United States, p. 25.
> > [1]Richard Barksdale and Keneth Kinnamon, Black Writers of America (New York: Macmillan, 1972), p. 222.
> > [2]Sterling A. Brown and others, eds., The Negro Caravan New York: The Citadel Press, 1941. p. 290.

[3]Carter G. Woodson, ed., The Mind of the Negro as Reflected in his letters, (New York: Negro University Press, 1926, 1929), p. 500.

WHITFIELD, Vantile (Motojicho).
DRAMA
The Creeps (one act), 1969.
In Sickness and in Health (one act), 1966.

WHITMAN, Albery Allson. Born 30 May 1851 in Mumfordsville, Kentucky. Died 29 June 1901. Education: Was graduated from Wilberforce University. Career: Whitman was forced to begin working at an early age because his parents died when he was 12 years old. His first jobs included working on a farm near his birthplace, in the "plough shop" of A. T. Beadle and Company, and as a railroad construction worker. He later taught school in Ohio and Kentucky for short periods; was Elder of the African Methodist Episcopal Church in Ohio and Kansas; served as financial agent at Wilberforce University, and was influential in establishing many churches.[1]
POETRY
Drifted Leaves: A Collection of Poems, n.d., n.p., 1890.
Essays on the Ten Plagues and Other Miscellaneous Poems. 1871.
An Idyl of the South. New York: The Metaphysical Publishing Co., 1901. (Epic poem.)
Leelah Misled. Elizabethtown, Ky.: Richard LaRue, Printer, 1873.
Not a Man, and Yet a Man. Springfield, Ohio: Republic Printing Co., 1877.
The Rape of Florida. St. Louis, Mo.: Nixon, Jones Printing Co., 1884.
Twasinta's Seminoles, or, Rape of Florida. St. Louis, Mo.: Nixon-Jones Printing Co., 1885; rev. ed. 1890.
The World's Fair Poem: The Freedman's Triumphant Song. Atlanta, Ga.: Holsey Job Printery, 1893.
(Anthologies): Brown, Davis and Lee, Negro Caravan; Calverton, Anthology of American Negro Literature; Patterson, International Library of Negro Life and History, Literature and Art; Robinson, Early Black American Poets; White and Jackson, An Anthology of Verse by American Negroes.
BIOGRAPHY AND CRITICISM ON WHITMAN
Braithwaite, William S. "Rev. Whitman's Idyll." Colored American (January-February 1902): 246.
Brawley. Negro Genius, pp. 11-16.
_____. The Negro in Literature and Art, pp. 45-49.
_____. "Three Negro Poets: Horton, Mrs. Harper and Whitman." Journal of Negro History 2 (October 1917): 384-392.
Brown, Davis and Lee. Negro Caravan, p. 297.
Dictionary of American Biography, pp. 138-139.
Jackson and White. An Anthology of Verse by American Ne-

groes, pp. 236-237.

Kerlin. Negro Poets and Their Poems, pp. 33, 35-36, 345.

Loggins. The Negro Author, pp. 336-341.

Payne, Daniel Alexander. Recollections of Seventy Years, 1888; reprint ed. New York: Arno, 1968, pp. 238-239.

Robinson. Early Black American Poets, pp. 178, 193-196.

Sherman, Joan R. "Albery Allson Whitman: Poet of Beauty and Manliness." CLA Journal 15 (December 1971): 126-144.

Simmons. Men of Mark, pp. 1122-1126.

Wagner. Black Poets of the United States, pp. 25-26, 128.

[1]Dumas Malone, ed., Dictionary of American Biography, (New York: Charles Scribner's Sons, 1936), pp. 138-139.

WHITMORE, Terry.
With Richard Weber. Memphis-Nam-Sweden. Garden City, N.Y.: Doubleday, 1971.

WHITNEY, Elvie.
DRAMA
Center of Darkness, 1968.
Pornuff, 1969.
Up a Little Higher, 1968.

WHITSITT, Joyce see WANGARA, Malaiko Ayo

WIDEMAN, John E. Born 14 June 1941 in Washington, D.C. Education: B.A., University of Pennsylvania (Ben Franklin Scholar), 1963; B.Phil., New College, Oxford (Rhodes Scholar), 1966; attended the University of Iowa, Creative Writing Workshop, 1966-67. Currently living in Philadelphia, Pennsylvania. Career: Taught American Literature at Howard University, Summer 1965; and at the University of Pennsylvania since 1967, taught creative writing seminars, freshman literature and Black literature. He has also served as administrator/teacher in an 18-month curriculum planning, teacher-training institute sponsored by NDEA. As a member of the National Humanities Faculty, has served as consultant in numerous states since 1969. Member: Rhodes Scholar Selection Committee for Pennsylvania (Middle Atlantic States Final); Board of Directors, American Association of Rhodes Scholars; Admissions Committee, University of Pennsylvania. Awards, Honors: Phi Beta Kappa; Two Year Captain Basketball/Thouron Fellowship (awarded for two years study in England); Creative Writing Prize for contribution to the University literary magazine (University of Pennsylvania); Kent Fellow, University of Iowa; Rhodes Scholar, New College, Oxford, 1963-66.

CRITICISM BY WIDEMAN
"Black Writer's Views on Literary Lions and Values." Negro Digest 17 (January 1968): 21.
"Charles W. Chesnutt: The Marrow of Tradition." The American Scholar 42 (Winter 1972-73).

NOVELS
    A Glance Away. New York: Harcourt, Brace, World, 1967.
    Hurry Home. New York: Harcourt, Brace, World, 1970.
    The Lynchers. New York: Harcourt, Brace, World, 1973.
POETRY
    (Periodical), Black World, September 1973.
SHORT STORY
    (Periodical): The American Scholar, Autumn 1971.
BIOGRAPHY AND CRITICISM ON WIDEMAN
    Journal of Negro History 48 (January 1963): 66.
    Knight, H. "Rhodes Scholar Family." Negro Digest 12
      (May 1963): 11-16.
    O'Brien. Interviews with Black Writers, pp. 213-223.
REVIEWS: A Glance Away
    Ebert, R. American Scholar 36 (Autumn 1967): 682.
    Caldwell, S. F. Saturday Review, 21 October 1967, p. 36.
    Roskolenko, H. New York Times Book Review, 10 Septem-
      ber 1967, p. 56.
The Lynchers
    New York Times Book Review, 29 April 1973, p. 25; 10
      June 1973, p. 40.
    Walker, Jim. Black Creation 5 (Fall 1973): 42-43.

WIGGINS, Bernice Love. Born 1897.
    POETRY Tuneful Tales. El Paso, Texas: n.p., 1925.

WIGGINS, Walter, Jr.
    NOVEL Dreams in Reality of the Undersea Craft. New York:
      Pageant, 1954.

WILDS, Myra Viola.
    POETRY
      Thoughts of Idle Hours. Nashville, Tenn.: The National
      Baptist Publishing Board, 1915.
    REVIEW: Thoughts of Idle Hours
      White and Jackson. An Anthology of Verse by American Ne-
      groes, p. 237.

WILEY, Electa.
    POETRY (Anthology): Boyd, Poems by Blacks, II.

WILKINS, Patricia Ann see BROWNE, Patricia Wilkins

WILKINSON, Brenda. Born in 1946 in Moultrie, Georgia. Educa-
    tion: Attended Hunter College. Currently living in Bronx, New
    York. Career: Began poetry readings in grammar school
    classrooms on a non-professional level in 1972; has continued
    readings with junior and senior high students. Member: Sonia
    Sanchez's Writers Workshop at Countée Cullen Library in Har-
    lem.
    SHORT STORY
      (Anthology): Sanchez, We Be Word Sorcerers.

WORK IN PROGRESS
A Collection of Children's poetry and a novel.
INTERJECTIONS
"I started writing about two years ago out of a personal
need--most of which came out blue. Now that I've gotten most
of the hurt out, I've moved on to other things. I've been cele-
brating with children beginning with my own two (girls 5 and 2).
I've done several poems, short stories, prose pieces that are
warm, humorous, entertaining, and always with a statement.
This has been my main concentration. The novel I'm doing is
for and about young people too. I'm a product of the last of
the southern segregated schools and I'm trying to re-build them
in print, so my younger sisters and brothers can see the joy
we had in our schools, and in general give a picture of growing
up during the fifties in Georgia."

WILKINSON, Henry Bertram.
POETRY
Idle Hours: A Volume of Verse Touching Various Topics.
New York: F. H. Hitchcock, 1927.
Shady Rest. New York: F. H. Hitchcock, 1928.
Desert Sands. London: Stockwell, 1933.
Transitory. Boston: n.p., 1941.
BIOGRAPHY ON WILKINSON
The New Writer's Who's Who, Number 11; Specially Pre-
pared and with Photographs. London: Author H. Stock-
well, Ltd., 1934. (Contains a short biography of Henry
B. Wilkinson.)

WILKS, Peter.
DRAMA
The Long-Game Mefy.
The Soul of Willy.

WILLIAMS, Ann see DEE, Ruby

WILLIAMS, Chancellor. Born in 1902.
NOVELS
Have You Been to the River? New York: Exposition, 1952.
The Raven. Philadelphia: Dorrance, 1943.

WILLIAMS, Clarence.
DRAMA Bottomland, 1927.

WILLIAMS, Delores.
POETRY
(Anthology): Watkins, Black Review No. 2.
(Periodical): Black Creation, Spring 1972.

WILLIAMS, Donald Ray. Born 2 February 1948 in Los Angeles,
California. Education: A.B., San Diego State University, 1970;
credential, San Diego State University, 1972. Currently living
in Los Angeles, California. Career: "I have spent the early

adulthood of my life going to school. I've washed dishes, I've
been a janitor and worked at various odd jobs to support my education. But I will never forget my job of loading mail trucks.
It introduced me to a wide variety of people, trying to get the
most out of their lives. During my incarceration in school, I
was able to put my energies into the field of Speech Pathology,
and through this association I will be doing my own research into the field of the Black Dialect. I was able to obtain my freedom from school through Literature, specifically Black Literature. I was motivated to write. And I have been writing seriously for five years. The publishing has been slow, but the
pleasure of expressing myself as a Black man has been significant. Writing for me is the opportunity and challenge of repre-
senting Black people in Literature as people."
WRITINGS
   (Periodicals): Inter-racial Voice, October-November 1971;
      Beau-Cocoa, January 1973.
WORK IN PROGRESS
   A non-fiction work for children and a novel, "In the Name of
   the Lord."

WILLIAMS, Edward G. Born 3 November 1929 in Fayetteville, North
   Carolina. Education: A.A., Virginia State College, Norfolk Division, 1950; also attended the College of the City of New York
   and New York University College of Continuing Education. Currently living in New York City. Career: Supervisor of staff of
   typists, United Nations, New York, 1959-63; traffic manager in
   promotion department and writer of promotional material, New
   York Herald Tribune, 1963-67; director of traffic department,
   S. R. Leon Advertising Agency, 1967. Freelance Writer of fic-
   tion and non-fiction, 1967 to present. Currently conducting a
   Writer's Workshop at Daytop Village (a drug rehabilitation pro-
   gram in New York City) under the auspices of the New York Chap-
   ter of P.E.N.
NON-FICTION
   (Newspaper): Christian Science Monitor.
NOVEL
   Not Like Niggers. New York: St. Martin's Press, 1969.
SHORT STORY
   (Anthology): Shuman, A Galaxy of Black Writing.
WORK IN PROGRESS
   A history of the Dance Theatre in Harlem, tentatively entitled
   "Like the Phoenix: Dance Theatre of Harlem." A drama-
   tization of a short story, "Great Day for a Funeral."

WILLIAMS, Edward W. Career: A minister in Washington, D.C. [1]
   POETRY The Views and Meditations of John Brown. Washing-
      ton, D.C.: n.p., 1893. (Pamphlet.)
         [1]Newman Ivey White and Walter Clinton Jackson, An An-
      thology of Verse by American Negroes (Durham, N.C.:
      Moore, 1968), p. 237. Includes a paragraph of critical
      comments.

Edward G. Williams

WILLIAMS, Egbert Austin (Bert Williams). <u>Born</u> 1878 in Antigua,
West Indies. <u>Died</u> 1922. <u>Career</u>: Williams was one of the first
Black men to achieve recognition as a stage personality.   He
teamed with George Walker, and they became a highly popular attraction in vaudeville.   They also starred in their own All-Negro
Musical revues which triumphantly toured the United States[1] and
Great Britain.   In London, one of the revues, <u>In Dahomey</u>, was
chosen to be given as a command performance for King Edward
VII.   When Walker was incapacitated, Bert Williams performed
alone and became one of the highest salaried performers in
vaudeville.   He later starred in the famed Ziegfeld Follies for

many years. [2] Williams wrote many of the comedy songs he
sang with unrivaled success.
DRAMA
  With Alex Rogers and J. A. Shipp. Mr. Lode of Koal, 1909.
  With George Walker. Sons of Ham, 1899.
POETRY
  Sewell, Eugene, ed. "Bert" Williams; Poetry and a Short
    Story, n.p., 1923. (Schomburg Collection.)
BIOGRAPHY AND CRITICISM ON WILLIAMS
  Adams. Great Negroes Past and Present, p. 132.
  Baskin and Runes. Dictionary of Black Culture, p. 472.
  Cantor, E. "Bert Williams--The Best Teacher I Ever Had."
    Ebony 13 (January 1958): 103-106.
  Fletcher, Tom. ...100 Years of the Negro in Show Business.
    New York: Burdge, 1954.
  Isaacs. The Negro in the American Theatre, pp. 32-42.
  Monfried, W. "Bert Williams: The Modern Pagliaccio."
    Negro Digest 11 (November 1961): 28-32. (Reprinted from
    the Milwaukee Journal.)
  Negro History Bulletin (January 1939).
  Patterson. International Library of Negro Life and History:
    Music and Art, p. 125.
  Robinson. Historical Negro Biographies, pp. 143-144.
  Rollins. Famous Negro Entertainers, pp. 105-107.
  Rowland, Mabel, ed. Bert Williams, Son of Laughter. New
    York: The English Crafters, 1923.
  Sanders, O. E. "Command Performance of Williams and
    Walker before the King and Queen." Negro Digest 11
    (March 1962): 16-21.
  Wolf, Rennold. The Greatest Comedian on the American
    Stage; a Real Life Story of Bert Williams, A Negro, who
    also has the distinction of being "the most modest actor in
    America." n.p., 1912.
  Workers of the Writers' Program of the Work Projects Ad-
    ministration in New York City. The Theatre: Research
    Studies. New York: n.p., 1938-40.
      [1]Wade Baskin and Richard N. Runes, Dictionary of
    Black Culture. (New York: Philosophical Library, 1973),
    p. 472.
      [2]Wilhelmina S. Robinson, Historical Negro Biographies
    (New York: Publishers Co., 1969), pp. 143-144.

WILLIAMS, Ellwoodson.
  DRAMA
    Mine Eyes Have Seen the Glory, 1970.
    Voice of the Gene, 1969.

WILLIAMS, Florence.
  POETRY The Guiding Light. Nashville, Tenn.: National Baptist
    Training School Board, 1963.

WILLIAMS, Frank B.
  POETRY Fifty Years of Freedom, 1913.

WILLIAMS, George Washington. Born 16 October 1849 in Bedford
Springs, Pennsylvania. Died 4 August 1891. Education: A.B. ,
Howard University 1868; M.A. , Newton Theological Seminary,
1874; attended Cincinnati Law School. Career: Enlisted in the
Union Army at the age of 14 in 1862; served as lieutenant-col-
onel in the Mexican Army; was ordained as a minister, 11 June
1874, and during his career as a minister, wrote an 80-page
history of the church, but no copy has survived; founded two
newspapers, The Commoner in Washington, and The Southern
Review in Cincinnati; was appointed Internal Revenue Storekeeper
by the Secretary of the Treasury; practiced law in Ohio; served
in the Ohio State Legislature and as a minister in Haiti; was appointed to the Federal Internal Revenue by President Hayes.
Awards, Honors: Was admitted to the Ohio Bar, 1881 and the
Massachusetts Bar, 1883. [1]
NON-FICTION
   1862--Emancipation--1884. The Negro as a Political Prob-
      lem. Boston: A. Mudge & Son, Printers, 1884.
   The Ethics of War, 1884.
   History of the Negro Race in America from 1619 to 1880.
      New York and London: G. P. Putnam's Sons, 1888.
   A History of the Negro Troops in the War of Rebellion.
      New York: Harper, 1888.
   Memorial Day. The Ethics of War. Newton, Mass.: Printed
      at the Office of the Graphic, 1884. (Oration.)
   An Open Letter to Leopold, 1890.
   Report Upon the Congo State and Country to the President of
      the Republic of the U.S. , 1886.
   (Anthologies): Davis and Redding, Cavalcade; Miller, Back-
      ground to Blackamerican Literature; Levitt, Afro-American
      Voices.
   (Periodical): Cincinnati Commercial.
BIOGRAPHY AND CRITICISM ON WILLIAMS
   Adams. Great Negroes Past and Present, p. 56.
   Brawley. Negro Genius, pp. 106-110.
   Brown, Davis and Lee. The Negro Caravan, p. 863.
   Burke and Howe. American Authors and Books.
   Butcher, Phillip. "George W. Cable and George Washington
      Williams: An Abortive Collaboration." Journal of Negro
      History 53 (October 1968): 334-344.
   Davis. American Negro Reference Book, pp. 142-151.
   Franklin, John Hope. "George Washington Williams, Histor-
      ian." The Journal of Negro History 31 (January 1946).
   Johnson and Malone. Dictionary of American Biography,
      1929-1937.
   Miller. Backgrounds to American Literature, pp. 245-255,
      768.
   National Encyclopedia.
   "Notes on George Washington Williams." Negro History Bulle-
      tin 30 (October 1967): 12.
   Ploski. Reference Library of Black America.
   Robinson. Historical Negro Biographies, pp. 144-145.
   Simmons. Men of Mark, pp. 549-566.

INTERJECTIONS
"Not as the blind panegyrist of my race, nor as the partisan
apologist, but from a love for 'the truth of history,' I have
striven to record the truth, the whole truth, and nothing but the
truth.   I have not striven to revive sectional animosities or
race prejudices.   I have avoided comment so far as it was con-
sistent with a clear exposition of the truth.   My whole aim has
been to write a thoroughly trustworthy history, and what I have
written, if it have no other merit, is reliable. "[2]
        [1]Dumas Malone, Dictionary of American Biography (New
York: Charles Scribner's Sons, 1936), p. 264.
        [2]Richard Barksdale and Keneth Kinnamon, Black Writers
of America (New York: Macmillan, 1972), pp. 257-259.

WILLIAMS, Harold.
DRAMA With the Right Seed My Plant Will Grow Green.

WILLIAMS, Henry Roger. Born 1869. Died 1929. Career: Medical Doctor.
    NON-FICTION
        The Blighted Life of Methuselah. Nashville, Tenn.: National
        Baptist Publishing Board, 1908.
    POETRY
        Are We Free? Mobile, Ala.: n.p., 1928.
        The Christ Is a Negro. Mobile, Ala.: n.p., 1923.
        Heart Throbs--Poems of Race Inspiration. Mobile, Ala.:
        Gulf City Printing Co., 1923.

WILLIAMS, Jeanette Marie.
    POETRY Soul of a Sapphire. Chicago: Free Black Press,

WILLIAMS, Jerome Ardell.
    The Tin Box: A Story of Texas Cattle and Oil. New York:
        Vantage, 1958.

WILLIAMS, Jim.
    CRITICISM
        "The Need for a Harlem Theatre." Freedomways 3 (1963);
            also in Patterson, An Anthology of the Negro in American
            Theater.
        "Pieces on Black Theatre and the Black Theatre Worker."
            Freedomways 9 (Spring 1969): 146-155.
        "Survey of Afro-American Playwrights." Freedomways 10
            (1970): 26-45.
    NON-FICTION
        (Periodical): Freedomways, Spring 1965.
    POETRY
        (Periodicals): Freedomways, Spring 1962; Spring 1963;
            Spring 1964; Spring 1965; Spring 1966.

WILLIAMS, John Alfred. Born 5 December 1925 in Jackson, Mis-
    sissippi. Career: See Shockley and Chandler, Living Black
    American Authors, pp. 172-173; Ploski, Reference Library of

Black Americans, pp. 36-37.
CRITICISM BY WILLIAMS
"Black Writer's Views of Literary Lions and Values." Negro Digest 17 (January 196 8): 46.
"The Harlem Renaissance: Its Artists, Its Impact, Its Meaning." Black World 20 (November 1970): 17-18.
"The Literary Ghetto." In Hemenway, The Black Novelist, pp. 227-230.
"The Manipulation of History and Fact: An Ex-Southerner's Apologist Tract for Slavery and the Life of Nat Turner: or, William Styron's Faked Confessions." In Clarke, William Styron's Nat Turner, pp. 45-49.
"The Negro in Literature Today." Ebony 8 (September 1963): 73-76.
"Problems of the Negro Writer." Saturday Review, 1963; reprinted in Bigsby, The Black American Writer, vol. 1.
DRAMA
Reprieve for All God's Children.
EDITOR
With Charles F. Harris. Amistad 1. New York: Random House, 1970†.
With Charles F. Harris. Amistad 2. New York: Random House, 1971†.
The Angry Black. New York: Lancer, 1962.
Beyond the Angry Black. New York: Lancer, 1962; New York Cooper Square, 1962*; New York: New American Library, 1971†. (A reissue of The Angry Black with new material.)
NON-FICTION
Africa: Her History, Lands and People Told with Pictures. New York: Cooper Square, 1963*†.
Flashbacks: A Twenty-Year Diary of Article Writing. Garden City, N.Y.: Doubleday, 1973*. (Includes material published in Authors Guild Bulletin, February/March 1972; Cavalier, September, November 1963; Holiday, August, September 1964; January, March, June 1967; Nickel Review, 1969; Swank, 1961; Herald Tribune Sunday magazine, 25 April 1965; Nugget, December 1962; Amistad 1, edited by Williams and Harris; The Immigrant Experience: The Anguish of Becoming an American, edited by Thomas Wheeler; Yardbird Reader, I.)
The King God Didn't Save: Reflections on the Life and Death of Martin Luther King. New York: Coward, McCann & Geoghegan, 1970*.
With Charles Obukar. The Modern African. London: MacDonald & Evans, 1965.
The Most Native of Sons: A Biography of Richard Wright. Garden City, N.Y.: Doubleday, 1970*†.
This Is My Country Too. New York: New American Library, 1964†. (Portions first appeared in Holiday magazine.)
(Anthology): Reed, Yardbird Reader I.
(Periodicals): Negro Digest, September 1965; August 1967; November 1969.

NOVELS
The Angry Ones. New York: Ace, 1960; New York: Pocket Books, 1970†.

Captain Blackman: A Novel. Garden City, N.Y.: Doubleday, 1972*.

The Man Who Cried I Am. Boston: Little, Brown, 1967*; New York: New American Library, 1972†. Excerpt in Davis and Redding, Cavalcade; Reed, 19 Necromancers from Now.

Night Song. New York: Farrar, Straus & Cudahy, 1961; New York: Pocket Books, 1970†. Excerpt in Ford, Black Insights.

Sissie. New York: Farrar, Straus & Cudahy, 1963.

Sons of Darkness, Sons of Light: A Novel of Some Probability. Boston: Little, Brown, 1969*; New York: Pocket Books, 1970†.

POETRY
(Anthology): Major, The New Black Poetry.

(Periodical): Partisan Review 35 (Spring 1968).

SHORT STORIES
(Anthologies): Adoff, Brothers and Sisters; Baker, Black Literature in America; Emanuel and Gross, Dark Symphony; Hills and Hills, How We Live; Hughes, Best Short Stories by Negro Writers; Kearns, Black Identity; King, Black Short Story Anthology; Margolies, A Native Sons Reader; Patterson, An Introduction to Black Literature in America; Simmons and Hutchinson, Black Culture; Singh and Fellowes, Black Literature in America; Williams, Beyond the Angry Black.

(Periodical): Negro Digest, January 1963.

BIOGRAPHY AND CRITICISM ON WILLIAMS
Algren, Nelson. "Remembering Richard Wright." Nation 192 (28 January 1961): 85-86.

Beauford, Fred. "John A. Williams: Agent Provocateur." Black Creation 2 (Summer 1971): 4-6.

Fleming, Robert E. "The Nightmare Level of The Man Who Cried I Am." Contemporary Literature 14 (Spring 1973): 186-196.

Kent. "Outstanding Works," pp. 311-314.

Henderson, David. "The Man Who Cried I Am: A Critique." In Gayle, Black Expression.

Klotman, P. R. "Examination of the Black Confidence Man in Two Black Novels: The Man Who Cried I Am and dem." American Literature 44 (January 1973).

Leonard, John. "Author at Bay." New York Times Book Review, 29 October 1967, p. 66.

O'Brien, John. "Art of John A. Williams." American Scholar (Summer 1973): 489-494.

_____. Interviews with Black Writers, pp. 225-244.

_____. "Seeking a Humanist Level: Interview with John A. Williams." Arts in Society 10 (Spring-Summer 1973): 94-99.

Peavy, Charles D. "Four Revolutionary Novels, 1899-1969."

Journal of Black Studies 1 (December 1970): 219-223.
Smith, Anneliese H. "A Pain in the Ass: Metaphor in John
A. Williams' The Man Who Cried I Am." Studies in Black
Literature 3 (Autumn 1972): 25-27.
Walcott, Ronald. "The Man Who Cried I Am: Crying in the
Dark." Studies in Black Literature 3 (Spring 1972): 24-32.
_____. "The Early Fiction of John A. Williams." CLA
Journal 16 (December 1972): 198-213.
Whitlow. Black American Literature, pp. 179-183.

WILLIAMS, John M.
POETRY (Anthology): Lincoln University Poets.

WILLIAMS, Lucy Ariel see HOLLOWAY, Lucy A. Williams

WILLIAMS, Mance.
POETRY (Anthology): Hughes, New Negro Poets: USA.

WILLIAMS, Marshall.
DRAMA A Tear for Judas, 1970.

WILLIAMS, Rene. Born 1951 in New Orleans.
POETRY (Anthology): Shuman, A Galaxy of Black Writing.

WILLIAMS, Richard L.
Parson Wiggin's Son. New York: Carlton, 1964.

WILLIAMS, Sandra Beth (Auransia). Born October 1948 in New
Haven, Connecticut. Education: Attended Temple University,
Yale University, Philadelphia Dance Academy. The New York
Library and the cinema also were important educational factors
in her life. Currently living in Madison, Connecticut. Career:
Mainly a playwright, but has also worked in other literary
genres; has acted with the Long Wharf Theatre in New Haven,
Connecticut, and with the Afro-American Arts Theatre in Philadelphia where she also served as director of a Movement Workshop. Directed the Black Dramatic Workshop at Temple, and
had her own radio program at Temple University. She has been
a professional dancer with the Arthur Hall Afro-American Dance
Ensemble, and had the singing lead in a 1972 Street Theatre
Production in New York. She has had poetry readings in Philadelphia, New York, and Buffalo. She is presently teaching creative writing. Awards, Honors: Awarded a CAPS grant for two
of her plays, 1972.
DRAMA
    The Family.
    Hey Nigger Can You Dig Her.
    Jest One Mo.
    Sunshine.
    Zodiac Zenith.
POETRY
    (Anthology): Giovanni, Night Comes Softly.
    (Periodical): Journal of Black Poetry, Winter-Spring, 1970;
    Stylus.

Sandra Beth Williams

INTERJECTIONS
"The essence of life is in creativity; that is man's inherent sexuality in his romance with nature. As a Black Artist, I am striving for a return of the coveted birthright of Egypt and Ethiopia; all of our grandeur and splendour touching in communion with the rest of the universe in perfection."

WILLIAMS, Sherley Anne.
    CRITICISM Give Birth to Brightness: A Thematic Study in
        Neo-Black Literature. New York: Dial, 1972.

WILLIAMS, Vincent.
    POETRY
        (Anthology): Murphy, Negro Voices.
        (Periodical): Opportunity, April 1937.

WILLIAMSON, Harvey M. Born 29 January 1908 in Shelby, Mississippi. Education: A.B., (Magna Cum Laude) Western Reserve University, 1949; M.A., Western Reserve University, 1949; M.A., Western Reserve University, 1952. Currently living in Cleveland, Ohio. Career: City Clerk, City of Cleveland, 1937-40; customs inspector, U.S. Air Corps, 1942-45; teacher, Cleveland public schools, 1949; Principal, R. B. Hayes Schools (Cleveland), 1962-70; Principal, Longwood School (Cleveland), 1970 to present. Member: City Club of Cleveland; President, Phillis Wheatley Association; President, Alumni Association, Western Reserve University, 1970-72; Phi Beta Kappa; Phi Delta Kappa; various educational associations. Awards, Honors: Board of Governors, Western Reserve University, 1962-68, and Board of Overseers, 1968-70; President, Phi Delta Kappa, Western Reserve University, 1964; Alumnus of the Year, 1964; poetry prize, 1948, and prose award, 1931, Cleveland College of Western Reserve University.
    CRITICISM
        (Periodical): "The Gilpin Players." Crisis, 1935.
    POETRY
        (Anthology): Murphy, Negro Voices.
        (Periodicals): Crisis, April, May, September, 1934; May,
            November 1937.
    SHORT STORIES
        (Periodicals): Crisis, November 1934; Story Magazine, October 1936.
    INTERJECTIONS
    "When I retire in the not too distant future, I'll probably turn my hand to writing for my own pleasure again."

WILSON, Alice T. Born 15 July 1908 in Virginia. Education: Attended Margaret M. Nursing School and the National Academy of Radio and Television Broadcasting. Currently living in Washington, D.C. Career: Presently writing country and western songs. Member: National Platform Association. Awards, Honors: Citations from Senators Taft, Barkley, and McCarthy, and from President Kennedy.

SCREENPLAY AND POETRY
How an American Poet Made Money and Forget-Me-Not. New
York: Pageant, 1968.

WILSON, Art. Born in San Diego, California.
POETRY (Anthology): Coombs, We Speak as Liberators.

WILSON, August. Born 1945.
POETRY
(Anthology): Adoff, The Poetry of Blackamerica.
(Periodicals): Black Lines, Summer 1971; September 1972;
also published in Connection.

WILSON, Cal.
DRAMA The Pet Shop, 1965.

WILSON, Carl Thomas David.
NOVEL The Half Caste. Ilfracombe, England: A. H. Stockwell, 1964.

WILSON, Charles P. Born 1885 in Iowa. Career: Was incarcer-
ated in the Missouri Penitentiary for a period of time. Was a
printer and theatrical performer.[1]
POETRY
(Anthology): Kerlin, Negro Poets and Their Poems.
BIOGRAPHY AND CRITICISM ON WILSON
Kerlin. Negro Poets and Their Poems.
[1]Robert T. Kerlin, Negro Poets and Their Poems
(Washington, D.C.: Associated, 1923).

WILSON, Ernest J., Jr. Born 1920 in Greenwich, Connecticut.
POETRY (Anthology): Hughes and Bontemps, The Poetry of
the Negro: 1746-1970.

WILSON, Floria McCullough. Born 20 November 1927 in Andrews,
South Carolina. Education: B.A., Allen University, 1953.
Currently living in Columbia, South Carolina. Career: Associa-
mentary education teacher at B-C #1 in West Columbia, South
Carolina. Member: South Carolina National Education Associa-
tion; N.A.A.C.P; Queen Easter Chapter, Order of Eastern Star.
POETRY
Not By Bread Alone. New York: Carlton, 1970.
UNPUBLISHED WORK
"The Face in the Mirror."
INTERJECTIONS
"Our civilization is facing old and new problems which should
be taken seriously by every living thinking being. We are facing an energy crisis, air and water pollution, political problems,
racial problems, sexual problems. Isn't it time that we began
to fear self extinction; that a future civilization may someday
view our skeletal remains with the same awe that we feel as we
view the remains of the dinosaurs and other prehistoric animals
who failed or were unable to control their environment?"

WILSON, Frank H. Born in New York City. Career: Spent 12
  years in vaudeville as an organizer and a baritone singer.
  First played Joe in O'Neill's play, All God's Chillun Got Wings,[1]
  and continued to star in many shows.
  DRAMA
    Back Home Again.
    Brother Mose: A Comedy of Negro Life with Music and Spir-
      ituals. (Original title, Meek Mose.) In Mantle and Burns
      Best Plays of 1927-28.
    Confidence (one act), 1922.
    The Frisco Kid.
    The Good Sister Jones.
    Sugar Cain (one act). In Opportunity 4 (June 1926): 181-184,
      201-203.
    Walk Together Chillun.
  BIOGRAPHY ON WILSON
    Bond. The Negro and the Drama, pp. 76, 109-110, 166-167.
    Davis. The American Negro Reference Book, pp. 832, 833,
      835.
    Hughes and Bontemps. Black Magic, pp. 108, 109, 113, 123,
      220, 300, 338.
    Mitchell. Black Drama, pp. 52-53.
    Opportunity 4 (June 1926), 188; 5 (March 1927): 86-87.
      [1]Opportunity 4 (June 1926): 188.

WILSON, Langford.
  DRAMA
    The Calico Cat and the Gingham Dog, 1969.
    The Hot L Baltimore.

WILSON, Pat.
  NOVEL The Sign of Keola. New York: Carlton, 1961.

WILSON, Ted. Born 1 September 1943 in New York City. Educa-
  tion: Central State College, 1961-62; Hunter College, 1962-64;
  School of Visual Arts, 1967-68. Currently living in Bronx, New
  York. Career: Teaches Black Literature and Creative Writing.
  Currently working on a recording of poetry and music, "Time
  and Space (No More Blues)."
  POETRY
    (Anthology): Jones and Neal, Black Fire.
  INTERJECTIONS
    "I am interested in researching Black American and African
  folklore with emphasis on various religions and rites which are
  originally African and now practiced in the U.S. and Latin Amer-
  ican countries."

WILSON, Welford.
  POETRY
    (Periodical): Crisis, November 1937.
  SHORT STORIES
    (Periodical): Opportunity, January, August 1942.

WILSON, Wilbert R.
POETRY Travels of the 20th Century and Beyond: Poems.
New York: Carlton, 1971.

WIMBERLI, Sigmonde (Kharlos Tucker). Born 1938.
POETRY
Ghetto Scenes: Poems. Chicago: Free Black Press, 1968.
(Anthologies): Brooks, Jump Bad; Brown, Lee and Ward,
To Gwen with Love.

WINSTON, Bessie Brent.
POETRY
Alabaster Boxes. Washington, D.C.: Review & Herald Pub-
lishing Assoc., 1947.
Life's Red Sea, and Other Poems. Washington: Review &
Herald Publishing Assoc., 1950.

WINSTON, Harry.
SHORT STORY (Anthology): Ford and Faggett, Best Short Stories by Afro-American Writers.

WITHERSPOON, James William.
POETRY A Breath of the Muse. Columbia, S.C.: Hampton,
1927.

WITHERSPOON, Naomi Long see MADGETT, Naomi Long

WOOBY, Philip.
NOVEL Nude to the Meaning of Tomorrow: A Novel of a Lonely Search. New York: Exposition, 1959.

WOOD, Lillian E.
NOVEL Let My People Go. Philadelphia: A.M.E. Book Concern, 1922.

WOOD, Odella Phelps.
NOVEL
High Ground. New York: Exposition, 1945.
POETRY
Recaptured Echoes. New York: Exposition, 1944.
CRITICISM ON WOOD
Hughes. The Negro Novelist, pp. 125-126.

WOODS, Barbara A.
SHORT STORY (Anthology): Mayfield, Ten Times Black.

WOODS, William B.
NOVEL Lancaster Triple Thousand: A Novel of Suspense.
New York: Exposition, 1956.

WOODSON, Jon. Born in 1944.
POETRY (Anthology): Davis and Redding, Cavalcade.

WOOTEN, Charles R. (Oblivious). Born 6 August 1949 in Lumber-
ton, North Carolina. Education: B.A., North Carolina State
University, 1971. Currently living in Dunn, North Carolina.
Career: Manager of a Sears retail store in Crabtree Valley
Mall, Raleigh, North Carolina, 1972 to present; also a musician
and a writer. Now moving from free verse toward the novel
form.
POETRY
    (Anthology): Shuman, A Galaxy of Black Writing.
INTERJECTIONS
    "I once stated to a friend, 'I'm not anti-white, just pro-Black
in expressing my feelings on the subject. But there was bitter-
ness, contempt, and a desire to show whites I was as good, or
better than they.... It's changed a little. I've mellowed quite
a bit from my 'experience.' In many cases, it is well that I
simply can believe in myself, and in my ability (to think, to do,
to know).
    "If I must live by something, and we all must...I choose the
best of the old, the most rational of the new...and the hope of
Oblivious."

WORK, J. W.
    POETRY
        (Anthologies): Kenricks, Afro-American Voices; Young, Black
            Experience.
        (Periodical): Crisis, 1920.

WORTHAM, Anne.
    POETRY
        Silence. New York: Pageant, 1965.
        (Periodical): Crisis, December 1945.

WRIGHT, Beatrice.
    POETRY
        Color Scheme: Selected Poems. New York: Pageant, 1957.
        (Periodical): Opportunity, Summer 1948.

WRIGHT, Bruce McMarion. Born 19 December 1918 in Princeton,
New Jersey. Education: "The nigger experience in white Amer-
ica's sideshow." Also--A.B., Lincoln University, 1942; addi-
tional study at Yale University Law School, 1950, and New
School of Social Research, 1951. Currently living in New York
City. Career: Rewrite editor, university newspaper, Lincoln
University, 1941; private lawyer, associated with various law
firms, 1949-67; General Counsel, The Human Resources Admin-
istration of the City of New York, 1967-70; Judge, Criminal
Court of the City of New York, 1970 to present. Member:
Association of the Bar of the City of New York; Urban League
of Greater New York; National Conference of Black Lawyers;
Legal Aid Society; College for Human Services; The Fortune So-
ciety; Yale Moot Court of Appeals, Chief Justice. Awards, Honors: Annual Judicial Award, National Bar Association, 1972;
Cited by Region I of the National Bar Association, March 1972;

LL.D. , Lincoln University, 1973; Conspicuous Service Cross,
New York, 1947; Cited by Neighborhood Board No. 3 of Harlem
for distinguished community service, 1970; Cited twice for heroic action against the enemy and awarded the Purple Heart twice,
U.S. Army, World War II.

CRITICISM
    "The Negritude Tradition in Literature." Studies in Black
        Literature 3 (Spring 1972): 1-3.
    "The Poetry of Léopold Sédar Senghor." Freedomways.
    Also published an article on Derek Walcott in Shango, The
        Magazine of the Caribbean 1 (1973).

EDITOR
    With Langston Hughes. Lincoln University Poets. New York:
        Fine Editions, 1954.

POETRY
    From the Shaken Tower. Cardiff, Wales: W. Lewis, 1944.
    (Anthologies): Adams, Conn and Slepian, Afro-American Lit-
        erature: Poetry; Adoff, The Poetry of Black America;
        Bontemps, American Negro Poetry; Hughes and Bontemps,
        The Poetry of the Negro: 1746-1970; Hughes and Wright,
        The Lincoln University Poets; Pool, Beyond the Blues;
        Singh and Fellowes, Black Literature in America; Vojka,
        Cernosska Poesie; Thorsten Jonsson, Mork Song (Stock-
        holm: Bonniers Forlag, 1949).
    Also published in the North Carolina Central University Law
        Review, 1973; The Student Lawyer, 1973; Judicature, June
        1973; National Bar Association Bulletin, 1973.

WORK IN PROGRESS
    "Selected Poems"--to be published in a French-English bi-
        lingual edition in Dakar, Senegal, with an introduction by
        President Léopold Sédar Senghor.

INTERJECTIONS
    "Life itself is an impression, although a fleeting one. I quite
agree with Ionesco, that happiness is an illusion, a pantomime,
acted out in a theatre of the absurd, with a script in an unknown
language. While an optimist thinks that this is the best of all
possible lives in the best of all possible worlds, as a pessimist,
I believe the optimist may just be right--alas. Art is that which
one thinks it is; it is an emotional aberration which sometimes
infects the mob and thus creates popularity and money for the
one thus made an 'artist.' "

WRIGHT, Charles Stevenson. Born 4 June 1932 in New Franklin,
    Missouri. Education: Attended public school in Missouri and
    Lowney Handy Writers Colony in Marshall, Illinois. Career:
    Wrote column, "Wright's World," for the Village Voice, 1967-
    1973. Presently working on a play, a screenplay, non-fiction,
    and a novel.

CRITICISM BY WRIGHT
    "Black Writer's Views on Literary Lions and Values." Ne-
        gro Digest 17 (January 1968): 15.

DRAMA
    Something Black.

Charles Wright

NON-FICTION
Absolutely Nothing to Get Alarmed About. New York: Farrar, Straus, 1973*.
(Periodicals): New York Times, 16 August 1973; Vogue, July 1973.
NOVELS
The Messenger. New York: Farrar, Straus, 1963.
The Wig: A Mirror Image. New York: Farrar, Straus & Giroux, 1966*.
SHORT STORIES
(Anthologies): Hughes, The Best Short Stories by Negro Writers; Patterson, An Introduction to Black Literature in America; Robinson, Nommo.
(Periodicals): Negro Digest, August 1968.
BIOGRAPHY AND CRITICISM ON WRIGHT
Foster, F. S. "Charles Wright: Black, Black Humorist." CLA Journal 15 (September 1973): 44-53.
O'Brien. Interviews with Black Writers, pp. 245-257.
Sedlack, Robert P. "Jousting with Rats: Charles Wright's The Wig." Satire Newsletter 7 (Fall 1969): 37-39.

WRIGHT, Jay. Born 25 May 1935 in Albuquerque, New Mexico.
Education: Studied at University of New Mexico; B.A., University of California-Berkeley; M.A., Rutgers University; additional work at Union Theological Seminary. Currently living in Penicuik, Scotland. Career: Poet-in-residence, Talledega University, Tougaloo University, Texas Southern University, and Dundee University; Hodder Fellow in Playwrighting, Princeton University.
POETRY
Death as History. Milbrook, N.Y.: Kriya Press, 1967.
Homecoming Singer. New York: Corinth, 1971.
(Anthologies): Adoff, The Poetry of Black America; Chapman, New Black Voices; Henderson, Understanding the New Black Poetry; Hughes, New Negro Poets: USA; Jones and Neal, Black Fire; Jordan, Soulscript; Patterson, An Introduction to Black Literature in America; Randall and Burroughs, For Malcolm; Schreiber, 31 New American Poets; Wilentz and Weatherly, Natural Process.
(Periodicals): Black World, April, September 1971; Journal of Black Poetry, Summer 1972; Negro American Literature Forum, Spring 1972; Negro Digest, February, September-October 1968; September 1969; also published in Evergreen Review, Hiram Poetry Review, The Nation.
REVIEWS: Homecoming Singer
Black World (September 1973): 90.
New York Times Book Review, 3 December 1972, p. 84.

WRIGHT, Julius C.
POETRY Poetic Diamonds. Montgomery, Ala.: W.E. Allred Printing Co., 1906.

WRIGHT, Nathan.
POETRY The Song of Mary. Boston: Humphries, 1958.

WRIGHT, Richard. Born 4 September 1908 on a plantation near Na-
tchez, Mississippi. Died 28 November 1960. Education: Completed the ninth grade in Jackson, Mississippi. This ended his
formal education.[1] Career: Wright's working career began
early because of his unstable childhood which can be attributed
to a broken home and his being shifted from relative to relative
for support. He even spent some time in an orphanage. As a
young man, he worked on unskilled jobs in Jackson, Mississippi,
Memphis, and Chicago, and became a clerk in the Chicago post
office in 1929; later, he became a worker at the South Side Chicago Boy's Club; a publicity agent for the Federal Negro Theatre; publicity agent for a white Federal Experimental Theatre;
an acting supervisor of the Federal Writer's Project;[2] and a
contributing editor for New Masses.[3] Also in Chicago, he was
elected secretary of the John Reed Club in 1932 and joined the
Communist Part shortly afterwards; however, in 1944, he for-
mally severed his membership.[4]
    Wright went to New York in 1937 and in addition to working
with the Federal Writers Project and having several books and
articles published, he collaborated with Paul Green on the drama
version of Native Son. The play was a Broadway hit in 1941. In
1950, Wright made Native Son into a film in Argentina and
starred in it, but the movie was a failure because of Wright's
poor acting.[5]
    The last 14 years of Wright's life were spent abroad. He be-
came an expatriate American in Paris, but also traveled, lectured, and visited in numerous countries, including Italy, Germany, Spain and some countries in Africa. His involvement in
the countries that he visited was incredible! For example, he
wrote radio dramas for German radio, helped organize the Société Africaine de Culture, and as a reporter, covered the Ban-
dung Conference in Asia in 1955.[6]
    He died of a heart attack 28 November 1960.
SELECTED ARTICLES AND ESSAYS BY WRIGHT
    (For a more complete listing, refer to the bibliographies
        listed below.)
    "Birth of Bigger Thomas." Crisis 48 (September 1942): 24-
        28.
    "Black Boyhood." Time, 5 March 1945, p. 944.
    "Early Days in Chicago. " Negro Digest 8 (July 1950: 52-
        68.
    "The God That Failed." In The Negro Since Emancipation,
        pp. 115-127.
    Edited by Harvey Wish. Englewood Cliffs, N. J. : Prentice-
        Hall, 1964.
    "Forerunner and Ambassador." New Republic 103 (24 Oc-
        tober 1940): 600. (Review of The Big Sea by Langston
        Hughes.)
    "How Bigger Was Born. " Saturday Review, 1 June 1940, pp.
        3-4, 17-20; also published in Literature for Our Time,

pp. 326-333. Edited by Leonard Stanley Brown and others.
New York: Holt, 1947; Native Son, New York: Harper &
Row, 1966. Also published in book form, New York:
Harper, 1940.

"Inner Landscape." New Republic, 5 August 1940, p. 195.
(Review of The Heart Is a Lonely Hunter by Carson Mc-
Cullers.)

"Men in the Making." Modern Writing, pp. 377-381. Edited
by Willard Thorp and Margaret Thorp. New York: American Book, 1944.

"Negro Tradition in the Theatre." Daily Worker, 15 October
1937, p. 5.

"Negro Writers Launch Literary Quarterly." San Antonio
Register (Texas), 10 July 1937, p. 4. Also published in
Daily Worker, 8 June 1937, p. 7.

"Reader's Right: Writer Asks Bread for Negroes." New
York Post, 5 April 1938, p. 20. (Letters to the Editors.)

"What Do I Think of the Theatre." New York World Telegram, 22 March 1941.

AUTOBIOGRAPHY
Black Boy. New York: Harper, 1945; New York: New American Library, 1963; Harper & Row, 1964 and 1966*†.

DRAMA
With Paul Green. Native Son, A Biography of a Young American. New York: Harper, 1941.

NON-FICTION
Black Power. New York: Harper, 1954; London: Dobson,
1956.

The Color Curtain. Cleveland: World, 1956; London: Dobson,
1956.

Pagan Spain. New York: Harper, 1957; London: The Bodley
Head, 1960.

12 Million Black Voices; Folk History of the Negro in the
United States. New York: Viking, 1941; London: Drummond,
1947; New York: Arno, 1969*.

White Man Listen. Garden City, N.Y.: Doubleday, 1957†.

NOVELS
Lawd Today. New York: Walker, 1963; New York: Hearst
Corp., 1963.

The Long Dream. Garden City, N.Y.: Doubleday, 1958; London: Angus & Robertson, 1960; Chatham, N.J.: Chatham
Bookseller, 1969*; New York: Ace Books†.

Native Son. New York: Harper, 1940, 1957, 1966, 1969*†;
New York: Modern Library, 1942; New York: New American Library, 1961, 1964.

The Outsider. New York: Harper, 1953; Harper & Row,
1969*†.

Savage Holiday. New York: Avon, 1954; Universal Publishing
& Distributing, 1965†.

PREFACES, INTRODUCTIONS, FOREWORDS, ETC.
For a complete listing, refer to:
Fabre, Michel. The Unfinished Quest of Richard Wright.
New York: Morrow, 1973, pp. 631-632.

Webb, Constance. Richard Wright: A Biography. New York:
G. P. Putnam's, 1968, pp. 428-429.

SHORT STORIES

Eight Men. Cleveland: World, 1961; New York: Avon, 1961;
New York: Pyramid†.

Uncle Tom's Children. New York: Harper, 1938; Harper &
Row, 1965, 1969*†; New York: New American Library,
1963.

Bright and Morning Star. New York: International, 1938. Also published in New Masses 27 (10 May 1938): 97-99, 116-
124, and in Wright's Uncle Tom's Children.

WRITINGS PUBLISHED IN ANTHOLOGIES

Wright's work can be found in most anthologies of Black literature. A partial listing is provided below:

Adams, Conn and Slepian, Afro-American Literature: Poetry,
Adoff, The Poetry of Black America; Baker, Black Litera-
ture in America; Barksdale and Kinnamon, Black Writers
of America; Bontemps, American Negro Poetry; Brown,
Davis and Lee, The Negro Caravan; Chapman, Black
Voices; Crossman, The God That Failed; Davis and Red-
ding, Cavalcade; Emanuel and Gross, Dark Symphony; Fad-
erman and Bradshaw, Speaking for Ourselves; Ford, Black
Insights; Hayden, Burrows and Lapides, Afro-American Lit-
erature: An Introduction; Hemenway, The Black Novelist;
Hughes, The Best Short Stories by Negro Writers; Jordan,
Soulscript; Kearns, Black Identity; Kendricks and Levitt,
Afro-American Voices: 1770's-1970's; Margolies, A Native
Sons Reader; Moon, Primer for White Folks; Wish, The
Negro Since Emancipation.

BIBLIOGRAPHIES ON WRIGHT

Abcarian, Richard, ed. Richard Wright's Native Son: A
Critical Handbook. Belmont, Calif.: Wadsworth, 1970, pp.
255-261.

Atlanta University Center for African and African-American
Studies. CAAS Bibliographies. Atlanta: Atlanta University,
1970.

Bakish, David. Richard Wright. New York: Ungar, 1973, pp.
107-109.

Bone, Robert A. Richard Wright. Minneapolis: University of
Minnesota Press, 1969.

Brignano, Russell Carl. Richard Wright; An Introduction to
the Man and His Works. Pittsburgh: University of Pittsburgh Press, 1970, pp. 191-198.

Bryer, Jackson. "Richard Wright: A Selected Check List of
Criticisms." Wisconsin Studies in Contemporary Literature
1 (Fall 1960): 22-33.

Fabre, M. and E. Margolies. "Richard Wright: A Bibliography."
Bulletin of Bibliography 24 (January 1965): 131-133, 137.

_____. The Unfinished Quest of Richard Wright. New York:
Morrow, 1973, pp. 625-638.

_____, and Edward Margolies. "A Bibliography of Richard
Wright's Works." New Letters 38 (Winter 1971): 155-169.

Gibson, Donald B. "Richard Wright: A Bibliographic Essay."

CLA Journal 12 (June 1969): 361-365.

_____, ed. Five Black Writers: Essays on Wright, Ellison, Baldwin, Hughes and Leroi Jones. New York: New York University Press, 1970, pp. 303-305.

Kinnamon, Keneth. Emergence of Richard Wright; A Study in Literature and Society. Urbana: University of Illinois Press, 1972, pp. 163-189.

McCall, Dan. The Example of Richard Wright. New York: Harcourt, Brace & World, 1969.

McDowell, Robert and George Fortenberry. "A Checklist of Books and Essays about American Negro Novelists." Studies in the Novel 3 (Summer 1971): 234-236.

Margolies, Edward. The Art of Richard Wright. With a preface by Harry T. Moore. Carbondale: Southern Illinois University Press, 1969.

Webb, Constance. Richard Wright: A Biography. New York: Putnam, 1968, pp. 423-429.

SELECTED BIOGRAPHY AND CRITICISM ON WRIGHT
(For a more complete listing, check the bibliographies listed above.)

Baker, Houston A., Jr., ed. Twentieth Century Interpretations of Native Son. Englewood Cliffs, N.J.: Prentice-Hall, 1973.

Basso, Hamilton. "Thomas Jefferson and the Black Boy." New Yorker, 10 March 1945, pp. 86-89.

Bland, Edward. "Social Forces Shaping the Negro Novel." Negro Quarterly 1 (1945): 241-248.

Brewster, Dorothy. "From Phyllis Wheatley to Richard Wright." Negro Quarterly 1 (1945): 80-83.

Brown, Sterling. "The Negro Author and His Publishers." Negro Quarterly 1 (1945): 7-20.

Bryant, Jerry H. "Politics and the Black Novel." Nation, 20 December 1971, pp. 660-662.

Burns, B. "Gertrude Stein on Race, Racists, and Racism." Sepia 2 (July 1971): 56-62.

Cayton, Horace. "Frightened Children of Frightened Parents." Twice a Year 12-13 (Spring-Summer, Fall-Winter 1945): 262-269.

Davis, A. P. "Outsider as a Novel of Race." Midwest Journal 7 (Winter 1955-56): 320-326.

Delpech, Jeanine. "An Interview with Native Son." Crisis 57 (November 1950): 625-626, 678

"Discussion of R. Wright's Novel Native Son." Phylon 23 (Fourth Quarter 1962): 364-368.

"The Education of the Negro in Richard Wright's Black Boy." Journal of Negro Education 35 (Spring 1966): 195-198.

Faris, Kenneth. "A Small Portrait of Richard Wright." Negro History Bulletin 25 (March 1962): 155-156.

Ford, Nick Aaron. "Juvenile Delinquent Becomes Famous Writer." Revue Afro-Americain, 22 (January 1949): 5.

Giles, James E. "Richard Wright's Successful Failure: A New Look at Uncle Tom's Children." Phylon 4 (September 1973): 256-266

Green, Gerald. "Back to Bigger." Kenyon Review 28 (1966): 521-539.

Hester, Sister Mary. " 'The Juggler' by Richard Wright." English Journal 54 (1965): 880-881.

Hill, Herbert, Moderator. "Reflections on Richard Wright." Anger, and Beyond. New York: Harper & Row, 1966.

Isaacs, H. R. "Five Writers and Their African Ancestors." Phylon 21 (Fall-Winter 1960): 243-265, 317-336.

Kennedy, James G. "The Content and Form of Native Son." College English 34 (November 1972): 269-286.

Knipp, Thomas, ed. Richard Wright: Letters to Joe C. Brown. With an Introduction. Kent, Ohio: Kent State University Library Occasional Papers, 1968.

Lawson, L. A. "Cross Damon, Kierkegaardian Man of Dread." CLA Journal 14 (March 1971): 298-316.

Lehan, Richard. "Existentialism in Recent American Fiction." Texas Studies in Literature and Language 1 (Summer 1959): 181-202.

Margolies, Edward. "Richard Wright: Native Son and Three Kinds of Revolution." Native Sons. New York: J. B. Lippincott, 1969.

"Native Son Filmed in Argentina; Screen Version of Best Selling Novel Is Most Frank Movie Yet Made about U.S. Negro Problem." Ebony 6 (January 1951): 82-86.

"Native Son: The Personal, Social and Political Background." Phylon 30 (First Quarter 1969): 66-72.

Ray, David and Robert N. Farnsworth, eds. Richard Wright: Impressions and Perspectives. Ann Arbor: University of Michigan Press, 1973.

Reilly, John. "Insight and Protest in the Works of Richard Wright." Dissertation Abstracts, XXVIII, 4185A-6A (Washington University).

"Return of the Native Son: Photo Editorial." Ebony 7 (December 1951): 100-101.

"Richard Wright, Writer, 52, Dies." New York Times, 30 November 1960, 37.

Riesman, David. "Marginality, Conformity, and Insight." Phylon 14 (Third Quarter 195-): 241-257.

Rosenthal, Jean. "Native Son--Backstage." Theatre Arts 25 (June 1941): 407-408.

Sherr, P. C. "Richard Wright, The Expatriate Pattern." Black Academy Review 2 (Spring-Summer 1971): 81-89.

Sillen, Samuel. "Bigger Thomas on the Boards." New Masses 39 (8 April 1941): 27-28.

Singh, Raman L. "The Black Novel and Its Tradition." Colorado Quarterly 20 (Summer 1971): 1.

Widmer, Kingsley. "The Existential Darkness: Richard Wright's The Outsider." Wisconsin Studies in Contemporary Literature 1 (Fall 1960): 13-21.

Winslow, H. F. "Beyond the Seas--an Uneasy World." Crisis 62 (February 1955): 77-80.

"World Mourns the Death of Richard Wright." Jet, 15 December 1960, pp. 18-19.

[1]Blyden Jackson, "Black Boy from America's Black Belt and Urban Ghettos," CLA Journal 12 (June 1969): 293.
[2]Ibid., p. 298.
[3]Maxine Block, ed., Current Biography (New York: Wilson, 1940, p. 885.
[4]Jackson, pp. 299-302.
[5]"Richard Wright, Writer, 52, Dies," New York Times, 30 November 1960, p. 37.
[6]Jackson, pp. 304-305.

WRIGHT, Sarah E. Born in Wetipquin, Maryland. Education: Howard University, University of Pennsylvania, Cheyney State Teachers College, New School for Social Research. Currently living in New York City. Career: Has worked in printing and publishing since 1953; has taught arts and crafts. "One of my continuing occupations is that of housekeeper in my own home. I feel most strongly that this job--occupation if you will--is and should be classified and emphasized as socially useful work of a most exacting nature, for it is one of the most critically pro-nounced activities given to the sustaining and enhancement of human life.... Housekeepers and Homemakers are workers. Much of my writing does, and will continue, to reflect this con-cern." Member: Harlem Writers' Guild, Inc.; P.E.N. Ameri-can Center and International; a MacDowell Colony Fellow. Awards, Honors: This Child's Gonna Live was selected by The New York Times Book Review as one of the most outstanding books of 1969; The Baltimore Sun selected it for its 1969 Read-ability Award.

CRITICISM
    "The Negro Woman in American Literature." Freedomways
        6 (Winter 1966): 8-10.
    "Roadblocks to the Development of the Negro Writer." The
        American Negro Writer and His Roots.
NOVEL
    This Child's Gonna Live. New York: Delacorte, 1969*; New
        York: Dell, 1971†.
POETRY
    With Lucy Smith. Give Me a Child. Philadelphia: Kraft,
        1955.
    (Anthologies): Adoff, The Poetry of Black America; Hughes
        and Bontemps, The Poetry of the Negro, 1746-1970; Pool,
        Beyond the Blues; Lowenfels, Poets of Today.
    (Periodical): Freedomways, Summer 1965.
WORK IN PROGRESS
    Novel: a sequel to This Child's Gonna Live.
    Poetry: a collection of poems tentatively entitled, "Why Do
        I Have Corns on My Feet?"
INTERJECTIONS
    "Tell it like it damn sure is, was and ought to be. With the
thought always in mind of making the sublime manifest in the execution of a piece of work. I look forward to the day when writers--in fact all artists--recognize themselves as producers

of products which are used and consumed and come together in
a union to ensure sensible compensation for their labor. The
production of art is work. Serious creative writing is work."
BIOGRAPHY AND CRITICISM ON WRIGHT
Contemporary Authors, 37/40.
Whitlow. Black American Literature, pp. 162-165.
REVIEW: This Child's Gonna Live.
Amini, Johari. Negro Digest 18 (August 1965): 51-52.

WRIGHT, TheArthur.
POETRY (Periodical): Black World, December 1973; March
1974.

WRIGHT, Zara.
Black and White Tangled Threads. Chicago: Barnard & Miller,
1920.
Kenneth. Chicago: By the Author, 1920.

-Y-

YANCEY, Bessie Woodson.
POETRY (Anthologies): Murphy, Negro Voices; Weisman and
Wright, Black Poetry for All Americans.

YARBROUGH, Camille. Born in Chicago, Illinois. Education:
"Six years of world travel studying humanity"; studied acting
and voice in New York and Australia; studied voice at Roosevelt
College in Chicago. Currently living in New York City. Career: Starred in the New York and national tour production,
To Be Young, Gifted and Black," in James Weldon Johnson's
Trumpets of the Lord, in the TV special "Caught in the Middle,"
in the film Shaft, in New York Public Theatre's productions of
Cities in Bezique and Sambo. Toured the New York high
schools in a program of improvisations and scene study; appeared in television commercials. Toured South America, Canada, and the United States as a singer; spent nine months as
dance instructor at Southern Illinois University's Performing
Arts Training Center in East St. Louis, under the direction of
Katherine Dunham in whose dance company she began her career. In 1972, singer Nina Simone performed a complete program of her songs and poetry at New York's Philharmonic Hall
and on tour. She has also appeared in Ellis Haizlip's NET program, "Soul!" and was invited to participate in the cultural festival, "Soul at the Center," at New York's Lincoln Center.
INTERJECTIONS
"The artist should "function in the tradition of the 'grio,' the
African oral historian, preacher, teacher, social catalyst who
uses song, rhyme, dance, and mime to illuminate and perpetu-
ate, to revitalize and redirect the culture which he or she
serves."

Camille Yarbrough

YEISER, Idabelle.
 POETRY Moods. Philadelphia: Colony Press, 1937.

YERBY, Frank. Born 5 September 1916 in Augusta, Georgia. Ca-
 reer: See Contemporary Authors; Current Biography, 1946.
 CHILDREN AND YOUNG ADULTS
  Bride of Liberty. Garden City, N.Y.: Doubleday, 1954; New
   York: Pyramid, 1971†.
 NOVELS
  Benton's Row. New York: Dial, 1954*; New York: Dell,
   1969†.

Captain Rebel. New York: Dial, 1956; New York: Dell, 1972†.

The Dahomean. New York: Dial, 1971*; New York: Dell, 1972†.

The Devil's Laughter. New York: Dial, 1953; New York: Dell, 1972†.

Fairoaks. New York: Dial, 1957*; New York: Dell, 1969†.

Floodtide. New York: Dial, 1950; New York: Dell, 1967†.

The Foxes of Harrow. New York: Dial, 1946*; New York: Dell, 1972†. Excerpt in Negro Digest, June 1946.

The Garfield Honor. New York: Dial, 1961*; New York: Dell, 1973†.

Gillian. New York: Dial, 1960*; New York: Dell, 1972†.

The Girl from Storyville. New York: Dial, 1972†.

The Golden Hawk. New York: Dial, 1948; New York: Dell, 1972†.

Griffin's Way. New York: Dial, 1962*; New York: Dell, 1972†.

Jarrett's Jade. New York: Dial, 1959; New York: Dell, 1972†.

Judas, My Brother: The Story of the Thirteenth Disciple. New York: Dial, 1968*; New York: Dell, 1970†.

An Odor of Sanctity: A Novel of Medieval Moorish Spain. New York: Dial, 1965*; New York: Dell, 1972†.

The Old Gods Laugh: A Modern Romance. New York: Dial, 1964*; New York: Dell, 1973†.

Pride's Castle. New York: Dial, 1949*; New York: Dell, 1968†.

The Saracen Blade. New York: Dial, 1952; New York: Pocket Books, 1965†; New York: Dell, 1973†.

The Serpent and the Staff. New York: Dial, 1958; New York: Dell, 1972†.

Speak Now: A Modern Novel. New York: Dial, 1969*; New York: Dell, 1970†.

The Treasure of Pleasant Valley. New York: Dial, 1955; New York: Dell, 1973†.

The Vixens. New York: Dial, 1947*; New York: Dell, 1972†; excerpt in Negro Digest, March 1948.

The Voyage Unplanned. New York: Dial, 1974*.

A Woman Called Fancy. New York: Dial, 1951*; New York: Dell, 1971†.

POETRY

(Anthologies): Bontemps, American Negro Poetry; Faderman and Bradshaw, Speaking for Ourselves; Hughes and Bontemps, The Poetry of the Negro, 1746-1970.

(Periodicals): Challenge, September 1934; May 1935; January 1936.

SHORT STORIES

(Anthologies): Clarke, American Negro Short Stories; Hughes, Best Short Stories by Negro Writers; James, From These Roots; Mirer, Modern Black Stories; Patterson, An Introduction to Black Literature in America; Singh and Fellowes, Black Literature in America; Turner, Black American Literature: Fiction; Watkins and David, To Be a Black Woman.

(Periodicals): Common Ground, Summer 1945; Harper's Mag-
azine, May 1944; Phylon, Fourth Quarter 1944; Tomorrow,
January 1946.
BIOGRAPHY AND CRITICISM ON YERBY
Bardolph. The Negro Vanguard, pp. 219, 373, 378, 379-
380, 381.
Bone. The Negro Novel in America, pp. 167-169.
Breit, Harvey. "Frank Yerby." The Writer Observed.
New York: World, 1965.
Ford. "Four Popular Negro Novelists." Phylon 15 (1954):
29-39.
Fuller, Hoyt W. "Famous Writer Faces a Challenge."
Ebony 21 (June 1966): 188-190, 192-194.
Gloster, Hugh M. "The Significance of Frank Yerby."
Crisis 55 (1948): 12-13.
"The Golden Corn: He Writes to Please." Time, 29 No-
vember 1954, p. 97.
Hughes. The Negro Novelist, pp. 149-159, 236-238.
Jet, 16 June 1960, pp. 4-5. (Interview.)
"Mystery Man of Letters." Ebony 10 (February 1955): 31-32,
35-38.
Robinson. Historical Negro Biographies, p. 267.
Turner, Darwin T. "Frank Yerby as Debunker." Massa-
chusetts Review 9 (1968): 569-577; also in Hemenway,
The Black Novelist, pp. 62-71.
Yerby, Frank. "How and Why I Write the Costume Novel."
Harper's Magazine, 1959; reprinted in Writing in America.
New Brunswick, N.J.: Rutgers University Press, 1960.

YOUNG, Al (Albert James Young). Born 31 May 1939 in Ocean
Springs, Mississippi. Education: Attended the University of
Michigan, 1957-1961; B.A. in Spanish, University of California
at Berkeley, 1969; Advanced Fiction Writing, Stanford University, 1966-67. Career: Disk jockey, professional musician,
lab assistant, yard clerk for the Southern Pacific Railroad, medical photographer, Spanish tutor, personnel interviewer, book reviewer, actor (TV documentary about Archie Moore). Writing
instructor, San Francisco Museum of Art's Teen Workshop Project, 1966-69; writing instructor and linguistic consultant for the
Berkeley/Oakland Neighborhood Youth Corps. Held the Edward
H. Jones Lectureship in Creative Writing at Stanford University,
1969-73. Founded and edited the avant-garde review, Lovelet-
ter (mid-1960s), which received awards from the National Arts
Council; serves as West Coast editor of Changes; edits, with
Ishmael Reed, the biennial anthology, Yardbird Reader. Has
served as lecturer and speaker at numerous universities throughout the country, and has read from his work at the invitation of
the Academy of American Poets in Manhattan, Cooper Union
Forum, and the YW/YMHA Poetry Series in New York. Presentations of his work have been broadcast by Pacifica Radio Network and by KQED-TV, the P.B.S. affiliate in San Francisco.
Has travelled extensively in the United States as well as in Canada, Mexico, the Azores, Portugal, Spain, and France. Wrote

Al Young (credit: Christa Fleischmann)

a treatment for Peter Brown of the Stigwood Corporation, 1972,
for a projected dramatic film based on the ascendence of "Soul"
music in the U. S. 1950 to present. Member: Authors Guild;
Writers Guild of America/West; Authors League; American Association of University Professors; American Civil Liberties Union. Awards, Honors: Stegner Fellowship in Creative Writing,
1966-67; Joseph Henry Jackson Award, 1969; National Arts
Council Awards for Poetry and Editing, 1968 and 1969.
INTRODUCTION BY YOUNG
      (Anthology): Reed et al. , Yardbird Reader, vol. 1.
NON-FICTION
      (Periodicals): Audience, California Living, San Francisco
      Fault (now defunct); San Francisco Chronicle; New Times.
NOVELS
      Snakes. New York: Holt, Rinehart & Winston, 1970*; New
         York: Dell, 1972†. Excerpt in Nickel Review, 11 May
         1970; Reed, 19 Necromancers from Now.
      Who Is Angelina? New York: Holt, Rinehart & Winston, forth-
         coming.
POETRY
      Dancing: Poems. New York: Corinth, 1969†.
      Some Recent Fiction. San Francisco: San Francisco Book Co. ;
         Boston: Houghton Mifflin, forthcoming.
      The Song Turning Back Into Itself. New York: Holt, Rinehart
         & Winston, 1971†.
      (Anthologies): Adoff, The Poetry of Black America; Chapman,
         New Black Voices; Colley and Moore, Starting with Poetry;
         Coombs, We Speak as Liberators; Major, The New Black
         Poetry; Miller, Dices and Black Bones; Reed, Yardbird
         Reader I; Simmons and Hutchinson, Black Culture; Wilentz
         and Weatherly, Natural Process; Williams, Contemporary
         Poetry in America.
SHORT STORIES
      (Anthology): Chapman, New Black Voices.
      Also published in Rolling Stone, Evergreen Review, Essence,
         Encore, Massachusetts Review, Chicago Review, Changes,
         Place, Journal of Black Poetry.
BIOGRAPHY AND CRITICISM ON YOUNG
      Contemporary Authors, 29/32.
      O'Brien. Interviews with Black Writers, pp. 259-269.
REVIEWS: Snakes
      Davis, L. J. Book World, 17 May 1970.
      Henden, Josephine. Saturday Review, 22 August 1970.
      Levin, Martin. New York Times Book Review, 17 May 1970.
      Sissman, L. E. New Yorker, 11 July 1970.
INTERJECTIONS
      " 'Fighters fight and writers write,' says veteran novelist
Chester Himes. I write to fight off the loneliness of being alive
as well as to share with others a bit of the joy and complexity
that is also a part of our mutually endured condition. "

YOUNG, Alexander.
      POETRY (Anthology): Murphy, Ebony Rhythm.

YOUNG, Clarence III.
    DRAMA Perry's Mission, 1970.

YOUNG, Frank A.
    POETRY (Anthology): Murphy, Negro Voices.

YOUNG, Otis.
    DRAMA Right On Brother, 1969.

YOUNGER, Martin.
    DRAMA
        Courting.
        A String of Periods.

-Z-

ZAYD.
    POETRY Cornbread & Potato Salad. Elkins Park, Pa. : Uhuru,
        1971.

ZUBENA, Sister (Cynthia Conley).
    POETRY
        Calling All Sisters. Chicago: Free Black Press, 1970.
        Om Black. Chicago: By the Author, 1971.
        (Periodical): Journal of Black Poetry, Summer 1972.

ZUBER, Ron.
    DRAMA Three X Love.

GENERAL BIBLIOGRAPHY

Abcarian, R. and M. Klotz, eds. Literature: The Human Experience. New York: St. Martin's 1973. (Anthology.)

Abdul, Raoul, ed. The Magic of Black Poetry. New York: Dodd, Mead, 1972. (Anthology.)

Abrahams, Roger. Deep Down in the Jungle: Negro Narrative Folklore from the Streets of Philadelphia. Chicago, Ill.: Aldine, 1970.

Abramson, Doris E. "Negro Playwrights in America." Columbia Forum 12 (Spring 1969): 11-17.

_____. Negro Playwrights in the American Theatre 1925-1959. New York: Columbia University Press, 1969.

Adams, Elsie and Mary L. Briscoe. Up Against the Wall, Mother: On Women's Liberation. Beverly Hills, Calif.: Glencoe, 1971. (Anthology.)

Adams, Russell L., ed. Great Negroes Past and Present. Chicago: Afro-Am, 1969.

Adams, William, Peter Conn and Barry Slepian, eds. Afro-American Literature: Drama, Fiction, Non-Fiction and Poetry. 4 vols. Boston: Houghton Mifflin, 1970. (Anthology.)

Adelman, Irving and Rita Dworkin. The Contemporary Novel: A Checklist of Critical Literature on the British and American Novel Since 1945. Metuchen, N.J.: Scarecrow, 1972.

Adoff, Arnold, ed. Black on Black. New York: Macmillan, 1968. (Anthology.)

_____. Black Out Loud: An Anthology of Modern Poems by Black Americans. New York: Macmillan, 1970. (Anthology.)

_____. Brothers and Sisters: Modern Stories by Black Americans. New York: Macmillan, 1970. (Anthology.)

_____, ed. City in All Directions. New York: Macmillan, 1969. (Anthology.)

799

_____, ed. I Am the Darker Brother: An Anthology of Modern Poems by Negro Americans. New York: Macmillan, 1968. (Anthology.)

_____, ed. The Poetry of Black America. New York: Harper & Row, 1972. (Anthology.)

Afro-Arts Anthology. Newark, N.J.: Jihad, 1967.

Alexander, Naledi Nnakintu. "Report on the National Black Theatre." In People's Theatre in America, pp. 320-325. Edited by Karen Malpede Taylor, New York: Drama Book Specialists, 1972.

Alexander, Rae P., ed. Young and Black in America. New York: Random House, 1972. (Anthology.)

Alhamisi, Ahmed and Harun Kofi Wangara, eds. Black Arts: An Anthology of Black Creations. Detroit: Black Arts, 1969.

Allen, Samuel. "Negritude and Its Relevance to the American Negro Writer." In The American Negro Writer and His Roots, pp. 8-20.

Allen, William G., ed. Wheatley, Banneker and Horton: With Selections from the Poetical Works of Wheatley and Horton, and the Letter of Washington to Wheatley, and of Jefferson to Banneker. Boston: D. Laing, Jr., 1849.

Altenbernd, Lynn, ed. Exploring Literature. New York: Macmillan, 1970.

Amann, Clarence A. "Three Negro Classics: An Estimate." Negro American Literature Forum 4 (1970): 113-119.

"American Negro Repertory Players." Ebony 5 (October 1950): 52-54.

The American Negro Writer and His Roots: Selected Papers from the First Conference of Negro Writers. New York: American Society of African Culture, 1960.

American Society of African Culture. Pan-Africanism Reconsidered. Berkeley: University of California, 1962.

Anderson, Jervis. "Black Writing: The Other Side." Dissent 15 (May-June 1968): 233-242.

Anselment, Carol and Donald B. Gibson, eds. Black and White Stories of American Life. New York: Washington Square, 1971. (Anthology.)

Anthology: Black Writers Workshop. Introduction by Don L. Lee. Kansas City, Mo.: KRIZNA Publications, 1970.

General Bibliography

Anthology of Our Black Selves. Newark, N.J.: Jihad, 1969.

Aptheker, Herbert. A Documentary History of the Negro People in
the United States. New York: Citadel, 1951.

_____. "Afro-American Superiority: A Neglected Theme in the
Literature." Phylon 31 (Winter 1970): 336-343.

Arden, Eugene. "The Early Harlem Novel." Phylon 20 (1959):
25-31.

Arnez, Nancy L. "Racial Understanding Through Literature." English Journal 58 (1969): 56-61.

_____ and Clara B. Anthony. "Contemporary Negro Humor as
Social Satire." Phylon 29 (Winter 1968): 339-346.

Aruri, N. and E. Ghareeb, eds. Enemy of the Sun: Poetry of the
Palestinian Resistance. Washington, D.C.: Drum & Spear, 1970.

Aubert, Alvin. "Black American Poetry: Its Language and the Folk
Tradition." Black Academy Review 1 and 2 (Spring-Summer):
408-416.

Austin, Gerlyn E. "The Advent of the Negro Actor on the Legiti-
mate Stage in America." Journal of Negro Education 35 (Summer 1966): 237-245.

Austin, Lettie J., Lewis W. Fenderson and Sophia P. Nelson, eds.
The Black Man and the Promise of America. Glenview, Ill.:
Scott, Foresman, 1970.

Bailey, Leaonead, ed. Broadside Authors. Detroit: Broadside,
1974.

Bailey, P. "Is the Negro Ensemble Company Really Black Theater?"
Negro Digest 17 (April 1968): 16-19.

_____ et al. "Report on Black Theatre." Negro Digest 18 (April 1969): 20-32; 19 (April 1970): 25-37, 42, 85, 98; Black World
20 (April 1971): 4-26, 95-96; 21 (April 1972): 31-36.

_____ et al. "Talking of Black Art, Theatre, Revolution and Na-
tionhood." Black Theatre no. 5 (1971): 18-37.

Baker, D. G. "From Apartheid to Invisibility: Black Americans in
Popular Fiction, 1900-1960. Midwest Quarterly 13 (July 1972):
365-385.

Baker, Houston A., Jr., ed. Black Literature in America. New
York: McGraw-Hill, 1971.

Baldwin, James. "Theatre: The Negro In and Out." Negro Digest

15 (April 1966): 37-44.

Bambara, Toni Cade, ed. Tales and Stories for Black Folks. Garden City, New York: Doubleday, 1971.

Baraka, Imamu Amiri (LeRoi Jones). "The Black Aesthetic." Negro Digest 18 (September 1969): 5-6.

Barbour, Floyd, ed. The Black Power Revolt: A Collection of Essays. Boston: Porter Sargent, 1968.

_____, ed. The Black Seventies. New York: Porter Sargent, 1970.

Barcus, F. Earle and Jack Levin. "Role Distance in Negro and Majority Fiction." Journalism Quarterly 43 (1966): 709-714.

Bardolph, Richard. The Negro Vanguard. New York: Rinehart, 1959.

Barksdale, Richard K. "Alienation and the Anti-Hero in Recent American Fiction." CLA Journal 10 (1966): 1-10.

_____. "Trends in Contemporary Poetry." Phylon 19 (Winter 1958): 408-416.

_____. "Urban Crisis and the Black Poetic Avant-Garde." Negro American Literature Forum 3 (1969): 40-44.

_____ and Keneth Kinnamon, eds. Black Writers of America: A Comprehensive Anthology. New York: Macmillan, 1972.

Baron, Virginia O., ed. Here I Am. New York: Dutton, n.d. (Anthology.)

Barrow, William. "New Theatre in Detroit--Introducing the Concept." Negro Digest 12 (May 1963): 76.

Barton, Rebecca C. Witnesses for Freedom: Negro Americans in Autobiography. New York: Harper, 1948. (Anthology.)

Baskin, Wade and Richard Runes. Dictionary of Black Culture. New York: Philosophical Library, 1973.

Battle, Sol, ed. Ghetto '68. New York: Panther House, 1968.

Baylor, Robert and Brenda Stokes, eds. Fine Frenzy: Enduring Themes in Poetry. New York: McGraw-Hill, 1972. (Anthology.)

Beier, Ulli, ed. Black Orpheus. New York: McGraw Hill, 1965.

Beja, Morris. "It Must Be Important: Negroes in Contemporary American Fiction." The Antioch Review 24 (1964): 323-336.

Belcher, Fannin S. "Negro Drama, Stage Center." Opportunity 17 (1939): 292-295.

_____. "The Negro Theatre: A Glance Backward." Phylon 11 (1950): 121-126.

Bell, Bernard W., ed. Modern and Contemporary Afro-American Poetry. Boston: Allyn & Bacon, 1972.

_____. "New Black Poetry: A Double-Edged Sword." CLA Journal 15 (September 1971): 37-43.

Bennett, Lerone, J. Before the Mayflower: A History of the Negro in America, 1619-1964. Baltimore, Md.: Penguin, 1964.

_____. Pioneers in Protest. Baltimore: Penguin, 1969.

Bennett, M. W. "Negro Poets." Negro History Bulletin 9 (1946): 171-172, 191.

Bennett, Stephen B. and William W. Nichols. "Violence in Afro-American Fiction: An Hypothesis." Modern Fiction Studies 17 (1971): 221-228.

Berceanu, Vera. "The Harlem Renaissance." Contemporanul 10 (July 1970): 9.

Berger, Art. "Negroes with Pens." Mainstream 16 (July 1963): 3-6.

Bergman, Peter M. The Chronological History of the Negro in America. New York: Harper & Row, 1969.

Berrigan, Philip, ed. A Punishment for Peace. New York: Macmillan, 1969. (Anthology.)

Berry, Faith. "Voice for the Jazz Age, Great Migration, or Black Bourgeoisie." Black World 20 (November 1970): 10-16.

Bessie, Alvah. "New Negro Theater." New Masses 24 (September 1940), p. 23.

Bibliographic Survey: The Negro in Print. Washington, D.C.: The Negro Bibliographic Research Center, 1965--.

Bigsby, C. W. E., ed. The Black American Writer, 2 vols. Baltimore, Md.: Penguin, 1969; Deland, Fla.: Everett Edwards, 1969.

_____. "Black Drama in the Seventies." Kansas Quarterly 3 (Spring 1971): 1-20.

_____, ed. Confrontation and Commitment: A Study of Contempo-

rary American Drama, 1959-1966.   Columbia: U. of Missouri
Press, 1969.

_____.   "From Protest to Paradox: The Black Writer at Mid-
Century." In the Fifties, edited by Norman Podhoretz.   New
York: Farrar, Straus, 1964.

_____.   "Three Black Playwrights: Loften Mitchell, Ossie Davis,
Douglas Turner Ward." In Bigsby, The Black American Writer,
vol. 2, pp. 137-155.

Birnbaum, Henry.   "The Poetry of Protest." Poetry 94 (1959): 408-
413.

Black on Black.   Stanford, Calif.: Black Student Union, 1967.

Black Poets Write On! An Anthology of Black Philadelphia Poets.
Philadelphia: Black History Museum Committee, 1970. (Anthology.)

A Black Quartet: Four New Black Plays.   Introduction by Clayton
Riley.   New York: New American Library, 1970.

"The Black Theater." Drama Review 12 (Summer 1968): entire issue.

"Black Theatre at the Crossroads: Old Formulas or New Directions?" Negro Digest 17 (April 1968): entire issue.

"Black Writers' Views on Literary Lions and Values." Negro Digest 17 (January 1968): 10-48, 81-89.   (Symposium.)

Bland, Edward.   "Racial Bias and Negro Poetry." Phylon 53
(1944): 328-333.

_____.   "Social Forces Shaping the Negro Novel." Negro Quarter-
ly 1 (Fall 1942): 241-248.

Bluestein, Gene.   "Blues as a Literary Theme." Massachusetts Review 8 (Autumn 1967): 593-617.

Bond, Frederick W.   The Negro and the Drama; 1944.   College
Park, Md.: McGrath, 1969.

_____.   The Negro's God, as Reflected in His Literature.   New
York: Negro Universities Press, 1969.

Bone, Robert A.   "American Negro Poetry: On the Stage and in the
Schools." Teachers College Record 68 (February 1967): 435-440.

_____.   "American Negro Poets: A French View." Tri-Quarter-
ly no. 4 (1965): 185-195.

_____.   The Negro Novel in America.   New Haven: Yale University Press, 1966.

Bontemps, Arna. "American Negro Poetry." Crisis 70 (1963): 509.

_____, ed. American Negro Poetry. New York: Hill & Wang,
1963. (Anthology.)

_____. "The Black Renaissance of the Twenties." Black World
20 (November 1970): 5-9.

_____, ed. Golden Slippers: An Anthology of Negro Poetry for
Young Readers. New York: Harper, 1941.

_____. "The Harlem Renaissance." Saturday Review of Litera-
ture, 22 March 1947, pp. 12-13, 44.

_____, ed. The Harlem Renaissance Remembered. New York:
Dodd, Mead, 1972.

_____. "Negro Poets, Then and Now." Phylon 11 (1950): 355-
360.

Boroff, David, ed. The State of the Nation. Englewood Cliffs,
N. J.: Prentice-Hall, 1966.

Botkin, B. A., ed. Folk-say: A Regional Miscellany, 1929-32.
4 vols. Norman: University of Oklahoma, 1929-32.

Boyd, Sue Abbot, ed. Poems by Blacks. 2 vols. Fort Smith,
Ark.: South & West, 1971, 1972.

Boyer, Jill Witherspoon, ed. The Broadside Annual 1973. Detroit:
Broadside, 1973.

Boyers, Robert. "Culture, Politics and Negro Writers." Salma-
gundi 1 (1965): 71-80.

Boyle, Kay, ed. 365 Days: A Book of Short Stories. New York:
Harcourt, Brace, 1936.

Bradley, Gerald. "Goodbye Mister Bones--The Emergence of Negro
Themes and Characters in American Drama." Drama Critique
12 (Spring 1964); 78.

Braithwaite, William S., ed. Anthology of Magazine Verse for 1926.
Boston: B. J. Brimmer, 1926.

_____. "The Negro in Literature." Crisis 28 (September 1924):
204-210.

_____. "Some Contemporary Poets of the Negro Race." Crisis
17 (1919): 275-280.

Brasmer, William and Dominick Consolo, eds. Black Drama: An Anthology. Columbus, Ohio: Charles E. Merrill, 1970.

Brawley, Benjamin. Early Negro American Writers, 1935; Freeport, N. Y.: Books for Libraries, 1968.

_____. Negro Builders and Heroes. Chapel Hill, University of North Carolina Press, 1937.

_____. The Negro Genius: A New Appraisal of the Achievement of the American Negro in Literature and the Fine Arts. New York: Dodd, Mead, 1940.

_____. "The Negro in American Literature." Bookman (October 1922): 137-141.

_____. The Negro in Literature and Art. New York: Duffield, 1930.

_____. "The Negro Literary Renaissance." Southern Workman 56 (April 1927): 177-180.

_____, ed. New Era Declamations. Sewannee, Tenn.: The University Press, 1918.

_____. "The Promise of Negro Literature." Journal of Negro History (January 1934): 53-59.

Breman, Paul. "Poetry Into the Sixties." In Bigsby, The Black American Writer, vol. 2, pp. 99-109.

_____, ed. Sixes and Sevens: An Anthology of New Poetry. London: Breman, 1962.

_____, ed. You Better Believe It. Baltimore, Md.: Penguin, 1973. (Anthology.)

_____ and Rosey Pool, eds. Ik zag hoe zwart ik was. Den Haag: Daamen: 1958.

Brewer, J. Mason, ed. American Negro Folklore. Chicago: Quadrangle Books, 1968.

_____, ed. Heralding Dawn: An Anthology of Verse, by (!) Selected and Edited, With a Historical Summary on the Texas Negroes' Versemaking. Dallas, Tex.: June Thomason, 1936.

Brinnin, J. M. and B. Read. Twentieth Century Poetry: American and British. New York: McGraw, 1967.

Broderick, Frances L., ed. Negro Protest Thought in the Twentieth Century. Indianapolis: Bobbs-Merrill, 1966. (Anthology.)

Bronz, Stephen H. <u>Roots of Negro Consciousness: The 1920's Three Harlem Renaissance Authors.</u> New York: Libra, 1964.

Brooks, A. Russell. "The Comic Spirit and the Negro's New Look." <u>CLA Journal</u> 6 (September 1962): 35-43.

_____. "The Motif of Dynamic Change in Black Revolutionary Poetry." <u>CLA Journal</u> 15 (September 1971): 7-17.

Brooks, Gwendolyn, ed. <u>The Black Position.</u> Detroit: Broadside, 1971. (Anthology.)

_____, ed. <u>A Broadside Treasury, 1965-1970.</u> Detroit: Broadside, 1971. (Anthology.)

_____, ed. <u>Jump Bad: A New Chicago Anthology.</u> Detroit: Broadside, 1971.

_____. "Poets Who Are Negro." <u>Phylon</u> 11 (1950): 312.

Brooks, Mary E. "Reactionary Trends in Recent Black Drama." <u>Literature and Ideology</u> (Montreal) 10 (1970): 41-48.

Brown, Hallie Q., ed. <u>Homespun Heroines and Other Women of Distinction.</u> Xenia, Ohio; Aldine, 1926.

Brown, Lloyd. "Which Way for the Negro Writer?" <u>Masses & Mainstream</u> 4 (March 1951): 53-63; 4 (April 1951): 50-59.

Brown, Lloyd W. "Black Entities: Names as Symbols in Afro-American Literature." <u>Studies in Black Literature</u> 1 (Spring 1970): 16-44.

_____, ed. <u>The Black Writer in Africa and the Americas.</u> Los Angeles: Hennessey & Ingalls, 1973.

_____. "The Expatriate Consciousness in Black American Literature." <u>Studies in Black Literature</u> 3 (Summer 1972): 9-11.

_____. "The West Indian as an Ethnic Stereotype in Black American Literature." <u>Negro American Literature Forum</u> 5 (1971): 8-14.

Brown, Patricia L., Don L. Lee and Francis Ward, eds. <u>To Gwen with Love: An Anthology Dedicated to Gwendolyn Brooks.</u> Chicago: Johnson, 1971. (Anthology.)

Brown, Sterling A. "The American Race Problem as Reflected in American Literature." <u>Journal of Negro Education</u> 8 (1939): 275-290.

_____, ed. American Stuff: An Anthology of Prose and Verse by Members of the Federal Writers Project. New York: Viking, 1937.

_____. "The Blues." Phylon 13 (1952): 286-292.

_____. "A Century of Negro Portraiture in American Literature." Massachusetts Review 7 (Winter 1966): 73-96.

_____. "The Negro Author and His Publisher." Quarterly Review of Higher Education Among Negroes 9 (July 1941): 140-146.

_____. "Negro Folk Expression: Spirituals, Seculars, Ballads, and Songs." Phylon 14 (1953): 45-61.

_____. Negro Poetry and Drama and The Negro in American Fiction. New York: Atheneum, 1969.

_____. "The New Negro in Literature (1925-1955)." In The New Negro Thirty Years Afterward, pp. 57-72. Edited by Rayford W. Logan et al. Washington, D.C.: Associated, 1955.

_____. "Our Literary Audience." Opportunity (February 1930): 42-46, 61.

_____, Arthur P. Davis and Ulysses Lee, The Negro Caravan. New York: Arno, 1970. (Anthology.)

Bryson, Clarence F. and James H. Robinson, eds. Dundo: An Anthology of Poetry by Cleveland Negro Youth. Cleveland, Ohio: The January Club, 1931.

Bullins, Ed. "Black Theatre Groups: A Directory." Drama Review 12 (Summer 1968): 172-175.

_____. "Black Theatre Notes." Black Theatre no. 1 (1968): 4.

_____, ed. New Plays from the Black Theatre. New York: Bantam, 1969.

_____. "A Short Statement on Street Theatre." Drama Review 12 (Summer 1968): 93.

_____. "Theatre of Reality." Negro Digest 15 (April 1966): 60-66.

Bullock, Penelope. "The Mulatto in American Fiction." Phylon 6 (1945): 78-82.

Burkhart, Robert and Francis X. Davey, eds. Perspectives on Our Time: Issues and Essays. Boston: Houghton Mifflin, 1970. (Anthology.)

Burma, John H. "Humor as a Technique in Race Conflict. American Sociological Review (December 1946): 710-715.

Burning Spear: An Anthology of Afro-Saxon Poetry. Washington, D.C.: Jupiter Hammon Press, 1963.

Butcher, Margaret Just. The Negro in American Culture, 1956; New York: Mentor, 1971.

Butcher, Philip. "The Younger Novelists and the Urban Negro." CLA Journal 4 (1961): 196-203.

Byars, J. C., Jr., ed. Black and White: An Anthology of Washington Verse. Washington, D.C.: Crane, 1927.

Byrd, James W. "Stereotypes of White Characters in Early Negro Novels." CLA Journal 1 (1957): 28-35.

Cade, Toni, ed. The Black Woman: An Anthology. New York: New American Library, 1970.

_____, ed. Tales and Stories for Black Folks. Garden City, N.Y.: Doubleday, 1971. (Anthology.)

Cahill, Susan and Michele F. Cooper, comps. The Urban Reader. Englewood Cliffs, N.J.: Prentice-Hall, 1971. (Anthology.)

Calverton, Victor Francis. "The Advance of Negro Literature." Opportunity 4 (February 1926): 54-55.

_____. Anthology of American Negro Literature. New York: Modern Library, 1929.

_____. "The Growth of Negro Literature." In Negro Anthology, p. 78. Edited by Nancy Cunard. New York: Frederick Ungar, 1970.

_____. The Liberation of American Literature. New York: Octagon 1932.

_____. "The Negro and American Culture." Saturday Review of Literature, 21 September 1940, pp. 3-4.

_____. "The Negro's New Belligerent Attitude." Current History (September 1929): 1081-1088.

_____. "The New Negro." Current History, (February 1926): 694-698.

Campbell, Dick. "Is There a Conspiracy Against Black Playwrights?" Negro Digest 17 (April 1968): 11-15.

Carolina Magazine 59 (April 1929): entire issue.

Carroll, Paul, ed. The Young American Poets. Chicago: Follett, 1968. (Anthology.)

Cartey, Wilfred. "Four Shadows of Harlem." Negro Digest 18 (August 1969): 22-25.

Cary, Elisabeth L. "A New Element in Fiction." The Book Buyer 23 (1901): 26-28.

Cassill, R. V., ed. Intro #3. New York: Bantam, 1970. (Anthology.)

Cayton, H. R. "Ideological Forces in the Work of Negro Writers." Negro Digest 15 (July 1966): 53-63; also in Hill, Anger, and Beyond.

Chace, William M. and Peter Collier, eds. Justice Denied: The Black Man in White America. New York: Harcourt, Brace & World, 1970. (Anthology.)

Chamberlain, John. "The Negro as Writer." The Bookman 70 (1930): 603-611.

Chambers, Bradford. Chronicles of Negro Protest. New York: Parents' Magazine Press, 1968.

_____ and Rebecca Moon, eds. Right On! Anthology of Black Literature. New York: New American Library, 1970.

Chametzky, Jules and Sidney Kaplan, eds. Black and White in American Culture. Amherst: University of Massachusetts Press, 1969.

Chandler, G. Lewis. "A Major Problem of Negro Authors in Their March Toward Belles-Lettres." Phylon 11 (1950): 383-386.

_____. "Coming of Age: A Note on American Negro Novelists." Phylon 9 (1948): 25-29.

Chapman, Abraham. "Black Poetry Today." Arts in Society 5 (1968): 401-408.

_____, ed. Black Voices. New York: New American Library, 1968.

_____. "The Harlem Renaissance in Literary History." CLA Journal 11 (September 1967): 38-58.

_____. The Negro in American Literature and a Bibliography By and About Negro Americans. Oshkosh, Wis.: Wisconsin Council of Teachers of English, 1966.

_____, ed. New Black Voices. New York: New American Library, 1972.

Charters, Samuel B. The Poetry of the Blues. New York: Oak, 1963.

Cherry, Gwendolyn, Ruby Thomas and Pauline Willis. Portraits in Color: The Lives of Colorful Negro Women. New York: Pageant, 1962.

Chesnutt, Charles W. "Post-Bellum--Pre-Harlem." Crisis (June 1931): 193-194.

Child, Maria L. Freedman's Book. New York: Arno, 1968.

Childress, Alice, ed. Black Scenes. Garden City, N.Y.: Double-day, 1971. (Anthology.)

Chrisman, Robert and Nathan Hare, eds. Contemporary Black Thought: The Best of the Black Scholar. Indianapolis: Bobbs-Merrill, 1973. (Anthology.)

Christmas, Walter. Negroes in Public Affairs and Government. Yonkers: Educational Heritage, 1966.

Clark, Admont, ed. The Real Imagination: An Introduction to Po-etry. Chicago: Science Research Associates, 1972. (Anthology.)

Clarke, John Henrik, ed. American Negro Short Stories. New York: Hill & Wang, 1966. (Anthology.)

_____, ed. Harlem: Voices from the Soul of Black America. New York: New American Library, 1970. (Anthology.)

_____. "The Neglected Dimensions of the Harlem Renaissance." Black World 20 (November 1970): 118-129.

_____. "The Origin and Growth of Afro-American Literature." Negro Digest 17 (December 1967): 54-67.

_____. "Transition in the American Negro Short Story." Phylon 21 (Winter 1960): 360-366.

_____, ed. William Styron's Nat Turner. Boston: Beacon, 1968.

Clay, Eugene. "The Negro and American Literature." Internation-al Literature no. 6 (June 1935): 75-89.

_____. "The Negro in Recent American Literature." In Ameri-can Writers' Congress, pp. 145-153. Edited by Henry Hart. New York: International, 1935.

Coleman, Edward Maceo, ed. Creole Voices: Poems in French by Free Men of Color. Washington, D.C.: Associated, 1945. (First published in 1845 as Les Cenelles, Armand Lanusse, comp.).

Coleman, Mike and Imamu Amiri Baraka. "What Is Black Theatre?" Black World 20 (April 1971): 32-36.

Collier, Eugenia W. "Heritage from Harlem." Black World 20 (November 1970): 52-59.

Conrad, Earl. "American Viewpoint: Blues School of Literature." Chicago Defender, 22 December 1945, p. 11.

Cook, Mercer and Stephen Henderson. The Militant Black Writer in Africa and the United States. Madison: University of Wisconsin Press, 1969.

Cooke, M. G., ed. Modern Black Novelists. Englewood Cliffs, N.J.: Prentice-Hall, 1971.

Coombs, Orde, ed. We Speak as Liberators. New York: Dodd, Mead, 1970. (Anthology.)

_____, ed. What We Must See. New York: Dodd, Mead, 1971. (Anthology.)

Cornish, Sam and Lucian W. Dixon, eds. Chicory: Young Voices from the Black Ghetto. New York: Association, 1969. (Anthology.)

Corrigan, Robert A. "Afro-American Fiction: A Checklist 1853-1970." Midcontinent American Studies Journal 11 (Fall 1970): 114-135.

Corrington, J. W. and M. Williams, eds. Southern Writing in the Sixties. Baton Rouge: Louisiana State University Press, 1967.

Cory, E. L. "Fiction by Negro Writers." Book Buyer 23 (1901): 26.

Cothran, Tilman C. "White Stereotypes in Fiction by Negroes." Phylon (1950): 252-256.

Cotton, L. J. "The Negro in the American Theatre." Negro History Bulletin (May 1960): 172.

_____, ed. New Black Playwrights. New York: Avon, 1970. (Anthology.)

Couch, William, Jr. "The Problem of Negro Character and Dramatic Incident." Phylon 11 (1950): 127-133.

Crocker, Edith, ed. Young and Black. New York: Grosset & Dunlap, 1971. (Anthology.)

Cromwell, Otelia, Lorenzo Dow Turner and Eva B. Dykes, eds. Readings from Negro Authors. New York: Harcourt, Brace, 1931.

Cruse, Harold. The Crisis of the Negro Intellectual. New York: Morrow, 1967.

Cullen, Countée, ed. Caroling Dusk: An Anthology of Verse by Negro Poets. New York: Harper & Row, 1927.

Cunard, Nancy, ed. Negro Anthology, 1934; Edited and abridged with introduction by Hugh Ford. New York: Frederick Ungar, 1970.

Cuney, Waring, Langston Hughes and Bruce McM. Wright, eds. Lincoln University Poets: Centennial Anthology. New York: Fine Editions, 1954.

Cunningham, James. "The Case of the Severed Life-line." Negro Digest 18 (October 1969): 23-28.

Curry, Gladys J. Viewpoints from Black America. New York: Prentice-Hall, 1970. (Anthology.)

Danner, Margaret, ed. The Brass Horse. Richmond: Virginia Union University, 1968. (Anthology.)

_____, ed. Regroup. Richmond: Virginia University Press, 1969. (Anthology.)

Dannett, Sylvia G. Liebovitz. Profiles of Negro Womanhood. 2 vols. Yonkers: Educational Heritage, 1964.

David, Jay, ed. Black Joy. Chicago: Cowles, 1971. (Anthology.)

Davis, Allison. "Our Negro Intellectuals." Crisis (August 1928): 268-269, 284-286.

Davis, Arthur P. From the Dark Tower: Afro-American Writers from 1900 to 1960. Washington, D.C.: Howard University Press, 1974.

_____. "Growing Up in the New Negro Renaissance: 1920-1935." Negro American Literature Forum 2 (1968): 53-59.

_____. "Integration and Race Literature." Phylon 17 (Summer 1956): 141-146.

_____. "The New Black Poetry of Hate." CLA Journal 13 (1970): 382-391.

_____. "Trends in Negro American Literature (1940-65)." In Emanuel and Gross, Dark Symphony, pp. 519-526.

_____ and J. Saunders Redding, ed. Cavalcade: Negro Ameri-

can Writing from 1760 to the Present. Boston: Houghton Mifflin,
1971. (Anthology.)

Davis, Charles T. and Daniel Walden, eds. On Being Black: Writings by Afro-American from Frederick Douglass to the Present.
Greenwich, Conn.: Fawcett, 1970. (Anthology.)

Davis, James Edward, ed. Spectrum in Black: Poems by 20th
Century Black Poets. Glenview, Ill.: Scott, Foresman, 1971.
(Recording.)

Davis, John P. American Negro Reference Book. Englewood Cliffs,
N. J.: Prentice-Hall, 1966.

Davis, K., ed. The Paradox of Poverty in America. New York:
H. W. Wilson, 1969.

Davis, Ossie. "The Flight from Broadway." Negro Digest 15 (Ap-
pril 1966): 14-19.

Daykin, Walter I. "Race Consciousness in Negro Poetry." Sociological and Social Research 20 (1936): 98-105.

_____. "Social Thought in Negro Novels." Sociological and So-
cial Research 19 (1935): 247-252.

DeArmond, Fred. "A Note on the Sociology of Negro Literature."
Opportunity 3 (1925): 369-371.

Debler, Lavinia G. Pioneers and Patriots. Garden City, N. Y.:
Doubleday, 1965.

"The Debut of the Younger School of Negro Writers." Opportunity
2 (May 1924): 143-144.

Dee, Ruby, ed. Glowchild: and Other Poems. New York: Third,
1972. (Anthology.)

Del Vizo, Hortensia Ruiz. Black Poetry of the America: A Bilingual Anthology. Miamia, Fla.: Ediciones Universal, 1972.
(Anthology.)

Demarest, David P. and Lois S. Lamdin. The Ghetto Reader. New
York: Random, 1970. (Anthology.)

Dennison, George. "Voices of the Dispossessed." Show 5 (May
1965): 28-33.

Dent, Thomas C. "The Free Southern Theater." Negro Digest 16
(April 1967): 40-44.

_____, Richard Schechner and Gilbert Moses, eds. The Free
Southern Theater by the Free Southern Theater. Indianapolis:

Bobbs-Merrill, 1969.

Deodene, Frank and William P. French. Black American Fiction Since 1952. Chatham, N.J.: Chatham, 1970.

Derby, Doris, Gilbert Moses and John O'Neal. "The Need for a Southern Free Theatre." Freedomways 4 (Winter 1964): 320.

Desdunes, R. L. Nos Hommes et Notre Histoire. Montreal: Arbour & DuPont, 1911. Translated by Sr. Dorothea O. McCants. Baton Rouge: Louisiana State University, 1973.

"Dialogue: The Free Southern Theatre." Tulane Drama Review 9 (Summer 1965): 63.

Dixon, Melvin. "Black Theater: The Aesthetics." Negro Digest 18 (July 1969): 41-44.

Dodge, Richard and Peter Lindblom, eds. Of Time and Experience: Literary Themes. n.p.: Winthrop, 1972. (Anthology.)

Dodson, Owen. "Playwrights in Dark Glasses." Negro Digest 17 (April 1968): 30-36.

Dover, Cedric. "Notes on Coloured Writing." Phylon 8 (1947): 213-224.

Drachler, Jacob. African Heritage. New York: Crowell-Collier, 1961.

Dreer, Herman, ed. American Literature by Negro Authors. New York: Macmillan, 1950.

Drotning, Philip and Wesley Smith, eds. Up from the Ghetto. New York: Cowles, 1970. (Anthology.)

Dubois, Jean. "An Introduction to Black American Poetry." English Journal 62 (May 1973): 718-722.

_____. "The Negro in Literature and Art." Annals of the American Academy of Political and Social Science (September 1913): 233-237.

Dumble, W. R. "A Footnote to Negro Literature." Negro History Bulletin 9 (1946): 82-84.

Dunaway, Philip. Turning Point: Fateful Moments that Revealed Men and Made History. New York: Random House, 1958.

Dybek, Caren. "Black Literature for Adolescents." English Journal 63 (January 1974): 64-67.

Dykes, Eva B. "The Poetry of the Civil War." Negro History

Bulletin (February 1944): 105.

Eastman, Arthur M. et al, eds. The Norton Anthology of Poetry.
New York: Norton, 1970.

Echeruo, M. J. C. "American Negro Poetry." Phylon 24 (Spring
1963): 63-68.

Echoes from the Gumbo: Writings and Works from the Workshops
of FST. New Orleans: Free Southern Theater, 1968. (Anthology.)

Edmonds, Randolph. "Black Drama in the American Theatre: 1700-
1970." The American Theatre: A Sum of Its Parts. New York:
Samuel French, 1971, 397-426.

_____. "Some Reflections on the Negro in American Drama."
Opportunity 8 (1930): 303-305.

Eisenberg, R. F., ed. Not Quite Twenty. New York: Holt, Rine-
Hart & Winston, 1971. (Anthology.)

Eisinger, Chester E. Fiction of the Forties. Chicago: University
Chicago Press 1963.

Elder, Lonne. "A Negro Idea Theatre." American Dialog 1 (July-
August 1964): 30-31.

Ellis, Eddie. "Revolutionary Theatre in Tune with the Folks." Liberator 15 (December 1965): 8.

Ellison, Martha. "Velvet Voices Feed on Bitter Fruit: A Study of
American Negro Poetry." Poet and Critic 4 (Winter 1967-1968):
39-49.

Ellison, Ralph. Shadow and Act. New York: New American Library,
1964.

Ellman, Richard and Robert O'Clair, eds. The Norton Anthology of
Modern Poetry. New York: Norton, 1973.

Ely, Effie Smith. "American Negro Poetry." Christian Century 40
(1923): 366-367.

Emanuel, James A. "America Before 1950: Black Writers' Views."
Negro Digest 18 (August 1969): 26-34, 67-69.

_____. "Blackness Can: A Quest for Aesthetics." In Gayle,
The Black Aesthetic.

_____. "The Invisible Men of American Literature." Books
Abroad 37 (1963): 391-394.

_____ and Theodore Gross, eds. Dark Symphony: Negro Literature in America. New York: Free Press, 1968.

Embree, Edwin. 13 Against the Odds. New York: Viking, 1945.

Eppse, Merl R. The Negro, Too, in American History. Chicago:
National Education, 1939.

Evans, Donald T. "Bring It All Back Home." Black World 20
(February 1971): 41-45.

Evans, Mari. "Contemporary Black Literature." Black World 19
(June 1970): 4, 93-94.

_____. "I'm With You." Negro Digest 17 (May 1968): 31-36,
77-80.

Fabio, Sarah Webster. "A Black Paper." Negro Digest 18 (July
1969): 26-31.

_____. "Tripping with Black Writing." In Gayle, The Black
Aesthetic.

Fabre, Genevieve E. "A Checklist: Thirteen Years of Black Plays."
Black World 23 (April 1974): 81-97.

Faderman, Lillian and Barbara Bradshaw, eds. Speaking for Ourselves. Glenview, Ill.: Scott, Foresman, 1969.

Farnsworth, T. A. "The Negro in American Literature." Contrast
1 (Summer 1960): 61-63.

Farrison, W. Edward. "Dialectology Versus Negro Dialect." CLA
Journal 13 (1969): 21-26.

_____. "What American Negro Literature Exists and Who Should
Teach It?" CLA Journal 13 (1970): 374-381.

Fenderson, Lewis H. "The New Breed of Black Writers and Their
Jaundiced View of Tradition." CLA Journal 15 (September 1971):
18-24.

Ferdinand, Val. "The Dashiki Project Theatre, We Are the Theater." Black Theater. no. 3 (1969): 4-6.

_____. "News from BlkArtSouth." Black Theatre. no. 4 (1970):
4.

Ferguson, Blanche E. Countée Cullen and the Harlem Renaissance. ✓
New York: Dodd, Mead, 1966.

Ferguson, Mary A. Images of Women in Literature. Boston:
Houghton Mifflin, 1972. (Anthology.)

Fidell, Estelle A.   Play Index: 1968-1972.   New York: H. W. Wilson, 1973.

Fieller, Leslie A.   Waiting for the End.   New York: Stein & Day, 1964.

Fishel, Leslie H., Jr. and Quarles, Benjamin, eds.   The Black American: A Documentary History.   New York: Morrow, 1970; Glenview, Ill.: Scott, Foresman, 1967.

Fleming, Robert.   "Playing the Dozens in the Black Novel."   Studies in Black Literature 3 (Autumn 1972): 17-22.

Fletcher, Tom.   The Tom Fletcher Story: 100 Years of the Negro in Show Business!   New York: Burdge, 1954.

Foley, Martha.   Best American Short Stories, 1961- .   Boston: Houghton Mifflin, annual.

Foner, Philip S., ed.   The Voice of Black America.   New York: Simon & Schuster, 1972.

Fontaine, William T.   "The Mind and Thought of the Negro of the United States as Revealed in Imaginative Literature, 1876-1940."   Southern University Bulletin (March 1942): 5-50.

_____.   "Toward a Philosophy of the American Negro Literature."   Présence Africaine.   nos. 24-25 (February-May 1959): 165-176.

Ford, Clebert.   "Black Nationalism and the Arts."   Liberator 4 (February 1964): 14.

_____.   "The Negro and the American Theatre."   Liberator 3 (May 1963): 6.

Ford, Nick Aaron.   Annual "Critical Survey of Significant Belles Lettres by and about Negroes."   Phylon 22 (1961): 119-134; 23 (1962): 128-138; 24 (1963): 123-234; 25 (1964): 123-234.

_____, ed.   Black Insights: Significant Literature by Black Americans, 1760 to the Present.   Waltham, Mass.: Ginn, 1971. (Anthology.)

_____.   "Black Literature and the Problem of Evaluation."   College English 32 (1971): 536-547.

_____.   "A Blueprint for Negro Authors."   Phylon 11 (1950): 374-377.

_____.   "Confessions of a Black Critic."   Black World 20 (June 1971): 30-43.

_____.   The Contemporary Negro Novel, A Study in Race Relations. Boston: Meador, 1936.

_____. "Four Popular Negro Novelists." Phylon 15 (1954): 29-
39.

_____. "The Negro Novel as a Vehicle of Propaganda." Quarter-
ly Review of Higher Education Among Negroes 9 (1941): 135-139.

_____ and H. L. Faggett, eds. Best Short Stories by Afro-American Writers, 1924-1950. Boston: Meador, 1950.

_____, Donald B. Gibson and Charles A. Ray. "Black Literature:
Problems and Opportunities." CLA Journal 13 (1969): 10-20.

Fox, Hugh and Sam Cornish, eds. The Living Underground: An Anthology of Contemporary American Poetry. East Lansing, Mich.:
Ghost Dance Press, 1969.

Frankenberg, Lloyd. Invitation to Poetry. Garden City, N.Y.:
Doubleday, 1956. (Anthology.)

Frazier, E. Franklin. "A Folk Culture in the Making." Southern
Workman (June 1928): 195-199.

Freedman, Francis S., ed. The Black American Experience: A
New Anthology of Black Literature. New York: Bantam, 1970.

French, Warren. "A Montage of Minorities: Some Waspish Re-
marks." Kansas English 55 (December 1969): 6-13.

Fuller, Hoyt W. "Black Images and White Critics." Negro Digest
19 (November 1969): 49-50.

_____. "Black Theater in America." Negro Digest 17 (April
1968): 83-93.

_____. "Contemporary Negro Fiction." Southwest Review 50
(1965): 321-335.

_____. "The Negro Writer in the United States." Ebony 20 (No-
vember 1964): 126-134.

_____. "Of Integrity, Hope and Dead Dialogue." New School
Bulletin 23 (12 May 1966): 1.

_____. "Perspectives." Negro Digest and Black World, monthly
columns.

_____. "Reverberations from a Writers' Conference." African
Forum 1 (1966): 11-20.

_____. "The So-Called Harlem Renaissance." Black World 20
(November 1970): 4, 65, 130.

_____, ed. "A Survey: Black Writers' Views on Literary Lions and Values." Negro Digest 17 (January 1968): 10-48, 81-89.

_____, ed., "The Task of the Negro Writer as Artist." Negro Digest 14 (April 1965): 54-70, 72-79.

_____. "Up in Harlem: New Hope." Negro Digest 14 (October 1965): 49-50.

Fullinwider, S. P. The Mind and Mood of Black America: 20th Century Thought. Homewood, Ill.: Dorsey, 1969.

Furay, Michael. "Africa in Negro American Poetry to 1929." African Literature Today 2 (1969): 32-41.

Gaffney, Floyd. "The Black Actor in Central Park." Negro Digest 16 (April 1967): 28-34.

_____. "Black Theatre: Commitment and Communication." Black Scholar 1 (June 1970): 10-15.

_____. "A Hand Is on the Gate in Athens." Educational Theatre Journal 21 (May 1969): 196-201.

Gale, Zona. "The Negro Sees Himself." Survey 54 (1925): 300-301.

Gant, L. "New Lafayette Theatre." Drama Review 16 (December 1972): 46-55.

Garland, Phyl. "Skill and Maturity Mark Negro Writer of Today." Pittsburgh Courier, 17 September 1960, sec. 3, p. 4.

Garner, Nat et al. The Negro Hero. New York: Scholastic, 1970. (Anthology.)

Garrett, DeLois. "Dream Motif in Contemporary Negro Poetry." English Journal 59 (1970): 767-770.

Garrett, Naomi M. "Racial Motifs in Contemporary American and French Negro Poetry." West Virginia University Philological Papers 14 (1963): 80-101.

Gassner, John and Clive Barnes. Best American Plays 1963-1967. New York: Crown, 1971.

Gayle, Addison, Jr., ed. The Black Aesthetic. Garden City, N.Y.: Doubleday, 1971.

_____, ed. Black Expression: Essays by and About Black Americans in the Creative Arts. New York: Weybright & Talley, 1969.

_____. "Black Literature and the White Aesthetic." Negro Digest 18 (July 1969): 32-39.

_____. The Black Situation. New York: Horizon, 1970.

_____, ed. Bondage, Freedom and Beyond: The Prose of Black Americans. Garden City, N.Y.: Doubleday, 1971. (Anthology.)

_____. "Cultural Nationalism: The Black Novel and the City." Liberator 9 (July 1969): 14-17.

_____. "Cultural Strangulation: Black Literature and the White Aesthetic." Negro Digest 18 (July 1969): 32-39.

_____, "The Harlem Renaissance: Towards a Black Aesthetic." Midcontinent American Studies Journal 11 (Fall 1970): 78-87.

_____. "The Politics of Revolution: Afro-American Literature." Black World 21 (June 1972): 4-12.

Gerald, Carolyn. "The Black Writer and His Role." Negro Digest 18 (January 1969): 42-48.

_____. "What Lies Ahead for Black Americans?" Negro Digest 19 (November 1969): 24-29.

Gerard, Albert. "Humanism and Negritude: Notes on the Contemporary Afro-American Novel. Diogenes. no. 37 (Spring 1962): 115-133.

Gibson, Donald B., ed. Five Black Writers: Essays on Wright, Ellison, Baldwin, Hughes and Jones. New York: New York University Press, 1970.

_____, ed. Modern Black Poets. Englewood Cliffs, N.J.: Prentice-Hall, 1973.

Gibson, Richard. "A No to Nothing." Kenyon Review 13 (1951): 252-255.

Gill, John, ed. New American and Canadian Poetry. Boston: Beacon, 1971. (Anthology.)

Giovanni, Nikki, ed. Night Comes Softly: Anthology of Black Female Voices. New York: Nik-Tom Publications, 1970.

Gleeson, Patrick, ed. First Reader of Contemporary Poetry. Columbus: Charles E. Merrill, 1969. (Anthology.)

Glicksberg, Charles I. "The Alienation of Negro Literature." Phylon 11 (1950): 49-58.

_____. "Bias, Fiction, and the Negro." Phylon 13 (1952), 127-135.

_____. "For Negro Literature: The Catharsis of Laughter."
Forum 108 (1947): 450-456.

_____. "The God of Diction." Colorado Quarterly 7 (1958):
207-220.

_____. "Negro Americans and the African Dream." Phylon ⌡
(Fourth Quarter 1947): 323-330.

_____. "The Negro Cult of the Primitive." Antioch Review 4 ⌡
(1944): 47-55.

_____. "Negro Fiction in America." South Atlantic Quarterly
45 (1946): 477-488.

_____. "Negro Poets and the American Tradition." Antioch Re-
view 6 (1946): 243-253.

_____. "Race and Revolution in Negro Literature." Forum 107
(1947): 300-308.

Gloster, Hugh M. Negro Voices in American Fiction. Chapel Hill:
University of North Carolina Press, 1948.

_____. "The Negro Writer and the Southern Scene." Southern
Packet 4 (January 1948): 1-3.

_____. "Race and the Negro Writer." Phylon 11 (1950): 369-
371.

Gold, Herbert. Fiction of the Fifties: A Decade of American Writing. New York: Doubleday, 1961. (Anthology.)

Gold, Robert S. The Rebel Culture. New York: Dell, 1970.

Goldstein, Rhoda L., ed. Black Life and Culture in the United
States. New York: T. Y. Crowell, 1971.

Goncalves, Joe. "The Mysterious Disappearance of Black Arts
West." Black Theatre. no. 2 (1969): 23-25.

_____. "West Coast Drama." Black Theatre. no. 4 (1970): 27.

Good, Charles Hamlin. "The First American Literary Movement."
Opportunity 10 (1932): 76-79.

Gordon, Edward, et al, eds. American Literature. Boston: Ginn,
1964. (Anthology.)

_____. The Study of Literature. Boston: Ginn, 1970. (Anthol-
ogy.)

_____. Types of Literature. Boston: Ginn, 1970. (Anthology.)

Gordon, Eugene. "Negro Novelists and the Negro Masses." New
Masses. 8 (July 1933): 16-20.

_____. "Social and Political Problems of the Negro Writer."
In American Writers' Congress, pp. 141-145. Edited by Henry
Hart. New York: International, 1935.

Gordon, John and L. Rust Hills, eds. New York, New York: The
City as Seen by Masters of Art and Literature. New York:
Showcrest, 1965.

Greaves, Griselda, ed. Burning Thorn. New York: Macmillan,
1971. (Anthology.)

Green, Elizabeth Lay. The Negro in Contemporary American Literature: An Outline for Individual and Group Study. Chapel Hill:
University of North Carolina Press, 1928.

Greene, Lorenzo Johnston. The Negro in Colonial New England.
New York: Atheneum, 1969.

Greenwood, Frank. "Cry in the Night." Liberator 3 (September
1963): 18.

Greever, G. "The Negro in Literature." Dial (Chicago): 8 June
1916, pp. 531-532.

Gregory, Horace and Mary Zaturenska. "The Negro Poet in America." A History of American Poetry, 1900-1940. New York:
Harcourt, Brace, 1964.

Gregory, Montgomery. "The Drama of Negro Life." In The New
Negro, pp. 153-160. Edited by Alain Locke. New York: A &
C Boni, 1925.

Grimes, Alan and Janet Owen. "Civil Rights and the Race Novel."
Chicago Jewish Forum 15 (1956): 12-15.

Gross, Ronald, ed. Open Poetry. New York: Simon & Schuster,
1972. (Anthology.)

Gross, Seymour L. "Stereotype to Archetype: The Negro in American Literary Criticism." In Images of the Negro in American
Literature, pp. 1-26. Edited Seymour L. Gross and John Edward Hardy. Chicago: University of Chicago Press, 1966.

Gross, Theodore L. The Heroic Ideal in American Literature.
New York: Free Press, 1971.

_____. "The Idealism of Negro Literature in America." Phylon
30 (1969): 5-10.

_____, ed. A Nation of Nations: Ethnic Literature in America.

New York: Free Press, 1971. (Anthology.)

_____. "Our Mutual Estate: The Literature of the American Negro." Antioch Review 28 (1968): 293-303.

Hagopian, John V. "Mau-Mauing the Literary Establishment." Studies in the Novel 3 (1971): 135-147.

_____. "Negro American Authors." Contemporary Literature 10 (1969): 416-420.

Hanau, D. "Ghetto Theatre: Vital Drama or Social Therapy?" Community 26 (April 1967): 7-10.

"Harlem, Mecca of the New Negro." Survey 6 (March 1925): entire issue.

Harper, Michael, ed. Heartblows: Black Veils. Urbana: University of Illinois Press, forthcoming.

Harris, Henrietta. "Building a Black Theatre." Drama Review 12 (Summer 1968): 157-158.

Harris, Jessica B. "National Black Theatre." Drama Review 16 (December 1972): 39-45.

Harrison, Paul Carter. The Drama of Nommo. New York: Grove, 1972.

_____, ed. Kuntu Drama. New York: Grove, 1974. (Anthology.)

Hartman, Dennis, ed. National Poetry Anthology, 1963, 1964, 1967. Los Angeles: National Poetry Press, 1963, 1964, 1967.

Haskins, Jim, ed. Black Manifesto for Education. New York: Morrow, 1973. (Anthology.)

Haslam, Gerald W. "The Awakening of American Negro Literature 1619-1900." In Bigsby, The Black American Writer.

_____, ed. Forgotten Pages of American Literature. Boston: Houghton Mifflin, 1970. (Anthology.)

_____. "Two Traditions in Afro-American Literature." Research Studies, A Quarterly Publication of Washington State University 37 (September 1969): 183-193.

Hatch, James V. Black Image on the American Stage: A Bibliography. New York: Drama Book Specialists, 1970.

_____. "White Folks Guide to 200 Years of Black and White Drama." Drama Review 16 (December 1972): 5-24.

_____ and Ted Shine, eds. Black Theatre USA: 1847-1974.
New York: Free Press, 1974.

_____ and Victoria Sullivan. Plays by and About Women. New
York: Random House, 1973.

Hatch/Billops Oral History Collection, Stage I, Stage II, and Stage
III. New York: Video Educational Workshop, 54 East 11th St.,
1974. (Includes over 100 interviews.)

Hayden, Robert, ed. Kaleidoscope: Poems by American Negro Poets. New York: Harcourt, Brace & World, 1967.

Hayden, Robert,David J. Burrows and Frederick R. Lapides, eds.
Afro-American Literature: An Introduction. New York: Harcourt
Brace Jovanovich, 1971 (Anthology.)

Haynes, Helen, ed. Voices of the Revolution. Philadelphia: Philadelphia Print Club, 1967. (Anthology.)

Haywood, Charles. "Negro Minstrelsy and Shakespearean Burlesque."
In Folklore and Society: Essays in Honor of Benjamin A. Botkin,
pp. 77-92. Edited by Bruce Jackson. Hatboro, Pa.: Folklore
Associates, 1966.

Heath, Phoebe Anne. "Negro Poetry as an Historical Record."
Vassar Journal of Undergraduate Studies 3 (May 1928): 34-52.

Heermance, J. Noel. "The Modern Negro Novel." Negro Digest
13 (May 1964): 66-76.

Hemenway, Robert, ed. The Black Novelist. Columbus: Charles E.
Merrill, 1970.

Henderson, David. Anthology of the 60's. New York: Dutton, n.d.

_____, ed. Umbra Anthology, 1967-1968. New York: Umbra,
1967.

Henderson, Stephen, ed. Understanding the New Black Poetry:
Black Speech and Black Music as Poetic References. New York:
Morrow, 1973. (Anthology and Criticism.)

Hentoff, Nat. "The Other Side of the Blues." In Anger, and Beyond: The Negro Writer in the United States, pp. 76-85. Edited
by Herbert Hill. New York: Harper & Row, 1966.

Hicklin, Fannie E. F. The American Negro Playwright, 1920-64.
Madison: University of Wisconsin, 1965.

Hicks, Jack, ed. Cutting Edges: Young American Fiction for the
Seventies. New York: Holt, Rinehart & Winston, 1973. (Anthology.)

Hieatt, Kent A. and William Park, eds. College Anthology of British and American Poetry, 2nd ed. Boston: Allyn & Bacon, 1972.

Hill, Herbert, ed. Anger, and Beyond: The Negro Writer in the
United States. New York: Harper & Row, 1966.

_____. "The Negro Writer and the Creative Imagination." Arts
in Society 5 (1968): 244-255.

_____. "The New Directions of the Negro Writer." Crisis 70
(1963): 205-210.

_____, ed. Soon, One Morning: New Writing by American Ne-
groes, 1940-1962. New York: Knopf, 1968.

Hill, J. Newton. "The Achievement of the Negro in Drama." Negro History Bulletin 12 (February 1949): 100-102, 119.

Hill, Roy L. The Rhetoric of Racial Revolt. Denver: Golden Bell,
1964.

Hilliard, Robert L. "Desegregation in Educational Theatre." Journal of Negro Education 26 (Fall 1957): 509-513.

_____. "The Drama and American Negro Life." Southern The-
atre 10 (Winter 1966): 12-13.

Hills, Penny Chapin and L. Rust Hills. How We Live: Contemporary Life in Contemporary Fiction, vols. 1 and 2. New York:
Collier, 1968. (Anthology.)

Hoffman, William H., ed. New American Plays, vols. 2 and 3.
New York: Hill & Wang, 1968, 1969.

Hogan, Homer, ed. Poetry of Relevance. Toronto: Methuen, 1970.
(Anthology.)

Hollo, Anselm, ed. Negro Verse. London: Vista, 1964. (Anthology.)

Holmes, Eugene C. "Problems Facing the Negro Writer Today."
New Challenge 2 (Fall 1937): 69-75.

Hoopes, Ned. Stories to Enjoy. rev. ed. New York: Macmillan,
1970. (Anthology.)

Hopkins, Tobie, ed. Soul Going Home (An Anthology): Los Angeles, 1969.

Horne, Frank S. "Black Verse." Opportunity 2 (1924): 330-332.

Houston, Helen R. "Contributions of the American Negro to American Culture: A Selected Checklist." Bulletin of Bibliography.

26 (July-September 1969): 71-83.

Howe, Florence and Ellen Bass. No More Masks: An Anthology of
Poems by Women. Garden City, N.Y.: Doubleday, 1973.

Huggins, Kathryn. "Aframerican Fiction." Southern Literary Messenger 3 (1941): 315-320.

Huggins, Nathan Irvin. Harlem Renaissance. New York: Oxford
University Press, 1971.

Hughes, Carl M. The Negro Novelist 1940-1950. New York: Citadel Press, 1953.

Hughes, Douglas A., ed. From a Black Perspective: Contemporary Black Essays. New York: Holt, Rinehart & Winston, 1970.
(Anthology.)

Hughes, Langston, ed. The Best Short Stories by Negro Writers:
An Anthology from 1899 to the Present. Boston and Toronto:
Little, Brown, 1967.

_____, ed. The Book of Negro Humor. New York: Dodd, Mead,
1966. (Anthology.)

_____. "Harlem Literati of the Twenties." Saturday Review of
Literature, 22 June 1940, pp. 13-14.

_____. "The Negro Artist and the Racial Mountain." Nation,
23 June 1926, pp. 692-694.

_____, ed. New Negro Poets: U.S.A. Bloomington: Indiana
University Press, 1964.

_____. A Pictorial History of the Negro in America. New York:
Crown, 1956.

_____, ed. La Poesie Negro-Americaine: Edition Bilingual.
Paris: Seghers, 1966.

_____. "The Twenties: Harlem and Its Negritude." African
Forum 1 (Spring 1966): 11-20.

_____ and Arna Bontemps, eds. Book of Negro Folklore. New
York: Dodd, Mead, 1958.

_____ and _____, eds. The Poetry of the Negro, 1746-1970.
Garden City, N.Y.: Doubleday, 1970.

_____ and Milton Meltzer. Black Magic: A Pictorial History of
the Negro in American Entertainment. Englewood Cliffs, N.J.:
Prentice-Hall, 1967.

Hurston, Zora Neale. The Negro in the American Theatre. New York: Theatre Arts, 1947; originally published in Theatre Arts 26 (1942): 492-543.

_____. "What White Publishers Won't Print." Negro Digest 5 (April 1947): 85-89.

Isaacs, Harold R. "Five Writers and Their African Ancestors." Phylon 21 (Fall 1960): 243-265; 21 (Winter 1960): 317-336.

_____. The New World of Negro Americans. London: Phoenix House, 1964.

Jackson, Blyden. "The Blithe Newcomers: A Resume of Negro Literature in 1954." Phylon 16 (Spring 1955): 5-12.

_____. "The Case for American Negro Literature." Michigan Alumnus Quarterly Review 61 (1955): 161-166.

_____. "The Continuing Strain: Resume of Negro Literature in 1955." Phylon 17 (Spring 1956): 35-40.

_____. "An Essay in Criticism." Phylon 11 (1950): 338-343.

_____. "Faith Without Works in Negro Literature." Phylon 12 (1951): 378-388.

_____. "Full Circle." Phylon 9 (1948): 30-35.

_____. "A Golden Mean for the Negro Novel." CLA Journal 3 (1959): 81-87.

_____. "The Negro's Image of the Universe as Reflected in His Fiction." CLA Journal 4 (1960): 22-31.

_____. "The Negro's Negro in Negro Literature." Michigan Quarterly Review 4 (1965): 290-295.

_____. "A Survey Course in Negro Literature." College English 35 (March 1974): 631-636.

Jackson, Esther Merle. "The American Negro and the Image of the Absurd." Phylon 23 (1962): 359-371.

_____. "A 'Tragic Sense' of the Negro Experience." Freedomways 7 (Winter 1967): 16-25.

Jackson, Kathryn. "LeRoy Jones and the New Black Writers of the Sixties." Freedomways 9 (Summer 1969): 232-246.

Jackson, Miles M. "Significance Belles Lettres by and About Negroes Published in 1962." Phylon 26 (Fall 1965): 216-227.

Jacobs, George W. "Negro Authors Must Eat." The Nation 128 (1929): 710-711.

Jahn, Janheinz. A Bibliography of Neo-African Literature from Africa, America, and the Caribbean. New York: Praeger, 1965.

_____. Neo-African Literature: A History of Black Writing. New York: Grove, 1968.

_____. "World Congress of Black Writers." Black Orpheus: A Journal of African and Afro-American Literature. no. 1 (September 1957): 39-40, 46.

James, Charles L. From the Roots: Short Stories by Black Americans. New York: Dodd, Mead, 1970. (Anthology.)

Jarrett, Thomas. "Recent Fiction by Negroes." College English 16 (1954): 85-91.

_____. "Toward Unfettered Creativity: A Note on the Negro Novelist's Coming of Age." Phylon 11 (1950): 313-317.

Jeffers, Lance. "Afro-American Literature, The Conscience of Man." Black Scholar 2 (January 1971): 47-53.

Jefferson, Miles M. "The Negro on Broadway." Phylon, 1945-1957, annual feature.

Jewett, Arno, ed. Discovering Literature. Boston: Houghton Mifflin, 1968. (Anthology.)

Johnson, Alicia L., ed. Black Art Creations, 1970. Carbondale, Ill.: n.p., 1970.

Johnson, Charles S., ed. Ebony and Topaz: A Collectanea. New York: National Urban League, 1927.

_____. "Jazz Poetry and Blues." Carolina Magazine 68 (May 1928): 16-20.

_____. "The Negro Enters Literature." Carolina Magazine 57 (May 1927): 3-9, 44-48.

_____. "The Negro Renaissance and Its Significance." In The New Negro Thirty Years Afterward, pp. 80-88. Edited by Rayford W. Logan et al. Washington, D.C.: Associated, 1955.

_____. "The Rise of the Negro Magazine." Journal of Negro History (January 1928): 7-21.

Johnson, Guy B. "Recent Literature on the Negro: Journal of Social Forces 12 (January 1925).

Johnson, Helen Armstead. "Playwrights, Audiences and Critics."
Negro Digest 19 (April 1970): 17-24.

Johnson, James Weldon. Black Manhattan. New York: Atheneum,
1969.

_____, ed. The Book of American Negro Poetry. New York:
Harcourt Brace, 1931. (Anthology.)

_____, ed. The Book of American Negro Spirituals. New York:
Viking, 1947.

_____. "The Dilemma of the Negro Author." American Mercury
(December 1928): 477-481.

_____. "Race Prejudice and the Negro Artist." Harper's Month-
ly Magazine (November 1928): 769-776.

Johnson, Lemuel. The Devil, the Gargoyle and Buffoon: The Negro as Metaphor in Western Literature. Port Washington, N.Y.:
Kennikat Press, 1971.

Jones, Iva G. "Research in Afro-American Literature." CLA
Journal 15 (December 1971): 240-244.

Jones, Junemary. "Teaching Afro-American Literature." Illinois
English Bulletin 57 (February 1970): 1-10.

Jones, LeRoi (Imamu Amiri Baraka). "The Black Aesthetic." Negro Digest 18 (September 1969): 5-6.

_____. Blues People: Negro Music in White America. New
York: Morrow, 1963.

_____. "Foreword." Black Fire: An Anthology of Afro-Amer-
ican Writing. Edited by LeRoi Jones and Larry Neal. New
York: Morrow, 1968, pp. xvii-xviii.

_____. Home: Social Essays. New York: Morrow, 1966.

_____. "In Search of the Revolutionary Black Theatre." Negro
Digest 15 (April 1966): 20-24.

_____. "The Myth of a Negro Literature." Saturday Review,
20 April 1963, pp. 20-21.

_____. "Philistinism and the Negro Writer." In Hill Anger, and
Beyond, pp. 51-61.

_____. "What the Arts Need Now." Negro Digest 16 (April
1967): 5-6.

_____ and Larry Neal, eds. Black Fire: An Anthology of Afro-

American Writing. New York: Morrow, 1968.

Jordan, June, ed. Soulscript: Afro-American Poetry. Garden City, N.Y.: Doubleday, 1970. (Anthology.)

_____ and Terri Bush, eds. Voice of the Children. Holt, Rinehart & Winston, 1970. (Anthology.)

_____ and _____, eds. Voice of the Children: Writings by Black and Puerto Rican Young People. New York: Washington Square Press, 1974.

Joseph, Stephen M., ed. The Me Nobody Knows: Children's Voices from the Ghetto. New York: Avon, 1969.

Jurges, Oda, comp. "Selected Bibliography." Drama Review 12 (Summer 1968).

Katz, William L., ed. Eyewitness: The Negro in American History. New York: Pitman, 1967.

Kearns, Francis E. Black Experience: An Anthology of American Literature for the 1970's. New York: Viking, 1970.

_____, ed. Black Identity. New York: Holt, Rinehart & Winston, 1970. (Anthology.)

Keller, Frances Richardson. "The Harlem Literary Renaissance." ✓ North American Review 5 (May 1968): 29-34.

Keller, Joseph. "Black Writing and the White Critic." Negro American Literature Forum 3 (1969): 103-110.

Kelly, Ernece, ed. Points of Departure. New York: John Wiley, 1972. (Anthology.)

Kendricks, Ralph, and Claudette Levitt, eds. Afro-American Voices: 1770's-1970's. New York: Oxford Book Co., 1970. (Anthology.)

Kent, George E. Blackness and the Adventure of Western Culture. Chicago: Third World, 1972.

_____. "Ethnic Impact in American Literature: Reflections on a Course." CLA Journal 11 (1967): 24-37.

_____. "Struggle for the Image: Selected Books by or About Blacks During 1971." Phylon 33 (Winter 1972): 304-323.

Kerlin, Robert T. "Conquest by Poetry." Southern Workman 56 (1927): 282-284.

_____. Contemporary Poetry of the Negro. Hampton, Va.: Hampton Institute Press, 1923. (Anthology.)

_____. A Decade of Negro Self-Expression. Charlottesville,
Va.: Michie, 1928.

_____. Negro Poets and Their Poems. Washington, D.C.: As-
sociated, 1923.

_____. "A Pair of Youthful Negro Poets." Southern Workman
53 (1924): 178-181. (Cullen and Hughes.)

_____. "Present Day Negro Poets." Southern Workman 49
(1920): 543-548.

_____. "Singers of New Songs." Opportunity 4 (1926): 162-164.

_____. The Voice of the Negro. New York: Arno, 1968. (An-
thology.)

Kessler, Sidney H. "American Negro Literature: A Bibliographical Guide." Bulletin of Bibliography. 21 (1955).

_____. "Collectors, Scholars, and Negro Literature." Midwest
Journal 7 (1954): 222-234.

Kgositsile, K. W. "Paths to the Future." In Gayle, The Black
Aesthetic.

_____. "Towards Our Theatre: A Definitive Act." Negro Di-
gest 16 (April 1967): 14-16.

Kilgore, James C. "The Case for Black Literature." Negro Digest 18 (July 1969): 22-25, 66-69.

_____. "Toward the Dark Tower." Black World 19 (June 1970):
14-17.

Killens, John Oliver. "Another Time When Black Was Beautiful."
Black World 20 (November 1970): 20-36.

_____. "The Black Writer and Revolution." Arts in Society 5
(1968): 395-399.

_____. "Broadway in Black and White." African Forum 1 (Win-
ter 1966): 66-76.

_____. "Opportunities for Development of Negro Talent." In
The American Negro Writer and His Roots, pp. 64-70.

Kimball, Robert and William Bolcom. Reminiscing with Sissle and
Blake. New York: Viking, 1973.

King, Woodie, Jr. "Black Theatre: Present Condition." Drama
Review 12 (Summer 1968): 117-124.

_____. "Black Theatre: Weapon for Change." Negro Digest 19 (April 1970): 10-15, 86-87.

_____, ed. Blackspirits: A Festival of New Black Poets in America. New York: Vintage, 1972.

_____. "The Dilemma of a Black Theater." Negro Digest 19 (April 1970): 10-15, 86-87.

_____ and Earl Anthony, eds. Black Poets and Prophets: The Theory, Practice, and Esthetics of the Pan-Africanist Revolution. New York: New American Library, 1972. (Anthology.)

_____ and Ron Milner, eds. Black Drama Anthology. New York: New American Library, 1971.

Kinnamon, Keneth. "Afro-American Literature, the Black Revolution, and Ghetto High Schools." English Journal 59 (1970): 189-194.

_____. "Native Son: The Personal, Social and Political Background." Phylon 30 (Spring 1969): 68-72.

Kinneman, John A. "The Negro Renaissance." Negro History Bulletin 25 (1962): 200, 197-199.

Kjersmeier, Carl. "Negroes as Poets." Crisis 30 (1925): 186-189.

Klotman, Phyllis R. "The White Bitch Archetype in Contemporary Black Fiction." Bulletin of the Midwest Modern Language Association. 6 (Spring 1973): 96-110.

Knight, Etheridge, ed. Black Voices from Prison. New York: Pathfinder, 1970. (Anthology.)

Knox, George. "The Negro Novelist's Sensibility and the Outsider Theme." Western Humanities Review 11 (Spring 1957): 137-148.

Knudson, Rozanne and P. K. Ebert, eds. Sports Poems. New York: Dell, 1971.

Kochman, Thomas, ed. Rappin' and Stylin' Out: Communication in Urban Black America. Urbana: University of Illinois Press, 1972. (Anthology.)

Koppell, L. S. et al. Live Poetry: Thoughts for the Seventies. New York: Holt, Rinehart & Winston, 1971. (Anthology.)

Kostelanetz, Richard, ed. In Youth. New York: Ballentine Books, 1972.

_____, ed. The Young American Writers. New York: Funk & Wagnalls, 1967. (Anthology.)

_____ et al., eds. Fourth Assembling. Brooklyn: Assembling, 1973.

Kreymborg, Alfred. An Anthology of American Poetry. New York: Tudor, 1941.

"Krigwa Players' Little Negro Theatre." Crisis 33 (1926): 134-136.

Lamplugh, G. R. "Image of the Negro in Popular Magazine Fiction, 1875-1900" Journal of Negro History 43 (April 1972): 276-291.

Lane, Pinkie Gordon, ed. Discourses in Poetry, 6th Annual edition. Fort Smith, Ark.: South & West, 1972. (Anthology.)

_____, ed. Poems by Blacks, Vol. 3, Fort Smith, Ark.: South & West, forthcoming.

Lane, Ronnie M., ed. Facing the Whirlwind: Anthology of Michi-Black Poets. n.p.: Pilot, 1973.

Lanusse, Armand, comp. Les Cenelles, New Orleans, 1945. See Coleman, Edward Maceo.

Larson, Charles. "African Afro-American Literary Relations: Basic Parallels." Negro Digest 19 (December 1969): 35-42.

Larson, Charles R. "Three Harlem Novels of the Jazz Age." Critique 11 (1969): 66-78.

Lash, John S. "The American Negro in American Literature: A Selected Bibliography of Critical Materials." Journal of Negro Education 15 (1946): 722-730.

_____. "The Anthologist and the Negro Author." Phylon 8 (1947): 68-76.

_____. "Critical Summary of Literature by and About Negroes." Phylon 18 (1957): 7-24; 19 (1958): 143-154, 247-275; 20 (1959): 115-131; 21 (1960): 111-123.

_____. "On Negro Literature." Phylon 6 (1945): 240-247.

_____. "The Race Consciousness of the American Negro Aughor." Toward a Re-examination of an Orthodox Critical Concept." Social Forces 28 (October 1949): 24-34.

_____. "The Study of Negro Literary Expression." Negro History Bulletin 9 (June 1946): 207-211.

_____. "What Is 'Negro Literature'?" College English 9 (1947): 37-42.

Lask, Thomas, ed. New York Times Book of Verse. New York:

Macmillan, 1970. (Anthology.)

Lawrence, Ruth, ed. Rhyme 'N' Rhythm Song Writers and Poets of Today. New York: Haven Press, 1947. (Anthology.)

_____. Songwriters and Poets of America. New York: Haven Press, 1945. (Anthology.)

Lawson, Hilda J. "The Negro in American Drama (Bibliography of Contemporary Negro Drama)." Bulletin of Bibliography 17 (1940): 7-8, 27-30.

Lazier, Gil. "The Next Stage: Youth Theatre for the Ghetto." Record 69 (February 1968): 465-467.

Lee, Don L. "Black Critics." Black World 19 (September 1970): 24-30.

_____. "Black Poetry: Which Direction?" Negro Digest 17 (September-October 1968): 27-32.

_____. "Directions for Black Writers." Black Scholar 1 (December 1969): 53-57.

_____. Dynamite Voices: Black Poets of the 1960's. Detroit: Broadside, 1971.

Lee, Ulysses. "Criticism at Mid-Century." Phylon 11 (Fourth Quarter, 1950): 328-337.

Lehan, Richard. "Existentialism in Recent American Fiction: The Demonic Quest." Texas Studies in Literature and Language 1 (1959): 181-202.

Leonard, Claire. "Dark Drama." Negro Digest 2 (August 1944): 81-82.

Lester, Julius. "The Arts and the Black Revolution." Arts in Society 5 (1968): 229.

Lev, Donald, ed. HNY Anthology. New York: Otherplanet Publications, 1972.

Leverton, Denise, ed. Out of the War Shadow: 1968 Peace Calendar. War Resisters League, 1968. (Anthology.)

Lewis, Theophilus. "The Frustration of Negro Art." Catholic World 155 (April 1942): 51-57.

_____. "Negro Actors in Dramatic Roles." America, 17 (September 1966): 298-300.

Lieber, Todd M. and Maurice J. O'Sullivan. " 'Native Sons?'

Black Students on Black Literature." Negro American Literature
Forum 5 (1971): 3-7.

Liebman, Arthur. "Patterns and Themes in Afro-American Literature." English Record 20 (February 1970): 2-12.

Lief, Leonard and James F. Light. The Modern Age: Literature.
New York: Holt, Rinehart & Winston, 1972. (Anthology.)

Lincoln University Poets. See Cuney, Waring.

Little, Stuart W. Off-Broadway: The Prophetic Theater. New
York: Coward, McCann & Geoghegan, 1972.

Littlejohn, David. Black on White: A Critical Survey of Writing by
American Negroes. New York: Grossman, 1966.

Llorens, David. "What Contemporary Black Writers Are Saying."
Nommo 1 (Winter 1969): 24-27.

_____. "Writers Converge at Fisk University." Negro Digest
15 (June 1966): 54-68.

Locke, Alain. "American Literary Tradition and the Negro." Modern Quarterly 3 (1926): 215-222.

_____. "Art or Propaganda?" Harlem: A Forum of Negro Life
(November 1928): 12.

_____. "Beauty Instead of Ashes." Nation, 18 April 1928, pp.
432-434.

_____. "Black Truth and Black Beauty." Opportunity (January
1933): 14-18.

_____. "Broadway and the Negro Drama." Theatre Arts 25
(1941): 745-752.

_____. Four Negro Poets. New York: Simon & Schuster, 1927.
(McKay, Toomer, Hughes, and Cullen.)

_____. "The Message of the Negro Poets." Carolina Magazine
58 (May 1928): 5-15.

_____. "The Negro and the American Theatre." In Theatre:
Essays on the Arts of the Theatre, pp. 290-303. Edited by Edith
J. R. Isaacs. 1927.

_____. "The Negro in American Literature." New World Writ-
ing 1. New York, 1952, pp. 18-33.

_____. "The Negro's Contribution to American Art and Litera-
ture." Annals of the American Academy of Political and Social

Science 140 (1928): 234-247.

_____. "The Negro's Contribution to American Culture." Jour-
nal of Negro Education 8 (1939): 521-529.

_____, ed. The New Negro: An Interpretation. New York: Al-
bert Charles Boni, 1925. (Anthology.)

_____. "Retrospective Review of the Literature of the Negro."
Opportunity, 1929, 1931-42; Phylon, 1947-1953.

_____. "Self-Criticism: The Third Dimension in Culture." Phy-
lon 11 (1950): 391-394.

_____. "Steps Toward the Negro Theatre." Crisis 25 (1922):
66-68.

_____. "This Year of Grace." Opportunity (February 1931):
48-51.

_____ and Montgomery Gregory, eds. Plays of Negro Life: A
Source Book of Native American Drama. New York: Harper,
1927. (Anthology.)

Loggins, Vernon. The Negro Author: His Development in America
to 1900. Port Washington, N.Y.: Kennikat, 1964.

Lomax, Alan and Raoul Abdul, eds. 3000 Years of Black Poetry.
New York: Dodd, Mead, 1970. (Anthology)

Lomax, Michael L. "Fantasies of Affirmation: The 1920's Novel
of Negro Life." CLA Journal 16 (December 1972): 232-246.

Loney, G. "The Negro and the Theatre." Educational Theatre
Journal 20 (May 1968): 231-233.

Long, Richard A. "Crisis of Consciousness." Negro Digest 17
(May 1968): 88-92.

_____ and Eugenia W. Collier. Afro-American Writing: An Anthology of Prose and Poetry. New York: New York University
Press, 1972.

Lottman, Herbert. " 'The Action Is Everywhere the Black Man
Goes.' " The New York Times Book Review, 21 April 1968,
pp. 6-7, 48-49.

Lovell, John, Jr. Black Song: The Forge and the Flame. New
York: Macmillan, 1972.

_____. "Black Renaissance." American Dialog 5 (1968): 30-31.

_____. "Drama: Double Take." Crisis (November 1947): 334-
335.

_____. "New Curtains Going Up." Crisis 54 (October 1947): 305-309, 315.

_____. "Round-Up: The Negro in the American Theatre (1940-1947)." Crisis 54 (July 1947): 212-217.

Lowenfels, Walter, ed. In the Time of Revolution: Poems from the Third World in America. New York: Random House, 1969. (Anthology.)

_____, ed. Poets of Today. New York: International, 1964. (Anthology.)

_____, ed. Where Is Vietnam? American Poets Respond. Garden City, N.Y.: Doubleday, 1967. (Anthology.)

_____. "The White Literary Syndicate." Liberator 10 (March 1970): 8.

Lyons, Thomas T. Black Leadership in American History. Menlo Park, Calif.: Addison-Wesley, 1971.

McCullough, Frances, ed. Earth, Air, Fire and Water. New York: Coward-McCann & Geoghegan, 1970. (Anthology.)

McDonnell, Thomas. "The Emergence of the Negro in Literature." The Critic 20 (December 1961-January 1962): 31-34.

McDowell, Robert E. "Mothers and Sons." Prairie Schooner 44 (Winter 1969-1970): 256.

McElroy, Hilda and Richard A. Willis. "Published Works of Black Playwrights in the United States, 1960-1970." Black World 21 (April 1970): 92-98.

McFarland, Philip, et al., eds. Moments in Literature. Boston: Houghton Mifflin, 1972. (Anthology.)

McKay, Alex and John MacKenzie, eds. What Does It Take? Menlo Park: Addison-Wesley, 1972. (Anthology.)

McMaster, R. J., ed. Points of Light. Ontario: Longmans, 1971. (Anthology.)

McPherson, James M., et al. Blacks in America: Bibliographical Essays. Garden City, N.Y.: Doubleday, 1971.

Mahadi, M.A., ed. Third World Poets Speak the Truth. New York: Third World Publications, 1970.

Mahoney, John and John Smittroth, eds. The Insistent Present. Boston: Houghton Mifflin, 1970. (Anthology.)

Main, C. F., ed. College Book of Verse. Belmont, Calif.: Wadsworth, 1970. (Anthology.)

Major, Clarence, ed. The New Black Poetry. New York: International, 1969. (Anthology.)

Majors, M. A. Noted Negro Women, 1893; Freeport, N.Y.: Books for Libraries, 1971.

Marcus, Samuel, ed. An Anthology of Revolutionary Poetry. New York: Active, 1929.

Marcus, Steven. "The American Negro in Search of Identity. Commentary 16 (1953): 456-463.

Margolies, Edward. "The Image of the Primitive in Black Letters." Midcontinent American Studies Journal 11 (Fall 1970): 67-77.

_____. Native Sons: A Critical Study of Twentieth-Century Negro American Authors. Philadelphia: J. P. Lippincott, 1968.

_____, ed. A Native Sons Reader. Philadelphia: Lippincott, 1970.

Markholt, Ottilie. "White Critics, Black Playwrights." Negro Digest 14 (April 1967): 54.

Marshall, C. and J. A. Myers, Jr., eds. Designs for Reading Poems. Boston: Houghton Mifflin, 1969. (Anthology.)

Maund, Alfred. "The Negro Novelist and the Contemporary American Scene." Chicago Jewish Forum 12 (Fall 1954): 28-34.

May, John R., S.J. "Images of Apocalypse in the Black Novel." Renascence 23 (1970): 31-45.

Mayfield, Julian. "Into the Mainstream and Oblivion." In The American Negro Writer and His Roots. pp. 29-34.

_____. "Tale of Two Novelists." Negro Digest 14 (June 1965): 70-72.

_____, ed. Ten Times Black: Stories from the Black Experience. New York: Bantam, 1970. (Anthology.)

Mays, Benjamin E. The Negro's God as Reflected in His Literature, 1938; reprint ed., New York: Negro Universities Press, 1969.

Meier, August. Negro Thought in America, 1880-1915. Ann Arbor, Mich.: University of Michigan Press, 1963.

_____. "Some Reflections on the Negro Novel." CLA Journal

2 (1959): 168-177.

Meltzer, Milton. In Their Own Words: The History of the American Negro. New York: T. Y. Crowell, 1964.

Messner, Gerald, ed. Another View: To Be Black in America.
New York: Harcourt, Brace & World, 1970. (Anthology.)

Metcalf, George R. Black Profiles. New York: McGraw Hill, 1968.

Mezu, S. Okechukwu, ed. Modern Black Literature. Buffalo: Black
Academy Press, 1971. (Anthology.)

Michel, L. A., ed. Headway: A Thematic Reader. New York:
Holt, Rinehart & Winston, 1970. (Anthology.)

_____, ed. Way Out: A Thematic Reader. New York: Holt,
Rinehart & Winston, 1968. (Anthology.)

Miller, Adam David, ed. Dices or Black Bones: Black Voices of
the Seventies. Boston: Houghton Mifflin, 1970. (Anthology.)

_____. "It's a Long Way to St. Louis: Notes on the Audience
for Black Drama." Drama Review 12 (Summer 1968): 147-150.

_____. "News from the San Francisco East Bay." Black The-
atre, no. 4 (1970): 5.

Miller, Elizabeth W. and Mary L. Fisher. The Negro in America:
A Bibliography. Cambridge: Harvard University Press, 1970.

Miller, Larry. "Spirit House." Black Theatre, no. 2 (1969): 34.

Miller, Ruth, ed. Backgrounds to Blackamerican Literature.
Scranton: Chandler, 1971.

_____. Blackamerican Literature: 1760-Present. Beverly Hills,
Calif.: Glencoe Press, 1971.

Miller, Wayne Charles. A Gathering of Ghetto Writers. New York:
New York University Press, 1972.

Miller, William C., and Stephanie L. Miller. "All Black Showcase:
The Effectiveness of a Negro Theatre Production." Educational
Theatre Journal 21 (May 1969): 202-204.

Millian, Bruce E. "Detroit Repertory Theatre." Black Theatre,
no. 2 (1969): 4-5.

Mills, Ralph, ed. Contemporary American Poetry. New York:
Random House, 1972. (Anthology.)

Milner, Ronald. "Black Magic: Black Art." Negro Digest 16 (April 1967): 8-12.

_____. "Black Theater--Go Home." Negro Digest 17 (April 1968): 5-10.

Mirer, Martin, ed. Modern Black Stories. Woodbury, N.Y.: Barron, 1971.

Mitchell, Loften. "Black Drama." Negro Digest 16 (April 1967): 75-87.

_____. Black Drama: The Story of the American Negro in the Theater. New York: Hawthorne, 1967.

_____. "Harlem, My Harlem." Black World 20 (November 1970): 91-97.

_____. "The Negro Theatre and the Harlem Community." Freedomways 3 (1963): 384-394.

_____. "The Negro Writer and His Materials." In The American Negro Writer and His Roots, pp. 55-60.

_____. "On the 'Emerging' Playwright." In Bigsby, The Black American Writer, pp. 129-136.

_____. "Three Writers and a Dream." Crisis 72 (1965): 219-223.

Molette, Carlton W., II. "The First Afro-American Theater." Negro Digest 19 (April 1970): 4-9.

Monaco, Richard, ed. New American Poetry. New York: McGraw-Hill, 1973. (Anthology.)

Monroe, Harriet. "Negro Sermon Poetry." Phylon 30 (1923): 291-293.

Moon, Bucklin. "A Literature of Protest." The Reporter, 6 (December 1949): 35-37.

_____, ed. Primer for White Folks. Garden City, N.Y.: Doubleday, 1946. (Anthology.)

Moore, Gerald. "Poetry in the Harlem Renaissance." In Bigsby, The Black American Writer, vol. 2, pp. 67-76.

Morgan, Fred. Here and Now II. New York: Harcourt Brace Jovanovich, 1972.

Morpurgo, J. E. "American Negro Poetry." Fortnightly 168 (July 1947): 16-24.

Morris, Lloyd. "The Negro 'Renaissance.'" Southern Workman 58 (1930): 82-86.

Morrison, Allan. "A New Surge in the Arts." Ebony 22 (August 1967): 134-138.

Morton, Lena Beatrice. Negro Poetry in America. Boston: Stratford, 1925.

Mulder, Arnold. "Wanted: A Negro Novelist." The Independent 112 (1924): 341-342.

Muraskin, William. "An Alienated Elite: Short Stories in The Crisis, 1910-1950." Journal of Black Studies 1 (1971): 282-305.

Murphy, Beatrice M., ed. Ebony Rhythm: An Anthology of Contemporary Negro Verse. New York: Exposition, 1948.

_____. Negro Voices. New York: Henry Harrison, 1938. (Anthology.)

_____. Today's Negro Voices: An Anthology of Young Negro Poets. New York: Messner, 1970.

Murray, Albert. The Omni-Americans: New Perspectives on Black Experience and American Culture. New York: Outerbridge, 1970.

_____. "Something Different, Something More." In Hill, Anger, and Beyond, pp. 112-137.

Murray, J. P. "Black Movies/Black Theatre." Drama Review (December 1972): 55-61.

Musgrave, Marian E. "Patterns of Violence and Non-Violence in Pro-Slavery and Anti-Slavery Fiction." CLA Journal 16 (June 1973): 426-437.

_____. "Triangles in Black and White: Interracial Sex and Hostility in Black Literature." CLA Journal 14 (1971): 444-451.

Myers, Carol. "A Selected Bibliography of Recent Afro-American Writers." CLA Journal 16 (March 1973): 377-382.

Neal, Larry. "Any Day Now: Black Art and Black Liberation." Ebony 24 (August 1969): 54-58.

_____. "The Black Arts Movement." Drama Review 12 (Summer 1968): 28-39.

_____. "Cultural Nationalism and Black Theatre." Black Theatre, no. 1. (1968): 8-10.

_____. "Toward a Relevant Black Theatre." Black Theatre, no. 4 (1970): 14-15.

"Negro Novelists--Blazing the Way in Fiction." Negro History

Bulletin (December 1938): 1-2, 22.

"Negro Playwrights." Ebony 14 (April 1959): 95-96.

"Negro Writing: A Literature of Protest." American Writing Today: Its Independence and Vigor. Edited by Allan Angoff. New
York: New York University Press, 1957.

Nelson, John H. The Negro Character in American Literature.
Lawrence, Kansas: University of Kansas Journalism Press, 1926.

New York Public Library. Dictionary of the Schomburg Collection
of Negro Literature and History. 9 vols. Boston: G. K. Hall,
1962; supplement 1965.

Nicholas, Xavier, ed. Poetry of Soul. New York, 1971.

Nichols, Charles H., Jr. "The Forties: A Decade of Growth."
Phylon 11 (1950): 377-380.

Nicolas, Denise. "View from the Free Southern Theatre." Liberator 6 (July 1966): 20.

Nower, Joyce. "Foolin' Master." Satire Newsletter 7 (Fall 1969):
5-10.

_____. "The Traditions of Negro Literature in the United States."
Negro American Literature Forum 3 (1969): 5-12.

O'Brien, John, ed. Interviews with Black Writers. Liveright,
1973.

_____. "Let Us Have a New American Theatre." Negro Digest
13 (March 1964): 44.

Oden, Gloria. "Literature and Politics--The Black Investment."
New School Bulletin, 16 November 1965, pp. 1, 4.

Oliver, Clinton and Stephanie Sills, eds. Contemporary Black Drama. New York: Scribners, 1971.

Oliver, Paul. Blues Fell This Morning: The Meaning of the Blues.
New York: Horizons, 1960.

_____. Conversation with the Blues. New York: Harcourt,
Brace, 1969.

Oliver, Walter, et al., eds. New Worlds of Reading. New York:
Harcourt, Brace, 1969.

O'Neal, John. "Motion in the Ocean: Some Political Dimensions of
the Free Southern Theatre." Drama Review 12 (Summer 1968):
70-77.

_____. "Problems and Prospects." Negro Digest 15 (April 1966): 4-12.

Orman, Roscoe. "The New Lafayette Theatre." Black Theatre, no. 2 (1969): 5-6; no. 4 (1970): 6; no. 5 (1971): 12-13.

Osofsky, Gilbert. "Symbols of the Jazz Age: The New Negro and Harlem Discovered." American Quarterly 17 (1965): 229-236.

Ottley, Roi and William J. Weatherby. The Negro in New York. New York: Oceana, 1967.

"Our Prize Winners and What They Say of Themselves." Opportunity 4 (1926): 188-189.

Ovington, Mary White. Portraits in Color, 1927. Freeport, N.Y.: Books for Libraries, 1971.

Owens, Rochelle, and Michael Feingold, eds. Spontaneous Combustion: Eight New American Plays. New York: Winter House, 1972.

Oxley, Thomas L. G. "Survey of Negro Literature 1760-1926." The Messenger 9 (February 1927): 37-39.

Page, James. "Black Literature." English Journal 62 (May 1973): 709-716.

Palms 1 (October 1926): entire issue.

Park, Robert E. "Negro Race Consciousness as Reflected in Race Literature." American Review (September-October 1923): 505-516.

Parker, John W. "The Emergence of Negro Fiction." Negro History Bulletin 12 (October 1948): 12, 18.

Parks, Carole A. "Phillis Wheatley Comes Home: Report on a Poetry Festival." Ebony 23 (February 1974): 93-95.

Parone, Edward, ed. Collision Course. New York: Random House, 1968.

Patterson, Lindsay, ed. Anthology of the American Negro in the Theatre. Washington, D.C.: Associated, 1967.

_____, ed. Black Theater: A Twentieth Century Collection of the Work of Its Best Playwrights. New York: Dodd, Mead, 1971. (Anthology.)

_____, ed. An Introduction to Black Literature in America from 1746 to the Present. New York: Publishers, 1968. (Anthology.)

_____, ed. The Negro in Music and Art. New York: Publishers, 1969.

_____, ed. A Rock Against the Wind: Black Love Poems. New York: Dodd, Mead, 1973. (Anthology.)

Pawley, Thomas. "The First Black Playwrights." Black World 21 (April 1972): 16-24.

Peavy, Charles D. "The Black Revolutionary Novel, 1899-1969." Studies in the Novel 3 (1971): 180-189.

_____. "Satire and Contemporary Black Drama." Satire Newsletter 7 (Fall 1969): 40-48.

Perkins, Eugene, ed. Black Expression: An Anthology of New Black Poets. Chicago: Conda, 1967.

_____. "The Changing Status of Black Writers." Black World 19 (June 1970): 18-23, 95-98.

Ploski, Harry A., ed. Negro Almanac. New York: Bellwether, 1967.

_____ and Ernest Kaiser. The Negro Almanac. New York: Bellwether, 1971.

_____, Otto J. Lindenmeyer and Ernest Kaiser, eds. Reference Library of Black America. Chicago: Afro-Am Press, 1971.

Poetry Broadcast (An Anthology Composed for Radio Programs.) Exposition, 1946.

Poland, Albert and Bruce Mailman, eds. The Off, Off-Broadway Book: The Plays, People, Theatre. New York: Bobbs-Merrill, 1972.

Pool, Rosey, ed. Beyond the Blues: New Poems by American Negroes. Kent, England: Hand and Flower Press, 1962. (Anthology.)

_____. "The Discovery of American Negro Poetry. Freedomways 3 (1963): 46-51.

_____. "Fling Me Your Challenge." Negro Digest 15 (December 1965): 54-60.

_____, ed. Ik ben de Nieuwe Neger. Den Haag: Bakker, 1965. (Anthology.)

_____ and Paul Breman, eds. Ik Zag hoe Zwart ik was. Den Haag: Bakker, 1958. (Anthology.)

Porter, Dorothy B. "Early American Negro Writings: A Bibliographical Study." Papers of the Bibliographical Society of America 39 (1945): 192-268.

_____. North American Poets: A Bibliographical Checklist of
Their Writings, 1760-1944. Hattiesburg, Miss.: The Book Farm,
1945.

_____. A Working Bibliography on the Negro in the United
States. Ann Arbor: University Microfilms, 1968.

Potter, Vilma R. "New Politics, New Mothers." CLA Journal 16
(December 1972): 247-255.

Powell, Anne. "The Negro in Federal Theatre." Crisis 43 (November 1936): 340-341.

Preminger, Alex, Frank H. Warnhand, and O. B. Hardison, Jr.,
eds. "Negro Poetry." Encyclopedia of Poetry and Poetics.
Princeton: Princeton University Press, 1965.

Prideaux, Tom. "Living Healing Kind of Theatre--Free Southern
Theatre." Life, 16 September 1966, p. 24.

Primus, Marc, ed. Black Theatre: A Resource Directory. New
York: The Black Theatre Alliance, 1564 Broadway #701, n.d.

Quarles, Benjamin, ed. Blacks on John Brown. Urbana: University of Illinois Press, 1972.

Querry, Ronald and Robert E. Fleming. "A Working Bibliography
of Black Periodicals." Studies in Black Literature 3 (Summer
1972): 31-36.

Ramsaran, J. A. "The 'Twice-Born' Artists' Silent Revolution."
Black World 20 (May 1971): 58-68.

Randall, Dudley. "The Black Aesthetic in the Thirties, Forties and
Fifties." In Gayle, The Black Aesthetic.

_____, ed. Black Poetry: A Supplement to Anthologies Which
Exclude Black Poets. Detroit: Broadside, 1969.

_____, ed. The Black Poets. New York: Bantam, 1971. (An-
thology.)

_____. "Ubi Sunt and Hic Sum." Negro Digest 14 (September
1965): 73-76.

_____. "White Poet, Black Critic." Negro Digest 14 (February
1965): 46-48.

_____ and Margaret Burroughs, eds. For Malcolm: Poems on

the Life and the Death of Malcolm X. Detroit: Broadside, 1967.
(Anthology.)

Reardon, William R. and Thomas D. Pawley, eds. The Black
Teacher and the Dramatic Arts. New York: Negro University
Press, 1970.

Record, Wilson. "The Negro as Creative Artist." Crisis 72
(1965): 153-158, 193.

_____. "The Negro Writer and the Communist Party." In Bigs-
by, The Black American Writer, vol. 1, pp. 217-228.

Reddick, L. D. "No Kafka in the South." Phylon 11 (1950): 380-
383.

Redding, Saunders. "American Negro Literature." American Scholar 18 (1949): 137-148.

_____. "The Black Arts Movement in Negro Poetry." Ameri-
can Scholar 42 (Spring 1973): 330-335.

_____. "The Black Revolution in American Studies." American
Studies: An International Newsletter 9 (Autumn 1970): 3-9.

_____. "Literature and the Negro." Contemporary Literature
9 (1968): 130-135.

_____. The Lonesome Road. Garden City, N.Y.: Doubleday,
1958.

_____. "The Negro Author: His Publisher, His Public and His
Purse." Publishers Weekly, 24 March 1945, pp. 1284-1288.

_____. "The Negro Writer and American Literature." In Hill,
Anger, and Beyond, pp. 1-19.

_____. "The Negro Writer--Shadow and Substance." Phylon 11
(1950): 371-373.

_____. "Negro Writing in America." New Leader, 16 May 1950,
pp. 8-10.

_____. "The Problems of the Negro Writer." Massachusetts
Review 6 (Autumn-Winter 1964-65): 57-70.

_____. "Since Richard Wright." African Forum 1 (Spring 1966):
21-31.

_____. They Came in Chains. Philadelphia: Lippincott, 1950.

_____. To Make a Poet Black. Chapel Hill: University of North
Carolina Press, 1939.

Redkey, Edwin S.   Black Exodus.   New Haven: Yale University
Press, 1969.

Redmond, Eugene.   "The Black American Epic: Its Roots, Its
Writers."   Black Scholar 2 (January 1971): 15-22.

_____, ed.   Sides of the River: A Mini-Anthology of Black Writ-
ing.   Oberlin, Ohio: By the Author, 1969.

Reed, Ishmael, ed.   19 Necromancers from Now: An Anthology of
Original American Writing for the 70's.   Garden City, N.Y.:
Doubleday, 1970.

_____ et al., eds.   Yardbird Reader, vol. 1.   Berkeley: Yardbird Publishing Cooperative, 1972.   (Anthology.)

Reid, Ira DeA.   "The Literature of the Negro: A Social Scientist's
Appraisal."   Phylon 11 (1950): 388-390.

Riach, Douglas C.   "Blacks and Blackface on the Irish Stage, 1830-
60."   Journal of American Studies 7 (December 1973): 231-242.

Riach, William A. D.   " 'Telling It Like It Is':   An Examination of
Black Theatre as Rhetoric."   Quarterly Journal of Speech.   56
(1970): 179-186.

Richards, Stanley, ed.   The Best Short Plays of 1970.   Philadelphia:
Chilton, 1970.   (Anthology.)

Richardson, Ben A.   Great American Negroes.   New York: T. Y.
Crowell, 1945.

Richardson, Jack.   "The Black Arts."   New York Review of Books
19 (December 1968), pp. 10-13.

Richardson, Willis, ed.   Plays and Pageants from the Life of the
Negro.   Washington, D.C.: Associated, 1930.   (Anthology.)

_____ and May Miller, eds.   Negro History in Thirteen Plays.
Washington, D.C.: Associated, 1935.   (Anthology.)

Riddell, Hugh J.   "New Negro Playwrights Group Formed in Harlem."   Daily Worker 27 July 1940, p. 7.

Rideout, Walter B.   The Radical Novel in the United States, 1900-
1954.   Cambridge: Harvard University, Press, 1956.

Riley, Phillip.   "Negro Theatre."   Encore 7 (November-December
1960): 11.

Robinson, Wilhelmina S.   Historical Negro Biographies.   New York:
Publishers, 1969.

Robinson, William H. Early Black American Poets. Dubuque,
Iowa: Wm. C. Brown, 1969.

_____. Early Black American Prose. Dubuque, Iowa: Wm. C.
Brown, 1970.

_____, ed. Nommo: An Anthology of Modern African and Black
American Literature. New York: Macmillan, 1972.

Rochon, Noel J., ed. No Big Thing. New Orleans: Moret Press,
1967. (Anthology.)

Rodgers, Carolyn M. "Black Poetry--Where It's At." Negro Digest 18 (September 1969): 7-16.

_____. "Breakforth, In Deed." Black World 19 (September
1970): 13-22.

_____. "The Literature of Black." Black World 19 (June 1970):
5-11.

_____. "Uh Nat'chal Thang--The WHOLE TRUTH--US." Black
World 20 (September 1971): 4-14.

Rollins, Charlemae, ed. Christmas Gif'. Chicago: Follett, 1963.
(Anthology.)

_____. Famous American Negro Poets. New York: Dodd, Mead,
1965.

_____. They Showed the Way: Forty American Negro Leaders.
New York: Crowell, 1964.

Romers, Patricia, ed. I, Too, Am American: Documents from
1619 to the Present. New York: Publishers, 1968. (Anthology.)

Rosenthal, M. L. The New Modern Poetry: New York: Macmillan,
1967. (Anthology.)

Rourke, Constance. "Tradition for a Negro Literature." In
Rourke, Roots of American Culture, pp. 262-274.

Rousseve, Charles B. The Negro in Louisiana: Aspects of His History and His Literature. New Orleans: 1927.

Rowell, Charles H. "A Bibliography of Bibliographies for the Study
of Black American Literature and Folklore." Black Experience,
A Southern University Journal 55 (June 1969): 95-111.

Russell, F. A., ed. Ted Malone's Scrapbook. Camden, N.J.:
Bookman, 1941.

Salisbury, Harrison E., ed. The Eloquence of Protest: Voices of the Seventies. Boston: Houghton Mifflin, 1972.

Sanchez, Sonia, ed. 360 Degrees of Blackness Coming at You.
n.p.: 5X Publishing Co., 1971.

_____, ed. We Be Word Sorcerers: 25 Stories by Black Amer-
icans. New York: Bantam, 1973.

"Satire and Humor in Black American Literature." Satire Newsletter 7 (1969): entire issue.

Savre, Nora. "New York's Black Theatre." New Statesman, 25
October 1968, p. 556.

Schechner, Richard. "Free Theatre for Mississippi." Harper 231
(October 1965): 11.

Schomburg, Arthur A. A Bibliographical Checklist of American Negro Poetry. New York: Charles F. Heartman, 1916.

Schreiber, Ron, comp. 31 New American Poets. New York: Hill
& Wang, 1969.

Schroeder, R. J. "Free Southern Theatre." Commonweal, 18
March 1966, p. 696.

Schuck, Barry. "Philadelphia's Black Drama Season '67-'68."
Black Theatre, no. 2 (1969): 34-35.

Schulberg, Budd. "Black Phoenix: An Introduction." Antioch Review 27 (Fall 1967): 277-284.

_____, ed. From the Ashes: Voices of Watts. New York:
New American Library, 1967. (Anthology.)

Schuyler, George S. "The Negro Art Hokum." Nation 122 (1926):
652-663.

_____. "The Van Vechten Revolution." Phylon 11 (1950): 362-
368.

_____. "What's Wrong with Negro Authors." Negro Digest 8
(May 1950): 3-7.

Scott, Nathan A., Jr. "Judgment Marked by a Cellar: The American Negro Writer and the Dialectic of Despair." Denver Quarterly 2 (Summer 1967): 5-35.

"The Scribes." Sing, Laugh, Weep: A Book of Poems by the
Scribes. St. Louis: Press, 1944.

Segnitz, Barbara and Carol Rainey, eds. Psyche: The Feminine
Poetic Consciousness. New York: Dial, 1973. (Anthology.)

Shapiro, Karl. "The Decolonization of American Literature." Wilson Library Bulletin 29 (June 1965): 842-853.

Shea, J. Vernon. Strange Barriers. New York: Lion Library, 1955. (Anthology.)

Sherr, P. C. "Change Your Luck: A Negro Satirizes White America." Phylon 32 (Fall 1971): 281-289.

Shih, Hsien-yung. "Impressions of American Negro Literature." Chicago Review, no. 4 (1966): 107-112.

Shockley, Ann A. and Sue Chandler. Living Black American Authors: A Biographical Dictionary. New York: Bowker, 1973.

Shuman, R. Baird, ed. A Galaxy of Black Writing. Durham, N.C.: Moore, 1970. (Anthology.)

_____, ed. Nine Black Poets. Durham, N.C.: Moore, 1968. (Anthology.)

Simmons, Gloria M., Helene D. Hutchinson, eds., under the direction of Henry E. Simmons. Black Culture: Reading and Writing Black. New York: Holt, Rinehart & Winston, 1972.

Simmons, Rev. Wm. J. Men of Mark: Eminent, Progressive and Rising. New York: Arno, 1968.

Singh, Raman K. "The Black Novel and Its Tradition." Colorado Quarterly 20 (Summer 1971): 23-29.

_____ and Peter Fellowes, eds. Black Literature in America: A Casebook. New York: T. Y. Crowell, 1970. (Anthology.)

Smith, Arthur L. "Socio-Historical Perspectives of Black Oratory." Quarterly Journal of Speech 56 (1970): 264-269.

_____, ed. Rhetoric of Black Revolution. Boston: Allyn & Bacon, 1969. (Anthology.)

Smith, Michael. More Plays from Off Off-Broadway. Indianapolis: Bobbs-Merrill, 1972.

Smith, William Gardner. "The Negro Writer: Pitfalls and Compensations." Phylon 11 (1950): 297-303.

Smitherman, Geneva. "The Power of the Rap: The Black Idiom and the New Black Poetry." Twentieth Century Literature 19 (October 1973): 259-274.

Solotaroff, Theodore. Writers and Issues. New York: New American Library, 1972.

Soul Session: Anthology of the B. C. D.   Newark, N.J.: Jihad, 1969.

Spradling, Mary Mace, ed.   In Black and White: Afro-Americans in Print.   Kalamazoo, Mich.: Kalamazoo Library System, 1971.

Stanford, Barbara Dodds, ed.   I, Too, Sing America: Black Voices in American Literature.   New York: Hayden, 1971.   (Anthology.)

Starke, Juanita.   "Symbolism of the Negro College in Three Recent Novels."   Phylon 17 (1956): 365-373.

Stein, M. L.   Blacks in Communication.   New York: Julian Messner, 1972.

Sterling, Dorothy.   "The Soul of Learning."   English Journal 57 (1968): 166-180.

_____ and Benjamin Quarles.   Lift Every Voice: The Lives of Booker T. Washington, W. E. B. Du Bois, Mary Church Terrell, and James Weldon Johnson.   Garden City, N.Y.: Doubleday, 1965.

Stern, Frederick C.   "Black Lit, White Crit?"   College English 35 (March 1974): 637-658.

Stewart, James T.   "The Development of the Black Revolutionary Artist."   In Hemenway, The Black Novelist, pp. 134-144.

Stone, J. and D. DeNevi.   Teaching Multi-Cultural Populations.   New York: Van Nostrand Reinhold, 1971.

Sutherland, E.   "Theatre of the Meaningful."   Nation, 19 October 1966, p. 254.

Swados, Harvey.   "The Writer in Contemporary American Society."   In Hill, Anger, and Beyond, pp. 62-75.

"Symposium: The Negro in the American Theatre."   Negro Digest 2 (July 1962): 52.

"Symposium: The Negro's Role in American Culture."   Negro Digest 2 (March 1962): 5.

"Symposium: The Negro Writer in America."   Negro Digest 12 (June 1963): 54.

Symposium: The Task of the Negro Writer as Artist.   Negro Digest 14 (April 1965): 54.

Takai, Ronald T.   Violence in the Black Imagination: Essays and Documents.   New York: G. P. Putnam's, 1972.

Talbot, William.   "Every Negro in His Place--The Scene On and

Off Broadway." Drama Critique 12 (Spring 1964): 92.

Tatham, Campbell. "Double Order: The Spectrum of Black Aesthetics." Midcontinent American Studies Journal 11 (Fall 1970):
88-100.

Taussig, Charlotte E. "The New Negro as Revealed in His Poetry."
Opportunity (April 1927): 108-111.

Taylor, Jeanne A. "On Being Black and Writing for Television."
Negro American Literature Forum 4 (1970): 79-82.

Teer, Barbara Ann. "To Black Artists, With Love." Negro Digest 18 (April 1969): 4-8.

Ten: An Anthology of Detroit Poets. Fort Smith, Ark.: South &
West, 1968.

Thomas, Will. "Negro Writers of Pulp Fiction." Negro Digest 8
(July 1950): 81-84.

Thompson, Era Bell. "Negro Publications and the Writer." Phylon 11 (1950): 304-305.

Thompson, T. "Burst of Negro Drama." Life, 29 May 1964, pp.
62A-70.

Thornhill, G. C. "Negro Becomes Literary Contributor." Poet
Lore 39 (1928): 431-435.

Thorpe, Earl E. Black Historians. New York: Morrow, 1971.

Three Negro Plays. Hammondsworth, England: Penguin, 1969.
(Hughes, Jones, Hansberry.)

Thurman, Wallace. "Negro Artists and the Negro." New Republic
31 August 1927, pp. 37-39.

_____. "Negro Poets and Their Poetry." Bookman 67 (1928):
555-561.

_____. "Nephews of Uncle Remus." The Independent, 24 (Sep-
tember 1927): 296-298.

Tillman, Nathaniel P. "The Threshold of Maturity." Phylon 11
(1950): 387-388.

Tischler, Nancy M. Black Masks: Negro Characters in Modern
Southern Fiction. University Park: Pennsylvania State University
Press, 1969.

Tobin, Terence. "Karamu Theatre 1915-1964--Its Distinguished
Past and Present Achievement." Drama Critique 12 (Spring 1964):
86.

Toppin, Edgar A. A Biographical History of Blacks in America since 1528. New York: David McKay, 1969.

Trent, Toni. "Stratification Among Blacks by Black Authors." Negro History Bulletin 34 (December 1971): 179-181.

Trott, Geri. "Black Theatre." Harper's Bazaar 101 (August 1968): 150-153.

Troupe, Quincy, ed. Watts Poets: A Book of New Poetry and Essays. Los Angeles: House of Respect, 1968. (Anthology.)

Turco, Lewis, ed. Poetry: An Introduction Through Writing. Reston, Va.: Reston, 1973. (Anthology.)

Turner, Darwin T. "Afro-American Literary Critics." Black World 19 (July 1970): 54-67.

_____. Afro-American Writers. New York: Appleton-Century-Crofts, 1970. (Bibliography.)

_____, ed. Black American Literature: Essays, Poetry, Fiction, Drama. Columbus: Charles E. Merrill, 1970. (Anthology.)

_____, ed. Black Drama in America: An Anthology. Greenwich, Conn.: Fawcett, 1971.

_____. "The Black Playwright in the Professional Theatre of the United States of America, 1858-1949." In Brasmer and Consolo, Black Drama: An Anthology, pp. 1-18.

_____. "Literature and Society's Values." English Journal 60 (1971): 577-586.

_____. "The Negro Dramatist's Image of the Universe." CLA Journal 5 (1961): 106-120.

_____. "The Negro Novel in America: In Rebuttal." CLA Journal 10 (December 1966): 122-134.

_____. "The Negro Novelist and the South." Southern Humanities Review 1 (Winter 1967): 21-29.

_____. "Negro Playwrights and the Urban Negro." CLA Journal 12 (September 1968): 19-25.

_____. "Past and Present in Negro Drama." Negro American Literature Forum 2 (1968): 26-27.

_____. "The Teaching of Afro-American Literature." College English 31 (1970): 666-670.

_____ and Jean M. Bright, eds. Images of the Negro in America. Boston: Heath, 1965.

_____ et al., eds. Voices from the Black Experience: African and Afro-American Literature. Boston: Ginn, 1972.

Turner, Lorenzo D. "Anti-Slavery Sentiment in American Literature Prior to 1865." Journal of Negro History 14 (1929): 371-492.

Turner, Sherry. "An Overview of the New Black Arts." Freedomways 9 (1969): 156-163.

Turpin, Waters E. "The Contemporary American Negro Playwright." CLA Journal 9 (September 1965): 19-20.

_____. "Four Short Fiction Writers of the Harlem Renaissance --Their Legacy of Achievement." CLA Journal 11 (1967): 59-72.

Tuttleton, James W. "The Negro Writer as Spokesman." In Bigsby, The Black American Writer, vol. 1, pp. 245-259.

Valenti, Suzanne. "The Black Diaspora: Negritude in the Poetry of West Africans and Black Americans." Phylon 34 (December 1973): 390-398.

Van Doren, Carl. "The Younger Generation of Negro Writers." Opportunity (May 1924): 144-145.

Vas Dias, R., ed. Inside Outer Space. New York: Anchor, n.d. (Anthology.)

Villard, Oswald Garrison. "Negro Literature." Literary Review 3 (1923): 797-798.

Wagner, Jean. Black Poets of the United States: from Paul Laurence Dunbar to Langston Hughes. Chicago: University of Illinois Press, 1973.

Walker, Margaret. "New Poets." Phylon 11 (1950): 345-354.

_____. "The Humanistic Tradition of Afro-American Literature." American Libraries 1 (October 1970): 849.

Walrond, Eric and Rosey Pool, eds. Black and Unknown Bards: A Collection of Negro Poetry. Aldington (England): Hand & Flower Press, 1958.

Walser, Richard. The Black Poet. New York: Philosophical Library, 1967.

Ward, Douglas Turner. "Needed: A Theater for Black Themes." Negro Digest 17 (December 1967): 34-39.

Ward, Theodore. "Five Negro Novelists: Revolt and Retreat."
Mainstream 1 (Winter 1947): 100-110.

Warfel, Harry R. American Novelists of Today. Westport, Conn.:
Greenwood, 1951.

Watkins, Mel, ed. Black Review No. 1 and No. 2. New York:
Morrow, 1971.

_____. "The Black Revolution in Books." New York Times
Book Review 10 August 1969: 8.

_____ and Jay David, eds. To Be a Black Woman: Portraits in
Fact and Fiction. New York: Morrow, 1970. (Anthology.)

Watkins, Sylvester C., ed. Anthology of American Negro Literature. New York: Modern Library, 1944.

Weales, Gerald C. The Jumping-Off Place: American Drama in
the 1960's. New York: Macmillan, 1969.

Weimer, David R. "Black Realities and White: The City and the
Imagination Gap." Southwest Review 54 (1969): 105-119.

Weisman, Leon and Elfreda S. Wright, eds. Black Poetry for All
Americans. New York: Globe, 1971. (Anthology.)

Welburn, Ron, ed. Dues: An Annual of New Earth Writing. vols.
1 and 2. New York: Emerson Hall, 1974.

Wesley, Charles H. Quest for Equality: from Civil War to Civil
Rights. New York: Publishers, 1968.

Wessling, Joseph H. "Pressures on the Black Intellectual." Negro
American Literature Forum 3 (Winter 1970): 117-118.

Wetherill, Julie K. "The Negro as Producer of Literature." The
Chautauquan 15 (1892): 224-225.

White, Newman I. "American Negro Poetry." South Atlantic Quarterly 20 (1921): 304-322.

_____. "Racial Feeling in Negro Poetry." South Atlantic Quar-
terly 21 (1922): 14-21.

_____ and Walter Clinton Jackson, eds. An Anthology of Verse
by American Negroes. Durham, N.C.: Moore, 1968.

Whiteman, Maxwell. A Century of Fiction by American Negroes,
1853-1952. A Descriptive Bibliography. Philadelphia: Press of
Maurice Jacobs, 1955.

Whitlow, Roger. Black American Literature: A Critical History.

Chicago: Nelson Hall, 1973.

Wilentz, Ted and Tom Weatherly, eds. Natural Process: An Anthology of New Black Poetry. New York: Hill & Wang, 1970.

Wilkerson, Doxey A. "Negro Culture: Heritage and Weapon." Masses and Mainstream 2 (August 1949): 3-24.

Wilkerson, Margaret. "Black Theatre in California." Drama Review (December 1972): 25-38.

Williams, George W. History of the Negro Race in America. New York: Arno, 1968.

Williams, Jim. "The Need for a Harlem Theatre." Freedomways 3 (Summer 1963): 307-311.

_____. "Pieces on Black Theatre and the Black Theatre Work." Freedomways 9 (1969): 146-155.

_____. "Survey of Afro-American Playwrights." Freedomways 10 (1970): 26-45.

Williams, John A., ed. The Angry Black. New York: Lancer, 1962. (Anthology.)

_____, ed. Beyond the Angry Black. New York: Cooper Square, 1966. (Anthology.)

_____. "The Harlem Renaissance: Its Artists, Its Impact, Its Meaning." Black World 20 (November 1970): 17-18.

_____. "Negro in Literature Today." Ebony 8 (September 1963): 73-76.

_____ and Charles F. Harris, eds. Amistad 1, 2. New York: Vintage Books, 1970, 1971.

Williams, Kenny J. They Also Spoke: An Essay on Negro Literature in America, 1787-1930. Nashville: Townsend, 1970.

Williams, Miller, ed. Contemporary Poetry in America. New York: Random, 1973. (Anthology.)

Williams, Ora. American Black Women in the Arts and Social Sciences: A Bibliographic Survey. Metuchen, N.J.: Scarecrow, 1973.

Williams, Paulette, ed. Phat Mama, vol. 1. New York: P.N., Inc., 1970.

Williams, Sherley Ann. Give Birth to Brightness: A Thematic Study in Neo-Black Literature. New York: Dial, 1972.

Willis, Richard A. and Hilda McElroy. "Published Works of Black
    Playwrights in the United States, 1960-1970." Black World (Ap-
    ril 1972): 92-98.

Witherspoon, Jill, ed. The Broadside Annual, 1973. Detroit:
    Broadside, 1973. (Anthology.)

Woodson, Carter G., ed. The Mind of the Negro as Reflected in
    Letters Written During the Crisis, 1800-1860. New York: Negro
    Universities Press, 1969.

_____. The Negro in Our History. Washington: Associated,
    1966.

_____, ed. Negro Orators and Their Orations. Washington,
    D.C.: Associated, 1925.

_____ and Charles H. Wesley. The Negro in Our History.
    Washington, D.C.: Associated, 1922.

Woolridge, Nancy. "English Critics and the Negro Writers." Phy-
    lon 15 (1954): 139-146.

Work, Monroe N. A Bibliography of the Negro in Africa and Amer-
    ica. New York: Octagon Books, 1965.

_____. "The Spirit of Negro Poetry." Southern Workman 37
    (1908): 73-77.

Wormley, Beatrice F. and Charles W. Carter, eds. An Anthology
    of Negro Poetry by Negroes and Others. Trenton, N.J.: n.p.,
    1937.

Wright, Bruce McM. "The Negritude Tradition in Literature."
    Studies in Black Literature 3 (Spring 1972): 1-3.

Wright, Nathan, Jr. What Black Educators Are Saying. New York:
    Hawthorne Books, 1970. (Anthology.)

Wright, Richard. "Blueprint for Negro Writing." New Challenge 1
    (1937): 53-65.

Writers' Program. Cavalcade of the American Negro. Compiled by
    the Workers of the Writers' Program of the Work Projects Ad-
    ministration in the State of Illinois. Chicago: Diamond Jubilee Ex-
    position Authority, 1940.

Yellin, Jean Fagan. The Intricate Knot: The Negro in American
    Literature, 1776-1863. New York: New York University Press,
    1971.

Young, Alfred Fabian, ed. Dissent. DeKalb: Northern Illinois Uni-
    versity Press, 1968. (Anthology.)

Young, Carlene, ed. <u>Black Experience: Analysis and Synthesis.</u> San Rafael, Calif.: Leswing Press, 1972.

Appendix A

BLACK CRITICS, HISTORIANS, EDITORS

Abdul, Raoul
Alexander, Naledi
    Nnakintu
Alhamisi, Ahmed
Allen, Samuel
Anderson, Jervis
Anthony, Clara B.
Arnez, Nancy L.
Aruri, Naseer
Aubert, Alvin
Austin, Lettie J.

Bailey, Leaonead
Bailey, Peter
Baker, Houston A.
Baldwin, James
Bambara, Toni Cade
Baraka, Imamu Amiri (LeRoi
    Jones)
Barbour, Floyd B.
Barksdale, Richard K.
Battle, Sol
Belcher, Fannin S.
Bell, Bernard W.
Bennett, Lerone
Berry, Faith
Bond, Frederick W.
Bond, Julian
Bontemps, Arna
Boyer, Jill Witherspoon
Braithwaite, William S.
Brawley, Benjamin
Brewer, J. Mason
Brooks, A. Russell
Brooks, Gwendolyn
Brooks, Mary E.
Brown, Hallie Q.
Brown, Lloyd W.
Brown, Patricia L.
Brown, Sterling A.
Bullins, Ed

Burroughs, Margaret
Butcher, Margaret Just
Butcher, Philip

Cartey, Wilfred
Cassill, R. V.
Cathran, Tilman C.
Cayton, Horace R.
Chandler, G. Lewis
Chesnutt, Charles W.
Childress, Alice
Chrisman, Robert
Clarke, John Henrik
Collier, Eugenia W.
Cook, Mercer
Cooke, M. G.
Coombs, Orde
Cornish, Sam
Couch, William Jr.
Cromwell, Otelia
Cruse, Harold
Cullen, Countée
Cuney, Waring
Cunningham, James

Danner, Margaret
Davis, Allison
Davis, Arthur P.
Davis, Charles T.
Davis, Ossie
Dee, Ruby
Dennison, George
Dent, Thomas C.
Dodson, Owen
Dreer, Herman
Du Bois, W. E. B.
Dykes, Eva B.

Echeru⊙ M. J. C. (African)

Edmonds, Randolph
Elder, Lonnie
Ellison, Ralph
Emanuel, James A.
Evans, Donald T.
Evans, Mari

Fabio, Sarah Webster
Farrison, W. Edward
Fenderson, Lewis H.
Ferdinand, Val
Ferguson, Blanche E.
Ford, Nick Aaron
Frazier, E. Franklin
Fuller, Hoyt W.

Gant, L.
Garrett, Naomi M.
Gassner, John & Cleve
Gayle, Addison
Gerald, Carolyn
Ghareeb, Edmund
Gibson, Donald B.
Gibson, Richard
Giovanni, Nikki
Gloster, Hugh M.
Gold, Herbert
Goncalves, Joe
Gray, Val
Gregory, Montgomery
Gross, Seymour L.
Gross, Theodore L.

Hare, Nathan D.
Harper, Michael
Harris, Charles F.
Harris, Henrietta
Harrison, Paul Carter
Hayden, Robert
Henderson, David
Henderson, Stephen
Hill, Herbert
Hill, Leslie
Holder, Geoffrey
Horne, Frank S.
Huggins, Nathan I.
Hughes, Langston
Hurston, Zora N.

Iman, Yusef

Jackson, Blyden
Jackson, Esther Merle
Jackson, Miles M.
Jarrett, Thomas
Jeffers, Lance
Johnson, Alicia L.
Johnson, Charles S.
Johnson, Helen A.
Johnson, James Weldon
Johnson, Lemuel A.
Jones, Harry L.
Jordan, June

Kelly, Ernece
Kent, George
Kgositsile, W. Keorapetse
Kilgore, James C.
Killens, John O.
King, Woodie
Knight, Etheridge

Lamming, George
Lane, Pinkie Gordon
Lanusse, Armand
Lash, John S.
Lee, Don L.
Lee, Ulysses
Lester, Julius
Lewis, Theophilus
Lincoln, C. Eric
Llorens, David
Locke, Alain
Lomax, Michael L.
Long, Richard A.
Lovell, John Jr.

McPherson, James M.
Major, Clarence
Marvin X
Mayfield, Julian
Mays, Benjamin E.
Miller, Adam
Milner, Ronald
Mitchell, Loften
Molette, Carlton W., II
Murphy, Beatrice M.
Murray, Albert

Murray, James Patrick
Musgrave, Marian A.

Neal, Larry
Nelson, Alice Dunbar
Nelson, Sophia P.
Nicholas, Xavier
Nichols, Charles H. Jr.
Nicolas, Denise

Oden, Gloria
Oliver, Clinton
O'Neal, Frederick

Parks, Carole A.
Patterson, Lindsay
Pawley, Thomas
Perkins, Eugene
Porter, Dorothy B.
Primus, Marc

Quarles, Benjamin

Randall, Dudley
Rashidd, Naima
Reddick, L. D.
Redding, Saunders
Redmond, Eugene
Reed, Ishmael
Reid, Ira DeA.
Richardson, Willis
Riley, Clayton
Rivers, Conrad Kent
Robinson, William H.
Rodgers, Carolyn
Rogers, J. A.
Rollins, Charlemae

Sanchez, Sonia
Schomburg, Arthur A.
Schuyler, George S.
Scott, Nathan A. Jr.
Shockley, Ann A.
Sills, Stephanie
Smith, Arthur L.
Smith, William Gardner
Smitherman, Geneva
Stewart, James T.
Still, William

Taylor, Jeanne A.
Teer, Barbara Ann
Thomas, Will
Thompson, Era Bell
Thurman, Wallace
Tillman, Nathaniel P.
Toppin, Edgar A.
Trent, Toni
Troupe, Quincy
Turner, Darwin T.
Turner, Lorenzo D.
Turpin, Waters E.

Walden, Daniel
Walker, Margaret
Walrond, Eric
Wangara, Harun Kofi
Ward, Douglas Turner
Ward, Theodore
Watkins, Mel
Watkins, Sylvester
Welburn, Ron
Wesley, Charles H.
West, Hollie I.
Wilentz, Ted
Wilkerson, Doxey A.
Williams, George W.
Williams, John A.
Williams, Ora
Williams, Paulette
Williams, Sherley Ann
Winslow, H. F.
Witherspoon, Jill
Woodson, Carter G.
Woolridge, Nancy
Work, Monroe N.
Wright, Bruce McM.
Wright, Nathan Jr.
Wright, Richard

Appendix B

WHITE CRITICS, HISTORIANS, EDITORS

Abrahams, Roger D.
Abramson, Doris E.
Adoff, Arnold
Altenbernd, Lynn
Angoff, Allan
Anselment, Carol
Aptheker, Herbert

Bardolph, Richard
Bayliss, John F.
Beier, Ulli
Bigsby, C. W. E.
Birnbaum, Henry
Bluestein, Gene
Bone, Robert A.
Botkin, B. A.
Boyd, Sue Abbott
Boyle, Kay
Brasner, William
Breman, Paul
Burkhart, Robert E.

Calverton, Victor F.
Carroll, Paul
Chapman, Abraham
Clark, Admont
Consolo, Dominick
Cunard, Nancy

Davy, Francis X.
Deodene, Frank
Dodds, Barbara

Eastman, Arthur M.

Fabre, Genevieve E.
Fabre, Michel

Fiedler, Leslie A.
Foley, Martha
French, Warren

Gale, Zona
Gregory, Horace
Gross, Ronald

Hagopian, John V.
Hatch, James V.
Hemenway, Robert
Hentoff, Nat
Hicks, Jack
Hieatt, Kent A.
Hollo, Anselm
Howe, Florence
Howe, Irving
Hughes, Carl M.

Jahn, Janheinz
James, Charles L.

Katz, William L.
Kearns, Frances
Kerlin, Robert T.
Kinnamon, Keneth
Kinneman, John A.
Klotman, Phyllis R.
Kostelanetz, Richard

Lask, Thomas
Levertov, Denise
Liebman, Arthur
Littlejohn, David
Loggins, Vernon
Lowenfels, Walter

Margolies, Edward
Meier, August
Miller, Ruth
Monroe, Harriet
Moon, Bucklin
Moore, Gerald
Myers, Carol

Oliver, Paul

Park, Robert E.
Parone, Edward
Ploski, Harry A.
Pool, Rosey E.

Record, Wilson
Rosenthal, M. L.
Rourke, Constance

Salisbury, Harrison E.
Schechner, Richard
Schulberg, Budd
Shapiro, Karl
Shuman, R. Baird
Swados, Harvey

Van Doren, Carl
Villiard, Oswald Garrison

Wagner, Jean
White, Newman I.